CHILTON'S Repair and Tune-Up Guide

Pinto

1971-77

ILLUSTRATED

Prepared by the

Automotive Editorial Department

Chilton Book Company

Chilton Way

Radnor, Pa. 19089

215—687-8200

CHILTON BOOK COMPANY RADNOR, PENNSYLVANIA

Published in Radnor, Pa. by Chilton Book Company
and simultaneously in Ontario, Canada
by Thomas Nelson & Sons, Ltd.

Manufactured in the United States of America

1234567890 6543210987

Chilton's Repair & Tune-Up Guide: Pinto 1971–77
ISBN 0-8019-6607-8 Pbk.

Library of Congress Catalog Card No. 76-57311

ACKNOWLEDGMENTS

Chilton Book Company expresses appreciation to the following for their generous assistance:

Ford Motor Company
Dearborn, Michigan

Murphy Ford Company
Chester, Pennsylvania

George Ruggiere Ford
Devon, Pennsylvania

Although the information in this guide is based on industry sources and is as complete as possible at the time of publication, the possibility exists that the manufacturer made later changes which could not be included here. While striving for total accuracy, Chilton Book Company cannot assume responsibility for any errors, changes, or omissions that may occur in the compilation of this data.

Contents

Chapter 1

General Information and Maintenance

Introduction

This book is designed to aid the Pinto owner in performing maintenance, tune-ups, and repairs on his automobile. It is intended for both the inexperienced and those initiated in auto repairing. Since this book contains information on very simple operations and the more complex ones, the user will not outgrow the book as he conquers easy repairs and is ready to progress to more difficult ones.

Several things were assumed of you while the repair procedures in this guide were being written and they are listed here so you will be aware of them. It was assumed that you own, or are willing to purchase, a basic set of hand tools. For many repair operations, the factory has suggested a special tool to perform the repairs. If it was at all possible, a conventional tool was substituted for the special tool in these cases. However, there are some operations which cannot be done without these tools. To perform these jobs correctly it will be necessary to order the tool through your local Ford dealer's parts department.

Two basic rules of automobile mechanics also deserve reviewing here. Whenever the left side of the car is referred to, it is meant to specify the driver's side of the car. Likewise, the right side of the car means the passenger's side of the car. Also, most screws and bolts are removed by turning counterclockwise and tightened by turning clockwise.

Before you perform any repairs, read the entire section in the book that deals with that job. In many places a description of the system in question is provided. By reading this first and then reading the repair procedure, you will understand the function of the system you will be working on and what is entailed in the repair procedure, before you start the job. This will help to avoid problems and also enable you to learn about your car while you are working on it.

While every effort was made to make this book as simple, yet as detailed as possible, there is no substitute for personal experience. You can gain the confidence and feel for mechanical things required to perform auto repairs only by doing them yourself. If you take your time and concentrate on what you are doing, you will be surprised at how fast you can learn.

Serial Number Identification

VEHICLE IDENTIFICATION NUMBER

The official vehicle identification number for title and registration purposes is stamped on a metal tag which is attached to the top of the instrument panel. The tag is visible through the windshield and is located on the driver's side of the instrument panel. An explanation of the codes which make up the vehicle identification number is given below under "Vehicle Certification Label."

Vehicle Identification Number

VEHICLE CERTIFICATION LABEL

The vehicle certification label is attached to the left door pillar. The top half of the label contains the name of the vehicle manufacturer, the vehicle consecutive unit number, the month and year of manufacture, and the manufacturer's certification statement. Federal Law requires that this information be posted on the vehicle.

The bottom half of the vehicle certification label contains the vehicle identification number, the body type code, the exterior paint color code, the interior trim color and material code, the rear axle code, the transmission code, and the district and special order codes.

The first number in the vehicle identification number is the model year of the car (1—1971, 2—1972), the second digit is the assembly plant code for the plant in which the vehicle was built, the third and fourth digits are the body serial code (sedan, station wagon), the fifth digit is the engine code which identifies the type of engine installed in the vehicle, and the last six numbers are the consecutive unit numbers which start at 100,001 for the first car of a model year built at each assembly plant.

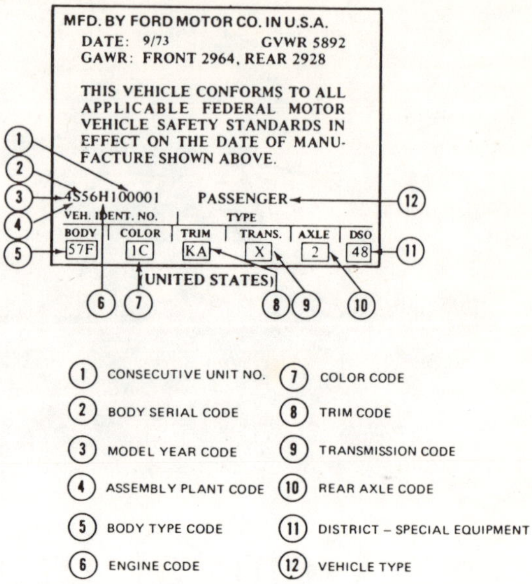

Vehicle certification label

Certification Label Codes

Assembly Plant Codes

R	San Jose
T	Metuchen
X	St. Thomas

Engine Codes

W	4 cylinder, 1600 cc engine
X	4 cylinder, 2000 cc engine
Y	4 cylinder, 2300 cc engine
Z	6 cylinder, 2800 cc engine

Rear Axle Ratio Codes

7	3.18 : 1 (1971–72 and 1976)
G	3.55 : 1 (1971–72)
7	3.40 : 1 (1973–76)
6	3.00 : 1 (1976)

Transmission Codes

5	4 speed manual transmission
E	4 speed manual transmission
W	C4 automatic transmission
V	C3 automatic transmission

Oil and Fuel Recommendations

FUEL

Your Pinto is designed to run on 91 octane (Research Method) gasoline when adjusted to factory specifications. The use of premium or high-test gasolines is not required. Octane is a measure of the resistance to knocking of a gasoline. Premium gasolines have a higher octane rating than regular gasoline. Your engine requires only a high enough octane rating to prevent it from pinging or knocking when you accelerate your car. So, if your engine does not ping on regular, you are wasting your money by buying premium gasoline, because it cannot make your car run any better. If your car does ping on regular, chances are your ignition timing is out of adjustment. See chapter two to learn how to adjust it. If your ignition timing is adjusted to specifications, try another brand of gasoline. Whatever the cause, never run your Pinto for extended periods with the engine pinging, for this can severely damage your engine.

In order to meet the 1975 emissions standards, a majority of the 1975 and all 1976 and later Pintos will be equipped with a catalytic converter integrated into the exhaust system. If so equipped, lead-free gasoline must be used. Failure to do so may result in costly repairs to the system.

OIL

Two factors must be considered when choosing an oil: quality and viscosity. Oil quality is determined by its sequence test rating. These tests were established by the American Petroleum Institute (API) to determine oil quality. Each test has a two-letter symbol to identify it. You can find these letters somewhere on the label of a can of oil. There are usually quite a few of these symbols on a can of oil, but you only need concern yourself with two symbols: MS or SE (SE preferred). If the oil contained in the can could not pass these tests, it is not good enough for your engine.

Oil viscosity refers to its thickness.

Oil Sequence Test Symbol

5W oil is a very thin oil which is good for low-temperature operation. 40W oil is a thicker oil which is preferred for warmer weather. There are two types of oil viscosity ratings, multiviscosity and single viscosity. Single viscosity oil retains the same flow characteristics under all temperature conditions, while multiviscosity oil is thin when cold, but thickens when its temperature rises. Generally speaking, single viscosity oil is slightly less expensive than multiviscosity oil, but it is not as flexible. On a cold winter morning you need a thin oil to allow the engine to turn over freely while you are trying to start it. However, you need a thicker oil if you are going to cruise at 60 miles per hour (mph). In this situation, multiviscosity oil is definitely preferred.

See the "Lubricant Specifications" chart in this chapter for viscosity recommendations based on ambient (outside) temperature.

Whatever type of oil you choose to use, avoid switching brands frequently, as not all brands are compatible with each other.

If you use a good oil and change it at the proper intervals, oil additives are not needed.

Preventive Maintenance

Preventive maintenance is just what its name implies, periodic maintenance services that are performed to prevent a component from wearing out or failing unexpectedly. It is far better to occasionally check the oil level in your engine at your leisure than to have your engine burn up in the middle of a snow storm 50 miles from home because you ran out of oil. What was once a 30 second job has now become a several hundred dollar engine overhaul.

If preventive maintenance is performed faithfully, your Pinto will be more economical to operate, more reliable, safer, and more fun to drive because it will be in top shape. Your Pinto will treat you the same way you treat it. If you take care of it properly, it will give you many miles of care-free driving. However, if you run it into the ground and never perform any maintenance on it, it will let you know about it.

ROUTINE MAINTENANCE

Oil Level

Oil level should be checked frequently. To check the oil level, raise the hood and position the hood support rod. Pull the oil dipstick from the engine and wipe it clean. Insert the dipstick in the engine until it is fully seated in the dipstick tube, then remove it and check the reading. On 1600 cubic centimer (cc) engines, the oil on the dipstick should be between the "Min" and "Max" marks, and on 2000 cc and 2300 cc engines, the oil on the dipstick should be between the "Add 1" and "safe" marks. If the oil is between these marks it is OK. Do not overfill the engine. Allow the engine to sit for five minutes before checking the oil level if it has been running.

Coolant Level

Check the coolant level in the radiator every couple of weeks while the engine is cold. With the engine cold, the coolant level should be about two inches (2 in.) below the filler neck on the radiator. This allows for coolant expansion when the engine warms. If only a small amount of coolant is needed, plain water can be added without fear of greatly diluting your antifreeze. Avoid removing the radiator cap when the engine is warm, as this will only allow the coolant in the radiator to spill out onto the pavement. If the engine is overheated, you run the risk of seriously burning yourself by removing the radiator cap. See the cooling system section of chapter three to learn how to deal with overheating cooling systems.

To check the coolant level, press downward on the radiator cap and, at the same time, turn it to the left.

Battery Fluid

The electrolyte level in the battery should be checked every few weeks. Remove the battery caps and check to see if the fluid level in the battery is up to the split rings in the bottom of the filler wells. If it is not, you can top it off with plain water unless you live in an area known to have hard water. If you do live in one of these areas, you should use distilled water. Fill the battery only to the split rings in the bottom of the filler wells. If you overfill the battery, the electrolyte will run out onto the pave-

1600 cc dipstick

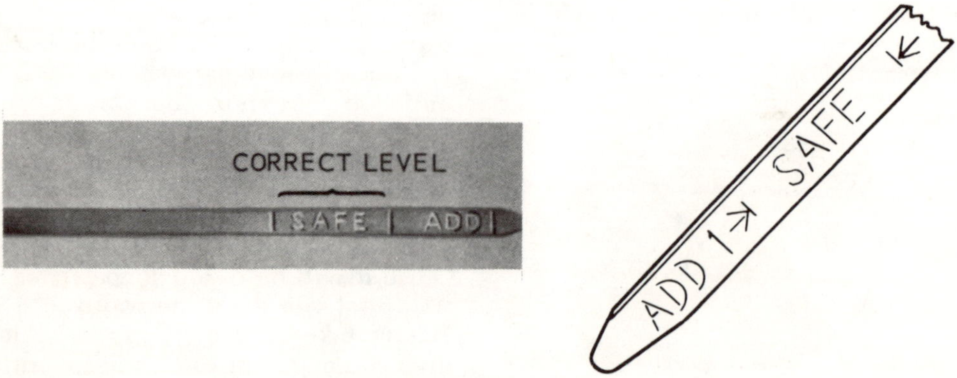

2000, 2300, 2800 cc dipstick

Checking the battery level

ment and you will be left with a battery full of plain water. Never light a match or use an open flame near the top of the battery, as the battery gives off *highly explosive* hydrogen gas.

Automatic Transmission Fluid Level

Check the automatic transmission fluid level about once a month. To check the fluid, the engine must be warmed up and idling in Park. Pull the dipstick out, wipe it off, and reinsert it into the filler tube. If the level is between the safe marks on the dipstick, do not add any fluid. It is possible to harm the transmission by overfilling it. If the transmission should need fluid, use only *Type F* automatic transmission fluid. Never use Type A or Dexron automatic transmission fluid in a Ford car.

NOTE: *Some 1974–75 Pintos equipped with the C3 automatic transmission have had slippage problems and the shifting may be softer than normal. These difficulties may be caused by too much fluid in the unit. If you suspect this, check the fluid level. If the level is correct, have the transmission checked by a dealer.*

Checking automatic transmission fluid

Tire Pressures

Check the air pressure in your tires about once a month while the tires are cold. If you check tire pressure when the tires are warm, you wil get a false reading, since tire pressure increases with tire temperature. A decal located on your glove box door will tell you the proper tire pressure for your car. A tire pressure gauge must be used to check tire pressure, as the low profile tires on your car may look low on air when they are not.

While you are checking the air pressure in your tires, check the tread wear on the tires. The tread of the tire should be wearing evenly across the tire. Excessive wear in the center of the tread indicates overinflation. Excessive wear on the outer corners of the tread indicates underinflation. An irregular wear pattern is usually an indication of improper front end alignment or improper wheel balance. A front end that is out of alignment will usually pull the car to one side of a flat road if the steering wheel is released while driving the car. Improper wheel balance is usually accompanied by vibration at high speed. When the front wheels are out of balance they will usually produce vibration in the steering wheel, while rear wheels that are out of balance usually produce vibration in the floor pan of the car. In any case, the source of the irregular tire wear must be found and corrected, or the tires will be ruined. A common occurrence is that the front end becomes misaligned, causing irregular tire wear. The irregular tire wear causes the wheels to become unbalanced.

To prolong tire life, the tires should be rotated on the car every 5,000 miles. An obvious exception to this is snow tires. If you equip your car with studded snow

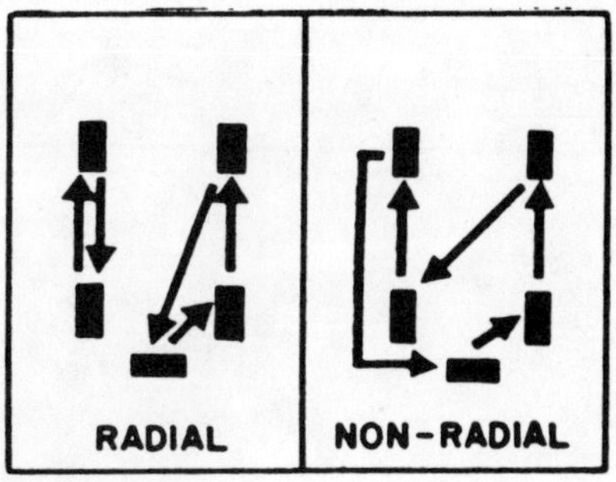

Tire rotation pattern

Capacities

Year	ENGINE No. Cyl Displacement (Cu In.)	Engine ■ Crankcase Add 1 Qt For New Filter	TRANSMISSION Pts To Refill After Draining: Manual 3-Speed	Manual 4-Speed	Automatic	Drive Axle (pts)	Gasoline Tank (gals)	COOLING SYSTEM (qts) With Heater	With A/C
'71–'72	4-98 (1600 cc)	3	—	2.5	—	2.2	11①	7.75	—
	4-122 (2000 cc)	4	—	2.5	16	2.2	11①	8.50	8.50
'73	4-98.6 (1600 cc)	3	—	2.8	—	2.2	11①	7.80	—
	4-122 (2000 cc)	4	—	2.8	16	2.2	11①	8.50	8.50
'74	4-122 (2000 cc)	4	—	2.8	16	3.0	11①	8.50	8.50
	4-140 (2300 cc)	4③	—	2.8	16	3.0	11①	8.80	9.29
'75–'77	4-140 (2300 cc)	4③	—	2.8	16②	2.2④	13⑤	8.7	9.0
	6-170.8 (2800 cc)	4.5③	—	2.8	16②	2.2④	13⑤	12.5	13.2

① Wagon—12 gals
② 14 with C4
③ Add only ½ qt for new filter
④ 4–4½ for 8 in. axle
⑤ 14 for station wagon

tires, always install them on the same side of the car. If a studded snow tire that was used on the left rear wheel one year is installed on the right rear wheel the next year, the result will be studs pulling out of the tire.

If your car is equipped with radial ply tires never mix with belted, and/or bias ply tires. It is also important that radials be periodically rotated from the front to the rear. No other method should be used.

Power Steering Reservoir Fluid

At the recommended intervals in the maintenance schedule, the fluid level in the power steering reservoir (if so equipped) should be checked. Run the engine until the fluid reaches operating temperature. Turn the steering wheel from lock-to-lock several times to relieve the system of any trapped air. Turn off the engine. Check the level on the reservoir dipstick. The level must be maintained on the crosshatch pattern between the Full mark and the end of the dipstick. Top up as necessary with ATF Type F.

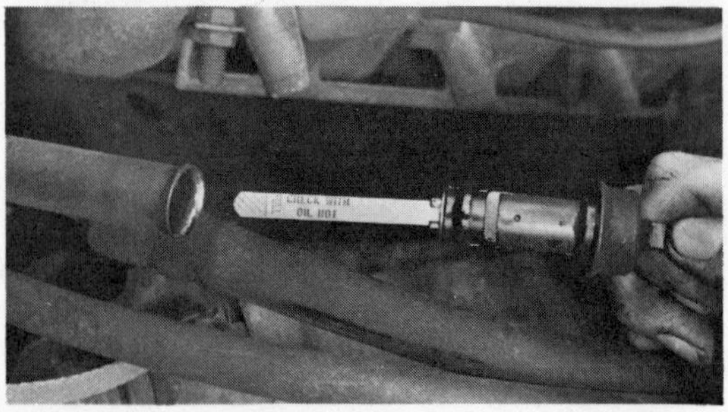

Checking the power steering fluid level

UNDER-HOOD MAINTENANCE

Master Cylinder Fluid Level

Push the master cylinder cap retaining clip off the left side of the cap with a screwdriver. Remove the cap and gasket.

Checking the brake fluid level

The brake fluid in the master cylinder should be within ¼ in. of the top of the master cylinder. If it is not, top it off with a high-quality, extra heavy-duty brake fluid. If the master cylinder is repeatedly low on fluid, there is a leak in the brake system. See chapter nine.

Crankcase Filter

Remove the top from the air cleaner. Remove the crankcase filter from the small pocket on the side of the bottom half of the air cleaner. Install a new filter in the pocket. Install the top of the air cleaner, aligning the arrows on 1600 cc air cleaners.

Removing the crankcase filter

Crankcase Oil Filler Breather Cap—

1600 cc Engine Only

Remove the oil filler cap from the front of the valve cover and disconnect the hose from the cap. Immerse the cap in a pan filled with mineral spirits or other suitable solvent. Agitate the cap in the pan, then remove and shake it dry. Connect the hose to the cap and install it on the valve cover.

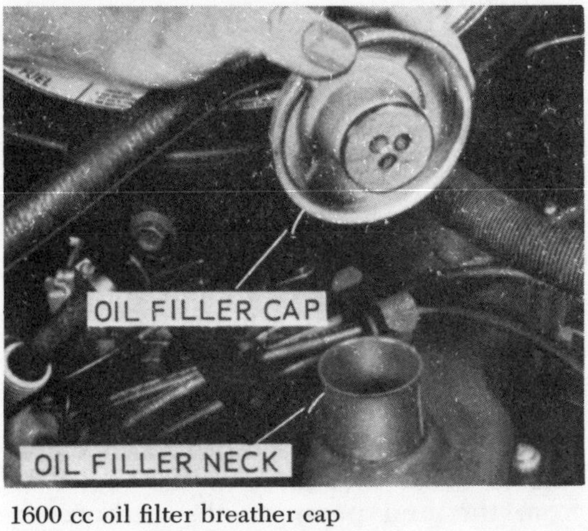

1600 cc oil filter breather cap

Oil and Oil Filter Change

Run the engine until it has reached normal operating temperature. Stop the engine. Place a drain pan under the engine oil pan and remove the oil drain plug. When all the oil has drained out of the engine, install the drain plug and tighten it to 15–20 ft lbs of torque. Do not overtighten the drain plug. Place the drain pan under the oil filter. An oil filter removal tool bought from your local auto parts store can be used to remove the oil filter. These tools are very inexpensive and make the job much easier. It will be necessary to install a rubber insert into the tool to use it on 1600 cc engines since their oil filters are smaller than normal. When the filter has been removed, wipe the oil filter mounting flange, on the engine, clean. Apply a film of engine oil to the gasket on the top of the new oil filter. Install the filter on the engine and tighten it until the gasket contacts the filter flange on the engine. Tighten the filter by hand an additional ½ turn. Do not overtighten the filter or use the filter tool to tighten it as this could cause the filter to leak.

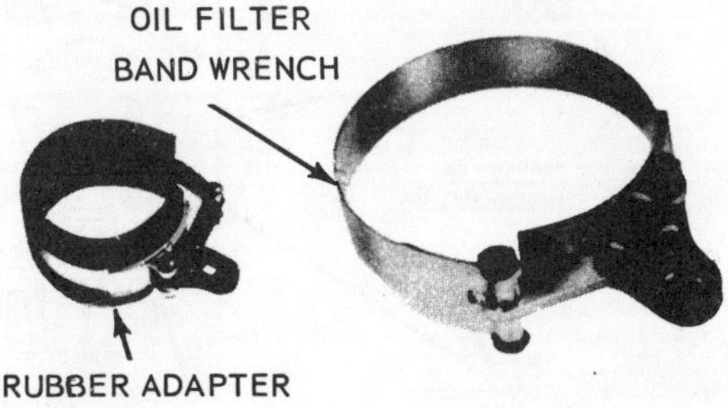

Oil filter removal tool

Consult the capacities chart at the end of this chapter for the correct amount of oil to put in the engine, then remove the oil filler cap and pour in the oil. Start the engine and allow it to idle. The oil pressure light on the instrument panel should go out after the engine has been running for a couple of seconds. Check the drain plug and the oil filter for leaks.

Carburetor Air Filter Replacement

Remove the top of the air cleaner from the air cleaner assembly by unsnapping the retainer clips and removing the wing nuts on 2000 cc engines. Discard the old air filter and wipe out the inside of the

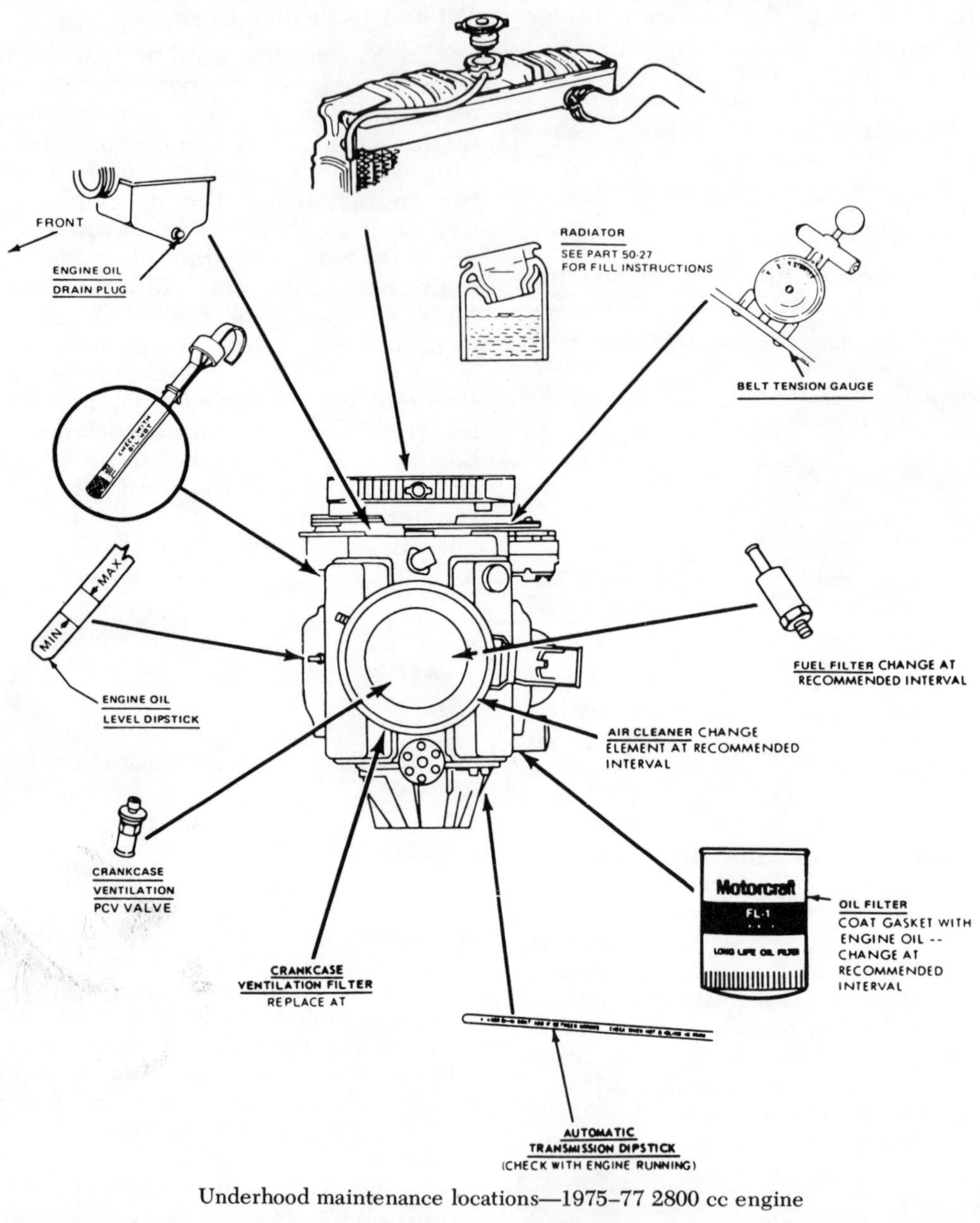

Underhood maintenance locations—1975–77 2800 cc engine

air cleaner and housing and the bottom of the air cleaner top. Install a new air filter in the air cleaner housing and install the top on the air cleaner. Some 2000 cc engines are equipped with a smaller inner filter, in addition to the regular air filter. This inner filter does not require service.

Fuel Filter Replacement

1600 cc Engines

On the 1600 cc engines, the fuel filter is in the fuel line located below the battery. Access to the filter can be made easier by removing the battery, however it is not necessary.

Locate the fuel filter in the fuel line and loosen the screws in the filter clamps. Remove the fuel lines from the old filter and install the new filter in the lines. Make sure the arrow on the filter points toward the line to the carburetor. Tighten the filter clamps and install the battery.

2000 cc Engine—1971–73

Locate the fuel filter in the fuel line from the fuel pump to the carburetor. Squeeze the tabs on the fuel filter

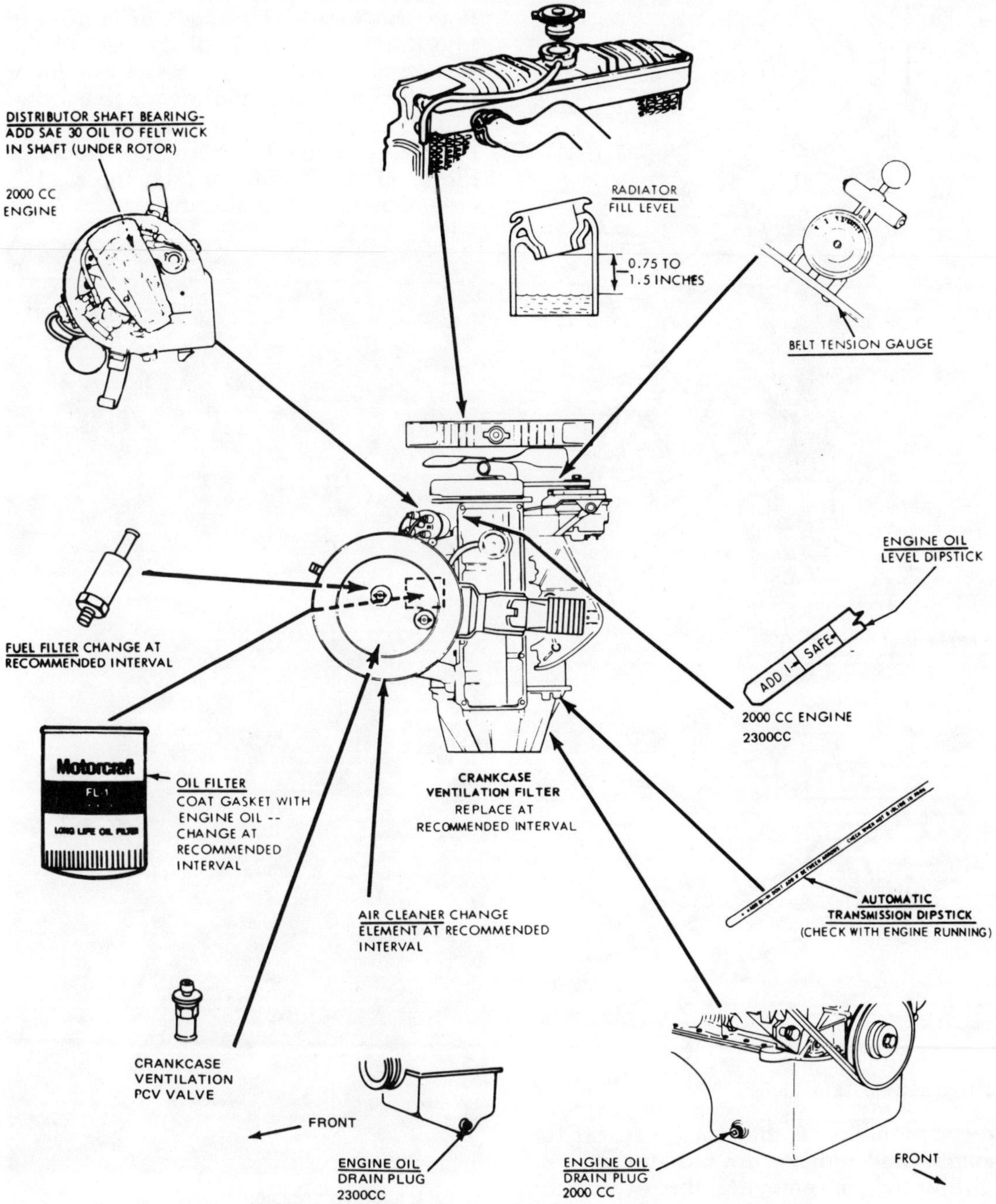

1974–77 2000 cc and 2300 cc, underhood maintenance locations

clamps together and move the clamps away from the filter. Remove the old filter from the fuel line and install a new one. Compress the tabs on the fuel filter clamps and position the clamps on the fuel lines near the filter.

1974–77 All Engines

Remove the air cleaner. Loosen the clamp securing the inlet hose to the fuel filter and unscrew the filter from the carburetor. Install a new filter and connect the fuel inlet hose and clamp. Tighten the filter and crimp the clamp securely. Start the engine and check for fuel leaks.

Flushing Cooling System

If the coolant is extremely dirty, add a good flushing additive to the radiator and run the engine the amount of time

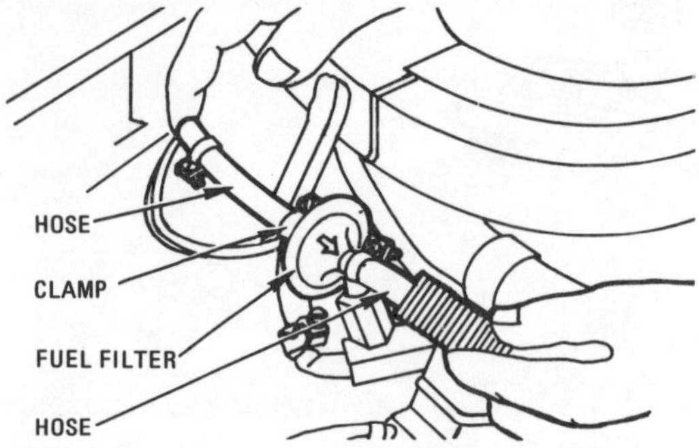

1600 cc fuel filter

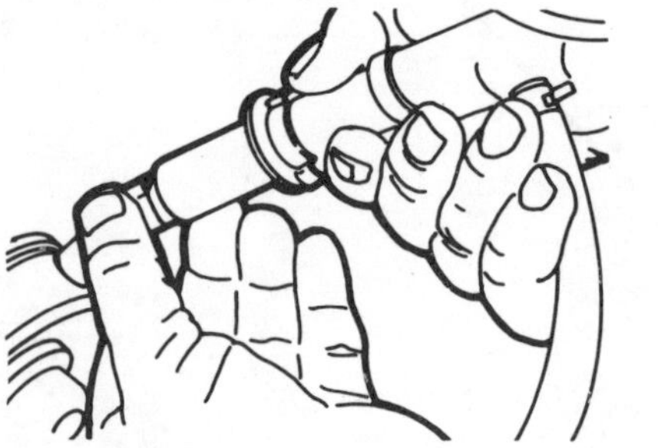
2000 cc fuel filter

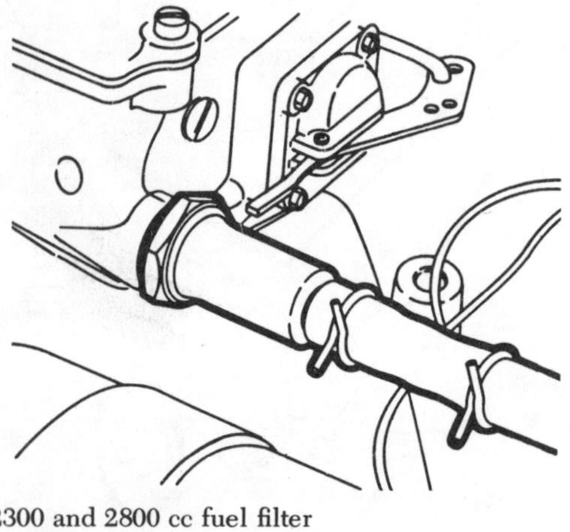
2300 and 2800 cc fuel filter

recommended on the can. Turn off the engine and remove the radiator cap. Be careful when removing the cap if the engine is hot. Open the petcock in the bottom of the radiator by turning its ears in a counterclockwise direction. When all the coolant has drained out of the system, insert a garden hose into the radiator cap opening. Turn the water on in the hose and start the engine. Allow the engine and the hose to run until the water coming out of the radiator is clean. Turn off the engine and remove the hose. Allow the water to drain out of the system, then close the radiator petcock. Pour the required amount of antifreeze into the radiator and fill the rest of the system with water. Run the engine for at least five minutes to allow air to escape. Fill the radiator to 1 in. below the filler neck and turn off the engine. Recheck the level in the radiator after the car has been driven a short distance.

Radiator petcock

Checking fan belt tension

Drive Belt Inspection and Adjustment

Inspection

Inspect all drive belts for excessive wear, cracks, glazed condition, noise, fraying or broken cords.

1. Press firmly on the belt approximately at the middle of the free span.
2. Belt deflection for all belts with a free span of less than 12 inches should be between ⅛ inch and ¼ inch.

Adjusting the fan belt

3. Belt deflection for all belts with a free span greater than 12 inches should be between ⅛ inch and ½ inch.

ADJUSTMENTS

Power Steering—2800 cc

1. Loosen the three bolts in the three elongated adjusting slots.
2. Turn the adjusting nut until the belt tension is 110 lbs, adjust a new belt (one run less than 10 minutes) to 140 lbs. If a tension gauge is not available press downward at the middle of the free span and the deflection should be approximately ¼ inch.

Thermactor (Air Pump)

1. Loosen the bolt in the slot in the bracket.
2. Move the thermactor out until the belt tension is 110 lbs, adjust a new belt (one run less than 10 minutes) to 140 lbs. If a tension gauge is not available press downward at the middle of the free span and the deflection should be approximately ¼ inch.

Alternator—All Engines

Belt tension adjustment is very critical. A belt that is too tight will cause premature bearing wear. A belt that is too loose will slip and stop the alternator from producing its full output. Therefore, it is recommended that a belt tension gauge is used for this adjustment.

NOTE: *The thermactor belt also drives the alternator on V6 models.*

1. Loosen the alternator attaching bolts.
2. Attach a belt tension gauge to the alternator belt.
3. Position a pry bar against the front of the alternator housing.

CAUTION: *Do not apply pressure to any other part of the alternator.*

Tighten the belt to 110 lbs. Adjust a new belt (one run less than 10 minutes) to 140 lbs. If a belt tension gauge is not available, an approximate adjustment can be made by tightening the alternator belt until it has about ¼ in. free-play when pushed downward at a center point between the alternator pulley and the water-pump pulley.

5. Tighten the alternator mounting bolts.

Thermactor (air pump) adjusting bolt

A/C Compressor—All Engines

The air conditioner drive belt is adjusted by adjusting an idler pulley.

1. Reach down with a ⁹⁄₁₆ inch open end wrench and loosen the lock bolt just enough to be able to move the pulley.
2. Insert a pry bar between the two pulleys. To increase tension on the belt, push upward on the handle. This will move the idler pulley down and away from the engine.
3. Tighten the belt to 110 lbs, adjust a new belt (one run less than 10 minutes) to 140 lbs. If a belt tension gauge is not available an approximate adjustment can be made by tightening the A/C belt until it has about ¼ in. free-play when pushed downward at a center point between the two pulleys.
4. Tighten the lock bolt and pivot bolt.

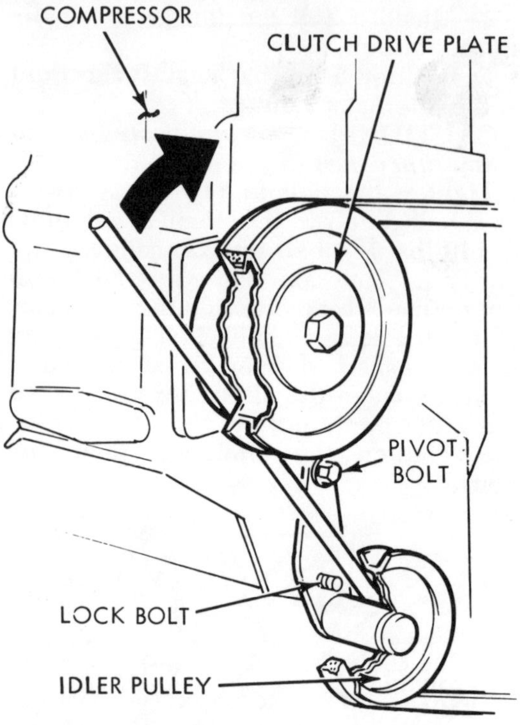

A/C compressor adjustment

UNDER-CAR MAINTENANCE

Manual Transmission and Rear Axle Fluid Level Check

Working under the car, use a ⅜ in. ratchet wrench without a socket to remove the plug from the transmission or rear axle. The location of the plug and the proper lubricant level are shown in the accompanying illustration. To check the fluid level, straighten out a cotter pin, then bend one end of the cotter pin 90° about 2 in. from the end. Insert the bent end into the filler plug hole and use it as a dipstick. If lubricant is needed, consult the "Lubricant Specifications" chart in this chapter. Use a syringe to add fluid as required.

Lock Cylinder Lubrication

Partially insert the key into the lock and apply a small amount of aerosol lock lubricant into the lock cylinder. Insert the key the rest of the way into the lock and turn it several times to work the lubricant into the cylinder.

Hinge and Latch Lubrication

Apply white grease on a brush to the hood, door, and trunk lid or third door hinges and latches.

Front Suspension Ball Joint Lubrication

Raise the front of the car and support it with safety stands. If the car has been exposed to a temperature of 20 degrees Fahrenheit (20°F) or less, it must be parked in a heated garage until the ball joints will accept lubricant. Wipe all dirt from the top of the upper ball joints and the bottom of the lower ball joints. Using a 3/16 in. wrench, remove the grease plugs from the top of the upper ball joints and the bottom of the lower ball joints. Install grease fittings in these locations and, using a hand-operated, low-pressure grease gun, pump grease into the ball joints until the rubber seal on the joints can be seen or felt to swell. *Do not fill the joints until grease runs out of the seals as you will destroy the weather-tight seal.* Remove the grease fittings and reinstall the grease plugs. Do not leave the grease fittings in the ball joints as they will allow moisture to enter the ball joints, while the plugs will not.

Pushing, Towing, and Jump-Starting

PUSHING

Pintos equipped with a standard transmission can be push-started, although more than one car has received dented fenders and bumpers from this operation. To push start the car, turn the ignition switch on, depress the clutch pedal, put the transmission selector lever in third gear, and partially depress the gas pedal. As the car gains speed while being pushed, release the clutch pedal.

Pintos equipped with an automatic transmission cannot be push-started no matter how far or how fast they are pushed.

TOWING

If the transmission and rear axle are known to be OK, the vehicle can be towed with the rear wheels on the ground for distances under 15 miles at speeds less than 30 mph. If the transmission or rear is known to be damaged, or if the car is to be towed over 15 miles or over 30 mph, the car must be towed with

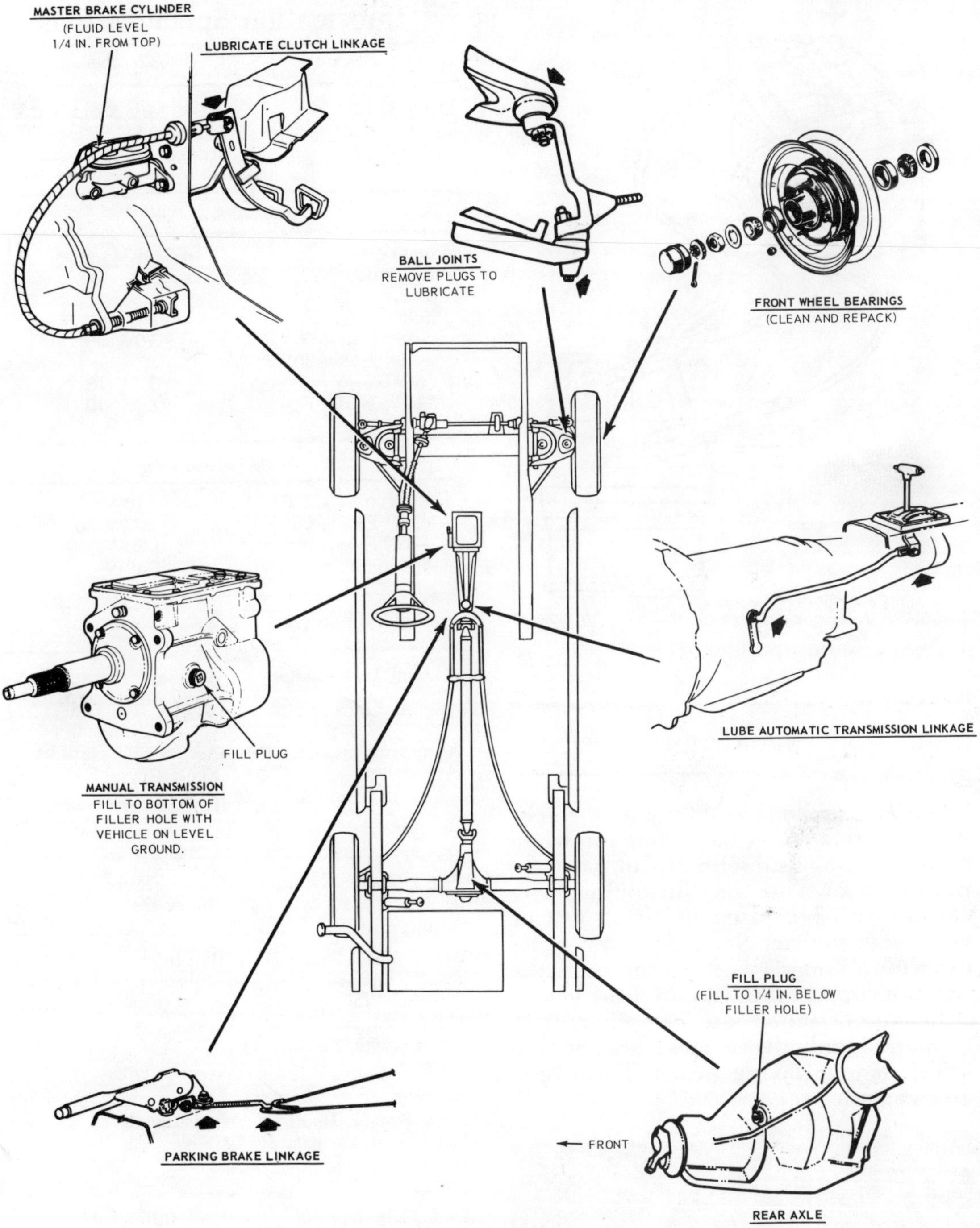

Chassis lubrication points

the rear wheels raised and the steering wheel locked so that the front wheels are in the straight-ahead position.

JUMP-STARTING

All cars can be jump-started from another car as long as the positive post on one battery is hooked to the positive post on the other battery, and likewise, negative to negative. This holds true even if the other car is positive ground (yours is negative ground). The positive battery terminal on your Pinto is the one closest to the front of the car.

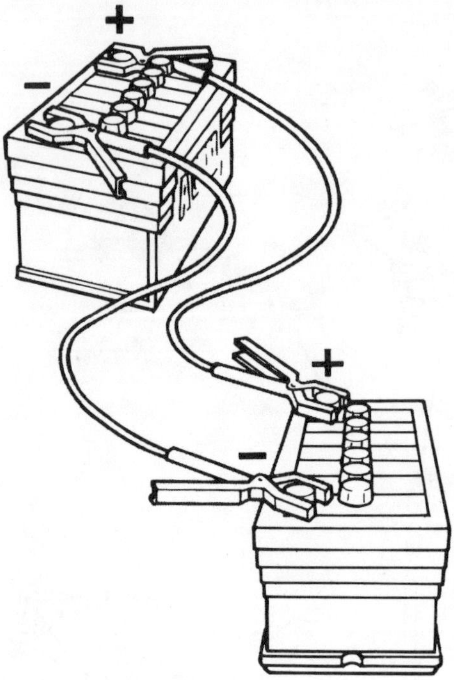

Connecting jumper cables

Jacking

The car can be jacked up with the scissors jack that came with your car when the jack is engaged with one of the body notches shown in the illustration. The car can also be raised by using a floor jack under the car. Never try to raise the car with a bumper jack, as the bumpers will not support the weight of the car.

Never get under the car when it is supported only by a jack; always use safety stands. Having a car fall on you is an awful way to go.

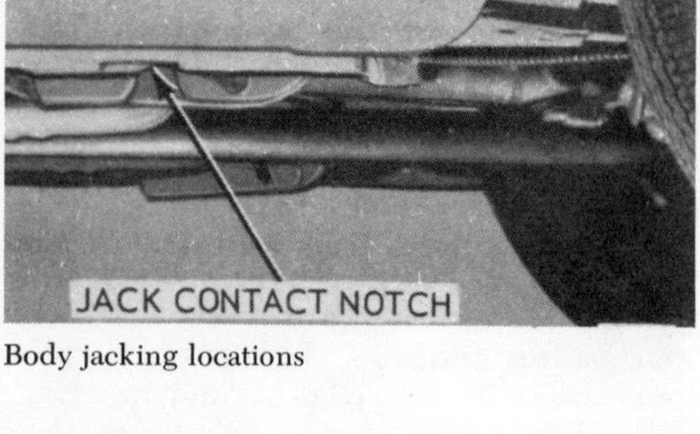

Body jacking locations

Lubrication Specifications

Item	*Type of Lubricant*
Motor Oil	6000 Mile Motor Oil (MS or SE Sequence tested)
Multiviscosity Oils	
When outside temperature is consistently	Use SAE Viscosity Number
Below +32° F	5W-30 *
−10° F to +90° F	10W-30
−10° F to +90° F (or above)	10W-40
Above +10° F	20W-40
Single Viscosity Oils	
10° F to +32° F	10W
+10° F to +60° F	20W-20
+32° F to +90° F	30W
Above 60° F	40W
Engine Oil Filter	6000 mile type
Manual Transmission	Standard Transmission Fluid—SAE 90
Automatic Transmission	Automatic Transmission Fluid—Type F
Rear Axle	Hypoid Gear Lube
Brake Master Cylinder	Brake Fluid Extra Heavy Duty
Front Wheel Bearings, Front Suspension, Steering Linkage, Ball Joints, and Transmission Shift Linkage	Ball Joint and Multipurpose Lube
Body Hinges, Hood Latch, and Auxiliary Catch	Polyethylene Grease
Lock Cylinders	Lock Lubricant
Steering Gear	Hypoid Gear Lube SAE 90
Cooling System Antifreeze	Ethylene Glycol Antifreeze/Coolant

* Where sustained driving and/or high-speed operation above 60 mph is anticipated, use the next heavier grade.

Maintenance Schedule

	Service Interval Number of months or thousands of miles, whichever comes first								
Maintenance Operation	*6*	*12*	*18*	*24*	*30*	*36*	*42*	*48*	*Sec Chapter Number*
UNDER HOOD									
Brake master cylinder fluid level—Check and add fluid if required	X	X	X	X	X	X	X	X	1
Transmission fluid level (automatic)—Check and add fluid if required	X	X	X	X	X	X	X	X	1
Carburetor idle speed and fuel mixture—Check and adjust	X	X	X	X	X	X	X	X	2
Deceleration valve—Check and adjust	X								4
Crankcase filter (in air cleaner)—Replace	X	X	X	X	X	X	X	X	1
Crankcase oil filter breather cap—Clean	X	X	X	X	X	X	X	X	1
Motor oil and oil filter—Change	X	X	X	X	X	X	X	X	1
Adjust valve clearance									
1600 cc (1.6 liter)	X	X	X		X	X	X		2
2000, 2800 cc (2.0, 2.8 liter)		X		X		X		X	2
Manifold exhaust bolts—Check torque	X								3
Manifold intake bolts—Check torque		X		X		X		X	3
Cooling system hoses—Inspect for deterioration, leaks, and loose hose clamps. Repair and/or replace as necessary		X		X		X		X	3
Carburetor air cleaner filter—Replace		X		X		X		X	1
Crankcase emission system—Clean hoses, tubes, and fittings. Replace PCV valve		X		X		X		X	4
Choke plate and linkage—Inspect and, if sticking, clean or correct as required		X		X		X		X	4
Fuel system filter—Replace and check fuel line connections for leaks		X		X		X		X	1
Drive belts—Check for tension and wear. Adjust as required		X		X		X		X	1
Ignition wiring (secondary)—Clean and inspect for damage. Replace as required		X		X		X		X	2
Spark plugs—Inspect, clean, adjust, and test. Replace as required		X		X		X		X	2
Distributor points—Check and adjust, or replace as required		X		X		X		X	2
Ignition timing—Check and adjust initial timing, mechanical and vacuum advances		X		X		X		X	2

Maintenance Schedule (cont.)

Maintenance Operation	*Service Interval Number of months or thousands of miles, whichever comes first* 6	12	18	24	30	36	42	48	*Sec Chapter Number*
UNDER HOOD									
Spark delay valve (if so equipped)—Replace		X		X		X		X	4
Fuel evaporation control canister—Replace				X				X	4
Electronic spark control system (if so equipped)—Check operation		X		X		X		X	4
Cooling system—Drain, flush, and replace coolant	Every 24 Months								1
Lubricate and check exhaust control valve		X		X		X			4
Check Thermactor system		X		X		X			4
Check and adjust throttle solenoid "off" speed	X								4
Check air cleaner temperature control and delay valve		X		X		X			4
Check EGR system (using leaded gas)—(if you are using unleaded gas, there is no scheduled maintenance required)		X		X		X		X	4
OUTSIDE VEHICLE									
Front wheel bearing—Clean and repack					X				9
Brake lines and lining—Check					X				9
UNDER VEHICLE									
Transmission fluid level (manual)—Check and add fluid if required	X	X	X	X	X	X	X	X	1
Clutch pedal free-play—Check and adjust linkage if required	X	X	X	X	X	X	X	X	6
Automatic transmission bands—Severe service adjustment	X		X			X			6
Automatic transmission bands—Adjust		X							6
Steering linkage joints—Check for abnormal looseness or damaged seals		X		X		X		X	8
Rear axle fluid level—Check and add fluid if required	X	X	X	X	X	X	X	X	1
LUBRICATION									
Body lock cylinders (door, ignition, glove box)—Lube	X	X	X	X	X	X	X	X	1
Hood hinges, latch, and auxiliary catch—Lube	X	X	X	X	X	X	X	X	1
Front suspension ball joints—Lube						X			1

NOTE: *1975 and later intervals are as follows: 5-15-20-30-35-40-45-48. These figures indicate months or miles, whichever comes first.*

Chapter 2

Tune-Up and Troubleshooting

Tune-Up Procedures

This section gives specific procedures on how to tune-up your Pinto. It is intended to be as complete and as basic as possible. Later in this chapter, there is another, more generalized section for tune-ups. Those who are familiar with the steps involved in a tune-up may wish to skip the following procedures and use the generalized section. However, it is felt that nothing would be lost by first reading over this section. Perhaps the best procedure to follow would be to read both sections before starting your tune-up.

SPARK PLUGS

The job of the spark plug is to ignite the air/fuel mixture in the cylinder as the piston approaches the top of the compression stroke. The ignited mixture then expands and forces the piston down on the power stroke. This turns the crankshaft which then turns the remainder of the drive train. If the transmission is in gear and the brakes are not applied, the vehicle will move.

The average life of a spark plug is approximately 12,000 miles. This is, however, dependent on the mechanical condition of the engine, the type of fuel that is used, and the type of driving conditions under which the car is used. For

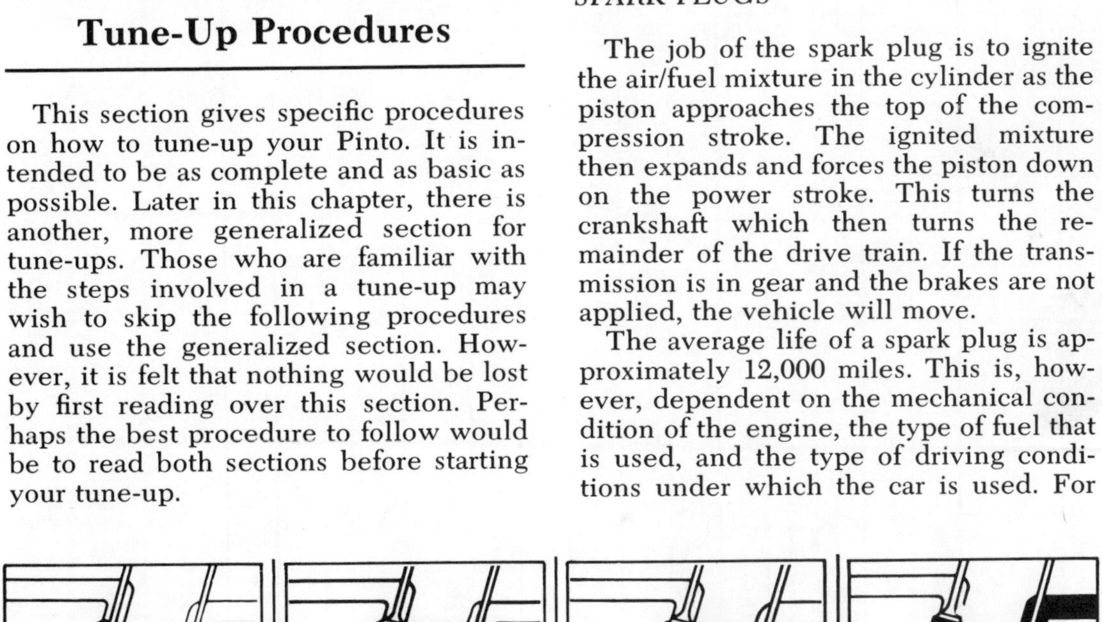

Four-stroke cycle of engine with spark plug ignition mixture in frame 3

Tune-up Specifications

When analyzing compression test results, look for uniformity among cylinders rather than specific pressures.

Year	ENGINE No. Cyl Displace-ment (cu in.)		SPARK PLUGS Type	SPARK PLUGS Gap (in.)	DISTRIBUTOR Point Dwell (deg)	DISTRIBUTOR Point Gap (in.)	IGNITION TIMING (deg) ▲ Man Trans	IGNITION TIMING (deg) ▲ • Auto Trans	VALVES Intake Opens ■ (deg)	Fuel Pump Pressure (psi)	IDLE SPEED (rpm) ▲ Man Trans	IDLE SPEED (rpm) ▲ Auto Trans
'71	4-79.6	(1600 cc)	AGR-22	.030	40	.025	12B	——	17	3½–5½	800/500③	——
	4-122	(2000 cc)	BRF-32①	②	40	.025	6B–10B	6B–10B	24	3½–5½	750/500③	650/500③
'72	4-97.6	(1600 cc)	AGR-22	.030	40	.025	12B	——	17	3½–5½	800/500③	——
	4-122	(2000 cc)	BRF-42	.034	40	.025	6B–10B	6B–10B	24	3½–5½	750/500③	650/500③
'73	4-97.6	(1600 cc)	AGR-32	.034	40	.025	12B	——	17	3½–5½	800/500③	——
	4-122	(2000 cc)	BRF-42	.034	40	.025	6B–10B	6B–10B	24	3½–5½	750/500③	650/500③
'74	4-122	(2000 cc)	BRF-42	.034	39	.025	6B④	6B④	24	3½–4½	750	650
	4-140	(2300 cc)	AGRF-52	.034	39	.025	6B	6B	22	3½–4½	750	650
'75	4-140	(2300 cc)	AGRF-52	.034	⑤	⑤	6B	6B (10B)	22	3½–5½	550	550
	6-170.8	(2800 cc)	AGR-42	.034	⑤	⑤	6B	10B (8B)	20	3½–5½	850	700
'76	4-140	(2300 cc)	AGRF-52	.034	⑤	⑤	6B @ 550 rpm	20B @ 550 rpm	22	5–7	850	750
	6-170.8	(2800 cc)	AGR-42	034	⑤	⑤	10B @ 700 rpm (8B @ 650 rpm)	12B (8B @ 700 rpm)⑥	20	3½–6	850	700
'77	4-140	(2300 cc)	AGRF-52	.034	⑤	⑤			22	5½–6½		
	6-170.8	(2800 cc)	AGR-42	.034	⑤	⑤			20	3½–5½		

▲ See text for procedure
■ All figures Before Top Dead Center
• Figures in parentheses are for California
NOTE: *Where figures listed on the engine tune-up sticker located under the hood disagree with those listed in the Tune-Up Specifications Chart, use engine sticker figures.*
① BRF-42 recommended service plug
② For BRF-32, set gap to .025 inches and for BRF-42, set gap to .034 inches
③ First figure is for idle speed with solenoid energized and automatic transmission in Drive, while the second figure is for idle speed with solenoid disconnected and automatic transmission in Neutral. Cars without a solenoid use lower figure.
④ 3B @ 650 rpm for California
⑤ Electronic ignition
⑥ With transmission in Drive
B Before Top Dead Center
—— Not applicable

some people, spark plugs will last 5,000 miles and for others, 15,000 or 20,000 miles.

Your Pinto came from the factory with resistor spark plugs. Resistor spark plugs help to limit the amount of radio frequency energy that is given off by the automotive ignition system. Radio frequency energy results in the annoying buzzing or clicking you sometimes hear on your radio or the jumping picture you see on your TV when a car pulls into the driveway in the middle of your favorite program.

The electrode end of the spark plug (the end that goes into the cylinder) is also a very good indicator of the mechanical condition of your engine. If a spark plug should foul and begin to misfire, you will have to find the condition that caused the plug to foul and correct it. It is also a good idea to occasionally give all the plugs the once-over to get an idea how the inside of your engine is doing. A small amount of deposit on a spark plug, after it has been in use for any period of time, should be considered normal. But a black liquid deposit on the plugs indicates oil fouling. You should schedule a few free Saturday afternoons to find the source of it. Because the combustion chamber is supposed to be sealed from the rest of the engine, oil on the spark plug means your engine is hemorrhaging. Don't worry, though, this only happens once in a while.

Removal

1. If the spark plug wires are not numbered as to their cylinder, place a piece of masking tape on each wire and number it.
2. Grasp each wire by the rubber boot at the end. Pull the wires from the spark plugs. If the boots stick to the plugs, remove them with a twisting motion. Do not attempt to remove the spark plug wires from the plugs by pulling on the wire itself as this will damage the spark plug wires.

Removing a spark plug wire boot

Removing a spark plug

3. Use a ⅝ in. socket to remove spark plugs with a type number prefix "A," i.e., AGR-32 or equivalent plug. If prefixed by "B," use a 13/16 in. socket.
4. If compressed air is available, blow off the area around each spark plug hole. Otherwise, use a rag or other suitable material and remove any loose particles from around each plug hole. In either case, make sure that foreign matter is not allowed to enter the cylinders.
5. Unscrew the plugs the rest of the way and remove them from the engine.

Inspection

Compare the condition of the spark plugs to the plugs shown in the accompanying illustration (see "Troubleshooting," subject 4.6). It should be remembered that any type of deposit will decrease the efficiency of the plug. If the plugs are not to be replaced, they should be thoroughly cleaned before installation. If the electrode ends of the plugs are not worn or damaged and if they are to be reused, wipe off the porcelain insulator on each plug and check for cracks or breaks. If either condition exists, the plug must be replaced.

If the plugs are judged reusable, have them cleaned on a plug cleaning machine (found in most service stations) or remove the deposits with a stiff wire brush.

Check the plug gap on both new and used plugs before installing them in the

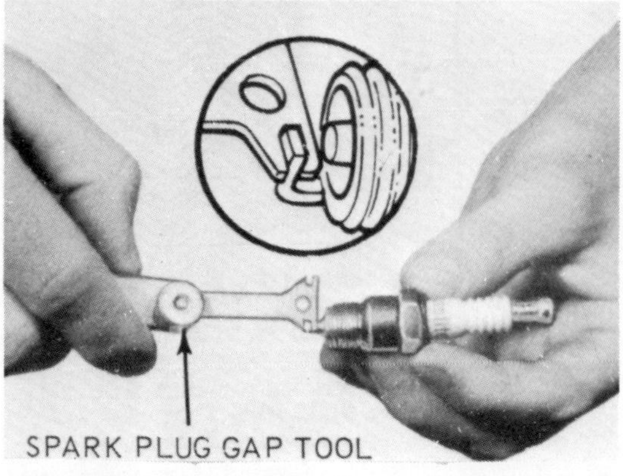

Adjusting spark plug gap

engine. The ground electrode must be parallel to the center electrode and the specified size wire gauge should pass through the opening with a slight drag. If the center or ground electrode has worn unevenly, level them off with a file. If the air gap between the two electrodes is not correct, open or close the ground electrode, with the proper tool, to bring it to specifications. Such a tool is usually provided with a gap gauge.

Installation

1. Insert the plugs into the engine and tighten them hand tight. Do not crossthread the plugs.
2. Tighten the plugs to the specified torque figure.
3. Install the spark plug wires on their respective plugs, making sure each wire is firmly connected.

BREAKER POINTS AND CONDENSER (1971–74 MODELS)

The points and condenser function as a circuit breaker for the primary circuit of the ignition system. The ignition coil must boost the 12 volts (V) of electrical pressure supplied to it by the battery to about 20,000 V in order to fire the spark plugs. To do this, the coil depends on the points and condenser for assistance.

The coil has a primary and a secondary circuit. When the ignition key is turned to the "on" position, the battery supplies voltage to the primary side of the coil which passes the voltage on to the points. The points are connected to ground to complete the primary circuit. As the cam in the distributor turns, the points open and the primary circuit collapses. The magnetic force in the primary circuit of the coil cuts through the secondary circuit and increases the voltage in the secondary circuit to a level that is sufficient to fire the spark plugs. When the points open, the electrical charge contained in the primary circuit jumps the gap that is created between the two open contacts of the points. If this electrical charge was not transferred elsewhere, the material on the contacts of the points would melt and that all-important gap between the contacts would start to change. If this gap is not maintained, the points will not break the primary circuit. If the primary circuit is not broken, the secondary circuit will not have enough voltage to fire the spark plugs. Enter the condenser.

The function of the condenser is to absorb the excessive voltage from the points when they open and thus prevent the points from becoming pitted or burned.

If you have ever wondered why it is necessary to tune-up your engine occasionally, consider the fact that the ignition system must complete the above cycle each time a spark plug fires. On a four-cylinder, four-cycle engine, two of the four plugs must fire once for every engine revolution. If the idle speed of your engine is 800 revolutions per minute (800 rpm), the breaker points open and close two times for each revolution. For every minute your engine idles, your points open and close 1,600 times ($2 \times 800 = 1{,}600$). And that is just at idle. What about at 65 mph? Lay that on somebody the next time they complain about having to replace their points after *only* 10,000 miles.

There are two ways to check breaker point gap: with a feeler gauge or with a dwell meter. Either way you set the points, you are adjusting the amount of time (in degrees of distributor rotation) that the points will remain open. If you adjust the points with a feeler gauge, you are setting the maximum amount the points will open when the rubbing block on the points is on a high point of the distributor cam. When you adjust the points with a dwell meter, you are measuring the number of degrees (of distributor cam rotation) that the points will remain closed before they start to open

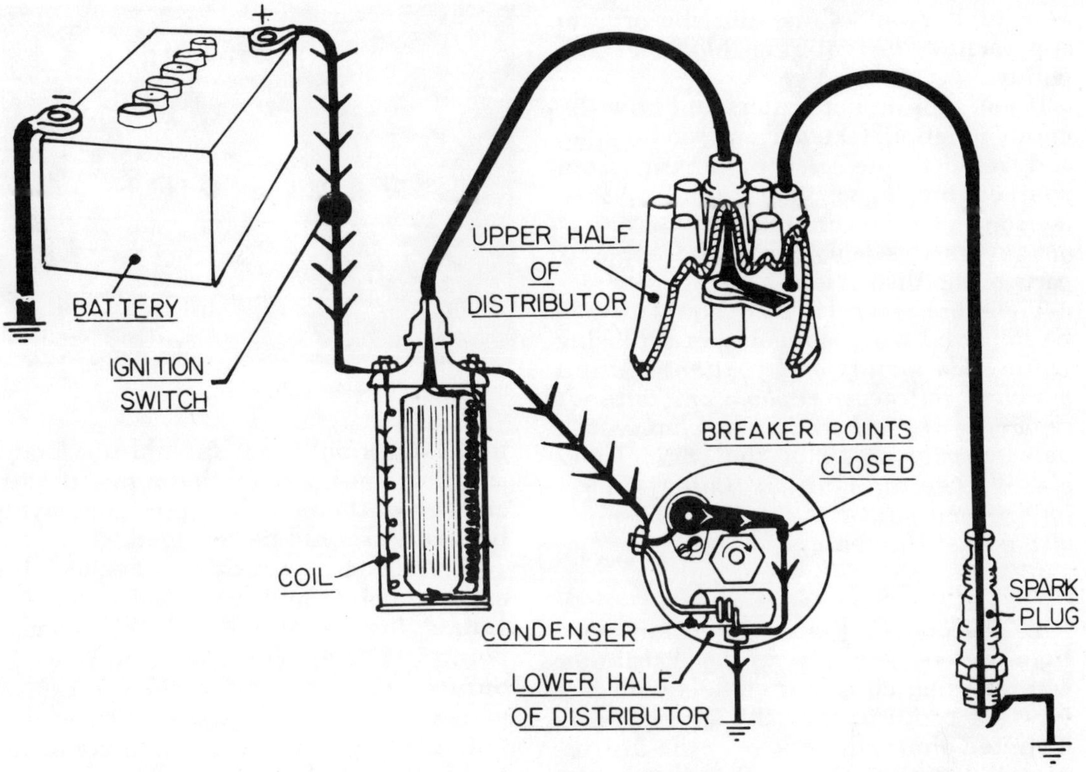

Primary side of ignition circuit is energized when breaker points are closed

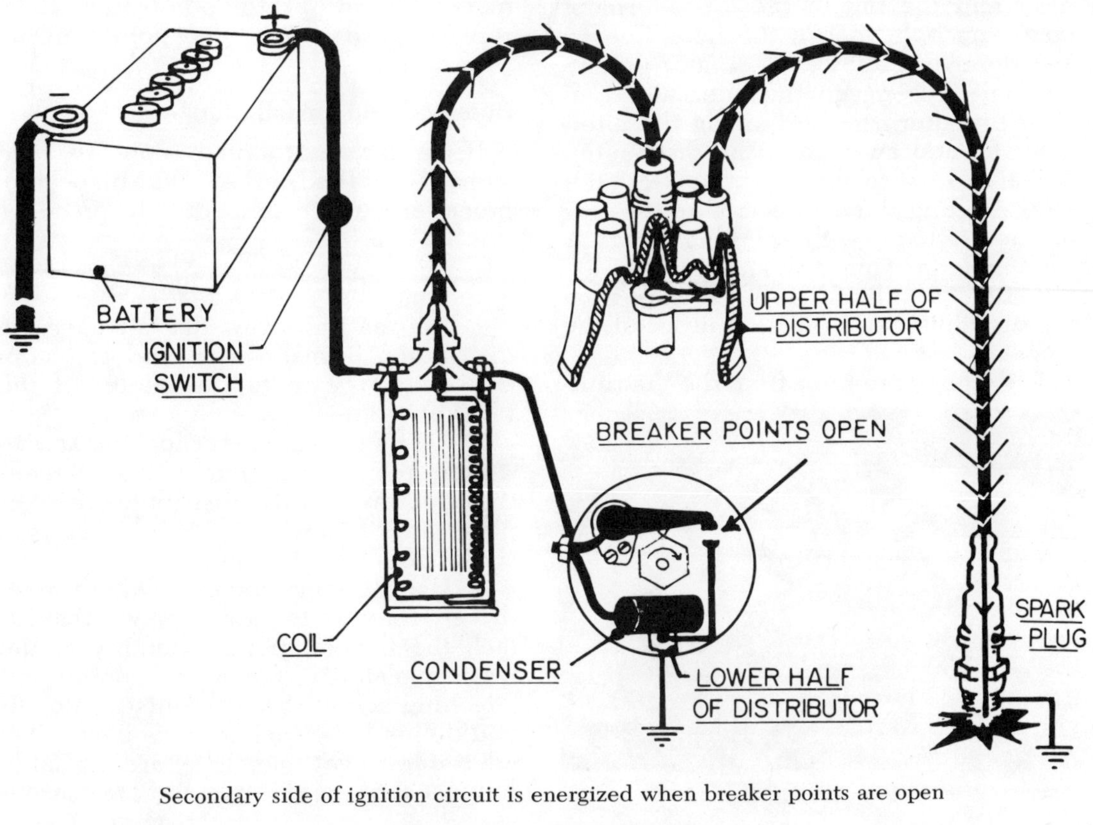

Secondary side of ignition circuit is energized when breaker points are open

as a high point of the distributor cam approaches the rubbing block of the points.

If you still do not understand how the points function, take a friend, go outside, and remove the distributor cap from your engine. Have your friend operate the starter (make sure the transmission is not in gear) as you look at the exposed parts of the distributor.

There are two rules that should always be followed when adjusting or replacing points. *The points and condenser are a matched set; never replace one without replacing the other. If you change the point gap or dwell of the engine, you also change the ignition timing. Therefore, if you adjust the points, you must also adjust the timing.*

Inspection

1. Disconnect the high-tension wire from the coil and unsnap the distributor cap retaining clips. On models with factory air conditioning, the alternator is mounted almost directly over the distributor. To gain access to the distributor, the alternator will have to be moved. Using the proper size wrench on the bolt head and the nut of the top alternator mounting bolt, loosen the bolt. Loosen and remove the lower alternator mounting bolt. Disengage the alternator belt from the alternator and swing the alternator up and away from the distributor. Be careful not to short out the alternator by contacting the connectors on the rear of the alternator with anything metallic. That includes your ring and watchband.

2. Remove the distributor cap from the distributor and position it out of the way.

3. Remove the rotor from the distributor shaft by pulling it straight up. Examine the condition of the rotor, if it is cracked or the metallic tip is excessively burned, it should be replaced.

Removing an outside mounted condenser

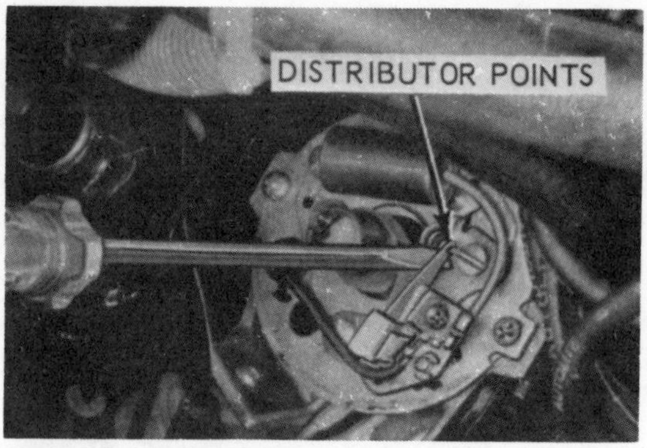

Inspecting breaker points

4. Place a screwdriver against the breaker points and pry them open. Examine the condition of the contact points. If they are excessively worn, burned, or pitted they should be replaced.

5. If the points are in good condition and not in need of replacement, proceed to the breaker point adjustment section which follows the breaker point replacement procedure. If the points need to be replaced, use the following point removal procedure.

Removal and Installation

If you have not already done so, read steps 1–3 of the breaker point inspection procedure which immediately precedes this section.

1600 CC AND 2300 CC

1. Loosen the screw that attaches the distributor primary wire and the condenser lead wire to the center of the breaker points.

2. Using a magnetic or locking screwdriver, remove the screw that attaches the condenser to the distributor breaker plate and remove the condenser and screw from the distributor.

3. Using a magnetic or locking screwdriver, remove the two screws that attach the breaker point assembly to the breaker plate and remove the points and attaching screws from the distributor. If you do not have such a screwdriver, it is advisable to get one. They are available in most auto parts stores and are reason-

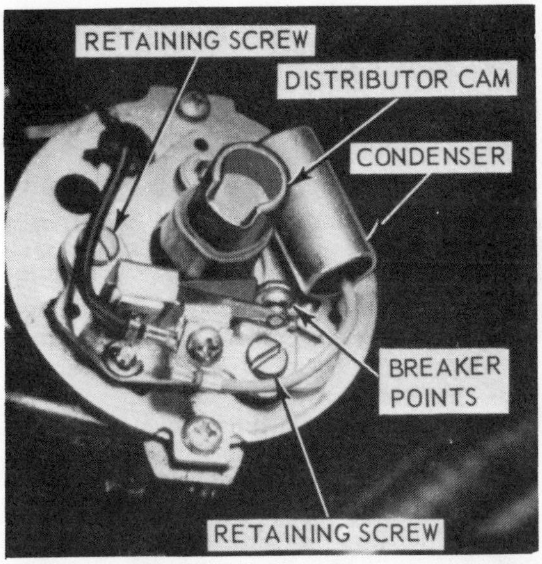

1600 cc and 2300 cc engine breaker points and condenser replacement

ably priced. The first time you are on your hands and knees trying to find one of those tiny screws from the distributor in the driveway, you will realize the value of this tool.

4. Wipe all dirt and grease from the distributor plate and cam with a lint-free rag.

5. Apply a small amount of special heat-resistant lube to the distributor cam. This lube is supplied with most breaker point kits. If you did not get this lube (usually in a small pull-apart capsule), buy some from a local auto parts store.

6. Position your new points on the breaker plate of the distributor, making sure the tab on the bottom of the points engages the indentation on the breaker plate. Install and tighten the breaker point attaching screws.

7. Position the distributor primary wire and the condenser lead wire on their attaching screw on the points and tighten the attaching screw. The connectors on the end of the wires must be parallel to each other and parallel to the ground when they are tightened. If this is not done, one of the connectors might contact the breaker plate and short out the primary side of the ignition. In most cases this will prevent the engine from starting.

8. Proceed to the breaker point adjustment section that follows.

2000 cc

1. Disconnect the condenser from the breaker points by pulling the breaker point wire from the condenser connector near the circumference of the distributor body.

2. Remove the breaker point attaching screw using a magnetic or locking screwdriver. If you do not have such a screwdriver it is advisable to get one. They are reasonably priced and available in most auto parts stores. The first time you have to remove the distributor from the engine to find the screw that fell inside it you will realize the value of this tool. If you are too frugal to purchase one, place something over the opening in the breaker plate and hope the screw doesn't get into the hole.

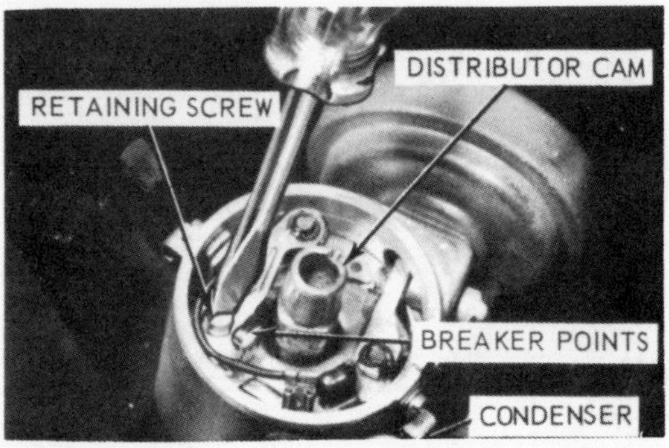

2000 cc engine breaker points and condenser replacement

3. Remove the breaker points from the distributor.

4. Remove the screw that attaches the condenser to the distributor body.

5. Grasp the condenser and wire and work the rubber grommet out of the distributor body.

6. Disconnect the ignition switch wire connector from the coil and disconnect the wire attached to the condenser from the coil.

7. Wipe all dirt and grease from the distributor plate and cam with a lint-free rag.

8. Apply a small amount of special heat-resistant lube to the distributor cam. This lube is included in most breaker point kits. If you did not get this lube (usually in a small pull-apart capsule), buy some from a local auto parts store.

9. Position the new condenser and

wire assembly on the side of the distributor and work the grommet into the distributor body.

10. Install the condenser attaching screw and position the end of the wire attached to the condenser on the post of the coil marked "dist."

11. Install the ignition switch wire on the coil post over the condenser wire.

12. If you have a locking screwdriver, position the breaker points in the distributor and install and tighten the attaching screw. If not, install the breaker point attaching screw in the slot in the points and install the points in the distributor. Do not allow the screw to fall into the hole in the breaker plate in the distributor. If the screw should fall down the hole, turn to chapter three, "Distributor Removal."

13. Firmly connect the breaker point wire to the condenser connector.

14. Proceed to the breaker point "Adjustment" section that follows.

Adjustment

WITH A FEELER GAUGE

1. If the two contact points of the breaker point assembly are not parallel, bend the stationary contact slightly to correct.

NOTE: *Bend only the bracket portion of the points, do not bend the other side.*

2. Turn the engine until the rubbing block on the points is on one of the four high points of the distributor cam. This can be accomplished either by having an assistant quickly turn the ignition switch to the "start" position and release it, or by placing the proper size wrench on the bolt in the center of the lower pulley on the front of the engine. If you choose the wrench on pulley method, turn the wrench *clockwise* (*to the right*). *Never turn the pulley counterclockwise on a 2000 cc engine as the camshaft drive belt could slip and alter the camshaft timing.*

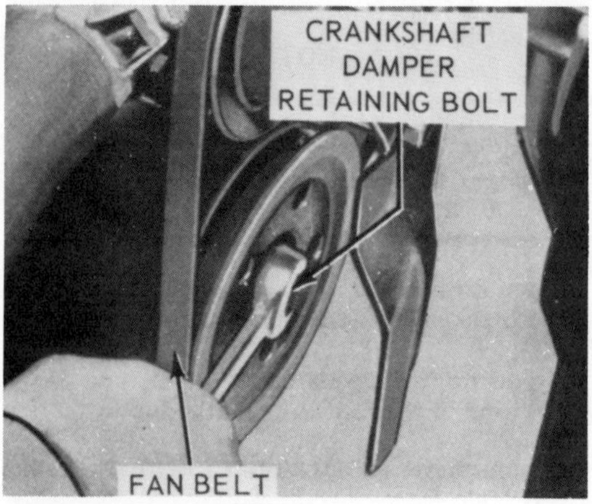

Turning crankshaft pulley

3. Insert the correct size feeler gauge between the open contacts of the points. To determine the correct feeler gauge size, see the point gap column on the "Tune-Up Specifications" chart in the front of this chapter. The gauge should fit between the contacts with a slight amount of drag. Always insert the gauge so that it is parallel with the contacts on the points.

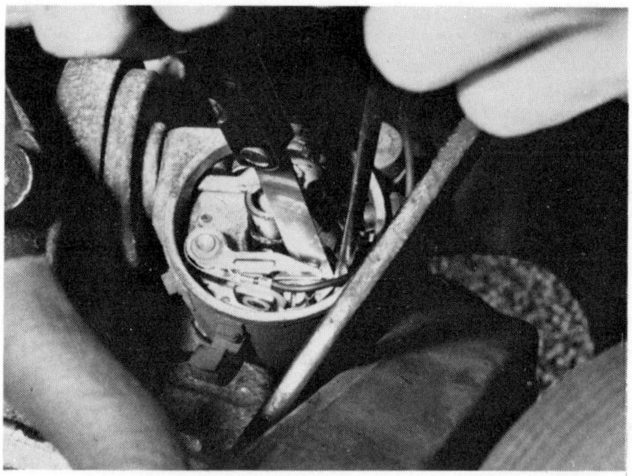
Adjusting the point gap

4. If the point gap is too large or too small, adjust as follows:

1600 cc, 2300cc—Slightly loosen the point attaching screws and insert a screwdriver in the notch in the breaker plate at the top of the points. Twist the

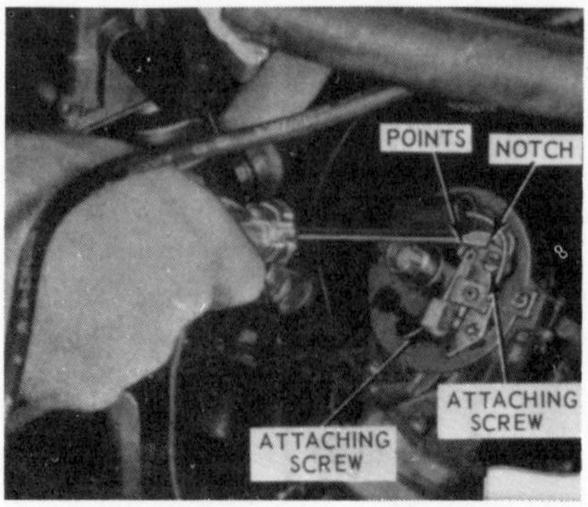

Adjusting point gap on the 1600 cc and 2300 cc engine

screwdriver to open or close the points as required. Tighten the breaker point attaching screws when the correct gap is obtained.

2000 cc—Slightly loosen the point attaching screw and insert a screwdriver blade between the boss on the breaker plate and the notch on the points. Twist the screwdriver to open or close the points as required. Tighten the breaker point attaching screw when the correct gap is obtained.

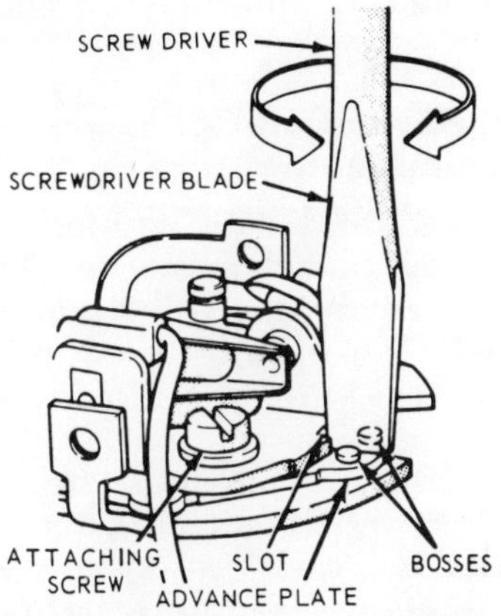

Adjusting point gap on the 2000 cc engine

5. Recheck the point gap to make sure it did not change when the breaker point attaching screws were tightened.

6. Push the distributor rotor onto the distributor shaft after aligning the tab inside the rotor with the notch on the shaft. Make sure the rotor is fully seated on the shaft.

7. Align the tab inside the base of the distributor cap with the notch in the lip of the distributor body opening. Install the cap on the distributor and make sure it is fully seated. Snap the distributor cap retaining clips into place on the side of the cap.

8. Install the coil high-tension wire. On models with air conditioning, after adjusting the ignition timing, install the alternator attaching bolts, install and adjust the air conditioner compressor belt, and tighten the attaching bolts on the alternator.

With a Dwell Meter

1. Adjust the points with a feeler gauge as described above.

2. Connect a dwell meter to the engine according to the manufacturer's instructions. One meter lead is connected to a metallic part of the vehicle to ground the meter. The other lead is connected to the distributor post marked "dist." To connect this lead, the ignition switch wire connector must be removed from the "dist" terminal, an adaptor installed and the ignition wire installed over the adaptor. If an adaptor is not available, a cotter pin may be substituted.

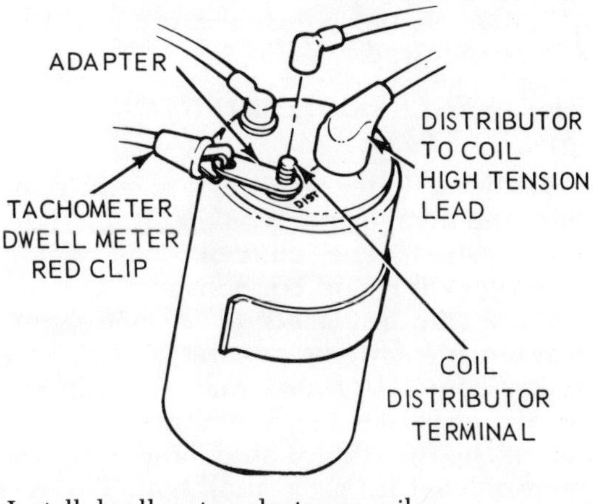

Install dwell meter adapter on coil

3. If the dwell meter has a set line on it, adjust the meter to zero the indicator.

4. Start the engine.

CAUTION: *When working on a vehicle with the engine running, the following precautions must be observed: Work only in a well-ventilated area. Be certain the transmission is in neutral and the parking brake firmly applied. Always keep your hands, clothing, and tools clear of the moving radiator fan.*

5. Observe the reading on the dwell meter. If your dwell meter does not have a scale for four-cylinder engines, multiply the eight-cylinder reading by two. If the reading is within the specified range, turn the engine "off" and disconnect the meter.

6. If the reading is above the specified range, the breaker point gap is too small. If the reading is below the specified range, the breaker point gap is too large. In either case, turn off the engine and close or open the point gap as required. Start the engine and recheck the dwell reading. When correct, turn off the engine and disconnect the meter.

7. Check and adjust the ignition timing as required.

BREAKERLESS DISTRIBUTOR (SOLID STATE)

1975 and later engines are equipped with the breakerless type electronic ignition system. The conventional contact breaker points and condenser in the distributor are replaced by a permanent magnet low-voltage generator. The generator consists of an armature with four or six gear-like teeth mounted on the top of the distributor shaft, and a permanent magnet inside a small coil. The coil is riveted in place to provide a preset air gap with the armature. The distributor base, cap, rotor and vacuum and centrifugal spark advance are about the same as the conventional system.

The distributor is wired to a solid state module in the engine compartment. Inside the module is an electronic circuit board which consists of inner connecting resistors, capacitors, transistors and diodes. The module senses a signal from the magnetic generator to perform the switching function of conventional points and it senses and controls dwell.

Unless a malfunction occurs, or the distributor is moved or replaced, the initial ignition timing remains constant. Because the low voltage coil in the distributor is riveted in position, the air gap adjustment with the gear tooth armature is not possible.

Module Test

If the electronic module is suspected of being defective, proceed as follows:

1. Without removing the existing module from the vehicle, unplug the connectors from the electronic module. Connect a known good module. The substitute module does not have to be fastened to the vehicle to operate properly.
2. Attempt to start the engine. If the engine starts and accelerates properly, proceed to step three. If the engine will still not start, the fault is in the wiring or other vehicle systems. Inspect and repair as necessary.
3. Reconnect the original module. Again attempt to start and run the engine. If the engine once again will not start, remove the original module and replace with a new one. If, however, the engine will now start and run on the original module, the module is not defective.
4. With the engine operating, check all connections in the primary wiring of the ignition system for such faults as poor wire crimp to terminal or improper engagement. The faculty connection will be observed when the engine misfires or stops. Correct as necessary. For more troubleshooting information, see Chapter 3.

Tachometer-to-Coil Connection—Electronic Ignition

The new solid state ignition coil connector allows a tachometer test lead with an alligator-type clip to be connected to the DEC (Distributor Electronic Control) terminal without removing the connector.

When engine rpm must be checked, install the tachometer alligator clip into the "TACH TEST" cavity as shown. If the coil connector must be removed, grasp the wires and pull horizontally until it disconnects from the terminals.

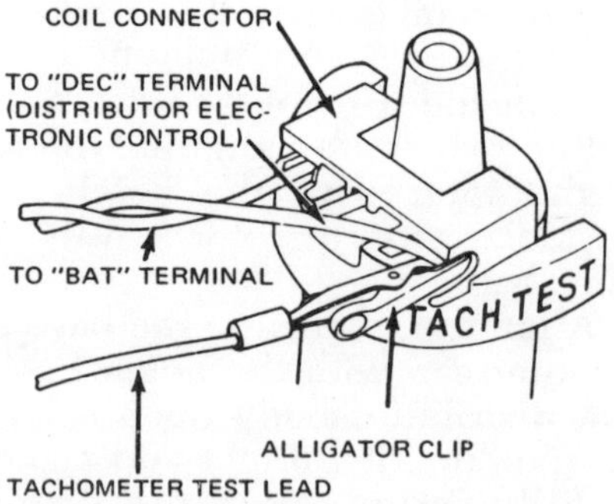

Attaching tachometer lead to coil connector

IGNITION TIMING

Ignition timing is the measurement in degrees of crankshaft rotation of the instant the spark plugs in the cylinders fire, in relation to the location of the piston, while the piston is on its compression stroke.

Ignition timing is adjusted by loosening the distributor locking device and turning the distributor in the engine.

Ideally, the air/fuel mixture in the cylinder will be ignited (by the spark plug)

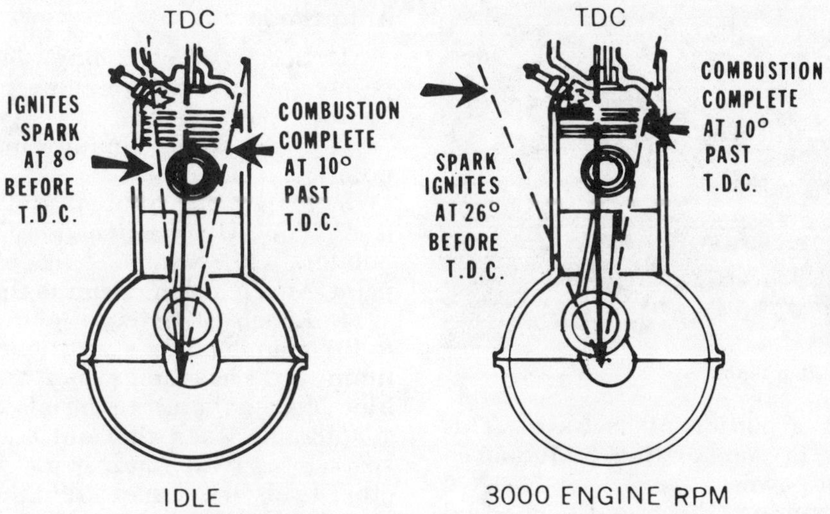

Ignition spark timing at idle and 3,000 rpm

and just beginning its rapid expansion as the piston passes top dead center (TDC) of the compression stroke. If this happens, the piston will be beginning the power stroke just as the compressed (by the movement of the piston) and ignited (by the spark plug) air/fuel mixture starts to expand. The expansion of the air/fuel mixture will then force the piston down on the power stroke and turn the crankshaft.

It takes a fraction of a second for the spark from the plug to completely ignite the mixture in the cylinder. Because of this, the spark plug must fire before the piston reaches TDC, if the mixture is to be completely ignited as the piston passes TDC. This measurement is given in degrees (of crankshaft rotation) *before* the piston reaches *top dead center* (BTDC). If the ignition timing setting for your engine is six degrees (6°) BTDC, this means that the spark plug must fire at a time when the piston for that cylinder is 6° before top dead center of its compression stroke. However, this only holds true while your engine is at idle speed.

As you accelerate from idle, the speed of your engine (rpm) increases. The increase in rpm means that the pistons are now traveling up and down much faster. Because of this, the spark plugs will have to fire even sooner if the mixture is to be completely ignited as the piston passes TDC. To accomplish this, the distributor incorporates means to advance the timing of the spark as engine speed increases.

The distributor in your Pinto has two means of advancing the ignition timing. One is called centrifugal advance and is actuated by weights in the distributor. The other is called vacuum advance and is controlled by that large circular housing on the side of the distributor.

In addition, some distributors have a vacuum-retard mechanism which is contained in the same housing on the side of the distributor as the vacuum advance. The function of this mechanism is to retard the timing of the ignition spark under certain engine conditions. This causes more complete burning of the air/fuel mixture in the cylinder and consequently lowers exhaust emissions.

Because these mechanisms change ignition timing, it is necessary to disconnect and plug the one or two vacuum lines from the distributor when setting the basic ignition timing.

If ignition timing is set too far advanced (BTDC), the ignition and expansion of the air/fuel mixture in the cylinder will try to force the piston down the cylinder while it is still traveling upward. This causes engine "ping," a sound which resembles marbles being dropped into an empty tin can. If the ignition timing is too far retarded (after, or ATDC), the piston will have already started down on the power stroke when the air/fuel mixture ignites and expands. This will cause the piston to be forced

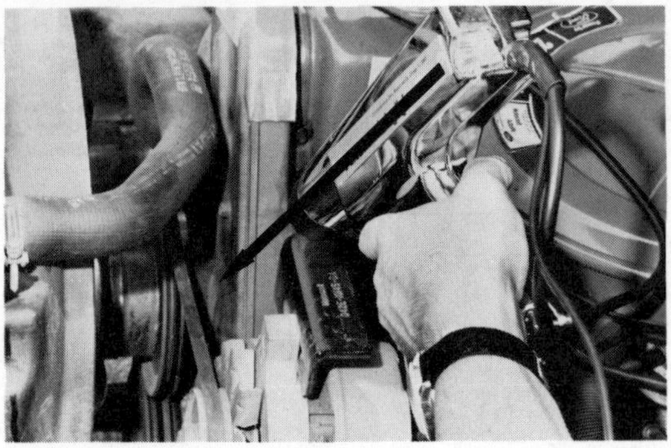

Checking ignition timing

down only a portion of its travel. This will result in poor engine performance and lack of power.

Ignition timing adjustment is checked with a timing light. This instrument is connected to the number one (no. 1) spark plug of the engine. The timing light flashes every time an electrical current is sent from the distributor, through the no. 1 spark plug wire, to the spark plug. The crankshaft pulley and the front cover of the engine are marked with a timing pointer and a timing scale. When the timing pointer is aligned with the "0" mark on the timing scale, the piston in no. 1 cylinder is at TDC of its compression stroke. With the engine running, and the timing light aimed at the timing pointer and timing scale, the stroboscopic flashes from the timing light will allow you to check the ignition timing setting of the engine. The timing light flashes every time the spark plug in the no. 1 cylinder of the engine fires. Since the flash from the timing light makes the crankshaft pulley seem stationary for a moment, you will be able to read the exact position of the piston in the no. 1 cylinder on the timing scale on the front of the engine.

If you have an inductive pick-up type timing light you may experience some difficulty in getting an accurate reading on a Pinto equipped with solid state ignition. To cure this, place a piece of rubber tubing over the spark plug wire and attach the timing light pick-up to this.

NOTE: *1972 California cars do not have a timing scale on the engine. Instead, they have a "V" notch to identify the correct ignition timing mark. When ignition timing is adjusted correctly on these engines, the timing pointer is aligned with the "V" notch.*

Adjustment

1. Locate the timing marks and pointer on the lower engine pulley and engine front cover.
2. Clean the timing marks and pointer.
3. Mark the proper timing mark (see "Tune-Up Specifications") and the pointer with white chalk or day-glo paint. Attach a tachometer to the engine.
4. Attach a timing light according to the manufacturer's instructions. If the timing light has three wires, one (usually blue or green) must be installed, with an adaptor, between the end of the no. 1 spark plug wire and spark plug. The other leads are connected to the positive (usually red lead) battery terminal and the negative (usually black lead) battery terminal.
5. Disconnect the one or two vacuum lines from the distributor. After removing the lines, plug the open end with the tip of a pencil or a golf tee.
6. Check to be sure the timing light wires are clear of the engine fan and start the engine.

CAUTION: *When working on a vehicle with the engine running, the following precautions must be observed: Work only in a well-ventilated area. Be certain the transmission is in Neutral and the parking brake firmly applied. Always keep your hands, clothing, and tools clear of the moving radiator fan.*

7. Adjust the carburetor to reduce the engine idle speed to specifications. See the idle speed adjustment procedure in this chapter.
8. Aim the timing light at the timing mark and pointer on the front of the

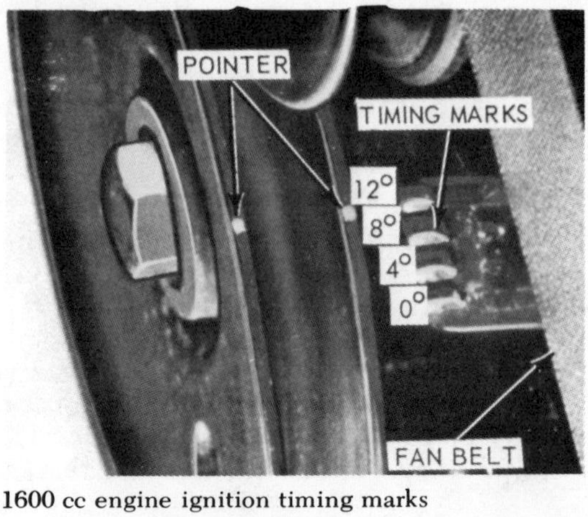

1600 cc engine ignition timing marks

2000 and 2300 cc engine ignition timing marks

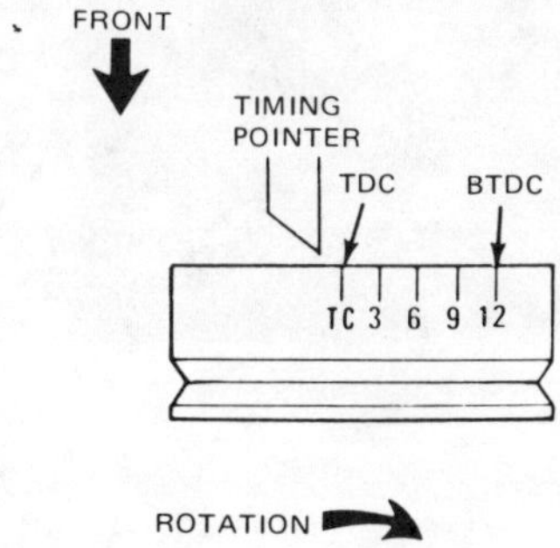

2800 cc timing marks

engine. If the marks you put on the timing mark and pointer are not aligned when the timing light flashes, turn off the engine and proceed to step nine. If the two marks do align, adjust the engine to normal idle speed, turn off the engine, and remove the test equipment.

9. On those models with a 1600 cc, 2300 cc, or 2800 cc engine, loosen the distributor lockscrew just enough that the distributor can be turned. On those models with a 2000 cc engine, loosen the distributor lock bolt just enough so the distributor can be turned.

NOTE: *The distributor lock bolt on the 2000 cc engine has a 13 mm metric head.*

The distributor lock bolt or screw is located at the base of the distributor where the distributor shaft enters the engine. Turn the distributor slightly in the direction of distributor rotor rotation to retard the spark. Turn the distributor slightly in the opposite direction of rotation to advance the spark. Tighten the lockscrew or bolt.

10. Start the engine and recheck the timing. If the timing mark and the pointer still do not align, repeat step nine.

11. Adjust the engine to normal idle speed, turn off the engine, and remove the test equipment.

VALVE ADJUSTMENT

All of the Pinto engines (except the 2300 cc) are equipped with mechanical valve lifters. The 2300 cc engine uses hydraulic lash adjusters which do not require routine adjustment. Those engines equipped with mechanical lifters however, should be adjusted at the recommended intervals (see Chapter 1).

Valve adjustment is one factor which determines how far the intake and exhaust valves will open into the cylinder.

If the valve clearance is too large, part of the lift of the camshaft will be used up in removing the excessive clearance, thus the valves will not be opened far enough. This condition has two effects, the valve train components will emit a tapping noise as they take up the excessive clearance, and the engine will perform poorly, since the less the intake valves open, the smaller the amount of air/fuel mixture that will be admitted to the cylinders. The less the exhaust valves open, the greater the back-pressure in the cylinder which prevents the proper air/fuel mixture from entering the cylinder.

If the valve clearance is too small, the intake and exhaust valves will not fully seat on the cylinder head when they close. When a valve seats on the cylinder head it does two things; it seals the combustion chamber so none of the gases in the cylinder can escape and it cools itself by transferring some of the heat it absorbed from the combustion process through the cylinder head and into the engine cooling system. Therefore, if the valve clearance is too small, the engine will run poorly (due to gases escaping from the combustion chamber), and the valves will overheat and warp (since they cannot transfer heat unless they are touching the seat in the cylinder head).

While all valve adjustments must be

as accurate as possible, it is better to have the valve adjustment slightly loose than slightly tight, as burnt valves may result from overly tight adjustments.

1600 cc

The engine must be at normal operating temperature to adjust the valves.

1. Start the engine and let it run until it reaches normal operating temperature. This operation requires a new valve cover gasket, so perhaps you can warm the engine by driving to the parts store to purchase one.
2. Turn off the engine and raise the hood. Be careful when touching any metal parts under the hood as they are going to be hot. Be particularly careful of the exhaust manifold.
3. If the spark plug wires are not numbered as to their cylinder, number them. Grasp the spark plug wires by the insulators and disconnect them from the plugs. Position the wires out of the way.
4. Remove the air cleaner.
5. Disconnect the carburetor solenoid wire at the connector near the rear of the valve cover.
6. Remove the screw that attaches the throttle cable to the valve cover.
7. Using a screwdriver, pry the end of the throttle cable off the stud on the carburetor. Position the throttle cable out of the way.
8. Pry the throttle linkage out of the carburetor arm with a screwdriver.
9. Remove the valve cover attaching screws and remove the valve cover from the engine.
10. Place a ⅝ in. wrench on the lower crankshaft pulley bolt and turn it in a clockwise direction until the no. 1 valve is fully depressed.

1600 cc engine valve identification

No. 1 valve depressed

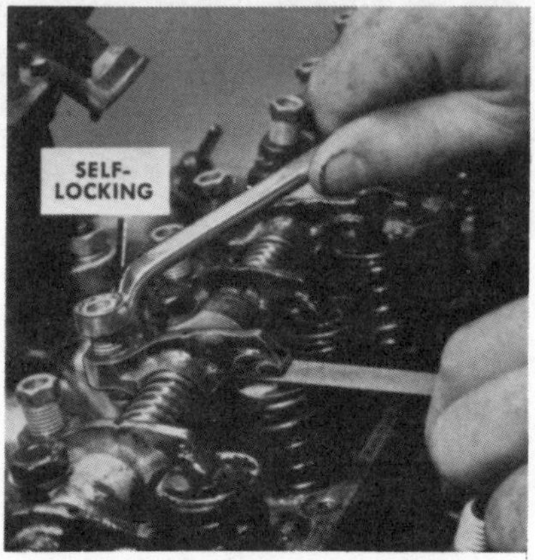

Valve clearance adjustments

11. Using a feeler gauge, check the clearance between the tip of the rocker arm and the top of the valve on valve no. 3. The clearance should be 0.010 in. If the clearance is not correct, turn the adjusting screw in or out to obtain the proper setting. Do not use an open-end wrench to turn the adjusting screw as this can damage it.
12. Check the clearance on valve no. 8; it should be 0.017 in.
13. Turn the engine with a wrench until the no. 2 valve is fully depressed. Check the clearance of valve no. 7; it should be 0.010 in.
14. Check the clearance of valve no. 5; it should be 0.017 in.
15. Turn the engine over with a wrench until no. 3 valve is fully depressed. Check the clearance of valve no. 6; it should be 0.010 in.
16. Check the clearance of valve no. 1, it should be 0.017 in.
17. Turn the engine with a wrench until no. 5 valve is fully depressed. Check the clearance of valve no. 2; it should be 0.010 in.

18. Check the clearance of valve no. 4; it should be 0.017 in.

19. Clean all old gasket material from the cylinder head and valve cover.

20. Position a new valve cover gasket on the cylinder head and install the valve cover.

21. Install the valve cover retaining screws and tighten them to 2.5–3.5 ft lbs.

22. Position the throttle cable in its bracket on the valve cover and install the cable retaining screw. Connect the carburetor solenoid wire.

23. Push the end of the throttle cable on the stud on the carburetor.

24. Attach the throttle linkage to the carburetor arm.

25. Install the spark plug wires on the proper plugs, making sure the boots are firmly seated on the plugs.

26. Install the air cleaner.

Valve Clearance Adjustment

1600 cc ENGINE—SET HOT

Valve Depressed	*Valves to Adjust to 0.010*	*0.017*
no. 1	no. 3	no. 8
no. 2	no. 7	no. 5
no. 3	no. 6	no. 1
no. 5	no. 2	no. 4

2000 cc

If the engine has been running and is hot, it must be allowed to cool before adjusting the valves.

1. Remove the air cleaner. After identifying the plug wire for each spark plug, disconnect and move them out of the way.

2. On models without air conditioning, remove the heater hose that is attached to the carburetor choke housing from the valve cover and move it out of the way. On cars with air conditioning, disconnect the carburetor choke heater hose from the heater hot water valve and move it out of the way.

3. Using a 11 mm socket wrench, remove the valve cover attaching screws. Note the position of the screws that have rubber-coated washers.

4. Remove the valve cover from the engine.

5. Place a ¾ in. wrench on the lower crankshaft pulley bolt and turn the wrench in a clockwise direction until the no. 1 valve is fully depressed (cam lobe pointing straight down).

NOTE: *Never turn the crankshaft pulley in a counterclockwise direction on a 2000 cc engine as the camshaft drive belt could slip and alter camshaft timing.*

6. Check the clearance between the no. 6 rocker arm and the cam. To do this, first place a screwdriver blade under the rocker arm retaining spring and snap the spring off the rocker arm until it hangs loose. Using a feeler gauge, check the clearance between the rocker arm and the cam. The correct clearance for no. 6 valve is 0.008 in. If the clearance is not correct, loosen the locknut with a ¾ in. wrench. Turn the adjusting screw in to increase clearance or out to decrease

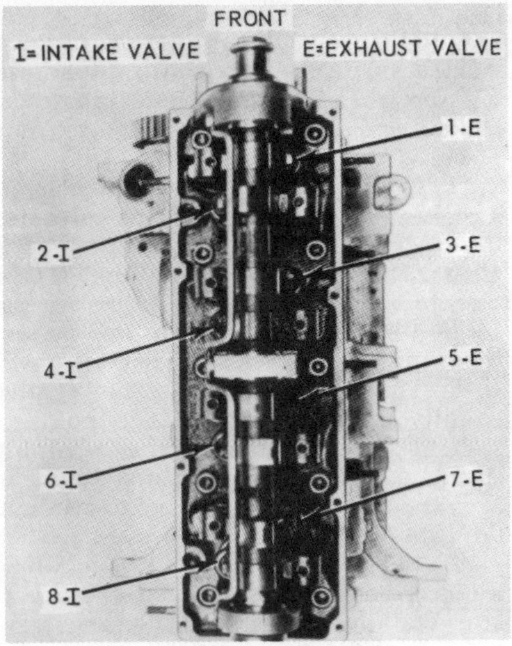

2000 cc engine valve identification

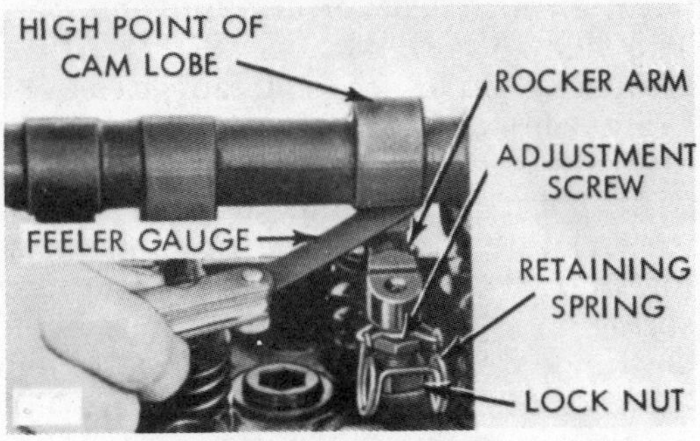

Valve clearance adjustment

clearance. When the adjustment is correct, tighten the adjusting screw locknut, making sure you do not turn the adjusting screw at the same time. Snap the rocker arm retaining spring back into place.

7. Check the clearance between no. 7 rocker arm and the cam, after releasing the rocker arm retaining spring. The clearance should be 0.010 in. If the clearance is not correct, adjust as described in step six. Snap the rocker arm retaining spring back into place.

8. Turn the engine until no. 2 valve is fully depressed (cam lobe pointing straight down). Release the retaining spring on no. 8 rocker arm and check the clearance between no. 8 rocker arm and the cam. The clearance should be 0.008 in. If the clearance is not correct, adjust as described in step six. Snap the rocker arm retaining spring back into place.

9. Release the retaining spring on no. 3 rocker arm and check the clearance between no. 3 rocker arm and the cam. The clearance should be 0.010 in. If the clearance is not correct, adjust as described in step six. Snap the rocker arm retaining spring back into place.

10. Turn the engine until the no. 3 valve is fully depressed (cam lobe pointing straight down). Release the retaining spring on no. 2 rocker arm and check the clearance between no. 2 rocker arm and the cam. The clearance should be 0.008 in. If the clearance is not correct, adjust as described in step six. Snap the rocker arm retaining spring back into place.

11. Release the retaining spring on no. 5 rocker arm and check the clearance between no. 5 rocker arm and the cam. The clearance should be 0.010 in. If the clearance is not correct, adjust as described in step six. Snap the rocker arm retaining spring back into place.

12. Turn the engine until no. 6 valve is fully depressed (cam lobe pointing straight down). Release the retaining spring on no. 4 rocker arm and check the clearance between no. 4 rocker arm and the cam. The clearance should be 0.008 in. If the clearance is not correct, adjust as described in step six. Snap the rocker arm retaining spring back into place.

13. Release the retaining spring from no. 1 rocker arm and check the clearance between the no. 1 rocker arm and the cam. The clearance should be 0.010 in. If the clearance is not correct, adjust as described in step six. Snap the rocker arm retaining spring back into place.

14. Clean all old gasket material from the cylinder head and the valve cover.

15. Position a new valve cover gasket on the cylinder head and install the valve cover on top of it. Install the valve cover attaching screws. Make sure the screws with rubber-coated washers are installed in their original location.

16. Tighten the six rear valve cover cap screws to 4–6 ft lbs working from the rear forward. Tighten the two vertical cap screws to 1–2 ft lbs. Tighten the two lateral cap screws to 4–6 ft lbs. Retighten the two vertical cap screws, this time to 4–6 ft lbs.

17. Connect the spark plug wires to the proper plugs.

18. On models without air conditioning, position the choke heater hose on the valve cover. On models with air conditioning, connect the choke heater hose to the heater hot water valve and replace any lost coolant.

19. Install the air cleaner.

Valve Clearance Adjustment

2000 cc ENGINE—SET COLD

Valve Depressed	*Valves to Adjust to 0.008*	*0.010*
no. 1	no. 6	no. 7
no. 2	no. 8	no. 3
no. 3	no. 2	no. 5
no. 6	no. 4	no. 1

1976 2800 cc Engine

1. Remove the air cleaner assembly and disconnect the negative battery cable.

2. Remove the Thermactor air by-pass valve and its mounting bracket.

3. Remove the two engine lifting eyes; remove the alternator drive belt, loosen the alternator mounting bolts and swing the alternator outward toward the fender.

4. Remove the plug wires and remove the rocker covers.

NOTE: *On 1975 models with the 2800 cc engine, the position of the distributor diaphragm may interfere with the removal of the rocker cover. This can be corrected as follows: Set the ignition timing at TDC. Remove the distributor hold-down bolt and clamp and turn the distributor assembly one tooth (20°) clockwise. The diaphragm housing should be pointing toward the rear face of the cylinder block. Reinstall the hold-down bolt and clamp, and reset the timing to the specification given on the underhood tune-up decal.*

5. When removing the rocker covers, remove or reposition any wires or hoses which might block the removal of the rocker covers.

6. Torque the rocker arm support bolts to 46 ft lbs.

7. Reconnect the battery cable, place the transmission in Neutral (manual) or Park (automatic), and apply the parking brake.

8. Place a finger on the adjusting screw of the intake valve rocker arm for cylinder No. 5. Cylinder numbering is shown under Firing Order at the start of the section. Valve arrangement, from front to rear, on the left bank is I-E-E-I-E-I; on the right it is I-E-I-E-E-I. You will be able to feel the rocker arm begin to move.

9. Use a remote starter switch to turn the engine over until you can just feel the valve begin to open. Now the cam is in position to adjust the intake and exhaust valves on the No. 1 cylinder.

10. Adjust the No. 1 intake valve so that a 0.014 in. feeler gauge has a slight drag, while a 0.015 in. feeler gauge is a tight fit. To decrease lash, turn the adjusting screw clockwise; to increase lash, turn the adjusting screw counterclockwise. There are no lockbolts to tighten as the adjusting screws are self-tightening.

CAUTION: *Do not use a step-type, "go-no go" feeler gauge. When checking lash, you must insert the feeler gauge and move it parallel with the crankshaft. Do not move it in and out perpendicular with the crankshaft as this will give an erroneous feel which will result in overtightened valves.*

11. Adjust the exhaust valve the same way so that an 0.018 in. feeler gauge has a slight drag, while a 0.019 in. gauge is a tight fit.

Valve Clearance Adjustment—2800 cc Engine (1976 Only)

Intake valve just opening	*Adjust both valves for this cylinder (Intake—0.014 in.; Exhaust—0.018 in.)*
5	1
3	4
6	2
1	5
4	3
2	6

12. The rest of the valves are adjusted in the same way, in their firing order (1-4-2-5-3-6), by positioning the cam according to the following chart:

13. Remove all the old gasket material from the cylinder heads and rocker cover gasket surfaces, and disconnect the negative cable from the battery.

14. Remove the spark plug wires and reinstall the rocker arm covers.

15. Reinstall any hoses and wires which were removed previously.

16. Reinstall the spark plug wires, the alternator drive belt, and the Thermactor air by-pass valve and its mounting bracket.

17. Reconnect the battery cable, replace the air cleaner assembly, start the engine, and check for leaks.

CARBURETOR

This section contains only carburetor adjustments as they normally apply to engine tune-up. Descriptions of the carburetor and complete adjustment procedures can be found in chapter four.

Idle Speed and Mixture Adjustment

1600 CC

1. Run the engine to bring it to normal operating temperature.

2. If you have not previously done so, check and adjust the ignition timing as required.

3. Attach a tachometer to the engine. Turn on the headlights and switch on the high beams.

4. Remove the air cleaner.

5. Start the engine and check the idle speed on the tachometer.

6. If the engine speed does not conform to the higher of the two idle speeds listed in the "Tune-Up Specifications"

chart, turn the adjusting nut on the bottom of the carburetor solenoid with a 3/8 in. wrench to correct it.

7. When the desired engine rpm has been obtained, disconnect the carburetor solenoid at the solenoid quick-disconnect.

8. Check the engine idle speed on the tachometer; it should now conform with the lower figure listed in the "Tune-Up Specifications" chart. If it does not, turn the curb idle adjusting screw to correct.

9. Reconnect the solenoid at the solenoid quick-disconnect.

10. Open the carburetor throttle plates slightly by depressing the throttle lever. When the throttle lever is depressed, the throttle solenoid plunger should extend and raise the engine idle speed to the higher figure given in the specifications table.

11. Using a screwdriver, turn the idle mixture adjustment screw inward and outward over the extent of its travel to obtain the smoothest idle.

12. Turn off the engine and install the air cleaner, leaving the tachometer attached.

13. Start the engine and recheck the engine idle speed. If it has changed, turn off the engine and remove the air cleaner. Start the engine and readjust the idle speed. Repeat as necessary.

14. Turn off the engine and disconnect the tachometer. Turn off the headlights.

1971–72 2000 cc Without Air Conditioning

1. Run the engine to bring it to normal operating temperature.

2. If you have not previously done so, check and adjust the ignition timing as required.

3. Attach a tachometer to the engine.

4. Remove the air cleaner.

5. Start the engine and turn on the headlights and switch on high beams.

6. Check the engine idle speed on the tachometer. If your Pinto is equipped with automatic transmission, securely block the wheels and check the idle speed with the transmission in Drive.

7. If the engine idle rpm does not conform with the specification given in the tune-up chart, turn the curb idle ad-

1600 cc engine throttle solenoid adjustment

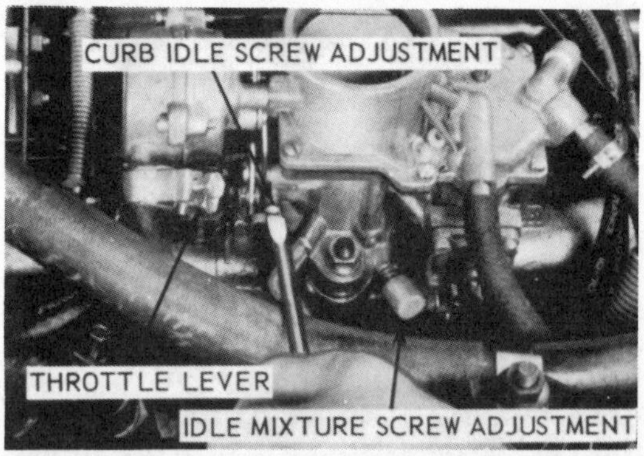

Curb idle speed and mixture adjustment

2000 cc engine curb idle speed and mixture adjustment

justing screw in or out to obtain the correct idle speed.

8. Using a screwdriver, turn the idle mixture adjusting screw inward and outward over the extent of its travel to obtain the smoothest idle.

9. Turn off the engine and install the air cleaner, leaving the tachometer attached.

10. Start the engine and recheck the idle speed. If it has changed, stop the engine and remove the air cleaner. Start the engine and readjust the idle speed. Repeat as necessary.

11. Stop the engine and disconnect the tachometer. Turn off the headlights.

1971–72 2000 cc With Air Conditioning

1. Follow the first five steps under 1971–72 2000 cc Without Air Conditioning.

2. Turn the air conditioner on. If equipped with automatic transmission, securely block the wheels and place the transmission in Drive.

3. Check the engine idle speed on the tachometer. If the idle speed does not conform with the higher figure given in the "Tune-Up Specifications chart, turn the adjusting nut on the bottom of the carburetor solenoid with a ⅜ in. wrench to correct. When the proper idle rpm has been obtained, disconnect the solenoid at the solenoid quick-disconnect. If equipped with automatic transmission, take the transmission selector lever out of Drive and put it in Neutral. Turn the air conditioner off.

4. Check the engine idle speed on the tachometer, it should conform with the lower figure given in the "Tune-Up Specifications." If it does not, turn the curb idle adjusting screw until it does.

5. Reconnect the solenoid at the solenoid quick-disconnect.

6. Open the carburetor throttle plates by slightly depressing the throttle lever. Turn the air conditioner on. If equipped with automatic transmission, securely block the wheels and place the transmission selector lever in Drive. When the throttle lever is depressed, the solenoid plunger should extend and raise the engine idle rpm to the higher figure given in the specifications table.

7. Using a screwdriver, turn the carburetor idle mixture adjusting screw inward and outward over the extent of its travel to obtain the smoothest idle.

8. Stop the engine and install the air cleaner, leaving the tachometer attached.

9. Start the engine and recheck the idle speed (A/C on, in Drive). If it has changed, turn off the engine and remove the air cleaner. Start the engine and readjust the idle speed. Repeat as necessary.

10. Turn off the engine and disconnect the tachometer. Turn the headlights off.

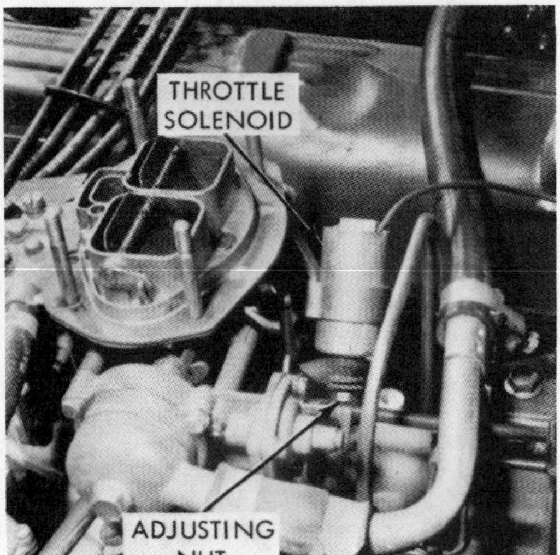

2000 cc engine throttle solenoid adjustment

1973–74 2000 cc and 2300 cc Engine

1. Remove the air cleaner assembly and plug the vacuum line.

2. Set the parking brake and block the wheels.

3. Attach a tachometer to the engine.

4. Start the engine and let it run until it reaches normal operating temperature.

5. Check the ignition timing to see that it is at the correct specification.

6. Make sure that the choke plate is fully open.

7. If equipped with automatic transmission, place the transmission in Drive.

8. If equipped with air conditioning, turn the A/C "off" on all 2300 cc engines and "on" on all 2000 cc engines.

9. Disconnect the decel valve line that connects to the carburetor.

10. Turn the hex nut on the end of the solenoid plunger in or out to obtain the higher figure given in the specification chart.

11. Disconnect the solenoid lead wire and place the automatic transmission in neutral.

12. Turn the hex nut on the end of the solenoid plunger in or out to obtain the lower figure given in the specification chart.

13. Connect the solenoid lead wire and open the throttle slightly to allow the solenoid plunger to extend.

14. Using a screwdriver turn the carb idle mixture adjusting screw inward and outward over the extent of its travel to obtain the smoothest idle.

15. Stop the engine, install the air cleaner and reconnect the vacuum line.

1975 and Later 2300 cc Engine

NOTE: *The recommended procedure for adjusting the idle mixture on 1975–76 Pintos involves addition of an artificial enrichment substance (propane), requiring special service equipment. The following are alternate procedures for mixture adjustment for 2300 cc and 2800 cc engines which can be used in place of the factory recommended method.*

1. Remove the air cleaner assembly and plug the vacuum line(s) at the source of the vacuum.

2. Set the parking brake and block the wheels.

3. Check the throttle and the choke linkage for freedom of movement.

4. Connect a tachometer to the engine.

5. Start the engine and warm up to the normal operating temperature.

Adjusting the idle speed

6. Reinstall any distributor vacuum lines that were removed and check the ignition timing.

7. Remove the EGR vacuum line at the valve and plug line.

8. If applicable, remove the spark delay valve and route the primary distributor advance vacuum signal directly to the primary distributor diaphragm (advance side). If the distributor has a secondary (retard) diaphragm, leave the vacuum connection intact.

9. Disconnect and plug the fuel deceleration valve hose (if so equipped) at the carburetor connection.

10. Turn the air conditioner off.

11. Put the automatic transmission in Drive and the manual transmission in Neutral.

12. On carburetors having a conventional curb idle adjusting screw only (no TSP), turn the screw in or out to obtain the specified curb idle rpm as shown in the vehicle specifications. Proceed to Step 17.

13. On those engines equipped with an anti-dieseling solenoid (TSP), adjust the curb idle speed to specifications with solenoid energized and fully extended, using the curb idle screw which contacts the solenoid plunger.

14. After adjusting the curb idle speed with the extended solenoid plunger, collapse the plunger by forcing the throttle

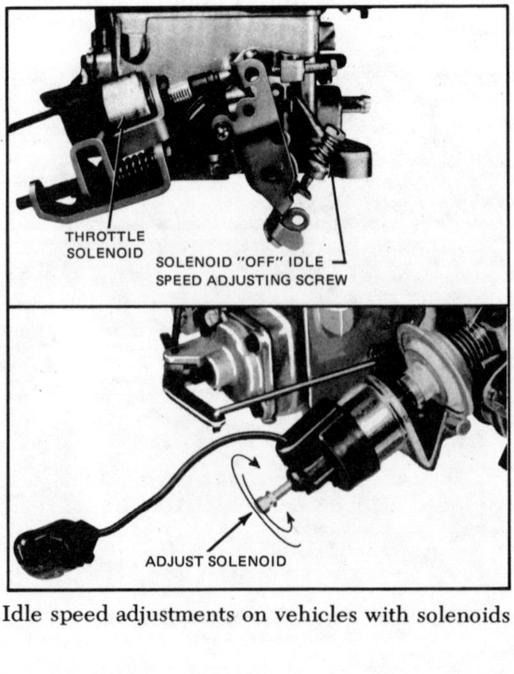

Idle speed adjustments on vehicles with solenoids

linkage against the plunger grasping the throttle lever and solenoid housing between the thumb and index finger to alleviate movement of the solenoid assembly position.

15. Adjust the TSP-off (lower curb idle) adjusting screw on the carburetor body to obtain the "lower" curb idle (TSP-off) rpm as listed in the vehicle specifications.

16. Open the throttle slightly to allow the solenoid plunger to extend.

17. Using a screwdriver turn the carburetor idle mixture adjusting screw inward and outward over the extent of its travel to obtain the smoothest idle.

NOTE: *On models equipped with catalytic converters, if you are experiencing the 'rotten egg' smell, this indicates your mixture is too rich. Lean out the mixture by turning the mixture screws in; if this doesn't work have the mixture checked and adjusted by a dealer or shop with the special tools.*

18. On applicable models, adjust the fuel deceleration valve to specifications each time the curb idle speed is reset. Connect decel valve for this check and balance of procedure.

19. Stop the engine and install the air cleaner and vacuum lines.

1975 AND LATER 2800 CC ENGINE

1. Remove the EGR vacuum line and air cleaner and plug both vacuum lines.

2. Place the transmission in Neutral and engage the parking brake.

3. Start the engine and bring to normal operation temperature.

4. Check the timing.

5. Remove spark delay valve (if so equipped) and route part throttle vacuum signal directly to advance side of distributor. If the distributor is a dual diaphragm model, leave manifold vacuum line connected to the retard side of distributor.

6. Turn the throttle arm adjusting screw on the carburetor body to obtain the lower TSP-off idle speed.

7. Raise the engine speed to 2,000 rpm and allow it to return to idle.

8. If applicable, wait at least 5 seconds for the dashpot to bottom out before checking curb idle speed. Place automatic transmission vehicles in Drive and manual transmission vehicles in Neutral. Turn the hex head adjusting screw on the TSP plunger to obtain the specified curb idle speed.

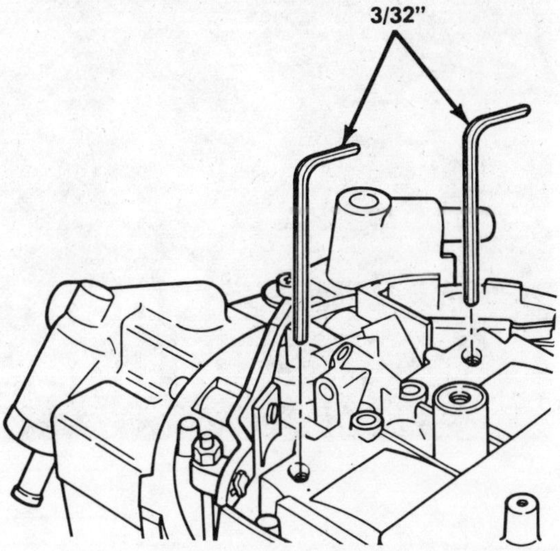

Air Adjusting screws on a variable venturi carburetor

9. If adjustment was necessary, repeat steps (10) and (11) until the proper idle speed is repeated.

10. Using a screwdriver turn the carburetor idle mixture adjusting screw inward and outward over the extent of its travel to obtain the smoothest idle. On the variable venturi carburetor, remove the air cleaner lid only, insert a 3/32 in. allen wrench into the air adjusting screws and turn clockwise (richen) or counterclockwise (lean). After you adjust the idle speed on a variable venturi carburetor, the internal vent must be adjusted. For this procedure, see Chapter 4.

NOTE: *On models equipped with catalytic converters, if you are experiencing the 'rotten egg' smell, this indicates your mixture is too rich. Lean out the mixture by turning the mixture screws in; if this doesn't work have the mixture checked and adjusted by a dealer or shop with the special tools.*

11. Stop the engine and reinstall the air cleaner and vacuum lines.

Deceleration Valve Adjustment

If the engine has a very rough idle or an excessively high idle speed, and a carburetor adjustment will not correct the problem, the problem could be caused by the deceleration valve. See Chapter 4.

Engine Tune-Up

Engine tune-up is a procedure performed to restore engine performance, deteriorated due to normal wear and loss of adjustment. The three major areas considered in a routine tune-up are compression, ignition, and carburetion, although valve adjustment may be included.

A tune-up is performed in three steps: *analysis*, in which it is determined whether normal wear is responsible for performance loss, and which parts require replacement or service; *parts replacement or service*; and *adjustment*, in which engine adjustments are returned to original specifications. Since the advent of emission control equipment, precision adjustment has become increasingly critical, in order to maintain pollutant emission levels.

Analysis

The procedures below are used to indicate where adjustments, parts service or replacement are necessary within the realm of a normal tune-up. If, following these tests, all systems appear to be functioning properly, proceed to the Troubleshooting Section for further diagnosis.

—Remove all spark plugs, noting the cylinder in which they were installed. Remove the air cleaner, and position the throttle and choke in the full open position. Disconnect the coil high tension lead from the coil and the distributor cap. Insert a compression gauge into the spark plug port of each cylinder, in succession, and crank the engine with the starter to obtain the highest possible reading. Record the readings, and compare the highest to the lowest on the compression pressure limit chart. If the difference exceeds the limits on the chart, or if all readings are excessively low, proceed to a wet compression check (see Troubleshooting Section).

Maxi. Press. Lbs. Sq. In.	*Min. Press. Lbs. Sq. In.*	*Max. Press. Lbs. Sq. In.*	*Min. Press. Lbs. Sq. In.*
134	101	188	141
136	102	190	142
138	104	192	144
140	105	194	145
142	107	196	147
146	110	198	148
148	111	200	150
150	113	202	151
152	114	204	153
154	115	206	154
156	117	208	156
158	118	210	157
160	120	212	158
162	121	214	160
164	123	216	162
166	124	218	163
168	126	220	165
170	127	222	166
172	129	224	168
174	131	226	169
176	132	228	171
178	133	230	172
180	135	232	174
182	136	234	175
184	138	236	177
186	140	238	178

Compression pressure limits
© Buick Div. G.M. Corp.)

—Evaluate the spark plugs according to the spark plug chart in the Troubleshooting Section, and proceed as indicated in the chart.

—Remove the distributor cap, and inspect it inside and out for cracks and/or carbon tracks, and inside for excessive wear or burning of the rotor contacts. If any of these faults are evident, the cap must be replaced.

—Check the breaker points for burning, pitting or wear, and the contact heel resting on the distributor cam for excessive wear. If defects are noted, replace the entire breaker point set.

—Remove and inspect the rotor. If the contacts are burned or worn, or if the rotor is excessively loose on the distributor shaft (where applicable), the rotor must be replaced.

—Inspect the spark plug leads and the coil high tension lead for cracks or brittleness. If any of the wires appear defective, the entire set should be replaced.

—Check the air filter to ensure that it is functioning properly.

Parts Replacement and Service

The determination of whether to replace or service parts is at the mechanic's discretion; however, it is suggested that any parts in questionable condition be replaced rather than reused.

—Clean and regap, or replace, the spark plugs as needed. Lightly coat the threads with engine oil and install the plugs. CAUTION: *Do not over-torque taper-seat spark plugs, or plugs being installed in aluminum cylinder heads.*

—If the distributor cap is to be reused, clean the inside with a dry rag, and remove corrosion from the rotor contact points with fine emery cloth. Remove the spark plug wires one by one, and clean the wire ends and the inside of the towers. If the boots are loose, they should be replaced.

If the cap is to be replaced, transfer the wires one by one, cleaning the wire ends and replacing the boots if necessary.

—If the original points are to remain in service, clean them lightly with emery cloth, lubricate the contact heel with grease specifically designed for this purpose. Rotate the crankshaft until the heel rests on a high point of the distributor cam, and adjust the point gap to specifications.

When replacing the points, remove the original points and condenser, and wipe out the inside of the distributor housing with a clean, dry rag. Lightly lubricate the contact heel and pivot point, and install the points and condenser. Rotate the crankshaft until the heel rests on a high point of the distributor cam, and adjust the point gap to specifications. NOTE: *Always replace the condenser when changing the points.*

—If the rotor is to be reused, clean the contacts with solvent. Do not alter the spring tension of the rotor center contact. Install the rotor and the distributor cap.

—Replace the coil high tension lead and/or the spark plug leads as necessary.

—Clean the carburetor using a spray solvent (e.g., Gumout Spray). Remove the varnish from the throttle bores, and clean the linkage. Disconnect and plug the fuel line, and run the engine until it runs out of fuel. Partially fill the float chamber with solvent, and reconnect the fuel line. In extreme cases, the jets can be pressure flushed by inserting a rubber plug into the float vent, running the spray nozzle through it, and spraying the solvent until it squirts out of the venturi fuel dump.

—Clean and tighten all wiring connections in the primary electrical circuit.

Additional Services

The following services *should* be performed in conjunction with a routine tune-up to ensure efficient performance.

—Inspect the battery and fill to the proper level with distilled water. Remove the cable clamps, clean clamps and posts thoroughly, coat the posts lightly with petroleum jelly, reinstall and tighten.

—Inspect all belts, replace and/or adjust as necessary.

—Test the PCV valve (if so equipped), and clean or replace as indicated. Clean all crankcase ventilation hoses, or replace if cracked or hardened.

—Adjust the valves (if necessary) to manufacturer's specifications.

Adjustments

—Connect a dwell-tachometer between the distributor primary lead and ground. Remove the distributor cap and rotor (unless equipped with Delco externally adjustable distributor). With the ignition off, crank the engine with a remote starter switch and measure the point dwell angle. Adjust the dwell angle to specifications. NOTE: *Increasing the gap decreases the dwell angle and vice-versa.* Install the rotor and distributor cap.

—Connect a timing light according to the manufacturer's specifications. Identify the proper timing marks with chalk or paint. NOTE: *Luminescent (day-glo) paint is excellent for this purpose.* Start the engine, and run it until it reaches operating temperature. Disconnect and plug any distributor vacuum lines, and adjust idle to the speed required to adjust timing, according to specifications. Loosen the distributor clamp and adjust timing to specifications by rotating the distributor in the engine. NOTE: *To advance timing, rotate distributor opposite normal direction of rotor rotation, and vice-versa.*

—Synchronize the throttles and mixture of multiple carburetors (if so equipped) according to procedures given in the individual car sections.

—Adjust the idle speed, mixture, and idle quality, as specified in the car sections. Final idle adjustments should be made with the air cleaner installed. CAUTION: *Due to strict emission control requirements on 1969 and later models, special test equipment (CO meter, SUN Tester) may be necessary to properly adjust idle mixture to specifications.*

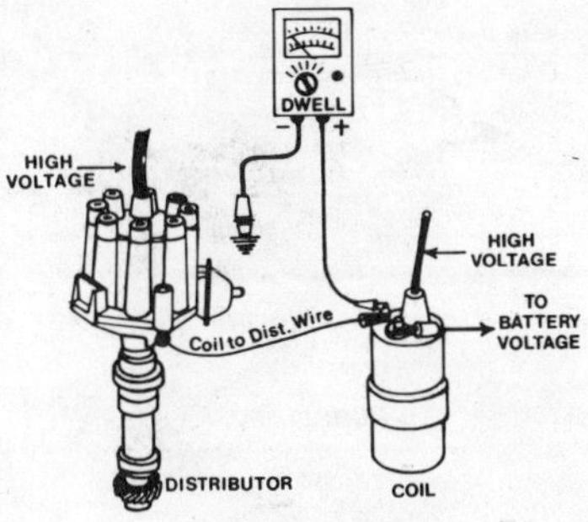

Dwell meter hook-up

Trouble-shooting

The following section is designed to aid in the rapid diagnosis of engine problems. The systematic format is used to diagnose problems ranging from engine starting difficulties to the need for engine overhaul. It is assumed that the user is equipped with basic hand tools and test equipment (tach-dwell meter, timing light, voltmeter, and ohmmeter).

Troubleshooting is divided into two sections. The first, *General Diagnosis*, is used to locate the problem area. In the second, *Specific Diagnosis*, the problem is systematically evaluated.

General Diagnosis

PROBLEM: *Symptom*	*Begin diagnosis at Section Two, Number* ———
Engine won't start:	
Starter doesn't turn	1.1, 2.1
Starter turns, engine doesn't	2.1
Starter turns engine very slowly	1.1, 2.4
Starter turns engine normally	3.1, 4.1
Starter turns engine very quickly	6.1
Engine fires intermittently	4.1
Engine fires consistently	5.1, 6.1
Engine runs poorly:	
Hard starting	3.1, 4.1, 5.1, 8.1
Rough idle	4.1, 5.1, 8.1
Stalling	3.1, 4.1, 5.1, 8.1
Engine dies at high speeds	4.1, 5.1
Hesitation (on acceleration from standing stop)	5.1, 8.1
Poor pickup	4.1, 5.1, 8.1
Lack of power	3.1, 4.1, 5.1, 8.1
Backfire through the carburetor	4.1, 8.1, 9.1
Backfire through the exhaust	4.1, 8.1, 9.1
Blue exhaust gases	6.1, 7.1
Black exhaust gases	5.1
Running on (after the ignition is shut off)	3.1, 8.1
Susceptible to moisture	4.1
Engine misfires under load	4.1, 7.1, 8.4, 9.1
Engine misfires at speed	4.1, 8.4
Engine misfires at idle	3.1, 4.1, 5.1, 7.1, 8.4

PROBLEM: *Symptom*	*Probable Cause*
Engine noises: ①	
Metallic grind while starting	Starter drive not engaging completely
Constant grind or rumble	*Starter drive not releasing, worn main bearings
Constant knock	Worn connecting rod bearings
Knock under load	Fuel octane too low, worn connecting rod bearings
Double knock	Loose piston pin
Metallic tap	*Collapsed or sticky valve lifter, excessive valve clearance, excessive end play in a rotating shaft
Scrape	*Fan belt contacting a stationary surface
Tick while starting	S.U. electric fuel pump (normal), starter brushes
Constant tick	*Generator brushes, shreaded fan belt
Squeal	*Improperly tensioned fan belt
Hiss or roar	*Steam escaping through a leak in the cooling system or the radiator overflow vent
Whistle	*Vacuum leak
Wheeze	Loose or cracked spark plug

①—It is extremely difficult to evaluate vehicle noises. While the above are general definitions of engine noises, those starred (*) should be considered as possibly originating elsewhere in the car. To aid diagnosis, the following list considers other potential sources of these sounds.

Metallic grind:
Throwout bearing; transmission gears, bearings, or synchronizers; differential bearings, gears; something metallic in contact with brake drum or disc.

Metallic tap:
U-joints; fan-to-radiator (or shroud) contact.

Scrape:
Brake shoe or pad dragging; tire to body contact; suspension contacting undercarriage or exhaust; something non-metallic contacting brake shoe or drum.

Tick:
Transmission gears; differential gears; lack of radio suppression; resonant vibration of body panels; windshield wiper motor or transmission; heater motor and blower.

Squeal:
Brake shoe or pad not fully releasing; tires (excessive wear, uneven wear, improper inflation); front or rear wheel alignment (most commonly due to improper toe-in).

Hiss or whistle:
Wind leaks (body or window); heater motor and blower fan.

Roar:
Wheel bearings; wind leaks (body and window).

Specific Diagnosis

This section is arranged so that following each test, instructions are given to proceed to another, until a problem is diagnosed.

INDEX

Group		*Topic*
1	*	Battery
2	*	Cranking system
3	*	Primary electrical system
4	*	Secondary electrical system
5	*	Fuel system
6	*	Engine compression
7	**	Engine vacuum
8	**	Secondary electrical system
9	**	Valve train
10	**	Exhaust system
11	**	Cooling system
12	**	Engine lubrication

*—The engine need not be running.
**—The engine must be running.

SAMPLE SECTION

Test and Procedure	*Results and Indications*	*Proceed to*
4.1—Check for spark: Hold each spark plug wire approximately 1/4″ from ground with gloves or a heavy, dry rag. Crank the engine and observe the spark.	→ If no spark is evident: →	4.2
	→ If spark is good in some cases: →	4.3
	→ If spark is good in all cases: →	4.6

DIAGNOSIS

1.1—Inspect the battery visually for case condition (corrosion, cracks) and water level.	If case is cracked, replace battery:	1.4
	If the case is intact, remove corrosion with a solution of baking soda and water (CAUTION: *do not get the solution into the battery*), and fill with water:	1.2
1.2—Check the battery cable connections: Insert a screwdriver between the battery post and the cable clamp. Turn the headlights on high beam, and observe them as the screwdriver is gently twisted to ensure good metal to metal contact.	If the lights brighten, remove and clean the clamp and post; coat the post with petroleum jelly, install and tighten the clamp:	1.4
	If no improvement is noted:	1.3

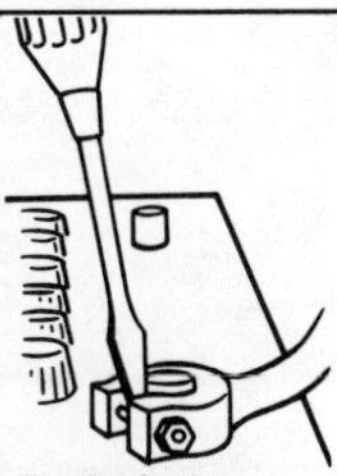

Testing battery cable connections using a screwdriver

1.3—Test the state of charge of the battery using an individual cell tester or hydrometer.

Spec. Grav. Reading	*Charged Condition*
1.260-1.280	Fully Charged
1.230-1.250	Three Quarter Charged
1.200-1.220	One Half Charged
1.170-1.190	One Quarter Charged
1.140-1.160	Just About Flat
1.110-1.130	All The Way Down

State of battery charge

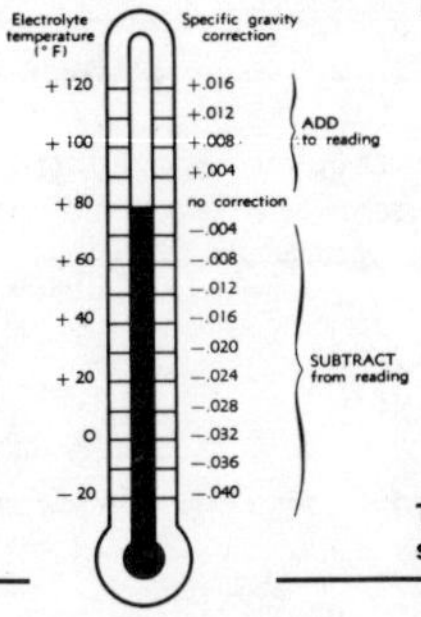

The effect of temperature on the specific gravity of battery electrolyte

If indicated, charge the battery. NOTE: *If no obvious reason exists for the low state of charge (i.e., battery age, prolonged storage), the charging system should be tested:* — 1.4

Test and Procedure	*Results and Indications*	*Proceed to*
1.4—Visually inspect battery cables for cracking, bad connection to ground, or bad connection to starter.	If necessary, tighten connections or replace the cables:	2.1

Tests in Group 2 are performed with coil high tension lead disconnected to prevent accidental starting.

Test and Procedure	*Results and Indications*	*Proceed to*
2.1—Test the starter motor and solenoid: Connect a jumper from the battery post of the solenoid (or relay) to the starter post of the solenoid (or relay).	If starter turns the engine normally:	2.2
	If the starter buzzes, or turns the engine very slowly:	2.4
	If no response, replace the solenoid (or relay).	3.1
	If the starter turns, but the engine doesn't, ensure that the flywheel ring gear is intact. If the gear is undamaged, replace the starter drive.	3.1
2.2—Determine whether ignition override switches are functioning properly (clutch start switch, neutral safety switch), by connecting a jumper across the switch(es), and turning the ignition switch to "start".	If starter operates, adjust or replace switch:	3.1
	If the starter doesn't operate:	2.3
2.3—Check the ignition switch "start" position: Connect a 12V test lamp between the starter post of the solenoid (or relay) and ground. Turn the ignition switch to the "start" position, and jiggle the key.	If the lamp doesn't light when the switch is turned, check the ignition switch for loose connections, cracked insulation, or broken wires. Repair or replace as necessary:	3.1
	If the lamp flickers when the key is jiggled, replace the ignition switch.	3.3

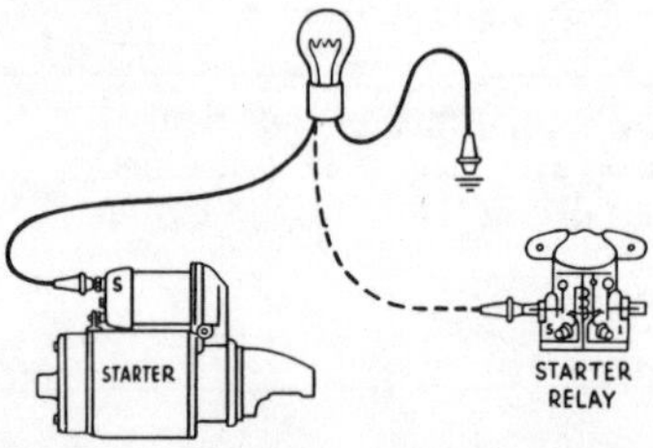

Checking the ignition switch "start" position

Test and Procedure	*Results and Indications*	*Proceed to*
2.4—Remove and bench test the starter, according to specifications in the car section.	If the starter does not meet specifications, repair or replace as needed:	3.1
	If the starter is operating properly:	2.5
2.5—Determine whether the engine can turn freely: Remove the spark plugs, and check for water in the cylinders. Check for water on the dipstick, or oil in the radiator. Attempt to turn the engine using an 18″ flex drive and socket on the crankshaft pulley nut or bolt.	If the engine will turn freely only with the spark plugs out, and hydrostatic lock (water in the cylinders) is ruled out, check valve timing:	9.2
	If engine will not turn freely, and it is known that the clutch and transmission are free, the engine must be disassembled for further evaluation:	Next Chapter

Tests and Procedures	*Results and Indications*	*Proceed to*
3.1—Check the ignition switch "on" position: Connect a jumper wire between the distributor side of the coil and ground, and a 12V test lamp between the switch side of the coil and ground. Remove the high tension lead from the coil. Turn the ignition switch on and jiggle the key.	If the lamp lights:	3.2
	If the lamp flickers when the key is jiggled, replace the ignition switch:	3.3
	If the lamp doesn't light, check for loose or open connections. If none are found, remove the ignition switch and check for continuity. If the switch is faulty, replace it:	3.3

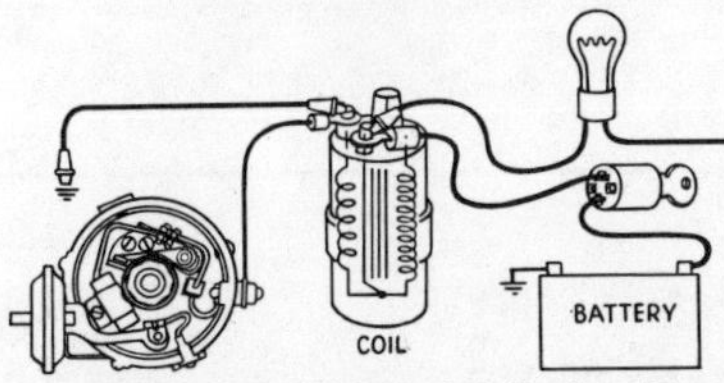

Checking the ignition switch "on" position

3.2—Check the ballast resistor or resistance wire for an open circuit, using an ohmmeter.	Replace the resistor or the resistance wire if the resistance is zero.	3.3
3.3—Visually inspect the breaker points for burning, pitting, or excessive wear. Gray coloring of the point contact surfaces is normal. Rotate the crankshaft until the contact heel rests on a high point of the distributor cam, and adjust the point gap to specifications.	If the breaker points are intact, clean the contact surfaces with fine emery cloth, and adjust the point gap to specifications. If pitted or worn, replace the points and condenser, and adjust the gap to specifications: NOTE: *Always lubricate the distributor cam according to manufacturer's recommendations when servicing the breaker points.*	3.4
3.4—Connect a dwell meter between the distributor primary lead and ground. Crank the engine and observe the point dwell angle.	If necessary, adjust the point dwell angle: NOTE: *Increasing the point gap decreases the dwell angle, and vice-versa.*	3.6
	If dwell meter shows little or no reading:	3.5

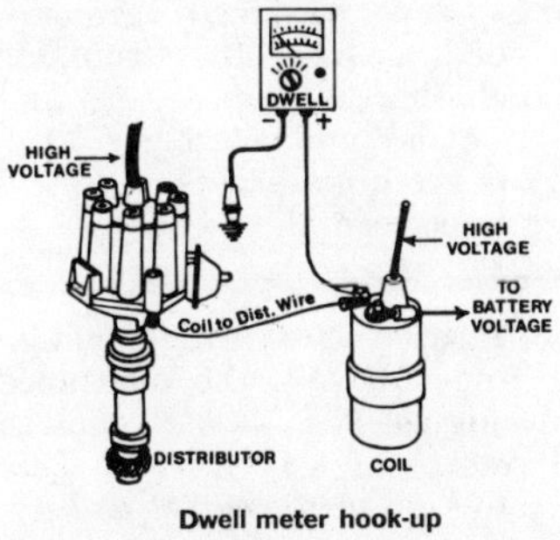

Dwell meter hook-up

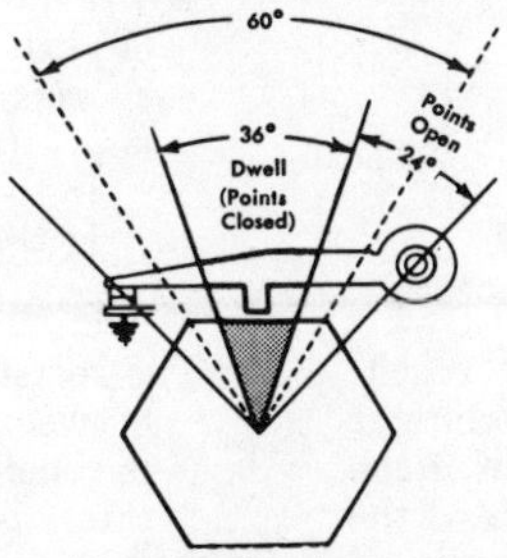

Dwell angle

3.5—Check the condenser for short: Connect an ohmmeter across the condenser body and the pigtail lead.	If any reading other than infinite resistance is noted, replace the condenser:	3.6

Checking the condenser for short

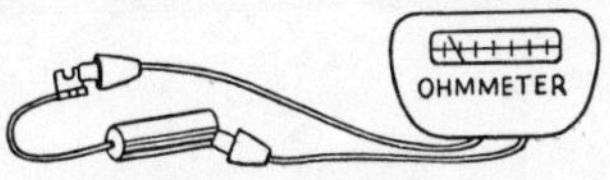

Test and Procedure	*Results and Indications*	*Proceed to*
3.6—Test the coil primary resistance: Connect an ohmmeter across the coil primary terminals, and read the resistance on the low scale. Note whether an external ballast resistor or resistance wire is utilized.	Coils utilizing ballast resistors or resistance wires should have approximately 1.0Ω resistance; coils with internal resistors should have approximately 4.0Ω resistance. If values far from the above are noted, replace the coil:	4.1

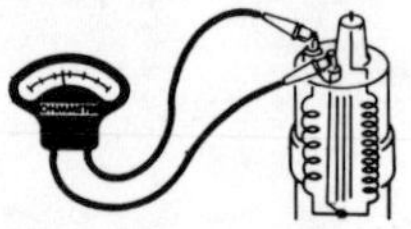

Testing the coil primary resistance

4.1—Check for spark: Hold each spark plug wire approximately ¼″ from ground with gloves or a heavy, dry rag. Crank the engine, and observe the spark.	If no spark is evident:	4.2
	If spark is good in some cylinders:	4.3
	If spark is good in all cylinders:	4.6
4.2—Check for spark at the coil high tension lead: Remove the coil high tension lead from the distributor and position it approximately ¼″ from ground. Crank the engine and observe spark. CAUTION: *This test should not be performed on cars equipped with transistorized ignition.*	If the spark is good and consistent:	4.3
	If the spark is good but intermittent, test the primary electrical system starting at 3.3:	3.3
	If the spark is weak or non-existent, replace the coil high tension lead, clean and tighten all connections and retest. If no improvement is noted:	4.4
4.3—Visually inspect the distributor cap and rotor for burned or corroded contacts, cracks, carbon tracks, or moisture. Also check the fit of the rotor on the distributor shaft (where applicable).	If moisture is present, dry thoroughly, and retest per 4.1:	4.1
	If burned or excessively corroded contacts, cracks, or carbon tracks are noted, replace the defective part(s) and retest per 4.1:	4.1
	If the rotor and cap appear intact, or are only slightly corroded, clean the contacts thoroughly (including the cap towers and spark plug wire ends) and retest per 4.1:	
	If the spark is good in all cases:	4.6
	If the spark is poor in all cases:	4.5
4.4—Check the coil secondary resistance: Connect an ohmmeter across the distributor side of the coil and the coil tower. Read the resistance on the high scale of the ohmmeter.	The resistance of a satisfactory coil should be between 4KΩ and 10KΩ. If the resistance is considerably higher (i.e., 40KΩ) replace the coil, and retest per 4.1: NOTE: *This does not apply to high performance coils.*	4.1

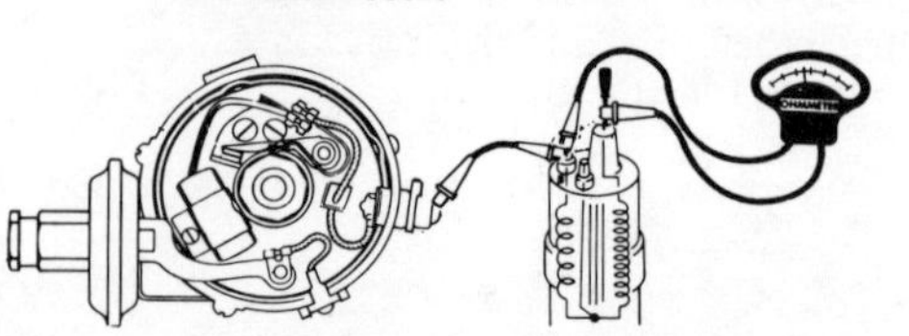

Testing the coil secondary resistance

Test and Procedure	*Results and Indications*	*Proceed to*
4.5—Visually inspect the spark plug wires for cracking or brittleness. Ensure that no two wires are positioned so as to cause induction firing (adjacent and parallel). Remove each wire, one by one, and check resistance with an ohmmeter.	Replace any cracked or brittle wires. If any of the wires are defective, replace the entire set. Replace any wires with excessive resistance (over 8000Ω per foot for suppression wire), and separate any wires that might cause induction firing.	4.6
4.6—Remove the spark plugs, noting the cylinders from which they were removed, and evaluate according to the chart below.	See below.	See below.

	Condition	*Cause*	*Remedy*	*Proceed to*
	Electrodes eroded, light brown deposits.	Normal wear. Normal wear is indicated by approximately .001″ wear per 1000 miles.	Clean and regap the spark plug if wear is not excessive: Replace the spark plug if excessively worn:	4.7
	Carbon fouling (black, dry, fluffy deposits).	If present on one or two plugs:		
		Faulty high tension lead(s).	Test the high tension leads:	4.5
		Burnt or sticking valve(s).	Check the valve train: (Clean and regap the plugs in either case.)	9.1
		If present on most or all plugs: Overly rich fuel mixture, due to restricted air filter, improper carburetor adjustment, improper choke or heat riser adjustment or operation.	Check the fuel system:	5.1
	Oil fouling (wet black deposits)	Worn engine components. NOTE: *Oil fouling may occur in new or recently rebuilt engines until broken in.*	Check engine vacuum and compression: Replace with new spark plug	6.1
	Lead fouling (gray, black, tan, or yellow deposits, which appear glazed or cinder-like).	Combustion by-products.	Clean and regap the plugs: (Use plugs of a different heat range if the problem recurs.)	4.7

	Condition	*Cause*	*Remedy*	*Proceed to*
	Gap bridging (deposits lodged between the electrodes).	Incomplete combustion, or transfer of deposits from the combustion chamber.	Replace the spark plugs:	4.7
	Overheating (burnt electrodes, and extremely white insulator with small black spots).	Ignition timing advanced too far.	Adjust timing to specifications:	8.2
		Overly lean fuel mixture.	Check the fuel system:	5.1
		Spark plugs not seated properly.	Clean spark plug seat and install a new gasket washer: (Replace the spark plugs in all cases.)	4.7
	Fused spot deposits on the insulator.	Combustion chamber blow-by.	Clean and regap the spark plugs:	4.7
	Pre-ignition (melted or severely burned electrodes, blistered or cracked insulators, or metallic deposits on the insulator).	Incorrect spark plug heat range.	Replace with plugs of the proper heat range:	4.7
		Ignition timing advanced too far.	Adjust timing to specifications:	8.2
		Spark plugs not being cooled efficiently.	Clean the spark plug seat, and check the cooling system:	11.1
		Fuel mixture too lean.	Check the fuel system:	5.1
		Poor compression.	Check compression:	6.1
		Fuel grade too low.	Use higher octane fuel:	4.7

Test and Procedure	*Results and Indications*	*Proceed to*
4.7—Determine the static ignition timing: Using the flywheel or crankshaft pulley timing marks as a guide, locate top dead center on the *compression* stroke of the No. 1 cylinder. Remove the distributor cap.	Adjust the distributor so that the rotor points toward the No. 1 tower in the distributor cap, and the points are just opening:	4.8
4.8—Check coil polarity: Connect a voltmeter negative lead to the coil high tension lead, and the positive lead to ground (NOTE: *reverse the hook-up for positive ground cars*). Crank the engine momentarily. 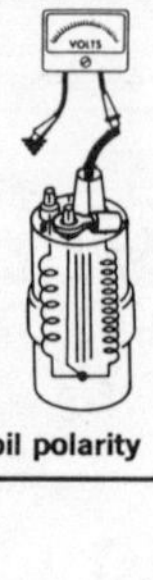 Checking coil polarity	If the voltmeter reads up-scale, the polarity is correct:	5.1
	If the voltmeter reads down-scale, reverse the coil polarity (switch the primary leads):	5.1

Test and Procedure	*Results and Indications*	*Proceed to*
5.1—Determine that the air filter is functioning efficiently: Hold paper elements up to a strong light, and attempt to see light through the filter.	Clean permanent air filters in gasoline (or manufacturer's recommendation), and allow to dry. Replace paper elements through which light cannot be seen:	5.2
5.2—Determine whether a flooding condition exists: Flooding is identified by a strong gasoline odor, and excessive gasoline present in the throttle bore(s) of the carburetor.	If flooding is not evident:	5.3
	If flooding is evident, permit the gasoline to dry for a few moments and restart. If flooding doesn't recur:	5.6
	If flooding is persistant:	5.5
5.3—Check that fuel is reaching the carburetor: Detach the fuel line at the carburetor inlet. Hold the end of the line in a cup (not styrofoam), and crank the engine.	If fuel flows smoothly:	5.6
	If fuel doesn't flow (NOTE: *Make sure that there is fuel in the tank*), or flows erratically:	5.4
5.4—Test the fuel pump: Disconnect all fuel lines from the fuel pump. Hold a finger over the input fitting, crank the engine (with electric pump, turn the ignition or pump on); and feel for suction.	If suction is evident, blow out the fuel line to the tank with low pressure compressed air until bubbling is heard from the fuel filler neck. Also blow out the carburetor fuel line (both ends disconnected):	5.6
	If no suction is evident, replace or repair the fuel pump:	5.6
	NOTE: *Repeated oil fouling of the spark plugs, or a no-start condition, could be the result of a ruptured vacuum booster pump diaphragm, through which oil or gasoline is being drawn into the intake manifold (where applicable).*	
5.5—Check the needle and seat: Tap the carburetor in the area of the needle and seat.	If flooding stops, a gasoline additive (e.g., Gumout) will often cure the problem:	5.6
	If flooding continues, check the fuel pump for excessive pressure at the carburetor (according to specifications). If the pressure is normal, the needle and seat must be removed and checked, and/or the float level adjusted:	5.6
5.6—Test the accelerator pump by looking into the throttle bores while operating the throttle.	If the accelerator pump appears to be operating normally:	5.7
	If the accelerator pump is not operating, the pump must be reconditioned. Where possible, service the pump with the carburetor(s) installed on the engine. If necessary, remove the carburetor. Prior to removal:	5.7
5.7—Determine whether the carburetor main fuel system is functioning: Spray a commercial starting fluid into the carburetor while attempting to start the engine.	If the engine starts, runs for a few seconds, and dies:	5.8
	If the engine doesn't start:	6.1

Test and Procedures	*Results and Indications*	*Proceed to*
5.8—Uncommon fuel system malfunctions: See below:	If the problem is solved:	6.1
	If the problem remains, remove and recondition the carburetor.	

Condition	*Indication*	*Test*	*Usual Weather Conditions*	*Remedy*
Vapor lock	Car will not restart shortly after running.	Cool the components of the fuel system until the engine starts.	Hot to very hot	Ensure that the exhaust manifold heat control valve is operating. Check with the vehicle manufacturer for the recommended solution to vapor lock on the model in question.
Carburetor icing	Car will not idle, stalls at low speeds.	Visually inspect the throttle plate area of the throttle bores for frost.	High humidity, 32-40° F.	Ensure that the exhaust manifold heat control valve is operating, and that the intake manifold heat riser is not blocked.
Water in the fuel	Engine sputters and stalls; may not start.	Pump a small amount of fuel into a glass jar. Allow to stand, and inspect for droplets or a layer of water.	High humidity, extreme temperature changes.	For droplets, use one or two cans of commercial gas dryer (Dry Gas) For a layer of water, the tank must be drained, and the fuel lines blown out with compressed air.

Test and Procedure	*Results and Indications*	*Proceed to*
6.1—Test engine compression: Remove all spark plugs. Insert a compression gauge into a spark plug port, crank the engine to obtain the maximum reading, and record.	If compression is within limits on all cylinders:	7.1
	If gauge reading is extremely low on all cylinders:	6.2
	If gauge reading is low on one or two cylinders:	6.2
	(If gauge readings are identical and low on two or more adjacent cylinders, the head gasket must be replaced.)	

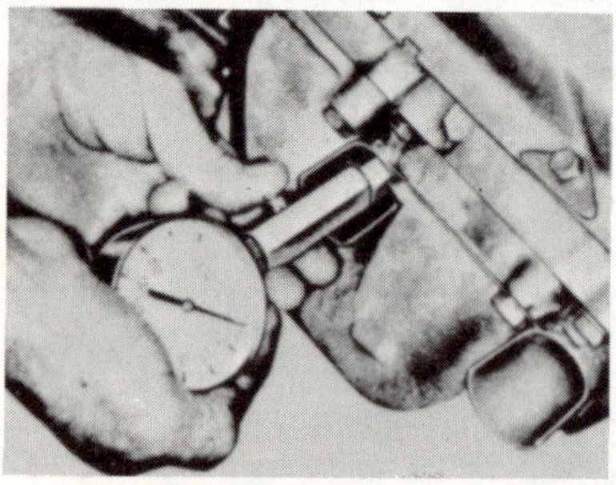

Testing compression
(© Chevrolet Div. G.M. Corp.)

Maxi. Press. Lbs. Sq. In.	*Min. Press. Lbs. Sq. In.*	*Maxi. Press. Lbs. Sq. In.*	*Min. Press. Lbs. Sq. In.*	*Max. Press. Lbs. Sq. In.*	*Min. Press. Lbs. Sq. In.*	*Max. Press. Lbs. Sq. In.*	*Min. Press. Lbs. Sq. In.*
134	101	162	121	188	141	214	160
136	102	164	123	190	142	216	162
138	104	166	124	192	144	218	163
140	105	168	126	194	145	220	165
142	107	170	127	196	147	222	166
146	110	172	129	198	148	224	168
148	111	174	131	200	150	226	169
150	113	176	132	202	151	228	171
152	114	178	133	204	153	230	172
154	115	180	135	206	154	232	174
156	117	182	136	208	156	234	175
158	118	184	138	210	157	236	177
160	120	186	140	212	158	238	178

Compression pressure limits
(© Buick Div. G.M. Corp.)

Test and Procedure	*Results and Indications*	*Proceed to*
6.2—Test engine compression (wet): Squirt approximately 30 cc. of engine oil into each cylinder, and retest per 6.1.	If the readings improve, worn or cracked rings or broken pistons are indicated:	Next Chapter
	If the readings do not improve, burned or excessively carboned valves or a jumped timing chain are indicated:	7.1
	NOTE: *A jumped timing chain is often indicated by difficult cranking.*	
7.1—Perform a vacuum check of the engine: Attach a vacuum gauge to the intake manifold beyond the throttle plate. Start the engine, and observe the action of the needle over the range of engine speeds.	See below.	See below

	Reading	*Indications*	*Proceed to*
	Steady, from 17-22 in. Hg.	Normal.	8.1
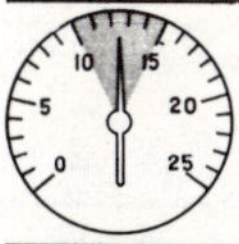	Low and steady.	Late ignition or valve timing, or low compression:	6.1
	Very low	Vacuum leak:	7.2
	Needle fluctuates as engine speed increases.	Ignition miss, blown cylinder head gasket, leaking valve or weak valve spring:	6.1, 8.3
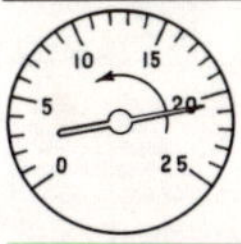	Gradual drop in reading at idle.	Excessive back pressure in the exhaust system:	10.1
	Intermittent fluctuation at idle.	Ignition miss, sticking valve:	8.3, 9.1
	Drifting needle.	Improper idle mixture adjustment, carburetors not synchronized (where applicable), or minor intake leak. Synchronize the carburetors, adjust the idle, and retest. If the condition persists:	7.2
	High and steady.	Early ignition timing:	8.2

Test and Procedure	*Results and Indications*	*Proceed to*
7.2—Attach a vacuum gauge per 7.1, and test for an intake manifold leak. Squirt a small amount of oil around the intake manifold gaskets, carburetor gaskets, plugs and fittings. Observe the action of the vacuum gauge.	If the reading improves, replace the indicated gasket, or seal the indicated fitting or plug: If the reading remains low:	8.1 7.3
7.3—Test all vacuum hoses and accessories for leaks as described in 7.2. Also check the carburetor body (dashpots, automatic choke mechanism, throttle shafts) for leaks in the same manner.	If the reading improves, service or replace the offending part(s): If the reading remains low:	8.1 6.1
8.1—Check the point dwell angle: Connect a dwell meter between the distributor primary wire and ground. Start the engine, and observe the dwell angle from idle to 3000 rpm.	If necessary, adjust the dwell angle. NOTE: *Increasing the point gap reduces the dwell angle and vice-versa.* If the dwell angle moves outside specifications as engine speed increases, the distributor should be removed and checked for cam accuracy, shaft endplay and concentricity, bushing wear, and adequate point arm tension (NOTE: *Most of these items may be checked with the distributor installed in the engine, using an oscilloscope*):	8.2
8.2—Connect a timing light (per manufacturer's recommendation) and check the dynamic ignition timing. Disconnect and plug the vacuum hose(s) to the distributor if specified, start the engine, and observe the timing marks at the specified engine speed.	If the timing is not correct, adjust to specifications by rotating the distributor in the engine: (Advance timing by rotating distributor opposite normal direction of rotor rotation, retard timing by rotating distributor in same direction as rotor rotation.)	8.3
8.3—Check the operation of the distributor advance mechanism(s): To test the mechanical advance, disconnect all but the mechanical advance, and observe the timing marks with a timing light as the engine speed is increased from idle. If the mark moves smoothly, without hesitation, it may be assumed that the mechanical advance is functioning properly. To test vacuum advance and/or retard systems, alternately crimp and release the vacuum line, and observe the timing mark for movement. If movement is noted, the system is operating.	If the systems are functioning: If the systems are not functioning, remove the distributor, and test on a distributor tester:	8.4 8.4
8.4—Locate an ignition miss: With the engine running, remove each spark plug wire, one by one, until one is found that doesn't cause the engine to roughen and slow down.	When the missing cylinder is identified:	4.1

Test and Procedure	*Results and Indications*	*Proceed to*
9.1—Evaluate the valve train: Remove the valve cover, and ensure that the valves are adjusted to specifications. A mechanic's stethoscope may be used to aid in the diagnosis of the valve train. By pushing the probe on or near push rods or rockers, valve noise often can be isolated. A timing light also may be used to diagnose valve problems. Connect the light according to manufacturer's recommendations, and start the engine. Vary the firing moment of the light by increasing the engine speed (and therefore the ignition advance), and moving the trigger from cylinder to cylinder. Observe the movement of each valve.	See below	See below

Observation	*Probable Cause*	*Remedy*	*Proceed to*
Metallic tap heard through the stethoscope.	Sticking hydraulic lifter or excessive valve clearance.	Adjust valve. If tap persists, remove and replace the lifter:	10.1
Metallic tap through the stethoscope, able to push the rocker arm (lifter side) down by hand.	Collapsed valve lifter.	Remove and replace the lifter:	10.1
Erratic, irregular motion of the valve stem.*	Sticking valve, burned valve.	Recondition the valve and/or valve guide:	Next Chapter
Eccentric motion of the pushrod at the rocker arm.*	Bent pushrod.	Replace the pushrod:	10.1
Valve retainer bounces as the valve closes.*	Weak valve spring or damper.	Remove and test the spring and damper. Replace if necessary:	10.1

*—When observed with a timing light.

Test and Procedure	*Results and Indications*	*Proceed to*
9.2—Check the valve timing: Locate top dead center of the No. 1 piston, and install a degree wheel or tape on the crankshaft pulley or damper with zero corresponding to an index mark on the engine. Rotate the crankshaft in its direction of rotation, and observe the opening of the No. 1 cylinder intake valve. The opening should correspond with the correct mark on the degree wheel according to specifications.	If the timing is not correct, the timing cover must be removed for further investigation:	

Test and Procedure	*Results and Indications*	*Proceed to*
10.1—Determine whether the exhaust manifold heat control valve is operating: Operate the valve by hand to determine whether it is free to move. If the valve is free, run the engine to operating temperature and observe the action of the valve, to ensure that it is opening.	If the valve sticks, spray it with a suitable solvent, open and close the valve to free it, and retest. If the valve functions properly: If the valve does not free, or does not operate, replace the valve:	 10.2 10.2
10.2—Ensure that there are no exhaust restrictions: Visually inspect the exhaust system for kinks, dents, or crushing. Also note that gasses are flowing freely from the tailpipe at all engine speeds, indicating no restriction in the muffler or resonator.	Replace any damaged portion of the system:	11.1
11.1—Visually inspect the fan belt for glazing, cracks, and fraying, and replace if necessary. Tighten the belt so that the longest span has approximately ½″ play at its midpoint under thumb pressure.	Replace or tighten the fan belt as necessary:	11.2

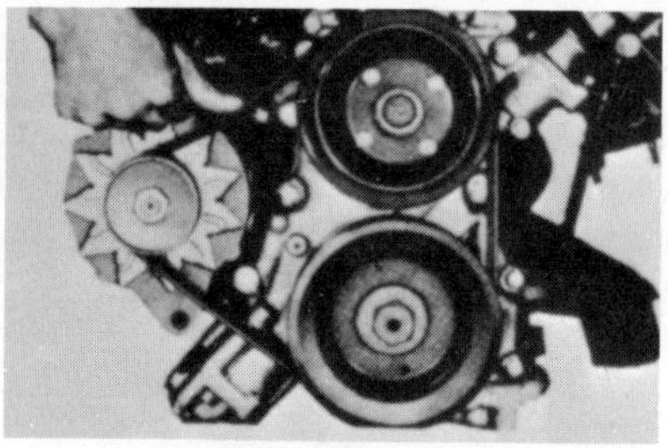

Checking the fan belt tension
(© Nissan Motor Co. Ltd.)

11.2—Check the fluid level of the cooling system.	If full or slightly low, fill as necessary: If extremely low:	11.5 11.3
11.3—Visually inspect the external portions of the cooling system (radiator, radiator hoses, thermostat elbow, water pump seals, heater hoses, etc.) for leaks. If none are found, pressurize the cooling system to 14-15 psi.	If cooling system holds the pressure: If cooling system loses pressure rapidly, reinspect external parts of the system for leaks under pressure. If none are found, check dipstick for coolant in crankcase. If no coolant is present, but pressure loss continues: If coolant is evident in crankcase, remove cylinder head(s), and check gasket(s). If gaskets are intact, block and cylinder head(s) should be checked for cracks or holes. If the gasket(s) is blown, replace, and purge the crankcase of coolant: NOTE: *Occasionally, due to atmospheric and driving conditions, condensation of water can occur in the crankcase. This causes the oil to appear milky white. To remedy, run the engine until hot, and change the oil and oil filter.*	11.5 11.4 12.6

Test and Procedure	*Results and Indication*	*Proceed to*
11.4—Check for combustion leaks into the cooling system: Pressurize the cooling system as above. Start the engine, and observe the pressure gauge. If the needle fluctuates, remove each spark plug wire, one by one, noting which cylinder(s) reduce or eliminate the fluctuation.  Radiator pressure tester (© American Motors Corp.)	Cylinders which reduce or eliminate the fluctuation, when the spark plug wire is removed, are leaking into the cooling system. Replace the head gasket on the affected cylinder bank(s).	
11.5—Check the radiator pressure cap: Attach a radiator pressure tester to the radiator cap (wet the seal prior to installation). Quickly pump up the pressure, noting the point at which the cap releases.  Testing the radiator pressure cap (© American Motors Corp.)	If the cap releases within ± 1 psi of the specified rating, it is operating properly:	11.6
	If the cap releases at more than ± 1 psi of the specified rating, it should be replaced:	11.6
11.6—Test the thermostat: Start the engine cold, remove the radiator cap, and insert a thermometer into the radiator. Allow the engine to idle. After a short while, there will be a sudden, rapid increase in coolant temperature. The temperature at which this sharp rise stops is the thermostat opening temperature.	If the thermostat opens at or about the specified temperature:	11.7
	If the temperature doesn't increase: (If the temperature increases slowly and gradually, replace the thermostat.)	11.7
11.7—Check the water pump: Remove the thermostat elbow and the thermostat, disconnect the coil high tension lead (to prevent starting), and crank the engine momentarily.	If coolant flows, replace the thermostat and retest per 11.6:	11.6
	If coolant doesn't flow, reverse flush the cooling system to alleviate any blockage that might exist. If system is not blocked, and coolant will not flow, recondition the water pump.	—
12.1—Check the oil pressure gauge or warning light: If the gauge shows low pressure, or the light is on, for no obvious reason, remove the oil pressure sender. Install an accurate oil pressure gauge and run the engine momentarily.	If oil pressure builds normally, run engine for a few moments to determine that it is functioning normally, and replace the sender.	—
	If the pressure remains low:	12.2
	If the pressure surges:	12.3
	If the oil pressure is zero:	12.3

Test and Procedure	*Results and Indications*	*Proceed to*
12.2—Visually inspect the oil: If the oil is watery or very thin, milky, or foamy, replace the oil and oil filter.	If the oil is normal: If after replacing oil the pressure remains low: If after replacing oil the pressure becomes normal:	12.3 12.3 —
12.3—Inspect the oil pressure relief valve and spring, to ensure that it is not sticking or stuck. Remove and thoroughly clean the valve, spring, and the valve body.  Oil pressure relief valve (© British Leyland Motors)	If the oil pressure improves: If no improvement is noted:	— 12.4
12.4—Check to ensure that the oil pump is not cavitating (sucking air instead of oil): See that the crankcase is neither over nor underfull, and that the pickup in the sump is in the proper position and free from sludge.	Fill or drain the crankcase to the proper capacity, and clean the pickup screen in solvent if necessary. If no improvement is noted:	12.5
12.5—Inspect the oil pump drive and the oil pump:	If the pump drive or the oil pump appear to be defective, service as necessary and retest per 12.1: If the pump drive and pump appear to be operating normally, the engine should be disassembled to determine where blockage exists:	12.1 Next Chapter
12.6—Purge the engine of ethylene glycol coolant: Completely drain the crankcase and the oil filter. Obtain a commercial butyl cellosolve base solvent, designated for this purpose, and follow the instructions precisely. Following this, install a new oil filter and refill the crankcase with the proper weight oil. The next oil and filter change should follow shortly thereafter (1000 miles).		

Chapter 3

Engine and Engine Rebuilding

Engine Electrical

DISTRIBUTOR

All of the Pinto engines are equipped with dual advance distributors. The distributor incorporates both centrifugal and vacuum ignition timing advance mechanisms. Centrifugal advance is controlled by weights contained in the distributor, under the breaker point mounting plate. As engine speed increases, centrifugal force moves the weights out from the distributor shaft and advances ignition timing. When the engine is operating under low-load conditions (light acceleration), the vacuum diaphram, which is mounted on the side of the distributor and attached to the breaker point mounting plate, moves the breaker point mounting plate, opposite the direction of distributor rotation and advances ignition timing.

Some models are also equipped with a vacuum retard mechanism. The retard mechanism is contained in the rear part of the vacuum diaphragm chamber. When the engine is operating under high-vacuum conditions (deceleration or idle), intake manifold vacuum is applied to the retard mechanism. The retard mechanism moves the breaker point mounting plate in the direction of distributor rotation and retards ignition timing. This is done to reduce engine exhaust emissions. More complete information on distributor controls which affect engine emission can be found in Chapter 4.

The 1600 cc distributor is mounted on the right side of the engine. The 2000 cc and 2300 cc on the left side front and the 2800 cc at the rear of the engine.

Removal

NOTE: *On early model 2000 cc engines equipped with air conditioning, it may be necessary to move the alternator out of the way to gain access to the distributor.*

Remove the lower alternator mounting bolt. Loosen the upper alternator mounting bolt and remove the alternator drive.

On the 2800 cc engine remove the air cleaner. On engines equipped with an air pump, remove one mounting bolt, and the drive belt; then, swing the pump to one side to allow access to the distributor. Disconnect the air pump, air filter, and lines if necessary.

1. Disconnect the high-tension and primary wires that run from the distributor to the coil.
2. Unsnap the two distributor cap retaining clamps and remove the distributor cap. Position it out of the way.
3. Using chalk or paint, carefully mark

the position of the distributor rotor in relation to the distributor housing, and the position of the distributor housing in relation to the engine block. When this is done, you should have a line on the distributor housing directly in line with the tip of the rotor, and another line on the engine block directly in line with the mark on the distributor housing. *This is very important because the distributor must be reinstalled in the exact same location it was removed from if correct ignition timing is to be maintained.*

4. Note the position of the vacuum line(s) on the vacuum diaphragm and then disconnect the line(s) from the distributor.

5. Remove the bolt that attaches the distributor to the engine block and remove the distributor from the engine.

NOTE: *On all engines except the 1600 cc, the oil pump is driven by a driveshaft which engages the bottom of the distributor shaft. If the oil pump driveshaft comes out of the engine when removing the distributor, coat the tip of the driveshaft with heavy grease and install it in the bottom of the distributor shaft when installing the distributor.*

CAUTION: *Do not disturb the engine while the distributor is removed. If you attempt to start the engine with the distributor removed, you will have to retime the engine.*

Installation

1. Install the rotor on the distributor shaft and align the tip of the rotor with the line that you made on the distributor housing.

2. With the rotor and housing aligned, insert the distributor into the engine while aligning the mark on the housing with the mark on the block.

NOTE: *Since the distributor is equipped with a spiral gear, the rotor will turn slightly as the gear on the distributor meshes with the gear on the camshaft or auxiliary shaft. Allow for this when installing the distributor by aligning the mark on the distributor with the mark on the block, but positioning the tip of the rotor slightly to the side of the mark on the distributor. On 1600 cc engines, the rotor will move to the right as it is installed. On all other engines, it will move to the left.*

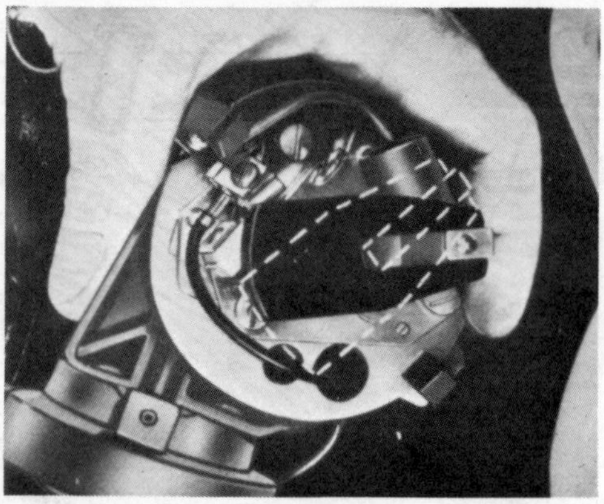

Movement of rotor while installing distributor

3. When the distributor is fully seated in the engine, install and tighten the distributor hold-down bolt.

4. Plug the vacuum line(s) to the distributor with a pencil or golf tee.

5. Align and install the distributor cap. Snap the cap retaining clamps into place.

6. Install the high-tension and primary wires on the coil.

7. Attach a timing light to the engine, start the engine, and check the ignition timing.

8. Turn off the engine, disconnect the timing light, and connect the vacuum line(s) to the distributor.

Installation When Engine Has Been Disturbed

If the engine was cranked with the distributor removed, it will be necessary to retime the engine. If you have installed the distributor incorrectly and the engine will not start, remove the distributor from the engine and start from scratch.

1. Hold the distributor close to the engine and install the cap on the distributor in its normal position.

2. Locate the no. 1 spark plug wire tower on the distributor cap.

3. Scribe a mark on the body of the distributor directly below the no. 1 spark plug wire tower on the distributor cap.

4. Remove the distributor cap from the distributor and move the distributor and cap out of the way.

5. Remove the no. 1 spark plug and crank the engine over until the no. 1 cyl-

Firing Order

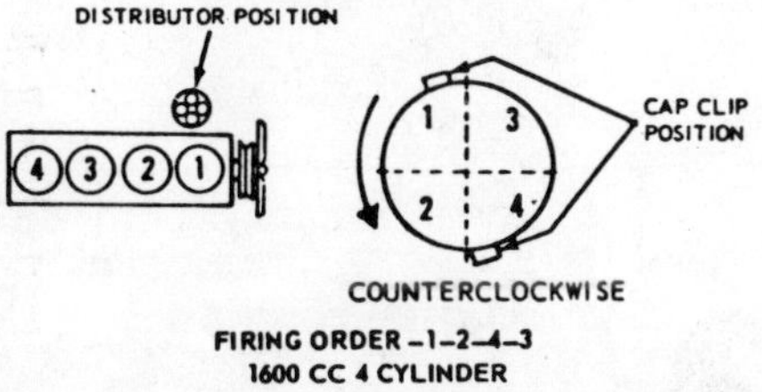

1600 cc distributor numbering and rotor rotation

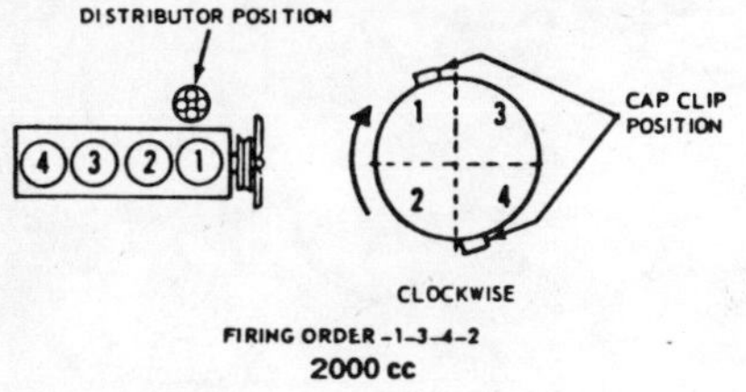

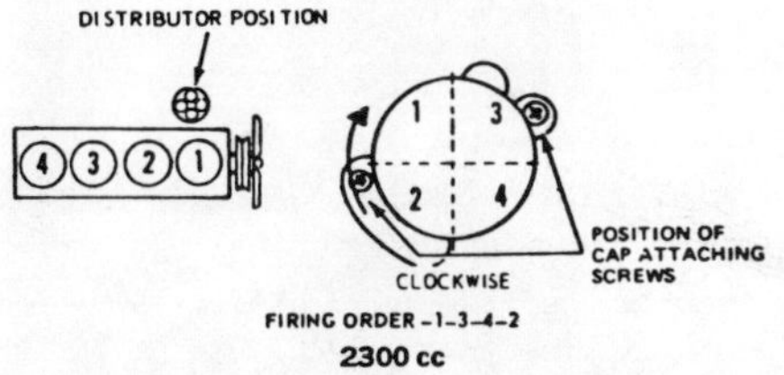

2000 and 2300 cc distributor numbering and rotor rotation

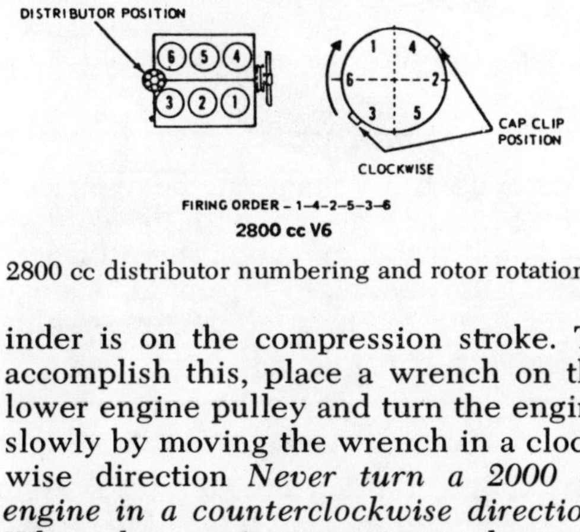

2800 cc distributor numbering and rotor rotation

inder is on the compression stroke. To accomplish this, place a wrench on the lower engine pulley and turn the engine slowly by moving the wrench in a clockwise direction *Never turn a 2000 cc engine in a counterclockwise direction.* When the no. 1 piston is on the compression stroke, air will be forced out of the no. 1 spark plug hole. When the no. 1 cylinder is on the compression stroke, continue to turn the engine over until the ignition timing pointer is aligned with the proper timing mark on the scale. The proper timing mark is the ignition timing figure given in the tune-up specifications in Chapter 2.

6. With the timing mark aligned, align the distributor rotor with the mark that was scribed on the distributor housing in step three.

7. Install the distributor in the engine keeping the rotor aligned with the mark. Since the distributor is driven by a spiral gear, the rotor will turn slightly as the distributor gear engages the camshaft or auxiliary shaft. Compensate for this by positioning the rotor slightly to the left of the mark on 1600 cc engines or slightly to the right of the mark on all other engines. Install and hand-tighten the distributor hold-down bolt.

8. Turn the distributor in the engine until the points just start to open. Tighten the distributor hold-down bolt.

9. Install the distributor cap and wires. Plug the vacuum lines to the distributor.

10. Attach a timing light and start the engine.

11. Check and adjust ignition timing.

12. Stop the engine, disconnect the timing light, and install the distributor vacuum line(s).

SOLID STATE IGNITION

Primary Circuit Testing

A breakdown or energy loss in the primary circuit can be caused by: defective primary wiring, loose or corroded connections, inoperative or defective magnetic pick-up coil assembly, or defective amplifier module.

A complete test of the primary circuit consists of checking the circuits in the ignition coil, the magnetic pick-up coil assembly and the amplifier module. Wiring harness checks will be included as a part of basic component circuit tests.

Always inspect connectors for dirt, corrosion or poor fit before assuming you have spotted a possible problem.

Troubleshooting

Make sure that the battery is fully charged before beginning tests. Perform a Spark Intensity Test. If no spark is observed, make sure that the high tension coil wire is good. Disconnect the three-

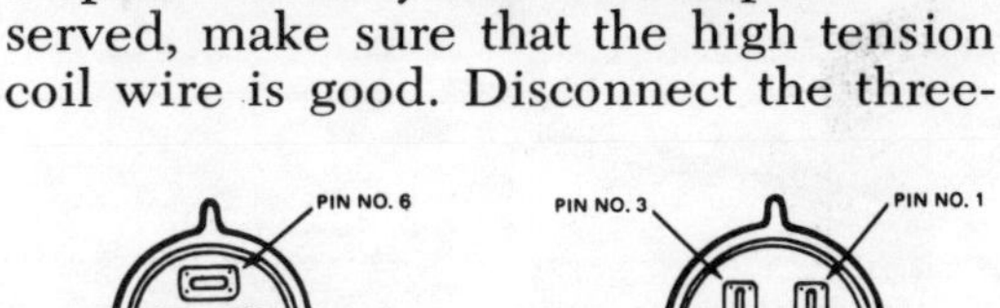

Electronic module connectors, harness side

way and four-way connectors at the electronic module.

The first trouble isolation test will be conducted on the harness terminals, with the electronic module disconnected from the circuit. The pin or socket numbers shown in the schematic correspond to those shown in the diagnosis tables.

Make the following tests using a sensitive volt-ohmmeter. These tests will direct you to the proper follow-up test to determine the actual problem.

If the circuit checks good at all these test points, connect a known good electronic module in place of the vehicle module and again perform the spark intensity test. If the substitution corrects the malfunction again reconnect the vehicle module and perform the spark intensity test. If the malfunction still exists, the problem is in the module and it must be replaced. If the problem is gone, it may be in the wiring connectors.

If the substitute module does not correct the problem, reconnect the original module and make repairs elsewhere in the system.

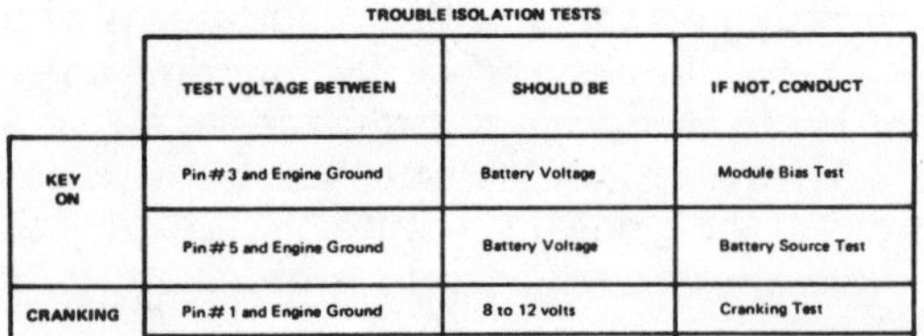

Electronic module schematic for solid state ignition

TROUBLE ISOLATION TESTS

	TEST VOLTAGE BETWEEN	SHOULD BE	IF NOT, CONDUCT
KEY ON	Pin # 3 and Engine Ground	Battery Voltage	Module Bias Test
	Pin # 5 and Engine Ground	Battery Voltage	Battery Source Test
CRANKING	Pin # 1 and Engine Ground	8 to 12 volts	Cranking Test
	Pin # 5 and Engine Ground	8 to 12 volts	Starting Circuit Test
	Pin # 7 and Pin # 8	½ volt A.C. or D.C. volt wiggle	Distributor Hardware Test

	TEST RESISTANCE BETWEEN	SHOULD BE	IF NOT, CONDUCT
KEY OFF	Pin # 7 and Pin # 8 Pin # 6 and Engine Ground Pin # 7 and Engine Ground Pin # 8 and Engine Ground	400 to 800 ohms 0 ohms more than 70,000 ohms more than 70,000 ohms	Magnetic Pick-up (Stator) Test
	Pin # 3 and Coil Tower Pin # 5 and Pin # 4	7000 to 13000 ohms 1.0 to 2.0 ohms	Coil Test
	Pin # 5 and Engine Ground	more than 10.0 ohms	Short Test
	Pin # 3 and Pin # 4	1.0 to 2.0 ohms	Resistance Wire

Solid state ignition troubleshooting chart

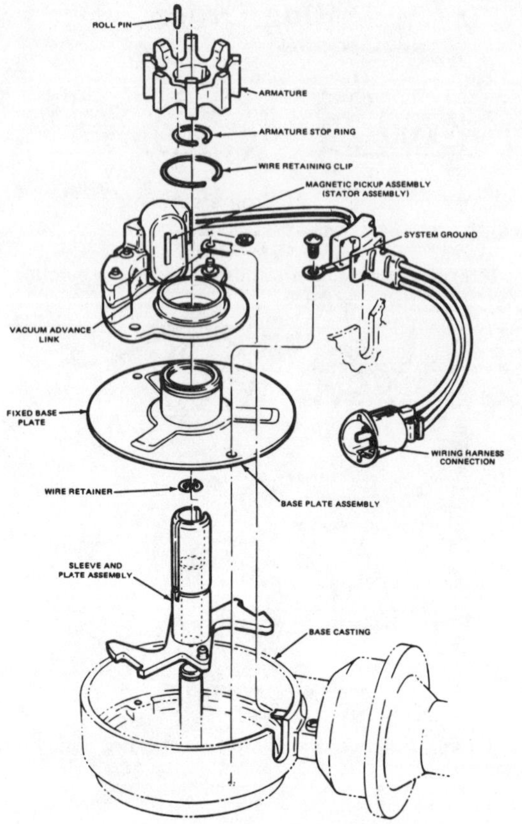

Exploded view of a solid state distributor

Module Bias Test

Measure the voltage at the indicated point to engine ground with the ignition key "on." If the voltage observed is less than battery voltage, repair the voltage feed wiring to the module for running conditions (rewire).

Battery Source Test

1. Connect the voltmeter leads from the battery terminal at the coil to engine ground, without disconnecting the coil from the circuit.
2. Install a jumper wire from the DEC terminal of the coil to a good engine ground.
3. Turn the lights and all accessories off.
4. Turn the ignition switch "on".
5. If the voltmeter reading is between 4.9 and 7.9 volts, the primary circuit from the battery is satisfactory.
6. If the voltmeter reading is less than 4.9 volts, check the following:
   a. The primary wiring for worn insu-

lation, broken strands, and loose or corroded terminals.

b. The resistance wiring for defects.

7. If the voltmeter reading is greater than 7.9 volts, the resistance wire should be replaced after verifying a defect.

CRANKING TEST

Measure the voltage at the indicated point to engine ground with the engine cranking. If the voltage observed is not 8 to 12 volts, repair the voltage feed to the module for starting conditions (white wire).

STARTING CIRCUIT TEST

If the reading is not between 8 and 12 volts on models through 1974 the ignition by-pass circuit is open or grounded from either the starter solenoid or the ignition switch to Pin 5. On 1975 and later models, the switch by-pass circuit is open or grounded from either the starter solenoid or the switch to socket 5, if the reading is under 6 volts. Check the primary connections at the coil.

DISTRIBUTOR HARDWARE TEST

1. Disconnect the three-wire weatherproof connector at the distributor pigtail.
2. Connect a D.C. voltmeter on a 2.5 volt scale to the two parallel blades. With the engine cranking, the meter needle should oscillate.
3. Remove the distributor cap and check for visual damage or misassembly.

   a. Sintered iron armature (4, 6 or 8-toothed wheel) must be tight on the sleeve, and the roll pin aligning the armature must be in position.

   b. Sintered iron stator must not be broken.

   Armature must rotate when the engine is cranked.
4. If the hardware is alright, but the meter doesn't oscillate, replace the magnetic pick-up assembly.

MAGNETIC PICK-UP TESTS

STARTING CIRCUIT TEST

If the reading is not between 8 and 12 volts on models through 1974 the ignition by-pass circuit is open or grounded from either the starter solenoid or the ignition switch to Pin 5. On 1975 and later models, the switch by-pass circuit is open or grounded from either the starter solenoid or the switch to socket 5, if the reading is under 6 volts. Check the primary connections at the coil.

DISTRIBUTOR HARDWARE TEST

1. Disconnect the three-wire weatherproof connector at the distributor pigtail.
2. Connect a D.C. voltmeter on a 2.5 volt scale to the two parallel blades. With the engine cranking, the meter needle should oscillate.
3. Remove the distributor cap and check for visual damage or misassembly.

   a. Sintered iron armature (4, 6 or 8-toothed wheel) must be tight on the sleeve, and the roll pin aligning the armature must be in position.

   b. Sintered iron stator must not be broken.

   c. Armature must rotate when the engine is cranked.
4. If the hardware is alright, but the meter doesn't oscillate, replace the magnetic pick-up assembly.

MAGNETIC PICK-UP TESTS

1. Resistance of pick-up coil measured between two parallel pins in the distributor connector must be 400–800 ohms.
2. Resistance between the third blade (ground) and the distributor body must be zero ohms.
3. Resistance between either parallel blade and engine ground must be greater than 70,000 ohms.
4. If any test fails, the distributor stator assembly is defective and must be replaced.
5. If the above readings are not the same as measured in the original test, check for a defective harness. If the readings are the same, proceed.
6. If these tests check alright, the signal generator portion of the distributor is working properly.

IGNITION COIL TEST

The breakerless ignition coil must be diagnosed separately from the rest of the ignition system.

1. Primary resistance must be 1.0–2.0 ohms, measured from the BAT to the DEC terminals.
2. Secondary resistance must be 7,000–13,000 ohms, measured from the

BAT or DEC terminal to the center tower of the coil.

3. If resistance tests are alright, but the coil is still suspected, test the coil on a coil tester by following the test equipment manufacturer's instructions for a standard coil. If the reading differs from the original test, check for a defective harness.

Short Test

If the resistance from Pin 5 to ground is less than 4 ohms, check for a short to ground at the DEC terminal of the ignition coil or in the wiring to that terminal.

Resistance Wire Test

Replace the resistance wire if it does not show a resistance of 1.3–1.4 ohms.

Adjustments

The air gap between the armature and magnetic pick-up coil in the distributor is not adjustable, nor are there any adjustments for the amplifier module. Inoperative components are simply replaced. Any attempt to connect components outside the vehicle may result in component failure.

Component Replacement

Magnetic Pick-Up Assembly Removal and Installation

1. Remove the distributor cap and rotor and disconnect the distributor harness plug.
2. Using a small gear puller or two screwdrivers, lift or pry the armature from the advance plate sleeve. Remove the roll pin.
3. Remove the large wire retaining clip from the base plate annular groove.
4. Remove the snap-ring which secures the vacuum advance link to the pick-up assembly.
5. Remove the magnetic pick-up assembly ground screw and lift the assembly from the distributor.
6. Lift the vacuum advance arm off the post on the pick-up assembly and move it out against the distributor housing.
7. Place the new pick-up assembly in position over the fixed base plate and slide the wiring in position through the slot in the side of the distributor housing.
8. Install the fine wire snap-ring securing the pick-up assembly to the fixed base plate.
9. Position the vacuum advance arm over the post on the pick-up assembly and install the snap-ring.
10. Install the grounding screw through the tab on the wiring harness and into the fixed base plate.
11. Install the armature on the advance plate sleeve making sure that the roll pin is engaged in the matching slots.
12. Install the distributor rotor cap.
13. Connect the distributor wiring plug to the vehicle harness.

CHARGING SYSTEM

The alternator charging system is composed of the alternator, the alternator regulator, the charging system warning light, the battery and a fuse link wire.

A failure of any component of the charging system can cause the entire system to stop functioning. Because of this, the charging system can be very difficult to troubleshoot when problems occur.

When the ignition key is turned to the "on" position, current flows from the battery, through the charging system indicator light on the instrument panel, to the voltage regulator, and to the alternator. Since the alternator is not producing any current, the alternator warning light comes on. When the engine is started, the alternator begins to produce current and the alternator light goes off. As the alternator turns and produces current, that current is divided in two ways: part to the battery to charge the battery and power the electrical components of the vehicle, and part to the alternator to enable it to increase its output. In this situation, the alternator is receiving current from the battery and from itself. A voltage regulator is wired into the current supply to the alternator to prevent it from receiving too much current which would cause it to put out too much current. Conversely, if the voltage regulator does not allow the alternator to receive enough current, the battery will not be fully charged and will eventually go dead.

The battery is connected to the alternator at all times, whether the ignition key is turned on or not. If the battery were shorted to ground, the alternator would also be shorted. This would damage the alternator. To prevent this, a fuse link is installed in the wiring between the battery and the alternator. If the battery is shorted, the fuse link melts, protecting the alternator.

Since the alternator, the alternator regulator, the charging system warning light, the battery and the fuse link are all interconnected, failure of one component can cause the others to become inoperative.

Troubleshooting

Portions of this section were written with the assistance of Mr. Chuck Belmont. There are many different types of charging system problems and most require expensive tools to diagnose. However, when one component of the system fails completely it is a little easier to locate the source of the problem. Therefore, we will deal only with a complete failure of the system which causes the battery to go dead. If the battery goes dead while the car is parked, but charges back up when the engine is run, the problem is a short in the car electrical system and not a charging system failure. Step one of this procedure will tell you how to determine if you have a short in the chassis electrical system.

You will need two testing instruments to use this section. They are both relatively cheap and readily available. The first is a current indicator. This device, when placed on a wire which has current passing through it, will measure the current in amps. The other is a test light. This is simply a pointed screwdriver which contains a light bulb and has a ground wire attached to it. When the pointed end is touched to an electrical component that has current running to it, and the ground wire is attached to a good ground, the light in the handle comes on.

This test works under three assumptions:

A: The battery is known to be good and fully charged.

B: The alternator belt is in good condition and adjusted to the proper tension.

C: All connections in the system are clean and tight.

NOTE: *In order for the current indicator to give a valid reading, the car must be equipped with battery cables which are of the same gauge size and quality as original equipment battery cables.*

1. Turn off all electrical components on the car. Make sure the doors of the car are closed. If the car is equipped with a clock, disconnect the clock by removing the lead wire from the rear of the clock. Disconnect the positive battery cable from the battery and connect the ground wire on a test light to the disconnected positive battery cable. Touch the probe end of the test light to the positive battery post. The test light should not light. If the test light does light, there is a short or open circuit on the car. See Chapter 5 for troubleshooting procedures for this problem.

2. Disconnect the voltage regulator wiring harness connector at the voltage regulator. Turn the ignition key to the "on" position. Connect the wire on a test light to a good ground (engine bolt). Touch the probe end of a test light to the ignition wire connector in the voltage regulator wiring connector. This wire corresponds to the I terminal on the regulator. If the test light goes on, the charging system warning light circuit is all right. If the test light does not come on and the warning light on the instrument panel is on, either the resistor wire, in parallel with the warning light, or the wiring to the voltage regulator is defective. If the test light does not come on and the warning light is not on, either the bulb is defective or the power supply wire from the battery through the ignition switch to the bulb has an open circuit. Connect the wiring harness to the regulator.

3. Examine the fuse link wire in the wiring harness from the starter relay to the alternator. If the insulation on the wire is cracked or split the fuse link may be melted. Connect a test light to the fuse link by attaching the ground wire on the test light to an engine bolt and touching the probe end of the light to the bottom of the fuse link wire where it splices into the alternator output wire. If the bulb in the test light does not light the fuse link is melted.

4. Start the engine and place a current indicator on the positive battery cable.

Turn off all electrical accessories and make sure the doors are closed. If the charging system is working properly, the gauge will show a charge of about five amps. If the system is not working properly, the gauge will show a draw of about five amps. A charge moves the needle toward the battery, a draw moves the needle away from the battery. Turn the engine off.

5. Disconnect the wiring harness from the voltage regulator at the regulator connector. Connect a male spade terminal (solderless connector) to each end of a jumper wire. Insert one end of the wire into the wiring harness connector which corresponds to the A terminal on the regulator. Insert the other end of the wire into the wiring harness connector which corresponds to the F terminal on the regulator. Position the connector with the jumper wire installed so that it cannot contact any metal surface under the hood. Position a current indicator gauge on the positive battery cable. Have an assistant start the engine. Observe the reading on the current indicator. Have your assistant *slowly* raise the speed of the engine to about 2000 rpm or until the current indicator needle stops moving, which ever comes first. *Do not run the engine for more than a short period of time in this condition. If the wiring harness connector or jumper wire become excessively hot during this test, turn off the engine and check for a grounded wire in the regulator wiring harness.* If the current indicator shows a charge of *about* 0–5 amps below the rated output of the alternator, the alternator is working properly. If the previous test showed a draw, the voltage regulator is defective. If the gauge does not show the proper charging rate, the alternator is defective.

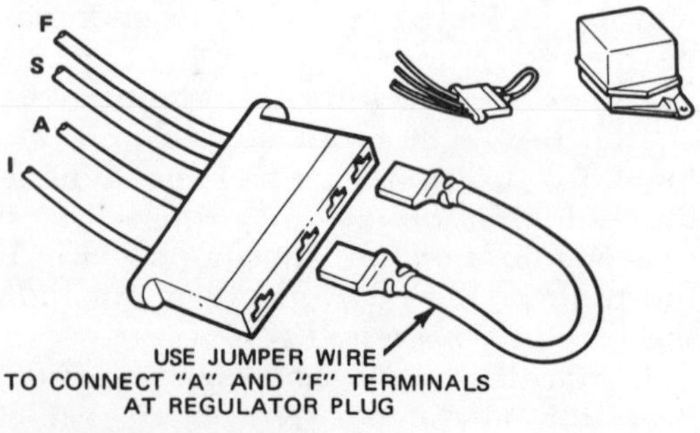

Jumper wire installation

Battery Rating

Batteries are now rated two ways, by a cold power rating number and a reserve capacity number. To determine the size battery you need, match your engine size (97, 122, 140 or 170 cu in.) to the cold power rating. The reserve capacity number will tell you how many minutes that particular battery will operate the ignition, lighting, wipers and defroster if your charging system should stop operating. A battery with a 140 cold power rating and a 120 reserve capacity rating would be for a Pinto 2300 cc engine, and would last for 120 minutes if the charging system should fail.

Charging System Precautions

Whenever working on an alternator charging system certain precautions must be followed.

It should be remembered that as long as a charged battery is connected to the circuit, voltage will be present at the alternator output terminal whether the engine is running or not.

Never run an engine with an alternator unless all the components of the charging system are connected.

Never short-out or ground a component of the system. Do not attempt to polarize the alternator.

If the vehicle is run for an extended period of time with a defective part in the charging system, it may be necessary to charge the battery at a very slow rate on a battery charger before the battery will accept a charge.

If another battery is connected to the vehicle to jump-start it, never use more than 12V.

Whenever jumping a vehicle with a booster battery (or another car) always connect positive to positive and negative to negative.

In order for an alternator charging system to work properly *all* connections in the system must be *clean* and *tight.*

Alternator Removal

While internal alternator repairs are possible, they require specialized tools and training. Therefore, it is advisable to replace a defective alternator, or have it repaired by a qualified shop.

1. Disconnect the negative battery cable from the battery.

2. Disconnect the wires from the rear of the alternator.
3. Loosen the alternator mounting bolts.
4. Remove the belt.
5. Remove the alternator mounting bolts and remove the alternator.

Alternator Installation

1. Position the alternator on the engine and install the attaching bolts.
2. Connect the wires on the rear of the alternator.
3. Position the belt on the alternator.
4. Adjust the alternator belt tension as described in Chapter 1.
5. Connect the negative battery cable.

Regulator

The regulator is a device which controls the output of the alternator. If the regulator did not limit the voltage output of the alternator, the excessive output could burn out components of the electrical system.

The voltage regulator is preset at the factory and is not adjustable

REMOVAL

1. Disconnect the negative battery cable from the battery.
2. Disconnect the wiring harness from the regulator.
3. Remove the regulator attaching screws and remove the regulator.

INSTALLATION

1. Position the regulator on the car and install the attaching screws.
2. Attach the wiring to the regulator.
3. Connect the negative battery cable.

Fuse Link

The fuse link is a short length of insulated wire contained in the alternator wiring harness, between the alternator and the starter relay. The fuse link is several wire gauge sizes smaller than the other wires in the harness. If a booster battery is connected incorrectly to the car battery or if some component of the charging system is shorted to ground, the fuse link melts and protects the alternator. The fuse link is attached to the starter relay. The insulation on the wire reads: Fuse Link. A melted fuse link can usually be identified by cracked or bubbled insulation. If it is difficult to determine if the fuse link is melted, connect a test light to both ends of the wire. If the fuse link is not melted, the test light will light showing that an open circuit does not exist in the wire.

REPLACEMENT

1. Disconnect the negative battery cable.
2. Disconnect the eyelet end of the link from the starter relay.
3. Cut the other end of the link from the wiring harness at the splice.
4. Connect the eyelet end of the new fuse link to the starter relay.

NOTE: *Use only an original equipment type fuse link, do not replace with standard wire.*

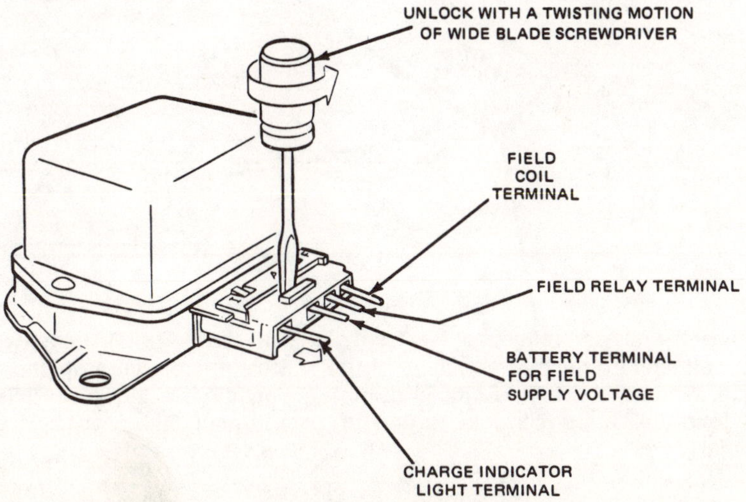

Voltage regulator

5. Splice the open end of the new fuse link into the wiring harness.

6. Solder the splice with rosin core solder and wrap the splice in electrical tape. This splice *must* be soldered.

7. Connect the negative battery cable.

STARTER

The positive engagement starter is connected to the battery (when the ignition key is turned to the "start" position) by a starter relay. When current is received from the battery, the starter drive engages the starter with the flywheel and turns the engine.

On models with an automatic transmission, a transmission-mounted neutral safety switch prevents the relay from being energized when the transmission selector lever is in any position but Park or Neutral.

Troubleshooting

For starting system troubleshooting see the troubleshooting section in Chapter 2.

For the neutral safety switch adjustment procedure see Chapter 6.

Alternator Specifications

Year	*Model No.*	*Amps*
'71	D0ZF-B	38
	D0AF-G	42
'72	D2ZF-AA	38
	D2AF-AA	42
	D2SF-AA	55
	D2AF-CA	61
	D20F-AA	65

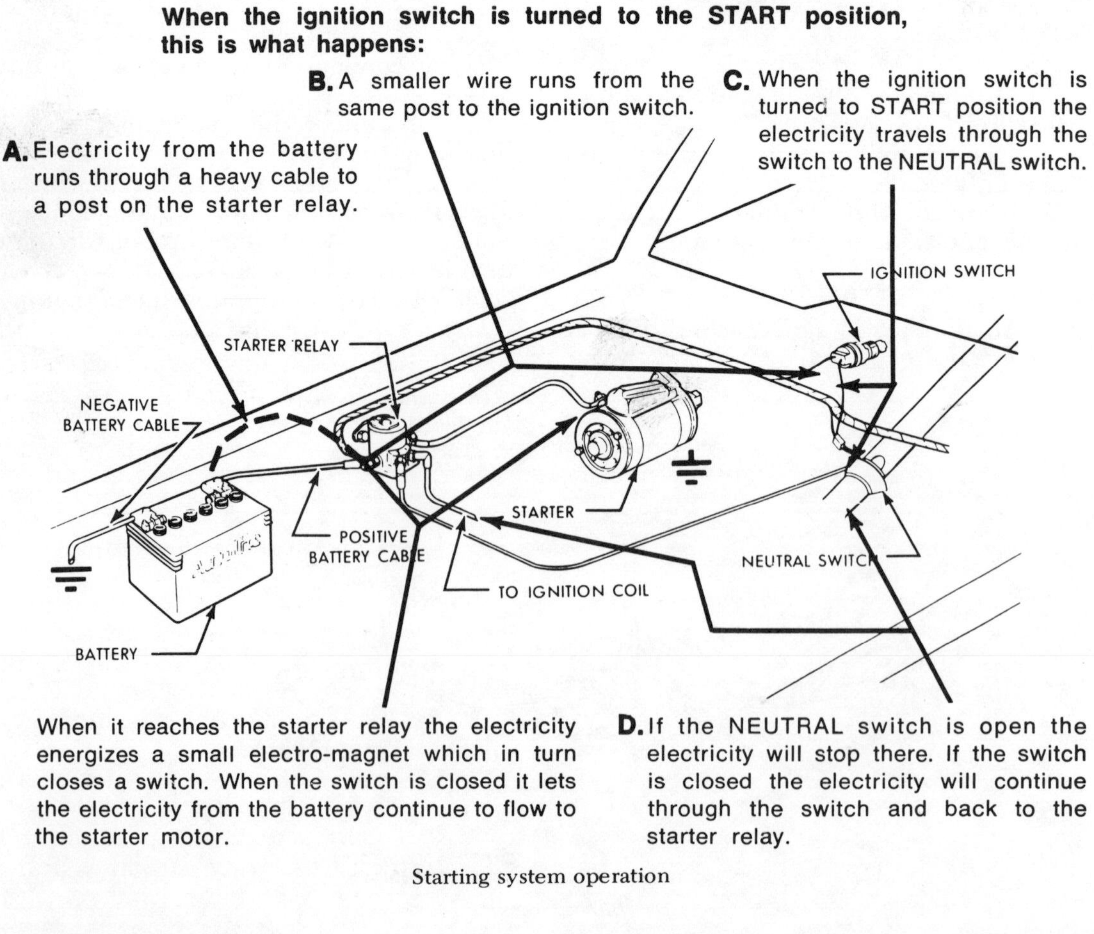

Starting system operation

Year	*Model No.*	*Amps*
'73	D2ZF-AC	38
	D20F-DB	42
	D20F-CB	61
	D2ZF-BA	61
	D2ZF-AB	70
'74–'75	D3ZF-AA,	38
	D4ZF-EA,	
	D42F-EA,	
	D42F-AA,	
	D4ZF-BA,	
	D32F-AA	
	D30F-EA,	61
	D32F-BA,	
	D32F-BA,	
	D42F-EA,	
	D3UF-AA,	
	D40F-DA,	
	D34F-AA	
	D30F-AA,	70
	D42F-AA,	
	D32F-AA,	
	D40F-EA,	
	D42F-CA,	
	D4ZF-AA	
	D52F-AA,	42
	D30F-FA,	

Year	*Model No.*	*Amps*
'74–'75	D3TF-CA	
'76–'77	D5AF-JA	40
	D5AF-AA	
	D5AF-BA	42
	D5AF-CA	60
	D5AF-LA	
	D30F-AA	70
	D4ZF-AA	
	D52F-BA	

Removal and Installation

1971–72 Engines

1. Raise the front of the vehicle and support it with jackstands.
2. Disconnect the cable from the starter.
3. Remove the attaching bolts and remove the starter from the engine.
4. Position the starter on the engine and install the starter attaching bolts hand tight.
5. Tighten the starter attaching bolts to 15–20 ft lbs while holding the starter squarely against its mounting.
6. Connect the cable to the starter.
7. Remove the jackstands and lower the vehicle.

1973 1600 cc Engine

1. Raise the front of the vehicle and support it with jackstands.
2. Remove the right steering gear housing clamp and grommet from the crossmember and loosen the left clamp bolts.
3. Disconnect the starter cable from the starter terminal.
4. Remove the three starter attaching bolts and remove the starter.
5. Place the starter into position and loosely install the three attaching bolts.

6. While holding the starter squarely against its mounting surface, tighten the bolts.

7. Tighten the bolts to 15–20 ft lbs.

8. Remove the jackstands and lower the vehicle.

1973 2000 cc Engine

1. Raise the front of the vehicle and support it with jackstands.

2. Disconnect the starter cable from the starter terminal.

3. Remove the three starter attaching bolts.

4. Turn the steering gear bellows clamp and remove the starter.

5. Place the starter into position and start the three attaching bolts.

6. While holding the starter squarely against its mounting surface, tighten the bolts.

7. Tighten the bolts to 15–20 ft lbs.

8. Connect the starter cable to the terminal.

9. Tighten the steering gear bellows clamp.

10. Remove the jackstands and lower the vehicle.

1974–76 All Engines

1. Disconnect the battery negative cable, raise the car and support it with jackstands.

2. Remove the four crossmember bolts and remove the crossmember.

3. Remove the flexible coupling clamping screw where it attaches to the steering gear.

4. Remove the bolts which connect the steering gear to the crossmember. Then disengage the steering gear from the flexible coupling and pull the gear down far enough to gain access to the starter motor.

5. Disconnect the starter cable, remove the starter bolts, and remove the motor.

6. Installation is the reverse of removal, but make sure that the steering gear is lined up properly when you replace it.

Starter Drive Replacement

1. Remove the starter from the engine.

2. Remove the brush cover band.

3. Remove the starter drive plunger lever cover.

4. Loosen the thru-bolts just enough to allow removal of the drive end housing and the starter drive plunger lever return spring.

5. Remove the pivot pin which attaches the starter drive plunger lever to the starter frame and remove the lever.

6. Remove the stop ring retainer and stop-ring from the armature shaft.

7. Remove the starter drive from the armature shaft.

8. Inspect the teeth on the starter drive. If they are excessively worn, inspect the teeth on the ring gear of the flywheel. If the teeth on the flywheel are excessively worn, the flywheel should be replaced.

9. Apply a thin coat of white grease

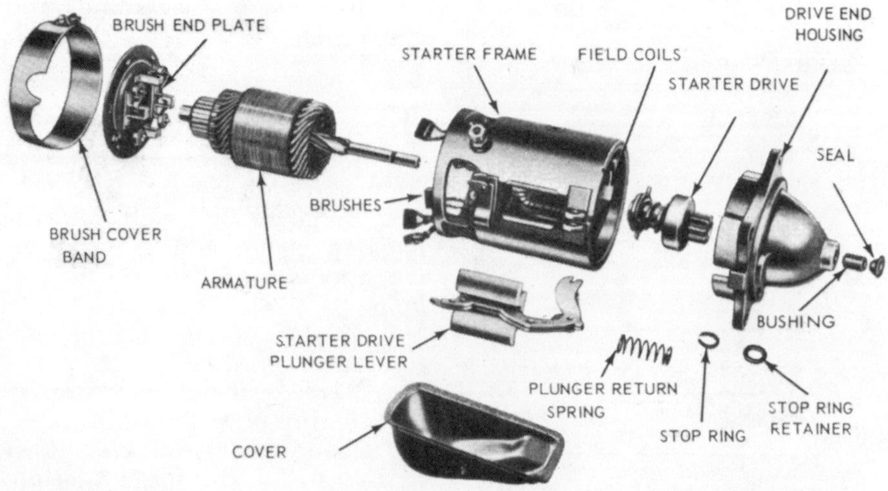

Exploded view of starter

to the armature shaft, in the area in which the starter drive operates.

10. Install the starter drive on the armature shaft and install a new stop-ring.

11. Position the starter drive plunger lever on the starter frame and install the pivot pin. *Make sure the plunger lever is properly engaged with the starter drive.*

12. Install a new stop ring retainer on the armature shaft.

13. Fill the drive end housing bearing bore ¼ full with grease.

14. Position the starter drive plunger lever return spring and the drive end housing to the starter frame.

15. Tighten the starter thru-bolts to 55–75 in. lbs.

16. Install the starter drive plunger lever cover and the brush cover band on the starter.

17. Install the starter.

BATTERY

Removal and Installation

1. Loosen the battery cable bolts and spread the ends of the battery cable terminals.
2. Disconnect the negative battery cable first.
3. Disconnect the positive battery cable.
4. Remove the battery hold-down.
5. Remove the battery from under the hood. *Be careful not to tip the battery and spill acid on yourself or the car during removal.*
6. Place the battery in its holder under the hood. *Use care not to spill the acid.*
7. Install the battery hold-down.
8. Install the positive battery cable first.
9. Install the negative battery cable.
10. Apply a *light* coating of grease to the cable ends.

Engine Mechanical

DESIGN

1600 cc

The 1600 cc engine is a modified version of the engine that was used in Cortinas for several years. The four-cylinder inline engine has overhead valves activated by mechanical valve lifters and a camshaft mounted in the block. The cylinder block and the cylinder head are cast iron. The intake manifold is cast aluminum. The intake manifold is mounted on the right side of the cylinder head and the exhaust manifold on the left side. This provides for a cross-flow of intake and exhaust gases through the cylinder head.

The pistons are made of aluminum alloy and are fitted to the steel connecting rods by full-floating piston pins. The cast iron crankshaft is supported by five main bearings with crankshaft end thrust being taken by the no. 3 bearing.

The combustion chamber is formed by a dish in the tops of the pistons, since the bottom of the cylinder head is flat.

The camshaft is chain driven at one-half engine speed by the crankshaft. A helical gear on the camshaft drives the distributor and oil pump, while the fuel pump is actuated by an eccentric on the cam.

The weight of the 1600 cc engine is 264 lbs.

NOTE: *The intake valves on the 1600 cc engine are aluminum-coated and cannot be refaced.*

2000 cc

The 2000 cc four-cylinder inline engine is equipped with an overhead camshaft. The camshaft is mounted on the top of the cylinder head in three bearings, and opens the valves by means of cam followers or rocker arms. The overhead camshaft eliminates the need for valve lifters and pushrods. The cylinder block and cylinder head are made of cast iron, while the intake manifold is aluminum. The intake and exhaust manifolds are mounted on opposite sides of the cylinder head, providing for a cross-flow of intake and exhaust gases through the cylinder head.

The pistons are made from an aluminum alloy with steel struts. The forged steel connecting rods are attached to the pistons by piston pins which are locked in place. The cast iron crankshaft is supported by five main bearings.

The camshaft is driven at one-half crankshaft speed by a fiberglass-reinforced rubber belt. An automatic timing belt tensioner maintains belt tension.

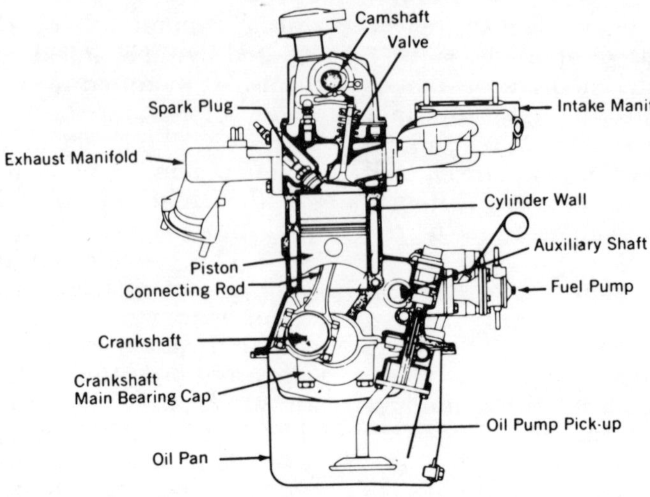

2000 cc engine

Since the camshaft is mounted on the top of the cylinder head, an auxiliary shaft was added to the engine to drive the oil pump, fuel pump and distributor. The auxiliary shaft is driven by the camshaft belt.

The weight of the engine is 297 lbs.

2300 cc

The 2300 cc engine is a 4 cylinder overhead cam engine. It uses a cross-flow cylinder head, with all intake ports on one side and all exhaust ports on the other. The block is cast iron and uses a five main bearing crankshaft. The camshaft is supported by four bearings. The main, connecting rod, camshaft and auxiliary shaft bearings are all replaceable. Hydraulic valve lash adjusters are used in the valve train which automatically regulate the rocker arm pivot height to maintain zero valve lash. The intake manifold is a die-cast aluminum type and uses a two barrel Holley/Weber carburetor. The camshaft is driven from the crankshaft by a fully enclosed belt. Compared to the 2000 cc engine, the 2300 cc engine uses a larger oil pump and water pump. The water pump and fan are separately driven from the crankshaft by a conventional V-belt, which also drives the alternator. A set of metric wrenches will be required to service the 2300 cc engine.

2800 cc

The 2800 cc engine is a V6 overhead valve design. The cylinder heads and engine block are made of cast iron. Four main bearings support the crankshaft. The distributor and the oil pump are driven by an eccentric at the front of the camshaft. The connecting rods are forged steel with replaceable copper-lead alloy insert bearings. The intake manifold is made from aluminum and has individual passages to the openings in the cylinder heads. The V6 has a full pressure lubrication system fed by a rotor type oil pump mounted at the rear of the crankcase.

ENGINE CAUTIONS

Both metric and standard threads are used in the engine and transmission. Since some metric threads are very similar to standard threads, it is possible to inadvertently install a standard bolt into a metric threaded hole. It is only after the bolt is tightened and the threads ruined that you may notice this mistake. Most metric attaching parts are color-coded blue. The best practice is to consult the accompanying illustration to learn the location of metric parts before starting any repair job. Use only metric tools to remove metric attaching parts.

If any repair operation requires the removal of a component of the air conditioning system (on vehicles so equipped), *do not disconnect the refrigerant lines.* If it is impossible to move the component out of the way with the lines attached, have the air conditioning system evacuated by a trained serviceman. *The air conditioning system contains freon under pressure. This gas can be very dangerous. Therefore, under no circumstances should an untrained*

General Engine Specifications

Year	Engine No. Cyl Displacement Cu In.	Carburetor Type	Advertised Horsepower @ rpm ■	Advertised Torque @ rpm (ft lbs) ■	Bore and Stroke (in.)	Advertised Compression Ratio	Oil Pressure @ 2050 rpm
'71	4-97.6	1 bbl	75 @ 5000	96 @ 3000	3.188 x 3.056	8.0 : 1	38
	4-122	2 bbl	100 @ 5600	120 @ 3600	3.575 x 3.029	8.6 : 1	50①
'72	4-97.6	1 bbl	54 @ 4600	80 @ 2400	3.188 x 3.056	8.0 : 1	38
	4-122	2 bbl	86 @ 5400	103 @ 3200	3.575 x 3.029	8.2 : 1	50①
'73	4-97.6	1 bbl	54 @ 4600	80 @ 2400	3.188 x 3.056	8.0 : 1	38
	4-122	2 bbl	86 @ 5400	103 @ 3200	3.575 x 3.029	8.2 : 1	50①
'74	4-122	2 bbl	86 @ 5400	103 @ 3200	3.575 x 3.029	8.2 : 1	50①
	4-140	2 bbl	102 @ 5200	122 @ 3200	3.781 x 3.126	8.4 : 1	50
'75	4-140	2 bbl	83 @ 4800	109 @ 2800	3.781 x 3.126	8.4 : 1②	50①
	6-170.8	2 bbl	97 @ 4400	138 @ 3200	3.66 x 2.70	8.2 : 1③	40–55①
'76–'77	4-140	2 bbl	92 @ 5000	121 @ 3000	3.781 x 3.126	9.0 : 1	40–60
	6-170.8	2 bbl	103 @ 4300	149 @ 2800	3.660 x 2.700	8.7 : 1	40–60
	6-170.8 (Calif.)	2 bbl	99 @ 4400	144 @ 2200	3.660 x 2.700	8.7 : 1	40–60

■ Beginning 1972, horsepower and torque are SAE net figures. They are measured at the rear of the transmission with all accessories installed and operating. Since the figures vary when a given engine is installed in different models, some are representative rather than exact.
① Oil pressure at 1500 rpm. ② 9.1 : 1 in 1976 ③ 8.7 : 1 in 1976

Valve Specifications

Year	Engine No.Cyl Displacement (cu in.)	Seat Angle (deg)	Face Angle (deg)	Spring Test Pressure (lbs @ in.)	Spring Installed Height (in.)	STEM TO GUIDE Clearance (in.)		STEM Diameter (in.)	
						Intake	Exhaust	Intake	Exhaust
'71	4-97.6	45	45	47 @ 1.26	1 17/64	.0008–.0030	.0017–.0039	.3100	.3100
	4-122	45	45	67 @ 1.42	1 13/32	.0015–.0015	.0015–.0025	.3149	.3149
'72	4-97.6	45	45	50 @ 1.26	1 17/64	.0008–.0027	.0017–.0036	.3102	.3093
	4-122	45	46	69 @ 1.42	1 13/32	.0008–.0025	.0018–.0035	.3163	.3153
'73	4-97.6	45	44	47 @ 1.263	1 17/64	.0008–.0027	.0017–.0036	.3102	.3093
	4-122	45	44	69 @ 1.418	1 13/32	.0008–.0025	.0018–.0035	.3163	.3153
'74	4-122	45	46	69 @ 1.418	1 13/32	.0008–.0025	.0018–.0035	.3163	.3153
	4-140	45	46	75 @ 1.560	1 9/16	.0006–.0023	.0006–.0023	.3424	.3415
'75–'77	4-140	45	46	75 @ 1.560	1 9/16	.0006–.0023	.0015–.0032	.3424	.3415
	6-170.8	45	45	64 @ 1.585	1 19/32	.0008–.0025	.0018–.0035	.3162	.3153

Crankshaft and Connecting Rod Specifications

All measurements are given in in.

Year	Engine No. Cyl Displacement (cu in.)	CRANKSHAFT Main Brg Journal Dia	CRANKSHAFT Main Brg Oil Clearance	CRANKSHAFT Shaft End-Play	CRANKSHAFT Thrust on No.	CONNECTING ROD Journal Diameter	CONNECTING ROD Oil Clearance	CONNECTING ROD Side Clearance
'71	97.6 (1600 cc)	2.1253–2.1261	.0004–.0018	.003–.011	3	1.9368–1.9376	.0004–.0024	.004–.010
	122.0 (2000 cc)	2.2432–2.2440	.0005–.0015	.004–.008	3	2.0464–2.0472	.0006–.0026	.004–.010
'72–73	97.6 (1600 cc)	2.1253–2.1261	.0005–.0016	.003–.011	3	1.9368–1.9376	.0004–.0024	.004–.010
	122.0 (2000 cc)	2.2432–2.2440	.0006–.0016	.003–.011	3	2.0464–2.0472	.0006–.0026	.004–.010
'74	122.0 (2000 cc)	2.2432–2.2440	.0006–.0016	.003–.011	3	2.0464–2.0472	.0006–.0026	.004–.010
	140.0 (2300 cc)	2.3982–2.3990	.0008–.0015	.004–.008	3	2.0465–2.0472	.0008–.0024	.0035–.0105
'75	140.0 (2300 cc)	2.3982–2.3990	.0008–.0026	.004–.008	3	2.0465–2.0472	.0008–.0015	.0035–.0105
	170.8 (2800 cc)	2.2433–2.2441	.0005–.0016	.004–.008	3	2.1252–2.1260	.0005–.0015	.004–.011
'76–'77	4-140 (2300 cc)	2.3982–2.3990	.0008–.0015	.004–.008	3	2.0464–2.0472	.0008–.0015	.0035–.0105
	6-170.8 (2800 cc)	2.2433–2.2441	.0008–.0015	.004–.008	3	2.1252–2.1560	.0006–.0015	.004–.011

Torque Specifications

All readings in ft lbs

Year	Engine No. Cyl Displacement (cu in.)	Cylinder Head Bolts	Rod Bearing Bolts	Main Bearing Bolts	Crankshaft Pulley Bolt	Flywheel to Crankshaft Bolts	MANIFOLD	
							Intake	Exhaust
'71–'74	97.6 (1600 cc)	65–70	30–35	65–70	24–28	50–55	12–15	15–18
	122.0 (2000 cc)	65–80	29–34	65–75	39–43	47–51	12–15	12–15①
'75–'77	140.0 (2300 cc)	80–90	30–36	80–90	80–114②	54–64	14–21	16–23
	170.8 (2800 cc)	65–80	21–25	65–75	92–103②	47–51	15–18	14–18

① 15–18 in 1974
② Crankshaft damper bolt

Ring Gap

All measurements are given in in.

Year	Engine	Top Compression	Bottom Compression
'71–'73	1600 cc	.009–.014	.009–.014
'71–'72	2000 cc	.019–.021	.019–.021
'73–'74	2000 cc	.015–.023	.015–.023
'74–'77	2300 cc	.010–.020	.010–.020
'74–'77	2800 cc	.015–.023	.015–.023

Year	Engine	Oil Control
'71–73	1600 cc	.009–.014
'71–74	2000 cc	.016–.055
'74–'77	2300 cc	.015–.055
'74–'77	2800 cc	.016–.055

Ring Side Clearance

All measurements are given in in.

Year	Engine	Top Compression	Bottom Compression
'71–'73	4-1600 cc	.0016–.0036	.0016–.0036
'71–'74	4-2000 cc	.0019–.0038	.0019–.0038
'74–'77	2300 cc	.0020–.0040	.0020–.0040
'75–'77	2800 cc	.0020–.0033	.0020–.0033

Year	Engine	Oil Control
'71–'73	1600 cc	.0018–.0038
'71–'74	2000 cc	Snug
'74–'77	2300 cc	Snug
'75–'77	2800 cc	Snug

person attempt to disconnect the air-conditioner refrigerant lines.

ENGINE REMOVAL AND INSTALLATION

1600 CC

1. Remove hood, after scribing match marks around hinges.
2. Disconnect battery cables.
3. Drain the cooling system.

NOTE: *Drain the engine block as well as the radiator.*

4. Disconnect the radiator hoses and remove the radiator.
5. Remove the air cleaner assembly.
6. Disconnect the heater hoses from the water pump and intake manifold.
7. Disconnect the throttle linkage.

8. Disconnect the oil pressure and water temperature sending unit wires. Disconnect the carburetor solenoid and coil wires. Disconnect the alternator wires.

NOTE: *It is a good idea to tag all these wires.*

9. Disconnect the exhaust pipe from the manifold and remove the hot air tubes.

10. Disconnect the fuel inlet line at the fuel pump.

NOTE: *Plug the line so that gas does not siphon from the tank.*

11. Disconnect the coil wires, then remove the spark plug wires and the distributor cap.

12. Jack up the front of the car and support on axle stands.

13. Disconnect the starter wires, and remove the starter and oil pan shield.

14. Remove the clutch cover. Drain the oil from the crankcase.

15. Lower the car to the floor.

16. Remove the clutch housing-to-engine bolts, then install lifting brackets and a chain hoist.

17. Disconnect the front motor mounts, while supporting the engine with a chain hoist.

18. Place an axle stand or wooden block under the transmission.

19. Raise the engine slightly, while pulling forward to separate the transmission input shaft from the clutch, and lift the engine out of the car.

20. Position the engine assembly in the engine compartment and start the transmission input shaft into the clutch disc. It may be necessary to adjust the position of the transmission if the transmission input shaft will not enter the clutch disc properly. If the engine hangs up after the shaft enters the clutch, turn the crankshaft pulley slowly with the transmission in gear until the splines on the input shaft mesh with the splines in the clutch disc.

21. Slide the engine rearward, making sure the flywheel upper cover plate engages the dowels on the clutch housing. Align the front motor mounts and the exhaust manifold with the exhaust pipe.

22. Install the front motor mount nuts and tighten them to 20–30 ft lbs.

23. Install and tighten the upper clutch housing-to-engine attaching bolts. Make sure the engine ground strap is secured by the upper left bolt.

24. Install the distributor cap and wires.

25. Connect the fuel line to the fuel pump.

Connecting chain hoist to engine

METRIC THREADS

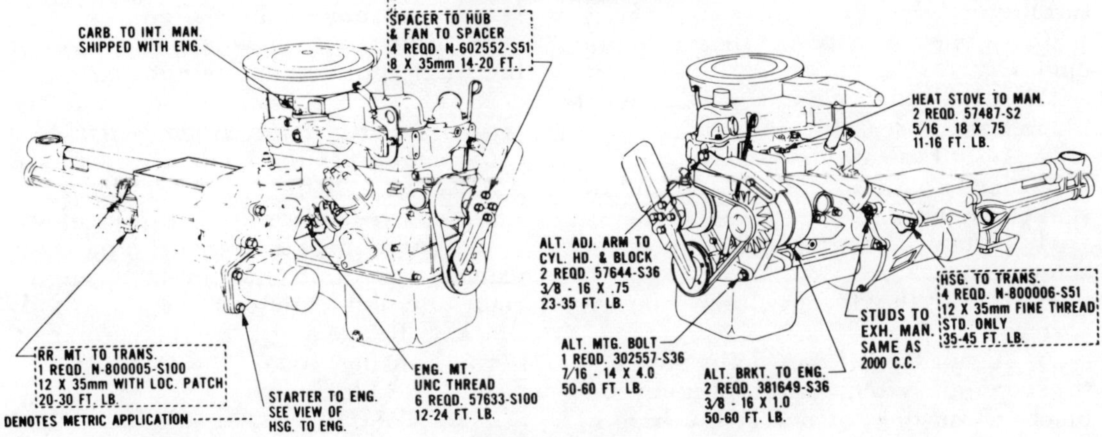

1600 cc. ENGINE

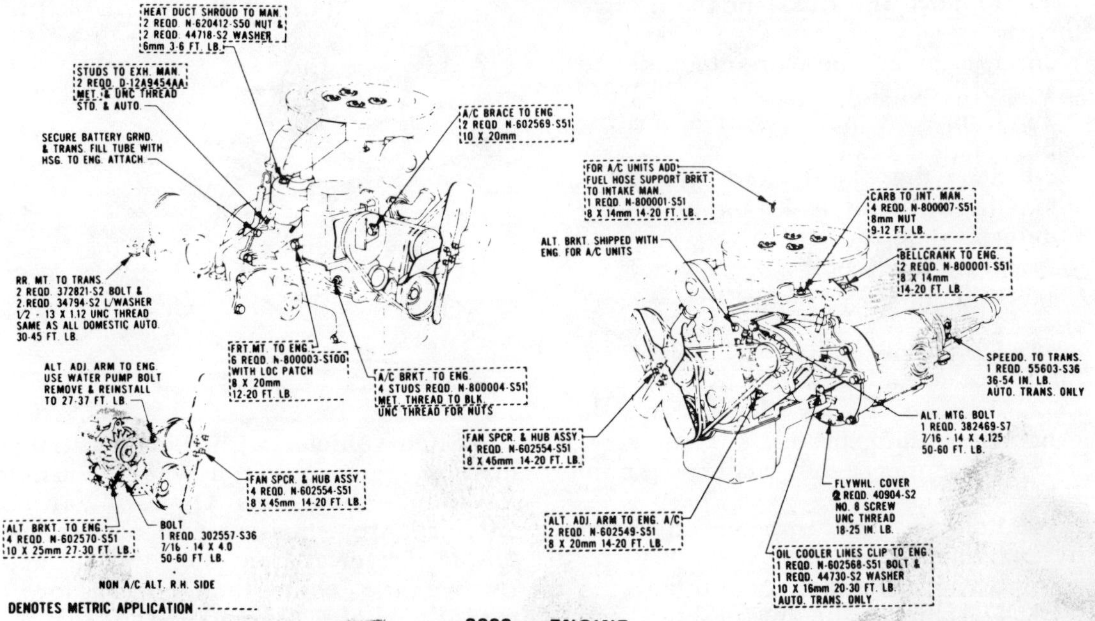

2000 cc. ENGINE

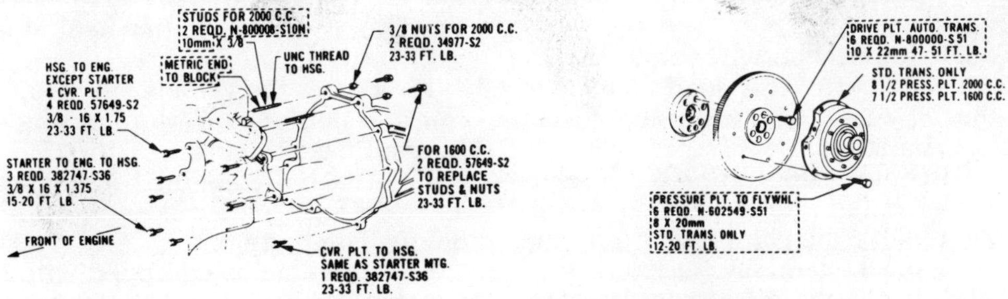

HOUSING TO ENGINE – 1600 C.C. AND 2000 C.C.

Metric bolt locations

26. Connect the oil pressure and water temperature sending unit wires. Connect the carburetor solenoid and distributor battery wires.

27. Connect the alternator wires.

28. Connect the exhaust pipe to the exhaust manifold and install the heat duct on the manifold.

29. Connect the throttle linkage to the carburetor.
30. Connect the heater hoses to the engine.
31. Install the radiator and connect the radiator hoses.
32. Install the air cleaner.
33. Jack up the front of the car and install jackstands.
34. Install the starter and connect the starter cable.
35. Install the lower clutch housing cover.
36. Install the oil pan drain plug and the cooling system drain plug in the block. Close the petcock at the base of the radiator.
37. Remove the jackstands and lower the car.
38. Fill the engine with oil and the radiator with coolant.
39. Connect the negative battery cable.
40. Start the engine and allow it to idle. Check for any leaks and adjust carburetor as required.
41. Install the hood.

2000 CC AND 2300 CC

1. Drain the engine of coolant and oil. Remove the hood.
2. Remove the air cleaner and the exhaust manifold shroud.
3. Disconnect the battery ground cable.
4. Remove the upper and lower hoses from the radiator.
5. Remove the radiator and fan.
6. Disconnect the heater hose from the water pump and carburetor choke fitting.
7. Disconnect the wires from the alternator and starter. It is good practice to tag these wires to prevent confusion during installation.
8. Disconnect the carburetor accelerator cable. If the vehicle has air conditioning, remove the compressor from the mounting bracket and lay it aside.

NOTE: *Leave the refrigerant lines attached.*

9. Disconnect the flexible fuel line from the fuel tank line and plug the fuel tank line.
10. Disconnect the coil primary wire and the water temperature and oil temperature sending units.
11. Jack up the vehicle, install safety stands and remove the starter.
12. Remove the flywheel (or converter housing) upper mounting nuts.

NOTE: *Two 10 mm x ⅜ in. studs are used to attach the upper housing to the engine. If the studs are removed, make sure they are reinstalled with the metric threads in the engine block.*

13. Disconnect the exhaust pipe at the exhaust manifold. Unbolt the engine right and left mount at the underbody bracket. Remove the flywheel (or converter housing) cover.

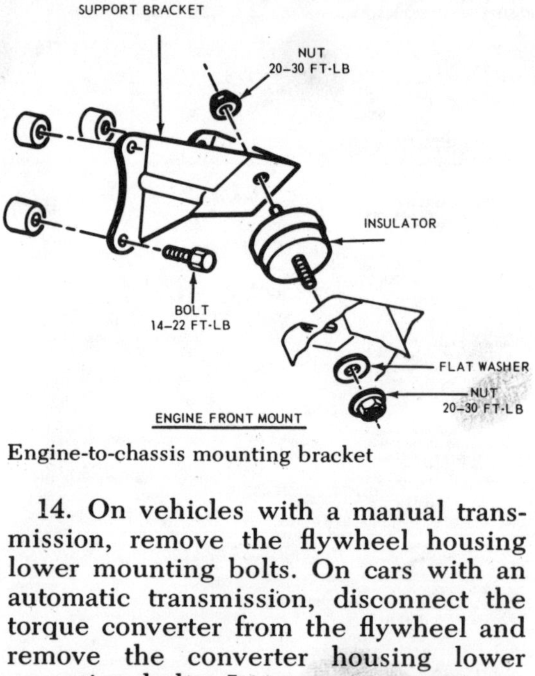

Engine-to-chassis mounting bracket

14. On vehicles with a manual transmission, remove the flywheel housing lower mounting bolts. On cars with an automatic transmission, disconnect the torque converter from the flywheel and remove the converter housing lower mounting bolts. It is necessary to turn the crankshaft pulley to gain access to the four converter-to-flywheel attaching nuts.
15. Lower the vehicle and support the transmission or converter housing with a hydraulic jack.
16. Attach the engine lifting apparatus and carefully pull the engine from the engine compartment.
17. On vehicles equipped with an automatic transmission, match-mark the flywheel and the torque converter so they may be rejoined at their original location.
18. Place a new gasket over the exhaust pipe.
19. Carefully lower the engine into the engine compartment. Be sure that

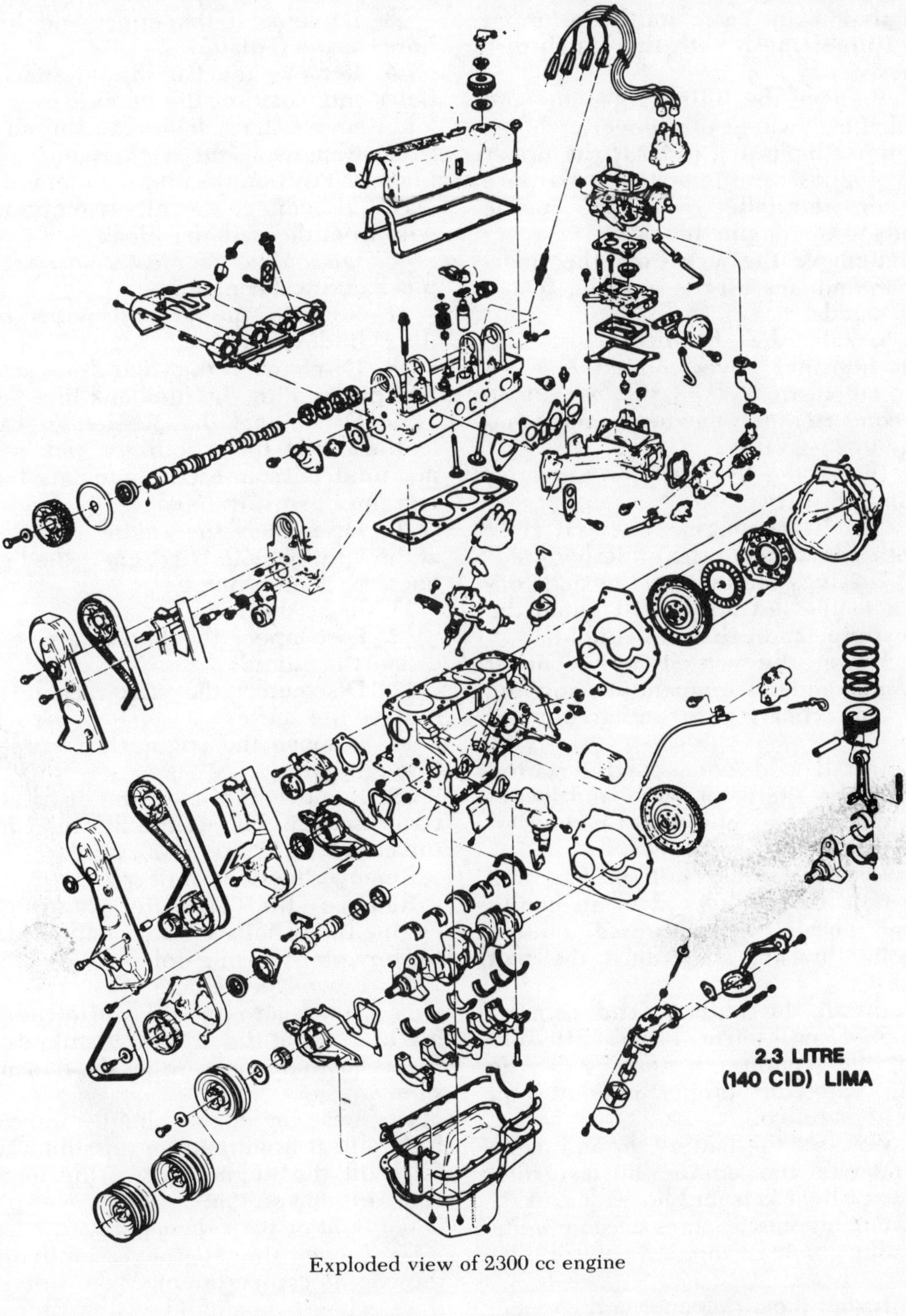

Exploded view of 2300 cc engine

the exhaust manifold studs are aligned with the holes in the exhaust pipe flange. On a vehicle with automatic transmission, start the converter pilot shaft into the crankshaft; while aligning the marks that were made previously. Make sure the studs on the flywheel engage the holes in the flywheel. On manual transmission cars, start the transmission drive gear into the clutch disc. It may be necessary to adjust the position of the transmission with relation to the engine if the input shaft fails to enter the clutch disc. If the engine hangs up after the shaft enters, turn the crankshaft slowly, in a clockwise direction, with the transmission in gear, until the input shaft splines mesh with the clutch disc splines.

20. Remove the lifting apparatus and install the flywheel (or converter housing) upper mounting nuts. If the upper housing studs were removed, make sure they are reinstalled with the metric threads in the engine block.

21. Remove the jack from the transmission and jack up the vehicle. Install safety stands.

22. Install the flywheel (or converter housing) lower mounting bolts. On an automatic transmission car, attach the converter to flywheel nuts and torque to 23–28 ft lbs.

23. Install the flywheel (or converter housing) dust cover.

24. Install the engine left and right mounting brackets to the underbody.

25. Unplug the fuel tank line and connect it to the flexible line. Tighten the exhaust pipe and exhaust manifold.

26. Lower the vehicle and connect the water and oil temperature sending units, coil primary wire, and accelerator cable.

27. Install and connect the starter. Connect the alternator wires and heater hose to the water pump and carburetor choke fitting.

28. Install the fan pulley, fan, and drive belt. On vehicles with air conditioning, install the compressor on the mounting bracket and adjust the belt tension.

29. Install the radiator and connect the upper and lower hoses. Fill and bleed the cooling system. Fill the engine with the proper amount and grade of engine oil.

30. Connect the battery ground cable and operate the engine at fast idle, checking all gaskets and hoses for leaks.

31. On automatic transmission vehicles, adjust the transmission control linkage.

32. Install the air cleaner and connect the crankcase ventilation hose.

33. Install the hood.

2800 cc V6

1. Disconnect the battery, drain the cooling system and remove the hood.

2. Remove the air cleaner and intake duct assembly. Remove any Thermactor pieces causing interference.

3. Disconnect the upper and lower hoses at the radiator.

4. Remove the fan shroud attaching bolts and position the shroud over the fan. Remove the radiator and shroud.

5. Remove the alternator and bracket. Position the alternator out of the way. Disconnect the alternator ground wire from the cylinder block.

6. Disconnect the heater hoses at the block and water pump.

7. Remove the ground wires from the cylinder block.

8. Disconnect the fuel line at the fuel pump. Plug the fuel tank line.

9. Disconnect the accelerator cable or linkage at the carburetor and intake manifold. Disconnect the automatic transmission downshift linkage.

10. Disconnect the engine wire loom at the ignition coil. Disconnect the brake booster vacuum line.

11. Raise the vehicle.

12. Disconnect the headpipes at the exhaust manifolds.

13. Disconnect the starter cable and remove the starter.

14. Remove the engine front support through-bolts.

15. Remove the converter inspection cover and disconnect the flywheel from the converter.

Remove the downshift rod.

Remove the converter housing-to-engine block bolts and the adapter plate-to-converter housing bolt.

16. Lower the vehicle.

17. Attach an engine hoist to the lifting brackets at the exhaust manifolds.

18. Position a jack under the transmission.

19. Raise the engine slightly and carefully pull it from the transmission. Carefully lift the engine out of the engine compartment so that the rear cover plate is not bent or parts damaged.

20. Lower the engine carefully into the engine compartment. Make sure that the exhaust manifolds are properly aligned with the headpipes. Start the converter pilot into the crankshaft.

21. Install the converter housing upper bolts, making sure that the dowels in the cylinder block engage the flywheel housing. Remove the jack from under the transmission.

22. Remove the lifting device from the engine.

23. Position the downshift rod on the transmission and engine.

24. Raise the vehicle.

25. Position the transmission linkage bracket and install the remaining converter housing bolts. Install the adapter plate-to-converter housing bolts. Install the converter-to-flywheel nuts and install the inspection cover. Connect the downshift rod on the transmission.

26. Install the starter and connect the cable.

27. Connect the muffler inlet pipes at the exhaust manifolds.

28. Install the engine front support through-bolts.

29. Lower the vehicle.

30. Install the ground wire. Install the engine wire loom and connect it to the ignition coil, then install the water temperature sending unit and oil pressure sending unit. Connect the brake booster vacuum line.

31. Install the accelerator linkage and connect the automatic transmission downshift rod. Connect the vacuum lines. Connect the fuel tank line at the fuel pump.

32. Connect the ground wire at the cylinder block. Install the heater hoses at the water pump and cylinder block.

33. Install the alternator and bracket. Connect the alternator ground wire to the cylinder block. Install the drive belt and adjust the belt tension.

34. Position the fan shroud over the fan. Install the radiator and connect the upper and lower radiator hoses. Install the fan shroud attaching bolts.

35. Fill and bleed the cooling system. Fill the crankcase with oil. Adjust the automatic transmission downshift linkage. Connect the battery.

36. Operate the engine at fast idle until it reaches normal operating temperature and check all gaskets and hose connections for leaks. Adjust the ignition timing and idle speed.

37. Install the air cleaner and intake duct. Install and adjust the hood.

VALVE ROCKER COVER AND ROCKER SHAFT—1600 CC

Removal and Installation

1. Raise the hood and remove the air cleaner.

2. Disconnect the spark plug wires from the plugs and position them out of the way.

3. Remove the valve cover attaching screws and remove the valve cover. If the rocker arm is not to be removed proceed to "Installation," step five.

4. Loosen each rocker shaft attaching bolt one turn at a time until all bolts are loose.

5. Remove the rocker shaft.

6. Position the rocker shaft on the cylinder head and align the pushrods with the rocker arm adjusting screws.

7. Starting from the front of the engine and working back, tighten each bolt one turn at a time until the rocker shaft is mounted on the cylinder head.

8. Tighten each bolt to 25–30 ft lbs.

9. Adjust the valves. See chapter two.

10. Clean all old gasket material from the rocker cover and the cylinder head and position a new gasket on the cylinder head.

11. Install the rocker cover and tighten the attaching screws.

12. Connect the spark plug wires and install the air cleaner.

VALVE ROCKER COVER AND ROCKER ARMS—2000 CC

Removal and Installation

1. Raise the hood and remove the air cleaner.

2. On models with air conditioning, remove the heater hose from the heater hot water valve.

3. Remove the valve cover attaching bolts and remove the valve cover.

NOTE: *Remember the location of the screws that have rubber-coated washers.*

If the rocker arms are not to be removed, proceed to "Installation," step three.

4. Rotate the crankshaft in a clockwise direction until the cam lobe (high point) for the rocker arm that is to be removed is pointing straight up.

5. Remove the rocker arm retaining spring from the rocker arm.

6. Depress the valve spring that corresponds to the rocker arm that is to be removed just enough to remove the rocker arm.

7. Repeat as required until all rocker arms are removed.
8. Position the rocker arm on the valve and adjusting screw and install the rocker arm retaining spring.
9. Adjust the valve clearance. See chapter two.
10. Clean all old gasket material from the rocker cover and the cylinder head.
11. Position a new valve cover gasket on the cylinder head and install and tighten the attaching screws as described in chapter two, under valve adjustment.
12. On models with air conditioning, install the heater hose on the hot water valve.
13. Install the air cleaner.

VALVE ROCKER COVER—2300 CC

Removal and Installation

1. Raise the hood and remove the air cleaner.
2. Remove any emission control equipment and associated parts that may be in the way.
3. Remove the four lower retaining screws first then the two front side screws.

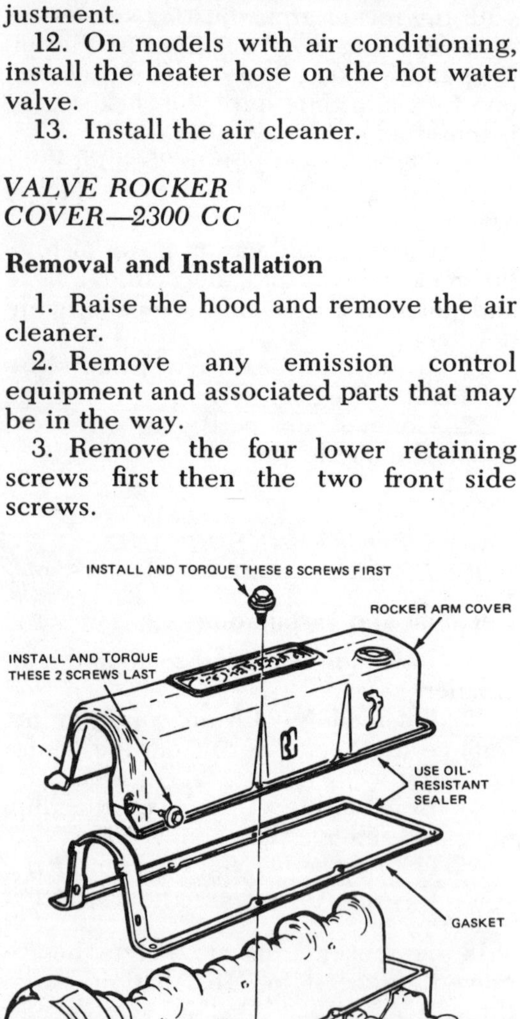

Valve rocker cover installation—2300 cc

4. Tap the cover just enough to break the seal and remove the cover.
5. Replace the valve cover gasket with a new one if necessary and coat either the surface of the gasket or the valve cover surface with an oil resistant sealer or gasket cement.
6. Install and tighten the four lower retaining screws first and the two front side screws last.
7. Replace any emission control equipment disconnected and install the air cleaner.

VALVE ROCKER ARM (CAM FOLLOWER) AND HYDRAULIC LASH ADJUSTER—2300 CC

Removal and Installation

1. Remove the valve cover and associated parts as required.
2. Rotate the camshaft so that the base circle of the cam is against the cam follower you intend to remove.
3. Remove the retaining spring from the cam follower, if so equipped.
4. Using special tool T74P-6565-B or a valve spring compressor tool for a 2300 cc engine, collapse the lash adjuster and/or depress the valve spring, as necessary, and slide the cam follower over the lash adjuster and out from under the camshaft.
5. Install the cam follower in the reverse order of removal. Make sure that the lash adjuster is collapsed and released before rotating the cam shaft.

VALVE ROCKER ARM COVER AND ROCKER ARM—2800 CC

> NOTE: *On some 1975 Pintos with the 2800 cc engine it is necessary to reposition the distributor to remove the valve cover. Refer to "Valve Adjustment" in Chapter 2 for this procedure.*

Removal and Installation

Remove emission control equipment as necessary to remove the cover.

1. Remove spark plug wires from spark plugs and rocker arm cover, using the proper plier-type tool to remove the boots from the plugs.
2. Remove throttle linkage to carburetor if it interferes with removal operation.
3. Remove rocker arm cover attaching screws. Tap rocker arm cover lightly to break gasket seal. Lift off rocker arm cover.

4. Remove rocker arm shaft stand retaining bolts by loosening the bolts two turns at a time, in sequence. Lift off rocker arm and shaft assembly and oil baffle.

5. Loosen the valve lash adjusting screws a few turns.

6. Apply engine oil to the assembly to provide initial lubrication.

7. Install oil baffle and rocker arm shaft assembly to the cylinder block and guide adjusting screws on to push rods.

8. Install and tighten rocker arm stand attaching bolts to specifications, two turns at a time, in sequence.

9. Adjust valve lash to cold specified setting.

10. Clean the valve rocker arm cover and cylinder head gasket surfaces. Coat one side of a new gasket with an oil-resistant sealer and lay cemented side of gasket on the cover. Install the cover, making sure the gasket seats evenly around the head. Tighten the cover attaching bolts.

11. Install parts removed to gain access to rocker arm and shaft assemblies.

12. Start engine and run until normal temperature is reached. Adjust valve lash to hot specified setting.

13. Run the engine at fast idle and check for oil leaks.

NOTE: *See Chapter 2 for valve adjustment.*

INTAKE MANIFOLD

Removal and Installation

ALL FOUR CYLINDER MODELS

1. Drain the cooling system.

2. Remove the air cleaner and disconnect the throttle linkage from the carburetor.

3. Disconnect the fuel and vacuum lines from the carburetor.

4. Disconnect the carburetor solenoid wire at the quick-disconnect.

5. Remove the choke water housing and thermostatic spring from the carburetor.

6. Disconnect the water outlet and crankcase ventilation hoses from the intake manifold.

7. Disconnect the deceleration valve-to-carburetor hose at the carburetor.

8. Remove the intake manifold attaching bolts and remove the manifold.

9. Clean all old gasket material from the manifold and cylinder head.

10. If the intake manifold is to be replaced by a new one, transfer all necessary components to the new manifold. Loosen the union fitting on the manifold and remove the deceleration valve from the intake manifold. Remove the deceleration valve adapter from the manifold by inserting a large allen wrench into the adapter and turning the adapter out of the manifold.

11. Apply water-resistant sealer to the intake manifold gasket and position it on the cylinder head.

12. Install the intake manifold attaching nuts and tighten them alternately and evenly to 15–18 ft lbs on a 1600 cc engine. On the 2000 and 2300 cc engine, follow the sequence given in the illustrations.

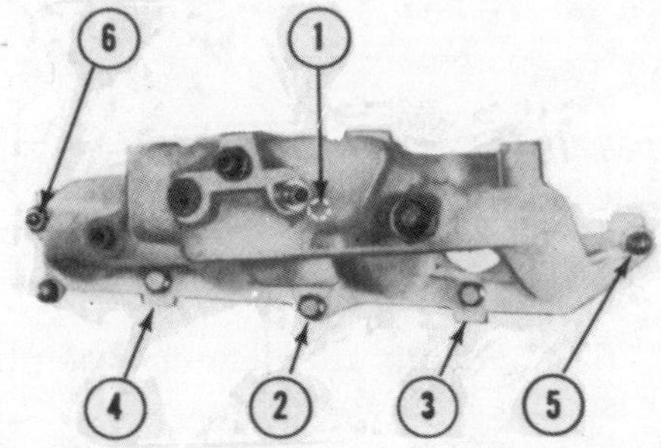

2000 cc intake manifold bolt tightening sequence. Torque to 12–15 ft lbs.

13. Connect the water and crankcase ventilation hoses to the intake manifold.

14. Connect the deceleration valve-to-carburetor hose to the carburetor.

15. Position the choke water housing and thermostatic spring on the carburetor and engage the end of the spring coil in the slot in the choke adjusting lever. Align the tab on the spring housing with the index mark on the choke housing. Tighten the choke water housing attaching screws.

16. Connect the carburetor solenoid wire.

17. Connect the fuel and vacuum lines to the carburetor.

18. Connect the throttle linkage to the carburetor.

19. Install the air cleaner and fill the cooling system.

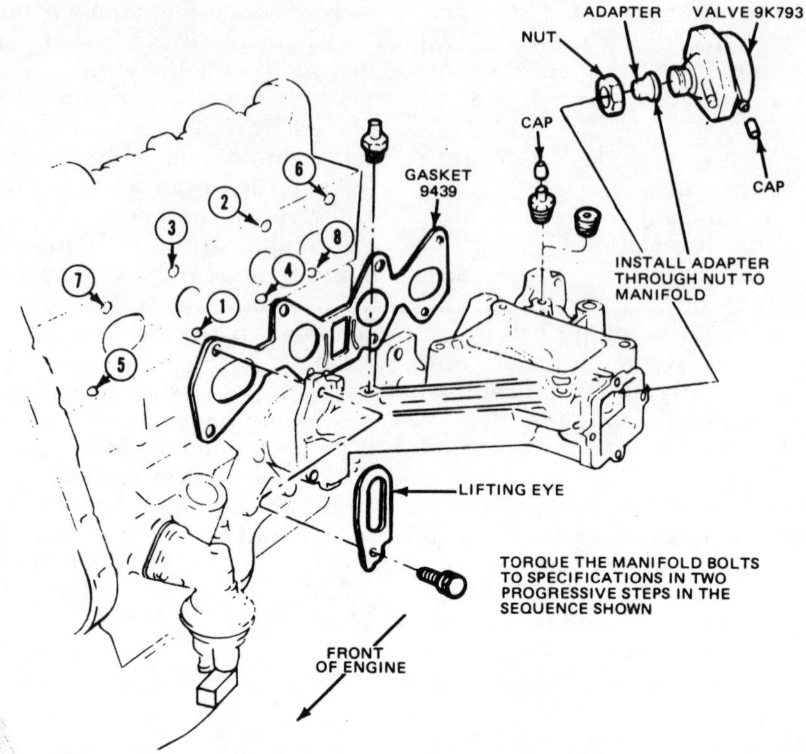

Installing 2300 cc intake manifold: step one—torque to 8 ft lbs; step two—torque to 16–23 ft lbs.

2800 cc V6

1. Remove the air cleaner assembly and disconnect the battery.

2. Disconnect the throttle cables.

3. Drain the cooling system. Disconnect and remove the hose from the water outlet to the radiator and the hoses and line from the water outlet to the water pump.

4. Remove the distributor cap and spark plug wires as an assembly. Disconnect the distributor wire and the vacuum line.

5. Mark the position of the distributor rotor and remove it.

6. Remove the fuel line and filter between the fuel pump and the carburetor and then remove the rocker arm covers and the EGR tube.

7. Remove the intake manifold bolts and nuts. Tap the manifold lightly with a plastic hammer to break the gasket seal, and then lift off the manifold.

8. Remove all the gasket material and dirt from the manifold and cylinder heads.

9. Apply sealing compound to the joining surfaces. Place the manifold gasket in place. (Make sure that the tap on the right bank of the cylinder head gasket fits into the cutout of the manifold gasket.)

10. Install the intake manifold. Tighten the attaching bolts until they are hand tight, and then tighten them, in sequence, to the proper torque.

NOTE: *Tightening bolt no. 7 with a torque wrench will require an attachment called a "crow's foot."*

11. Install the distributor so that the rotor is pointing to the mark made previously.

12. Connect the distributor wire and vacuum line.

13. Install the carburetor, fuel line, fuel filter, EGR tube, and the rocker arm covers.

14. Install the distributor cap and wires.

15. Install and adjust the carburetor linkage.

16. Install the air cleaner assembly and air cleaner tube to the carburetor. Connect the battery.

17. Adjust the ignition timing.

EXHAUST MANIFOLD

Removal and Installation

1600 CC

1. Remove the air cleaner.
2. Place a block of wood under the front of the exhaust pipe and disconnect the exhaust pipe from the exhaust manifold.
3. Remove the exhaust manifold attaching nuts and bolts and remove the exhaust manifold. Discard the old gaskets.
4. If a new manifold is to be installed, remove the heat shroud from the old manifold and install it on the new manifold.
5. Clean all old gasket material from the manifold and the cylinder head.
6. Install a new exhaust manifold gasket over the center studs on the cylinder head.
7. Position the exhaust manifold near the cylinder head and install the end exhaust manifold gaskets between the manifold and the head.
8. Install the manifold attaching nuts and bolts and tighten them alternately and equally to 15–18 ft lbs.
9. Connect the exhaust pipe to the exhaust manifold and remove the wood support from under the pipe.
10. Install the air cleaner.

2000 CC AND 2300 CC

1. Remove the air cleaner.
2. Remove the heat shroud from the exhaust manifold.
3. Place a block of wood under the exhaust pipe and disconnect the exhaust pipe from the exhaust manifold.
4. Remove the exhaust manifold attaching nuts and remove the manifold.
5. Install a light coat of graphite grease on the exhaust manifold mating

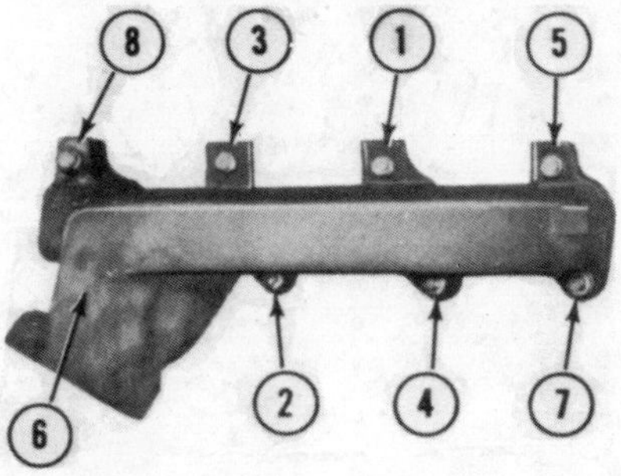

2000 cc exhaust manifold bolt tightening sequence. Torque to 12–15 ft lbs.

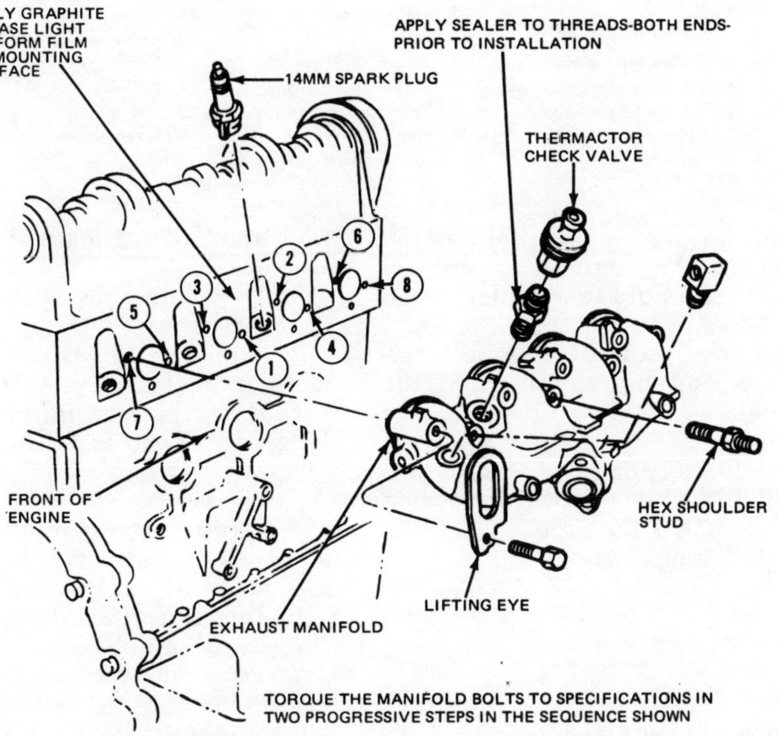

Installing 2300 cc exhaust manifold: step one—torque to 8 ft lbs; step two—torque to 16–23 ft lbs.

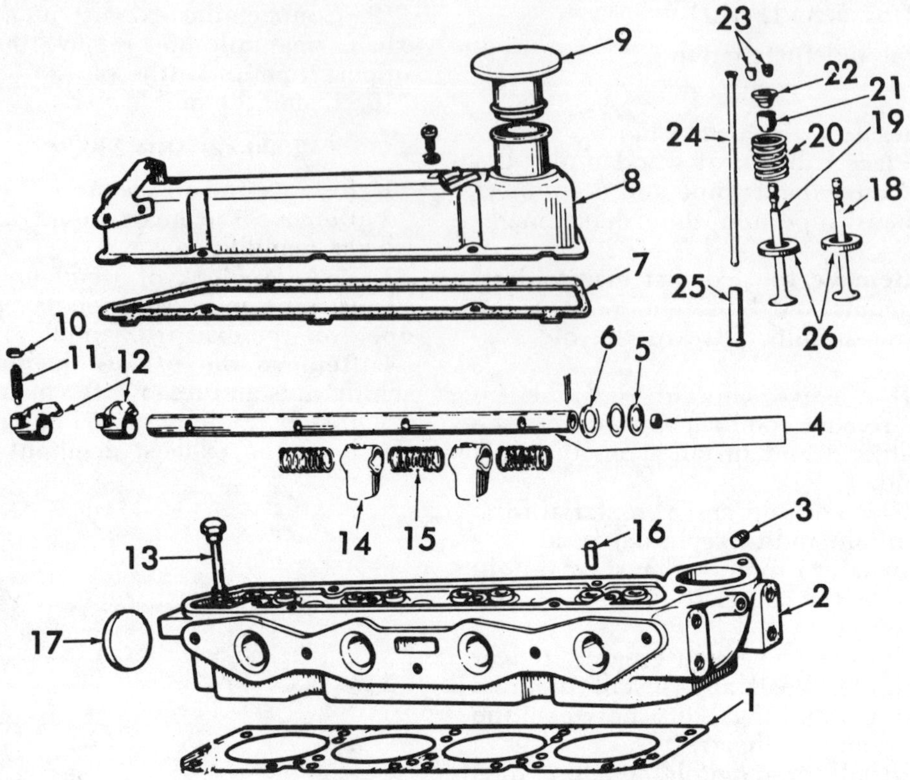

Cylinder head and valve system—1600 cc

1. Cylinder head gasket
2. Cylinder head
3. Plug
4. Rocker arm shaft
5. Spring type washer
6. Flat type washer
7. Valve cover gasket
8. Valve cover
9. Oil filler cap
10. Lock
11. Adjusting screw
12. Rocker arm
13. Bolt
14. Rocker shaft support
15. Rocker shaft spring
16. Valve guide bushing
17. Plug
18. Intake valve
19. Exhaust valve
20. Valve spring
21. Valve seal
22. Valve spring retainer
23. Valve spring key
24. Pushrod
25. Valve tappet
26. Insert valve seat

surface and position the manifold on the cylinder head. This engine does not use an exhaust manifold-to-cylinder head gasket.

6. Install the exhaust manifold attaching nuts and tighten them in the sequence shown in the illustration to 12–15 ft lbs.
7. Connect the exhaust pipe to the exhaust manifold and remove the wood support from under the pipe.
8. Install the air cleaner.

2800 CC V6

1. Remove the air cleaner.
2. Remove the four attaching nuts from the exhaust manifold shroud (right side only).
3. Disconnect the attaching nuts from the muffler inlet pipe.
4. Remove the exhaust manifold attaching nuts and remove the manifold.

NOTE: *These manifolds do not use gaskets. When installing the manifold, smear a light coat of graphite grease on the mating surfaces.*

5. Position the manifold on the studs and install the bolts hand tight then torque them evenly to the proper torque.
6. Install a new inlet pipe gasket and the attaching nuts.
7. Position the exhaust manifold shroud on the manifold and install the attaching nuts (right side).
8. Install the air cleaner.

CYLINDER HEAD

Removal and Installation

1600 CC

1. Remove the air cleaner.
2. Drain the cooling system.
3. Disconnect the fuel and vacuum lines from the carburetor.
4. Disconnect the spark plug wires from the plugs and position them out of the way.
5. Disconnect the heater and vacuum hoses from the intake manifold.
6. Disconnect the heater hoses from the choke housing.
7. Disconnect the wire from the engine temperature sending unit.
8. Disconnect the exhaust pipe from the exhaust manifold.
9. Disconnect the throttle linkage from the carburetor and disconnect the carburetor solenoid wire.
10. Remove the thermostat housing and the thermostat.
11. Remove the valve cover and gasket.
12. Loosen each rocker arm attaching bolt several turns at a time until they are loose, then remove the rocker arm.
13. Remove the pushrods and keep them in order so they may be installed in their original location when the engine is reassembled.
14. Using a 12 point metric socket, remove the cylinder head attaching bolts.
15. Remove the cylinder head from the engine with the intake and exhaust manifolds attached.

    NOTE: *Do not lay the cylinder head flat on its base as this may damage the spark plugs, valves or the sealing surface of the head.*
16. Clean the bottom of the head and the top of the cylinder block of all gasket material. If any debris gets into the cylinders, it must be removed before assembling the engine.
17. See the "Engine Rebuilding," section for cylinder head disassembly.
18. Position a new cylinder head gasket on the engine.
19. Install the cylinder head on the engine and install the cylinder head attaching bolts finger-tight.
20. Using a torque wrench, tighten the head bolts in the order shown in the illustration in the following steps:

    A—tighten all bolts to 5 ft lbs
    B—tighten all bolts to 20–30 ft lbs
    C—tighten all bolts to 50–55 ft lbs
    D—tighten all bolts to 65–70 ft lbs

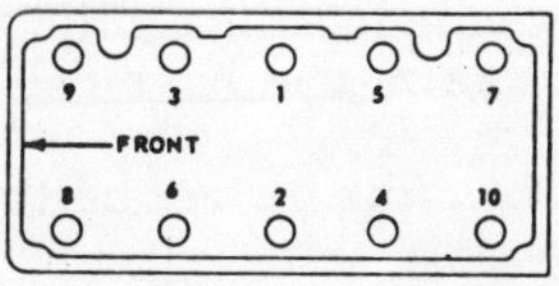

1600 cc cylinder head bolt tightening sequence

Install the pushrods in their original location in the engine.

21. Install the rocker shaft on the head and install the rocker shaft attaching bolts finger-tight.
22. Position the tips of the pushrods in the rocker arm adjusting screws and tighten each bolt several turns at a time until the rocker shaft is mounted on the cylinder head.
23. Tighten the rocker arm attaching bolts to 25–30 ft lbs.
24. Connect the exhaust pipe to the exhaust manifold.
25. Using a new gasket, install the thermostat and thermostat housing.
26. Connect the carburetor linkage and solenoid wire.
27. Connect the heater hose to the choke housing and the wire to the engine temperature sending unit.
28. Connect the heater and vacuum hoses to the intake manifold.
29. Connect the fuel and vacuum lines to the carburetor.
30. Fill the cooling system.
31. Adjust the valve clearance. See "Valve Adjustment" in chapter two.
32. Install the valve cover and air cleaner.

2000 CC AND 2300 CC

NOTE: *Removal of 2000 cc cylinder head bolts requires the use of a special 12 point "allen type" wrench. The cylinder head bolts on the 2300 cc engine are metric.*

1. Drain the cooling system.
2. Remove the air cleaner.
3. Remove the valve cover. Note the

location of the valve cover attaching screws that have rubber grommets.

4. Remove the intake and exhaust manifolds from the head. See the procedures for intake manifold and exhaust manifold removal.

5. Remove the camshaft drive belt cover. Note the location of the belt cover attaching screws that have rubber grommets.

6. Loosen the drive belt tensioner and remove the belt.

7. Remove the water outlet elbow from the cylinder head with the hose attached.

8. Using a 12 point special tool, remove the cylinder head attaching bolts.

9. Remove the cylinder head from the engine.

10. Clean all gasket material and carbon from the top of the cylinder block and pistons and from the bottom of the cylinder head.

11. Position a new cylinder head gasket on the engine and place the head on the engine.

NOTE: *If you encounter difficulty in positioning the cylinder head on the engine block, it may be necessary to install guide studs in the block to cor-*

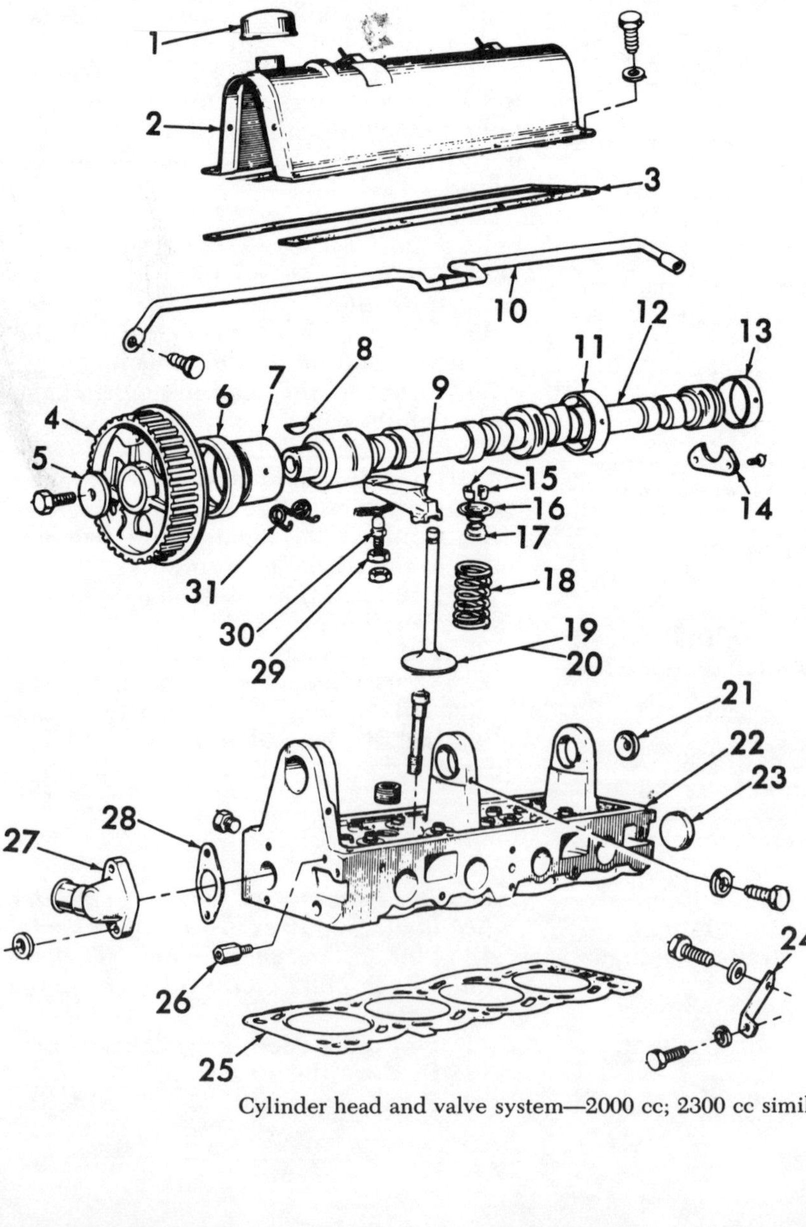

1. Oil filler cap
2. Valve cover
3. Valve cover gasket
4. Camshaft gear
5. Flat washer
6. Crankshaft front seal
7. Camshaft front bearings
8. Key
9. Follower arm (rocker arm)
10. Valve drive tube assembly
11. Center camshaft bearing
12. Camshaft
13. Camshaft bearing (rear)
14. Thrust plate
15. Valve key
16. Valve spring retainer
17. Valve stem seal
18. Valve spring
19. Intake valve
20. Exhaust valve
21. Sealing ring assembly
22. Cylinder head
23. Expansion plug
24. Bracket
25. Cylinder head gasket
26. Timing belt cover spacer
27. Water outlet
28. Water outlet gasket
29. Adjusting nut
30. Ball stud
31. Clip

Cylinder head and valve system—2000 cc; 2300 cc similar

rectly align the head and the block. To fabricate guide studs, obtain two new cylinder head bolts and cut their heads off with a hack saw. Install the bolts in the holes in the engine block which correspond with cylinder head bolt holes nos. 3 and 4, as identified in the cylinder head bolt tightening sequence illustration. Then, install the head gasket and head over the bolts. Install the cylinder head attaching bolts, replacing the studs with the original head bolts.

12. Using a torque wrench, tighten the head bolts in the sequence shown in the illustration in the following steps:

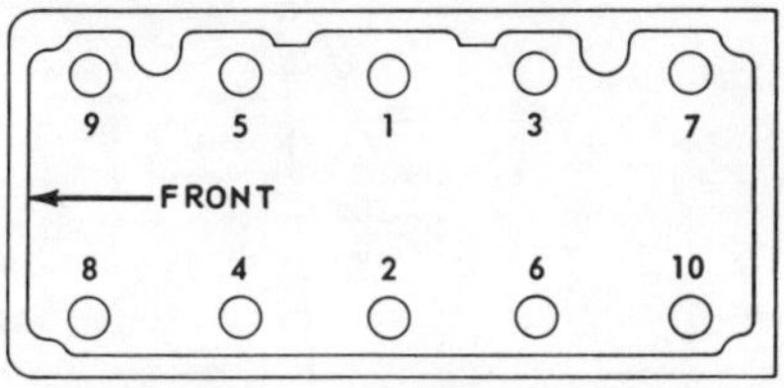

2000 cc cylinder head bolt tightening sequence

A—tighten all bolts to 14–29 ft lbs
B—tighten all bolts to 36–50 ft lbs
C—tighten all bolts to 65–80 ft lbs

13. Install the camshaft drive belt. See "Camshaft Drive Belt Installation."

14. Install the camshaft drive belt cover and its attaching bolts. Make sure the rubber grommets are installed on the bolts. Tighten the bolts to 6–13 ft lbs.

15. Install the water outlet elbow and a new gasket on the engine and tighten the attaching bolts to 12–15 ft lbs.

16. Install the intake and exhaust manifolds. See the procedures for intake and exhaust manifold installation.

17. Adjust valve clearance. See chapter two, "Valve Adjustment."

18. Install the air cleaner and the valve cover.

19. Fill the cooling system.

Disassembly and Assembly

1. Remove the rocker arms from the cylinder head as outlined earlier.

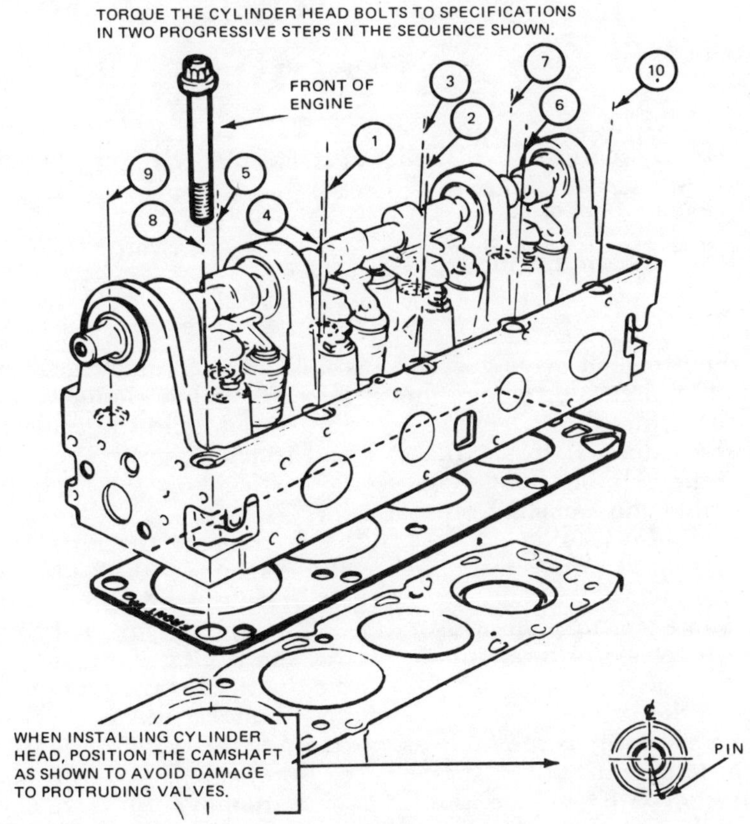

2300 cc cylinder head bolt tightening sequence: step one—torque to 60 ft lbs; step two—torque to 80–90 ft lbs.

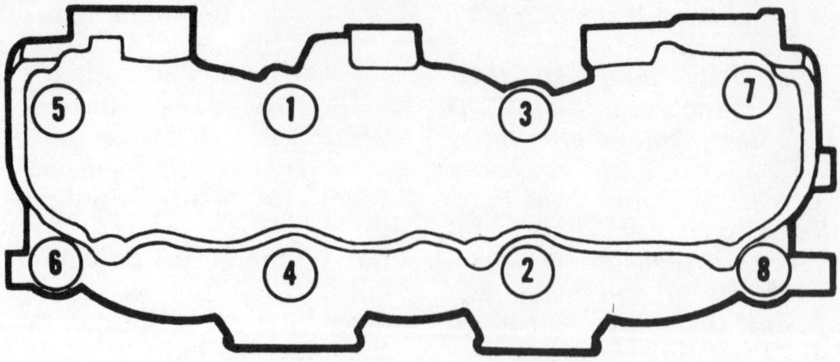

Cylinder head bolt torque sequence—2800 cc

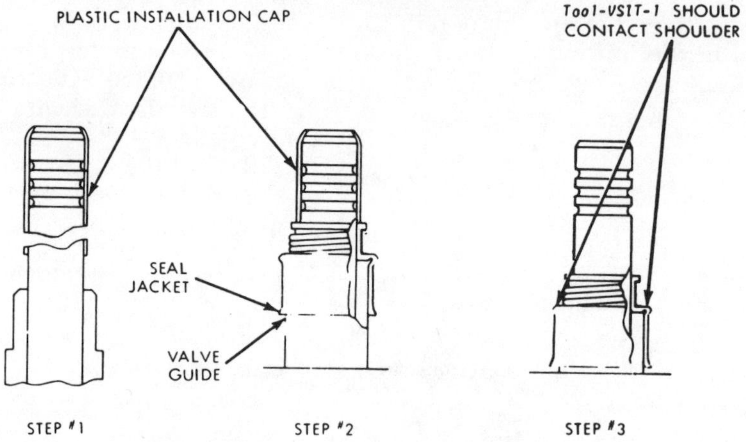

STEP #1 WITH VALVES IN HEAD. PLACE PLASTIC INSTALLATION CAP OVER END OF VALVE STEM.

STEP #2 START VALVE STEM SEAL CAREFULLY OVER CAP. PUSH SEAL DOWN UNTIL JACKET TOUCHES TOP OF GUIDE.

STEP #3 REMOVE PLASTIC INSTALLATION CAP. USE INSTALLATION TOOL-VSIT-1 OR SCREWDRIVERS TO BOTTOM SEAL ON VALVE GUIDE.

2000 and 2300 cc valve installation

2. Remove the camshaft drive gear attaching bolt and washer and remove the gear and belt guide plate.

3. Remove the camshaft thrust plate from the rear of the cylinder head.

4. Carefully slide the camshaft out of the rear of the cylinder head.

5. Remove the spark plugs from the head.

6. Using a valve spring compressor, remove the valve springs and retainers.

7. Remove the valve seals from the head and remove the valves.

Cylinder head assembly is the same as the procedure found in the "Engine Rebuilding" section with two exceptions. When installing the valve stem seals, follow the procedure given in the illustration for valve seal installation. If the camshaft was removed from the cylinder head, install it along with the camshaft thrust plate and the camshaft drive gear and attaching bolt.

2800 cc V6

1. Remove the air cleaner assembly and disconnect the battery and accelerator linkage. Drain the cooling system.

2. Remove the distributor cap with the spark plug wires attached. Remove the distributor vacuum line and distributor. Remove the hose from the water pump to the water outlet which is on the carburetor.

3. Remove the valve covers, fuel line and filter, carburetor, and the intake manifold.

4. Remove the rocker arm shaft and

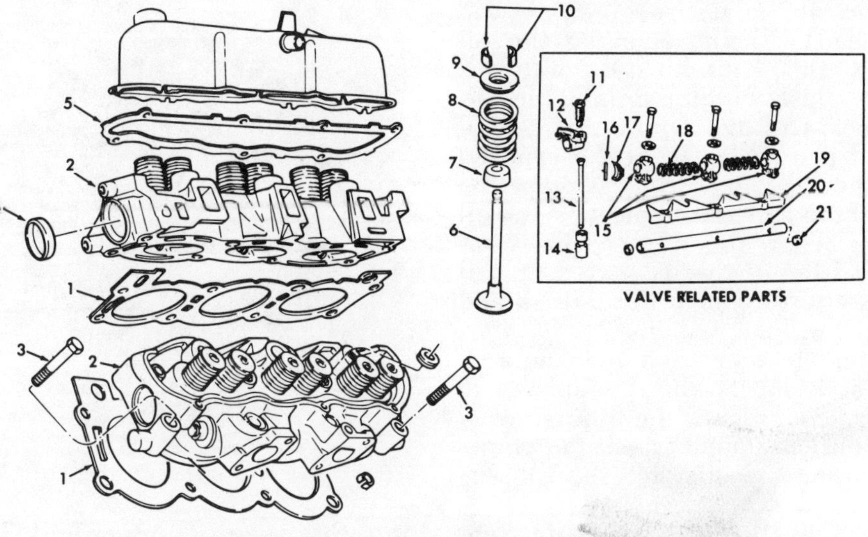

Cylinder head and valve system—2800 cc

1. Cylinder head gasket
2. Cylinder head
3. Head bolt
4. Plug
5. Valve cover gasket
6. Valves
7. Valve seal
8. Valve spring
9. Retainer
10. Valve key
11. Adjusting screw
12. Rocker arm
13. Pushrod
14. Valve tappet
15. Shaft support
16. Pin
17. Spring type washer
18. Rocker shaft spring
19. Oil Baffle
20. Rocker arm shaft
21. Plug

oil baffles. Remove the pushrods, keeping them in the proper sequence for installation.

5. Remove the exhaust manifold, referring to the appropriate procedures.

6. Remove the cylinder head retaining bolts and remove the cylinder heads and gaskets.

CAUTION: *Do not lay the cylinder head flat on its mating surface.*

7. Remove all gasket material and carbon from the engine block and cylinder heads.

8. Place the head gaskets on the engine block.

NOTE: *The left and right gaskets are not interchangeable.*

9. Install guide studs in the engine block. Install the cylinder head assemblies on the engine block one at a time. Tighten the cylinder head bolts in sequence, and in steps, 65–80 lbs.

10. Install the intake and exhaust manifolds.

11. Install the pushrods in the proper sequence. Install the oil baffles and the rocker arm shaft assemblies. Adjust the valve clearances.

12. Install the valve covers with new gaskets.

13. Install the distributor and set the ignition timing.

14. Install the carburetor and the distributor cap with the spark plug wires.

15. Connect the accelerator linkage, fuel line, with fuel filter installed, and distributor vacuum line to the carburetor. Fill the cooling system.

CYLINDER BLOCK FRONT COVER, TIMING CHAIN AND SPROCKET—1600 CC

Removal and Installation

1. Drain the cooling system.

2. Remove the radiator and water pump. See "Engine Cooling" in this chapter for removal procedure.

3. Remove the lower pulley attaching bolt.

4. Using a two-jawed puller, remove the lower engine pulley.

5. Remove the front cover attaching bolts.

NOTE: *The four front oil pan attaching bolts thread into the front cover and must be removed.*

6. Remove the front cover. If the oil pan gasket sticks to the front cover and tears when it is removed, the front por-

tion of the oil pan gasket sometimes can be replaced without removing the oil pan. To do this, cut both sides of the oil pan gasket flush with the front of the cylinder block. Cut the required portion of a new oil pan gasket to fit the exposed part of the oil pan. Firmly cement the portion of the gasket into place. If the oil pan leaks when the front cover is installed and the engine is started, it will be necessary to remove the oil pan and replace the oil pan gasket.

7. With the transmission in neutral, have an assistant tap the ignition key to the "on" position until the timing marks on the camshaft sprocket and the crankshaft sprocket are aligned (see illustration).

8. Remove the timing chain tensioner.

9. Remove the timing chain sprocket attaching bolts.

10. Slide the timing chain and the camshaft sprocket off the engine as an assembly.

NOTE: *The timing chain tensioner pad is designed so that two grooves wear into it as the engine accumulates mileage. Do not alter these grooves. If the chain is replaced, the pad should also be replaced.*

11. If a new oil dipstick is installed

Timing mark alignment—1600 cc

Timing gear alignment—2800 cc

into the cover, its upper end should be 4.90 in. from the base of the front cover.

12. Install the timing chain on the camshaft and crankshaft sprockets and align the timing marks.

13. Position the sprockets and timing chain on the engine. *Make sure the timing marks on the sprockets are aligned as shown in the illustration.*

14. Install the camshaft sprocket attaching bolts.

15. Coat the front cover gasket with oil-resistant sealer and position the gasket and the cover on the engine.

16. Install a large socket wrench or other suitable tool on the front of the crankshaft to center the front cover on the engine and install the front cover attaching bolts.

17. Tighten the bolts evenly to 5–7 ft lbs and remove the alignment tool.

18. Install the four front oil pan bolts and tighten them to 7–9 ft lbs.

19. Install the lower engine pulley and the water pump. Adjust the engine drive belts.

20. Install the radiator and fill the cooling system.

21. Start the engine and check for leaks.

Front Cover Oil Seal Replacement

While supporting the cover with several sockets as shown in the illustration, drive the old seal from the cover. To install the new seal, turn the cover over and again support with several sockets. Drive the new seal into the cover.

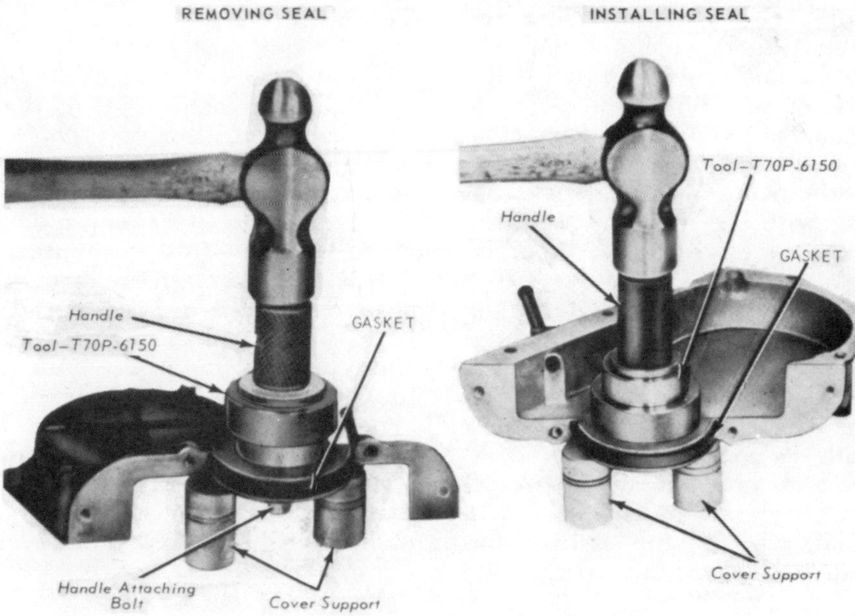

Removing and installing front cover oil seal

CAMSHAFT AND LIFTERS—1600 CC

The mechanical valve lifters are of an inverted mushroom design. The bottom portion of the lifters, which contact the camshaft, have a larger diameter than the top of the lifters, which ride in the lifter bores in the cylinder block. Because of this, it is necessary to remove the engine from the vehicle, remove most of the external components from the engine, and invert the engine to remove the camshaft and/or valve lifter.

The procedures for removing all of the necessary components are contained in this chapter. Therefore, the procedures will not be repeated here. Instead, this section will only list the components that must be removed.

Removal and Installation

1. Remove the engine from the vehicle and mount it on a work stand.
2. Remove the fuel and oil pumps.
3. Remove the distributor.
4. Remove the valve cover, rocker shaft, and pushrods.
5. Remove the cylinder block front cover and timing chain.
6. Place a drain pan under the engine and invert the the engine on the engine stand.
7. Remove the oil pan.
8. Remove the camshaft thrust plate and remove the camshaft.
9. Remove the lifters.

Installation is generally the reverse of the removal procedure, however several things should be kept in mind. When installing the timing chain and sprockets, make sure the timing marks are aligned. When installing the distributor use the procedure in this chapter for installing the distributor when the engine has been disturbed. If a new camshaft or valve lifter(s) have been installed, make a preliminary valve adjustment before starting the engine. After installing the engine and warming it up, adjust the valve clearance with the engine hot. For the valve adjustment procedure see chapter two.

CAMSHAFT DRIVE BELT—2000 CC AND 2300 CC

The correct installation and adjustment of the camshaft drive belt is mandatory if the engine is to run properly. The camshaft controls the opening of the engine valves through coordination of the movement of the camshaft and the crankshaft. When any given piston is on the intake stroke the corresponding intake valve must be open to admit air/fuel mixture into the cylinder. When the same piston is on the compression and power strokes, both valves in that cylinder must be closed. When the piston is on the exhaust stroke, the exhaust valve for that cylinder must be open. If the opening and closing of the valves is not coordinated with the movements of the pistons, the engine will run very poorly, if at all.

The camshaft drive belt also turns the engine auxiliary shaft. The distributor is driven by the engine auxiliary shaft. Since the distributor controls ignition timing, the auxiliary shaft must be coordinated with the camshaft and the crankshaft, since both valves in any given cylinder must be closed and the piston in that cylinder near the top of the compression stroke when the spark plug fires.

Due to this complex interrelationship between the camshaft, the crankshaft and the auxiliary shaft, the cogged pulleys on each component must be aligned when the camshaft drive belt is installed.

Troubleshooting

Should the camshaft drive belt jump timing by a tooth or two, the engine could still run; but very poorly. To visually check for correct timing of the crankshaft, auxiliary shaft, and the camshaft on the 2000 cc and 2300 cc engines, follow this procedure:

On 2000 cc engines, turn the crankshaft over until the two round locating holes in the camshaft pulley are visible from the rear side of the pulley, looking forward from the left-side of the car. When these two holes are parallel to the ground, the timing pointer on the crankshaft pulley should point to TDC. If the drive belt is dislocated, the crankshaft damper will be retarded or advanced 19° per cog on the belt.

NOTE: *If the engine you are working on does not have the two locating holes on the rear side of the camshaft pulley, then you will have to remove the drive belt cover and observe that when the crankshaft timing marks are aligned to TDC of the compression*

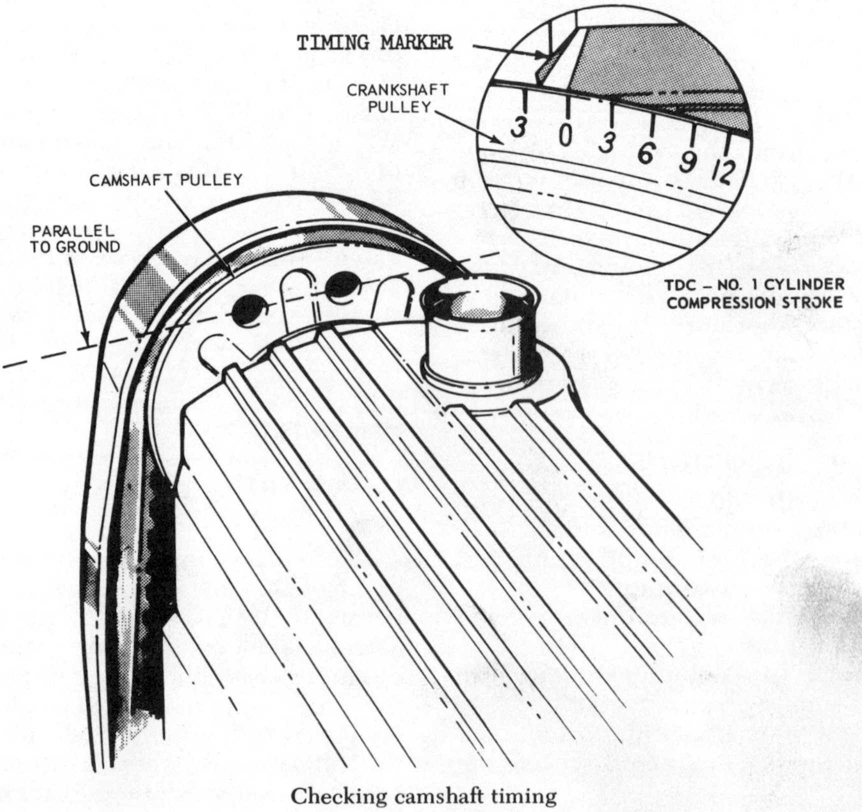

Checking camshaft timing

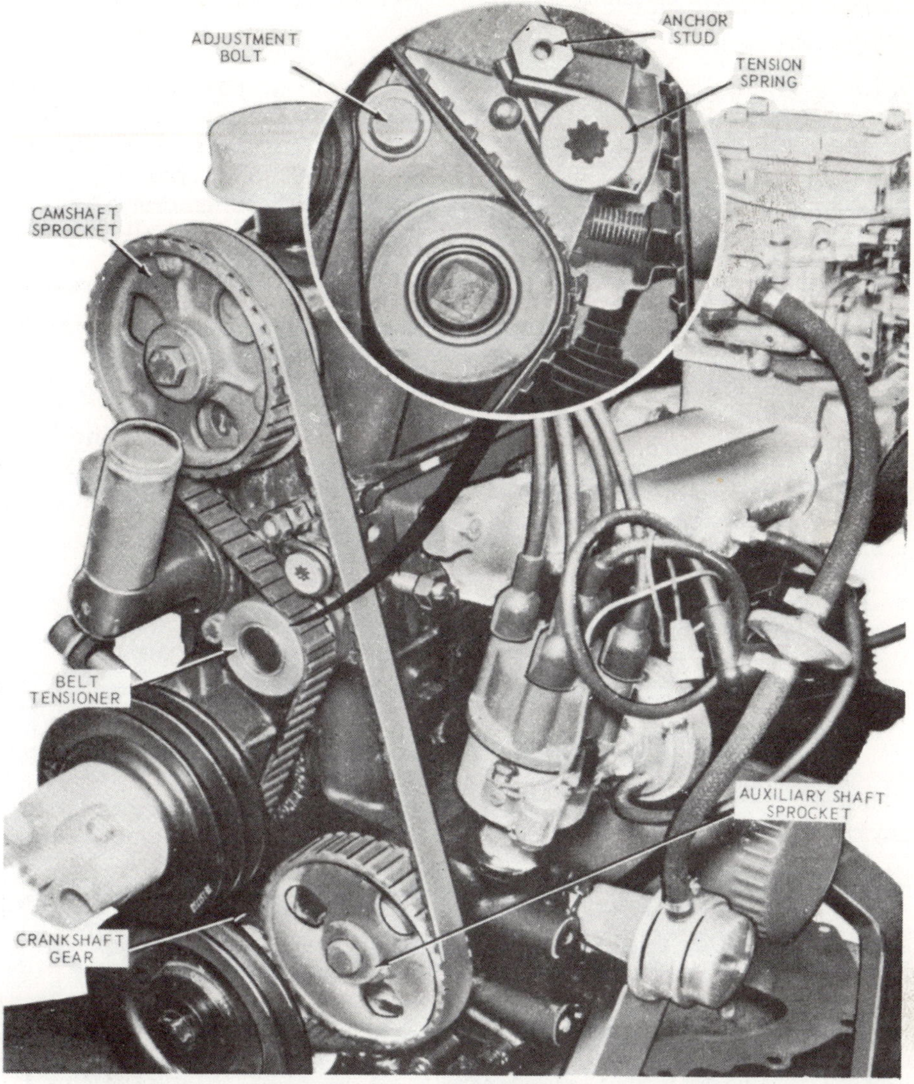

Camshaft drive train—2000 cc

stroke of the No. 1 cylinder, the distributor rotor is pointing to the index mark on the upper lip of the distributor housing which coincides with No. 1 spark plug tower, and the pointer on the camshaft pulley is aligned with the index mark on the cylinder head.

On 2300 cc engines, there is an access plug provided in the cam drive belt cover so that the camshaft timing can be checked without removing the drive belt cover.

1. Remove the access plug.
2. Turn the crankshaft until the timing marks on the crankshaft indicate TDC.
3. Make sure that the timing mark on the camshaft drive sprocket is aligned with the pointer on the inner belt cover. Also, the rotor of the distributor must align with the No. 1 cylinder firing position.

NOTE: *Never turn the crankshaft of any of the overhead cam engines in the opposite direction of normal rotation. Backward rotation of the crankshaft may cause the timing belt to slip and alter the timing.*

CAMSHAFT DRIVE BELT—2000 CC AND 2300 CC

Removal and Installation

1. Remove the camshaft drive belt cover.

2. Remove the distributor cap from the distributor and position it out of the way.

3. Using a wrench attached to the bolt on the crankshaft pulley, turn the wrench in a clockwise direction until the following conditions exist:

A—the timing pointer on the front of the engine is aligned with the "O" or "V" mark on the pulley.

B—the pointer on the camshaft sprocket is aligned with the ball in the belt guide plate.

C—the distributor rotor is aligned with the timing mark on the upper lip of the distributor housing.

NOTE: *If the drive belt has slipped and is out of timing, disregard this procedure.*

4. Loosen the drive belt tensioner bolt and move the tensioner as far to the left as possible. Tighten the tensioner adjustment bolt. This will remove the preload of the tensioner from the belt.

5. Remove the belt from the pulleys.

NOTE: *Do not rotate the camshaft, the crankshaft, or the auxiliary shaft while the belt is removed.*

6. If the timing marks on the camshaft, the crankshaft and the distributor were not aligned before the belt was re-

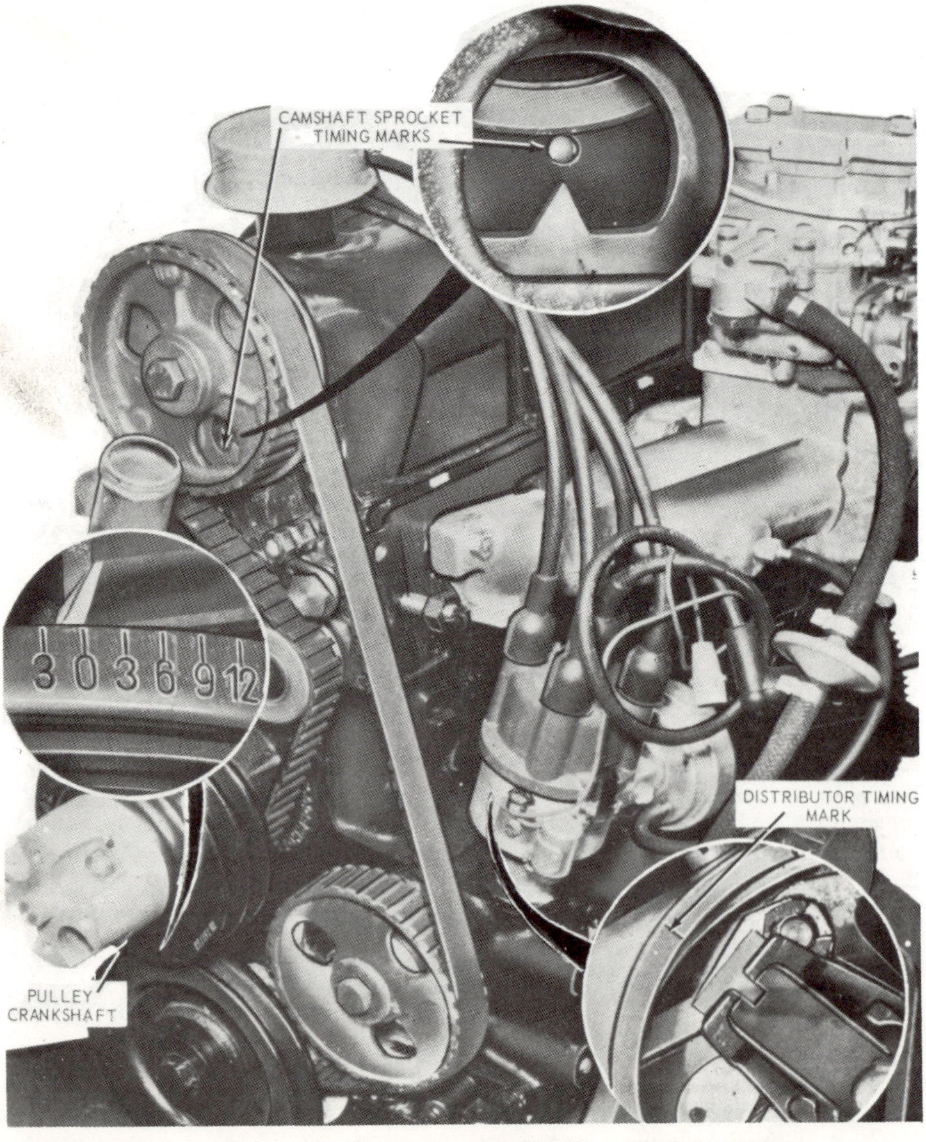

Pulley alignment for drive belt removal and installation—2000 cc

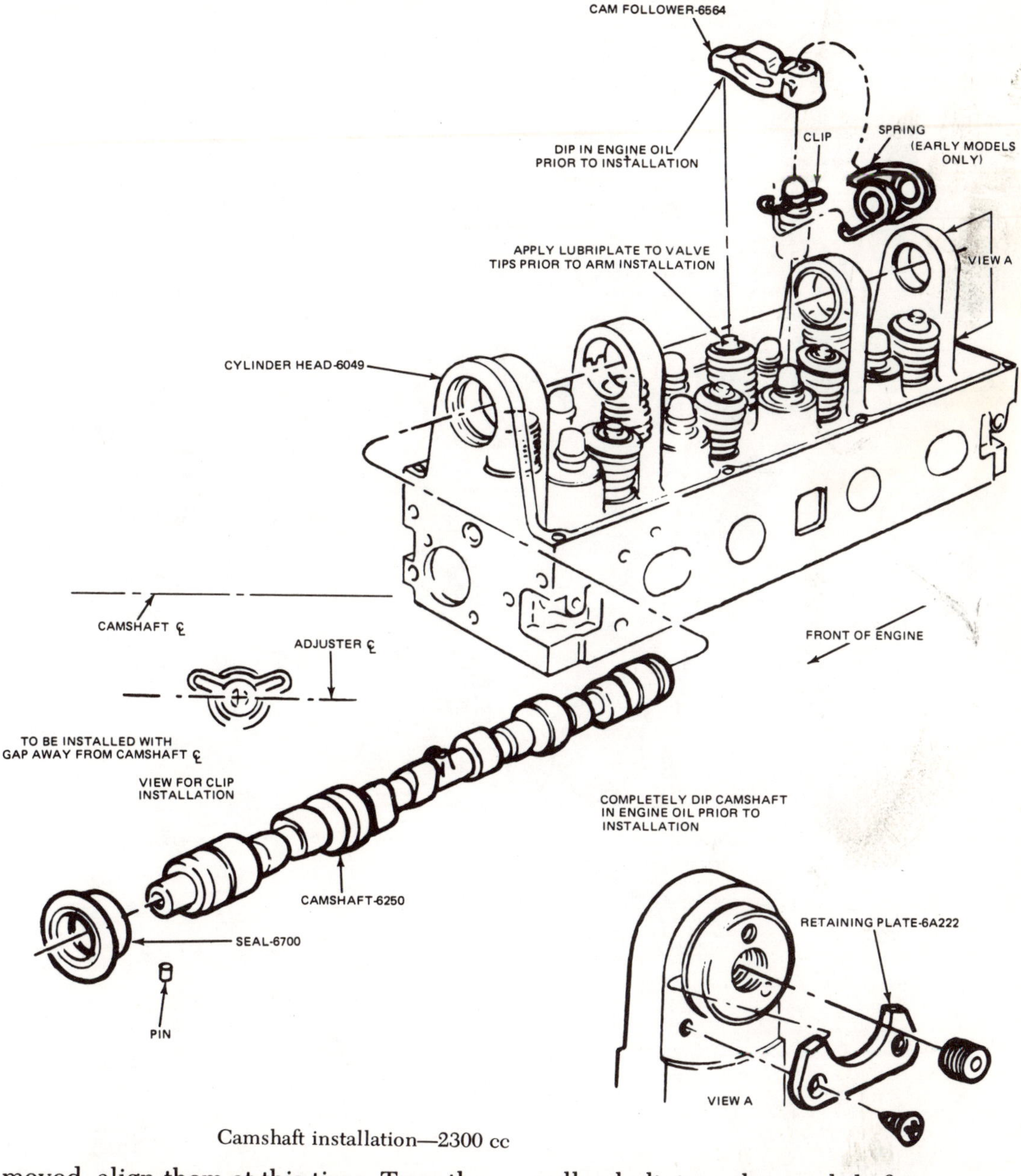

Camshaft installation—2300 cc

moved, align them at this time. Turn the crankshaft (A), the camshaft (B), or the auxiliary shaft (C) until the components are in the positions described in step three of the belt removal procedure.

7. Install the belt on the three sprockets, making sure the cogs on the belt fully engage the slots in the sprockets.

8. Loosen the tensioner adjustment bolt and allow the full spring pressure of the tensioner to force the tensioner against the belt.

9. Using a wrench on the crankshaft pulley bolt, turn the crankshaft two complete turns in a *clockwise* direction to remove all slack from the belt.

10. Continue to turn the crankshaft until the three marks described in step three of the belt removal procedure are aligned. If the belt has slipped, remove the belt and repeat the installation procedure.

11. Position the drive belt tensioner so there is no free play in the drive belt and tighten the tensioner adjustment bolt.

NOTE: *Do not overtighten the belt.*

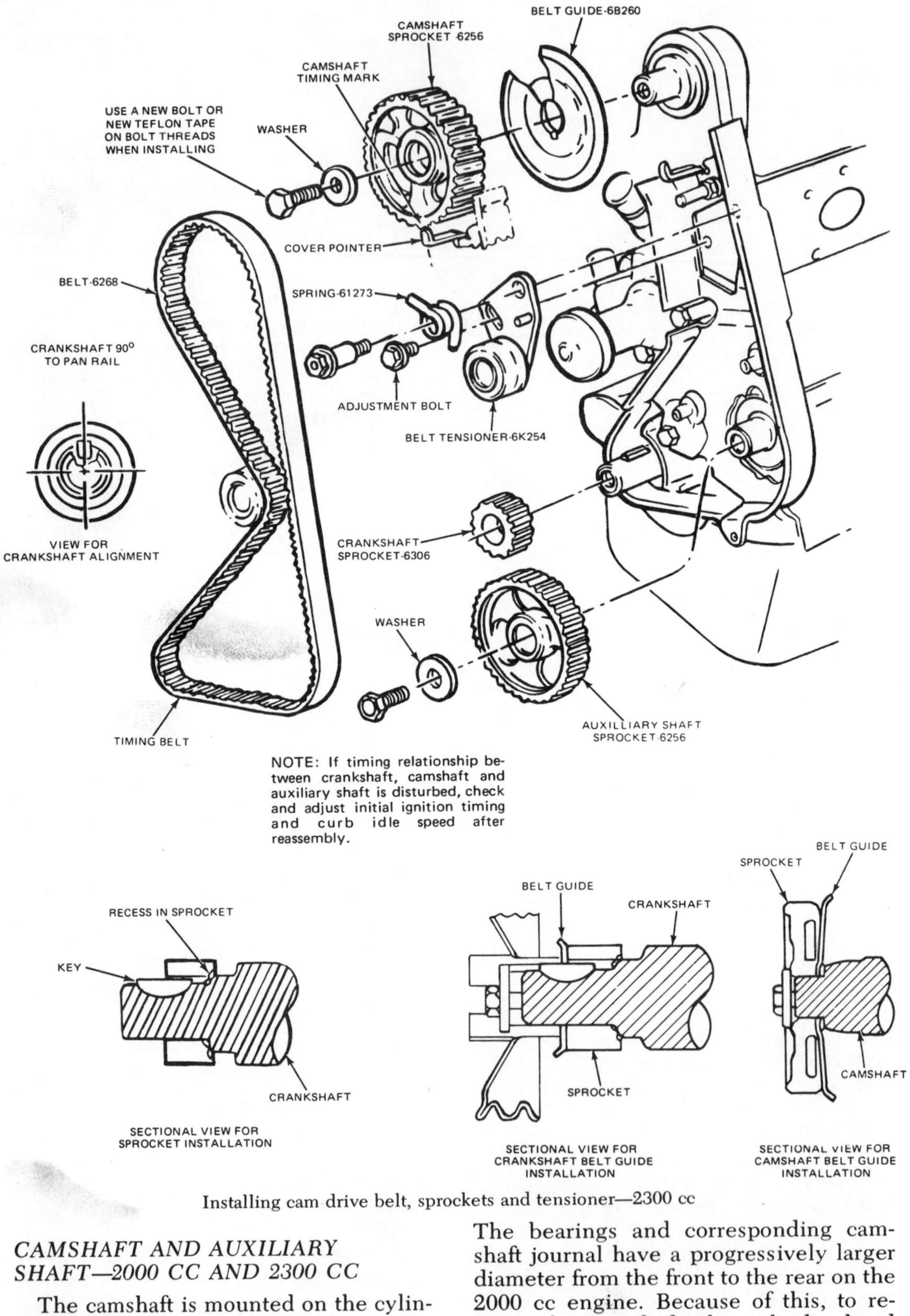

Installing cam drive belt, sprockets and tensioner—2300 cc

CAMSHAFT AND AUXILIARY SHAFT—2000 CC AND 2300 CC

The camshaft is mounted on the cylinder head in three circular bearings. The bearings are mounted in carriers that are an integral part of the cylinder head. The bearings and corresponding camshaft journal have a progressively larger diameter from the front to the rear on the 2000 cc engine. Because of this, to remove the camshaft, the cylinder head must be removed from the engine and the camshaft must be removed from the rear of the cylinder head. On the 2300 cc engine the camshaft is removed through the front of the cylinder head.

Removal and Installation

1. Remove the cylinder head as previously described.
2. Remove the rocker arms.
3. Remove the camshaft drive gear attaching bolt and washer, and remove the gear and belt guide plate.
4. Carefully slide the camshaft out of the rear of the cylinder head on the 2000 cc engine. On the 2300 cc engine, the camshaft is removed through the front of the cylinder head.
5. Reverse the removal procedure to install the camshaft and cylinder head.

NOTE: *Coat the camshaft with oil before sliding it into the cylinder head.*

CAUTION: *After any procedure requiring removal of the rocker arms on the 2300, each lash adjuster must be fully collapsed after assembly, then released. This must be done before the camshaft is turned.*

Auxiliary Shaft

1. Remove the camshaft drive belt cover.
2. Remove the drive belt. Follow all steps under "Camshaft Drive Belt Removal and Installation." Remove the auxiliary shaft sprocket. It may be necessary to use a puller to remove the sprocket.
3. Remove the distributor and fuel pump. Follow all steps under "Distributor Removal."
4. Remove the auxiliary shaft cover and thrust plate.
5. Withdraw the auxiliary shaft from the block.

NOTE: *The distributor drive gear and the fuel pump eccentric on the auxiliary shaft must not be allowed to touch the auxiliary shaft bearings during removal and installation. Completely coat the shaft with oil before sliding it into place.*

6. Slide the auxiliary shaft into the housing and insert the thrust plate to hold the shaft.
7. Install a new gasket and auxiliary shaft cover.
8. Fit a new gasket to the fuel pump and install the pump.
9. Insert the distributor and install the auxiliary shaft sprocket. Follow all steps under "Distributor Installation."
10. Align the timing marks and install the drive belt. Follow all steps under "Camshaft Drive Belt Removal and Installation."
11. Install the drive belt cover.
12. Check the ignition timing.

TIMING CASE COVER—2800 CC

Removal and Installation

1. Remove oil pan.
2. Drain the coolant. Remove the radiator and any other parts to provide necessary clearance.
3. Remove A/C compressor and bracket, if equipped.
4. Remove alternator, thermactor, and drive belt(s).
5. Remove the fan.
6. Remove the drive pulley from the crankshaft.
7. Remove the front cover retaining bolts. If necessary, tap cover lightly with a plastic hammer to break gasket seal. Remove front cover. If front cover plate gasket needs replacement, remove two screws and remove plate. If necessary, remove guide sleeves from cylinder block.
8. Clean the mating surfaces of gasket material. Apply sealing compound to the gasket surfaces on the cylinder block and back side of the front cover plate. Position the gasket and front cover plate on cylinder block. Temporarily install four front cover screws to position the gasket and cover plate in place. Install and tighten two cover plate attaching bolts then remove four screws that were temporarily installed.
9. If removed, fit new seal rings to the guide sleeves and, with no sealer used, insert the sleeves in the cylinder block with the chamfered side of the sleeve toward the front cover.
10. Apply sealing compound to front cover gasket surface. Place the gasket in position on front cover.
11. Place the front cover on the engine and start all retaining screws two or three turns. Center the cover by inserting tool in the oil seal.
12. Tighten the front cover attaching screws to specifications.
13. Install the belt drive pulley and

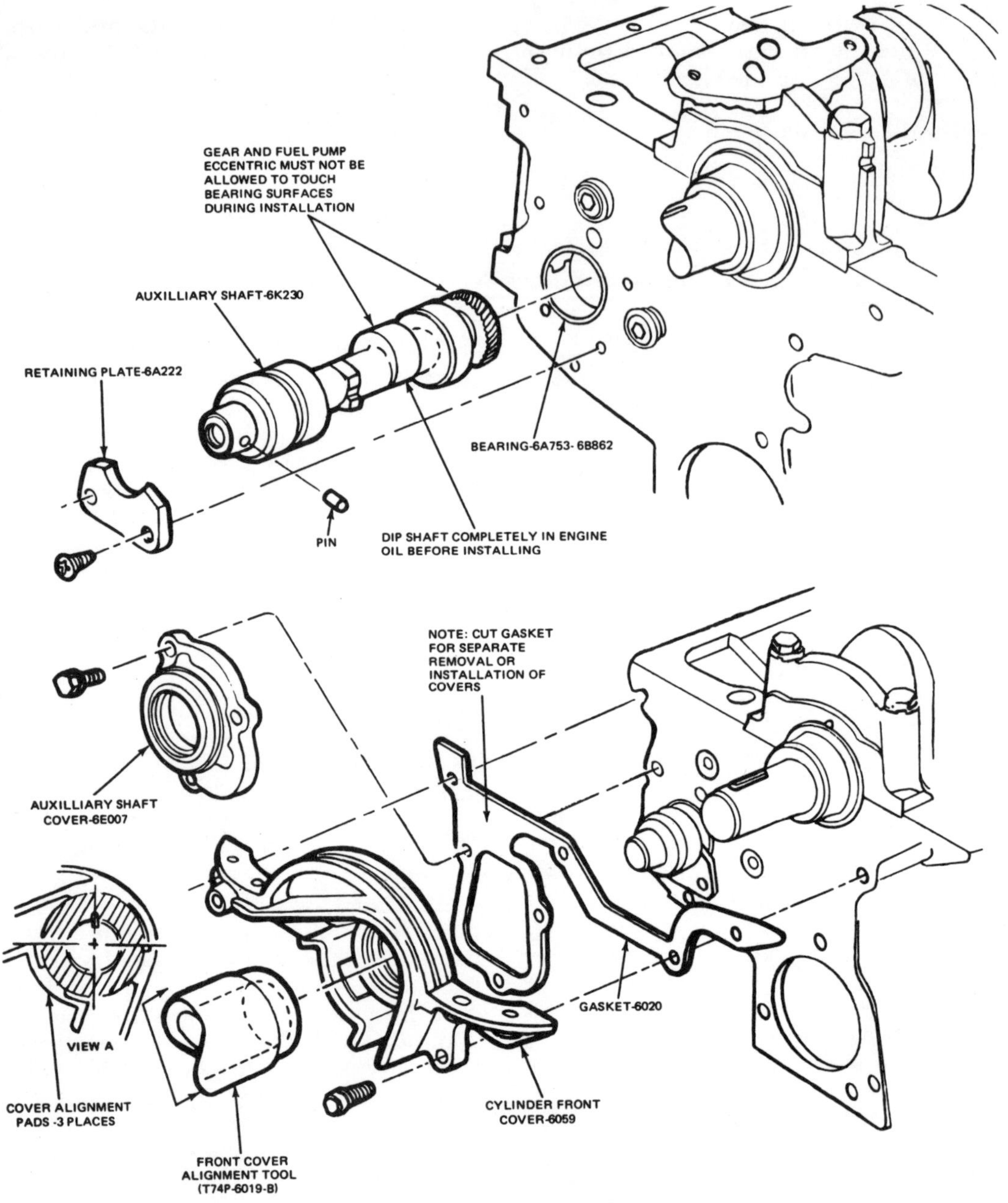

Installing auxiliary shaft and bearings and cylinder front cover—2300 cc

tighten the attaching bolt to specifications.

14. Install the oil pan.

15. Install the water pump, water hose, A/C compressor, alternator and drive belt(s). Adjust the drive belt tension to specifications.

16. Fill the cooling system to the proper level with the specified coolant.

17. Operate the engine at fast idle speed and check for coolant and oil leaks.

NOTE: *If the guide sleeves were removed, install them with new seal rings but do not use sealing compound.*

FRONT COVER OIL SEAL—2800 CC (FRONT COVER REMOVED)

Removal and Installation

1. Support the front cover to prevent damage while driving out the seal.

2. Drive out the seal from the front cover.

3. Support the front cover to prevent damage while installing the seal.

4. Coat the new front cover oil seal with a light grease. Install the new seal in the front cover.

VALVE LIFTERS—2800 CC

Removal and Installation

1. Remove the cylinder head and related parts.

2. Using a magnet, remove the valve lifters. Place them in a rack in sequence. If the lifters are stuck use a plier-type tool to remove them by rotating the lifters back and forth.

3. Clean and lubricate the valve lifters with heavy oil.

4. Install the lifters in their original sequence.

5. Install the cylinder head and related parts.

CAMSHAFT—2800 CC

Removal and Installation

1. Drain the coolant and remove the radiator, fan, spacer, water pump pulley and the drive belt.

2. Remove the distributor cap with spark plug wires as an assembly. Remove the distributor vacuum line, distributor, alternator, Thermactor, rocker arm covers, fuel line and filter, carburetor, EGR tube, and intake manifold. Remove the spark plug wire boots.

3. Drain the crankcase. Remove the rocker arm and the shaft assemblies. Lift out the pushrods and place in a marked rack so they can be reinstalled in the same location.

4. Remove the oil pan.

5. Remove the drive sprocket attaching bolt and slide the sprocket off the end of the shaft.

6. Remove the engine front cover and water pump as an assembly.

7. Remove the camshaft gear retaining bolt and slide the gear off the camshaft.

8. Remove the camshaft thrust plate and the screws.

9. Using a magnet, remove the valve lifters.

10. Carefully pull the camshaft from the block, avoiding any damage to the camshaft bearings. Remove the camshaft gear key and spacer ring.

11. Oil the camshaft journals with gear oil or assembly lube and apply it to the cam lobes.

12. Install the camshaft in the block, carefully avoiding damage to the bearing surfaces.

13. Install the spacer ring with the chamfered side toward the camshaft. Insert the camshaft key and install the thrust plate so that it covers the main oil gallery. Torque the attaching screws to specifications.

14. Check the camshaft for the specified end-play. The spacer ring and thrust plate are available in two thicknesses to permit adjusting the end-play.

15. Turn the camshaft and the crankshaft as necessary to align the timing marks and install the camshaft gear. Install the retaining washer and bolt and tighten to specifications.

16. Install the valve lifters to their original locations.

17. Install the engine front cover and water pump as an assembly.

18. Install the belt drive pulley and secure with washer and retaining bolt. Tighten the bolt to specifications.

19. Install the oil pan.

20. Apply a light grease to both ends of the pushrods. Install the valve pushrods in their original locations. moved.

21. Install the intake manifold.

22. Install the oil baffles and the rocker arm and shaft assemblies. Tighten the rocker arm stand bolts to specifications. Adjust the valves to specified cold setting.

23. Install the water pump pulley, fan spacer, fan, and the drive belt. Adjust the belt tension to specifications. Install the carburetor, EGR tube, fuel line and filter, alternator, Thermactor, distributor, distributor vacuum line, and distributor cap and wires. Install the radiator. Fill the cooling system to the proper level with the specified coolant. Adjust the ignition timing.

24. Install the rocker arm covers.

25. Run the engine and check the idle speed.

26. Run the engine at fast idle speed and check for coolant and oil leaks.

TIMING GEARS—2800 CC

Removal and Installation

1. Drain the cooling system and the crankcase. Remove the oil pan and the radiator.
2. Remove the cylinder front cover and water pump, drive belt, and camshaft following the procedures in this section.
3. Using a gear puller, remove the crankshaft gear. Remove the key from the crankshaft.
4. Place the spacer and thrust plate on the camshaft.
5. Install the key in the camshaft. Align the keyway in the gear with the key, then slide the gear onto the shaft, making sure that it seats tight against the spacer.
6. Check the camshaft end play. If not within specifications, replace the thrust plate.
7. Position the key in the crankshaft. Align the keyway and install the gear.
8. Install the cylinder front cover following the procedures in this section. Replace the oil pan and the radiator.
9. Fill the cooling system and crankcase.
10. Start the engine and adjust the ignition timing. Operate the engine at fast idle and check all hose connections and gaskets for leaks.

PISTON REMOVAL AND PISTON RING REPLACEMENT—ALL MODELS

1. Drain the cooling system and the crankcase.
2. Remove the cylinder head and manifolds as an assembly.
3. Remove the oil pan and oil pump.
4. Turn the crankshaft until the piston to be removed is at the bottom of its stroke.
5. Place a cloth on the head of the piston to be removed and, using a ridge reamer, remove the deposits from the upper end of the cylinder bore.

NOTE: *Never remove more than 1/32 in. from the ring travel area when removing the ridges.*

6. Mark all connecting rod bearing caps so they may be returned to their original location in the engine.
7. Remove the connecting rod caps.
8. Push the connecting rod and piston out through the top of the cylinder with the handle end of a hammer. Be careful not to damage the cylinder wall or crankshaft journal.
9. Using an internal micrometer, measure the bores both across the thrust faces of the cylinder and parallel to the axis of the crankshaft at a minimum of four locations equally spaced. The bore must not be out of round by more than 0.005 in. and it must not "taper" more than 0.010 in. "Taper" is the difference in wear between two bore measurements in any cylinder. See "Engine Rebuilding" for complete details.
10. If the cylinder bore is in satisfactory condition, place each ring in the bore in turn and square it in the bore with the head of the piston. Measure the ring-gap. If the ring-gap is greater than the limit, get a new ring. If the ring-gap is less than the limit, file the end of the ring to obtain the correct gap.
11. Check the ring side clearance by installing rings on the piston, and inserting a feeler gauge of the correct dimension between the ring and the lower land. The gauge should slide freely around the ring circumference without binding. Any wear will form a step on the lower land. Replace any pistons having high steps. Before checking the ring side clearance be sure the ring grooves are clean and free of carbon, sludge, or grit.
12. Space ring gaps at equidistant intervals around the piston circumference.

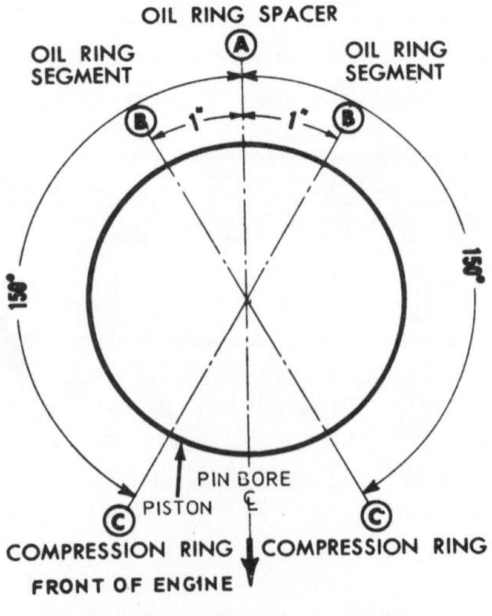

Correct piston ring gap spacing

Be sure to install the piston in its original bore. Install short lengths of rubber tubing over the connecting rod bolts to prevent damage to the rod journal. Install the ring compressor over the rings on the piston. Lower the piston and rod assembly into the bore until the ring compressor contacts the block. Using the wooden handle of a hammer, push the piston into the bore while guiding the rod onto the journal.

NOTE: *Arrows or notches on the pistons must point forward. On 1600 cc engines, the word FRONT faces forward.*

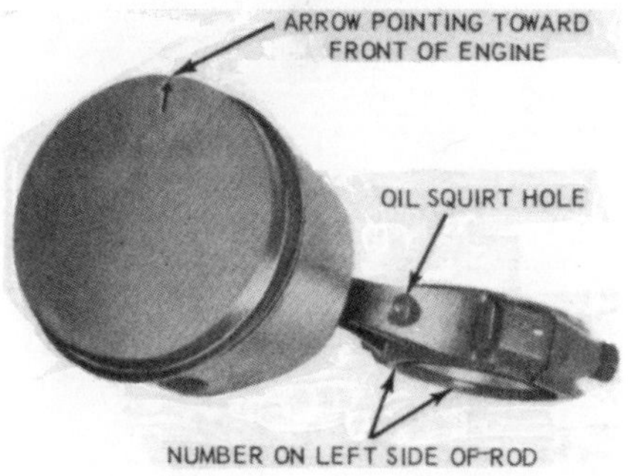

Correct piston and rod position—2000 cc and 2300 cc

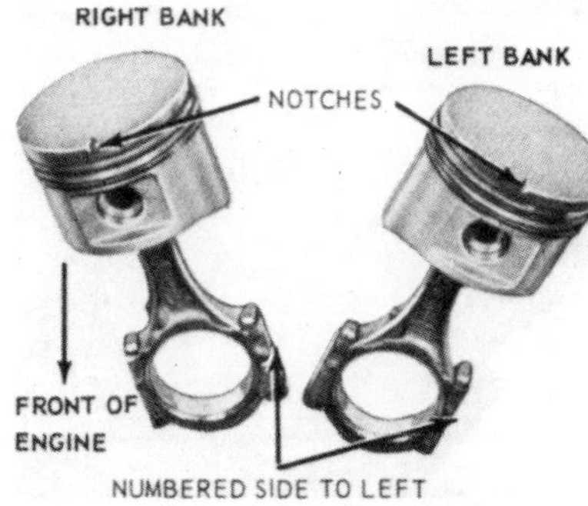

Correct piston and rod position—2800 cc

Engine Lubrication

NOTE: *The Brazilian-built 2300 cc engine has an oil restrictor pin in the oil gallery behind the pressure sender. This pin restricts oil pressure to the tappets during cold and full throttle operation. If the pin is removed, the valves will not seat properly. The Brazilian engine has a 900 through 922 series number on the white engine timing belt cover tag.*

OIL PAN

Removal and Installation

FOUR CYLINDER MODELS

1. Drain the crankcase.
2. Remove the oil dipstick.
3. On 1600 cc engines, disconnect the negative battery cable, remove the starter motor retaining bolts and remove the starter from the engine.
4. Disconnect the steering shaft connection from the rack and pinion.
5. Disconnect the rack and pinion from the crossmember and move it forward to provide clearance.
6. Remove the flywheel housing inspection cover.
7. Remove the oil pan attaching bolts and remove the pan.

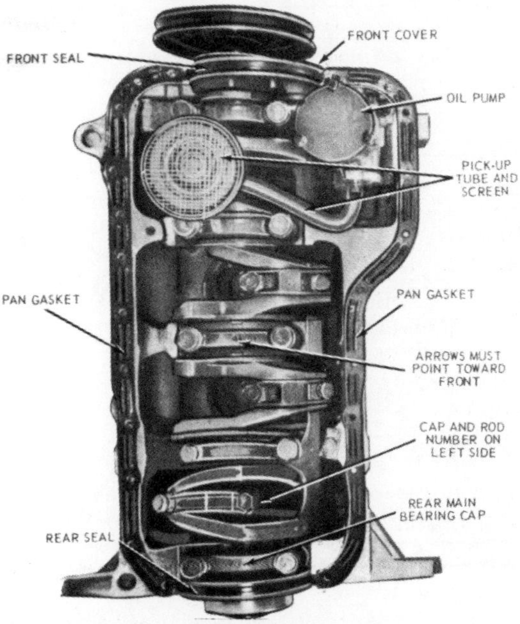

Oil pan gasket installation—2000 cc

8. Clean the gasket mounting surfaces of the block and pan.
9. Coat the block surface and the oil pan gasket with oil-resistant sealer and position the gasket on the bottom of the block.
10. Coat the oil pan front seal and the front cylinder cover with oil-resistant sealer and position the seal on the front cover. Make sure the ends of the seal contact the oil pan gasket.
11. Coat the rear oil pan seal with oil-resistant sealer and install the seal in the rear main bearing cap.

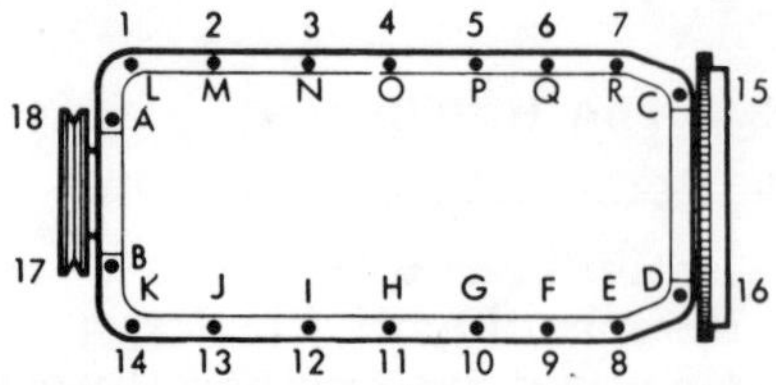

1600 cc oil pan bolt tightening sequence

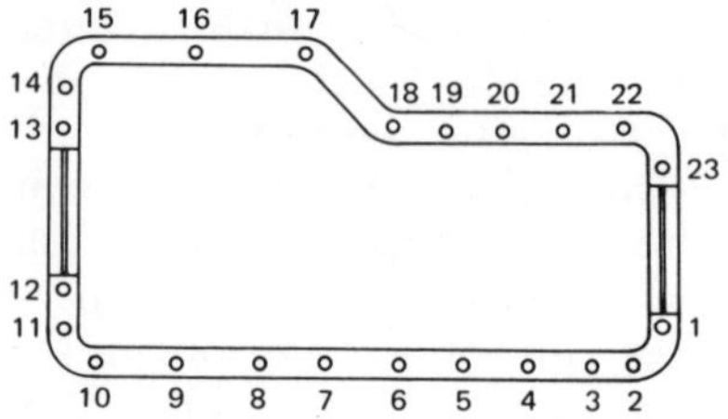

2000 cc oil pan bolt tightening sequence

12. Position the oil pan on the engine and install the attaching bolts finger-tight.

13. Tighten the oil pan attaching bolts in the sequence shown in the illustrations. On 1600 cc engines, follow the alphabetical sequence first, then the numerical sequence for each step of the tightening operation.

14. Tighten bolts in two steps:

A—tighten all bolts to 1–2 ft lbs.

B—on 1600 cc and 2300 cc engines, tighten all bolts to 6–8 ft lbs; on 2000 cc

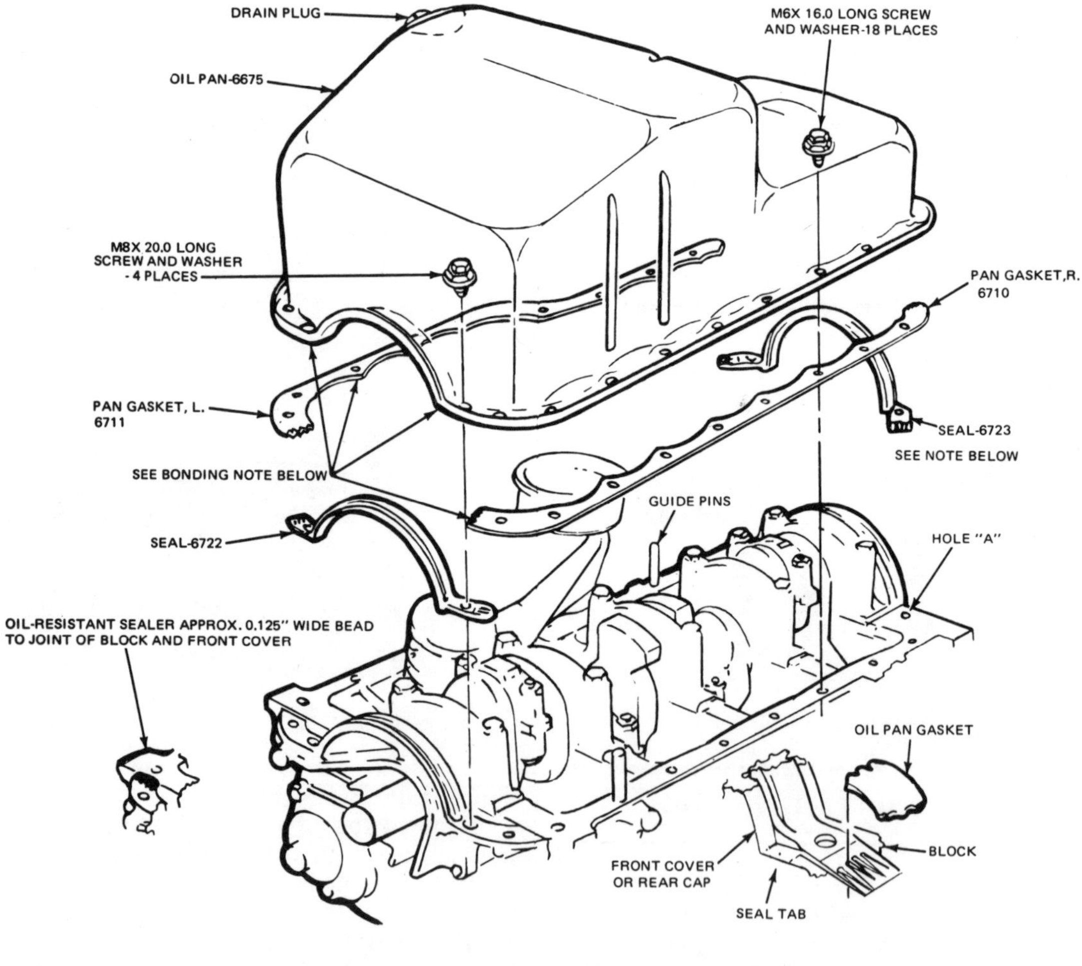

1. APPLY GASKET ADHESIVE EVENLY TO OIL PAN FLANGE AND TO PAN SIDE GASKETS. ALLOW ADHESIVE TO DRY PAST WET STAGE, THEN INSTALL GASKETS TO OIL PAN.
2. APPLY SEALER TO JOINT OF BLOCK AND FRONT COVER. INSTALL SEALS TO FRONT COVER AND REAR BEARING CAP AND PRESS SEAL TABS FIRMLY INTO BLOCK. BE SURE TO INSTALL THE REAR SEAL BEFORE THE REAR MAIN BEARING CAP SEALER HAS CURED.
3. POSITION 2 GUIDE PINS AND INSTALL THE OIL PAN. SECURE THE PAN WITH THE FOUR M8 BOLTS SHOWN ABOVE.
4. REMOVE THE GUIDE PINS AND INSTALL AND TORQUE THE EIGHTEEN M6 BOLTS, BEGINNING AT HOLE A AND WORKING CLOCKWISE AROUND THE PAN.

Oil pan installation—2300 cc

engines, tighten all bolts to 4–6 ft lbs.

15. Install the flywheel housing inspection cover.

16. Connect the rack and pinion to the crossmember and the steering shaft to the rack and pinion.

17. On 1600 cc engines, install the starter and the battery cable.

18. Install the dipstick and fill the crankcase with oil.

2800 cc V6

1. Remove the dipstick. Remove the bolts attaching the fan shroud to the radiator. Position the shroud over the fan. Disconnect the battery ground cable at the battery. Loosen the alternator bracket and adjusting bolts.

2. Raise the car and support it. Disconnect the automatic transmission cooler lines at the radiator. Disconnect the steering gear and power steering hoses if equipped, and unbolt the sway bar at the ends so that it can be rotated to give sufficient clearance.

3. Drain the crankcase.

4. Remove the splash shield. Remove the starter.

5. Remove the engine front support nuts.

6. Raise the engine and place wood blocks between the engine front supports and the chassis brackets.

7. Remove the oil pan attaching bolts and remove the oil pan.

8. Clean the gasket surfaces of the block and the oil pan. The oil pan has a two-piece gasket.

9. Coat the block surface and the oil pan gasket with sealer. Position the oil pan gaskets on the cylinder block.

10. Position the oil pan front seal on the cylinder front cover. Be sure that the tabs on the seal are over the oil pan gasket.

11. Place the end seals in position flush with the cylinder block oil pan rail, if previously removed. Position the oil pan rear seal on the rear main bearing cap. Be sure that the tabs on the seal are over the oil pan gasket.

12. Position the oil pan centered on the cylinder block. Install two bolts at both ends (front and rear) of the oil pan, then install the remaining bolts and tighten them to 5–7 ft lbs, starting with the bolt at the left front corner (looking from the rear) on the leading edge of the oil pan and working around the circumference of the pan.

13. Replace the converter housing or clutch cover.

14. Raise the engine and remove the wood blocks from between the engine supports and chassis brackets. Lower the engine and install the engine support nuts.

15. Replace the starter and splash shield. Reconnect the sway bar, install the power steering gear, and reconnect the automatic transmission cooler lines if they were disconnected.

16. Lower the car.

17. Install the alternator.

18. Connect the battery ground wire.

19. Install the fan shroud.

20. Install the dipstick. Fill the crankcase with oil. Start the engine and check for leaks.

OIL PUMP

Removal and Installation

1600 cc

The oil pump is mounted on the left side of the engine and is attached to the engine by three bolts. To remove the oil pump, remove the three mounting

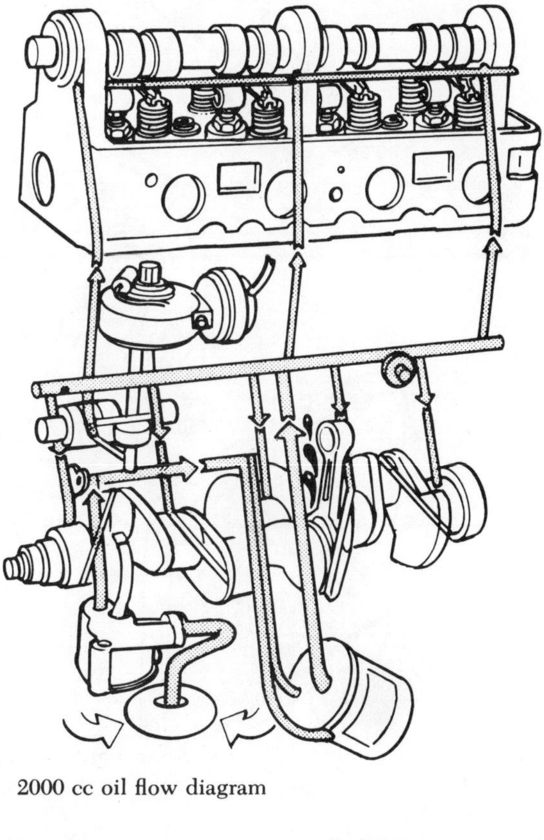

2000 cc oil flow diagram

screws and remove the oil pump and oil filter from the engine as an assembly. When installing the oil pump, use a new gasket and fill the pump and oil filter with engine oil to prime the pump.

2000 CC, 2300 CC, AND 2800CC

The oil pump is mounted on the bottom of the engine block and is enclosed by the oil pan. To remove the oil pump, remove the oil pan and remove the oil pump attaching bolts. On 2800 cc engines, first you must remove the bolt which attaches the pick-up screen to the main bearing cap. When installing the oil pump, use a new gasket and fill the pump with oil to prime the pump.

NOTE: *Under no circumstances should the three-bolt cover oil pump on a 2300 cc engine be disassembled. If the pump is found to be defective, it should be replaced as a unit. Four-bolt cover pumps (introduced in 1976) may be disassembled.*

CRANKSHAFT REAR OIL SEAL

The rear oil seal on 1600 cc engines is installed in a carrier which attaches to the rear of the crankshaft. The rear oil seal on all other engines is installed in the rear main bearing cap. Replacement of the seal on either of the engines requires removal of the transmission and flywheel. However, the removal and installation of the seal itself requires special tools. Therefore, it is recommended that this operation be left to authorized Ford shops which are equipped with the proper tools.

Engine Cooling

All of the Pinto engines are water-cooled by a water/antifreeze solution which passes from the radiator, through the lower radiator hose, through the

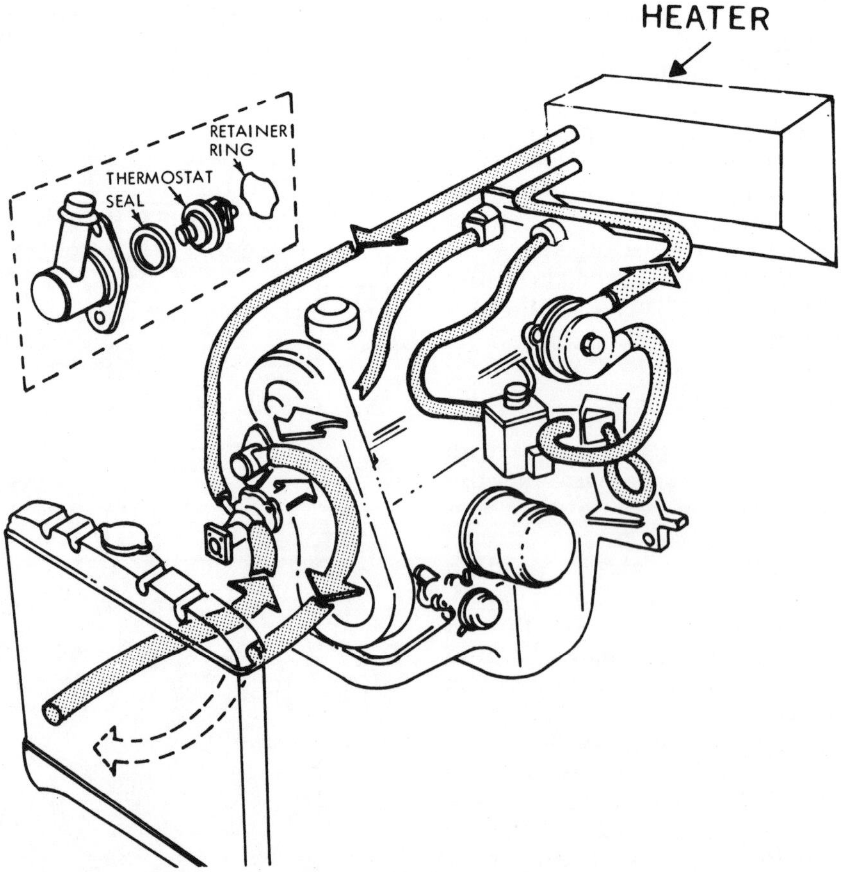

2000 cc cooling system

engine, past the engine thermostat, through the upper radiator hose, and returns to the radiator. As the hot solution passes through the radiator, outside air is drawn through the radiator by the engine fan and cools it. Heat is supplied to the interior of the car by bypassing a portion of the hot solution through a heater core which is located in the heater housing under the instrument panel. On the way to the heater core, this hot water/antifreeze solution first passes through the carburetor choke housing where it heats the choke thermostatic spring. As the engine warms and reaches normal operating temperature, the choke spring expands and opens the choke.

When the engine is cold, the thermostat, which is located in a housing between the top of the engine and the upper radiator hose, is closed and prevents the coolant in the engine from passing to the radiator. This causes the coolant in the engine to heat quickly, shortening the time required for the engine to reach its normal operating temperature. When the coolant reaches a predetermined temperature (183–190°F), the thermostat opens and the normal engine cooling cycle begins.

If your Pinto has an automatic transmission, the bottom section of the radiator in your car contains an automatic transmission oil cooler. Oil from the transmission is transported to the radiator by metal lines. As it passes through the radiator the oil is cooled and returned to the transmission.

TROUBLESHOOTING

Possible causes of cooling system problems listed in order of probable cause:

Engine Overheats

1. Low coolant level probably caused by a leak in the cooling system. Check all hoses, radiator, water pump and heater core for leaks. If no leaks are evident, have system pressure tested.
2. Slipping fan belt. Tighten a loose belt or replace it, if it is cracked or impregnated with foreign material.
3. Sticking thermostat—allow engine to cool, start engine, and fill with water. As the engine warms, look inside the radiator cap opening to see if the coolant level increases by several inches. If it does not, remove the thermostat and place it in a pan of water on the kitchen stove. Make sure the thermostat is completely immersed in water. As the water reaches 190°F, the thermostat should open. If you don't have a thermometer, keep in mind that water boils at 212°F, so the thermostat should open shortly before the water starts to boil.
4. Defective water pump. No real testing is possible. Observe the circulation of water through the radiator cap opening in the radiator. If the coolant has poor circulation and there is no blockage in the cooling system, a defective water pump is the probable cause. A defective water pump usually causes the engine to overheat in stop and go driving but will cool the engine when doing highway driving.
5. Dirty coolant or clogged cooling system. Have the cooling system reverse-flushed and install new coolant. If there is water in the engine oil, it indicates a leaking cylinder head gasket or a crack in one of the cooling system passages in the engine.
6. Defective radiator cap. Have the cap pressure-tested.
7. Retarded ignition timing. Reset the ignition timing.
8. Defective warning light system. Your engine is not really overheating; the warning light is just putting you on.

Engine Does Not Warm Up

1. Defective thermostat, that's all there is to it.

COOLING SYSTEM PRECAUTIONS

Use great care when removing the radiator cap from an overheated engine. The coolant in the engine is *very hot* and under *great pressure* when the engine overheats. Place several heavy rags over the radiator cap and release it very slowly. As soon as steam starts to come out of the cap or radiator overflow hose, *stop* and wait until the steam stops.

Never put cold water into a hot engine without having the engine running. If the engine is very hot, let it cool off first or use warm water, but in all cases, the engine must be running when water is added. Failure to heed this precaution may result in a cracked engine block.

RADIATOR

Removal and Installation

1. Open the petcock at the bottom of the radiator and drain the coolant into a pan. The radiator will drain faster if the cap is removed.
2. Disconnect the charcoal canister line from the clip on the radiator.
3. Disconnect the radiator hoses from the radiator.
4. If equipped with automatic transmission, disconnect the transmission oil cooler lines from the bottom of the radiator.
5. Position a block of wood under the radiator to support it and remove the radiator mounting bolts. If equipped with a fan shroud, position it rearward over the fan. Remove the radiator from beneath the hood.
6. Position the radiator in the car and install the radiator mounting bolts. If equipped with a fan shroud, make sure it is properly installed.
7. If equipped with an automatic transmission, attach the transmission oil cooler lines to the bottom of the radiator.
8. Connect the radiator hoses to the radiator. The hoses are easier to install if a *light* film of oil is spread inside the ends.
9. Attach the charcoal canister line to the clip on the radiator.
10. Close the petcock on the radiator and fill the radiator with coolant.

WATER PUMP

Removal and Installation

1. Drain the cooling system.
2. Disconnect the lower radiator hose and the heater hose from the water pump.
3. Loosen the alternator attaching and adjustment bolt and remove the belt.
4. Remove the fan attaching bolts and remove the fan and the water pump pulley. On 2000 and 2300 cc engines, remove the camshaft drive belt cover.
5. Remove the water pump attaching bolts and remove the pump from the engine.
6. Clean all old gasket material from the engine and the pump if it is to be reused.

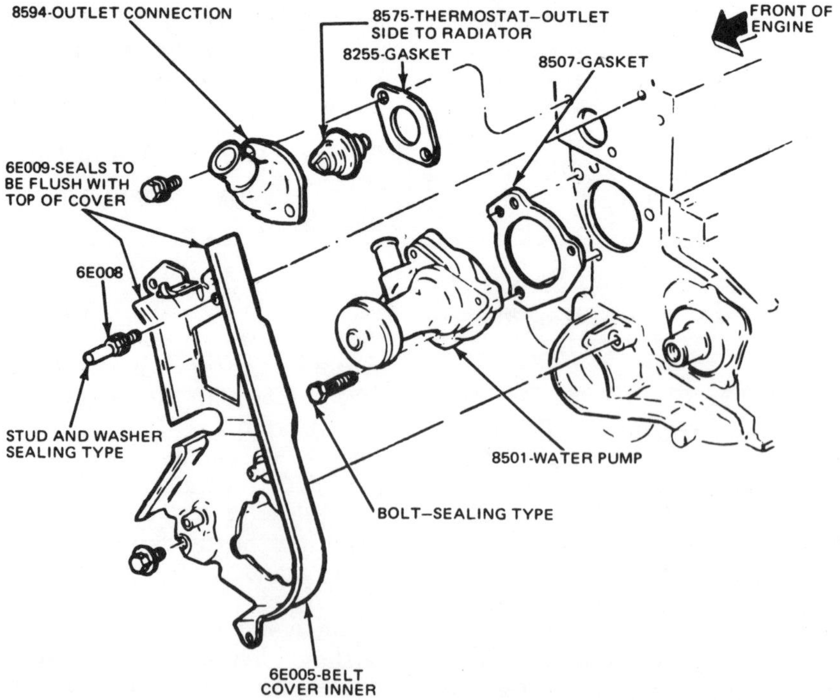

Water pump and thermostat installation—2300 cc

7. If a new water pump is being installed, transfer the heater hose fitting to the new pump.

8. Coat a new gasket with water-resistant sealer and position the pump and gasket on the engine.

9. Install the pump mounting bolts and tighten them. On 2000 cc engines, install the camshaft drive belt cover.

10. Install the fan and the water pump pulley.

11. Install the alternator drive belt and tighten the alternator mounting bolts.

12. Connect the lower radiator hose and the heater hose to the water pump.

13. Close the radiator petcock and fill the cooling system.

THERMOSTAT

Removal and Installation

1. Drain the cooling system.

2. On all engines except the 2800 cc V6, remove the thermostat housing attaching bolts at the upper radiator hose.

3. On the 2800 cc V6, remove the thermostat housing attaching bolts at the bottom of the water pump housing at the lower hose.

4. On the 1600 cc and 2000 cc engines, remove the retaining ring, thermostat, thermostat seal and gasket from the housing.

5. On the 2300 cc and 2800 cc engines lift the thermostat housing from the engine and remove the thermostat and gasket from the engine.

6. Clean all old gasket material from the engine and the thermostat housing.

7. Install the thermostat, gasket and seal, and retaining ring (2000 cc and 1600 cc only) in the thermostat housing. Coat the gasket with water-resistant sealer.

8. Install the housing attaching bolts and tighten them to 12–15 ft lbs.

9. Close the cooling system drains and fill the system.

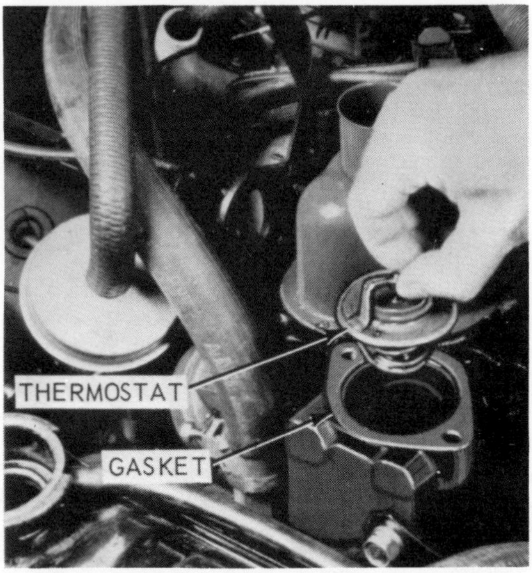

1600 cc thermostat installation

Engine Rebuilding

This section describes, in detail, the procedures involved in rebuilding a typical engine. The procedures specifically refer to an inline engine, however, they are basically identical to those used in rebuilding engines of nearly all design and configurations. Procedures for servicing atypical engines (i.e., horizontally opposed) are described in the appropriate section, although in most cases, cylinder head reconditioning procedures described in this chapter will apply.

The section is divided into two sections. The first, Cylinder Head Reconditioning, assumes that the cylinder head is removed from the engine, all manifolds are removed, and the cylinder head is on a workbench. The camshaft should be removed from overhead cam cylinder heads. The second section, Cylinder Block Reconditioning, covers the block, pistons, connecting rods and crankshaft. It is assumed that the engine is mounted on a work stand, and the cylinder head and all accessories are removed.

Procedures are identified as follows:

Unmarked—Basic procedures that must be performed in order to successfully complete the rebuilding process.

Starred (*)—Procedures that should be performed to ensure maximum performance and engine life.

Double starred (**)—Procedures that may be performed to increase engine performance and reliability. These procedures are usually reserved for extremely heavy-duty or competition usage.

In many cases, a choice of methods is also provided. Methods are identified in the same manner as procedures. The choice of method for a procedure is at the discretion of the user.

The tools required for the basic rebuilding procedure should, with minor exceptions, be those

TORQUE (ft. lbs.)*

U.S.

Bolt Diameter (*inches*)	*Bolt Grade (SAE)* 1 and 2	5	6	8	*Wrench Size (inches)* Bolt	Nut
1/4	5	7	10	10.5	3/8	7/16
5/16	9	14	19	22	1/2	9/16
3/8	15	25	34	37	9/16	5/8
7/16	24	40	55	60	5/8	3/4
1/2	37	60	85	92	3/4	13/16
9/16	53	88	120	132	7/8	7/8
5/8	74	120	167	180	15/16	1
3/4	120	200	280	296	1-1/8	1-1/8
7/8	190	302	440	473	1-5/16	1-5/16
1	282	466	660	714	1-1/2	1-1/2

Metric

Bolt Diameter (*mm*)	*Bolt Grade* 5D	8G	10K	12K	*Wrench Size (mm) Bolt and Nut*
6	5	6	8	10	10
8	10	16	22	27	14
10	19	31	40	49	17
12	34	54	70	86	19
14	55	89	117	137	22
16	83	132	175	208	24
18	111	182	236	283	27
22	182	284	394	464	32
24	261	419	570	689	36

*—Torque values are for lightly oiled bolts. CAUTION: Bolts threaded into aluminum require much less torque.

General Torque Specifications

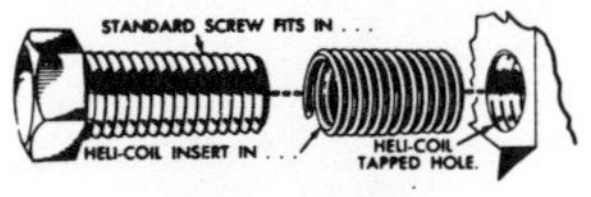

Heli-Coil installation
(© Chrysler Corp.)

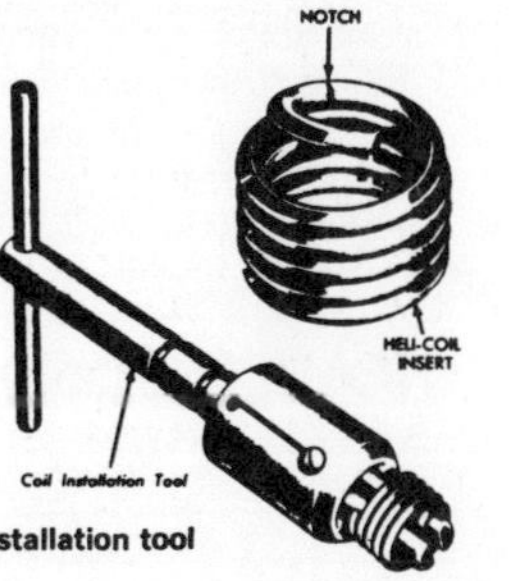

Heli-Coil and installation tool

Heli-Coil Insert Thread Size	Heli-Coil Insert Part No.	Heli-Coil Insert Insert Length (In.)	Drill Size	Tap Part No.	Insert. Tool Part No.	Extracting Tool Part No.
1/2 -20	1185-4	3/8	17/64(.266)	4 CPB	528-4N	1227-6
5/16-18	1185-5	15/32	Q(.332)	5 CPB	528-5N	1227-6
3/8 -16	1185-6	9/16	X(.397)	6 CPB	528-6N	1227-6
7/16-14	1185-7	21/32	29/64(.453)	7 CPB	528-7N	1227-16
1/2 -13	1185-8	3/4	33/64(.516)	8 CPB	528-8N	1227-16

Heli-Coil Specifications

included in a mechanic's tool kit. An accurate torque wrench, and a dial indicator (reading in thousandths) mounted on a universal base should be available. Bolts and nuts with no torque specification should be tightened according to size (see chart). Special tools, where required, all are readily available from the major tool suppliers (i.e., Craftsman, Snap-On, K-D). The services of a competent automotive machine shop must also be readily available.

When assembling the engine, any parts that will be in frictional contact must be pre-lubricated, to provide protection on initial start-up. Vortex Pre-Lube, STP, or any product specifically formulated for this purpose may be used. NOTE: *Do not use engine oil.* Where semi-permanent (locked but removable) installation of bolts or nuts is desired, threads should be cleaned and coated with Loctite. Studs may be permanently installed using Loctite Stud and Bearing Mount.

Aluminum has become increasingly popular for use in engines, due to its low weight and excellent heat transfer characteristics. The following precautions must be observed when handling aluminum engine parts:

—Never hot-tank aluminum parts.

—Remove all aluminum parts (identification tags, etc.) from engine parts before hot-tanking (otherwise they will be removed during the process).

—Always coat threads lightly with engine oil or anti-seize compounds before installation, to prevent seizure.

—Never over-torque bolts or spark plugs in aluminum threads. Should stripping occur, threads can be restored according to the following procedure, using Heli-Coil thread inserts:

Tap drill the hole with the stripped threads to the specified size (see chart). Using the specified tap (NOTE: *Heli-Coil tap sizes refer to the size thread being replaced, rather than the actual tap size*), tap the hole for the Heli-Coil. Place the insert on the proper installation tool (see chart). Apply pressure on the insert while winding it clockwise into the hole, until the top of the insert is one turn below the surface. Remove the installation tool, and break the installation tang from the bottom of the insert by moving it up and down. If the Heli-Coil must be removed, tap the removal tool firmly into the hole, so that it engages the top thread, and turn the tool counter-clockwise to extract the insert.

Snapped bolts or studs may be removed, using a stud extractor (unthreaded) or Vise-Grip pliers (threaded). Penetrating oil (e.g., Liquid Wrench) will often aid in breaking frozen threads. In cases where the stud or bolt is flush with, or below the surface, proceed as follows:

Drill a hole in the broken stud or bolt, approximately ½ its diameter. Select a screw extractor (e.g., Easy-Out) of the proper size, and tap it into the stud or bolt. Turn the extractor counterclockwise to remove the stud or bolt.

Magnaflux and Zyglo are inspection techniques used to locate material flaws, such as stress cracks. Magnafluxing coats the part with fine magnetic particles, and subjects the part to a magnetic field. Cracks cause breaks

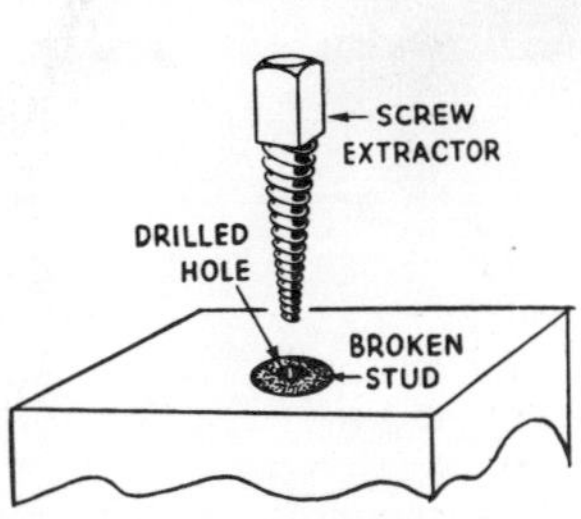

Screw extractor

in the magnetic field, which are outlined by the particles. Since Magnaflux is a magnetic process, it is applicable only to ferrous materials. The Zyglo process coats the material with a fluorescent dye penetrant, and then subjects it to blacklight inspection, under which cracks glow bright-

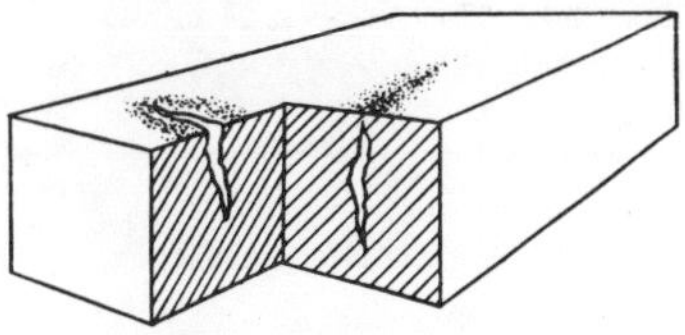
Magnaflux indication of cracks

ly. Parts made of any material may be tested using Zyglo. While Magnaflux and Zyglo are excellent for general inspection, and locating hidden defects, specific checks of suspected cracks may be made at lower cost and more readily using spot check dye. The dye is sprayed onto the suspected area, wiped off, and the area is then sprayed with a developer. Cracks then will show up brightly. Spot check dyes will only indicate surface cracks; therefore, structural cracks below the surface may escape detection. When questionable, the part should be tested using Magnaflux or Zyglo.

CYLINDER HEAD RECONDITIONING

Procedure	*Method*
Identify the valves:  Valve identification (© SAAB)	Invert the cylinder head, and number the valve faces front to rear, using a permanent felt-tip marker.
Remove the rocker arms:	Remove the rocker arms with shaft(s) or balls and nuts. Wire the sets of rockers, balls and nuts together, and identify according to the corresponding valve.
Remove the valves and springs:	Using an appropriate valve spring compressor (depending on the configuration of the cylinder head), compress the valve springs. Lift out the keepers with needlenose pliers, release the compressor, and remove the valve, spring, and spring retainer.
Check the valve stem-to-guide clearance:  Checking the valve stem-to-guide clearance (© American Motors Corp.)	Clean the valve stem with lacquer thinner or a similar solvent to remove all gum and varnish. Clean the valve guides using solvent and an expanding wire-type valve guide cleaner. Mount a dial indicator so that the stem is at 90° to the valve stem, as close to the valve guide as possible. Move the valve off its seat, and measure the valve guide-to-stem clearance by moving the stem back and forth to actuate the dial indicator. Measure the valve stems using a micrometer, and compare to specifications, to determine whether stem or guide wear is responsible for excessive clearance.
De-carbon the cylinder head and valves: 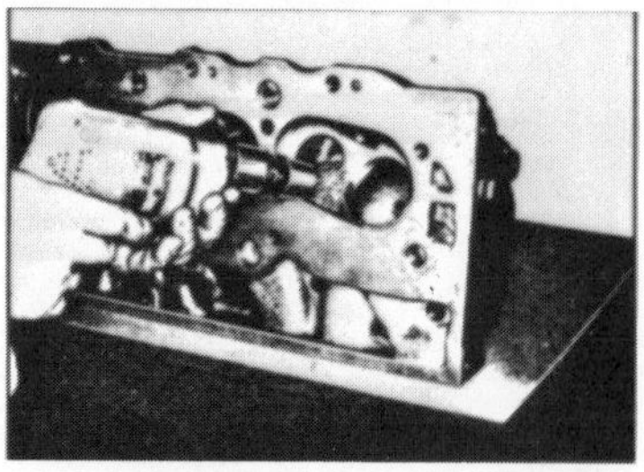 Removing carbon from the cylinder head (© Chevrolet Div. G.M. Corp.)	Chip carbon away from the valve heads, combustion chambers, and ports, using a chisel made of hardwood. Remove the remaining deposits with a stiff wire brush. NOTE: *Ensure that the deposits are actually removed, rather than burnished.*

Procedure	*Method*
Hot-tank the cylinder head:	Have the cylinder head hot-tanked to remove grease, corrosion, and scale from the water passages. NOTE: *In the case of overhead cam cylinder heads, consult the operator to determine whether the camshaft bearings will be damaged by the caustic solution.*
Degrease the remaining cylinder head parts:	Using solvent (i.e., Gunk), clean the rockers, rocker shaft(s) (where applicable), rocker balls and nuts, springs, spring retainers, and keepers. Do not remove the protective coating from the springs.
Check the cylinder head for warpage: 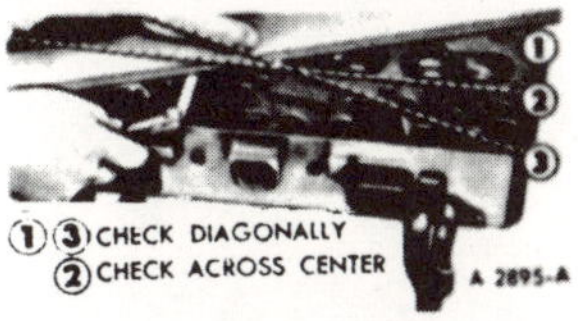 **Checking the cylinder head for warpage** (© Ford Motor Co.)	Place a straight-edge across the gasket surface of the cylinder head. Using feeler gauges, determine the clearance at the center of the straight-edge. Measure across both diagonals, along the longitudinal centerline, and across the cylinder head at several points. If warpage exceeds .003″ in a 6″ span, or .006″ over the total length, the cylinder head must be resurfaced. NOTE: *If warpage exceeds the manufacturers maximum tolerance for material removal, the cylinder head must be replaced.* When milling the cylinder heads of V-type engines, the intake manifold mounting position is altered, and must be corrected by milling the manifold flange a proportionate amount.
** Porting and gasket matching: 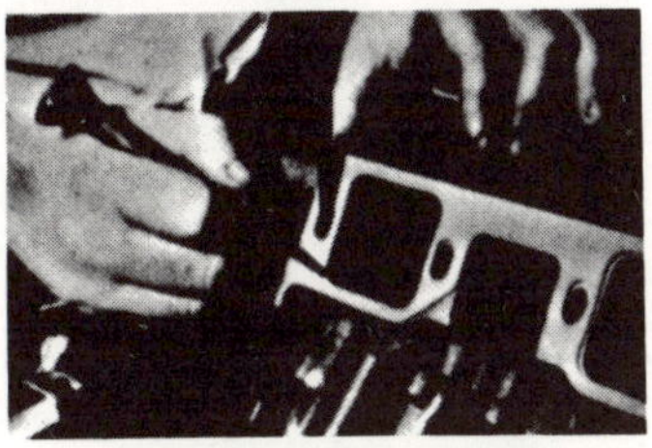 **Marking the cylinder head for gasket matching** (© Petersen Publishing Co.)  **Port configuration before and after gasket matching** (© Petersen Publishing Co.)	** Coat the manifold flanges of the cylinder head with Prussian blue dye. Glue intake and exhaust gaskets to the cylinder head in their installed position using rubber cement and scribe the outline of the ports on the manifold flanges. Remove the gaskets. Using a small cutter in a hand-held power tool (i.e., Dremel Moto-Tool), gradually taper the walls of the port out to the scribed outline of the gasket. Further enlargement of the ports should include the removal of sharp edges and radiusing of sharp corners. Do not alter the valve guides. NOTE: *The most efficient port configuration is determined only by extensive testing. Therefore, it is best to consult someone experienced with the head in question to determine the optimum alterations.*

Procedure	*Method*
** Polish the ports:	** Using a grinding stone with the above mentioned tool, polish the walls of the intake and exhaust ports, and combustion chamber. Use progressively finer stones until all surface imperfections are removed. NOTE: *Through testing, it has been determined that a smooth surface is more effective than a mirror polished surface in intake ports, and vice-versa in exhaust ports.*

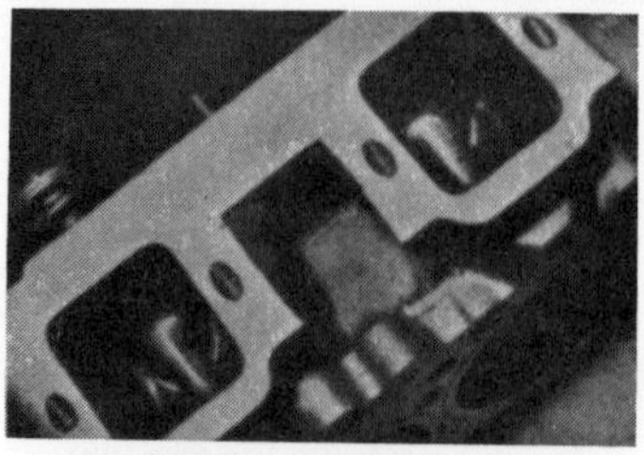

Relieved and polished ports
(© Petersen Publishing Co.)

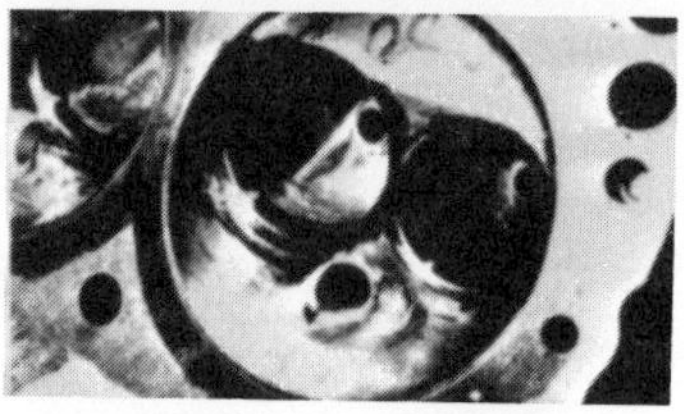

Polished combustion chamber
(© Petersen Publishing Co.)

* Knurling the valve guides:	* Valve guides which are not excessively worn or distorted may, in some cases, be knurled rather than replaced. Knurling is a process in which metal is displaced and raised, thereby reducing clearance. Knurling also provides excellent oil control. The possibility of knurling rather than replacing valve guides should be discussed with a machinist.

Cut-away view of a knurled valve guide
(© Petersen Publishing Co.)

Replacing the valve guides: NOTE: *Valve guides should only be replaced if damaged or if an oversize valve stem is not available.*	Depending on the type of cylinder head, valve guides may be pressed, hammered, or shrunk in. In cases where the guides are shrunk into the head, replacement should be left to an equipped machine shop. In other cases, the guides are replaced as follows: Press or tap the valve guides out of the head using a stepped drift (see illustration). Determine the height above the boss that the guide must extend, and obtain a stack of washers, their I.D. similar to the guide's O.D., of that height. Place the stack of washers on the guide, and insert the guide into the boss. NOTE: *Valve guides are often tapered or beveled for installation.* Using the stepped installation tool (see illustration), press or tap the guides into position. Ream the guides according to the size of the valve stem.

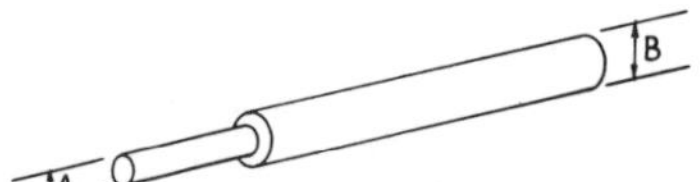

A-VALVE GUIDE I.D.
B-SLIGHTLY SMALLER THAN VALVE GUIDE O.D.

Valve guide removal tool

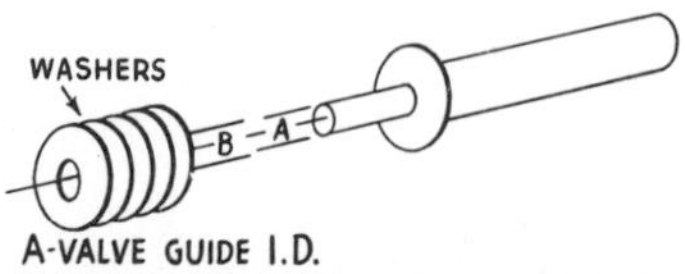

A-VALVE GUIDE I.D.
B-LARGER THAN THE VALVE GUIDE O.D.

Valve guide installation tool (with washers used during installation)

Procedure	Method
Replacing valve seat inserts:	Replacement of valve seat inserts which are worn beyond resurfacing or broken, if feasible, must be done by a machine shop.
Resurfacing (grinding) the valve face: 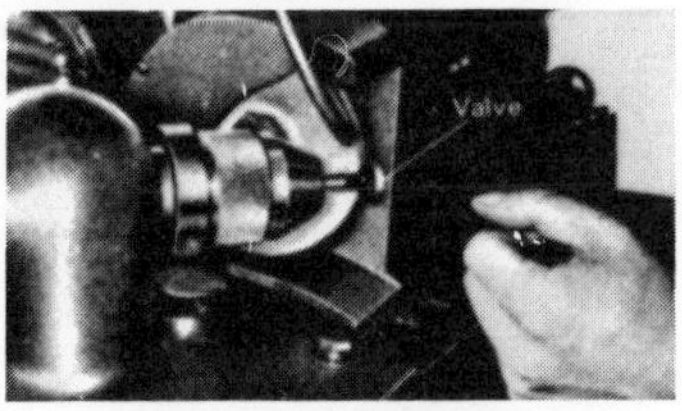 Grinding a valve (© Subaru) 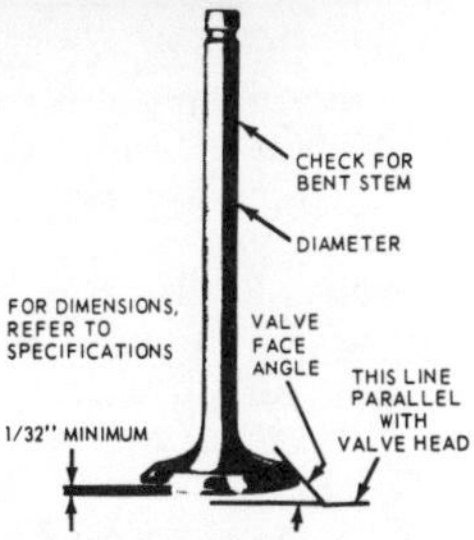 Critical valve dimensions (© Ford Motor Co.)	Using a valve grinder, resurface the valves according to specifications. CAUTION: *Valve face angle is not always identical to valve seat angle.* A minimum margin of 1/32" should remain after grinding the valve. The valve stem tip should also be squared and resurfaced, by placing the stem in the V-block of the grinder, and turning it while pressing lightly against the grinding wheel.
Resurfacing the valve seats using reamers:  Reaming the valve seat (© S.p.A. Fiat)  Valve seat width and centering (© Ford Motor Co.)	Select a reamer of the correct seat angle, slightly larger than the diameter of the valve seat, and assemble it with a pilot of the correct size. Install the pilot into the valve guide, and using steady pressure, turn the reamer clockwise. CAUTION: *Do not turn the reamer counter-clockwise.* Remove only as much material as necessary to clean the seat. Check the concentricity of the seat (see below). If the dye method is not used, coat the valve face with Prussian blue dye, install and rotate it on the valve seat. Using the dye marked area as a centering guide, center and narrow the valve seat to specifications with correction cutters. NOTE: *When no specifications are available, minimum seat width for exhaust valves should be 5/64", intake valves 1/16".* After making correction cuts, check the position of the valve seat on the valve face using Prussian blue dye.
* Resurfacing the valve seats using a grinder: 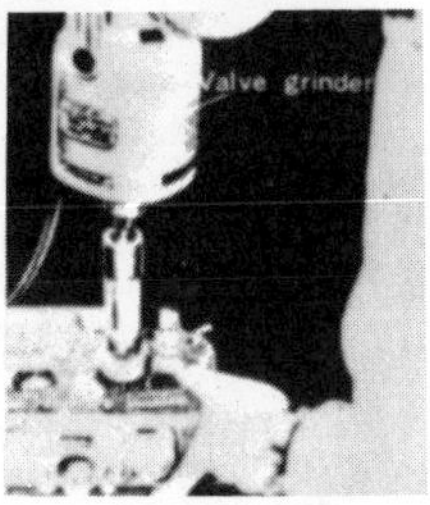 Grinding a valve seat (© Subaru)	Select a pilot of the correct size, and a coarse stone of the correct seat angle. Lubricate the pilot if necessary, and install the tool in the valve guide. Move the stone on and off the seat at approximately two cycles per second, until all flaws are removed from the seat. Install a fine stone, and finish the seat. Center and narrow the seat using correction stones, as described above.

Procedure	*Method*
Checking the valve seat concentricity:	Coat the valve face with Prussian blue dye, install the valve, and rotate it on the valve seat. If the entire seat becomes coated, and the valve is known to be concentric, the seat is concentric.
	* Install the dial gauge pilot into the guide, and rest the arm on the valve seat. Zero the gauge, and rotate the arm around the seat. Run-out should not exceed .002″.

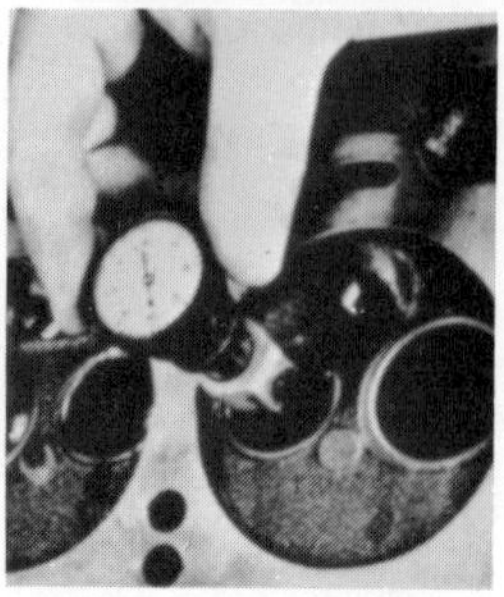

Checking the valve seat concentricity using a dial gauge (© American Motors Corp.)

* Lapping the valves: NOTE: *Valve lapping is done to ensure efficient sealing of resurfaced valves and seats. Valve lapping alone is not recommended for use as a resurfacing procedure.*	* Invert the cylinder head, lightly lubricate the valve stems, and install the valves in the head as numbered. Coat valve seats with fine grinding compound, and attach the lapping tool suction cup to a valve head (NOTE: *Moisten the suction cup*). Rotate the tool between the palms, changing position and lifting the tool often to prevent grooving. Lap the valve until a smooth, polished seat is evident. Remove the valve and tool, and rinse away all traces of grinding compound.
	** Fasten a suction cup to a piece of drill rod, and mount the rod in a hand drill. Proceed as above, using the hand drill as a lapping tool. CAUTION: *Due to the higher speeds involved when using the hand drill, care must be exercised to avoid grooving the seat.* Lift the tool and change direction of rotation often.

Hand lapping the valves

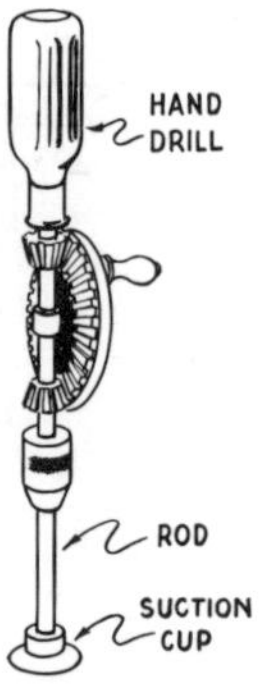

Home made mechanical valve lapping tool

Check the valve springs:	Place the spring on a flat surface next to a square. Measure the height of the spring, and rotate it against the edge of the square to measure distortion. If spring height varies (by comparison) by more than 1/16″ or if distortion exceeds 1/16″, replace the spring.
	** In addition to evaluating the spring as above, test the spring pressure at the installed and compressed (installed height minus valve lift) height using a valve spring tester. Springs used on small displacement engines (up to 3 liters) should be ± 1 lb. of all other springs in either position. A tolerance of ± 5 lbs. is permissible on larger engines.

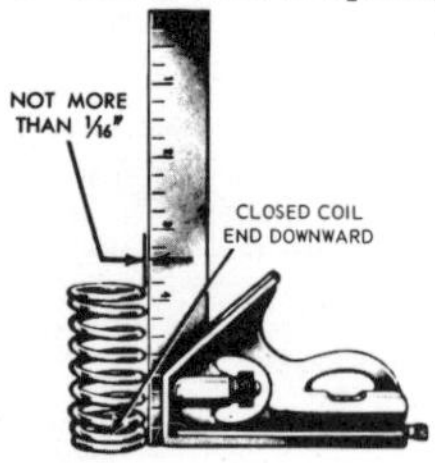

Checking the valve spring free length and squareness (© Ford Motor Co.)

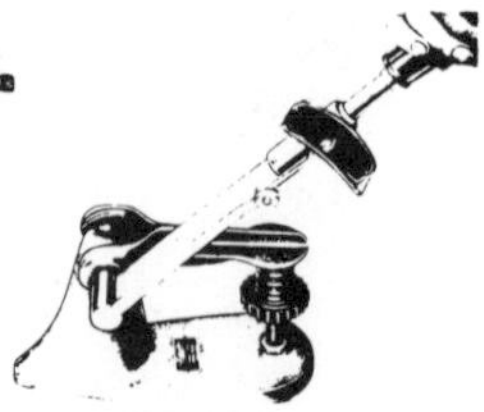

Checking the valve spring tension (© Chrysler Corp.)

Procedure	*Method*

* Install valve stem seals:

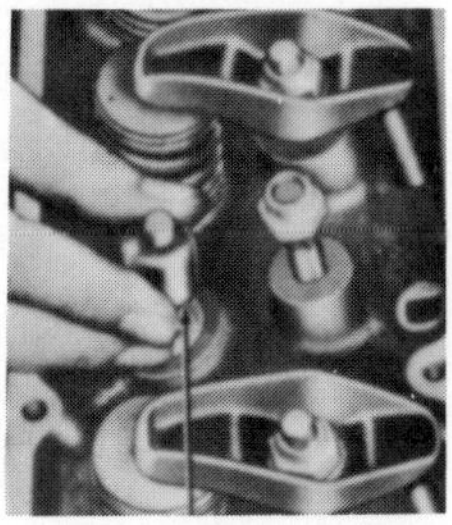

Valve stem seal installation
(© Ford Motor Co.)

* Due to the pressure differential that exists at the ends of the intake valve guides (atmospheric pressure above, manifold vacuum below), oil is drawn through the valve guides into the intake port. This has been alleviated somewhat since the addition of positive crankcase ventilation, which lowers the pressure above the guides. Several types of valve stem seals are available to reduce blow-by. Certain seals simply slip over the stem and guide boss, while others require that the boss be machined. Recently, Teflon guide seals have become popular. Consult a parts supplier or machinist concerning availability and suggested usages. NOTE: *When installing seals, ensure that a small amount of oil is able to pass the seal to lubricate the valve guides; otherwise, excessive wear may result.*

Install the valves:

Lubricate the valve stems, and install the valves in the cylinder head as numbered. Lubricate and position the seals (if used, see above) and the valve springs. Install the spring retainers, compress the springs, and insert the keys using needlenose pliers or a tool designed for this purpose. NOTE: *Retain the keys with wheel bearing grease during installation.*

Checking valve spring installed height:

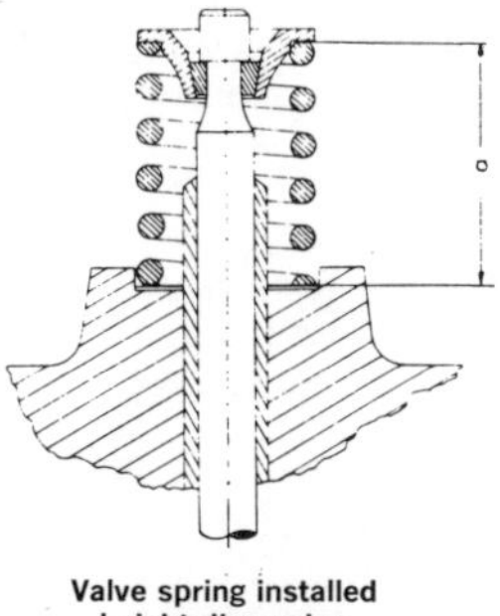

Valve spring installed height dimension
(© Porsche)

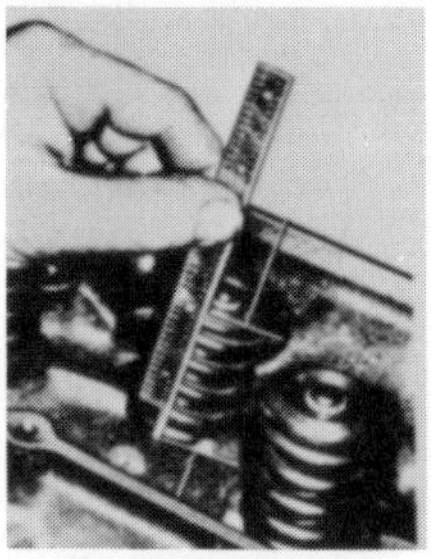

Measuring valve spring installed height
(© Petersen Publishing Co.)

Measure the distance between the spring pad and the lower edge of the spring retainer, and compare to specifications. If the installed height is incorrect, add shim washers between the spring pad and the spring. CAUTION: *Use only washers designed for this purpose.*

** CC'ing the combustion chambers:

** Invert the cylinder head and place a bead of sealer around a combustion chamber. Install an apparatus designed for this purpose (burette mounted on a clear plate; see illustration) over the combustion chamber, and fill with the specified fluid to an even mark on the burette. Record the burette reading, and fill the combustion chamber with fluid. (NOTE: *A hole drilled in the plate will permit air to escape*). Subtract the burette reading, with the combustion chamber filled, from the previous reading, to determine combustion chamber volume in cc's. Duplicate this procedure in all combustion

Procedure	*Method*
 CC'ing the combustion chamber (© Petersen Publishing Co.)	chambers on the cylinder head, and compare the readings. The volume of all combustion chambers should be made equal to that of the largest. Combustion chamber volume may be increased in two ways. When only a small change is required (usually), a small cutter or coarse stone may be used to remove material from the combustion chamber. NOTE: *Check volume frequently.* Remove material over a wide area, so as not to change the configuration of the combustion chamber. When a larger change is required, the valve seat may be sunk (lowered into the head). NOTE: *When altering valve seat, remember to compensate for the change in spring installed height.*
Inspect the rocker arms, balls, studs, and nuts (where applicable): 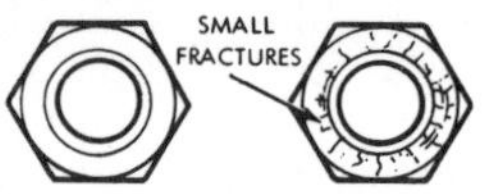 Stress cracks in rocker nuts (© Ford Motor Co.)	Visually inspect the rocker arms, balls, studs, and nuts for cracks, galling, burning, scoring, or wear. If all parts are intact, liberally lubricate the rocker arms and balls, and install them on the cylinder head. If wear is noted on a rocker arm at the point of valve contact, grind it smooth and square, removing as little material as possible. Replace the rocker arm if excessively worn. If a rocker stud shows signs of wear, it must be replaced (see below). If a rocker nut shows stress cracks, replace it. If an exhaust ball is galled or burned, substitute the intake ball from the same cylinder (if it is intact), and install a new intake ball. NOTE: *Avoid using new rocker balls on exhaust valves.*
Replacing rocker studs:  Reaming the stud bore for oversize rocker studs (© Buick Div. G.M. Corp.) 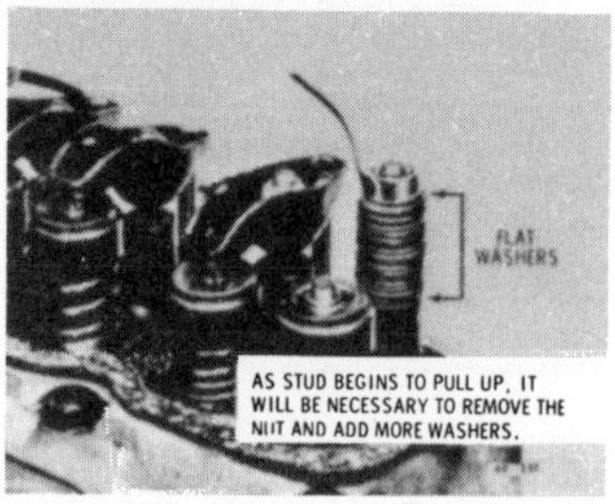 Extracting a pressed in rocker stud (© Buick Div. G.M. Corp.)	In order to remove a threaded stud, lock two nuts on the stud, and unscrew the stud using the lower nut. Coat the lower threads of the new stud with Loctite, and install. Two alternative methods are available for replacing pressed in studs. Remove the damaged stud using a stack of washers and a nut (see illustration). In the first, the boss is reamed .005-.006″ oversize, and an oversize stud pressed in. Control the stud extension over the boss using washers, in the same manner as valve guides. Before installing the stud, coat it with white lead and grease. To retain the stud more positively, drill a hole through the stud and boss, and install a roll pin. In the second method, the boss is tapped, and a threaded stud installed. Retain the stud using Loctite Stud and Bearing Mount.

Procedure	*Method*
Inspect the rocker shaft(s) and rocker arms (where applicable): 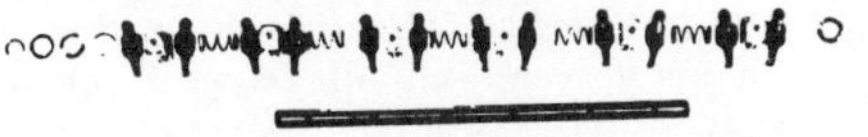 Disassembled rocker shaft parts arranged for inspection (© American Motors Corp.) 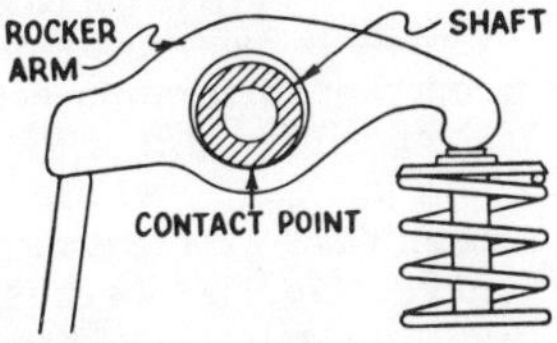 Rocker arm to rocker shaft contact	Remove rocker arms, springs and washers from rocker shaft. NOTE: *Lay out parts in the order they are removed.* Inspect rocker arms for pitting or wear on the valve contact point, or excessive bushing wear. Bushings need only be replaced if wear is excessive, because the rocker arm normally contacts the shaft at one point only. Grind the valve contact point of rocker arm smooth if necessary, removing as little material as possible. If excessive material must be removed to smooth and square the arm, it should be replaced. Clean out all oil holes and passages in rocker shaft. If shaft is grooved or worn, replace it. Lubricate and assemble the rocker shaft.
Inspect the camshaft bushings and the camshaft (overhead cam engines):	See next section.
Inspect the pushrods:	Remove the pushrods, and, if hollow, clean out the oil passages using fine wire. Roll each pushrod over a piece of clean glass. If a distinct clicking sound is heard as the pushrod rolls, the rod is bent, and must be replaced.
	* The length of all pushrods must be equal. Measure the length of the pushrods, compare to specifications, and replace as necessary.
Inspect the valve lifters: 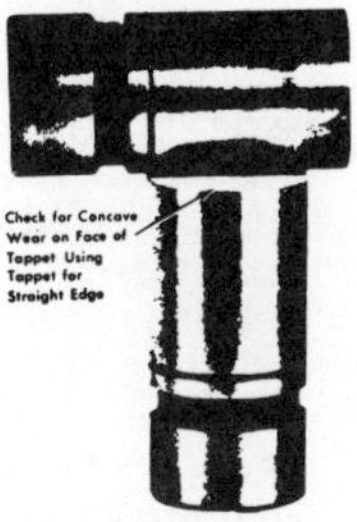 Checking the lifter face (© American Motors Corp.)	Remove lifters from their bores, and remove gum and varnish, using solvent. Clean walls of lifter bores. Check lifters for concave wear as illustrated. If face is worn concave, replace lifter, and carefully inspect the camshaft. Lightly lubricate lifter and insert it into its bore. If play is excessive, an oversize lifter must be installed (where possible). Consult a machinist concerning feasibility. If play is satisfactory, remove, lubricate, and reinstall the lifter.
* Testing hydraulic lifter leak down: 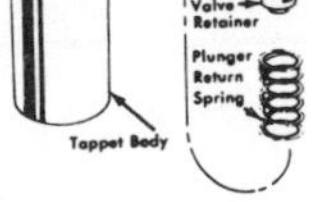 Exploded view of a typical hydraulic lifter (© American Motors Corp.)	Submerge lifter in a container of kerosene. Chuck a used pushrod or its equivalent into a drill press. Position container of kerosene so pushrod acts on the lifter plunger. Pump lifter with the drill press, until resistance increases. Pump several more times to bleed any air out of lifter. Apply very firm, constant pressure to the lifter, and observe rate at which fluid bieeds out of lifter. If the fluid bleeds very quickly (less than 15 seconds), lifter is defective. If the time exceeds 60 seconds, lifter is sticking. In either case, recondition or replace lifter. If lifter is operating properly (leak down time 15-60 seconds), lubricate and install it.

CYLINDER BLOCK RECONDITIONING

Procedure | *Method*

Checking the main bearing clearance:

Plastigage installed on main bearing journal
(© Chevrolet Div. G.M. Corp.)

Measuring Plastigage to determine main bearing clearance
(© Chevrolet Div. G.M. Corp.)

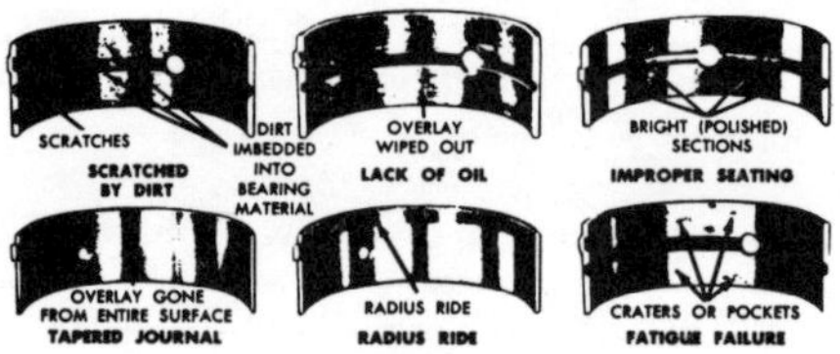

Causes of bearing failure
(© Ford Motor Co.)

Invert engine, and remove cap from the bearing to be checked. Using a clean, dry rag, thoroughly clean all oil from crankshaft journal and bearing insert. NOTE: *Plastigage is soluble in oil; therefore, oil on the journal or bearing could result in erroneous readings.* Place a piece of Plastigage along the full length of journal, reinstall cap, and torque to specifications. Remove bearing cap, and determine bearing clearance by comparing width of Plastigage to the scale on Plastigage envelope. Journal taper is determined by comparing width of the Plastigage strip near its ends. Rotate crankshaft 90° and retest, to determine journal eccentricity. NOTE: *Do not rotate crankshaft with Plastigage installed.* If bearing insert and journal appear intact, and are within tolerances, no further main bearing service is required. If bearing or journal appear defective, cause of failure should be determined before replacement.

* Remove crankshaft from block (see below). Measure the main bearing journals at each end twice (90° apart) using a micrometer, to determine diameter, journal taper and eccentricity. If journals are within tolerances, reinstall bearing caps at their specified torque. Using a telescope gauge and micrometer, measure bearing I.D. parallel to piston axis and at 30° on each side of piston axis. Subtract journal O.D. from bearing I.D. to determine oil clearance. If crankshaft journals appear defective, or do not meet tolerances, there is no need to measure bearings; for the crankshaft will require grinding and/or undersize bearings will be required. If bearing appears defective, cause for failure should be determined prior to replacement.

Checking the connecting rod bearing clearance:

Plastigage installed on connecting rod bearing journal
(© Chevrolet Div. G.M. Corp.)

Connecting rod bearing clearance is checked in the same manner as main bearing clearance, using Plastigage. Before removing the crankshaft, connecting rod side clearance also should be measured and recorded.

* Checking connecting rod bearing clearance, using a micrometer, is identical to checking main bearing clearance. If no other service

Procedure	*Method*
 Measuring Plastigage to determine connecting rod bearing clearance (© Chevrolet Div. G.M. Corp.)	is required, the piston and rod assemblies need not be removed.
Removing the crankshaft:  Connecting rod matching marks (© Ford Motor Co.)	Using a punch, mark the corresponding main bearing caps and saddles according to position (i.e., one punch on the front main cap and saddle, two on the second, three on the third, etc.). Using number stamps, identify the corresponding connecting rods and caps, according to cylinder (if no numbers are present). Remove the main and connecting rod caps, and place sleeves of plastic tubing over the connecting rod bolts, to protect the journals as the crankshaft is removed. Lift the crankshaft out of the block.
Remove the ridge from the top of the cylinder: 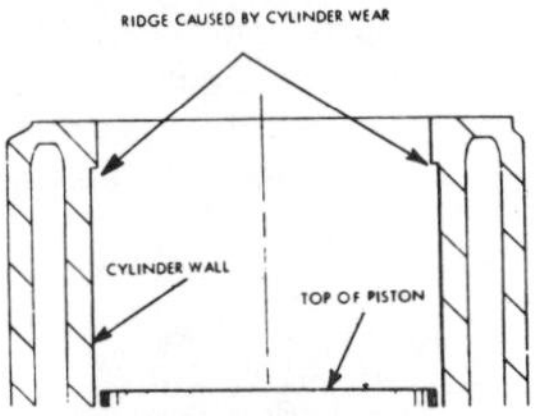 Cylinder bore ridge (© Pontiac Div. G.M. Corp.)	In order to facilitate removal of the piston and connecting rod, the ridge at the top of the cylinder (unworn area; see illustration) must be removed. Place the piston at the bottom of the bore, and cover it with a rag. Cut the ridge away using a ridge reamer, exercising extreme care to avoid cutting too deeply. Remove the rag, and remove cuttings that remain on the piston. CAUTION: *If the ridge is not removed, and new rings are installed, damage to rings will result.*
Removing the piston and connecting rod: 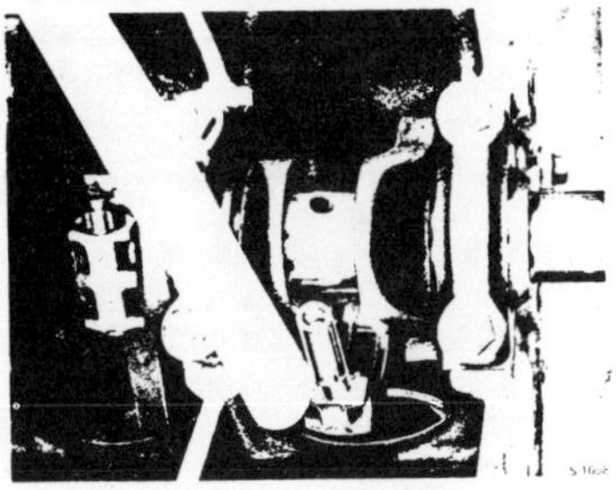 Removing the piston (© SAAB)	Invert the engine, and push the pistons and connecting rods out of the cylinders. If necessary, tap the connecting rod boss with a wooden hammer handle, to force the piston out. CAUTION: *Do not attempt to force the piston past the cylinder ridge* (see above).

Procedure	*Method*
Service the crankshaft:	Ensure that all oil holes and passages in the crankshaft are open and free of sludge. If necessary, have the crankshaft ground to the largest possible undersize.
	** Have the crankshaft Magnafluxed, to locate stress cracks. Consult a machinist concerning additional service procedures, such as surface hardening (e.g., nitriding, Tuftriding) to improve wear characteristics, cross drilling and chamfering the oil holes to improve lubrication, and balancing.
Removing freeze plugs:	Drill a hole in the center of the freeze plugs, and pry them out using a screwdriver or drift.
Remove the oil gallery plugs:	Threaded plugs should be removed using an appropriate (usually square) wrench. To remove soft, pressed in plugs, drill a hole in the plug, and thread in a sheet metal screw. Pull the plug out by the screw using pliers.
Hot-tank the block:	Have the block hot-tanked to remove grease, corrosion, and scale from the water jackets. NOTE: *Consult the operator to determine whether the camshaft bearings will be damaged during the hot-tank process.*
Check the block for cracks:	Visually inspect the block for cracks or chips. The most common locations are as follows: Adjacent to freeze plugs. Between the cylinders and water jackets. Adjacent to the main bearing saddles. At the extreme bottom of the cylinders. Check only suspected cracks using spot check dye (see introduction). If a crack is located, consult a machinist concerning possible repairs.
	** Magnaflux the block to locate hidden cracks. If cracks are located, consult a machinist about feasibility of repair.
Install the oil gallery plugs and freeze plugs:	Coat freeze plugs with sealer and tap into position using a piece of pipe, slightly smaller than the plug, as a driver. To ensure retention, stake the edges of the plugs. Coat threaded oil gallery plugs with sealer and install. Drive replacement soft plugs into block using a large drift as a driver.
	* Rather than reinstalling lead plugs, drill and tap the holes, and install threaded plugs.

Procedure	*Method*
Check the bore diameter and surface:	Visually inspect the cylinder bores for roughness, scoring, or scuffing. If evident, the cylinder bore must be bored or honed oversize to eliminate imperfections, and the smallest possible oversize piston used. The new pistons should be given to the machinist with the block, so that the cylinders can be bored or honed exactly to the piston size (plus clearance). If no flaws are evident, measure the bore diameter using a telescope gauge and micrometer, or dial gauge, parallel and perpendicular to the engine centerline, at the top (below the ridge) and bottom of the bore. Subtract the bottom measurements from the top to determine taper, and the parallel to the centerline measurements from the perpendicular measurements to determine eccentricity. If the measurements are not within specifications, the cylinder must be bored or honed, and an oversize piston installed. If the measurements are within specifications the cylinder may be used as is, with only finish honing (see below). NOTE: *Prior to submitting the block for boring, perform the following operation(s).*

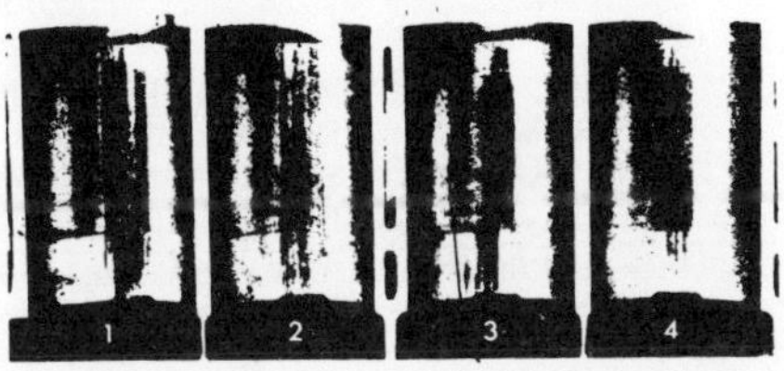

1, 2, 3 Piston skirt seizure resulted in this pattern. Engine must be rebored

4. Piston skirt and oil ring seizure caused this damage. Engine must be rebored

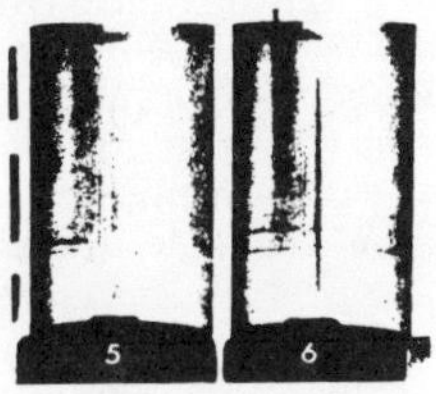

5, 6 Score marks caused by a split piston skirt. Damage is not serious enough to warrant reboring

7. Ring seized longitudinally, causing a score mark 1 3/16" wide, on the land side of the piston groove. The honing pattern is destroyed and the cylinder must be rebored

8. Result of oil ring seizure. Engine must be rebored

9. Oil ring seizure here was not serious enough to warrant reboring. The honing marks are still visible

Cylinder wall damage
(© Daimler-Benz A.G.)

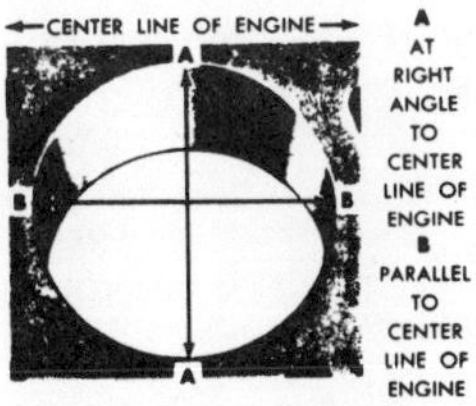

Cylinder bore measuring positions
(© Ford Motor Co.)

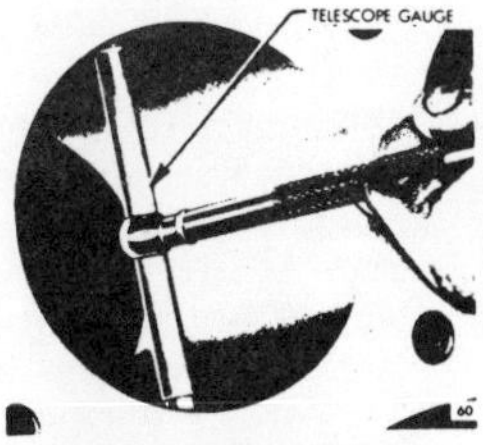

Measuring the cylinder bore with a telescope gauge
(© Buick Div. G.M. Corp.)

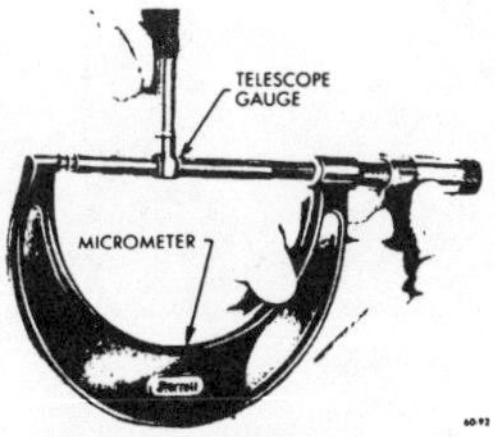

Determining the cylinder bore by measuring the telescope gauge with a micrometer
(© Buick Div. G.M. Corp.)

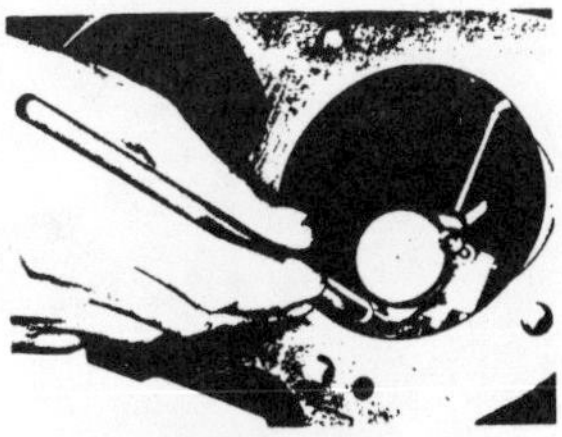

Measuring the cylinder bore with a dial gauge
(© Chevrolet Div. G.M. Corp.)

Procedure	*Method*
Check the block deck for warpage:	Using a straightedge and feeler gauges, check the block deck for warpage in the same manner that the cylinder head is checked (see Cylinder Head Reconditioning). If warpage exceeds specifications, have the deck resurfaced. NOTE: *In certain cases a specification for total material removal (Cylinder head and block deck) is provided. This specification must not be exceeded.*
* Check the deck height:	The deck height is the distance from the crankshaft centerline to the block deck. To measure, invert the engine, and install the crankshaft, retaining it with the center main cap. Measure the distance from the crankshaft journal to the block deck, parallel to the cylinder centerline. Measure the diameter of the end (front and rear) main journals, parallel to the centerline of the cylinders, divide the diameter in half, and subtract it from the previous measurement. The results of the front and rear measurements should be identical. If the difference exceeds .005", the deck height should be corrected. NOTE: *Block deck height and warpage should be corrected concurrently.*
Check the cylinder block bearing alignment:  **Checking main bearing saddle alignment** (© Petersen Publishing Co.)	Remove the upper bearing inserts. Place a straightedge in the bearing saddles along the centerline of the crankshaft. If clearance exists between the straightedge and the center saddle, the block must be alignbored.
Clean and inspect the pistons and connecting rods: 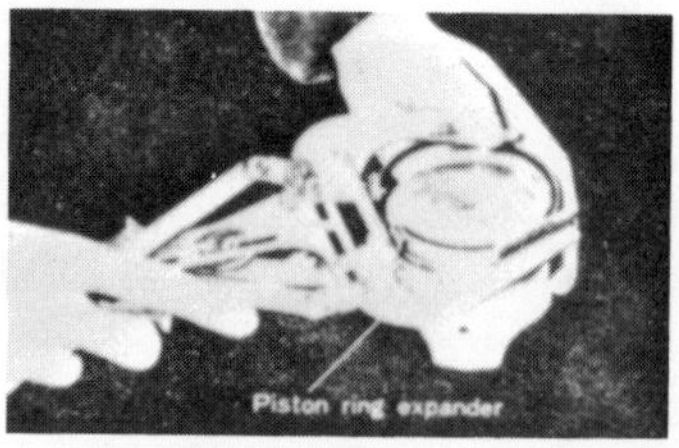 **Removing the piston rings** (© Subaru)	Using a ring expander, remove the rings from the piston. Remove the retaining rings (if so equipped) and remove piston pin. NOTE: *If the piston pin must be pressed out, determine the proper method and use the proper tools; otherwise the piston will distort.* Clean the ring grooves using an appropriate tool, exercising care to avoid cutting too deeply. Thoroughly clean all carbon and varnish from the piston with solvent. CAUTION: *Do not use a wire brush or caustic solvent on pistons.* Inspect the pistons for scuffing, scoring, cracks, pitting, or excessive ring groove wear. If wear is evident, the piston must be replaced. Check the connecting rod length by measuring the rod from the inside of the large end to the inside of the small end using calipers (see

Procedure	*Method*

Cleaning the piston ring grooves
(© Ford Motor Co.)

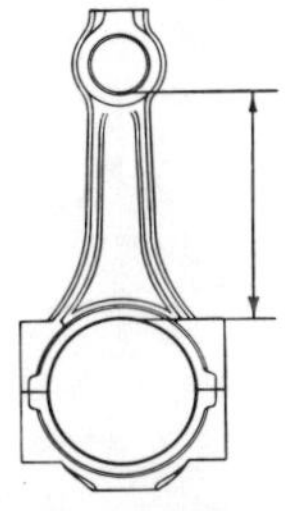
Connecting rod length checking dimension

illustration). All connecting rods should be equal length. Replace any rod that differs from the others in the engine.

* Have the connecting rod alignment checked in an alignment fixture by a machinist. Replace any twisted or bent rods.

* Magnaflux the connecting rods to locate stress cracks. If cracks are found, replace the connecting rod.

Fit the pistons to the cylinders:

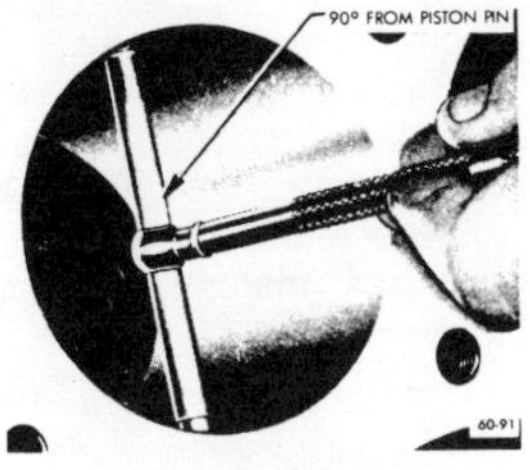

Measuring the cylinder with a telescope gauge for piston fitting
(© Buick Div. G.M. Corp.)

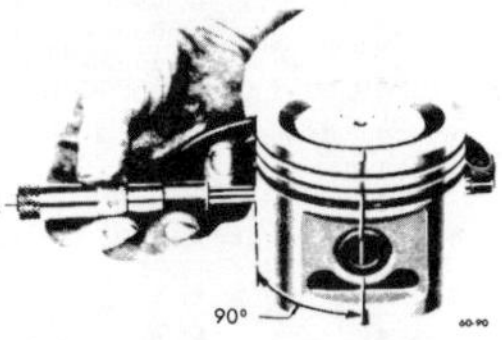

Measuring the piston for fitting
(© Buick Div. G.M. Corp.)

Using a telescope gauge and micrometer, or a dial gauge, measure the cylinder bore diameter perpendicular to the piston pin, 2½″ below the deck. Measure the piston perpendicular to its pin on the skirt. The difference between the two measurements is the piston clearance. If the clearance is within specifications or slightly below (after boring or honing), finish honing is all that is required. If the clearance is excessive, try to obtain a slightly larger piston to bring clearance within specifications. Where this is not possible, obtain the first oversize piston, and hone (or if necessary, bore) the cylinder to size.

Assemble the pistons and connecting rods:

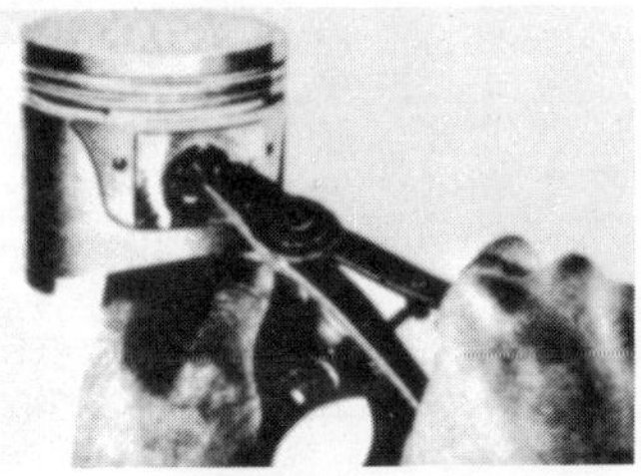
Installing piston pin lock rings
(© Nissan Motor Co., Ltd.)

Inspect piston pin, connecting rod small end bushing, and piston bore for galling, scoring, or excessive wear. If evident, replace defective part(s). Measure the I.D. of the piston boss and connecting rod small end, and the O.D. of the piston pin. If within specifications, assemble piston pin and rod. CAUTION: *If piston pin must be pressed in, determine the proper method and use the proper tools; otherwise the piston will distort.* Install the lock rings; ensure that they seat properly. If the parts are not within specifications, determine the service method for the type of engine. In some cases, piston and pin are serviced as an assembly when either is defective. Others specify reaming the piston and connecting rods for an oversize pin. If the connecting rod bushing is worn, it may in many cases be replaced. Reaming the piston and replacing the rod bushing are machine shop operations.

Procedure	*Method*

Clean and inspect the camshaft:

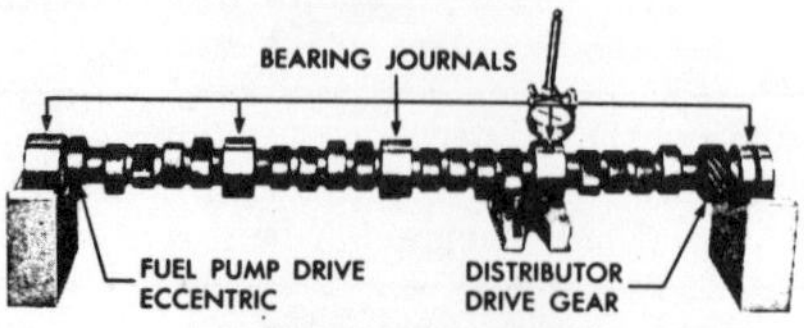

Checking the camshaft for straightness
(© Chevrolet Motor Div. G.M. Corp.)

Degrease the camshaft, using solvent, and clean out all oil holes. Visually inspect cam lobes and bearing journals for excessive wear. If a lobe is questionable, check all lobes as indicated below. If a journal or lobe is worn, the camshaft must be reground or replaced. NOTE: *If a journal is worn, there is a good chance that the bushings are worn.* If lobes and journals appear intact, place the front and rear journals in V-blocks, and rest a dial indicator on the center journal. Rotate the camshaft to check straightness. If deviation exceeds .001″, replace the camshaft.

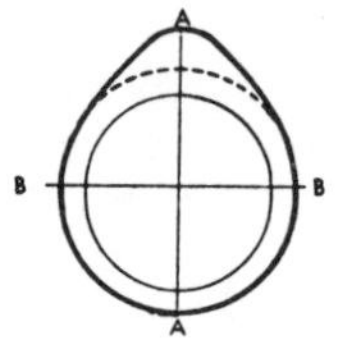

Camshaft lobe measurement
(© Ford Motor Co.)

* Check the camshaft lobes with a micrometer, by measuring the lobes from the nose to base and again at 90° (see illustration). The lift is determined by subtracting the second measurement from the first. If all exhaust lobes and all intake lobes are not identical, the camshaft must be reground or replaced.

Replace the camshaft bearings:

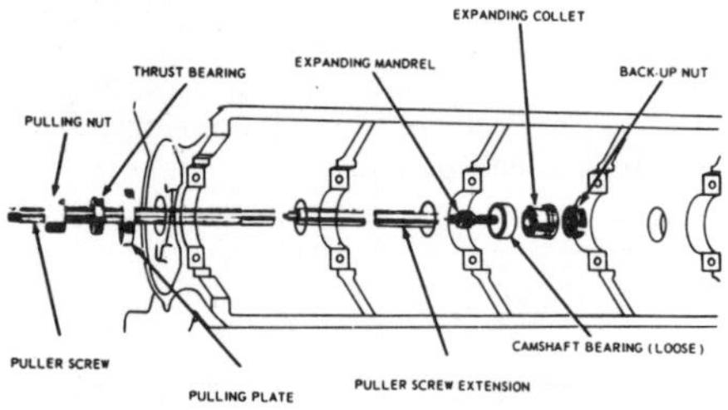

Camshaft removal and installation tool (typical)
(© Ford Motor Co.)

If excessive wear is indicated, or if the engine is being completely rebuilt, camshaft bearings should be replaced as follows: Drive the camshaft rear plug from the block. Assemble the removal puller with its shoulder on the bearing to be removed. Gradually tighten the puller nut until bearing is removed. Remove remaining bearings, leaving the front and rear for last. To remove front and rear bearings, reverse position of the tool, so as to pull the bearings in toward the center of the block. Leave the tool in this position, pilot the new front and rear bearings on the installer, and pull them into position. Return the tool to its original position and pull remaining bearings into position. NOTE: *Ensure that oil holes align when installing bearings.* Replace camshaft rear plug, and stake it into position to aid retention.

Finish hone the cylinders:

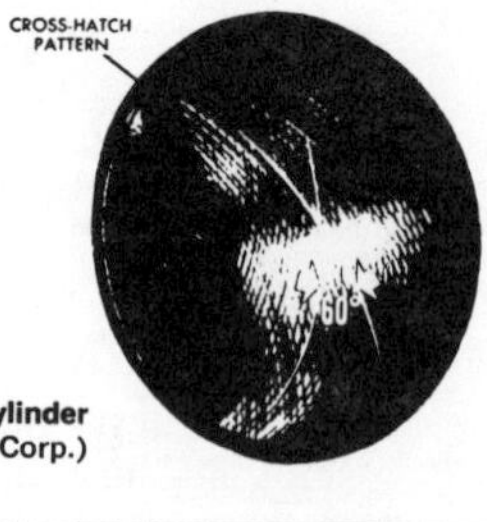

Finish honed cylinder
(© Chrysler Corp.)

Chuck a flexible drive hone into a power drill, and insert it into the cylinder. Start the hone, and move it up and down in the cylinder at a rate which will produce approximately a 60° cross-hatch pattern (see illustration). NOTE: *Do not extend the hone below the cylinder bore.* After developing the pattern, remove the hone and recheck piston fit. Wash the cylinders with a detergent and water solution to remove abrasive dust, dry, and wipe several times with a rag soaked in engine oil.

Procedure — *Method*

Check piston ring end-gap:

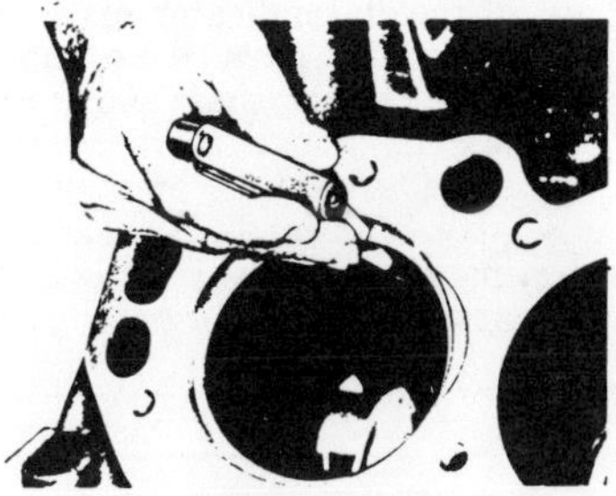

Checking ring end-gap
(© Chevrolet Motor Div. G.M. Corp.)

Compress the piston rings to be used in a cylinder, one at a time, into that cylinder, and press them approximately 1″ below the deck with an inverted piston. Using feeler gauges, measure the ring end-gap, and compare to specifications. Pull the ring out of the cylinder and file the ends with a fine file to obtain proper clearance. CAUTION: *If inadequate ring end-gap is utilized, ring breakage will result.*

Install the piston rings:

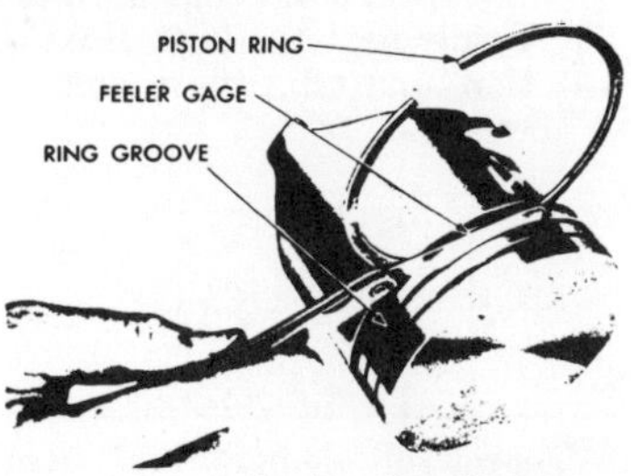

Checking ring side clearance
(© Chrysler Corp.)

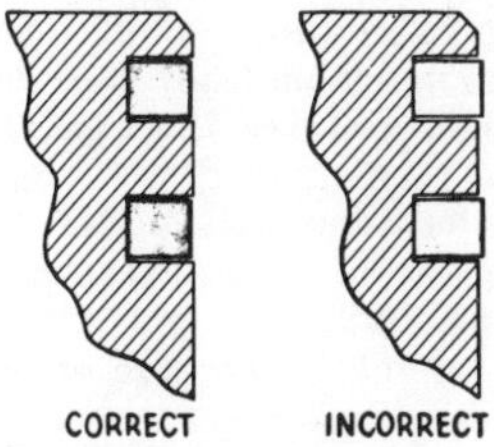

Piston groove depth

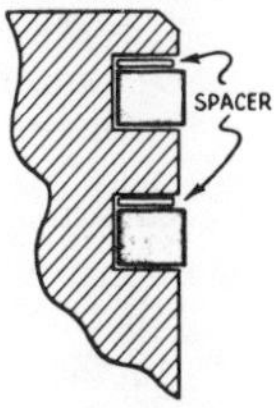

Correct ring spacer installation

Inspect the ring grooves in the piston for excessive wear or taper. If necessary, recut the groove(s) for use with an overwidth ring or a standard ring and spacer. If the groove is worn uniformly, overwidth rings, or standard rings and spacers may be installed without recutting. Roll the outside of the ring around the groove to check for burrs or deposits. If any are found, remove with a fine file. Hold the ring in the groove, and measure side clearance. If necessary, correct as indicated above. NOTE: *Always install any additional spacers above the piston ring.* The ring groove must be deep enough to allow the ring to seat below the lands (see illustration). In many cases, a "go-no-go" depth gauge will be provided with the piston rings. Shallow grooves may be corrected by recutting, while deep grooves require some type of filler or expander behind the piston. Consult the piston ring supplier concerning the suggested method. Install the rings on the piston, lowest ring first, using a ring expander. NOTE: *Position the ring markings as specified by the manufacturer (see car section).*

Install the camshaft:

Liberally lubricate the camshaft lobes and journals, and slide the camshaft into the block. CAUTION: *Exercise extreme care to avoid damaging the bearings when inserting the camshaft.* Install and tighten the camshaft thrust plate retaining bolts.

Check camshaft end-play:

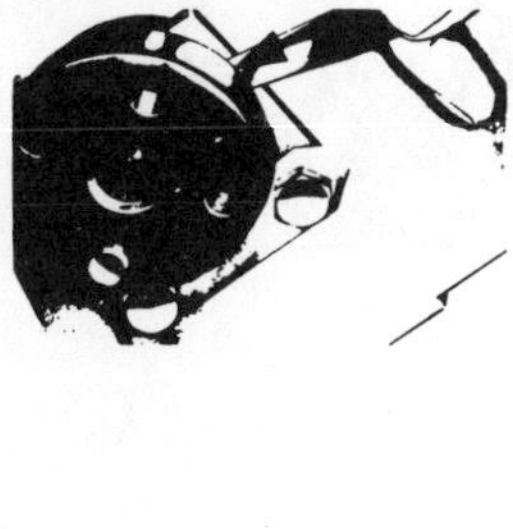

Checking camshaft end-play with a feeler gauge
(© Ford Motor Co.)

Using feeler gauges, determine whether the clearance between the camshaft boss (or gear) and backing plate is within specifications. Install shims behind the thrust plate, or reposition the camshaft gear and retest end-play.

Procedure	*Method*
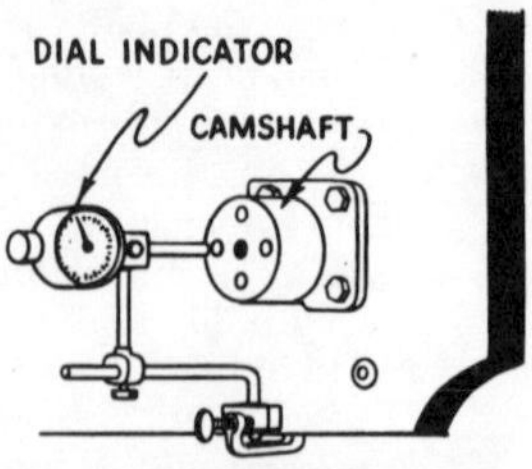 Checking camshaft end-play with a dial indicator	* Mount a dial indicator stand so that the stem of the dial indicator rests on the nose of the camshaft, parallel to the camshaft axis. Push the camshaft as far in as possible and zero the gauge. Move the camshaft outward to determine the amount of camshaft end-play. If the end-play is not within tolerance, install shims behind the thrust plate, or re-position the camshaft gear and retest.
Install the rear main seal (where applicable):  Seating the rear main seal (© Buick Div. G.M. Corp.)	Position the block with the bearing saddles facing upward. Lay the rear main seal in its groove and press it lightly into its seat. Place a piece of pipe the same diameter as the crankshaft journal into the saddle, and firmly seat the seal. Hold the pipe in position, and trim the ends of the seal flush if required.
Install the crankshaft: 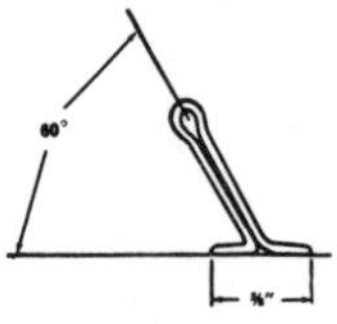 Home made bearing roll-out pin (© Pontiac Div. G.M. Corp.)  Removal and installation of upper bearing insert using a roll-out pin (© Buick Div. G.M. Corp.)	Thoroughly clean the main bearing saddles and caps. Place the upper halves of the bearing inserts on the saddles and press into position. NOTE: *Ensure that the oil holes align.* Press the corresponding bearing inserts into the main bearing caps. Lubricate the upper main bearings, and lay the crankshaft in position. Place a strip of Plastigage on each of the crankshaft journals, install the main caps, and torque to specifications. Remove the main caps, and compare the Plastigage to the scale on the Plastigage envelope. If clearances are within tolerances, remove the Plastigage, turn the crankshaft 90°, wipe off all oil and retest. If all clearances are correct, remove all Plastigage, thoroughly

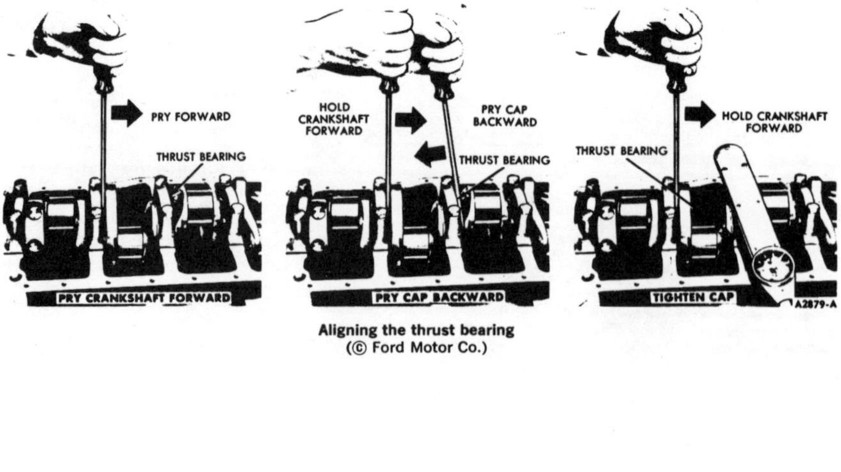

Aligning the thrust bearing
(© Ford Motor Co.)

Procedure	*Method*
	lubricate the main caps and bearing journals, and install the main caps. If clearances are not within tolerance, the upper bearing inserts may be removed, without removing the crankshaft, using a bearing roll out pin (see illustration). Roll in a bearing that will provide proper clearance, and retest. Torque all main caps, excluding the thrust bearing cap, to specifications. Tighten the thrust bearing cap finger tight. To properly align the thrust bearing, pry the crankshaft the extent of its axial travel several times, the last movement held toward the front of the engine, and torque the thrust bearing cap to specifications. Determine the crankshaft end-play (see below), and bring within tolerance with thrust washers.
Measure crankshaft end-play:  Checking crankshaft end-play with a dial indicator (© Ford Motor Co.)  Checking crankshaft end-play with a feeler gauge (© Chevrolet Div. (G.M. Corp.)	Mount a dial indicator stand on the front of the block, with the dial indicator stem resting on the nose of the crankshaft, parallel to the crankshaft axis. Pry the crankshaft the extent of its travel rearward, and zero the indicator. Pry the crankshaft forward and record crankshaft end-play. NOTE: *Crankshaft end-play also may be measured at the thrust bearing, using feeler gauges* (see illustration).
Install the pistons:	Press the upper connecting rod bearing halves into the connecting rods, and the lower halves into the connecting rod caps. Position the piston ring gaps according to specifications (see car section), and lubricate the pistons. Install a ring compresser on a piston, and press two long (8") pieces of plastic tubing over the rod bolts. Using the plastic tubes as a guide, press the pistons into the bores and onto the crankshaft with a wooden hammer handle. After seating the rod on the crankshaft journal, remove the tubes and install the cap finger tight. Install the remaining pistons in the same man-

Procedure	*Method*
**Tubing used as guide when installing a piston** (© Oldsmobile Div. G.M. Corp.) 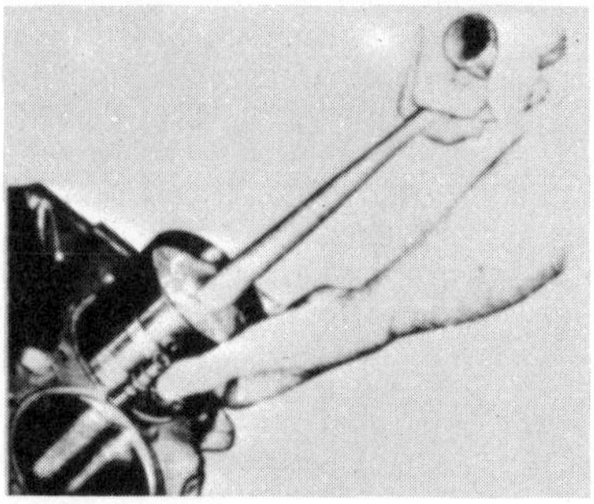**Installing a piston** (© Chevrolet Div. G.M. Corp.)	ner. Invert the engine and check the bearing clearance at two points (90° apart) on each journal with Plastigage. NOTE: *Do not turn the crankshaft with Plastigage installed.* If clearance is within tolerances, remove *all* Plastigage, thoroughly lubricate the journals, and torque the rod caps to specifications. If clearance is not within specifications, install different thickness bearing inserts and recheck. CAUTION: *Never shim or file the connecting rods or caps.* Always install plastic tube sleeves over the rod bolts when the caps are not installed, to protect the crankshaft journals.
Check connecting rod side clearance: 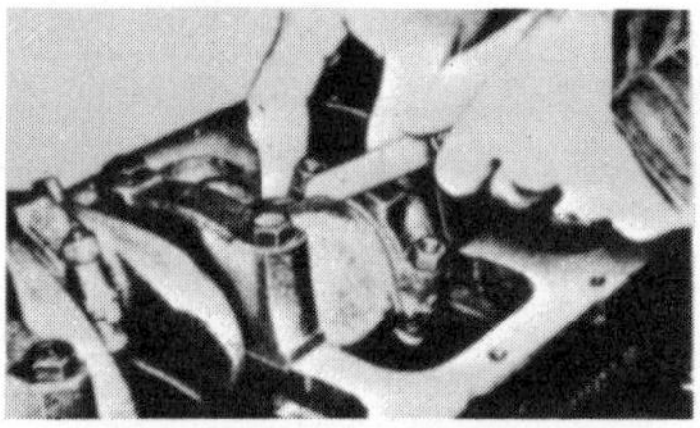**Checking connecting rod side clearance** (© Chevrolet Div. G.M. Corp.)	Determine the clearance between the sides of the connecting rods and the crankshaft, using feeler gauges. If clearance is below the minimum tolerance, the rod may be machined to provide adequate clearance. If clearance is excessive, substitute an unworn rod, and recheck. If clearance is still outside specifications, the crankshaft must be welded and reground, or replaced.
Inspect the timing chain:	Visually inspect the timing chain for broken or loose links, and replace the chain if any are found. If the chain will flex sideways, it must be replaced. Install the timing chain as specified. NOTE: *If the original timing chain is to be reused, install it in its original position.*

Procedure	*Method*
Check timing gear backlash and runout:  Checking camshaft gear backlash (© Chevrolet Div. G.M. Corp.)  Checking camshaft gear runout (© Chevrolet Div. G.M. Corp.)	Mount a dial indicator with its stem resting on a tooth of the camshaft gear (as illustrated). Rotate the gear until all slack is removed, and zero the indicator. Rotate the gear in the opposite direction until slack is removed, and record gear backlash. Mount the indicator with its stem resting on the edge of the camshaft gear, parallel to the axis of the camshaft. Zero the indicator, and turn the camshaft gear one full turn, recording the runout. If either backlash or runout exceed specifications, replace the worn gear(s).

Completing the Rebuilding Process

Following the above procedures, complete the rebuilding process as follows:

Fill the oil pump with oil, to prevent cavitating (sucking air) on initial engine start up. Install the oil pump and the pickup tube on the engine. Coat the oil pan gasket as necessary, and install the gasket and the oil pan. Mount the flywheel and the crankshaft vibrational damper or pulley on the crankshaft. NOTE: *Always use new bolts when installing the flywheel.* Inspect the clutch shaft pilot bushing in the crankshaft. If the bushing is excessively worn, remove it with an expanding puller and a slide hammer, and tap a new bushing into place.

Position the engine, cylinder head side up. Lubricate the lifters, and install them into their bores. Install the cylinder head, and torque it as specified in the car section. Insert the pushrods (where applicable), and install the rocker shaft(s) (if so equipped) or position the rocker arms on the pushrods. If solid lifters are utilized, adjust the valves to the "cold" specifications.

Mount the intake and exhaust manifolds, the carburetor(s), the distributor and spark plugs. Adjust the point gap and the static ignition timing. Mount all accessories and install the engine in the car. Fill the radiator with coolant, and the crankcase with high quality engine oil.

Break-in Procedure

Start the engine, and allow it to run at low speed for a few minutes, while checking for leaks. Stop the engine, check the oil level, and fill as necessary. Restart the engine, and fill the cooling system to capacity. Check the point dwell angle and adjust the ignition timing and the valves. Run the engine at low to medium speed (800-2500 rpm) for approximately ½ hour, and retorque the cylinder head bolts. Road test the car, and check again for leaks.

Follow the manufacturer's recommended engine break-in procedure and maintenance schedule for new engines.

Chapter 4

Emission Controls and Fuel System

Emission Controls

Automotive pollutants fall into three categories: crankcase fumes, terminal exhaust gases, and gasoline evaporation. Automotive manufacturers have developed ways to limit environmental pollutants that come from each of these sources and the equipment they use to obtain this end is commonly referred to as emission control equipment.

EMISSION CONTROL EQUIPMENT

1971 All Models

Closed positive crankcase ventilation.
Heated air cleaner.
Vapor control, canister storage.
Emission calibrated carburetor.
Emission calibrated distributor.
Dual diaphragm vacuum advance.
Decel enrichment valve.

1972 All Models

Closed positive crankcase ventilation.
Heated air cleaner.
Vapor control, canister storage.
Emission calibrated carburetor.
Emission calibrated distributor.
Decel enrichment valve.
Dual diaphragm vacuum advance (on all 1600 cc engines and 2000 cc engines with automatic transmission except Calif.).
Single diaphragm vacuum advance (on all Calif. 2000 cc engines. On 2000 cc manual transmission engines, outside Calif.).
Electronic spark control (2000 cc engines with automatic transmission, Calif. only).
Spark delay valve (on all Calif., manual transmission cars. On 2000 cc engines with manual transmission, outside Calif.).

1973 All Models

Closed positive crankcase ventilation.
Heated air cleaner.
Vapor control, canister storage.
Emission calibrated carburetor.
Emission calibrated distributor.
Single diaphragm vacuum advance (2000 cc engine only).
Spark delay valve (see vacuum diagrams).
Decel enrichment valve (2000 cc engine with manual transmission).
Fuel distribution plate (2000 cc engine with auto transmission).

1974 All Models

Electric assist choke.
Ported vacuum system.
Air pump—California only.

Closed positive crankcase ventilation.
Heated air cleaner.
Vapor control, canister storage.
Emission calibrated carburetor.
Emission calibrated distributor.
Single diaphragm vacuum advance.
Spark delay enrichment valve.
Decel enrichment valve.
Fuel distribution plate.
EGR-system.

1975 AND LATER

NOTE: *Specific application of these devices depends on engine and transmission options on your car, except where noted.*

Fuel Deceleration Valves

Spark Delay Valves—In '75, used only with 2300 cc engine and manual transmission combination and all 2800 cc engines. Not used on '76 four-cylinder engines.

Exhaust Heat Control Valve (HCV)—Only on the 2800 cc engine in '75; on all '76 engines, except 2300 cc.

Heated Air Intake System—All

Exhaust Gas Recirculation System—All

Evaporative Emissions Control Canister—All

Thermactor System—All

Transistorized Ignition—All

Catalytic Converter—In '75, used only on 2300 cc Calif. engine and all 2800 cc engines; on all '76 and later engines.

Dual Diaphragm Distributor

Electric Assisted Choke—All

Coolant Spark Control System—All

Cold Start Spark Advance System—1975 Calif. Pintos with 2.3 liter engine.

CRANKCASE EMISSION CONTROLS

Crankcase emission control equipment consists of an oil separator,

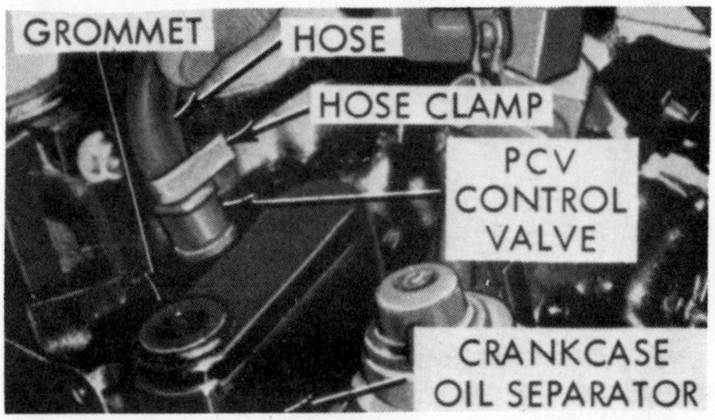

PCV valve and oil separator

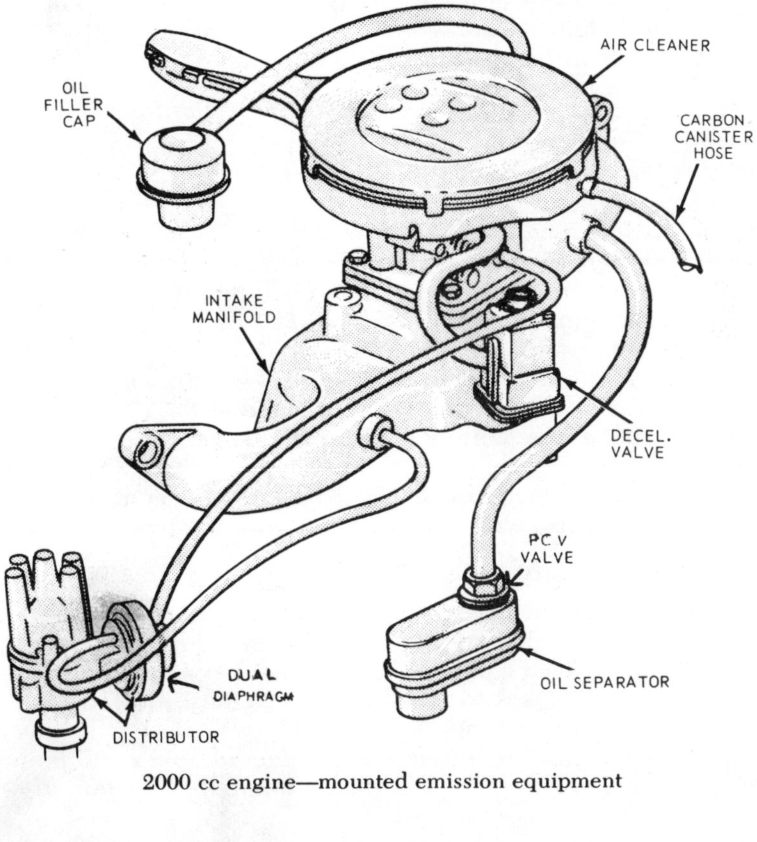

2000 cc engine—mounted emission equipment

mounted on the side of the engine block, a positive crankcase ventilation (PCV) valve, mounted on the top of the oil separator, a closed oil filler cap, and the hoses that connect this equipment.

When the engine is running, a small portion of the gases which are formed in the combustion chamber leak by the piston rings and enter the crankcase. Since these gases are under pressure, they tend to escape from the crankcase and enter the atmosphere. If these gases are allowed to remain in the crankcase for any period of time, they contaminate the engine oil and cause sludge to build up in the crankcase. If the gases are allowed to escape into the atmosphere, they pollute the air, with unburned hydrocarbons. The job of the crankcase emission control equipment is to recycle these gases back into the engine combustion chamber where they are reburned.

The crankcase gases are recycled in the following way: as the engine is running, clean, filtered air is drawn through the air filter and the oil filler cap and into the crankcase. As the air passes through the crankcase, it picks up the combustion gases and carries them out of the crankcase, through the oil separator, through the PCV valve, and into the intake manifold. As they enter the intake manifold, they are drawn into the combustion chamber where they are reburned.

The most critical component in the system is the PCV valve. This valve controls the amount of gases which are recycled into the combustion chamber. At low engine speeds, the valve is partially closed, limiting the flow of the gases into the intake manifold. As engine speed increases, the valve opens to admit greater quantities of the gases into the intake manifold. If the valve should become blocked or plugged, the gases will be prevented from escaping from the crankcase by the normal route. Since these gases are under pressure, they will find their own way out of the crankcase. This alternate route is usually a weak oil seal or gasket in the engine. As the gas escapes by the gasket, it also creates an oil leak. Besides causing oil leaks, a clogged PCV valve also allows these gases to remain in the crankcase for an extended period of time, promoting the formation of sludge in the engine.

Troubleshooting

With the engine running, pull the PCV valve and hose from the oil separator. Block off the end of the valve with your finger. Engine speed should drop at least 50 rpm when the end of the valve is blocked. If engine speed does not drop at least 50 rpm, the valve is defective and should be replaced.

Removal and Installation

1. Pull the PCV valve and hose from the oil separator.
2. Remove the PCV valve from the hose. Inspect the inside of the PCV valve hose. If it is dirty, disconnect it from the intake manifold and clean it.
3. If the PCV valve hose was removed, connect it to the intake manifold.
4. Connect the PCV valve to its hose.
5. Install the PCV valve in the oil separator.

EXHAUST EMISSION CONTROLS

Engine modifications to lower engine exhaust emissions fall into four categories; distributor controls, fuel system controls, exhaust system controls, and internal engine modifications. Internal engine modifications are not discussed since these are changes in the basic design of the engine.

Distributor Controls

NOTE: *See emission control equipment for application.*

Dual Distributor Diaphragm

The dual distributor diaphragm is a two-chambered housing which is mounted on the side of the distributor. The outer side of the housing is a distributor vacuum advance mechanism, connected to the carburetor by a vacuum hose. The purpose of the vacuum advance is to advance ignition timing according to the conditions under which the engine is operating. This device has been used on automobiles for many years now and its chief advantage is economical engine operation. The second side of the dual diaphragm is the side that has been added to help control engine exhaust emissions at idle.

The inner side of the dual diaphragm is connected by a vacuum hose to the intake manifold. When the engine is idling, intake manifold vacuum is high and carburetor vacuum is low. Under these conditions, intake manifold vacuum, applied to the inner side of the dual diaphragm, retards ignition timing to promote more complete combustion of the air fuel mixture in the engine combustion chambers.

Distributor-Vacuum Control Valve

The Ported Vacuum Switch (PVS) and the Electric Ported Vacuum Switch are basically sensing devices which are used as parts of other more complex systems. Coolant temperature controls them, allowing them to pass or stop vacuum. Vacuum either can be given or denied to the object connected to the switch depending upon whether or not the engine requires it to operate with reduced pollutants. The electric PVS has the capability to send an electric signal.

NOTE: *Consult the application chart for the correct vacuum schematic for any particular model, then check the schematic to see if the control valve is used on that model.*

The distributor vacuum control valve is a temperature-sensitive valve which screws into the water jacket of the engine. Three vacuum lines are attached to the vacuum control valve: one that runs from the carburetor to the control valve, one that runs from the control valve to the distributor vacuum advance (outer) chamber, and one that runs from the intake manifold to the distributor vacuum control valve.

During normal engine operation, vacuum from the carburetor passes through the top nipple on the distributor control valve, through the valve to the second nipple on the valve, and out the second nipple on the valve to the distributor vacuum advance chamber. When the engine is idling however, carburetor vacuum is very low, so there is little, if any, vacuum in the passageways described above.

If the engine should begin to overheat while idling, a check ball inside the distributor vacuum control which normally blocks off the third nipple of the valve (intake manifold vacuum) moves upward to block off the first nipple (carburetor vacuum). This applies intake manifold vacuum (third nipple) to the distributor vacuum advance chamber (second nipple). Since intake manifold vacuum is very high while the engine is idling, ignition timing is advanced by the application of intake manifold vacuum to the distributor vacuum advance chamber. This raises the engine idle speed and helps to cool the engine.

Spark Delay Valve (SDV)

The spark delay valve is a plastic, spring-loaded color coded valve which is installed in the vacuum line to the distributor advance diaphragm on most 1974 and later models.

Under heavy throttle application, the valve will close, blocking normal carburetor vacuum to the distributor. After the designated period of closed time, the valve opens, restoring the carburetor vacuum to the distributor. The following chart outlines the spark delay valve applications.

Valve Color	*ID #*	*Time Delay (seconds)* *Min*	*Max*
Black/Gray	1	1	4
Black/Brown	2	2	5
Black/White	5	4	12
Black/Yellow	10	5.8	14
Black/Blue	15	7	16
Black/Green	20	9	20
Black/Orange	30	13	24
Black/Red	40	15	28
White/Brown *	2	2	5
White/Green *	20	9	20

* Dual delay, all others are single delay

NOTE: *The black side of the valve always faces the vacuum source, the carburetor.*

Electronic Spark Control

NOTE: *See emission control equipment for application.*

Electronic spark control is a system which blocks off carburetor vacuum to the distributor vacuum advance mechanism under certain temperature and speed conditions. The electronic spark control system consists of four components: a temperature sensor, a speed sensor, an amplifier, and a distributor modulator vacuum valve. The system serves to prevent ignition timing advance (by blocking off carburetor vacuum from the distributor vacuum advance mechanism) until the car reaches a

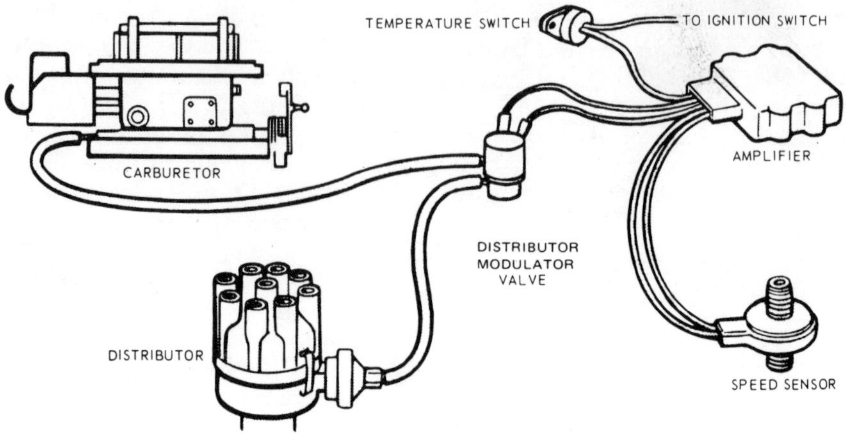

Electronic spark control system

speed of 35 mph when the ambient temperature is over 65°F.

The temperature sensor, which is mounted on the front face of the right door pillar, monitors the outside air temperature and relays this information to the amplifier. The amplifier, which is located under the instrument panel, controls the distributor modulator vacuum valve. The modulator valve, which is attached to the ignition coil mounting bracket, is connected into the carburetor vacuum line to the distributor, and is normally open. If the temperature of the outside air is below 48°F, the contacts in the temperature sensor are open and no signal is sent to the amplifier. Since no signal is sent to the amplifier, the amplifier does not send a signal to the distributor modulator valve, and the vacuum passage from the carburetor to the distributor vacuum advance remains open. When the outside temperature rises to 65°F or above, the contacts in the temperature sensor close and a signal is sent to the amplifier. The amplifier relays the message to the distributor modulator, which closes to block the vacuum passage to the distributor, preventing ignition timing advance.

When the ambient temperature is 65°F or above, ignition timing advance is prevented until the amplifier receives a signal from the speed sensor that the speed of the vehicle has reached 35 mph, and the distributor modulator vacuum valve can be opened to permit ignition timing advance.

The speed sensor is a miniature generator which is connected to the speedometer cable of the car. As the speedometer cable turns, the inside of the speed sensor turns with the speedometer cable. As the speed of the car increases, a rotating magnet in the speed sensor induces an electronic current in the stationary windings in the speed sensor. This current is sent to the amplifier. As the speed of the vehicle increases, the amount of current sent to the amplifier by the speed sensor increases proportionately. When the car reaches a speed of 35 mph, the amplifier signals the distributor modulator vacuum valve to open, allowing carburetor vacuum to be sent to the distributor vacuum advance chamber. This permits the ignition timing to advance.

It should be noted that this system operates only when the ambient temperature is 65°F or above, and then only when the speed of the car is below 35 mph.

Troubleshooting

Dual Diaphragm Distributor

1. Connect a timing light and start the engine.
2. Disconnect the vacuum hose from the outer distributor diaphragm. Plug the line with a golf tee or pencil.
3. Shine the timing light on the lower engine pulley and observe the position of the ignition timing marks.
4. Disconnect the vacuum hose from the rear vacuum diaphragm on the distributor and hold your finger over the line.
5. Again check the ignition timing. It should be advanced beyond the reading

obtained in step three. If it is not, the rear diaphragm on the distributor is defective or the vaçuum hose from the intake manifold is broken.

Distributor Vacuum Control Valve

1. Attach a tachometer and start the engine.
2. Observe the reading on the tachometer.
3. Disconnect the hose from the intake manifold to the control valve and plug it with a golf tee or pencil.
4. Again observe the reading on the tachometer. If it has not changed, the control valve does not have an internal vacuum leak. If it does change, replace the valve.
5. Reconnect the intake manifold hose to the vacuum valve.
6. Block the front of the radiator with cardboard and have a friend watch the warning light on the instrument panel.
7. As soon as the red warning light comes on, again observe the reading on the tachometer. It should be at least 100 rpm higher than the reading obtained in step two. If it is not, replace the vacuum control valve.
8. Remove the cardboard from in front of the radiator and allow the engine to cool off before stopping the engine.

Spark Delay Valve

1. Disconnect the vacuum hose that runs from the spark delay valve to the distributor at the spark delay valve. Connect a vacuum gauge to the end of the spark delay valve from which you just disconnected the vacuum hose.
2. Start the engine and quickly raise the speed of the engine to about 2000 rpm with the transmission in Neutral. As soon as you accelerate the engine, the vacuum gauge reading should drop to zero.
3. With the engine speed held steady at about 2000 rpm, observe the time in seconds required until the vacuum gauge reading moves up to at least 6 in. Hg.
4. If the time required is less than 20 seconds, the spark delay valve is functioning properly.
5. If the time required is less than two seconds, the valve is defective.
6. If the time required is more than 20 seconds, disconnect the vacuum gauge from the spark delay valve. Remove the carburetor-to-spark delay valve hose from the spark delay valve and connect the vacuum gauge to it.

Start the engine and raise the speed of the engine to about 2000 rpm. The vacuum gauge should show a reading of about 10–16 in. Hg. If it does not, there is a blockage in the carburetor vacuum port or the vacuum hose from the carburetor to the spark delay valve is plugged or broken.

Electronic Spark Control

System Operation Check

1. Raise the rear of the car until the rear wheels are clear of the ground by at least 4 in. Support the rear of the car with safety stands.

   CAUTION: *The rear of the car must be firmly supported during this test. If one of the rear wheels should come in contact with the ground while it is turning, the car will move forward very rapidly and unexpectedly.*
2. Disconnect the vacuum hose from the distributor vacuum advance chamber. This is the outer hose on cars with a dual diaphragm.
3. Connect the hose you just disconnected from the distributor to a vacuum gauge.
4. Pour hot water on the temperature-sensing switch to ensure that its temperature is above 65°F. The temperature sensor is located on the right door pillar.
5. Start the engine, apply the foot brake, and shift the transmission selector lever into Drive.
6. Slowly release the foot brake and allow the transmission to shift into high (third) gear.
7. Have a friend observe the vacuum gauge while you raise the speed of the engine until the speedometer reads 35 mph.
8. If the system is working properly, there should be no reading on the vacuum gauge until the speedometer reads 35 mph, at which time the vacuum gauge should show a reading.
9. If the vacuum gauge shows a reading below 35 mph, a component in the electronic spark control system is defec-

tive. If the vacuum gauge does not show a reading, even above 35 mph, there is either a defective component in the electronic spark control system, or there is a broken or clogged vacuum passage between the carburetor and the distributor.

Vacuum Passages Check

1. Disconnect the vacuum hose that runs from the carburetor to the distributor modulator vacuum valve at the vacuum valve. Connect the end of the hose that was just disconnected to a vacuum gauge. Start the engine and keep the transmission selector lever in either the Park or Neutral position. Raise the speed of the engine to about 1500 rpm and observe the reading on the vacuum gauge. If the vacuum gauge shows a reading, this section of the system is OK. If the vacuum gauge does not show a reading, either the vacuum port in the carburetor is plugged or the vacuum hose out of the carburetor is plugged or broken.

2. Reconnect the vacuum hose that was disconnected in step one. Disconnect the vacuum hose coming out of the distributor modulator vacuum valve and connect it to a vacuum gauge. Disconnect the lead wires that run to the distributor modulator. Start the engine and raise the speed of the engine to about 1500 rpm. If the vacuum gauge does not show a reading, the distributor modulator vacuum valve is defective.

3. On cars with air conditioning, reconnect the vacuum hose to the modulator valve but leave the wires to the valve disconnected. Disconnect the vacuum hose coming out of the second nipple on the distributor control valve. Start the engine and raise the speed of the engine to about 1500 rpm. If the vacuum gauge does not show a reading, the distributor control valve is defective or the hose leading to the valve is plugged or broken.

4. Reconnect all vacuum lines but leave the lead wires to the distributor modulator vacuum valve disconnected. Disconnect the vacuum hose to the distributor vacuum advance chamber. Connect this hose to a vacuum hose. Start the engine and raise the speed of the engine to about 1500 rpm. Observe the reading on the vacuum gauge. If the gauge does not show a reading, the hose to the distributor vacuum advance chamber is plugged or broken.

Component Testing Temperature Sensor

1. Disconnect the two wires that run to the temperature sensor. Pour hot water on the sensor to ensure that its temperature is above 65°F. Connect the two leads of an ohmmeter to the two leads from the temperature sensor. At temperatures above 65°F, the ohmmeter should show a reading. Cool the temperature sensor with ice to bring its temperature below 65°F. At temperatures below 49°F the ohmmeter should not show a reading. If the temperature sensor does not react this way, it is defective.

2. With the ignition switch turned on, connect the ground wire on a test light to a good metal ground and insert the probe of the light into the connector of the red and yellow wire running to the temperature sensor connector. If the test light does not light, either the wire is defective or the ignition switch is defective.

Component Testing Speed Sensor

1. Disconnect the wires running from the speed sensor connector. Connect the two leads on an ohmmeter to the two wires running to the speed sensor. At room temperature the ohmmeter should show a reading of about 40–60 ohms.

2. Disconnect the speed sensor from the speedometer cable. Connect one lead on a ohmmeter to the inside core of the speed sensor and the other to the body of the speed sensor. The ohmmeter should not show a reading.

3. If the speed sensor does not give these readings, it is defective.

Component Testing Distributor Modulator Vacuum Valve and Amplifier

If the system operation check showed that the electronic spark control system was not operating properly, and if the vacuum passages check OK, and the temperature and speed sensors check out OK, then the trouble is either in the modulator valve or the amplifier.

1. Pour hot water on the temperature

sensor to ensure that its temperature is above 65°F.

2. Disconnect the lead wires to the modulator valve at the quick-disconnect connector.

3. Turn the ignition switch on.

4. Connect the ground wire on a test light to a good ground and insert the probe end into the two wires leading to the connector to which the wires from the distributor modulator vacuum valve connect. If connecting to one of these wires lights the test light, and the electronic spark control system is not working correctly, the distributor modulator vacuum valve is defective. If connecting to one of these wires does not light the test light, the amplifier is defective.

Distributor Controls Replacement

DISTRIBUTOR DUAL DIAPHRAGM

1. Tag the two vacuum hoses that attach to the diaphragm and disconnect them.

2. Remove the distributor cap and remove the C-clip that attaches the diaphragm arm to the breaker point mounting plate. On 1600 cc engines, you must remove the breaker point mounting plate to disconnect the arm.

3. Remove the two screws that attach the diaphragm to the distributor housing and remove the diaphragm from the distributor.

4. Position the new diaphragm on the distributor and connect the hole in the diaphragm arm to the stud on the breaker point mounting plate.

5. Install the C-clip that retains the arm on the plate.

6. Install the distributor cap.

7. Install the two diaphragm attaching screws.

8. Connect the vacuum hoses to the diaphragm.

DISTRIBUTOR VACUUM CONTROL VALVE

1. Drain about one gallon (1 gal) of coolant out of the radiator.

2. Tag the vacuum hoses that attach to the control valve and disconnect them.

3. Unscrew and remove the control valve.

4. Install the new control valve.

5. Connect the vacuum hoses.

6. Fill the cooling system.

ESC TEMPERATURE SENSOR

1. Open the right door and remove the two screws that attach the temperature sensor to the right door pillar.

2. Disconnect the lead wires from the temperature sensor.

3. Connect the lead wires to the new sensor.

4. Position the sensor on the door pillar and install the attaching screws.

ESC SPEED SENSOR

1. Disconnect the lead wires from the sensor.

2. Disconnect the speed sensor from the speedometer cable.

3. Position the O-rings on both ends of the new speed sensor.

4. Connect both ends of the speedometer cable to the speed sensor.

5. Connect the lead wires to the speed sensor.

ESC AMPLIFIER

1. Locate the amplifier under the instrument panel, on the brake pedal mounting bracket.

2. Disconnect the wiring harness from the amplifier.

3. Remove the two amplifier attaching screws and remove the amplifier.

4. Position a new amplifier under the instrument panel and connect the wiring harness to it.

5. Install the two amplifier attaching screws.

ESC DISTRIBUTOR MODULATOR VACUUM VALVE

1. Tag the hoses that attach to the modulator and disconnect them from the amplifier.

2. Disconnect the lead wires from the modulator.

3. Remove the bolt that attaches the modulator to the ignition coil mounting bracket and remove the modulator.

4. Position the new modulator on the ignition coil mounting bracket and install the attaching bolt.

5. Connect the wires and hoses to the modulator.

Spark Delay Valve

1. Locate the spark delay valve in the distributor vacuum line and disconnect it from the line.
2. Install a new spark delay valve in the line, making sure the black end of the valve is connected to the line from the carburetor and the red end is connected to the line from the spark delay valve to the distributor.

Fuel System Controls

Fuel system modifications for the purpose of exhaust emission control consist of leaner carburetor mixtures, idle mixture limiter caps, a deceleration valve, heated intake air cleaner, and a EGR valve.

Carburetor Mixtures

All carburetors have been calibrated for leaner mixtures to decrease the amount of unburned hydrocarbons contained in the vehicle exhaust. Also, plastic limiter caps have been installed on the idle mixture adjusting screws. These caps limit the travel of the idle mixture screws, preventing them from being adjusted in such a way that the air/fuel mixture at idle would be excessively rich.

Deceleration Valve

When you quickly release the gas pedal on your Pinto, the rapid closing of the throttle plate(s) in the carburetor and resultant internal engine conditions cause engine exhaust emission levels to be very high during deceleration. To counteract these high emission levels, the Pinto is equipped with a deceleration valve.

The deceleration valve is a vacuum-actuated valve attached to the intake manifold of the engine. A hose connects the deceleration valve to the carburetor.

Since the throttle valve(s) in the base of the carburetor are closed during deceleration, very little air/fuel mixture from the carburetor enters the intake manifold during deceleration. This causes engine speed to drop very rapidly. This rapid closing of the throttle plates also causes a high-vacuum condition in the intake manifold. This high-vacuum condition opens the deceleration valve and draws a metered air/fuel mixture from the carburetor, through the connecting hose to the deceleration valve, through the deceleration valve and into the intake manifold. This additional air/fuel mixture then enters the combustion chamber and is burned. Due to this additional mixture, engine speed drops gradually instead of rapidly. This helps to lower engine exhaust emissions during deceleration.

As engine speed gradually decreases, intake manifold vacuum drops and the valve closes. The engine then operates on the normal idle mixture from the carburetor.

A large, white nylon adjusting screw in the top of the deceleration valve determines the amount of spring pressure that is applied to the poppet valve inside the deceleration valve. The amount of spring pressure determines how much vacuum is required to open the deceleration valve and how long it will remain open. This adjustment is critical. If too much spring pressure is exerted, the deceleration valve will not open and engine emissions will be high during deceleration. If too little spring pressure is exerted, the deceleration valve will open too soon and stay open too long; it may even remain open at all times. This will result in very high engine idle speeds and excessive fuel consumption. If the diaphragm in the deceleration valve becomes ruptured, additional air will be admitted into the intake manifold. This will cause a lean air/fuel mixture, rough engine idle, and poor throttle response.

Troubleshooting and Adjustment

NOTE: *A tachometer, a vacuum gauge, and a watch with a second hand are required to adjust the deceleration valve.*

A malfunctioning deceleration valve can be caused by three things: a leaking diaphragm, a defective poppet valve, or improper adjustment.

Diaphragm Test

NOTE: *A leaking diaphragm will cause rough engine idle.*

With the engine running, reach under the base of the deceleration valve and cover the small hole in the base of the valve with your finger. If the engine idle smoothes out or the speed of the engine decreases, the diaphragm is leaking and must be replaced.

Poppet Valve Test

If the engine has an excessively high idle speed and it is not caused by improper carburetor adjustment or binding carburetor linkage or throttle plates, the poppet valve in the deceleration valve may be defective. With the engine running, disconnect the air/fuel hose from the carburetor to the deceleration valve at the deceleration valve. Seal the opening from which the hose was disconnected with your finger. If the speed of the engine decreases noticeably when this opening is closed, the poppet valve is hanging open and must be replaced.

Decel Valve Adjustment

1. Set the engine ignition timing to specification. See chapter two for the procedure. Attach a tachometer to the engine.
2. Disconnect the air/fuel hose that runs from the carburetor to the deceleration valve at the carburetor and then plug the hose.
3. Connect a vacuum gauge to the engine. This can be done by removing a vacuum hose from the intake manifold and connecting the vacuum gauge to the fitting for the hose you remove.
4. Start the engine and adjust the carburetor idle mixture screw to obtain the highest reading possible on the vacuum gauge. See chapter two for idle mixture screw locations.

   NOTE: *Although this step calls for the carburetor to be adjusted to produce the highest possible reading on the vacuum gauge, the reading must not exceed 18.5 in. Hg for cars with a dual diaphragm (two vacuum hoses running to the distributor) distributor or 19.5 in. Hg for cars with a single diaphragm (one vacuum hose running to the distributor) distributor. If engine vacuum exceeds these values, it must be reduced or the deceleration valve will not function properly. If the vacuum is too high, and the ignition timing is set to specifications, readjust the carburetor idle mixture adjusting screw to obtain 18.5 or 19.5 in. Hg.*
5. Adjust the engine idle speed to specification. See chapter two.
6. Unplug the hose that was disconnected in step two and disconnect the vacuum gauge from the engine. Reconnect the vacuum hose that was removed to facilitate installation of the vacuum gauge.
7. Attach the air/fuel hose to the carburetor and then, using a tee fitting, connect the vacuum gauge into the air/fuel line between the carburetor and the deceleration valve.
8. Have a friend raise the speed of the engine to 3000 rpm and hold it at that for five seconds.
9. Have your friend quickly release the gas pedal while you observe the vacuum gauge and your watch. As soon as the gas pedal is released, the vacuum gauge should show a reading. A reading should hold on the gauge for two seconds and then the needle on the gauge should return to zero. If everything works out that way, your deceleration valve is working properly. If not proceed to step 10.
10. If the reading on the gauge remained for more than two seconds, you must turn the adjusting screw on the top of the deceleration valve "in." If the reading remained for less than two seconds, the adjusting screw must be turned OUTWARD. Before you can adjust the valve, however, you must fabricate an adjusting tool by grinding a ⅜ in.

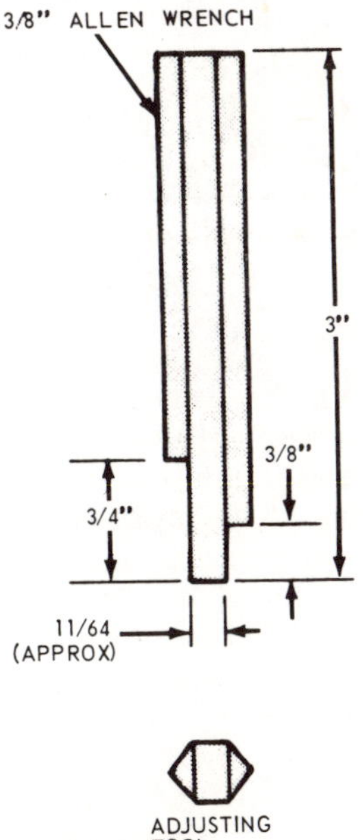

Dimensions for deceleration valve adjusting tool

allen wrench, or piece of hex rod, to the dimensions shown in the illustration.

11. Insert the tool into the deceleration valve nylon adjusting screw and turn in or out as required. If you have the new style valve, with the hidden adjusting screw, you must first pry the gray cover off the top of the deceleration valve to uncover the adjusting screw.

12. After adjusting the valve repeat steps 8, 9, and 10 to check the operation of the valve. If you are unable to adjust the valve to bring it within specifications, the valve must be overhauled or replaced.

Decel Valve Removal

1. Disconnect the air/fuel hose from the deceleration valve.
2. Loosen the union nut that attaches the deceleration valve to the intake manifold and remove the valve.

Poppet Valve Replacement

1. Loosen the four screws that hold the top cover on the deceleration valve while holding the cover in place with your hand.

   CAUTION: *The top cover is spring-loaded and could fly off if it is not held in place while the attaching screws are removed.*
2. Remove the top cover attaching screws and gradually release the spring pressure from the cover.
3. Remove the cover and its gasket.
4. Turn the valve over to remove the poppet valve and spring.
5. Install a new poppet valve in the housing and install the spring, gasket, and cover.

Diaphragm Replacement

1. Remove the four screws that attach the bottom cover to the deceleration valve and remove the cover.
2. Remove the diaphragm and spring retainer.
3. Install a new diaphragm and spring retainer in the bottom of the housing.
4. Install the bottom cover on the deceleration valve.

Installation

1. Position the deceleration valve on the intake manifold and tighten the union nut.
2. Connect the air/fuel hose to the valve.
3. Test and adjust the deceleration valve as required.

Heated Intake Air Cleaner

The heated air intake portion of the air cleaner consists of a thermostat and a spring-loaded temperature control door in the snorkel of the air cleaner. The temperature control door is located between the end of the air cleaner snorkel which draws in air from the engine compartment and the duct that carries heated air up from the exhaust manifold. When under hood temperature is below 90°F, the temperature control door blocks off under hood air from entering the air cleaner and allows only heated air from the exhaust manifold to be drawn into the air cleaner. When underhood temperature rises above 130°F, the temperature control door blocks off heated air from the exhaust manifold and allows only underhood air to be drawn into the air cleaner.

By controlling the temperature of the engine intake air this way, exhaust emissions are lowered and fuel economy is improved.

Troubleshooting

1. With the engine cold and underhood temperature below 90°F, check the position of the temperature door in the air cleaner. It should be in the up position, blocking off underhood air.
2. Immerse the air cleaner duct assembly in water after removing the air cleaner from the car. Raise the temperature to 130°F and allow the temperature to stabilize for five minutes. The temperature control door should be in the down position, blocking off heated air from the exhaust manifold.

If the temperature door does not react this way, and the door is not binding, replace the duct and valve assembly.

Cold Start Spark Advance System (CSSA)

Used in 1975 California Pintos with the 2300 cc engine, this system uses PVS switches to provide direct manifold vacuum to the distributor when the engine is cold, i.e., below 125°F. On most models, a check valve is used to maintain maximum, but on some this is replaced with a retard delay valve which inhibits vacuum for a time when the engine is hot. Testing the system consists of checking for vacuum leaks and testing the PVS and spark (retard) delay valve as previously outlined in this chapter.

Exhaust Gas Recirculation

Some models utilize an Exhaust Gas Recirculation System (EGR) to control oxides of nitrogen. On V6 engines, exhaust gases travel through the exhaust gas crossover passage in the intake manifold. A portion of these gases are diverted into a spacer which is mounted under the carburetor. The EGR control valve, which is attached to the rear of the spacer, consists of a vacuum diaphragm with an attached plunger which normally block off exhaust gases from entering the intake manifold. On 4 cylinder engines, an external tube carries exhaust manifold gases to the carburetor spacer. The EGR valve is controlled by a vacuum line from the carburetor.

The vacuum diaphragm opens the EGR valve permitting exhaust gases to flow through the carburetor spacer and enter the intake manifold where they combine with the fuel mixture and enter the combustion chambers. The exhaust gases are relatively oxygen-free, and tend to dilute the combustion charge. This lowers peak combustion temperature thereby reducing oxides of nitrogen.

EGR-CSC System

For 1976 and later models, the exhaust gas recirculation (EGR) system has been connected to the coolant spark control system (CSC). There are now two vacuum sources available to the distributor to aid driveability with either a hot or cold engine.

When the engine is cold (coolant temperature below 82°F), the PVS valve gives the distributor vacuum which is normally routed to the EGR valve. When coolant temperature rises above 95°F, the EGR valve receives its normal vacuum from the carburetor and the distributor receives vacuum through the other PVS valve and the SDV valve.

EGR Valve Service

Valves which are riveted cannot be disassembled. Valves which can be disassembled should be thoroughly cleaned and reassembled with extreme care not to enlarge orifices or bend any parts. Rebuilding is not recommended. Defective valves should be replaced.

Amplifier and other components are limited to replacement if defective.

EGR Valve Cleaning

Remove the EGR valve for cleaning. Do not strike or pry on the valve diaphragm housing or supports as this may damage the valve operating mechanism and/or change the valve calibration. Check orifice hole in the EGR valve body for deposits. A small hand drill of no more than 0.060 in. diameter may be used to clean the hole if plugged. Extreme care must be taken to avoid enlarging the hole or damaging the surface of the orifice plate.

Valves Which Cannot Be Disassembled

Valves which are riveted or otherwise permanently assembled should be replaced if highly contaminated; they cannot be cleaned.

Valves Which Can Be Disassembled

Separate the diaphragm section from the main mounting body. Clean the valve plates, stem, and the mounting plate, using a small power driven rotary type wire brush. Take care not to damage the parts. Remove deposits between stem and valve disc by using a steel blade or shim approximately 0.028 inch thick in a sawing motion around the stem shoulder at both sides of the disc.

The poppet must wobble and move axially before re-assembly.

Clean the cavity and passages in the main body of the valve with a power driven rotary wire brush. If the orifice plate has a hole less than 0.450 in., it must be removed for cleaning. Remove all loosened debris using shop compressed air. Reassemble the diaphragm section on the main body using a new gasket between them. Torque the attaching screws to specification. Clean the orifice plate and the counterbore in the valve body. Re-install the orifice plate using a small amount of contact cement to retain the plate in place during assembly of the valve to the carburetor spacer. Apply cement only to outer edges of the orifice plate to avoid restriction of the orifice.

EGR Supply Passages and Carburetor Spacer Cleaning

Remove the carburetor and carburetor spacer on engines so equipped. Clean the supply tube with a small power driven rotary type wire brush or blast cleaning equipment. Clean the exhaust gas passages in the spacer using a suitable wire brush and/or scraper. The machined holes in the spacer can be cleaned by using a suitable round wire brush. Hard encrusted material should be probed loose first, then brushed out.

EGR Exhaust Gas Channel Cleaning

Clean the exhaust gas channel, where applicable, in the intake manifold, using a suitable carbon scraper. Clean the exhaust gas entry port in the intake manifold by hand passing a suitable drill bit thru the holes to auger out the deposits. Do not use a wire brush. The manifold riser bore(s) should be suitably plugged during the above action to prevent any of the residue from entering the induction system.

Venturi Vacuum Amplifier System

All Pintos with EGR use a venturi vacuum amplifier. The amplifier is used to boost a relatively weak venturi vacuum signal in the throat of the carburetor into a strong intake manifold vacuum signal to operate the EGR valve. This device improves driveability by more closely matching venturi airflow and EGR flow.

The amplifier features a vacuum reservoir and check valve to maintain an adequate vacuum supply regardless of variations in engine manifold vacuum. Also used in conjunction with the amplifier, is a relief valve, which will cancel the output EGR vacuum signal whenever the venturi vacuum signal is equal to, or greater than, the intake manifold vacuum. Thus, the EGR valve may close at or near wide-open throttle acceleration, when maximum power is needed.

EXHAUST SYSTEM CONTROLS

Thermactor (Air Pump)

The "Thermactor" air injection system is used on all Ford vehicles intended for sale in California. A pump supplies air under pressure to the exhaust port near the exhaust valve, by either an external manifold or internal drilled passages. The oxygen in the fresh air plus the heat of the exhaust gases causes burning which converts exhaust gases to carbon dioxide and water vapor. The system consists of an air supply pump, external air manifold or cylinder head/exhaust manifold with drilled passages, air by-pass valve, check valve, hoses, clamps and brackets.

Testing and Troubleshooting System

Prior to testing the system, a test gauge adapter must be made. This can easily be done as follows.

Obtain:

1. ½ in. pipe tee.
2. ½ in. pipe, 2 in. long, threaded at one end.
3. ½ in pipe plug.
4. ½ in. reducer bushing.

Apply sealer to all threaded portions, thread plug and pipe into opposite ends of the tee and the reducer into the perpendicular orifice of the tee.

Drill an 11/32 hole through the center of the plug.

Attach pressure gauge with ¼ psi. increments to the bushing or adapter.

Preliminary Thermactor System Check

1. Check the belt for tension, remove the air cleaner, and check all components for wear.
2. With automatic transmissions in Park or manual transmissions in Neutral and the parking brake on, start the engine and warm it.
3. Stop the engine and connect a tachometer. Remove the air supply hose at the check valve (if there are two supply hoses, remove both).
4. Start and run the engine at 1,500 rpm. Place your hand over the open hose. If you don't feel any air, perform the "Pump Test."

Pump Test (air supply)

1. Operate engine at normal operating temperature. Inspect hoses and connections for leaks. Correct if necessary.
2. Check and adjust pump drive belt tension.
3. Disconnect air supply hose at

check valve. With more than one hose, plug one.

4. Insert adapter with gauge into the open air supply hose and clamp securely.

5. Connect a tachometer to the engine.

6. Start engine and operate at 1000 rpm.

7. Pressure reading should be at least 2¼ psi.

If 2¼ psi is not attained, replace the pump.

Check Valve Test

1. Operate engine until normal temperature is reached.
2. Disconnect air supply hose at the check valve.
3. Visually make certain that the valve plate is lightly seated and away from the manifolds.
4. Depress the valve plate with some kind of probe and release. It should return freely to its original position.
5. With the hose still connected, start and run the engine at 1,500 rpm and check for leakage at the check valve.

By-Pass Valve Test

1. Remove the hose connecting the by-pass valve to the check valve at the by-pass valve.
2. Place transmission in Neutral, apply the parking brake, start the engine and operate at normal idle speed.
3. Pinch off the vacuum line to the by-pass valve for 5–8 seconds, then release. Air flow should diminish or stop for a short time.
4. Remove the vacuum supply to the by-pass valve at the by-pass valve.
5. Insert a tee connection in the supply hose. Connect a gauge and a three inch hose to the remaining connections.
6. Plug the open end of the short hose. Start the engine and note the reading.
7. Unplug and connect the short hose. The reading should correspond to the first reading within 60 seconds. If not, replace the valve.

Service

Repairs on the system are limited to replacement except for replacement of the centrifugal filter fan. The fan can be removed by prying it off the shaft.

Catalytic Converter

All 1975 Pintos with the 2300 cc engine sold in California and all 2800 cc engines will be equipped with a catalytic converter(s) integrated into the exhaust system. All 1976 and later models are also equipped with catalytic converters. The function of the catalytic converter is to reduce hydrocarbon and carbon monoxide emission levels. Fundamentally, the catalyst enhances the conversion of the hydrocarbons to water vapor and carbon dioxide and carbon monoxide to carbon dioxide. Lead-free gasoline must be used in all cars equipped with the catalytic converter.

FUEL EVAPORATION CONTROLS

When liquid gasoline is subjected to heat, it expands and vaporizes. If this expansion and vaporization takes place in a conventional automobile gas tank, the fuel vapor escapes and pollutes the atmosphere once it has left the fuel tank. All Pintos are equipped with an evaporative emission control system to prevent gasoline vapors from entering the atmosphere.

The major components of this system are an expansion area in the gas tank, a foam-filled vapor separator which is mounted on the fuel tank, a carbon canister which stores fuel vapors, and hoses which connect this equipment.

As the gasoline in the fuel tank of a parked vehicle begins to expand due to heat, the vapor that forms moves to the top of the fuel tank. It leaves the fuel tank through the vapor separator. The vapor separator permits fuel vapors to leave the gas tank but prevents liquid gasoline from escaping. The fuel vapor enters the vapor separator outlet hose and passes through the hose to the carbon canister, which is mounted in the engine compartment. The vapor enters the canister passes through a charcoal filter, and then exits from the canister through its grated bottom. As the vapor passes through the carbon, it is cleansed of hydrocarbons, so that the air that passes out of the bottom of the canister is free of atmospheric pollutants.

When the engine is started, vacuum from the carburetor draws fresh air into the carbon canister. As the entering air passes through the carbon in the canister, it picks up the hydrocarbons that were deposited there. This gas mixture is then carried through a hose to the air cleaner. In the carburetor it combines with the incoming air/fuel mixture and enters the combustion chambers of the engine where it is burned.

Servicing

The 1971–72 canisters are small in size and should be replaced every 24,000 miles. It is also recommended that the hose to the air cleaner be replaced at the same time. To remove the canister, loosen and remove the mounting bracket and disconnect the purge hose.

1973 and later canisters are larger and do not have to be replaced unless they are leaking or damaged.

Fuel System

FUEL PUMP

All of the engines use a diaphragm-type mechanical fuel pump. All of the fuel pumps are mounted on the front, left-side of the engine, except on the 1600 cc engine where it is on the right side.

The fuel pump is operated by a lever running on an eccentric on the camshaft on the 1600 cc engine and on 1974 2000 cc and 2300 cc engines. All 1971–73 2000 cc engines and 2800 cc V6 engines have a pushrod operated fuel pump driven by an eccentric on the auxiliary shaft (2000 cc) or camshaft (2800 cc).

All of the fuel pumps are sealed and must be replaced when defective.

Troubleshooting

The fuel pump can fail in two ways; it can fail to provide a sufficient volume of gasoline under the proper amount of pressure to the carburetor, or it can develop an internal or external leak. An external leak will be very evident; not so with an internal leak. A quick check for an internal leak is to remove the oil dipstick and examine the oil on it. A fuel pump with an internal leak will leak fuel into the engine oil pan. If the oil on the dipstick is very thin and smells of gasoline, a defective fuel pump could be the cause.

PRESSURE TEST

Disconnect the fuel line from the carburetor and attach a pressure tester to the end of the line. Crank the engine over and note the reading on the tester. The reading should be 3.5 to 5.5 pounds per square inch (psi) from years 1971–74 and 3.5–4.5 psi on all 1975 and later models.

VOLUME TEST

Disconnect the fuel line from the carburetor and insert it into a one quart container and crank the engines to the specifications listed below.

1971–73

1600 cc, one pint in 38 sec. @ 500 rpm.
2000 cc, one pint in 43 sec. @ 500 rpm.

1974

2000 cc, one pint in 35 sec. @ 500 rpm.
2300 cc, one pint in 20 sec. @ 500 rpm.

1975 AND LATER

2300 cc, one pint in 25 sec. @ 500 rpm.
2800 cc, one pint in 25 sec. @ 500 rpm.

Replacement

1. Disconnect the fuel lines from the fuel pump and plug the inlet line from the gas tank to prevent gas leakage.
2. Remove the fuel pump retaining screws and remove the pump.
3. Remove the fuel pump actuating rod, if so equipped.
4. Clean all gasket mounting surfaces.
5. Install the fuel pump actuating rod, if so equipped.
6. Apply oil-resistant sealer to the fuel pump, position the pump on the engine and install the retaining screws.

NOTE: *Make sure that the fuel pump rocker arm is riding on the eccentric.*

7. Connect the fuel lines to the fuel pump, start the engine and check for leaks.

CARBURETORS

The carburetor is a seemingly mystical device mounted on the intake manifold which performs the following tasks; open and close its intake port to maintain a predetermined amount of gasoline in its reservoir, channel air into the engine through the air cleaner, atomize measured amounts of gasoline and introduce the vapor into the incoming air stream, provide metered amounts of air/fuel mixture to the deceleration valve while it is operating, act as a vacuum source for the distributor vacuum advance mechanism, and change the air/fuel mixture it supplies to the engine for normal warm weather driving, acceleration, maximum power, cold engine operation, and idling. It looks complicated because it is. There are, however, many carburetor adjustments and repairs that can be performed by those who have a certain amount of mechanical aptitude. Take your time, concentrate on what you are doing, and don't let it intimidate you. It's only a carburetor.

Float, Needle Valve and Seat

As previously stated, the carburetor contains a reservoir for gasoline. Two devices in the carburetor control the flow of gasoline into this reservoir: the needle valve and its seat, and the float. When fuel enters the carburetor, it passes around the needle valve, through the needle valve seat, and into the reservoir. As the level of the fuel in the carburetor increases, it contacts the float, moving the float upward. A tang on the end of the float contacts the needle valve and, as the float moves upward, the tang on the float pushes the needle valve into its seat, limiting the flow of gasoline into the engine. When the float reaches a predetermined level, the float tang pushes the needle valve completely into its seat, preventing any more gasoline from entering the carburetor. As the engine uses fuel from the carburetor, the float drops, allowing more fuel to enter the carburetor. If the float is adjusted in such a way that it does not close the needle valve when the reservoir is full, or if the needle

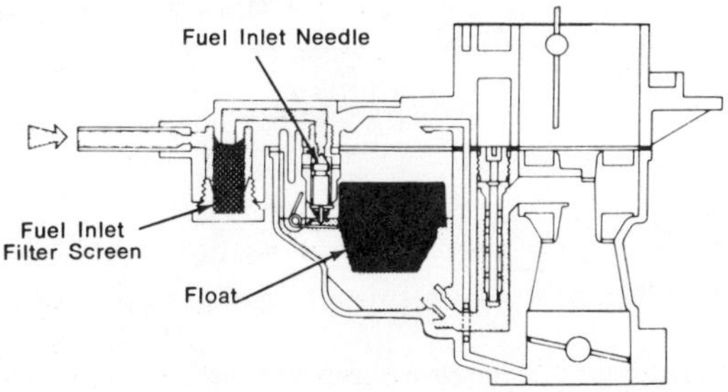

Carburetor fuel inlet system

valve does not completely seal on its seat, the reservoir will overfill and dump raw gasoline into the engine. If the float is adjusted to close the needle valve too soon, the reservoir will contain an insufficient supply of gasoline, and the engine will run lean under some conditions causing hesitation or stalling.

Main Metering System

When the engine is operating at a constant speed above idle, it is the passage of air through the center of the carburetor (throttle bore) and into the engine that draws fuel from the carburetor; the carburetor does not inject gasoline into the engine. This drawing of gas out of the carburetor is due to pressure, vacuum, and other such matters. The throttle plates control the flow of air through the carburetor. These are small discs mounted in the base of the carburetor. When the throttle plates are closed, no air can pass into the engine and, therefore, no gasoline can be drawn from the carburetor. The gas pedal of the car is connected to the throttle plates. When you push down on the gas pedal, you open the throttle plates. The further you push down on the gas pedal, the further you open the throttle plates. The greater the throttle plate opening, the greater the amount of air that can flow through the carburetor and into the engine.

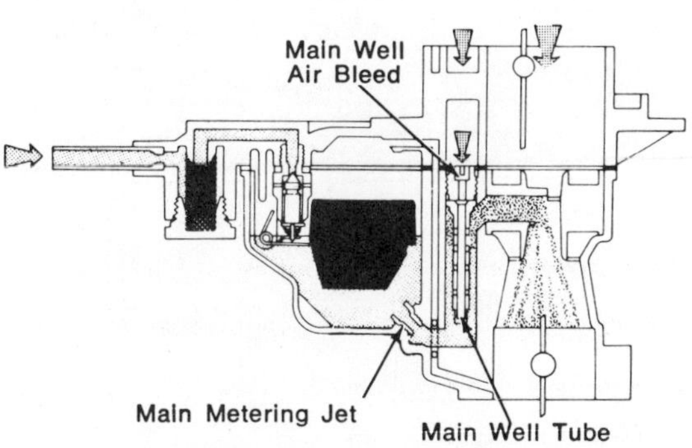

Carburetor main metering system

Gasoline on its way from the carburetor reservoir to the throttle bore, passes through metering jets which determine the amount of gasoline that will enter the throttle bore. These jets are screwed into an internal part of the carburetor housing. They are not adjustable. The only way the fuel supply to the engine can be increased is by changing the jets.

Power Valve—2000 cc and 2300 cc Only

Since the main metering jet determines the amount of fuel that can be drawn into the engine by the air passing through the carburetor throttle bore, the size of these jets must necessarily be a compromise. While smaller jets afford greater fuel economy (to a certain endpoint), larger jets provide better performance (once again, up to a certain point). Therefore, a jet size is picked that will give the best all-around performance. This compromise jet size cannot, however, supply a sufficient amount of fuel for wide-open throttle engine operation. Therefore, the carburetor contains a power valve to supplement the normal fuel supply to the engine during wide-open throttle. The power valve is normally closed but is allowed to open during conditions of low intake manifold vacuum. While it is open, additional fuel passes through the power valve circuit in the carburetor, bypassing the main metering jets, and combining with the normal fuel supply to enrich the air/fuel mixture supplied to the engine. If the power valve should become defective, it will open too soon, or remain partially open at all times, causing the air/fuel mixture to be too rich.

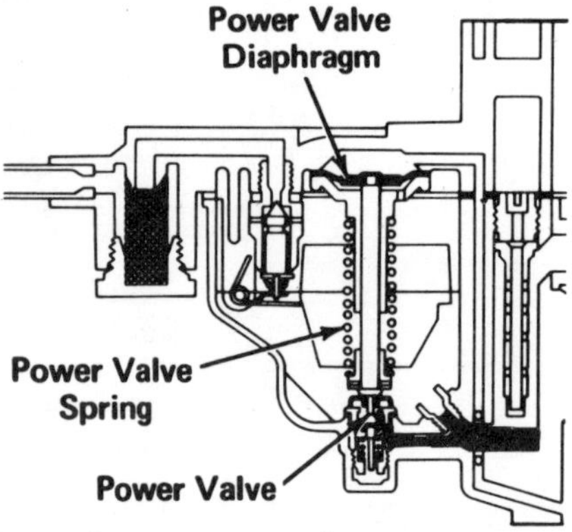

2000 cc carburetor power valve

Accelerator Pump

When you push down quickly on the gas pedal to accelerate, the throttle plates open rapidly. This means that the air flow through the carburetor increases suddenly. However, for a brief moment, this rapidly increased air flow cannot draw a proportionally increased amount of gas from the carburetor. To compensate for this, the carburetor contains an accelerator pump.

The accelerator pump is a diaphragm pump mounted on the body of the carburetor and connected by linkage to the carburetor throttle linkage. When the throttle linkage is depressed to accelerate the car, the movement of the throttle linkage produces a corresponding movement of the accelerator pump linkage. The movement of the accelerator pump linkage stretches the accelerator pump diaphragm; this forces a stream of gasoline into the throttle bore of the carburetor. This is the only time gasoline is actually injected into the engine and occurs only while the gas pedal is being depressed to give a greater throttle plate opening. The accelerator pump is completely mechanical in operation; its function is not dependent on the amount of air flowing through the carburetor. The purpose of the accelerator pump is to momentarily supplement the fuel flow from the carburetor during acceleration, thereby preventing a lean air/fuel mixture. If the accelerator pump system is not working properly, this lean condition will cause the engine to hesitate on acceleration. Accelerator pump problems can be caused by a defective diaphragm or spring, a defective check ball, binding linkage, or clogged passages in the system. A good way to check the operation of the accelerator pump system is to look into the top of the carburetor with the air cleaner removed and the engine stopped. Have a friend depress the gas pedal. A stream of gasoline should appear in the throttle bore of the carburetor as soon as the gas pedal moves and should continue until the gas pedal is fully depressed.

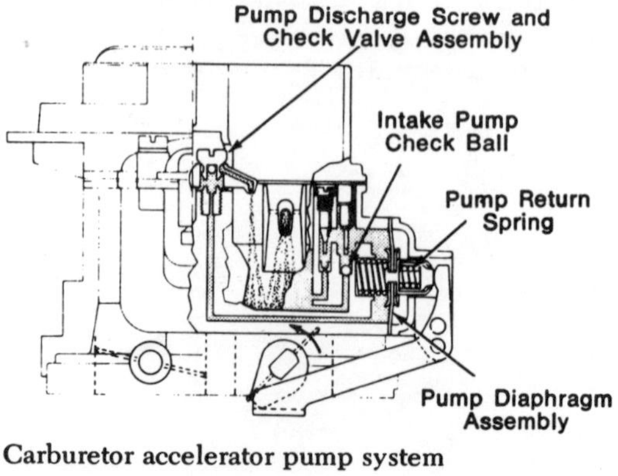

Carburetor accelerator pump system

Choke System

1971–73

During cold engine operation, the engine requires a richer air/fuel mixture. The choke system makes this richer mixture possible. The choke system consists of: a choke plate, which is mounted in the carburetor air intake horn; a temperature-sensitive coil spring, which is contained in the choke housing on the side of the carburetor; a choke plate vacuum pull-down device; a choke unloader tab; and a fast idle cam.

During choke operation, the choke plate closes to limit air flow into the carburetor and intake manifold vacuum pulls a proportionally greater fuel mixture into the engine than during hot engine operation.

Application of the choke is controlled by the choke spring. This coil spring is connected to the choke plate and expands when cold and contracts when hot. When the engine has not been running for a while, and ambient temperature is low, the coil spring expands and exerts spring pressure on the choke plate. When the gas pedal is depressed before starting the engine, this spring pressure forces the choke plate closed.

The fast idle cam is also attached, by linkage, to the choke plate. The fast idle cam is a stepped cam which is pulled up into its working position at the same time as the choke plate (when the accelerator pedal is depressed before starting the engine). A fast idle speed adjusting screw or tab, which is attached to the throttle shaft, contacts the cam and, by holding the throttle plates open, raises the idle speed of the engine to the required level.

Engine coolant passes through the choke coil spring housing while the engine is operating. As the engine reaches operating temperature, the increased temperature of the coolant causes the spring to contract. This removes spring pressure from the choke plate and allows the choke plate to return to the open position. This movement of the plate also disengages the fast idle cam and allows engine idle speed to return to normal.

The choke plate vacuum pull-down device opens the choke plate slightly when the engine has started and continues to function after the choke is off. On 1600 cc engines, the device consists of a piston which is contained in the choke housing. On 2000 cc engines, it consists of a diaphragm and spring which are contained in an extension on the choke housing. When the engine is running, intake manifold vacuum is applied to the diaphragm or piston. The diaphragm or piston then exerts a corresponding pull on the choke plate. When the engine is cold, and the choke coil spring is exerting pressure on the choke plate, the pull of the diaphragm or piston opens the choke plate slightly. After the engine has reached normal operating temperature, and the choke spring has contracted, the diaphragm or piston holds the choke plate in the full open position.

The choke unloader is a tab which is attached to the carburetor throttle shaft, opposite the fast idle adjusting screw. When the gas pedal is depressed to the full open position, the fast idle adjusting screw moves away from the fast idle cam and the unloader tab moves up to contact the cam. The cam, through its connecting linkage, then opens the choke plate partially. This allows additional air to enter the engine and serves to aid in starting a flooded engine.

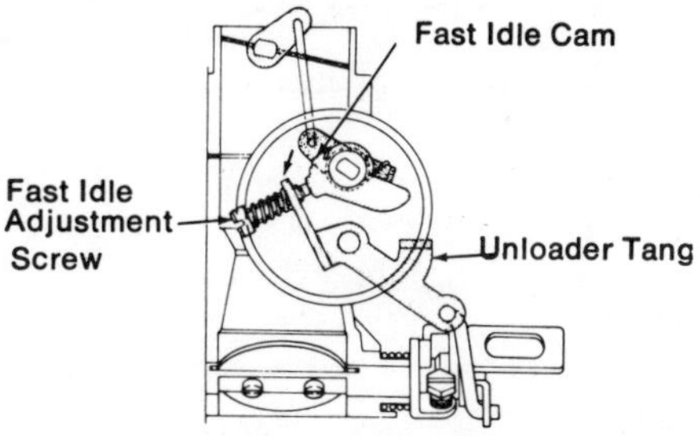

Carburetor fast idle cam and unloader tang

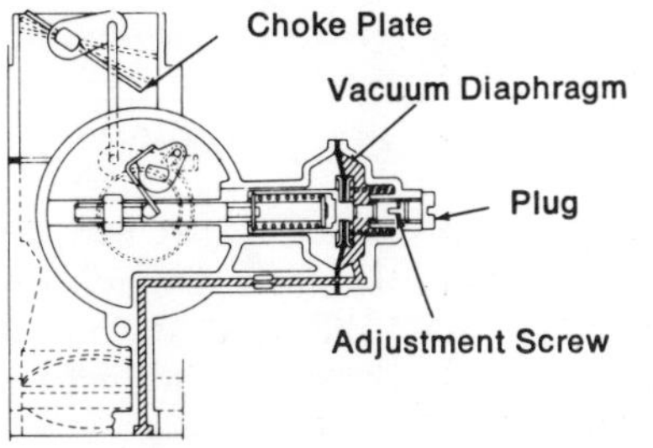

2000 cc carburetor vacuum pulldown

1974 and Later

Beginning in 1974 an electrically heated choke thermostatic spring housing was added to aid fast choke release and better emission characteristics during engine warmup. The system consists of a choke cap, thermostatic spring, bimetallic temperature sensing disc, and a ceramic heater powered from the stator tap of the alternator. Current is supplied from the center tap of the alternator under a constant rate to the temperature sensing switch. The system is grounded through a strap connected to the carburetor body. At temperatures below 60 degrees F, the switch remains open and no current is supplied. Above 60 degrees the switch closes and causes the spring to pull the choke open within 1–1½ minutes.

Application

See the specifications chart at the end of this chapter for applications and specifications.

Throttle Solenoid (Anti-dieseling Solenoid) Test

1. Turn the ignition key on and open the throttle. The solenoid plunger should extend (solenoid energize).
2. Turn the ignition off. The plunger should retract, allowing the throttle to close.

NOTE: *With the antidieseling solenoid deenergized, the carburetor idle speed adjusting screw must make contact with the throttle shaft to prevent the throttle plates from jamming in the throttle bore when the engine is turned off.*

3. If the solenoid is functioning properly and the engine is still dieseling, check for one of the following:
   a. High idle or engine shut off speed;
   b. Engine timing not set to specification;
   c. Binding throttle linkage;
   d. Too low an octane fuel being used.

   Correct any of these problems as necessary.
4. If the solenoid fails to function as outlined in Steps 1–2, disconnect the solenoid leads; the solenoid should deenergize. If it does not, it is jammed and must be replaced.
5. Connect the solenoid to a 12 V power source and to ground. Open the throttle so that the plunger can extend. If it does not, the solenoid is defective.
6. If the solenoid is functioning correctly and no other source of trouble can be found, the fault probably lies in the wiring between the solenoid and the ignition switch or in the ignition switch itself. Remember to reconnect the solenoid when finished testing.

Removal

1. Remove the air cleaner.
2. On 2000 cc and 2300 cc engines, remove the bolt that attaches the choke water housing to the carburetor and remove the water cover with the hoses attached. On 1600 cc engines, remove the three screws that attach the water housing to the carburetor. A small amount of engine coolant will run out from the water cover when it is removed.
3. Note the location of all fuel and vacuum hoses that attach to the carburetor, then disconnect them from the carburetor.
4. Disconnect the throttle linkage from the carburetor.
5. On all 1600 cc engines and those 2000 cc and 2300 engines with air conditioning, disconnect the throttle solenoid wire at the push-on connection.
6. On 1600 cc engines, remove the two nuts that attach the carburetor to the intake manifold. On 2000, 2300, and 2800 cc engines remove the four nuts that attach the carburetor to the intake manifold.

Installation

1. Inspect the carburetor base gasket. If it is damaged in any way, replace it. Clean any foreign matter from the base of the carburetor.
2. Position the carburetor on the intake manifold.
3. Install and tighten the carburetor attaching nuts.
4. Connect the vacuum and fuel lines to the carburetor.
5. Connect the throttle linkage to the carburetor.
6. Connect the choke water housing to the carburetor.

7. On models equipped with a throttle solenoid, connect the lead wire at the push-on connector.

8. Replace any coolant that was lost from the cooling system and install the air cleaner.

1250 CARBURETOR

Adjustments

Float Level Adjustment

1. Remove the air cleaner.
2. Disconnect the fuel line and the deceleration valve hose from the carburetor.
3. Remove the choke fast idle cam pivot screw.
4. Remove the screws that attach the choke water housing and thermostatic spring to the carburetor and disconnect the housing from the carburetor.
5. Remove the six screws and spring washers that attach the upper carburetor body to the main carburetor body.
6. Carefully lift the upper body and gasket from the main body of the carburetor.
7. Turn the upper body and gasket sideways, so that the fuel inlet tube is pointing straight upward and the float is hanging down.
8. Measure the distance between the bottom of the float and the bottom of the carburetor upper body gasket. The distance should be 1.20 in. If the distance is incorrect, bend the float tab that is resting on the bottom of the needle valve to correct it.

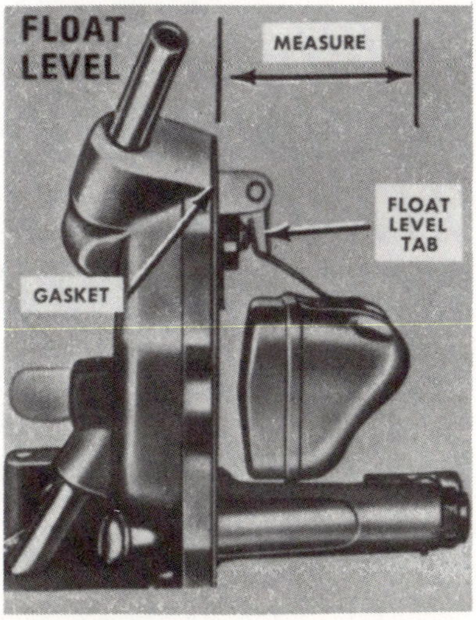

1250 float level adjustment

9. Turn the carburetor upperbody upward to its normal installed position.
10. Measure the distance between the bottom of the float and the bottom of the carburetor upper body gasket (float drop). The distance should be 1.40 in. If the distance is not correct, bend the drop tab to adjust it.

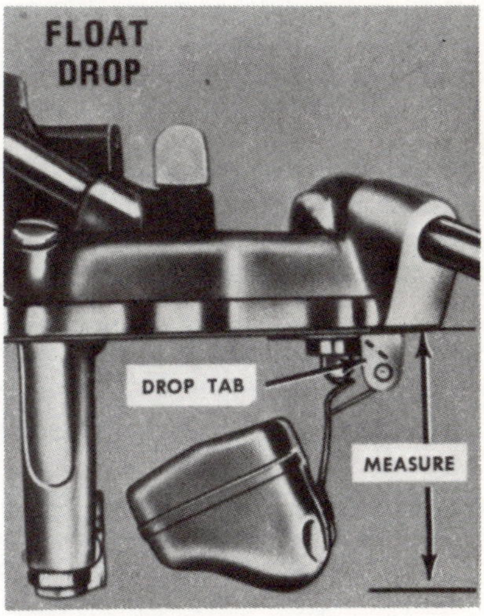

1250 float drop adjustment

11. Install the carburetor upper body on the carburetor main body.
12. Install the choke water housing and spring on the choke housing, making sure the tab in the end of the spring engages the slot in the choke control lever. Align the notch in the water housing with the large notch on the choke housing and install and tighten the attaching screws.
13. Position the fast idle cam on the carburetor and install its pivot screw.

Accelerator Pump Adjustment

1. Remove the air cleaner.
2. Back off the throttle stop screw two turns.
3. Push the bottom of the accelerator pump lever toward the rear of the car until it reaches the limit of its travel.
4. Using a feeler gauge, measure the clearance between the top end of the accelerator pump lever and the tab on the accelerator pump diaphragm that is

sticking out of the front of the accelerator pump cover. The clearance should be 0.065–0.070 in.

5. If the clearance is below this figure, close up the inverted U-bend in the far end of the accelerator pump control rod enough to correct the clearance. If the clearance is too large, open the inverted U-bend in the far end of the accelerator pump control rod enough to correct the clearance.

6. Turn the throttle stop screw inward two turns and install the air cleaner.

CHOKE ADJUSTMENTS

Thermostatic Coil Spring Adjustment

1. Remove the air cleaner.
2. Loosen the three screws that attach the choke water housing to the choke housing.
3. Turn the choke water housing to align the index mark on the water housing with the large index mark on the choke housing and tighten the water cover attaching screws. (See the specifications chart at the end of this chapter).

1250 choke spring adjustment

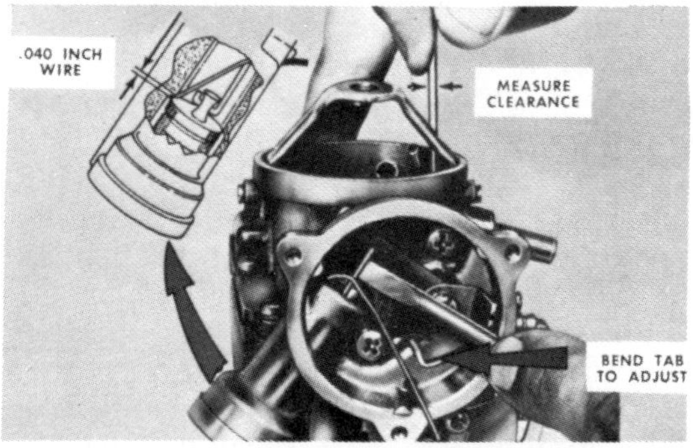

1250 choke vacuum pulldown adjustment

Choke Plate Vacuum Pull Down Adjustment

1. Remove the air cleaner.
2. Remove the three screws that attach the choke water housing to the choke housing.
3. Depress the choke piston assembly in the choke housing until the vacuum bleed slot in the wall of the piston housing is exposed.
4. Insert the bent tip of a piece of 0.040 in. (thick) wire into this slot, then raise the piston to trap the wire.
5. Close the choke plate in the top of the carburetor until it stops.
6. Partially open the throttle plates in the carburetor to disengage the fast idle screw from the fast idle cam.
7. Check the clearance between the bottom of the choke plate and the wall of the carburetor. It should be 0.064–0.085 in. (no. 51–46 drill bit).
8. If clearance is not within specifications, bend the tab on the end of the choke thermostatic lever to adjust it.
9. Remove the wire from the vacuum piston.
10. Install the choke water housing on the choke housing, making sure the tab on the end of the choke coil spring engages the slot in the choke control lever. Align the index mark on the water cover with the large index mark on the choke housing before tightening the water cover.

Choke Unloader Adjustment

1. Remove the air cleaner and fully depress the throttle control lever.
2. Measure the clearance between the bottom of the choke plate and the carbu-

retor wall. Clearance should be 0.210 in. (no. 4 drill bit).

3. If clearance is not within specifications, bend the fast idle cam tab to adjust it.

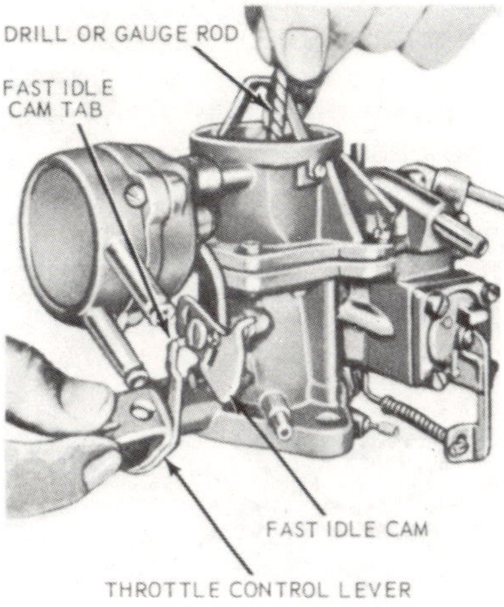

1250 choke unloader adjustment

Fast Idle Speed Adjustment

1. Remove the air cleaner and attach a tachometer to the engine.

2. Depress the throttle lever to open the throttle plates in the carburetor and position the fast idle adjusting tab on the second step of the fast idle cam. An arrow on the fast idle cam shows the proper tab contact location.

3. Start the engine and check the fast idle speed on the tachometer, it should be 1700 rpm.

4. If the fast idle speed is not correct, bend the fast idle tab to correct it. (See Specifications Chart.)

Idle Speed and Mixture Adjustment

See Chapter 2

Carburetor Repairs—1250 1V Carburetor

ACCELERATOR PUMP DIAPHRAGM REPLACEMENT

1. Remove the air cleaner.

2. Remove the four screws that attach the accelerator pump cover to the carburetor and move the cover away from the carburetor.

NOTE: *Hold your hand under the cover to catch the accelerator pump spring as you remove the cover.*

3. Remove the diaphragm from the pump cover.

4. Clean any foreign matter from inside the pump cover or from the face of the carburetor.

5. Position the pump spring, spring seat (if so equipped), and the diaphragm, and then install the pump cover.

6. Install and tighten the four cover attaching screws.

7. Install the air cleaner.

NEEDLE VALVE AND SEAT AND/OR FLOAT REPLACEMENT

1. Remove the air cleaner.

2. Disconnect the fuel line and the deceleration valve hose from the carburetor.

3. Remove the choke fast idle cam pivot screw.

4. Remove the screws that attach the choke water housing and thermostatic spring to the carburetor and disconnect the housing from the carburetor.

5. Remove the six screws and spring washers that attach the upper carburetor body to the main carburetor body.

6. Carefully lift the upper body and gasket from the main body of the carburetor.

7. Invert the carburetor upper body and knock out the float arm pivot pin. Remove the float and upper body gasket from the upper body.

8. Lift the needle valve from its seat, then unscrew the seat from the upper carburetor body.

9. If the small gas filter came out of the upper body, install it in the needle valve housing.

10. Install the needle valve seat in the upper body, using a *new* gasket. Tighten the seat to 15–30 in. lbs.

11. Install the needle valve in its seat, tapered end first.

12. Position the float on the upper body and install the float retaining pin. Set float level. See "Float Level Adjustment" earlier in this chapter.

13. Install the upper body and gasket. Install the choke fast idle cam pivot screw.

14. Install the choke water cover on

the choke housing, making sure the tab on the end of the coil spring engages the slot in the choke control lever. Align the index mark on the water cover with the large mark on the choke housing and tighten the three cover attaching screws.

15. Connect the fuel and deceleration valve hoses to the carburetor and install the air cleaner.

5200 CARBURETOR

Adjustments

Float Level Adjustment

1. Remove the air cleaner.
2. Disconnect the fuel and deceleration valve hoses from the carburetor.
3. Remove the small clip that attaches the choke rod to the choke plate

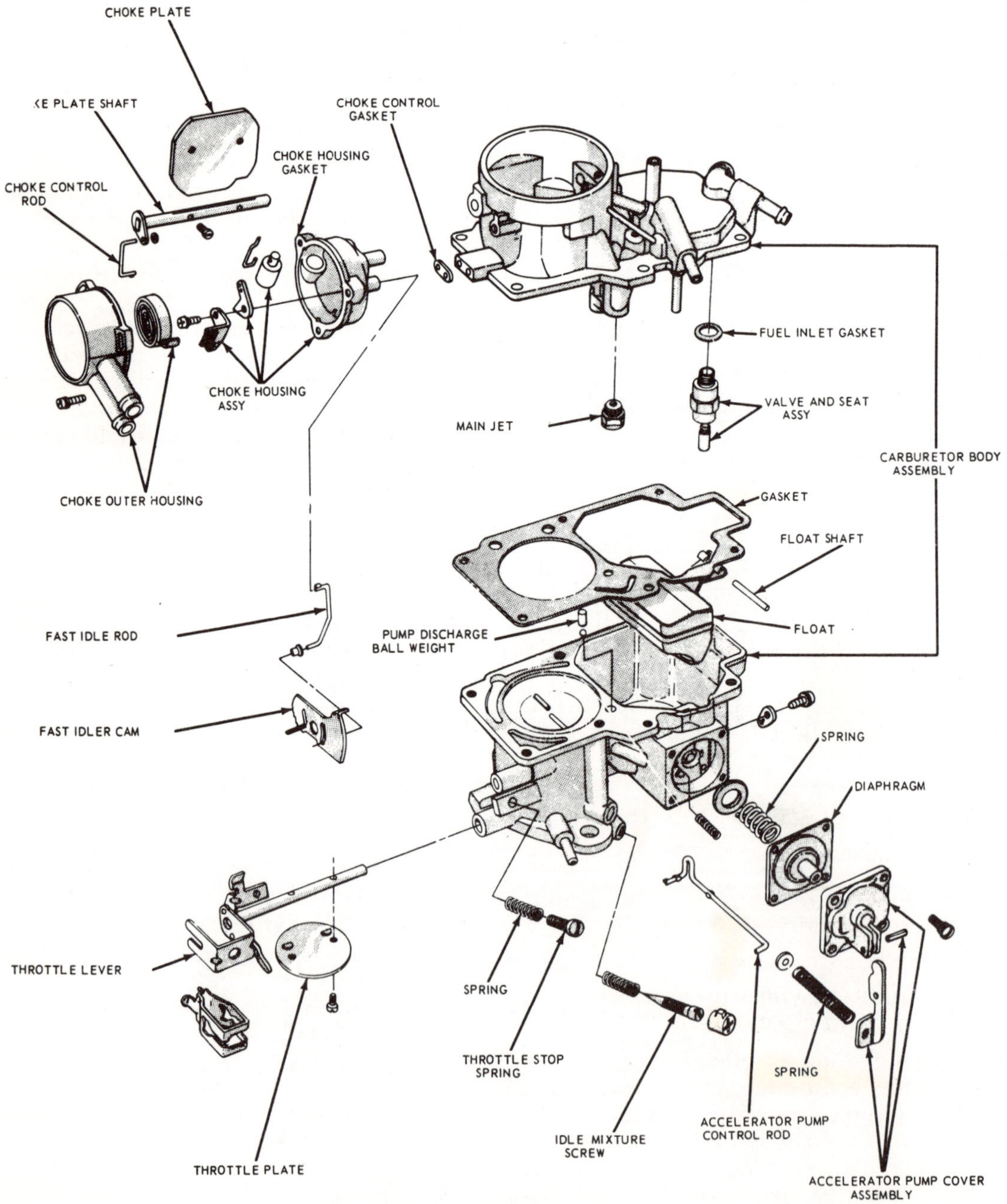

Exploded view of 1250 carburetor

shaft and disconnect the rod from the shaft.

4. Remove the screws that attach the upper body of the carburetor to the main body of the carburetor and carefully lift the upper body off the main body. Be careful not to tear the upper body gasket.

5. Turn the carburetor upper body upside down and measure the clearance between the bottom of each float and the bottom of the carburetor upper body. The clearance should be 0.420 in. (no. 58 drill bit).

6. If the clearance is incorrect, bend the float level adjusting tang to correct.

NOTE: *Both floats must be adjusted to the same clearance.*

7. With the upper body still in the inverted position, measure the clearance between the tang on the rear of the float mounting bracket and the bumper spring on the float pivot pin. The clearance should be 0.020–0.050 in. If the clearance is incorrect, bend the float drop tang to adjust.

NOTE: *Some very early models may not be equipped with this spring. On these carburetors, turn the upper body over to its normal position and allow the floats to drop. Measure the distance between the bottom of the float and the bottom of the upper housing. Distance should be 1.87 in. Bend the float drop tang on rear of float mounting bracket to adjust it.*

8. Position the upper body and gasket of the main body of the carburetor and connect the choke rod to the choke plate lever. Install the choke rod attaching clip in the hole in the rod.

9. Install the upper body attaching screws.

10. Connect the fuel and deceleration valve hoses to the carburetor.

11. Install the air cleaner.

CHOKE ADJUSTMENTS—1971–74

Fast Idle Cam Clearance

1. Remove the air cleaner.

2. Move the fast idle cam upward while holding the throttle shaft open to align the fast idle adjusting screw with the second step on the fast idle cam. Release the throttle shaft so the adjusting screw contacts the cam.

3. Insert a $^5/_{32}$ in. drill bit into the carburetor air horn and close the choke plate until the drill is trapped between the plate and the carburetor wall.

4. Check the clearance between the tang on the choke lever and the tab on the fast idle cam. Clearance should be 0.010 in. maximum. Bend choke lever tang as required to adjust clearance.

Choke Vacuum Pull-Down Adjustment

1. Remove the three screws from around the choke water cover that attach the cover to the choke housing. Do not remove the center water cover screw.

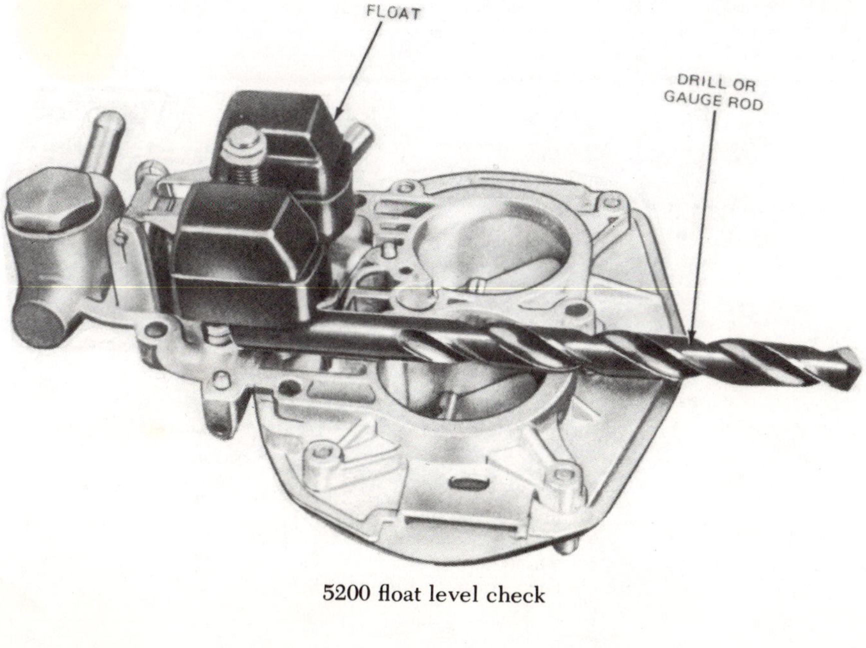

5200 float level check

2. Remove the water housing with the hoses attached.

3. Position the fast idle cam so the fast idle adjusting screw is contacting the highest step on the cam.

4. Using a screwdriver, push the vacuum diaphragm stem back into the diaphragm housing until it stops. Hold the stem in this position.

5. Insert a 15/64 in. drill bit into the air horn of the carburetor and apply light pressure to the choke plate to remove all slack. With the drill bit against the air

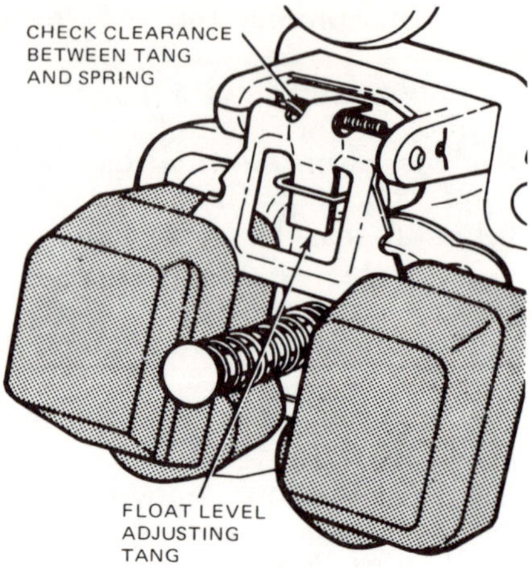

5200 float bumper spring clearance

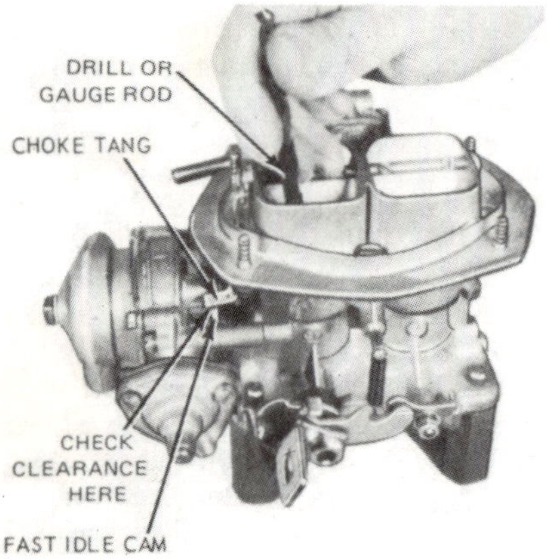

5200 fast idle cam clearance

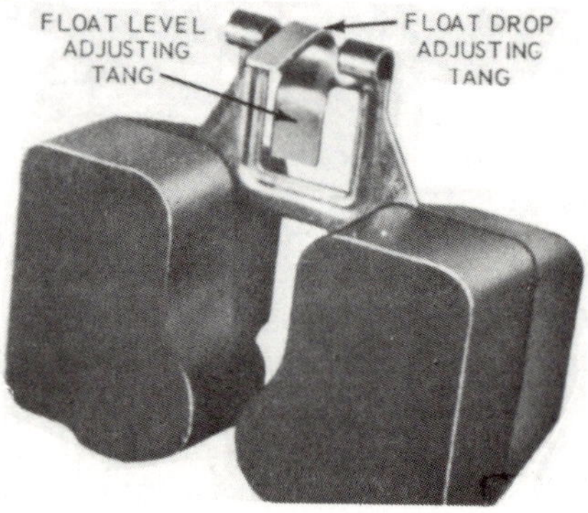

5200 float adjustment

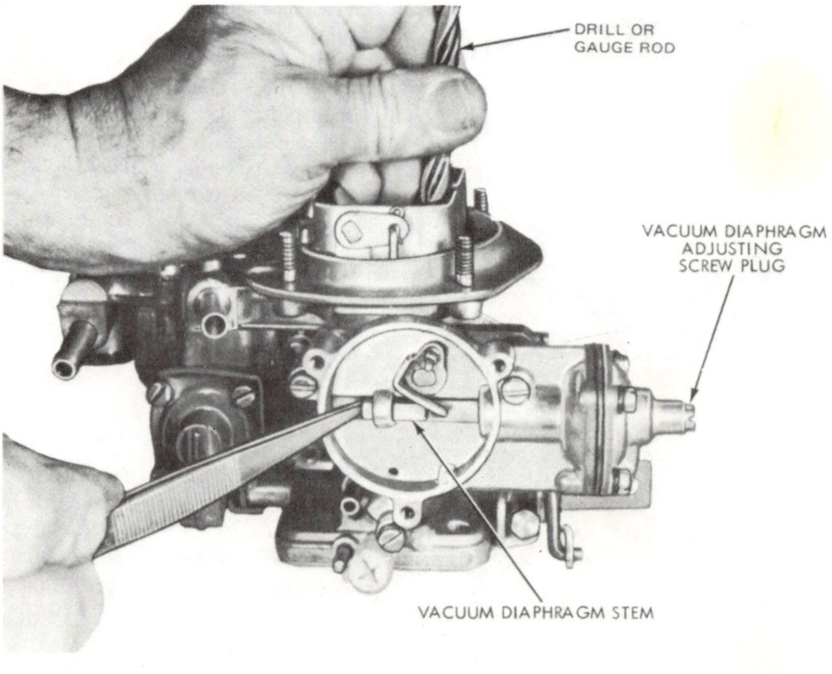

5200 choke vacuum pulldown adjustment

horn wall, the bottom of the choke plate should just contact the drill bit.

6. If the clearance is incorrect, remove the vacuum diaphragm adjusting screw plug and insert a screwdriver into the exposed hole, then adjust the screw inward or outward as required.

7. Install the choke water housing on the choke housing, making sure the tab on the end of the coil spring engages the slot in the choke housing shaft.

8. Install the three choke water housing attaching screws and tighten them fingertight. Adjust the thermostatic coil spring as described below.

Thermostatic Coil Spring Adjustment

1. Loosen the three screws that attach the choke water housing to the choke housing.

2. Turn the choke water housing as required to align the index mark on the water housing with the specified mark on the choke housing. If the choke cap setting is index, align the notch on the water cover with the large index mark in the center of the top of the choke housing. If the choke cap setting is one lean, align the notch on the water cover with the first small notch to the left of the large index mark on the choke housing. If the choke cap setting is one rich, align the notch on the water cover with the first small notch to the right of the large index mark on the choke housing. See the "Carburetor Specifications" chart in this chapter for choke specifications.

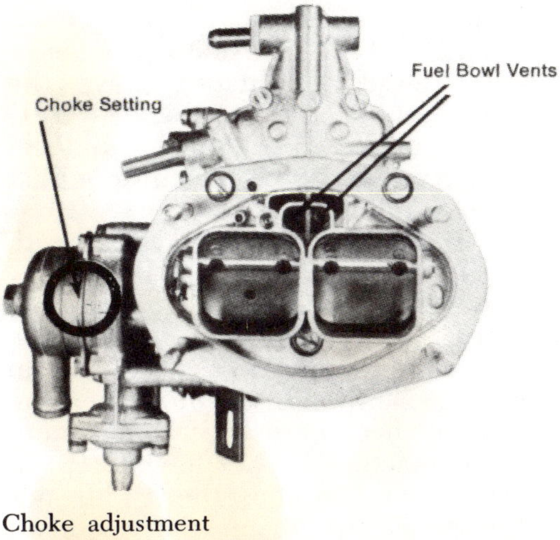

Choke adjustment

Choke Unloader Adjustment

1. Hold the carburetor throttle lever in the wide open position.

2. Insert a 9/32 in. drill bit (0.282 in.) into the air horn of the carburetor.

3. Apply light pressure to the choke plate to remove all slack.

4. With the drill bit against the carburetor wall, the bottom of the choke plate should just contact the drill. If it does not, bend the tab on the fast idle lever where it contacts the fast idle cam to correct it.

AUTOMATIC CHOKE (ELECTRIC)—
1975–76

Linkage Adjustment

With the engine shut off, perform the following operations:

1. Remove air cleaner, verify that vacuum hoses, solenoid and electric choke wire are properly connected and intact. Correct as required.

Function Check

1. Disconnect the stator lead at the choke cap terminal or at lead connector and connect it to one lead of a test lamp.

2. Connect the second test light lead to ground.

3. The light should glow at all times with engine running.

4. If light does not glow, either the alternator is not functioning or the automatic choke wire from the stator is an open circuit and should be repaired as necessary.

5. If the light glows, disconnect the test lead from ground and connect it to the choke lead connector.

6. If necessary, warm up engine to normal operating temperature:

a. Verify the engine coolant is flowing through the choke housing. The housing should get hot. If not, check hoses for restriction.

b. The choke unit should operate and the test lamp should glow. If not, the choke unit is defective and should be replaced.

7. If the light glows, an additional electrical check must be performed as outlined below. Remove test lamp.

a. Stop engine and record choke cap setting. Release cooling system pressure and disconnect the water hoses to the automatic choke housing.

b. Adapt the choke tester (LRE-34618) or equivalent to one of the automatic choke hose connections.

c. Cool the choke housing per the choke tester manufacturer's instructions until the bimetal closes the choke plate lightly in the air horn (maintain ¼ throttle opening while using choke tester). If the choke plate is not lightly closed after five minutes, tap plate lightly and continue. If choke plate does not close in 10 minutes, check for binding and correct as required.

d. Check the electrical continuity between the choke cap terminal or lead connector and ground at choke *bimetal* housing with an ohmmeter. (Be sure that the above conditions are met and that adequate connections are made with the ohmmeter leads.)

e. The resistance should be:

2300 cc—1.5–3.5 ohms
2800 cc—0.8–4.0 ohms

If not, the electric choke unit should be replaced. Repeat electric continuity check with new choke cap and correct as required.

8. Reinstall related system components to specifications. (Check coolant level, if required, reset choke cap setting to specifications on engine tune-up decal.)

Automatic Choke 1977

1977 models are equipped with a fully electric choke, there are no coolant connections to the choke housing. For procedures, see the choke procedures under the 2150 carburetor.

Fast Idle Speed Adjustment—1971–74

1. Connect a tachometer to the engine.
2. Depress the throttle lever to open the throttle plates in the carburetor and position the fast idle speed adjusting screw on the second step of the fast idle cam.
3. Start the engine and check the fast idle speed on the tachometer.
4. Fast idle speed should be 1600 rpm for cars with standard transmissions and 1800 rpm for cars with automatic transmissions.

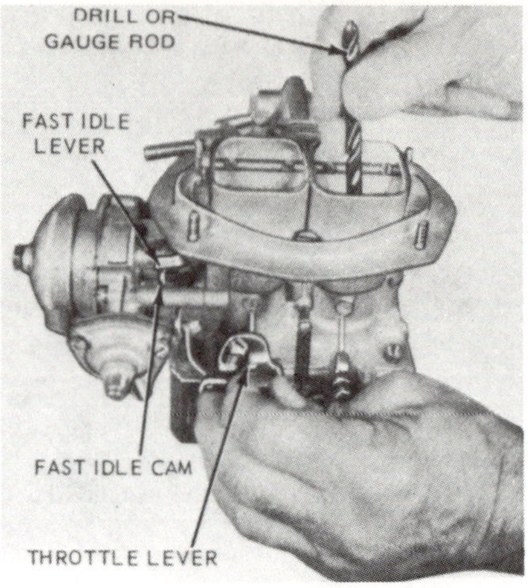

5200 choke unloader adjustment

5. If the speed is incorrect, turn the adjusting screw in or out to adjust.

Fast Idle Speed Adjustment—1975–77

1. Remove the air cleaner assembly and plug the vacuum line at the source of vacuum.
2. Set the parking brake and block the wheels.
3. Connect a tachometer to the engine.
4. Start the engine and warm up to normal operating temperature.
5. Reinstall any distributor vacuum lines that were removed and check the ignition timing.
6. Remove the EGR vacuum line at the valve and plug the line.
7. If applicable, remove the spark delay valve and route the primary distributor advance vacuum signal directly to the primary distributor diaphragm (advance side). If the distributor has a secondary (retard) diaphragm, leave the vacuum connection intact.
8. Disconnect and plug the fuel deceleration valve hose (if so equipped) at the carburetor connection.
9. Air conditioner, if so equipped, must be "off."
10. With the engine running at normal operating temperature and choke plate fully opened (automatic transmission in Park and manual in Neutral) set the throttle so that the fast idle adjustment screw contacts the kickdown step of the choke cam and adjust the fast idle adjusting screw to obtain the specified

rpm according to vehicle specifications.

11. Set the throttle to the high step of the choke cam and allow the engine to run approximately 5 seconds.

12. Rotate the choke cam until the fast idle adjustment screw contacts the kick-down step of the choke cam. After allowing the rpm to stabilize, recheck fast idle rpm and readjust if necessary by repeating Steps 10–12 until the specified fast idle speed is obtained and can be repeated.

13. Stop the engine and install air cleaner and vacuum lines.

5200 CARBURETOR

Carburetor Repairs

ACCELERATOR PUMP DIAPHRAGM REPLACEMENT

1. Remove the air cleaner.
2. Remove the four screws that attach the accelerator pump cover to the carburetor housing.
3. Move the accelerator pump cover away from the carburetor and twist it to disengage the pump lever from the throttle lever while holding your hand under the cover to catch the accelerator pump spring.
4. Remove the diaphragm from the pump cover.
5. Clean any foreign matter from the pump cover or from the face of the carburetor.
6. Engage the accelerator pump lever in the throttle lever, position a new diaphragm and the pump spring on the pump housing and install the pump cover and its attaching screws.
7. Tighten the pump cover attaching screws and install the air cleaner.

NEEDLE VALVE AND SEAT AND/OR FLOAT REPLACEMENT

1. Remove the air cleaner.
2. Disconnect the fuel and deceleration valve hoses from the carburetor.
3. Remove the small clip that attaches the choke rod to the choke plate shaft, and disconnect the rod from the shaft.
4. Remove the screws that attach the upper body of the carburetor to the main body of the carburetor and carefully lift the upper body off the main body. Do not tear the upper body gasket.
5. Turn the carburetor upper body upside down and tap out the float shaft.
6. Lift the float and needle valve from the upper body. Disengage the needle valve clip from the float tab and remove the needle valve from the float.
7. Unscrew the needle valve seat from the upper body.
8. To install new components, screw the needle valve seat into the upper body, using a *new* gasket. Tighten the seat to 15–30 in. lbs.
9. Connect the needle valve clip to the float tab and install the needle valve in its seat and the float in its housing.
10. Install the float shaft.
11. Adjust the float lever. See "Float Level Adjustment" earlier in this chapter.
12. Install the carburetor upper body on the main body and install the attaching screws.
13. Connect the choke rod to the choke plate shaft and install the retaining clip. Connect the fuel and deceleration valve hoses to the carburetor.
14. Install the air cleaner.

POWER VALVE REPLACEMENT

1. Remove the carburetor upper body as described in Steps 1–4 of the preceding float replacement operation.
2. Turn the upper body upside down and remove the three power valve diaphragm attaching screws.
3. Remove the power valve diaphragm from the upper body.
4. Position the power valve on the upper housing and, while holding the diaphragm in a horizontal position, install and tighten the diaphragm attaching screws.
5. Install the carburetor upper body and gasket on the carburetor main body and install and tighten the attaching screws.
6. Connect the choke rod to the choke plate shaft and install the retaining clip.
7. Connect the fuel and deceleration valve hoses to the carburetor and install the air cleaner.

Adjustments—2150 2V Carburetor

FLOAT LEVEL ADJUSTMENT—WET

1. Run the engine to normal operating temperature and stop the engine.

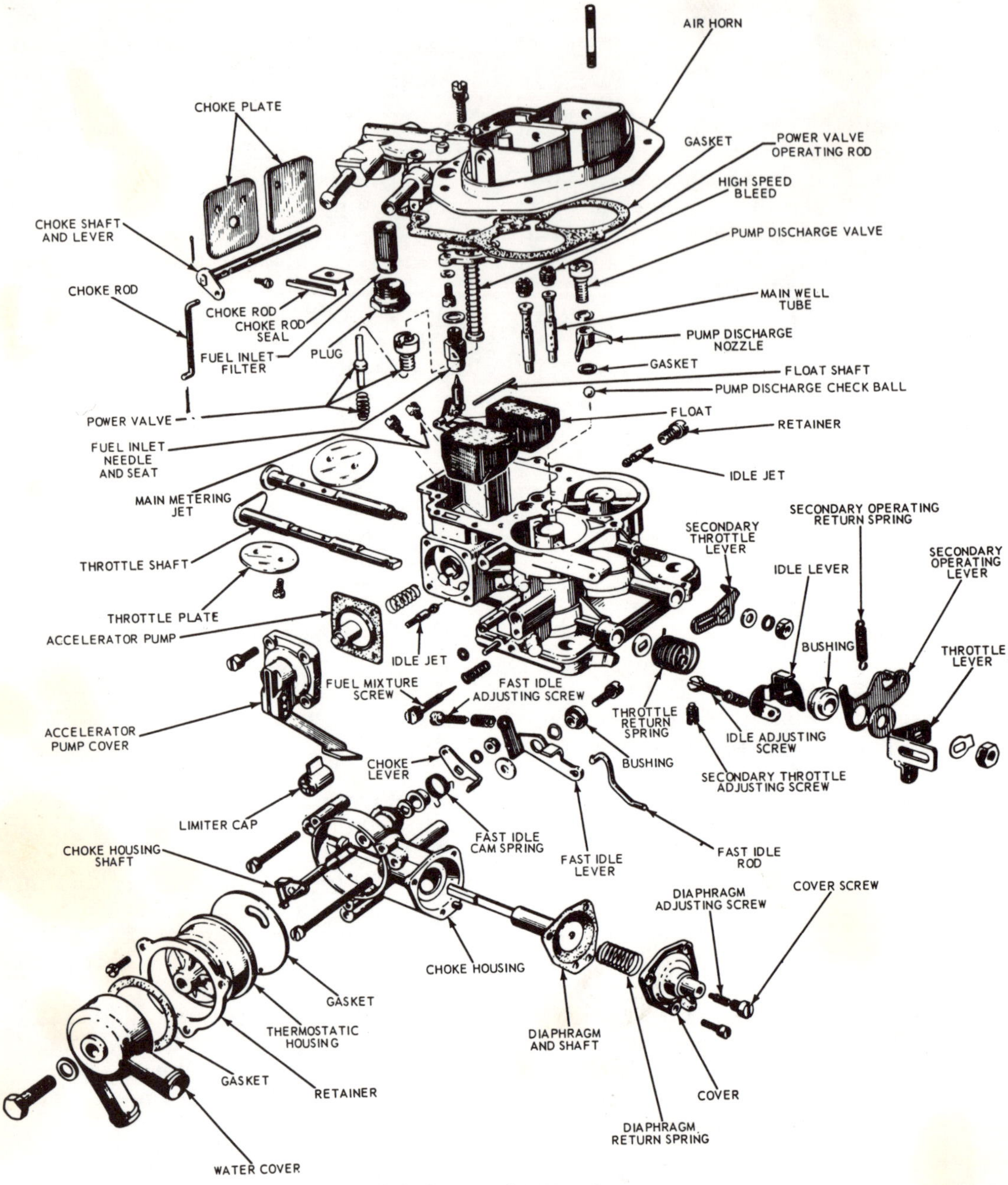

Exploded view of 5200 carburetor

2. Remove the air cleaner.

3. Remove the air horn attaching screws and the carburetor identification tag. Leave the air horn and gasket in position on the carburetor main body and start the engine. Let the engine idle a few minutes then remove the air cleaner stud and the air horn and gasket to provide access to the float assembly.

4. While the engine is idling use a standard depth scale to measure the vertical distance from the top machined surface of the carburetor main body to the level of the fuel in the fuel bowl. The measurement must be made at least a ¼ inch away from any vertical surface to assure an accurate reading. The fuel level should be measured at the point of contact of the float with the fuel. To raise the fuel level bend the flat tab contacting the fuel inlet valve upward and downward to lower it.

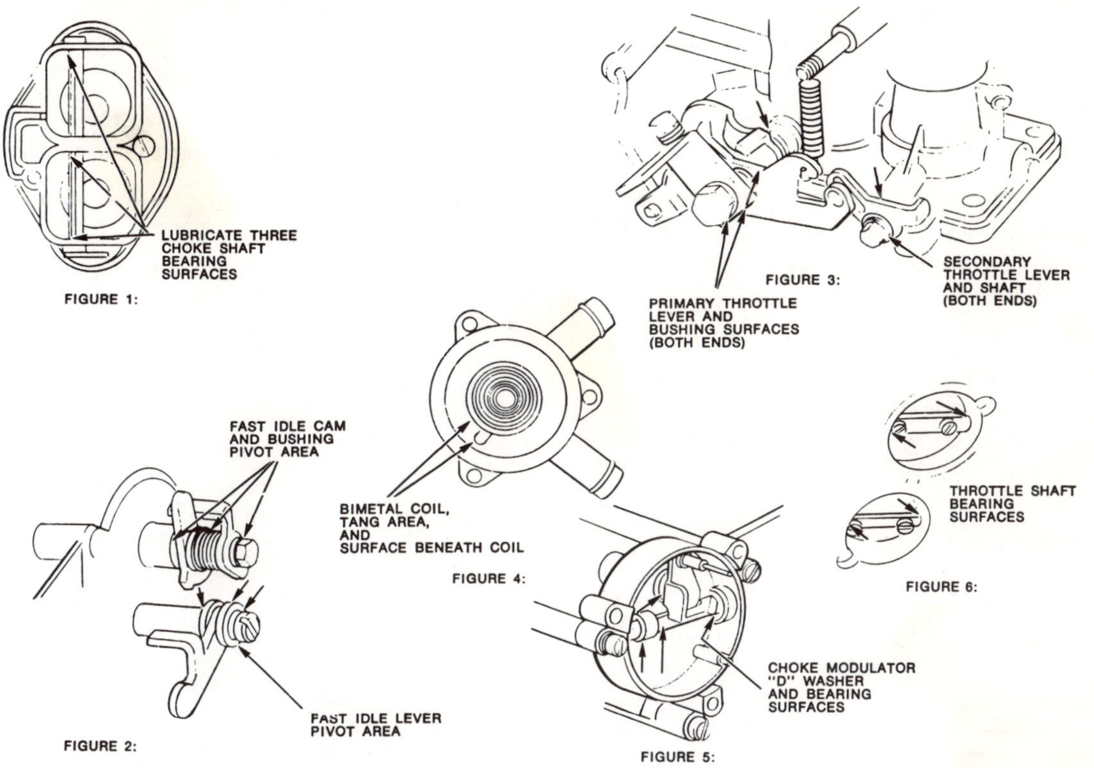

Carburetor lubrication locations

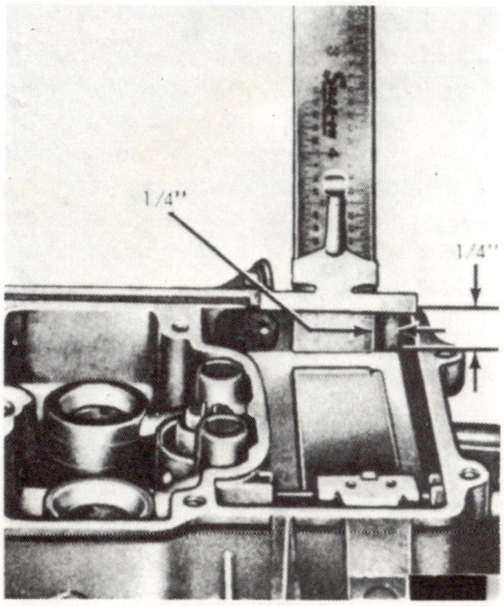

Fuel level (float) adjustment—wet

5. Install a new air horn gasket and install the air horn assembly.
6. Install the air cleaner anchor stud and install the air cleaner. (See "Carburetor Specifications" chart.)

Float Level Adjustment—Dry

The dry float adjustment is a preliminary fuel level adjustment only. The wet float adjustment must be made after the carburetor is mounted on the engine.

1. With the air horn removed, the air float raised and the inlet needle seated, check the distance between the top surface of the main body (gasket removed) and the surface of the float.
   a. Depress the float tab to seat the fuel inlet needle.
   b. Measure near the center of the

Fuel level (float) adjustment—dry

float around ⅛ inch from the free end.

c. Bend the tab on the float to adjust.

ELECTRIC CHOKE

Linkage Check

1. With the engine off, remove the air cleaner and make sure that the hold-down wingnut has not been over torqued and caused the A/C housing to interfere with the choke plate operation.

2. Make sure that the vacuum hoses, solenoid, and electrical choke wires are properly connected.

3. Check throttle system, choke plate, linkage and fast idle cam for freedom of operation.

Electrical Test

1. Disconnect the choke lead wire from the choke cap and connect a jumper wire between the choke cap terminal and the wire terminal. Start the engine.

2. Connect a test light between the connector of the choke lead wire and ground. If the light glows, current is available to the choke cap. The choke cap should be replaced. If the light does not glow, connect the test light between the alternator stator and the choke lead wire. If the light glows, replace the lead wire. If the light does not glow, the problem lies in the engine electrical circuit.

Automatic Choke Adjustment

The automatic choke has an adjustment to control its reaction to engine temperature.

1. Remove the air cleaner.

2. Remove the heater hose from the bracket (if so equipped).

3. Loosen the thermostatic spring housing clamp retaining screws.

4. Set the spring housing to the specified index mark and tighten the clamp attaching screws.

Automatic choke thermostatic spring housing adjustment

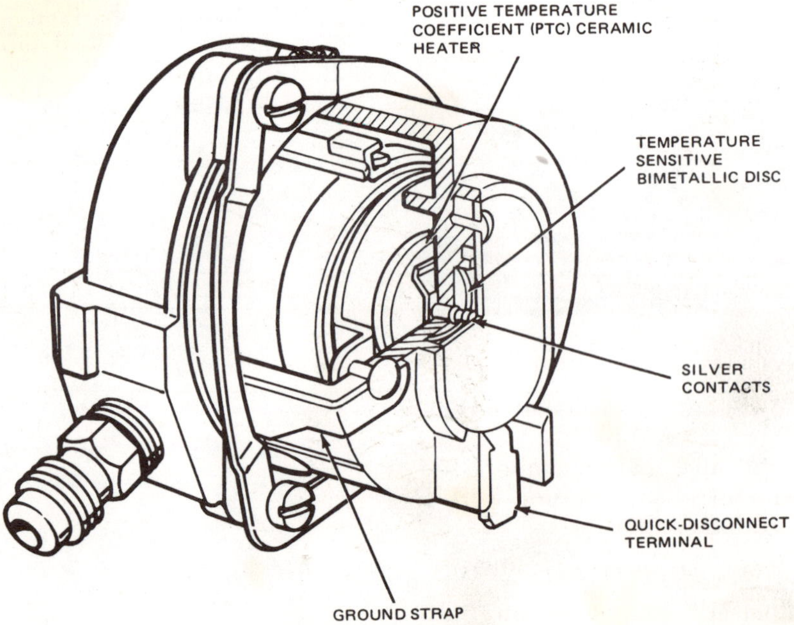

Electric assist choke

5. Replace the heater hose and air cleaner assembly.

Choke Plate Pulldown and Fast Idle Cam

The Model 2150 2V carburetor is equipped with a choke pulldown diaphragm assembly. Vacuum is metered to the diaphragm through internal passages in the carburetor, through a connecting external tube. As the vacuum bleeds through the orifices in the carburetor, the choke diaphragm pulls the choke plate to the pulldown position.

Choke Pulldown Check

1. Set the throttle on the fast idle cam top step.
2. Note the index position of the choke bimetallic cap. Loosen the retaining screws and rotate the cap 90 degrees in the rich (closing) direction.
3. Manually force the pulldown control diaphragm link in the direction of the applied vacuum or apply vacuum to the external vacuum tube to activate the pulldown motor.
4. Measure the vertical hard gauge clearance between the choke plate and the center of the carburetor air horn wall nearest the fuel bowl. Adjust the choke plate pulldown to specification by adjusting the diaphragm stop on the end of the choke pulldown diaphragm.
5. Set the choke bimetallic cap to specification.

Choke Pulldown Diaphragm Assembly Removal and Installation

1. Remove the air cleaner.
2. Disconnect the choke pulldown link by removing the rod retainer and pulling the rod out of the diaphragm link slot.
3. Remove the two (2) attaching screws from the bracket, disconnect the vacuum supply tube and remove the pulldown diaphragm.
4. Position the choke pulldown diaphragm mounting bracket against the main body casting and install the two (2) attaching screws.
5. Connect the vacuum supply tube to

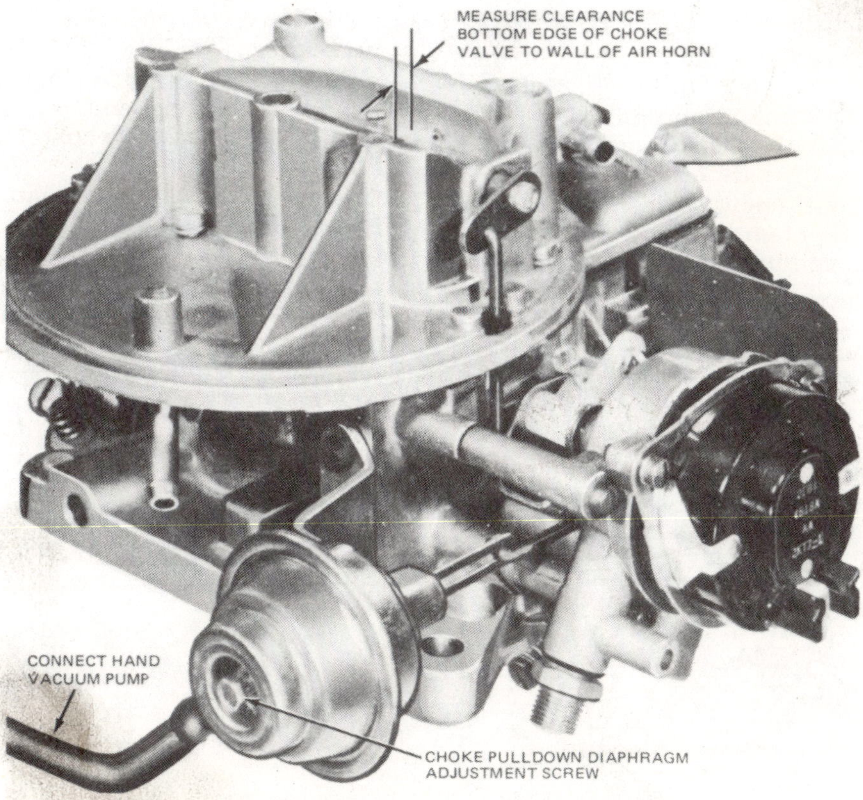

Adjusting choke plate pulldown

Choke pulldown diaphragm assembly

the correct vacuum base tube connection.

6. Insert the choke pulldown control rod through the slot in the diaphragm link and install the retainer clip over the end of the rod, in the slot.

7. Perform the automatic choke pulldown and fast idle cam adjustments as described in this chapter.

8. Install the air cleaner assembly.

Fast Idle Speed Adjustment

1. Remove the EGR vacuum line and air cleaner and plug both vacuum lines.

2. Check the ignition timing.

3. Place the transmission in Neutral and engage the parking brake.

4. Start the engine and bring to normal operation temperature.

5. Remove the spark delay valve (if so equipped) and route part throttle vacuum signal directly to advance side of distributor. If the distributor is a dual diaphragm model, leave the manifold vacuum line connected to the retard side of the distributor.

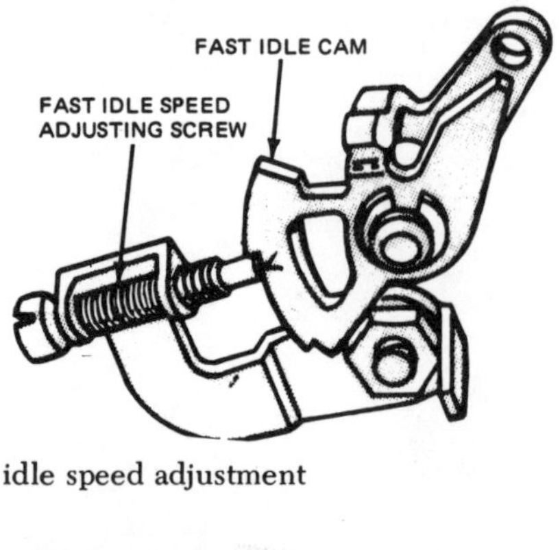

Fast idle speed adjustment

6. Set the throttle to the kickdown step on the choke cam and make sure the adjusting screw is against the shoulder of the kickdown step.

7. Adjust the rpm to specifications.

Repairs—2150 2V Carburetor

Accelerator Pump Diaphragm Removal and Installation

1. Remove the carburetor air horn to main body gasket.

   a. Remove the air cleaner and the air cleaner anchor screw.

   b. Disconnect the choke air tube at the carburetor.

   c. Remove the automatic choke plate operating rod that connects to the lever retainer.

   d. Remove the air horn attaching screws and washers and remove the air horn gasket.

2. Remove the accelerating pump operating rod retainer.

   a. Lift upward on the portion of the clip that snaps over the shaft and then disconnect the rod.

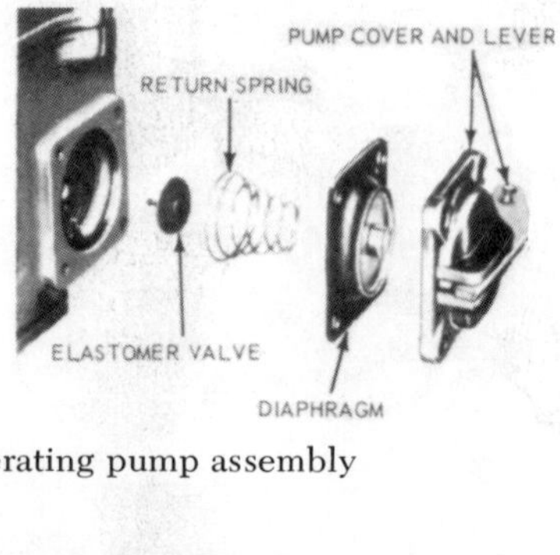

Accelerating pump assembly

b. Remove the pump cover diaphragm assembly and spring.

3. Position the new accelerating pump diaphragm assembly to the cover and place the cover and diaphragm assembly into position on the return spring and main body.

NOTE: *The large end of the spring must face the Elastomer valve. Install the cover screws finger tight. Push the accelerating pump plunger the full length of travel and tighten the cover screws.*

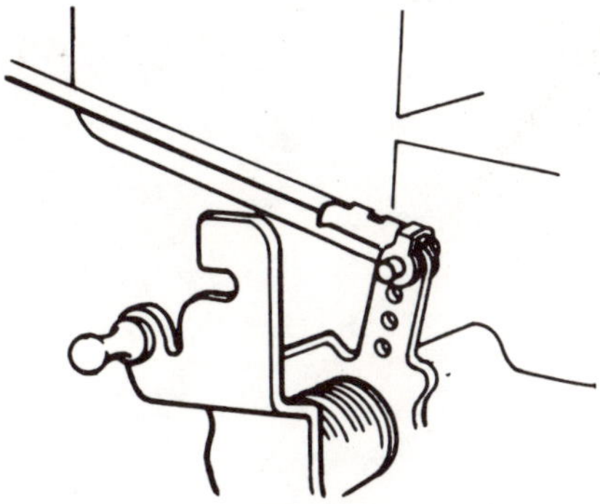

Accelerating pump stroke adjustment

4. Position the accelerating pump operating rod in the hole in the pump operating arm.

5. Adjust the accelerating pump stroke to specification by installing the pump rod in the proper hole in the overtravel lever. Position the rod retainer in the proper hole and insert the end of the rod through the hole in the retainer. Snap the end of the retainer over the rod.

6. Install the carburetor air horn and gasket.

a. Position the air horn on the main body and gasket so that the choke plate operating rod fits into the opening in the choke housing lever.

b. Install the choke plate rod retainer.

c. Install the air horn.

7. Connect the automatic choke clean air tube to the carburetor.

8. Install the air cleaner.

Float Needle Valve and Seat, Inlet Screen, or Main Jets Removal and Installation

1. Remove the air horn-to-main body gasket.

a. Remove the air cleaner and air cleaner anchor screw.

b. Disconnect the choke air tube at the carburetor.

c. Remove the automatic choke plate operating rod that connects to the lever retainer.

d. Remove the air horn attaching screws and washers and remove the air cleaner.

2. Pry the float shaft retainer from the fuel inlet seat with a screwdriver. Remove the float, float shaft retainer and fuel inlet needle assembly.

3. If required, remove the fuel inlet needle seat, filter screen, baffle and main jets with a jet wrench.

4. If removed, install the fuel inlet filter in the inlet valve seat bore. Install the valve seat, baffle and gasket. Install the inlet needle valve.

5. Slide the float shaft into the float lever and position the float shaft retainer on the float shaft.

6. Insert the float assembly into the fuel bowl and hook the float lever tab under the fuel inlet needle clip. Insert the float shaft into the guides at the sides of the fuel bowl.

7. Use a screwdriver and position the float shaft retainer on the groove of the fuel inlet needle seat.

8. Perform the dry float level adjustment described earlier in this chapter.

9. Install the air horn and gasket and related parts.

a. Position the air horn on the main body and gasket so that the choke plate operating rod fits into the opening in the choke housing lever.

b. Install the choke plate rod retainer.

c. Install the air horn.

d. Connect the automatic choke clean air tube to the carburetor.

e. Install the air cleaner.

10. Perform the wet float level adjustment described earlier in this chapter.

11. Adjust the idle fuel mixture and idle speed.

Carburetor Lubrication

Many pivot points on the carburetor are lubricated with a molybdenum—disulfide-base lubricant during manufacturing. This lubrication should

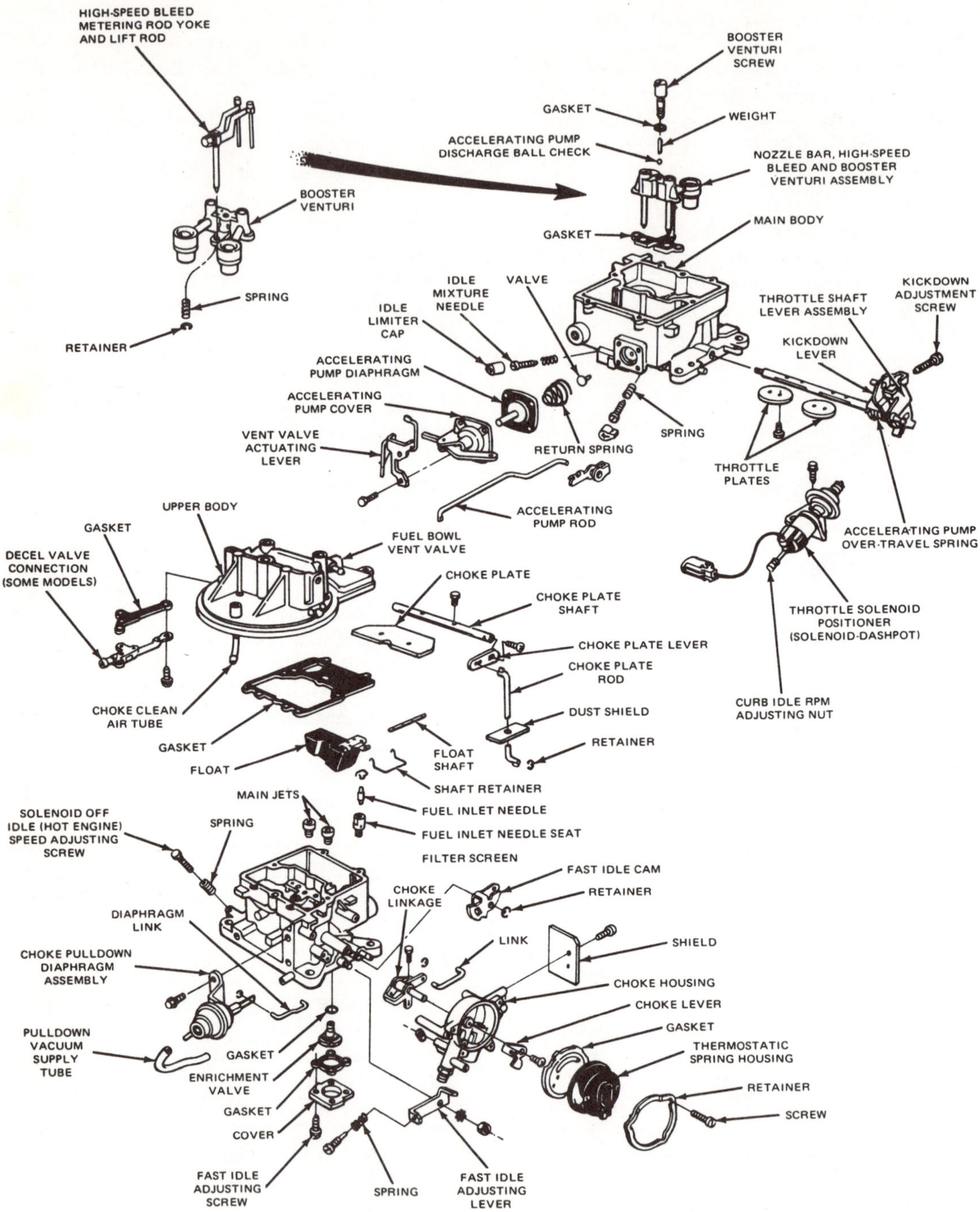

Exploded view of 2150 carburetor

be replenished according to the following schedule: every 12,000 miles, whenever solvent has been applied to the carburetor, or whenever a prelubricated part has been replaced. Molybdenum disulfide grease dries on application but retains its friction-resistant characteristics while also combatting contamination from dust, moisture, or fuel vapor. Only this type of lubricant should be used. *Never use conventional oil, or grease.*

The following areas should be lubricated: choke plate shaft (where it passes through the upper carburetor body), both ends of the choke rod, fast idle lever and choke lever pivot points, primary and secondary throttle levers, choke thermostatic coil spring end tang and the area on the housing behind the spring, choke housing shaft, and primary and secondary throttle shafts (where they pass through the base of the carburetor).

2700 CARBURETOR

The Motorcraft 2700 carburetor was introduced in 1977 for use on California 2800 cc engines. This carburetor is a variable venturi model which means that it is capable of changing the area of the venturi in relation to engine demand.

Adjustment

INTERNAL VENT

1. Set the emergency brake and let the engine warm up.
2. Set the idle speed to specifications.
3. Remove the air cleaner lid and place a .010 feeler gauge between the accelerator pump stem and the pump operating link.
4. Turn the nylon adjusting nut attached to the link to obtain the proper clearance.

NOTE: *This adjustment must be done whenever the idle speed is set.*

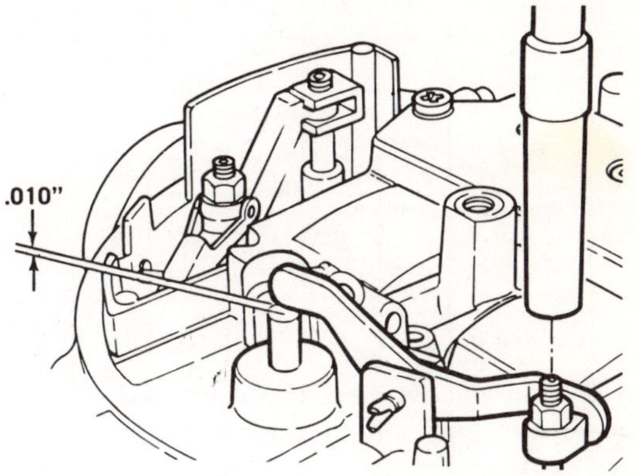

Internal vent adjustment, variable venturi carburetor

Carburetor Specifications

Engine								Fast Idle		
Cyl	Cu in.	Trans	Carb bbl	Carb Make & Type	Carb Part no.	Choke Setting	Choke Plate Pulldown (in.)	Cam Step	Spd (rpm)	Float Level (in.)
					1971					
4	97.6	Std	1	Autolite 1250	721F-9510-KFA	Index	.100	1st	2100	—
4	122.0	Std	2	Motorcraft 5200	D12F-9510-BA	Index	.236	2nd	1800	.420
4	122.0	Std	2	Motorcraft 5200	D12F-9510-EA	1 Rich	.236	2nd	1800	.420
4	122.0	Auto	2	Motorcraft 5200	D12F-9510-AA	Index	.236	2nd	1800	.420
4	122.0	Auto	2	Motorcraft 5200	D12F-9510-DA	1 Rich	.236	2nd	1800	.420
4	122.0	Std①	2	Motorcraft 5200	D12F-9510-CA	Index	.236	2nd	1800	.420
4	122.0	Auto①	2	Motorcraft 5200	D12F-9510-FA	1 Rich	.236	2nd	1800	.420
					1972					
4	97.6	Std	1	Motorcraft 1250	721F-9510-KFA, KFB	Index	.075	2nd	1700	1.20②
4	122.0	Auto	2	Motorcraft 5200	D22F-9510-AB	1 Lean	.236	2nd	1800	.420②
4	122.0	Auto	2	Motorcraft 5200	D22F-9510-AC	1 Lean	.236	2nd	1800	.420②
4	122.0	Auto①	2	Motorcraft 5200	D22F-9510-CB	1 Lean	.236	2nd	1800	.420②
4	122.0	Auto①	2	Motorcraft 5200	D22F-9510-AC	1 Lean	.236	2nd	1800	.420②
4	122.0	Std	2	Motorcraft 5200	D22F-9510-BB	1 Lean	.236	2nd	1600	.420②

4	122.0	Std	2	Motorcraft 5200	D22F-9510-BC	1 Lean	.236	2nd	1800	.420②
4	122.0	Std①	2	Motorcraft 5200	D22F-9510-DB	1 Lean	.236	2nd	1600	.420②
4	122.0	Std①	2	Motorcraft 5200	D22F-9510-BC	1 Lean	.236	2nd	1800	.420②
4	122.0	Auto (Calif.)	2	Motorcraft 5200	D22F-9510-EA	Index	.236	2nd	1800	.420②
4	122.0	Auto (Calif.)	2	Motorcraft 5200	D22F-9510-EB	Index	.236	2nd	1800	.420②
4	122.0	Auto (Calif.)①	2	Motorcraft 5200	D22F-9510-GA	Index	.236	2nd	1800	.420②
4	122.0	Auto (Calif)①	2	Motorcraft 5200	D22F-9510-EB	Index	.236	2nd	1800	.420②
					1973					
4	97.6	Std	1	Motorcraft 1250	K3LF-9510-KEA	Index	.075	Center	1700	1.20
4	122.0	Auto	2	Motorcraft 5200	D32F-9510-BB	Index	.158	Center	1800	.420
4	122.0	Std	2	Motorcraft 5200	D3ZF-9510-AB	Index	.158	Center	1600	.420
					1974					
4	2000	Man	2	Motorcraft 5200	D42TF-9510-EA	Index	.255	2nd	*	0.46
4	2000	Auto	2	Motorcraft 5200	D42F-9510-GA	Index	.236	2nd	*	0.46
4	2300	Man	2	Motorcraft 5200	D42E-9510-BA	1 Rich	.280	2nd	1500	0.46
4	2300	Auto	2	Motorcraft 5200	D42E-9510-AA	Index	.280	2nd	1500	0.46

Carburetor Specifications (cont.)

Engine Cyl	Engine Cu in.	Trans	Carb bbl	Carb Make & Type	Carb Part no.	Choke Setting	Choke Plate Pulldown (in.)	Fast Idle Cam Step	Fast Idle Spd (rpm)	Float Level (in.)
					1975					
4	2300	Man	2	Motorcraft 5200	D52E-DB, CA, BA, AA, CB, EA, AB, FA	1 Lean	0.198 @ 75°	Kick-down③	1800	0.46
6	2800	Auto	2	Motorcraft 2150	D5ZE-BC, DC, DF	2 Rich	0.145	Kick-down③	1600	3/8 in. Dry④
					1976					
4	2300	Auto (49 S)	2	Motorcraft 5200	D6EE-BA	1 Lean	0.288 @ 75°	Kick-down③	2000	0.46
4	2300	Man (Calif.)	2	Motorcraft 5200	D6EE-CA	1 Lean	0.278 @ 75°	Kick-down③	1500	0.46
4	2300	Auto (Calif.)	2	Motorcraft 5200	D6EE-DA	1 Lean	0.238 @ 75°	Kick-down③	1800	0.46
4	2300	Man (49 S)	2	Motorcraft 5200	D6EE-DA	1 Lean	0.275 @ 75°	Kick-down③	1500	0.46
6	2800	Auto (49 S)	2	Motorcraft 2150	D5ZE-BE, D6ZE-BA	3 Rich	0.145	Kick-down③	1600	3/8 in. Dry④
6	2800	Auto (Calif.)	2	Motorcraft 2150	D6ZE-DA	3 Rich	0.145	Kick-down③	1600	3/8 in. Dry④
					1977					
4	2300	Man (49 S)	2	Motorcraft 5200	D6EE-AA	—	—	—	—	—

4	2300	Man (Calif.)	2	Motorcraft 5200	D6EE-CA	—	—	—	—	—
6	2800	Auto (49 S)	2	Motorcraft 5200	D6EE-BA	—	—	—	—	—
6	2800	Auto (Calif.)	2	Motorcraft 5200	D6EE-AA	—	—	—	—	—
6	2800	Auto (49 S) No A/C	2	Motorcraft 2150	D7YE-AA	—	—	—	—	—
6	2800	Auto (49 S) A/C	2	Motorcraft 2150	D7YE-EA	—	—	—	—	—
6	2800	Auto (Calif.)	VV	Motorcraft 2700	D7ZE-BD	—	—	—	—	—

Engine CID	*Decal Code No.*	*Fast Idle RPM*
2000 cc	615	1600
2000 cc	722	1800

① With air conditioning
② Dry setting
③ Highest step of cam resting against stop
④ ¾ in. wet
49 S Forty Nine States version
VV Variable Venturi

Chapter 5

Chassis Electrical

Understanding and Troubleshooting Electrical Systems

For any electrical system to operate, it must make a complete circuit. This simply means that the power flow from the battery must make a complete circle. When an electrical component is operating, power flows from the battery to the component, passes through the component causing it to perform its function (lighting a light bulb), and then returns to the battery through the ground of the circuit. This ground is usually (but not always) the metal part of the car on which the electrical component is mounted.

Perhaps the easiest way to visualize this is to think of connecting a light bulb with two wires attached to it to your car battery. The battery in your car has two posts (negative and positive). If one of the two wires attached to the light bulb was attached to the negative post of the battery and the other wire was attached to the positive post of the battery, you

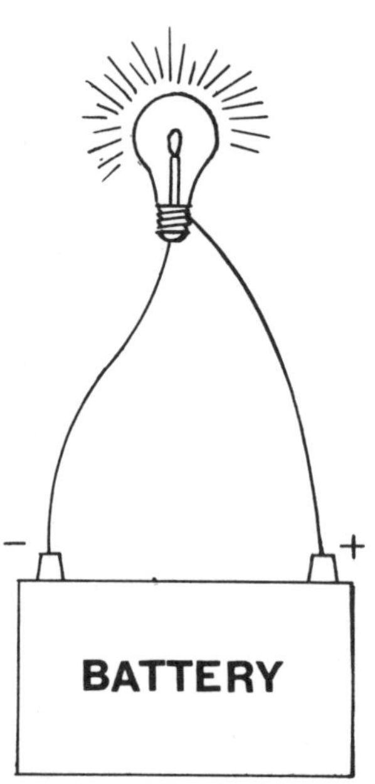

A complete circuit

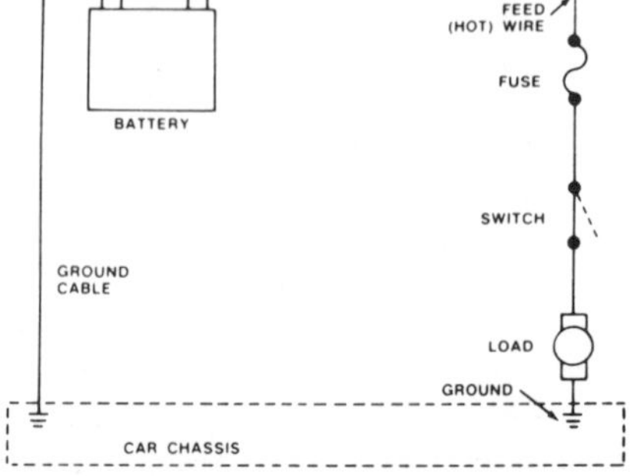

A simple automotive circuit

would have a complete circuit. Current from the battery would flow out one post, through the wire attached to it and then to the light bulb, where it would pass through causing it to light. It would then leave the light bulb, travel through the other wire, and return to the other post of the battery.

The normal automative circuit differs from this simple example in two ways. First, instead of having a return wire from the bulb to the battery, the light bulb returns the current to the battery through the chassis of the vehicle. Since the negative battery cable is attached to the chassis and the chassis is made of electrically conductive metal, the chassis of the vehicle can serve as a ground wire to complete the circuit. Secondly, most automotive circuits contain switches to turn components on and off as required.

There are many types of switches, but the most common simply serves to prevent the passage of current when it is turned off. Since the switch is a part of the circle necessary for a complete circuit, it operates to leave an opening in the circuit, and thus an incomplete or open circuit, when it is turned off.

Some electrical components which require a large amount of current to operate also have a relay in their circuit. Since these circuits carry a large amount of current, the thickness of the wire in the circuit (gauge size) is also greater. If this large wire were connected from the component to the control switch on the instrument panel, and then back to the component, a voltage drop would occur in the circuit. To prevent this potential drop in voltage, an electromagnetic switch (relay) is used. The large wires in the circuit are connected from the car battery to one side of the relay, and from the opposite side of the relay to the component. The relay is normally open, preventing current from passing through the circuit. An additional, smaller, wire is connected from the relay to the control switch for the circuit. When the control switch is turned on, it grounds the smaller wire from the relay and completes the circuit. This closes the relay and allows current to flow from the battery to the component. The horn, headlight, and starter circuits are three which use relays.

Did you ever notice how your instrument panel lights get brighter the faster your car goes? This happens because your alternator (which supplies the battery) puts out more current at speeds above idle. This is normal. However, it is possible for larger surges of current to pass through the electrical system of your car. If this surge of current were to reach an electrical component, it could burn it out. To prevent this from happening, fuses are connected into the current supply wires of most of the major electrical systems of your car. The fuse serves to head off the surge at the pass. When an electrical current of excessive power passes through the component's fuse, the fuse blows out and breaks the circuit, saving it from destruction.

The fuse also protects the component from damage if the power supply wire to the component is grounded before the current reaches the component.

Let us here interject another rule to the complete circle circuit. *Every complete circuit from a power source must include a component which is using the power from the power source.* If you were to disconnect the light bulb (from the previous example of a light bulb being connected to the battery by two wires) from the wires and touch the two wires together (please take my word for this; don't try it), the result would be shocking. You probably haven't seen so many sparks since the Fourth of July. A similar thing happens (on a smaller scale) when the power supply wire to a component or the electrical component itself becomes grounded before the normal ground connection for the circuit. To prevent damage to the system, the fuse for the circuit blows to interrupt the circuit—protecting the components from damage. Because grounding a wire from a power source makes a complete circuit—less the required component to use the power—this phenomenon is called a short circuit. The most common causes of short circuits are: the rubber insulation on a wire breaking or rubbing through to expose the current carrying core of the wire to a metal part of the car, or a shorted switch.

Some electrical systems on the car are protected by a circuit breaker which is, basically, a self-repairing fuse. When either of the above-described events takes place in a system which is protected by a circuit breaker, the circuit breaker opens the circuit the same way a fuse does. However, when either the short is removed from the circuit or the surge subsides, the circuit breaker resets itself and does not have to be replaced as a fuse does.

The final protective device in the chassis electrical system is a fuse link. A fuse link is a wire that acts as a fuse. It is connected between the starter relay and the main wiring harness for the car. This connection is under the hood, very near a similar fuse link which protects the engine electrical system. Since the fuse link protects all the chassis electrical components, it is the probable cause of trouble when none of the electrical components function, unless the battery is disconnected or dead. The procedure for replacing the fuse link is described in chapter three, in the "Engine Electrical" section.

Electrical problems generally fall into one of three areas:

1. The component that is not functioning is not receiving current.
2. The component itself is not functioning.
3. The component is not properly grounded.

Problems that fall into the first category are by far the most complicated. It is the current supply system to the component which contains all the switches, relays, fuses, etc.

The electrical system can be checked with a test light and a jumper wire. A test light is a device that looks like a pointed screwdriver with a wire attached to it. It has a light bulb in its handle. A jumper wire is a piece of insulated wire with an alligator clip attached to each end. To check the system you must follow the wiring diagrams found in this chapter. A wiring diagram is a road map of the car's electrical system.

If a light bulb is not working, you must follow a systematic plan to determine which of the three causes is the villain.

1. Turn on the switch that controls the inoperable bulb.
2. Disconnect the power supply wire from the bulb.
3. Attach the ground wire on the test light to a good metal ground.
4. Touch the probe end of the test light to the end of the power supply wire that was disconnected from the bulb. If the bulb is receiving current, the test light will go on.

NOTE: *If the bulb is one which works only when the ignition key is turned on (turn signal), make sure the key is turned on.*

If the test light does not go on, then the problem is in the circuit between the battery and the bulb. As mentioned before, this includes all the switches, fuses, and relays in the system. Turn to the wiring diagram and find the bulb on the diagram. Follow the wire that runs back to the battery. The problem is an open circuit between the battery and the bulb. If the fuse is blown and, when replaced, immediately blows again, there is a short circuit in the system which must be located and repaired. If there is a switch in the system, bypass it with a jumper wire. This is done by connecting one end of the jumper wire to the power supply wire into the switch and the other end of the jumper wire to the wire coming out of the switch. Again, consult the wiring diagram. If the test light lights with the jumper wire installed, the switch or whatever was bypassed is defective.

NOTE: *Never substitute the jumper wire for the bulb, as the bulb is the component required to use the power from the power source.*

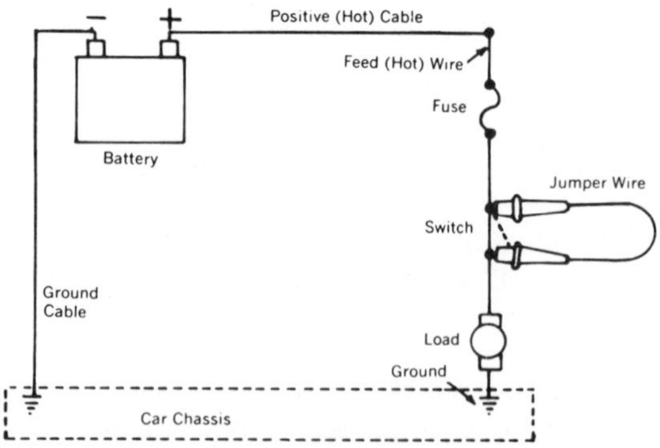

By-passing switch with jumper wire

5. If the bulb in the test light goes on, then the current is getting to the bulb that is not working in the car. This eliminates the first of the three possible causes. Connect the power supply wire

and connect a jumper wire from the bulb to a good metal ground. Do this with the switch which controls the bulb turned on, and also the ignition switch turned on if it is required for the light to work. If the bulb works with the jumper wire installed, then it has a bad ground. This is usually caused by the metal area on which the bulb mounts to the car being coated with some type of foreign matter.

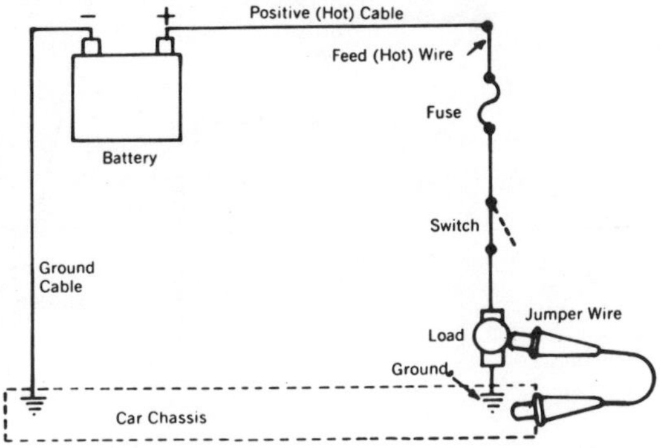

Check for a bad ground

6. If neither test located the source of the trouble, then the light bulb itself is defective.

The above test procedure can be applied to any of the components of the chassis electrical system by substituting the component that is not working for the light bulb. Remember that for any electrical system to work, all connections must be clean and tight.

HEATER–WITHOUT AIR CONDITIONING

The heater operates by bypassing a portion of the hot coolant from the engine through the heater core. Outside air passes through the core and the heater blower motor forces the warmed air into the car.

The heater core is located in the heater housing under the instrument panel. The heater core is like a miniature engine radiator. Coolant is passed through small corrugated fins in the heater core; air passes through the openings between these fins and removes heat from the coolant. The engine thermostat controls the temperature of the coolant that passes through the heater core.

The heater controls consist of a heater fan control, a temperature control, and a heater/defroster control. The heater fan switch is connected to a blower motor resistor which is mounted on the heater housing. The blower motor is also connected to this resistor. The resistor acts to control the amount of current that is supplied to the blower motor. When the fan control switch is moved from "low" to "high," the amount of resistance in the circuit is lowered and the speed of the blower motor increases.

The temperature control lever is connected by a cable to the temperature blend door on the heater housing. When the lever is in the "hot" position, all of the outside air entering the heater housing is routed through the heater core. When the lever is moved toward the "cool" position, a portion of the outside air is allowed to bypass the heater core. The bypassed air then combines with the air coming through the heater core to lower the temperature of the air entering the passenger compartment.

The heater/defroster control lever is connected by a cable to a door on the heater housing which controls the direction of the hot air coming out of the heater housing.

Heater Housing Assembly Removal

1. Drain the cooling system and disconnect the negative battery cable.
2. Disconnect the blower motor ground wire (black) at the engine side of the dash panel.
3. Disconnect the heater hoses at the engine block.
4. Remove the four nuts that attach the heater assembly to the dash, from the engine side of the dash.
5. Working inside the car, remove the glove box.
6. Disconnect the control cables from the heater.
7. Remove the snap-rivet that attaches the forward side of the defroster air duct to the heater assembly. Move the air duct back into the defroster nozzle and disengage it from the tabs on the heater box. Tilt the forward edge of the duct up and forward to disengage it from the nozzle and remove it from the left side of the heater assembly.
8. Remove the heater assembly-to-dash panel support bracket mounting

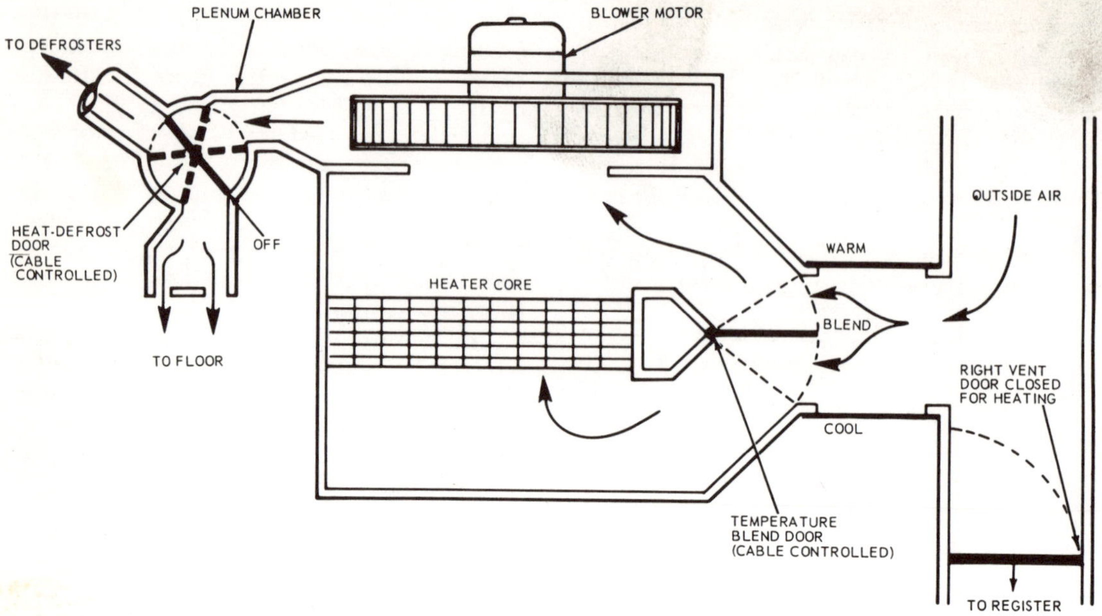

Heater airflow diagram

screw and remove the heater assembly. At the same time, pull the heater hoses through the dash panel. Then, disconnect the hoses from the heater core in the case.

Blower Motor Replacement

1. Remove the heater assembly.
2. Disconnect the blower motor lead wire from the resistor. Remove the four blower motor mounting plate attaching nuts and remove the motor wheel.

Heater Core Replacement

1. Remove the heater assembly.
2. Remove the compression gasket from the cowl air inlet and remove the 11 clips from the case. Separate the case and remove the heater core.

HEATER—WITH AIR CONDITIONING

Blower Motor Removal and Installation

1971–73

1. Disconnect the battery ground cable.
2. Remove the console and radio, if so equipped.
3. Remove the fuse panel retaining screw, separate the panel and electrical connector and remove both from the support bracket.
4. Remove the support bracket and position out of the way.
5. Remove the dash panel brace and set the fuse panel out of the way.
6. Disconnect all wiring and the two vacuum hoses.
7. Remove the cover plate from the A/C defrost plenum by removing the two retaining screws.
8. Remove the blower housing mounting stud nut and lock plate.
9. Turn the blower housing clockwise to unlock from the evaporator housing, and remove the blower housing. On 1972 models, remove the dash to steering column brace.
10. Cut the gaskets around the outlets at the break line.
11. Remove seven clips, and separate the left and right halves of the blower housing.
12. Remove the three blower motor housing plate retaining nuts, and remove the motor and wheel assembly.
13. Position the motor wheel assembly in the housing, and tighten the mounting plate retaining nuts.
14. Install new gaskets, and clip the two halves together, making sure the A/C heat door is positioned properly.
15. Rotate the blower motor counterclockwise to lock into the evaporator housing, and tighten the nut.

16. Reconnect the wiring and vacuum hoses.

17. On 1972 models, reinstall the fuse panel and dash panel brace. Reconnect the fuse panel electrical connector and retaining screw.

18. Attach the air distributor duct to the blower housing.

19. Attach the A/C defrost plenum with the lower cover plate and tighten retaining screws.

20. Reinstall the console and radio, and reconnect the battery ground cable.

1974 AND LATER

1. Remove the glove box.
2. Disconnect the blower motor lead and ground wires.
3. Remove the four retaining screws and remove the blower motor from the scroll portion of the evaporator.
4. Position blower motor in evaporator.
5. Insert and tighten the four retaining screws.
6. Connect the motor lead and ground wires.
7. Replace the glove box.

INSTRUMENT CLUSTER REMOVAL

1. Disconnect the negative battery cable. Reach under the dash and disconnect the speedometer cable by pressing on the flat surface of the connector while pulling the cable away from the speedometer head.
2. Remove the two screws that attach the top of the instrument cluster to the dash.
3. Slide the top of the instrument cluster forward and lift it up to disengage the mounting pins in the bottom of the instrument cluster from the brackets in the dash.
4. Reach inside the instrument cluster opening and disengage the multiple connector plug from the instrument cluster printed circuit by pushing in on the clips on the side of the connector and pulling it away from the cluster.
5. Remove the cluster from the dash.

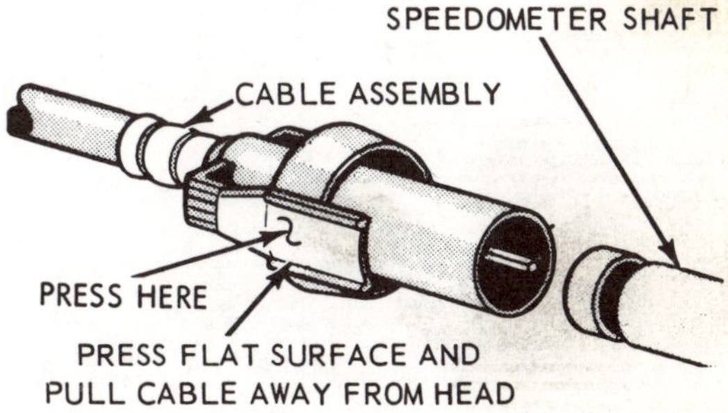

Disconnecting speedometer cable

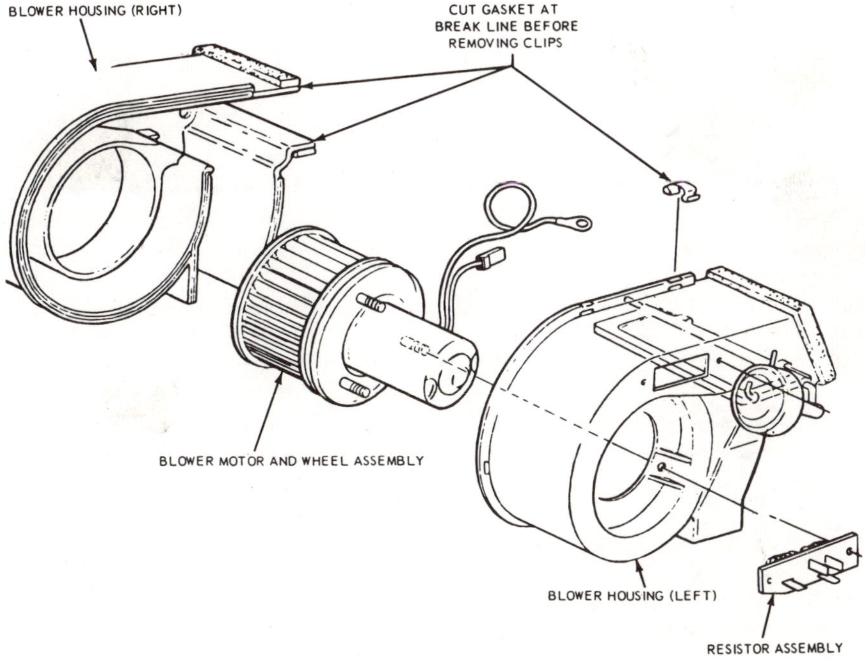

Blower motor removal

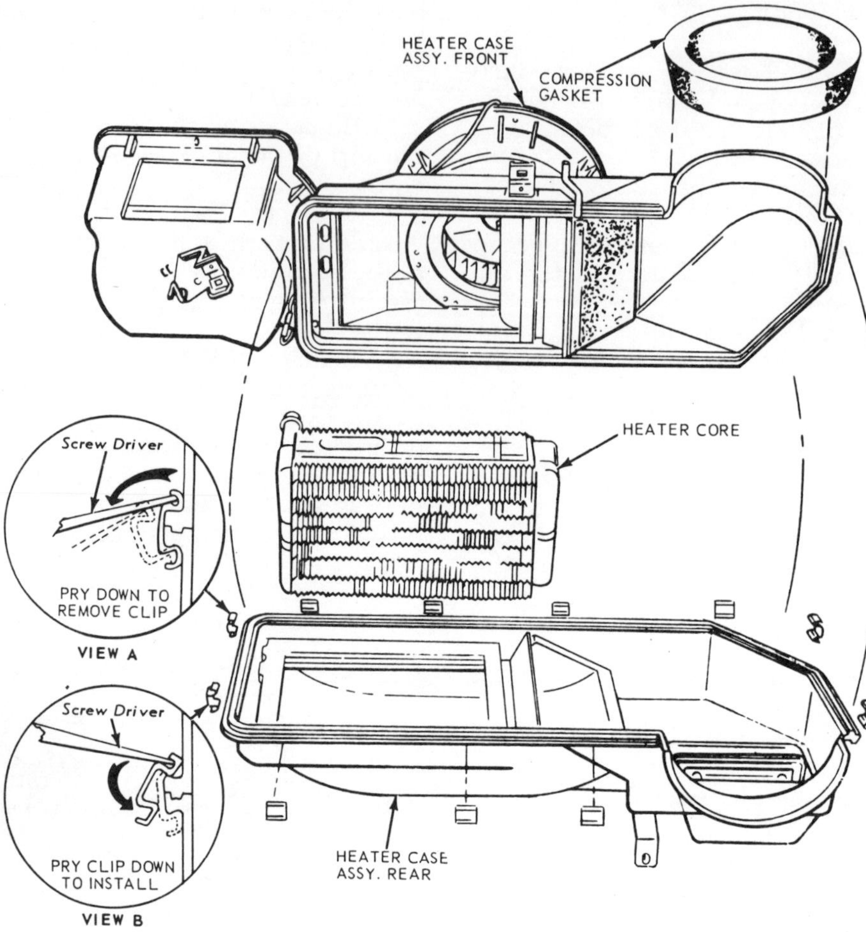

Heater core removal

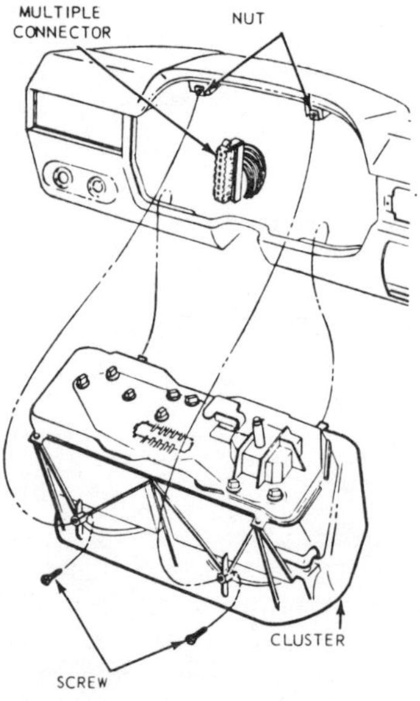

Removing instrument cluster

6. Reverse the above procedure to install.

HEADLIGHT SWITCH REMOVAL

1. Disconnect the battery ground cable.
2. Remove the instrument cluster.
3. Remove the headlight switch control knob, shaft, and retaining nut.
4. Disconnect the multiple connector from the switch and remove the switch from the instrument cluster opening.
5. Reverse the above procedure to install.

RADIO REMOVAL

1. Disconnect the negative battery cable.
2. Remove the bolt that mounts the radio to the radio support.

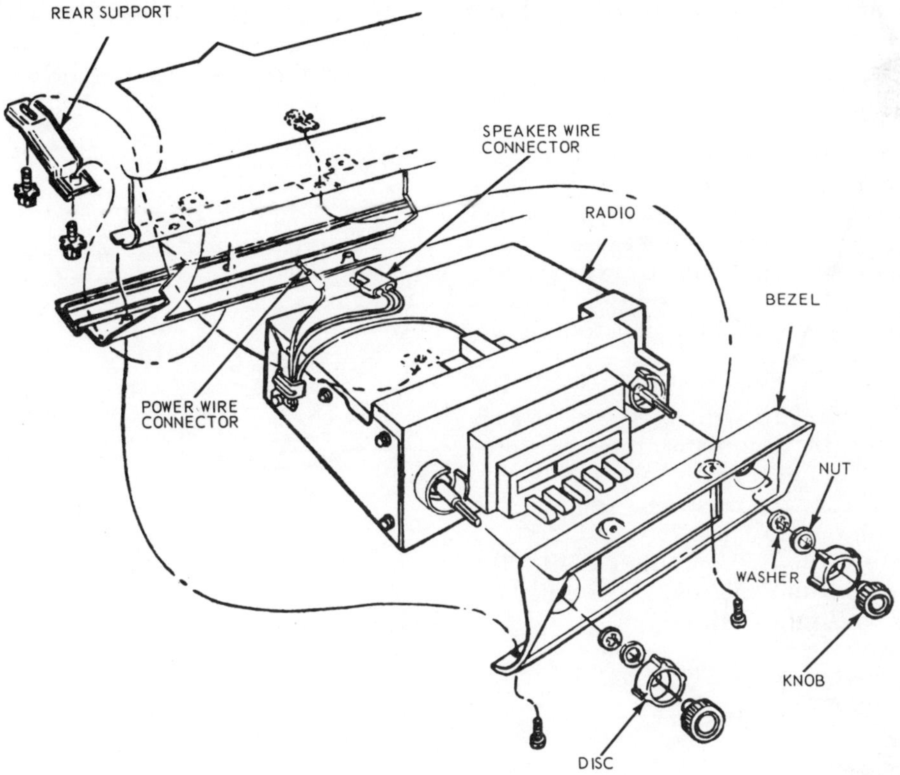

Radio removal

3. Remove the four screws attaching the radio cover bezel to the instrument panel.

4. Pull the radio from the instrument panel and disconnect the radio lead wires.

5. Remove the radio from the car.

6. Reverse the above procedure to install.

IGNITION SWITCH

The ignition switch is mounted on the steering column and is connected to the ignition lock cylinder by an actuating rod.

Removal and Installation

1. Disconnect the negative battery cable.

2. To gain access to the switch, remove the steering column shroud, and disconnect and lower the steering column from the brake support bracket.

3. Disconnect the switch wiring at the multiple connector.

4. Remove the two nuts that retain the ignition switch to the steering column.

5. Remove the pin that connects the switch plunger to the actuating rod and remove the switch.

6. When installing the ignition switch, both the switch and the ignition lock must be in the "lock" position. The manual parts can be held in place by turning the ignition lock cylinder to the "lock" position with the transmission in Park (automatic transmission) or Reverse (standard transmission). To hold the switch in the "lock" position, insert a pin in the hole on the top of the switch, after manually moving the switch to the lock position. The lock position is one detent back from the fully extended position.

7. Position the hole in the end of the switch plunger to the hole in the actuator and install the connecting pin.

8. Position the ignition switch on the steering column and install, but do not tighten, the retaining nuts.

9. Move the switch up and down on the steering column to find the midpoint of the actuating rod lash, then tighten the switch retaining nuts.

10. Remove the locking pin from the

switch and install the steering column and shroud.

IGNITION LOCK CYLINDER REPLACEMENT

NOTE: *See Chapter 10 for door lock cylinder replacement.*

1. Disconnect the negative battery cable.
2. Remove the steering wheel. See Chapter 8 for the procedure. Insert a stiff wire into the hole located in the lock cylinder housing.
3. Place the gear shift lever in Reverse on standard shift cars and in Park on cars with automatic transmissions, and turn the ignition key on.
4. Depress the wire and remove the lock cylinder and wire.
5. Insert the new cylinder into the housing and turn to "off." This will lock the cylinder into position.
6. Reinstall the steering wheel and pad.
7. Connect the negative battery cable.

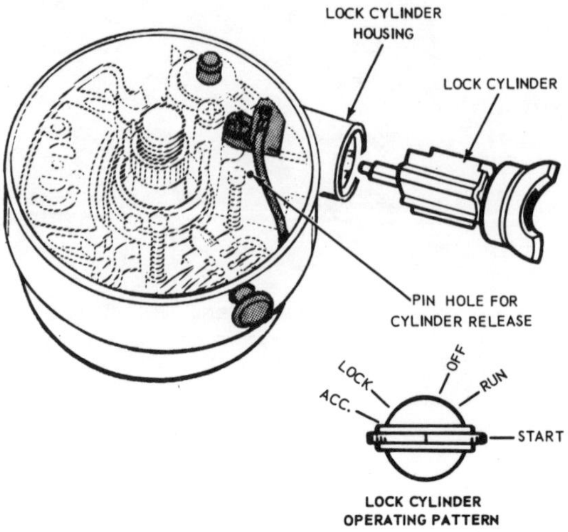

Lock cylinder removal

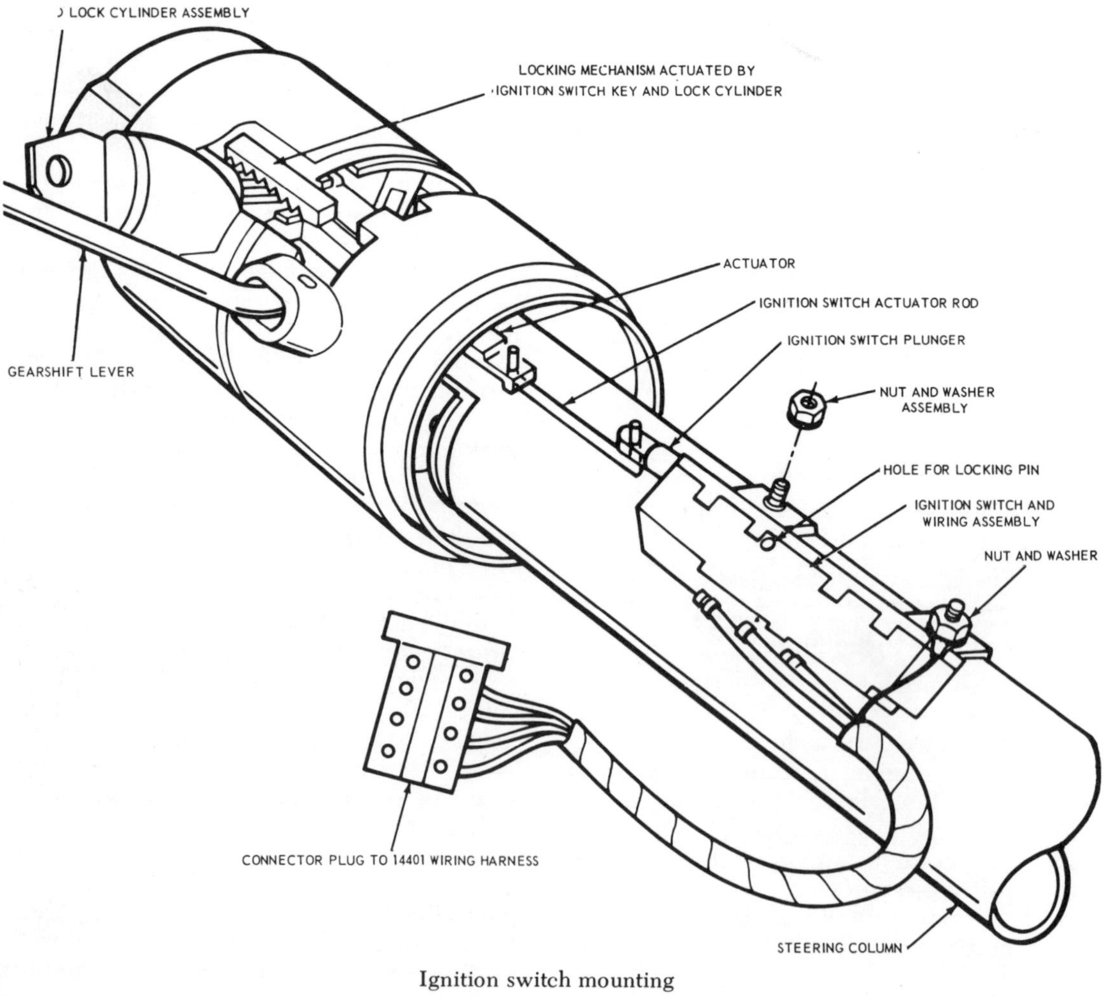

Ignition switch mounting

STOP LIGHT SWITCH REPLACEMENT

The stop light switch is located on the brake pedal.

1. Disconnect the wire connector from the switch.
2. Remove the pin that attaches the stop light switch to the brake pedal.
3. Move the switch assembly to the right and upward for removal.
4. Install a new switch on the pedal.
5. Install the retaining pin and connect the wires.

BACK-UP LIGHT SWITCH

Manual Transmission

The back-up light switch is located on the transmission. To remove it, raise the car with the transmission in neutral. Support the car with safety stands and remove the wire from the switch. Remove the switch from the transmission. Install a new switch and connect the wire. Remove the safety stands and lower the car.

Automatic Transmission

The back-up light switch is integral with the neutral safety switch. See chapter six.

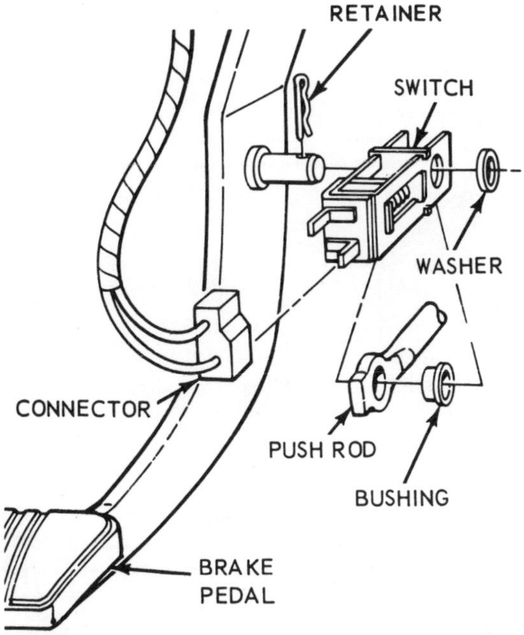

Stoplight switch removal

WINDSHIELD WIPERS

Motor Replacement

1. Loosen the two nuts and disconnect the wiper pivot shaft and link assembly from the motor drive arm ball.
2. Remove the three motor attaching screws and lower the motor away from the left side of the dash.
3. Disconnect the wiper motor wires and remove the wires.
4. To install, position the motor under the dash and install the wires. Operate the motor to be sure it is in the Park position.
5. Position the motor to the dash and install the retaining screws.
6. Position the wiper pivot shaft and link assembly to the motor drive arm ball and tighten the two nuts.

Wiper Blade Pivot Replacement

WITHOUT AIR CONDITIONING

1. Remove the windshield wiper arms and blades from the pivot shafts.
2. Loosen the two nuts retaining the wiper pivot shaft and link assembly to the motor drive arm ball.
3. Remove the three screws attaching each pivot shaft.
4. Remove the pivot shaft and link assembly from under the left side of the dash.
5. Reverse the above procedure to install. Operate the wiper motor before installing the wiper blades to be sure the pivots are in the Park position.

WITH AIR CONDITIONING

The blower motor and housing will have to be removed. See the instructions

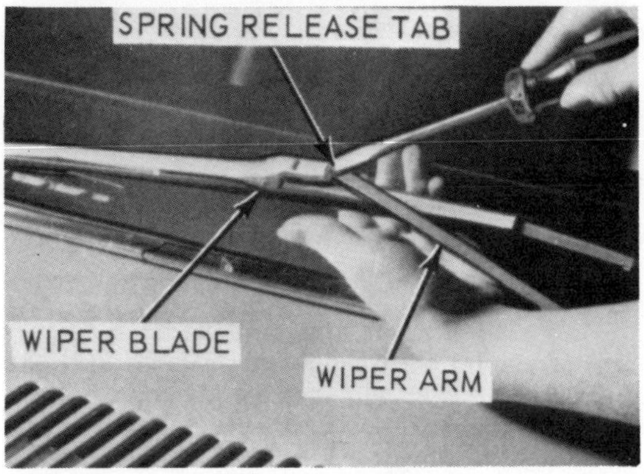

Removing windshield wiper blade

for blower motor removal with air conditioning then follow the procedure above.

Windshield Wiper Blade Replacement

To remove the wiper blades, lift up on the spring release tab on the wiper blade-to-wiper arm connector and pull the wiper blade off the wiper arm.

There are two types of replacement rubbers for the windshield wipers; one requires replacement of the entire wiper blade, but the other type allows replacement of only the rubber wiper blade insert.

If you have bought an entire replacement blade, simply snap it back into place on the wiper arm. If you have bought a rubber insert only, press the old rubber insert down, away from the wiper blade, to free it from the retaining clips on the ends of the wiper blades. Slide the insert from the blade. Position the new insert in the wiper blade, then bend it upward slightly to engage the retaining clips.

VEHICLE LIGHTING

Headlight Replacement

1. Remove the two headlight cover retaining screws and the cover.
2. Loosen, but do not remove, the three headlight retaining ring attaching screws.

NOTE: *Do not mistake the headlight adjustment screws for the three retaining ring screws.*

3. Rotate the headlight retaining ring to the left until the large openings in the attaching screw slots are aligned with

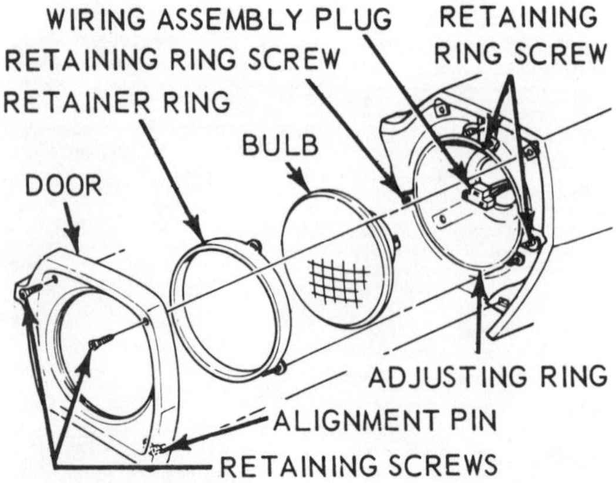

Headlight replacement

the heads of the screws. Remove the ring.

4. Pull the headlight toward the front of the car and disconnect the wiring connector from the headlight.
5. Connect the wire connector to a new headlight.
6. Position the headlight in the headlight pot making sure the tabs on the back of the headlight enter the slots in the pot.
7. Position the retaining ring on the retaining screws and turn the ring to the right. Tighten the screws.
8. Position the headlight cover and install the attaching screws.

Parking Lights, Turn Signals, and Stop Lights

All of these lighting functions are performed by four bulbs. The front parking lights and front turn signal bulbs are mounted in the parking light housing in the grille. Each of these dual-element bulbs performs two functions for their respective side of the car. To replace a bulb, raise the hood and twist the socket counterclockwise in its housing. When the socket has been removed, push down on the bulb and turn it counterclockwise to remove it from the socket.

The rear taillight, stop light, and turn signal functions are performed by dual-element bulbs on each side of the car. To replace a bulb, raise the trunk lid or rear door and turn the bulb socket counterclockwise. When the socket has been removed, push down on the bulb and turn it counterclockwise to remove it from the socket.

Back-Up Lights

To replace a back-up light bulb, raise the trunk lid or rear door and turn the bulb socket counterclockwise. To remove the bulb from the socket, push down on it and turn it counterclockwise.

License Plate Light

To replace the license plate bulb, remove the screw that attaches the lens and housing to the bottom of the bumper. Remove the lens and housing, push in on the bulb, and turn it counterclockwise to remove it.

Front Side Marker Light

To replace a front side marker bulb, reach up under the fender and turn the bulb socket counterclockwise to remove it from its housing. Pull the bulb *straight out* to remove it from the socket. Do not try to turn the bulb to remove it.

Rear Side Marker Light

The bulb replacement procedure is the same as the front marker light with the exception that the trunk lid or rear door must be raised to gain access to the bulb and socket.

Instrument Panel and Warning Lights

To replace any of these bulbs you will probably have to remove the instrument cluster from the instrument panel. However, if you are supple enough you may be able to remove the bulb from under the instrument panel without removing the cluster. (Disconnect the negative battery cable first.) See the accompanying illustration for bulb identification. Turn the socket counterclockwise to remove it from the instrument cluster. Pull the bulb *straight out* to remove it from the socket. Do not try to turn the bulb to remove it.

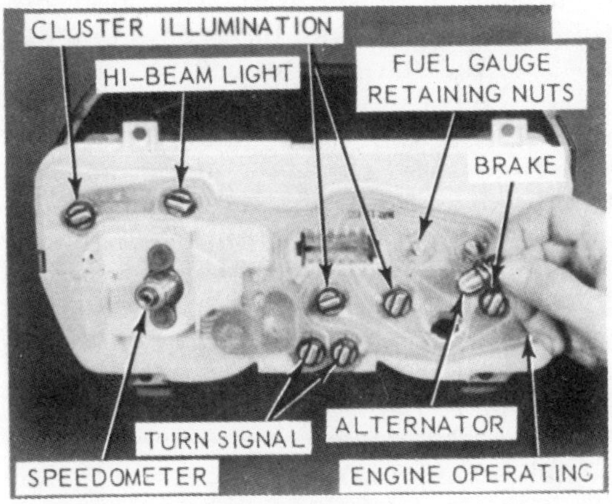

Rear view of instrument cluster

Dome Light

To gain access to the dome light bulb, pry the dome light lens out from the housing. After making sure the doors are closed and the headlight switch is not turned to the dome light "on" position, pry the bulb *straight out* of the housing.

Turn Signal Flasher and Emergency Flasher

The turn signal flasher is located behind the instrument panel directly over the glove box door opening. The emergency flasher is also in this location, slightly to the left of the turn signal flasher. When the turn signal or emergency flasher lights come on but fail to flash on and off, the flasher for that system is probably defective. To replace a flasher, open the glove box door and disconnect the flasher from the in-

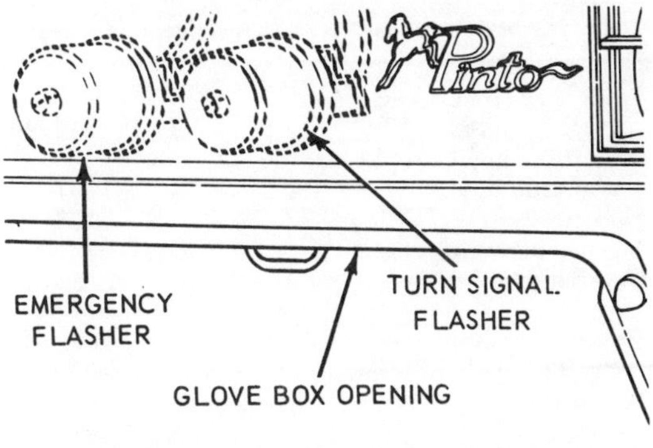

Turn signal and emergency flasher location

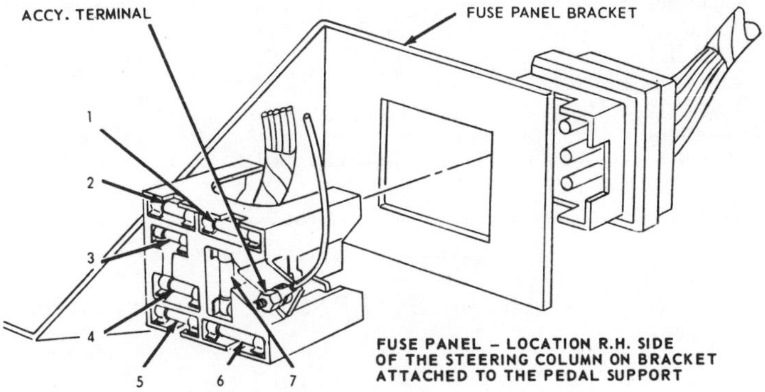

(1) (20 AMP.) HAZARD FLASHER, CIGAR LIGHTER & CLOCK FEED (CONSOLETTE ONLY)
(2) (14 AMP.) COURTESY, DOME LAMP & IGNITION KEY BUZZER
(3) (SPARE) NOT USED
(4) (14 AMP.) INDICATOR LAMPS, EMISSION CONTROL AND/OR CARBURETOR SOLENOID
(5) (14 AMP.) HEATER-DEFROSTERZ
NOTE: (30 AMP. FUSE) REQUIRED FOR AIR CONDITIONER
(6) (15 AMP.) BACK-UP LAMPS, RADIO, W/S WASHER & REAR WINDOW DEFOGGER
(7) (SPARE) (ACCY) NOT USED

Pinto fuse panel—1971–74

1	15 AMP FUSE (30 AMP FUSE)	HEATER BLOWER MOTOR (OPTIONAL A/C BLOWER MOTOR AND CLUTCH)
2	15 AMP FUSE	TURN SIGNAL, BACK UP LAMPS
3	7.5 AMP FUSE	RADIO
4	15 AMP FUSE	WINDSHIELD WASHER, REAR WINDOW DEFOGGER FEED, ELECTRIC REAR WINDOW DEFROSTER CONTROL AND INDICATOR, ANTI-THEFT MODULE
5	4 AMP FUSE	ILLUMINATION LAMPS FOR; INSTRUMENT PANEL CLUSTER, HEATER OR A/C CONTROL, RADIO, ASHTRAY, WINDSHIELD WIPER SWITCH
6	14 AMP FUSE	WARNING LAMPS FOR; ENGINE, BRAKES, FASTEN BELTS, LIFTGATE OPEN INDICATOR. POWER TO; SEAT BELT BUZZER AND MODULE, EMISSION CONTROL SOLENOIDS.
7	BLANK	
8	BLANK	
9	20 AMP FUSE	HORN, CIGAR LIGHTER
10	15 AMP FUSE	STOP LAMPS, HAZARD FLASHERS
11	15 AMP FUSE	DOME, MAP, GLOVE BOX, CARGO AND LUGGAGE COMPARTMENT LAMPS; KEY AND HEADLAMPS ON WARNING BUZZER; ANTI-THEFT HORN AND TRIGGER FEED; SEAT BELT MODULE
12	BLANK	

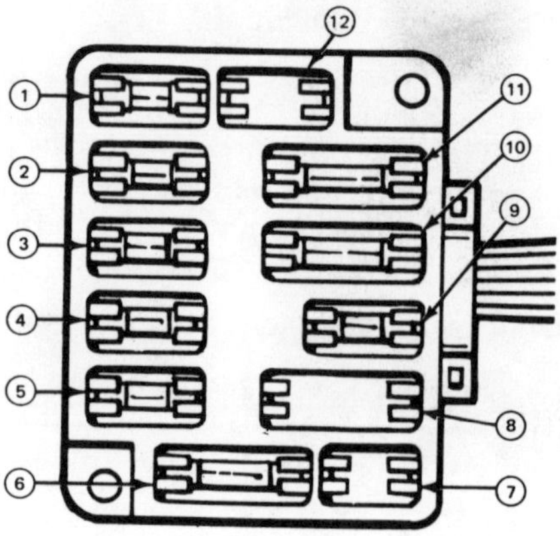

Pinto fuse panel—1975

strument panel by turning it and pulling toward the front of the car. Remove the push-on connector from the flasher.

FUSES

The fuses are located in the fuse box mounted under the instrument panel.

Light Bulb Specifications

Light Description	*Candlepower or Wattage*	*Trade No.*
Front turn signals and parking lights	3—32	1157 NA
Rear turn signal, stoplights, and taillights	3—32	1157
Back-up light	32	1156
License plate light	4	97
Dome light	6	212 and 212-1
Side marker lights	2	194
Instrument panel illumination	2	194
Hi-beam indicator	2	194
Turn signal indicator (dash)	2	194
Engine warning lights	2	194
Speedometer	2	194
Fuel Gauge	2	194
Radio light	1.9	1893
Auto trans selector	1.5	1445
Clock	3	1895
Headlights		
Cars built before 1/3/72	40—50	6012
Cars built after 1/3/72	50—60	6014

SEAT BELT/STARTER INTERLOCK SYSTEM

All 1974 and some 1975 Pintos are equipped with the Federally-required starter interlock system. The purpose of this system is to force the wearing of seat belts.

The system includes a warning light and buzzer (as in late 1972 and 1973), weight sensors in the front seats, switches in the outboard front seat belt retractors, and an electronic control module. The center front seat is tied into the warning light and buzzer system, but not into the starter interlock.

The electronic control module requires that the driver and right front passenger first sit down, then pull out their seat belts. If this is not done, the starter will not operate, but the light and buzzer will. The sequence must be followed each time the engine is started unless the driver and passenger have remained seated and buckled. If the seat belts have been pulled out and left buckled, the engine will not start. The switches in the retractors must be cycled for each start. If the belts are released after the start, the light and buzzer will operate.

If the system should fail, preventing starting, the interlock by-pass switch under the hood can be used. This switch permits one start without interference from the interlock system. This by-pass switch can also be used for servicing purposes.

Troubleshooting

If the starter will not crank or the warning buzzer will not shut off, perform the following checks:

Problem: Front seat occupant sits on a prebuckled seat belt.

Solution: Unbuckle the prebuckled belt, fully retract, extract, and then rebuckle the belt.

Problem: The front seat occupants are buckled, but the starter will not crank.

Solution: The unoccupied seat sensor switch stuck closed before the seat was occupied. Reset the unoccupied seat sensor switches by applying and then releasing 50 lbs or more of weight to the seat directly over the seat sensor switches.

Problem: Starter will not crank with a heavy parcel on the front seat.

Solution: Buckle the seat belt around the parcel somewhere else in the car. Unbuckle the seat belt when the parcel is removed from the front seat.

Problem: Starter will not crank due to starter interlock system component failure.

Solution: An emergency starter interlock override switch is located under the hood on the fender apron. Depress the red push button on the switch and release it. This will allow one complete cycle of the ignition key from Off to Start and back to Off. Do not tape the button down as this will result in deactivation of the override feature.

Disabling The Starter Interlock System

Cars built after October 29, 1974 are no longer required to have the interlock system. The system may be legally disabled on cars which have it, but the following procedure must be used:

1. Open the hood and locate the override switch and terminal connector attached to it.
2. Remove the number 32 wire(s) which are red with a light blue stripe, and the number 33 wire(s) which are white with pink dots. After cutting these wires, splice them together.
3. To remove the buzzer, remove the terminal connector from the buzzer and tape it to the wiring harness to prevent it from rattling. The buzzer now can be removed and discarded. Federal law requires that the warning light still be operable, so do not disconnect it.

Wiring Diagrams

NOTE: *1975 and later wiring diagrams were omitted due to their extreme length. The diagrams can be found in* Chilton's Wiring Diagram Manual.

Codes:

C, followed by a number (C15), indicates a connector. Number, followed letters (140 BK-P), indicates a circuit number and the color of the wire (black with pink stripe). Number, in parenthesis after the color code (16), indicates gauge size of the wire. G, followed by a number (G20), indicates a chassis ground connection. Four or five-digit number, followed by assy (9278 assy), indicates the Ford basic part number for the part.

WIRING COLOR KEY
PRIMARY COLORS

BLACK	BK
BROWN	BR
TAN	T
RED	R
PINK	PK
ORANGE	O
YELLOW	Y
DK GREEN	DG
LT GREEN	LG
DK BLUE	DB
LT BLUE	LB
PURPLE	P
GRAY	GY
WHITE	W
STRIPE	(S)
HASH	(H)
DOT	(D)

1971 Index

Component	*Location*
A/C clutch solenoid	K—29
Alternator	B—2
Alternator regulator	E—2
Battery	B—3
Cigar lighter	E—11
Clock	G—12
Constant voltage unit	H—10
Distributor	F—5
Flashers:	
Emergency warning	C—11
Turn signal	B—16
Fuel gauge	F—10
Fuel sender	H—9
Fuse panel	A—11 — A—24
Heater blower resistor	F—29
Horns	C—17
Ignition coil	C—4
Indicators:	
Alternator	F—3
Dual brake	J—5
Engine hot	K—2
High beam	H—16
Oil pressure	K—1
Turn signal	H—18 & H—20
Key reminder buzzer	D—17
Lamps:	
Back-up	J—28 & H—28
Brake warning	G—3
Dome lamp	B—14
Side marker lamps:	
Front	F—18 & H—19
Rear	G—22
Headlamps	J—17 & J—18
License plate lamp	K—22
Parking lamps	H—18 & G—20
Tail lamps	H—21 & H—23
Illuminations:	
Clock	K—12
Air cond blower switch	H—14
Instrument cluster	J—13
PRNDL	K—21
Motors:	
Defogger	G—25
Heater blower	F—29 — G29
Starter	B—7
Windshield wiper	E—21
Oil pressure sender	G—2
Radio	C—26
Safety fuse link	A—3 & A—4
Speaker	D—26
Starter motor relay	B—5
Switches:	
Back-up lamp	E—26 — G—28
Courtesy lamp:	
Front left	C—15
Front right	C—13
De-icing	G—30
Defogger	G—25
Dimmer foot	F—17
Dual brake warning	K—2
Emergency warning	B—20
Head light	F—13
Heater blower	D—29
Horn switch	D—16
Ignition	H—7
Limit (ac)	E—20
Neutral safety	E—7
Stop lamp	F—15
Turn signal	E—19, E—20 & C—20
Windshield wiper/wash	B—22 — C—24
Windshield washer pump	E—24
Key reminder switch	E—17
Radio supp capacitor	C—3
Noise supp choke	H—10

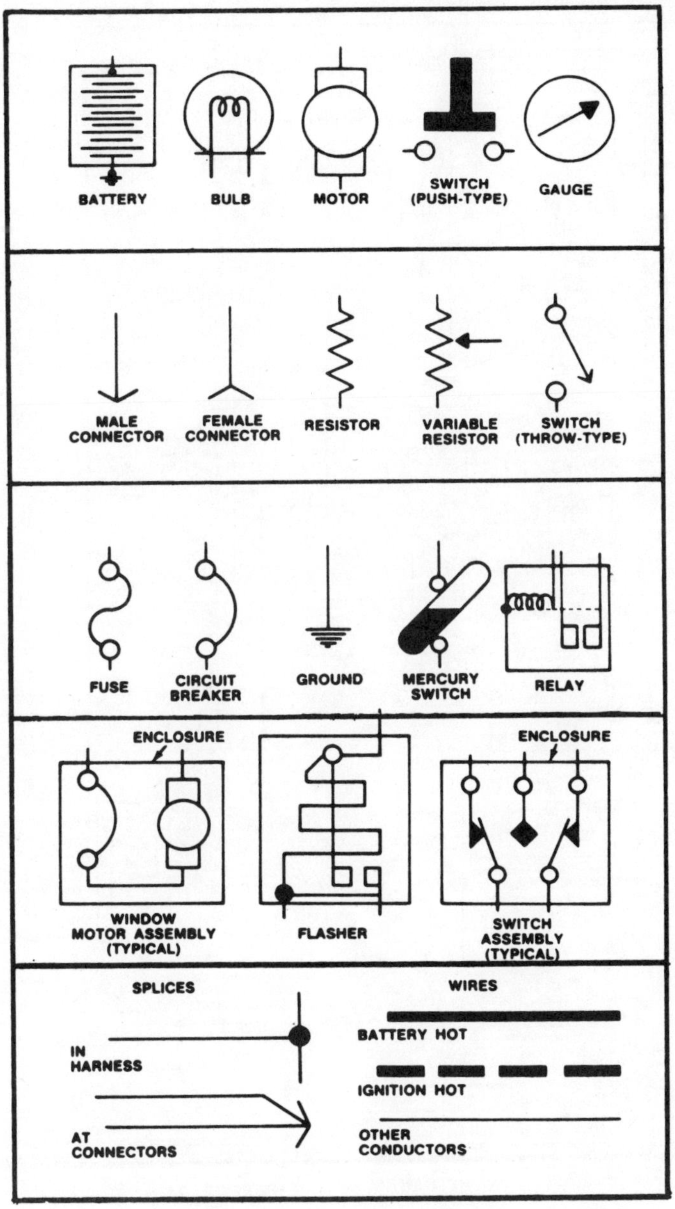

Symbols used in wiring diagram

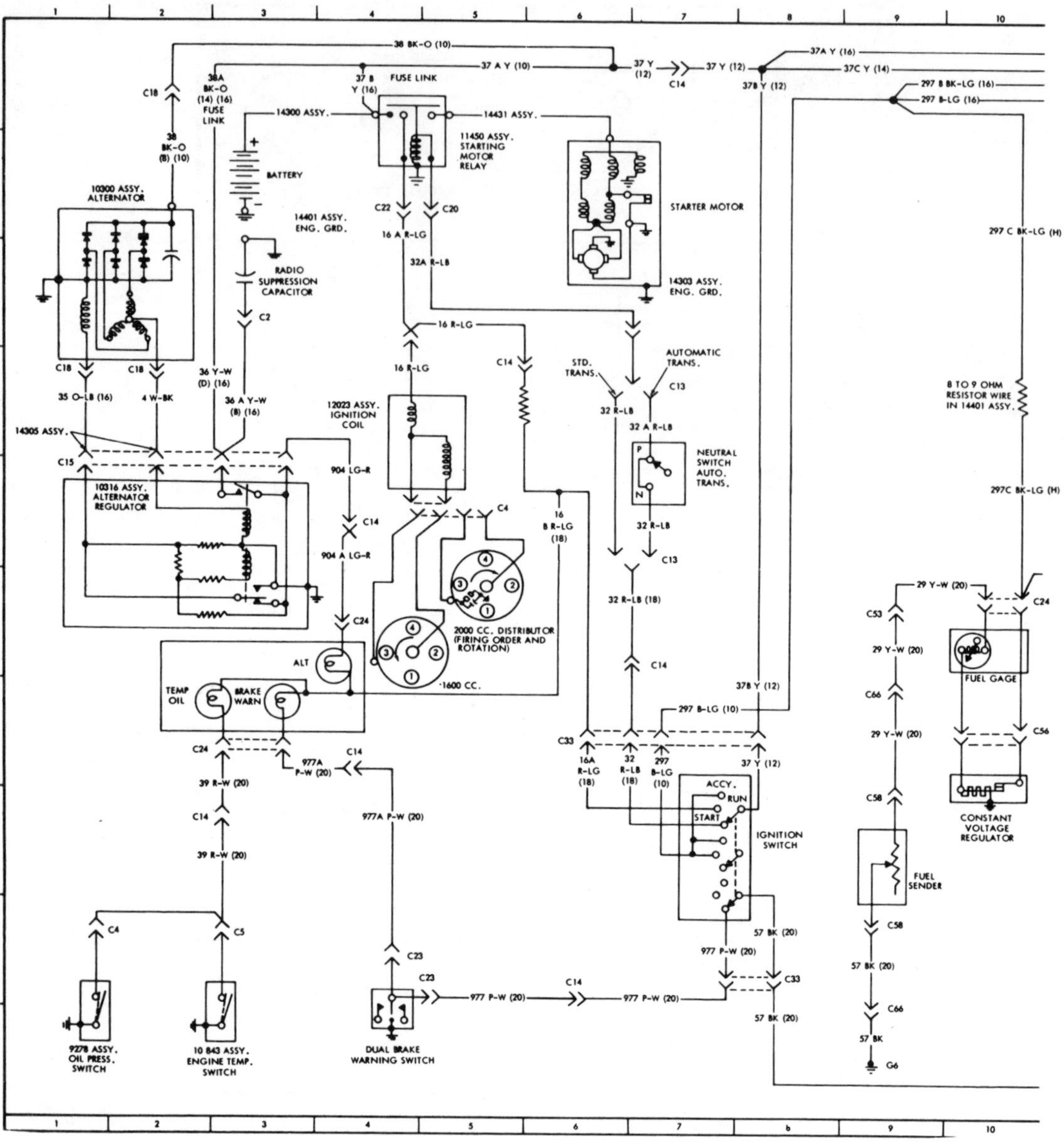

1971 Pinto wiring diagram

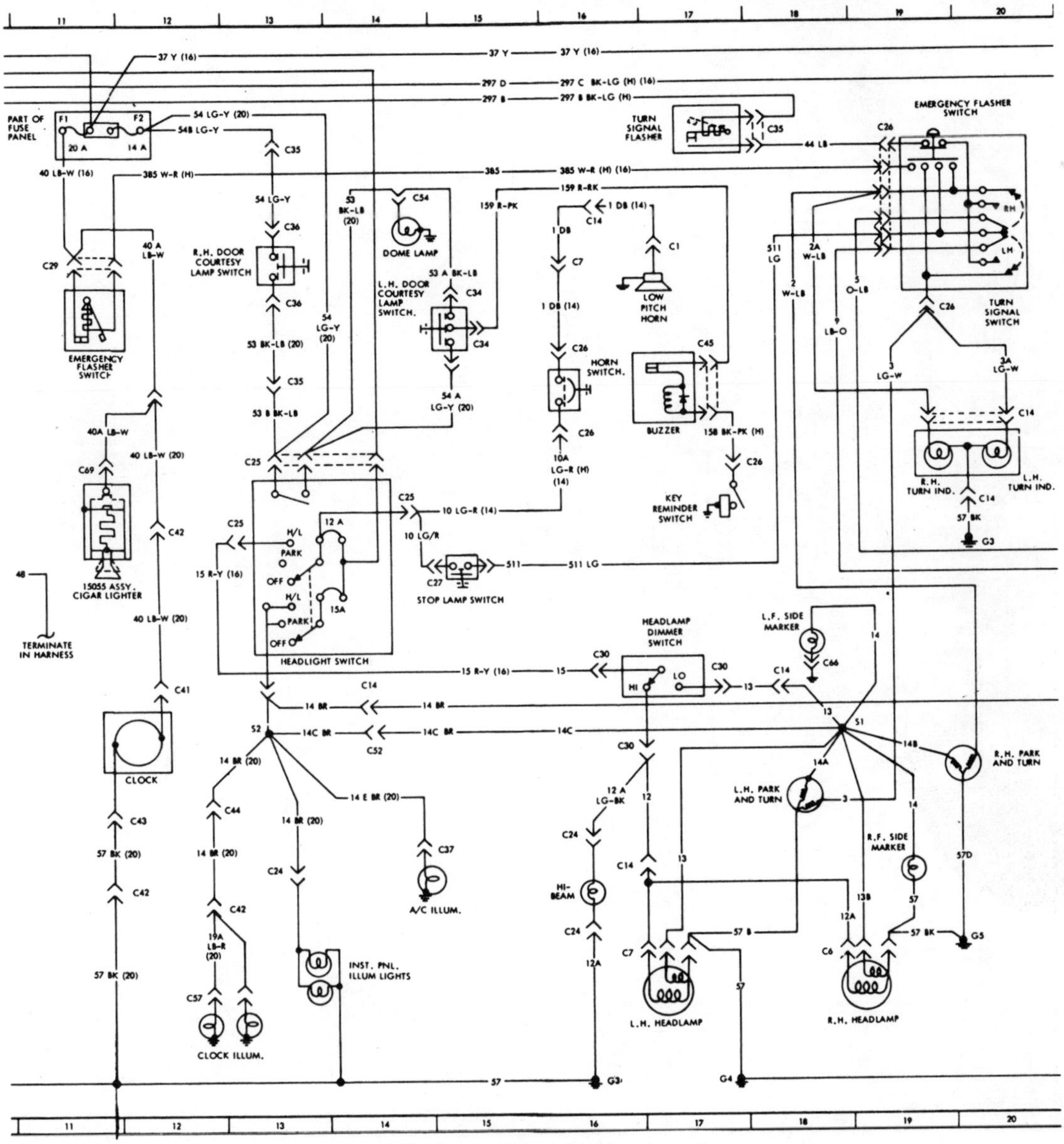

1971 Pinto wiring diagram (cont.)

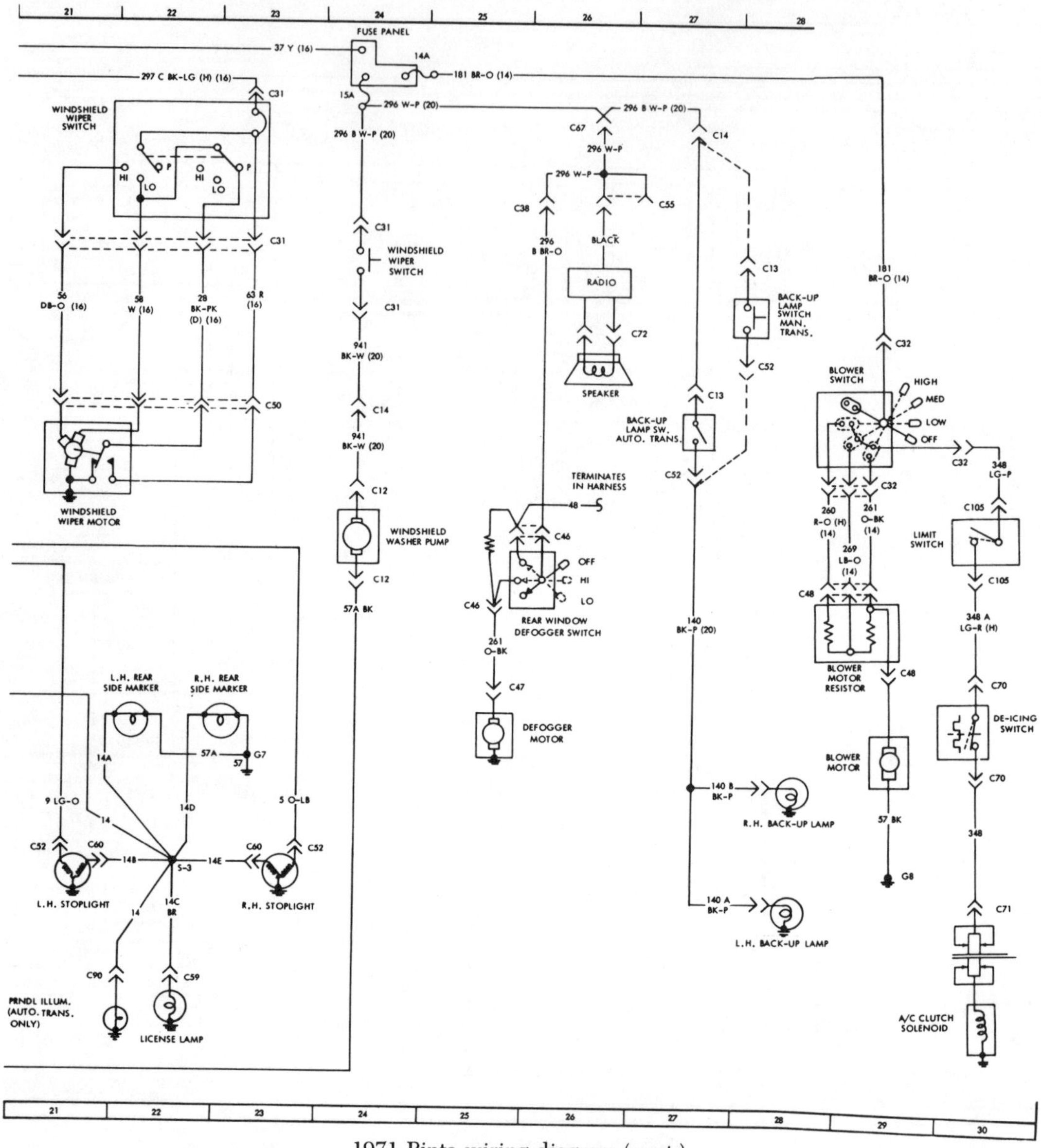

1971 Pinto wiring diagram (cont.)

1972 Index

Component	Location
Alternator	B—2
Battery	B—3
Cigar lighter	E—14
Clock	F—14
Alternator regulator	E—2
Distributor	F—5
Emission control solenoid	J—5
Electronic spark control modulator	K—8
Flashers:	
Emergency warning	D—13
Turn signal	C—20
Fuel gauge	D—12
Fuel sender	F—11
Sport lamp relay	H—37
Horns	F—20
Heated backlite relay	E—10
Ignition coil	D—5
Indicators:	
Heated backlite	F—9
Alternator	F—3
Dual brake	G—2
Engine hot	K—2
High beam	K—17
Oil pressure	G—2
Turn signal	J—18
Seat belt warning	K—12
Key reminder buzzer	E—20
Seat belt reminder buzzer	H—11
Lamps:	
Back-up	G—41
Cargo lamp	C—19
Dome lamp	D—18
Side marker lamps:	
Left front	G—21
Right front	J—23
Left rear	H—25
Right rear	H—26
Headlamps	K—20
License plate lamp	K—25
Parking lamps	J—21
Tail lamps	J—25
Sport lamps	G—32
Illuminations:	
Clock	K—16
Air cond blower switch	J—16
Instrument cluster	J—17
PRNDL	J—24
Motors:	
Defogger	H—38
Heater blower	G—43
Starter	B—7
Windshield wiper	E—24
Radio	D—39
Radio supp capacitor	C—3
Starter motor relay	B—5
Switches:	
Clutch	E—44
Back-up lamp	D—41
Courtesy lamp:	
Front left	D—18
Front right	D—16
Cargo lamp	C—19
De-icing	G—45
Defogger	G—38
Dimmer foot	G—20
Dual brake warning	K—3
Engine temp	H—2
Emergency warning	D—22
Head light	F—17
Heated backlite	C—10
Heater blower	D—43
Horn switch	F—19
Ignition	G—8
Seat sensor	H—14
Key reminder switch	F—20
Neutral safety	E—7
Oil pressure	H—1
Sport lamp	G—37
Stop lamp	C—18
Turn signal	D—22
Windshield wiper/wash	E—26
Windshield washer pump	F—25

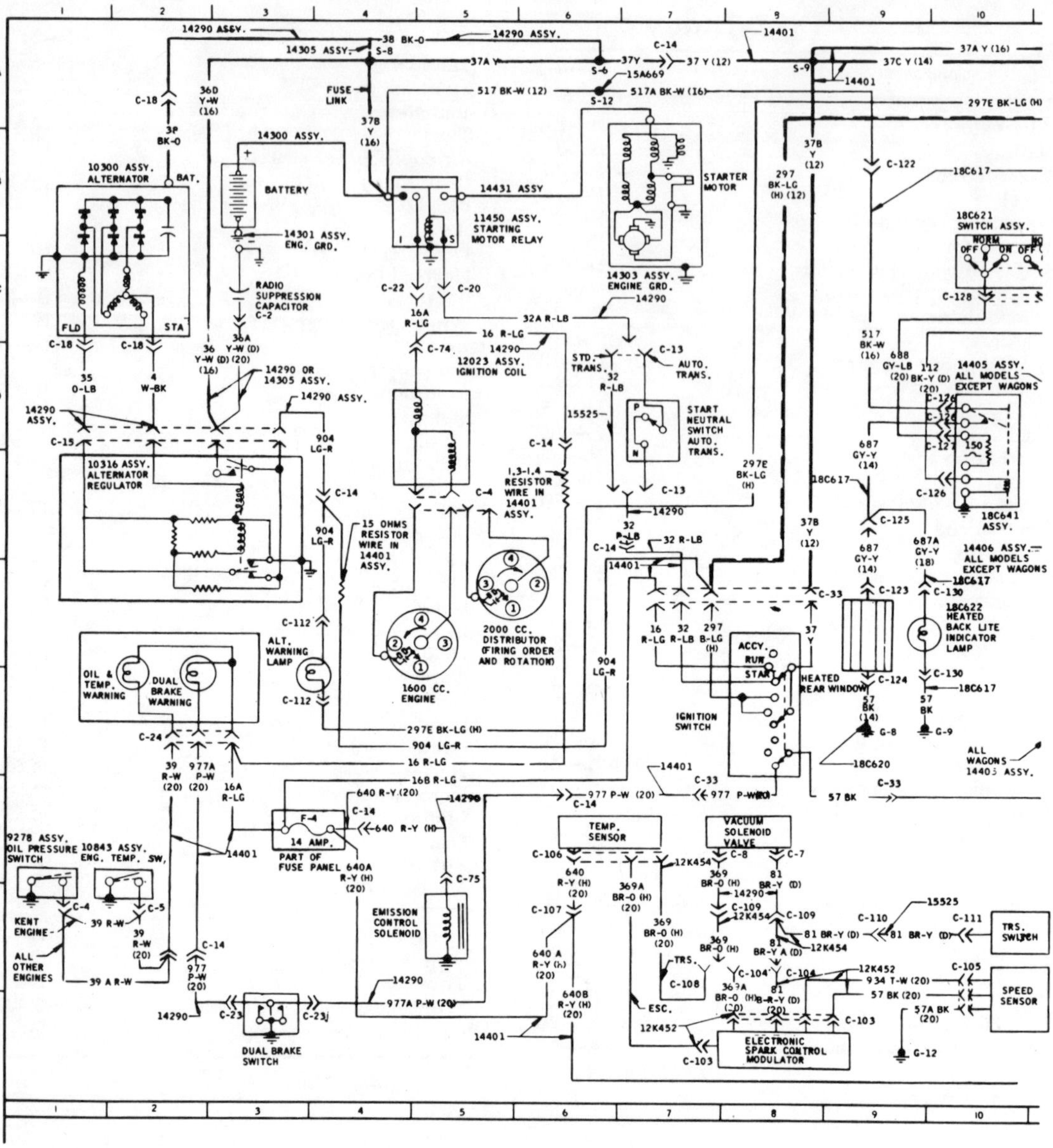

1972 Pinto wiring diagram

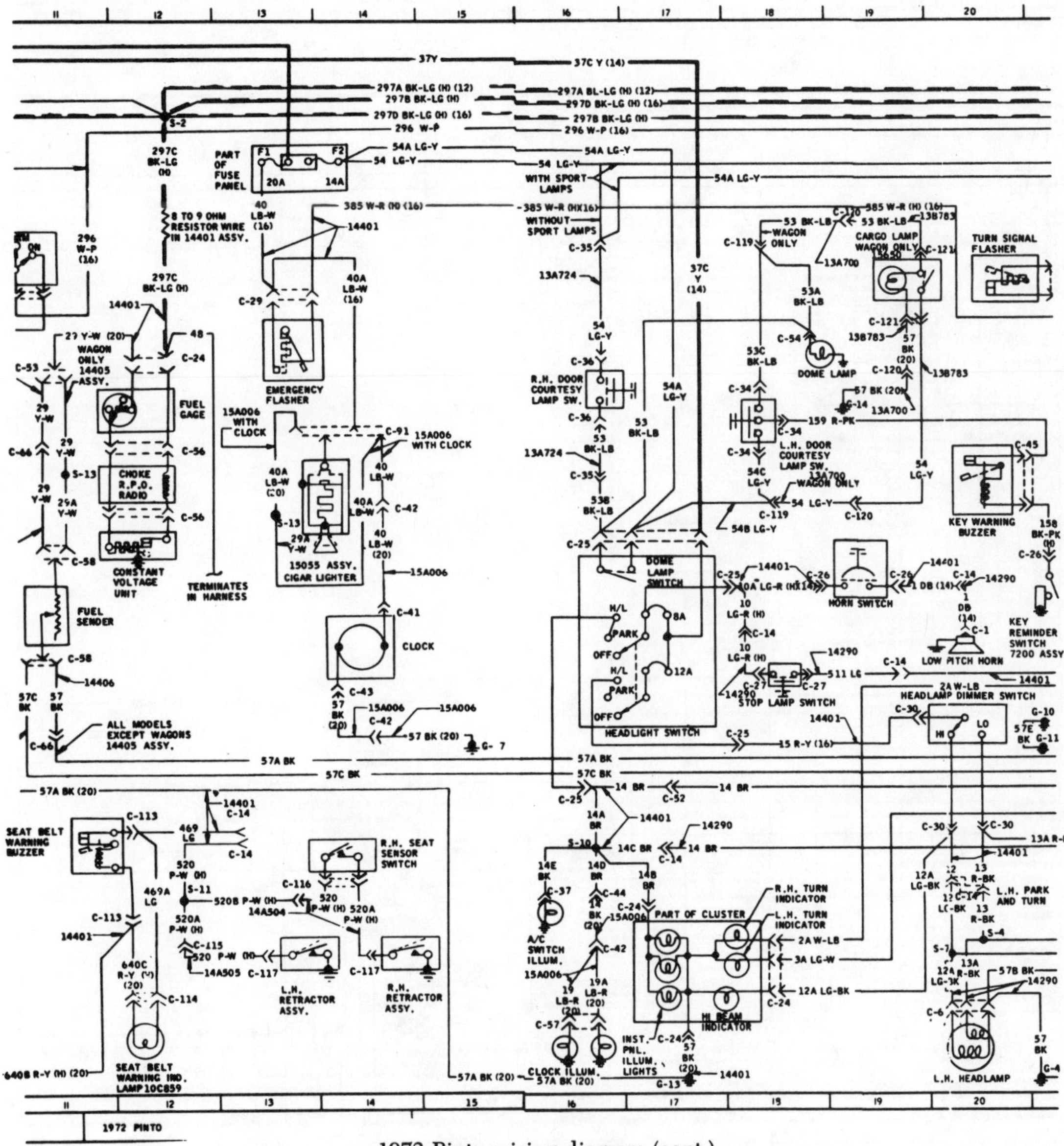

1972 Pinto wiring diagram (cont.)

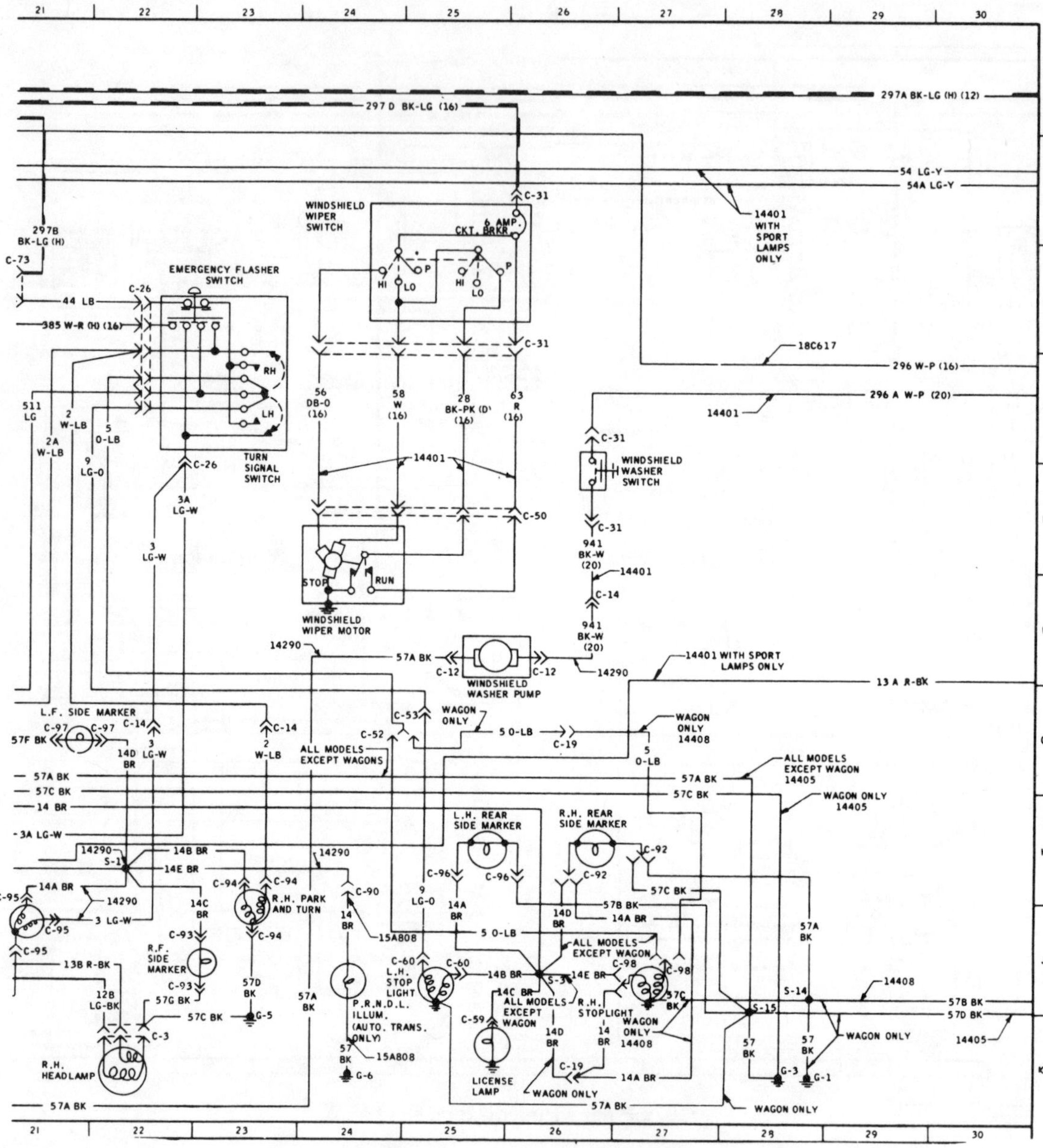

1972 Pinto wiring diagram (cont.)

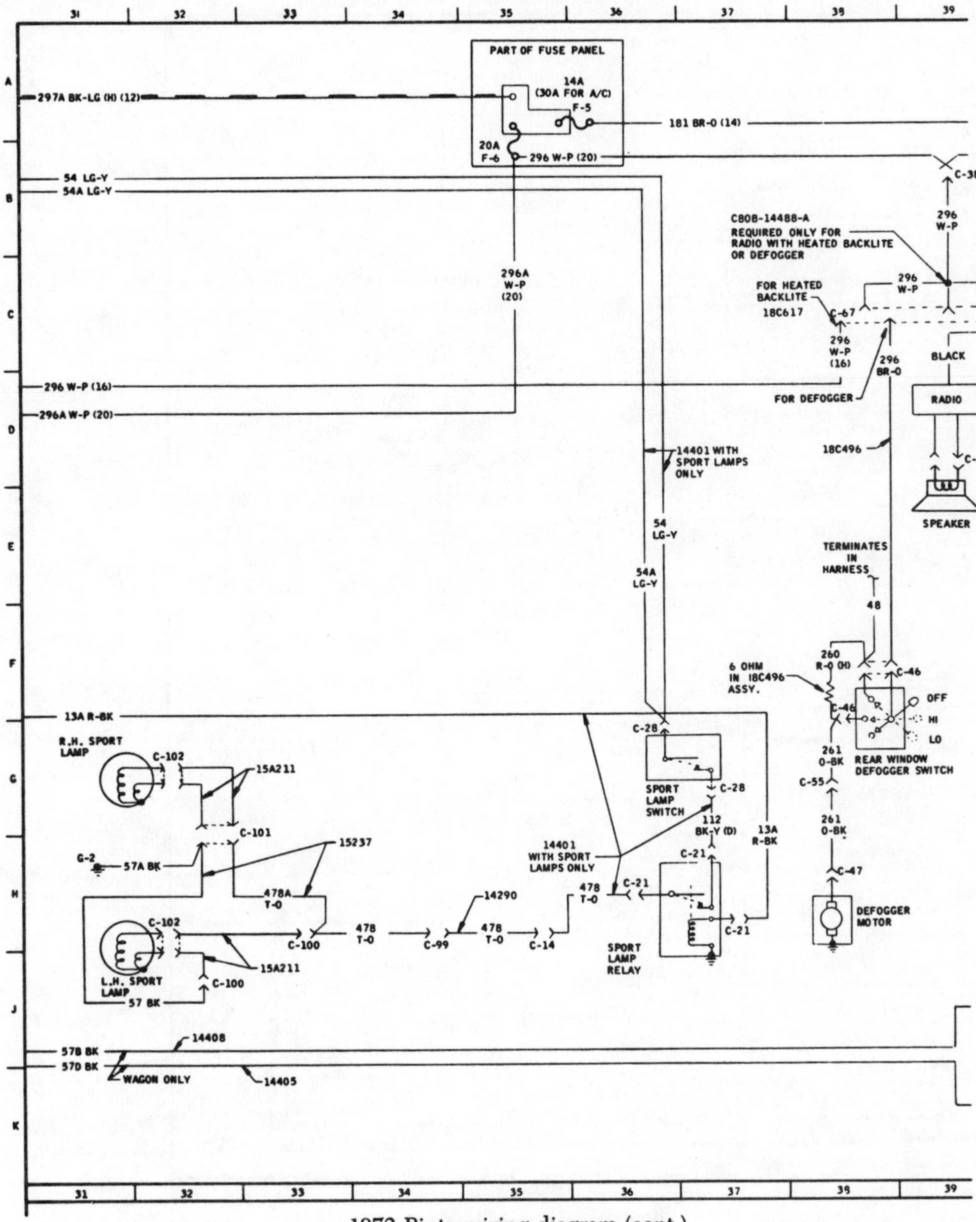

1972 Pinto wiring diagram (cont.)

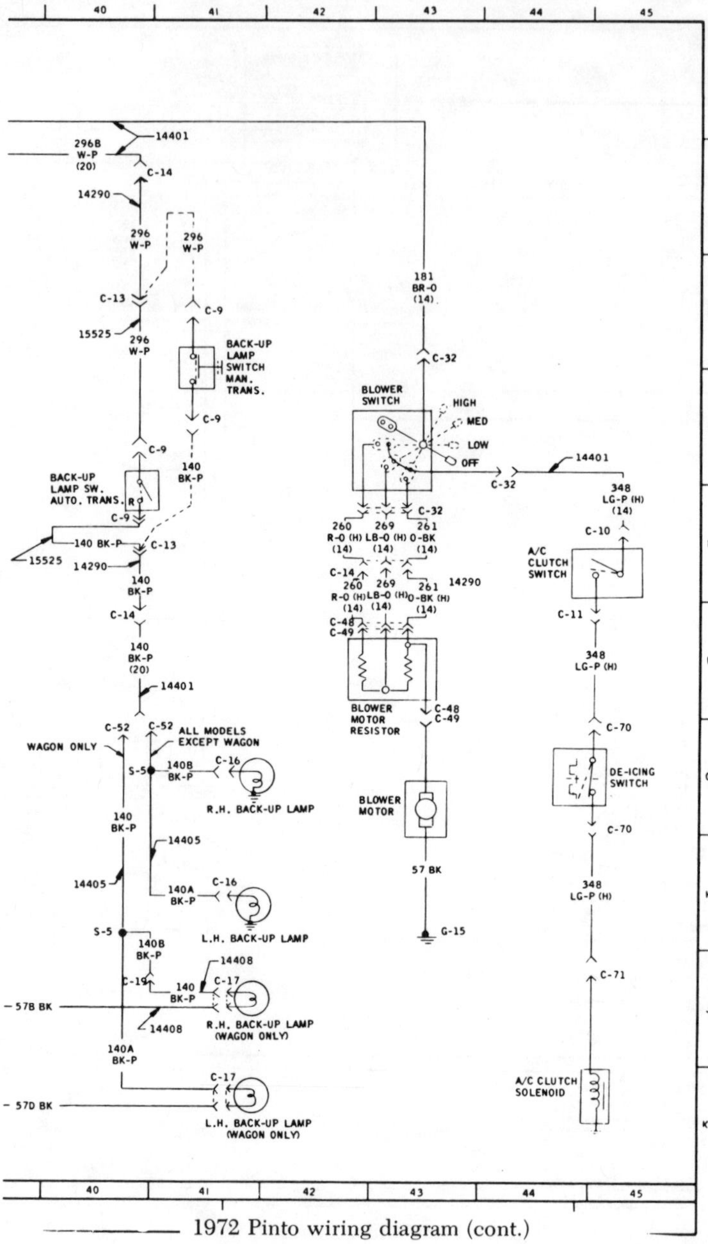

1972 Pinto wiring diagram (cont.)

1973 Index

Component	*Location*
A/C clutch solenoid	F—46
Alternator	A—3
Alternator 70 amp	A—1
Alternator regulator	F—2
Battery	C—5
Blower motor resistor A/C	D—45
Blower motor resistor heater	D—42
Cigar lighter	D—21
Constant voltage unit	F—20
Distributor 1600 cc	F—4
Distributor 2000 cc	E—4
Emission control solenoid	D—14
Flashers:	
Emergency warning	C—22
Turn signal	B—31
Fuel gauge	B—20
Fuel gauge sender	E—20
Heated backlite	E—9
Heated backlite relay	C—10
Horn	D—27
Ignition coil	E—5
Illuminations:	
A/C switch	E—21
Heater switch	E—22
Cluster	F—23
PRNDL	E—28
Immersion heater	E—47
Indicators:	
Alternator warning	A—18
Dual brake warning	C—13
Heated backlite	E—10
High beam	C—25
Oil pressure and temp warning	C—12
Seat belt warning	C—15, C—63
Turn signal	B—32, C—32
Key reminder buzzer	D—37
Lamps:	
Back-up:	
Sedan	C—35, C—36
Wagon	C—33
Cargo	D—38
Dome	E—38
Headlamps:	
LH	E—27
RH	E—25
License:	
Sedan	F—31
Wagon	F—34
Park and turn:	
LH	E—27
RH	E—25
Stop and turn:	
LH sedan	E—30
RH sedan	E—32
LH wagon	E—33
RH wagon	E—36
Side markers:	
LH front	E—28
RH front	E—26
LH rear sedan	E—30
RH rear sedan	E—31
LH rear wagon	E—34
RH rear wagon	E—35
Motors:	
Heater blower	E—42
Heater blower A/C	E—45
Starter	E—3
Windshield washer pump	F—24
Windshield wiper	E—23
Noise supp capacitor	E—3
Radio	D—40
Radio supp choke	E—20
Radio speaker	E—40
Seat belt actuator assy	A—60
Seat belt reminder buzzer	B—16, D—63
Starter interlock system	49—64
Starter motor relay	C—6, E—52
Switches:	
A/C blower	B—45
A/C clutch	C—46
De-icing	D—46
Door jambs:	
LH	C—37, A—63
RH	B—31
Dual brake warning	F—13
Emergency warning	B—30
Headlamp	B—28
Headlamp dimmer	B—25
Heated backlite	C—11
Heater blower	B—42
Horn	C—26
Ignition	E—18, E—55
Key reminder	F—37
Seat belt retractor:	
LH	F—14, F—62
RH	F—16, F—63
Oil pressure	F—11
Seat sensor	F—15, F—60
Start interlock and back-up lamp	B—18, D—58
Stoplamp	F—29
Turn signal	B—29
Transmission seat belt sensor	F—16, F—57
Water temperature	F—12
Windshield wiper and washer	C—23

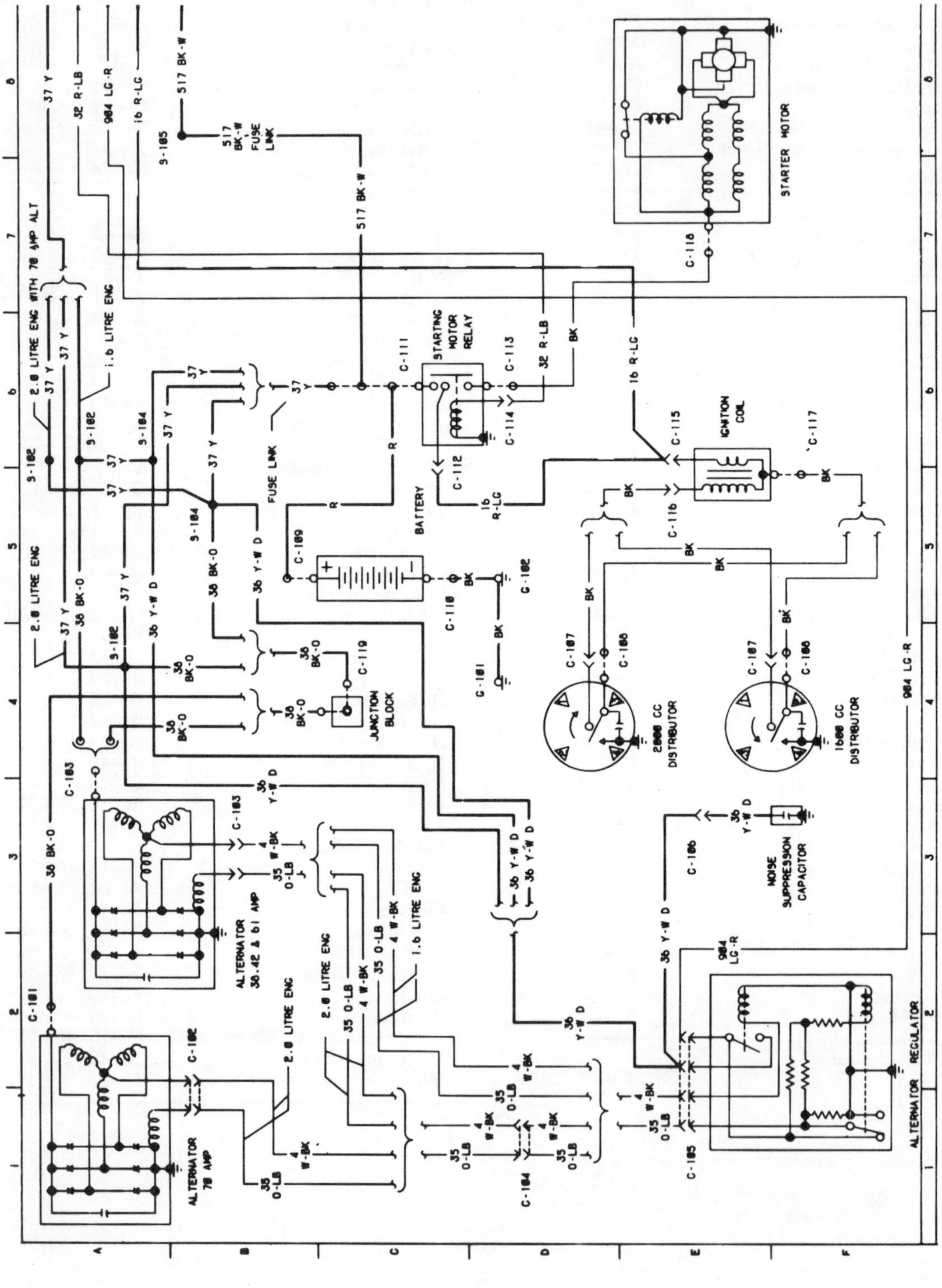

1973 Pinto Part 1

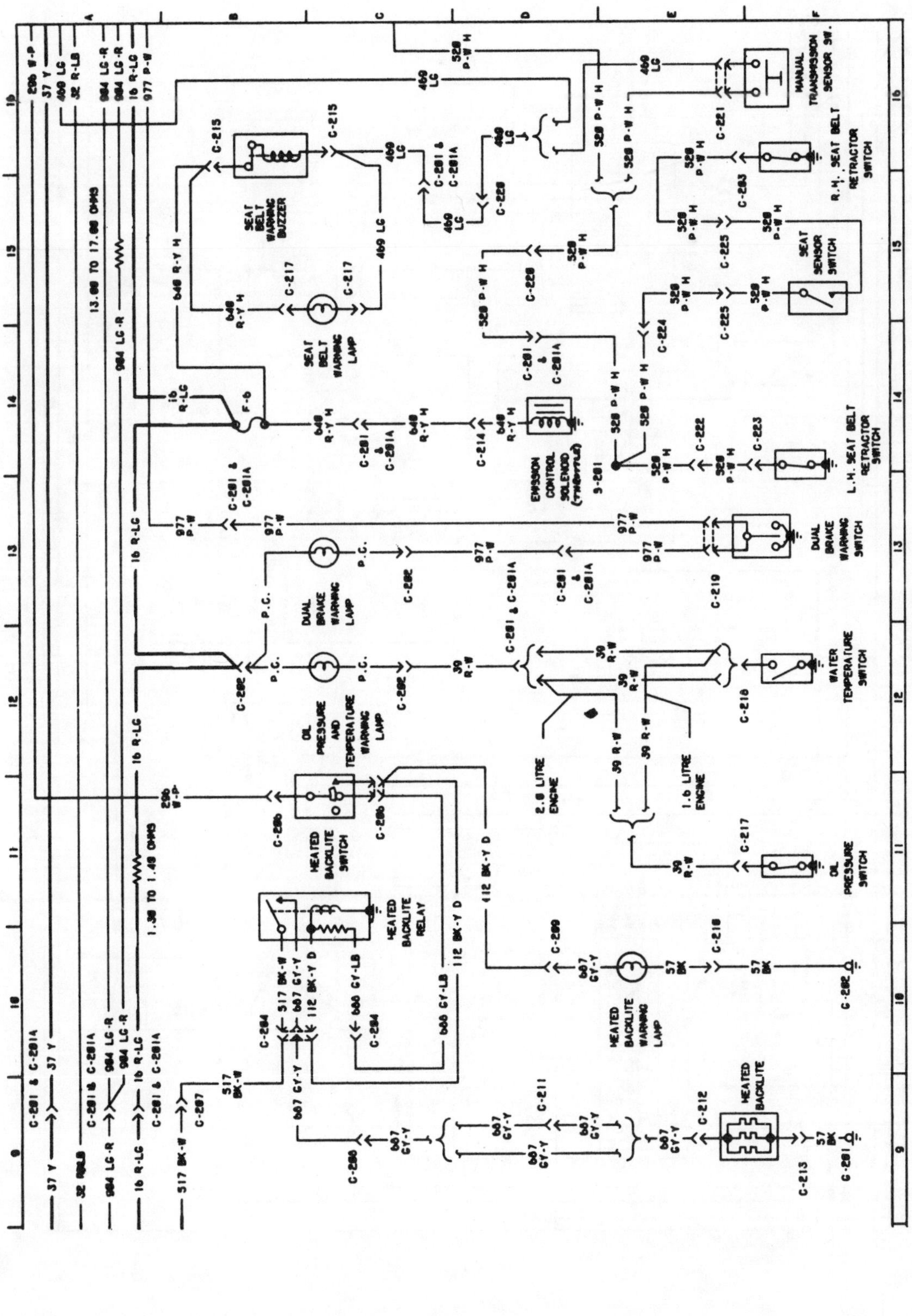

1973 Pinto Part 2

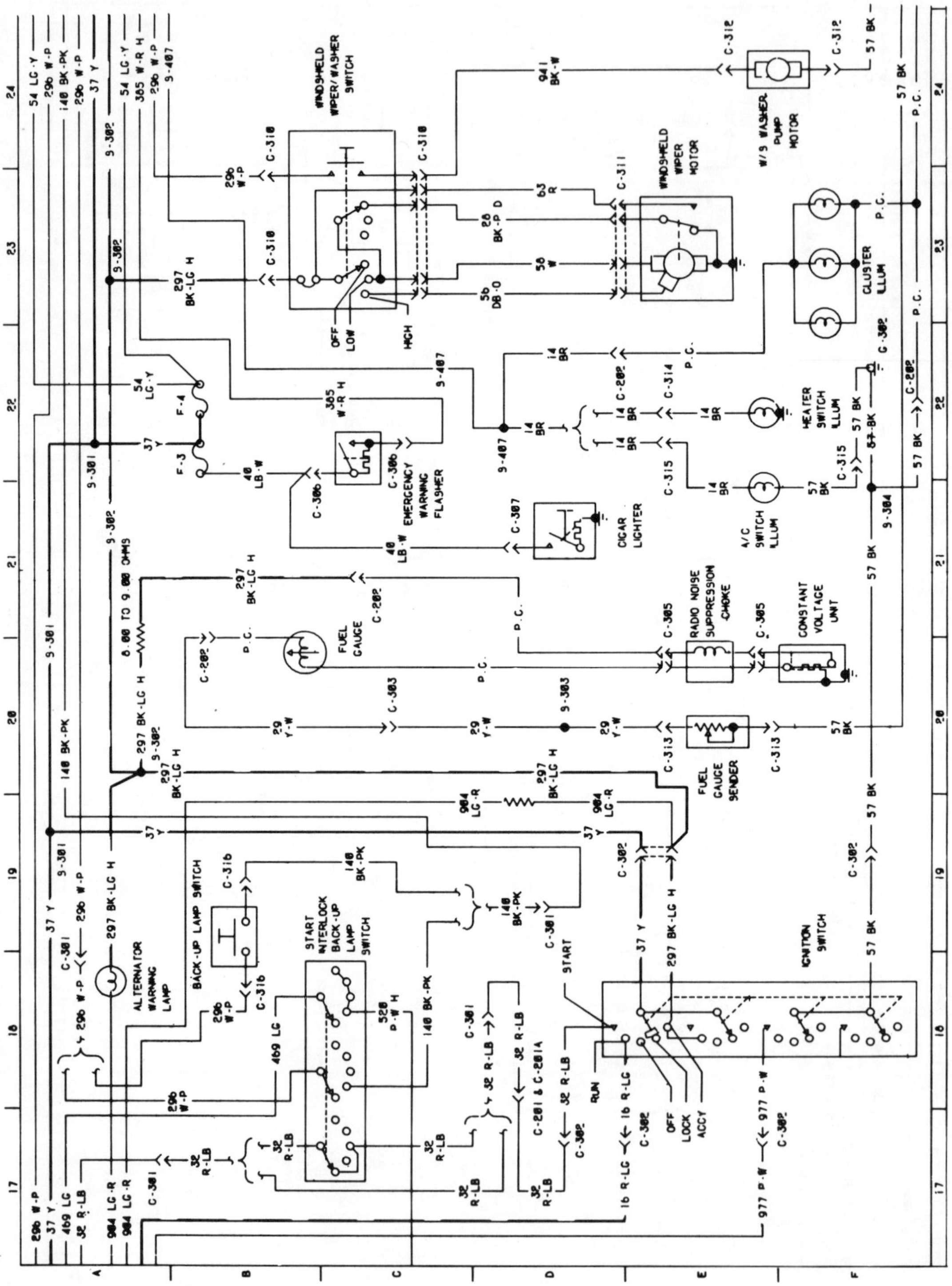

1973 Pinto Part 3

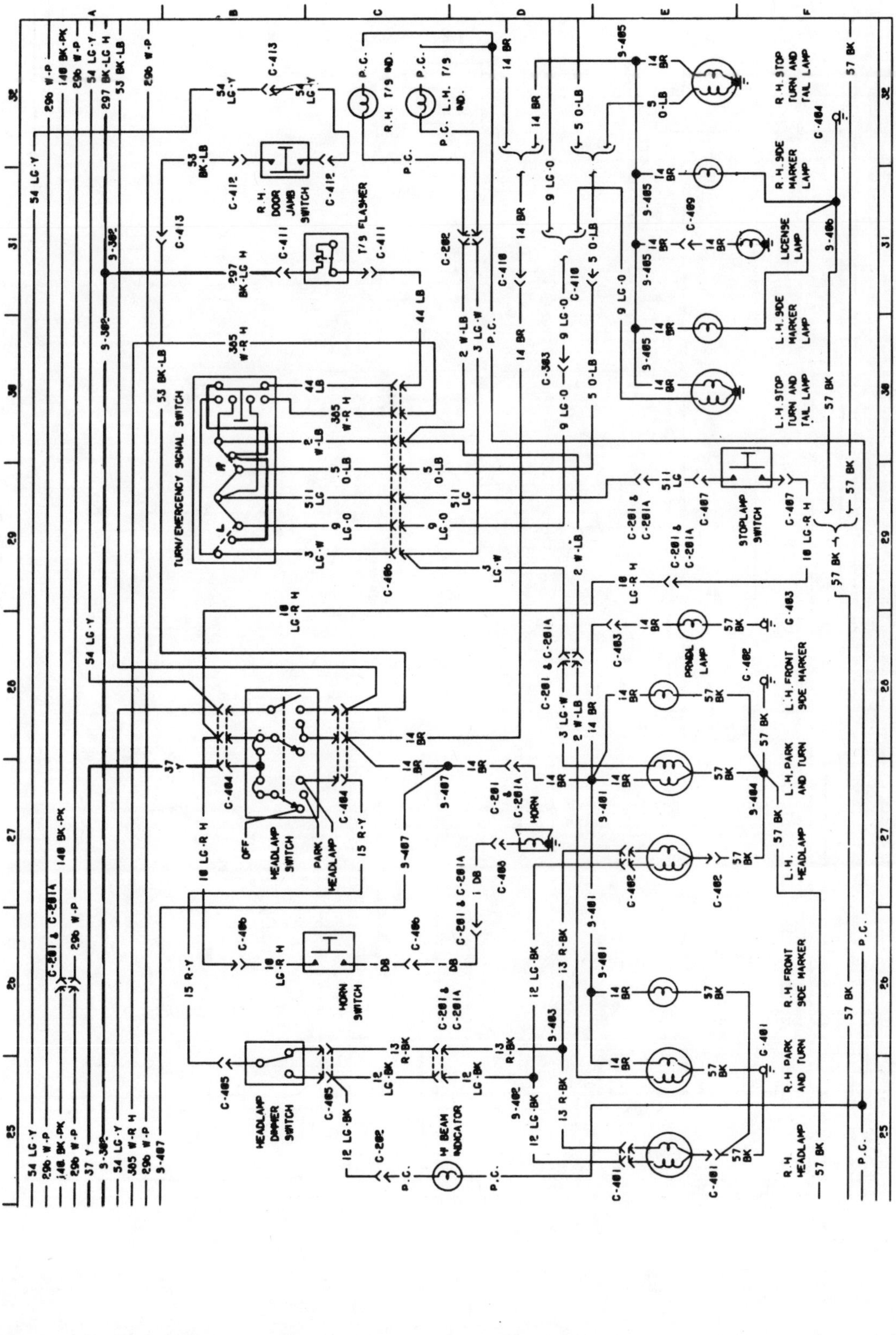

1973 Pinto Part 4

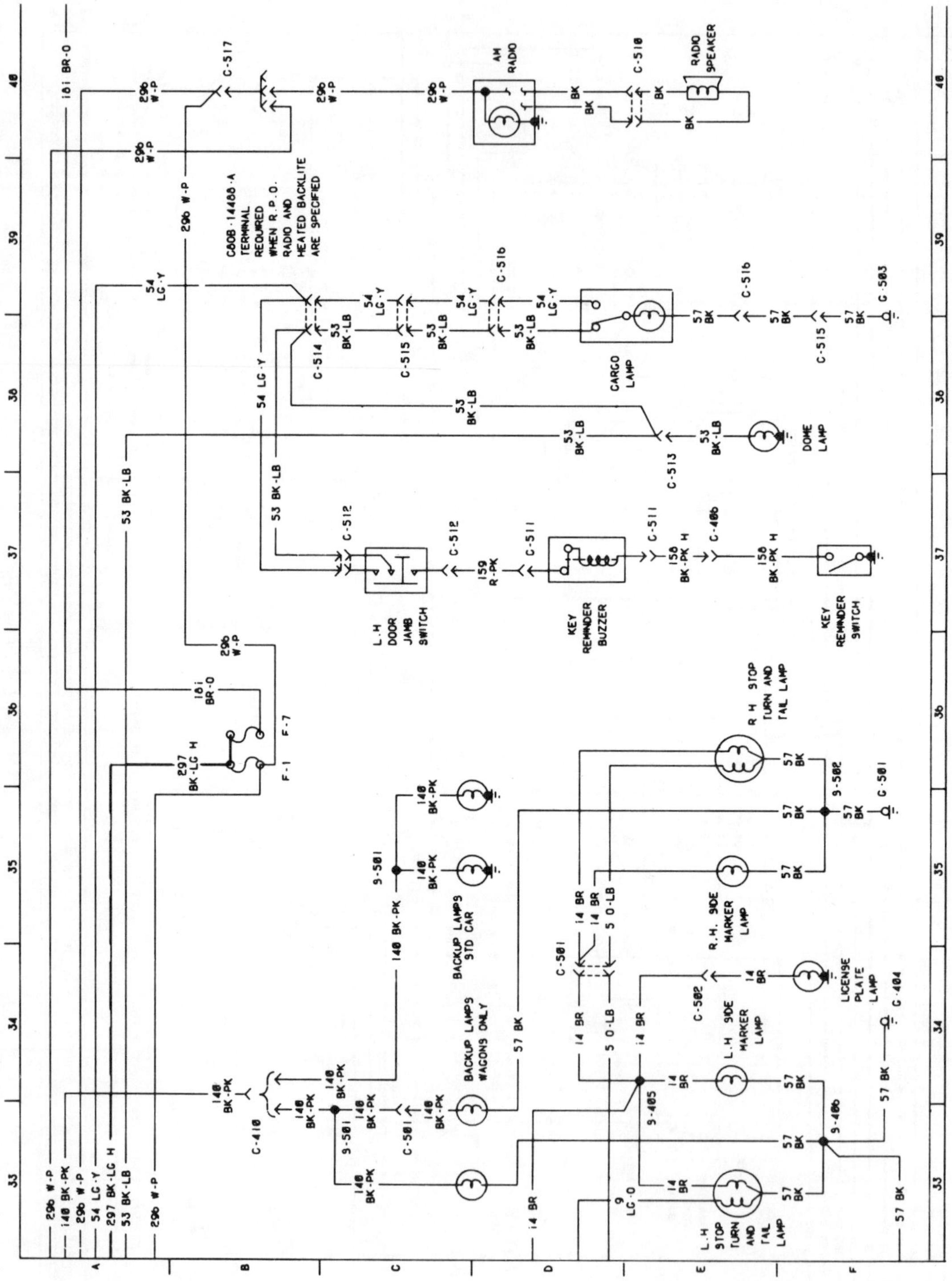

1973 Pinto Part 5

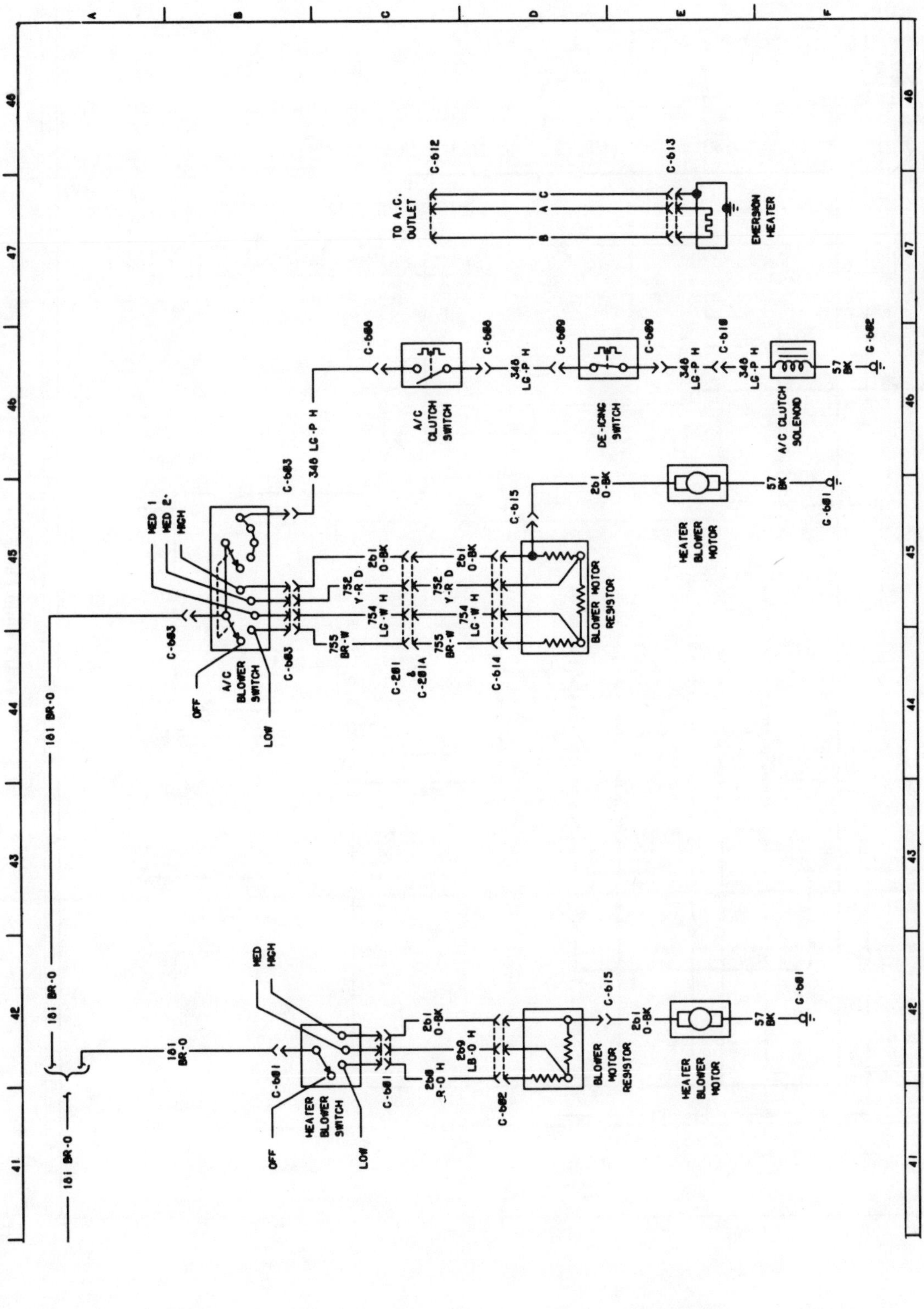

1973 Pinto Part 6

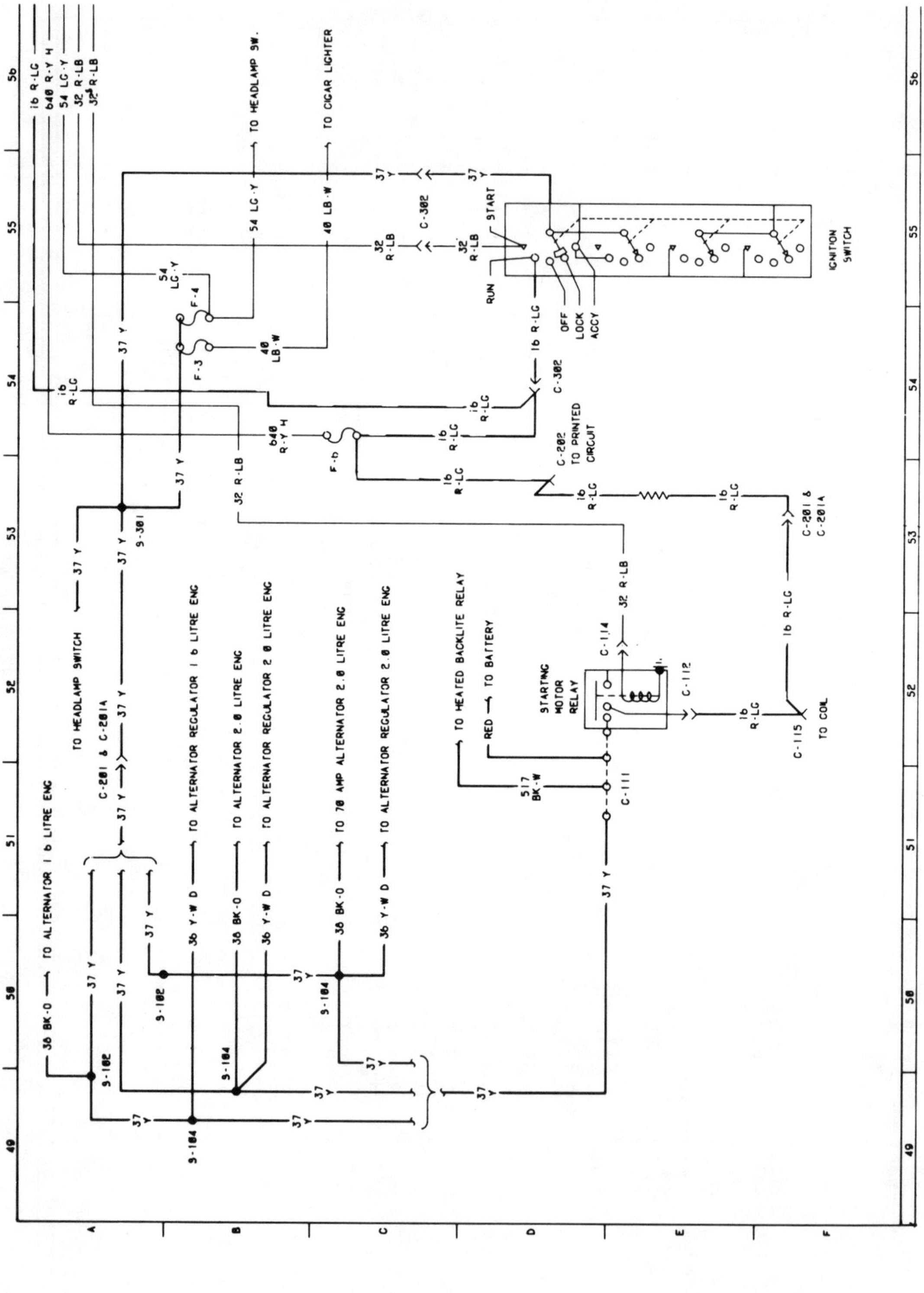

1973 Pinto Part 7

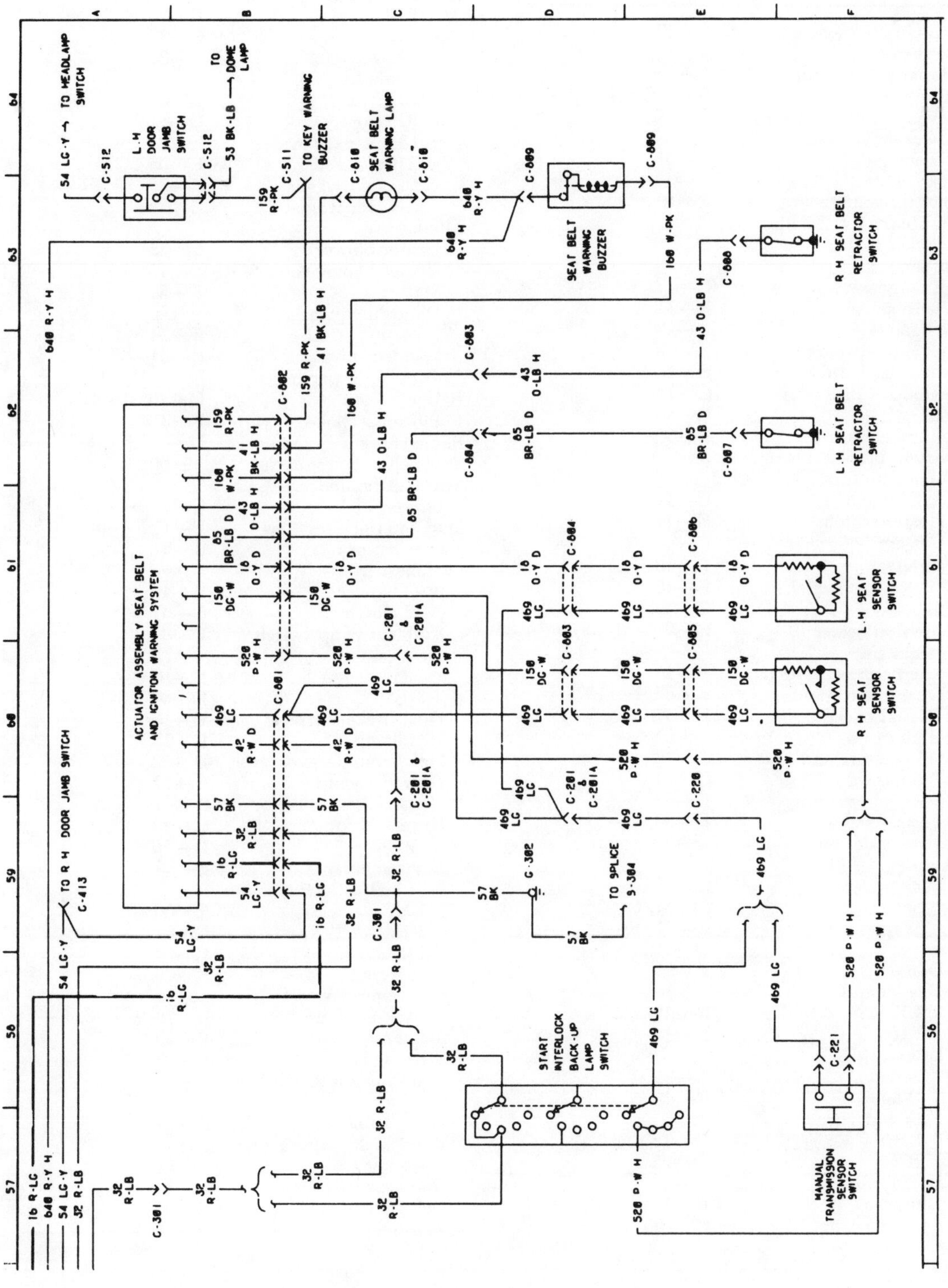

1973 Pinto Part 8

1974 Index

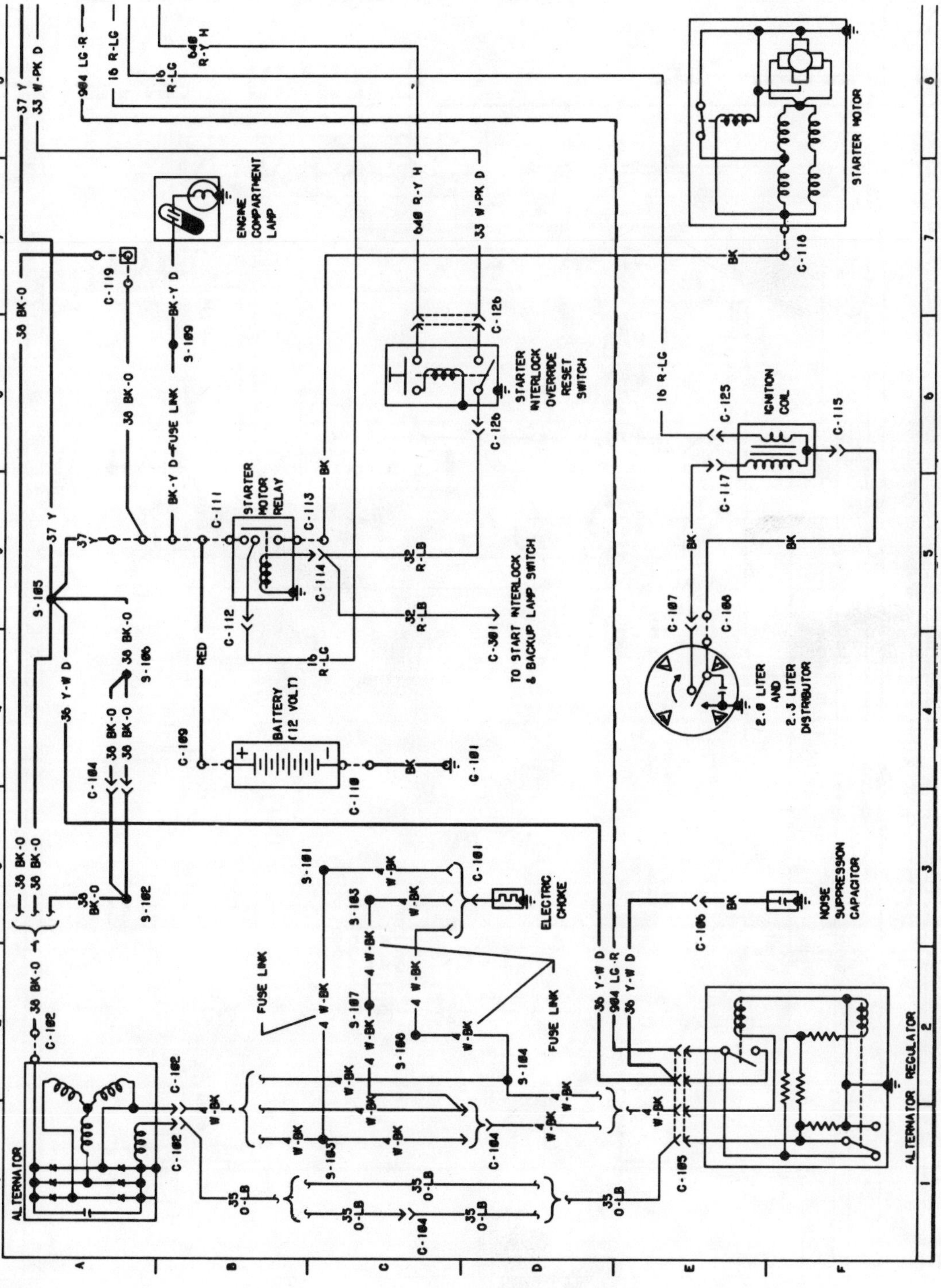

1974 Pinto Part 1

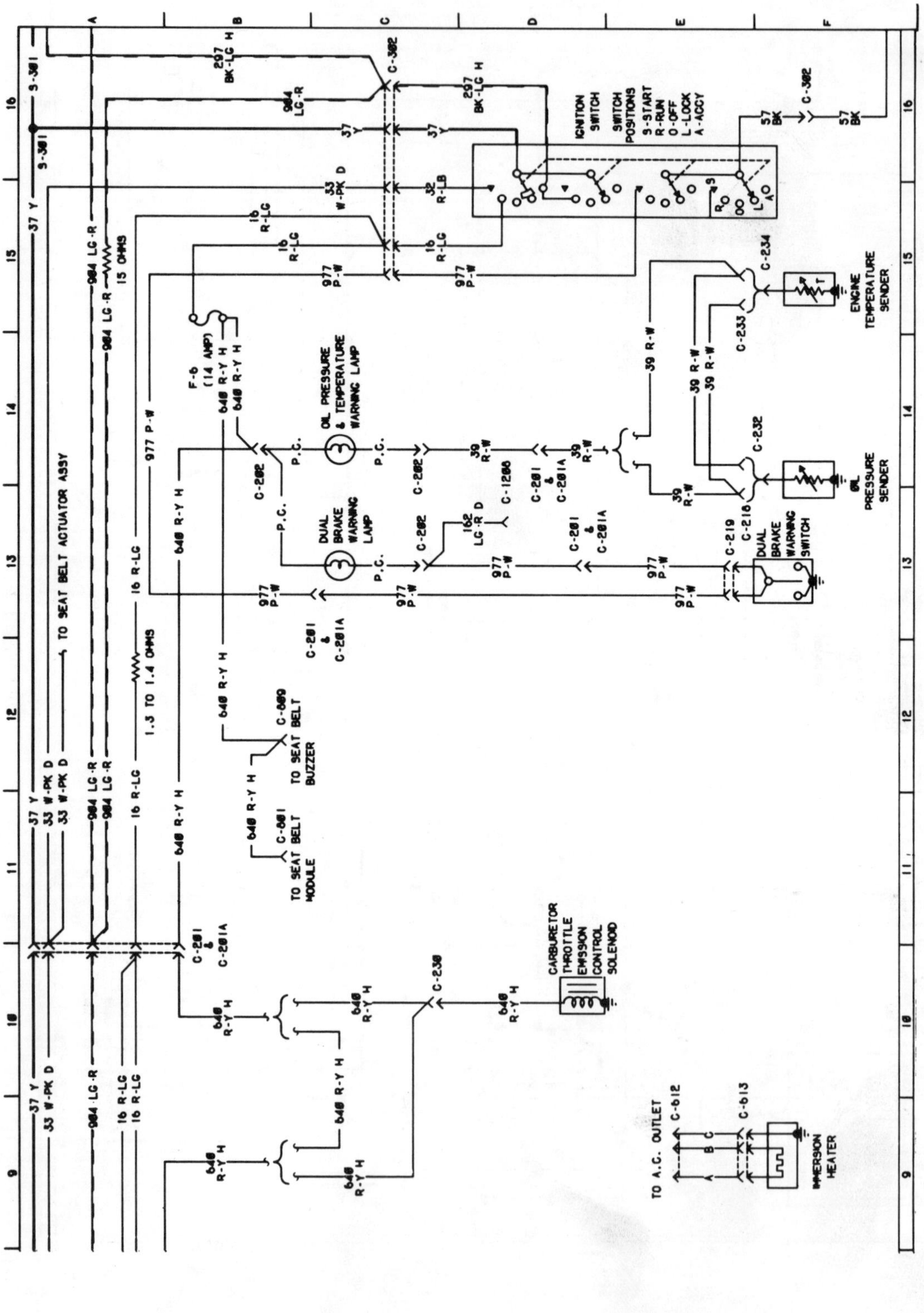

1974 Pinto Part 2

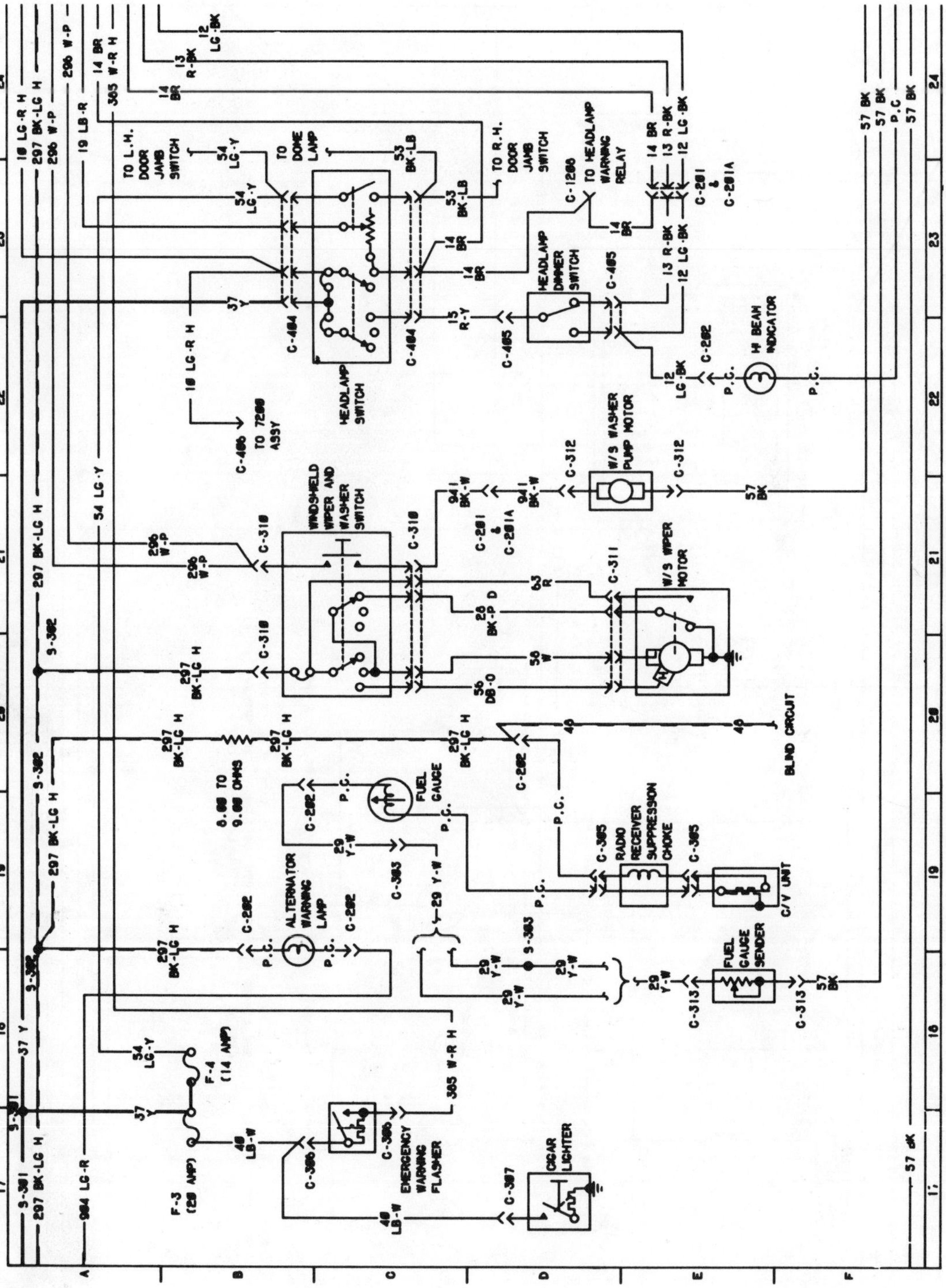

1974 Pinto Part 3

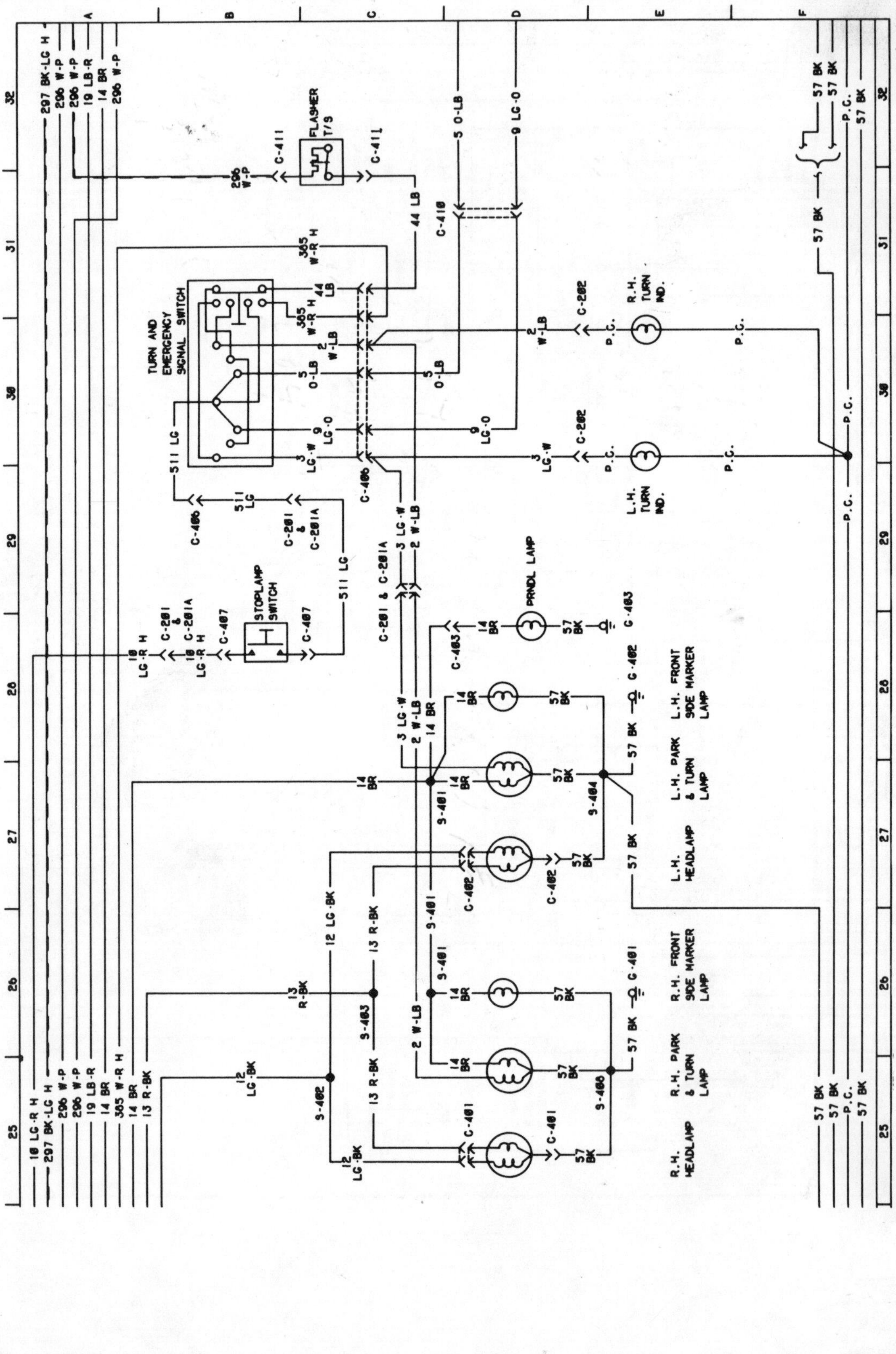

1974 Pinto Part 4

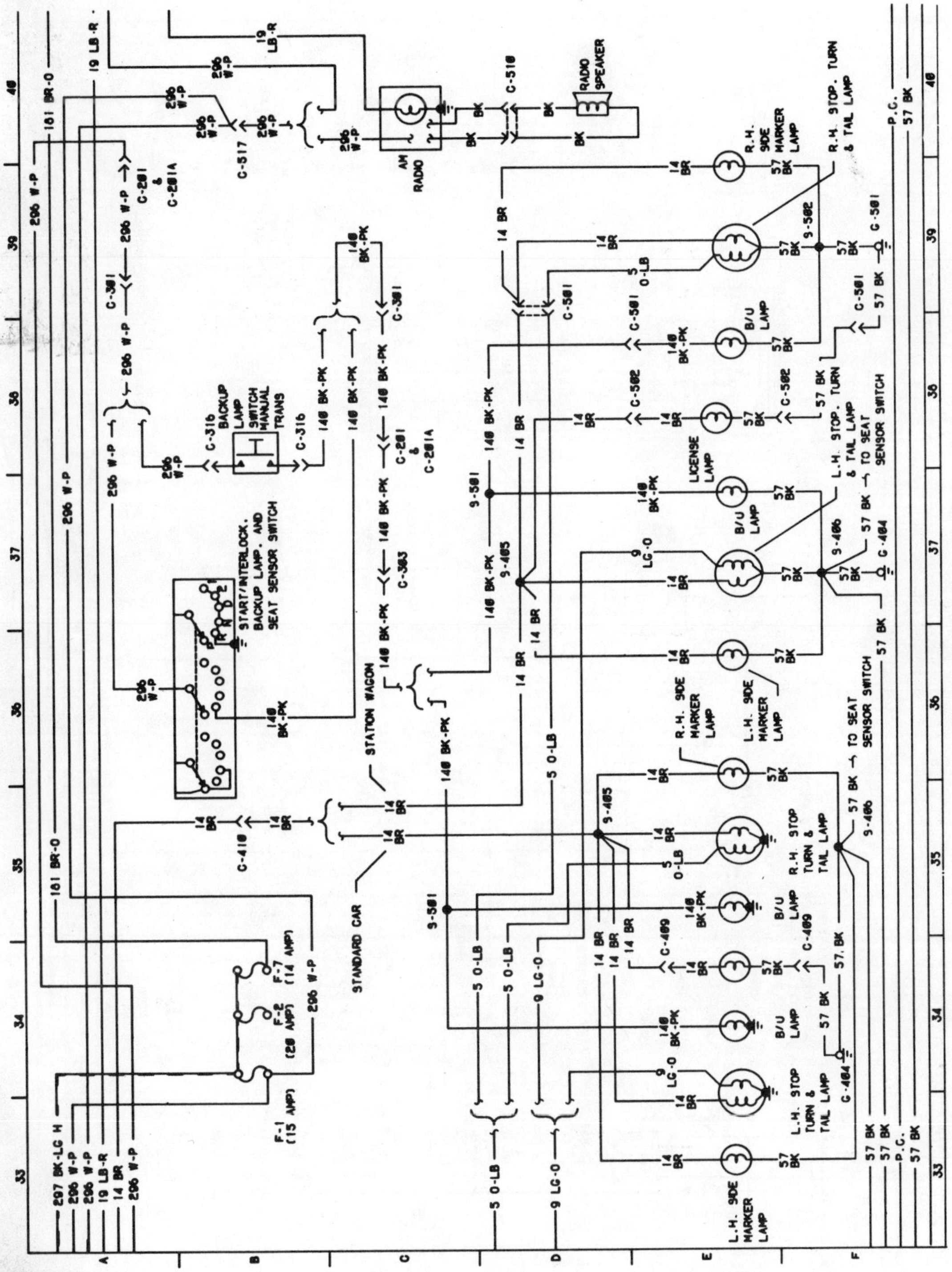

1974 Pinto Part 5

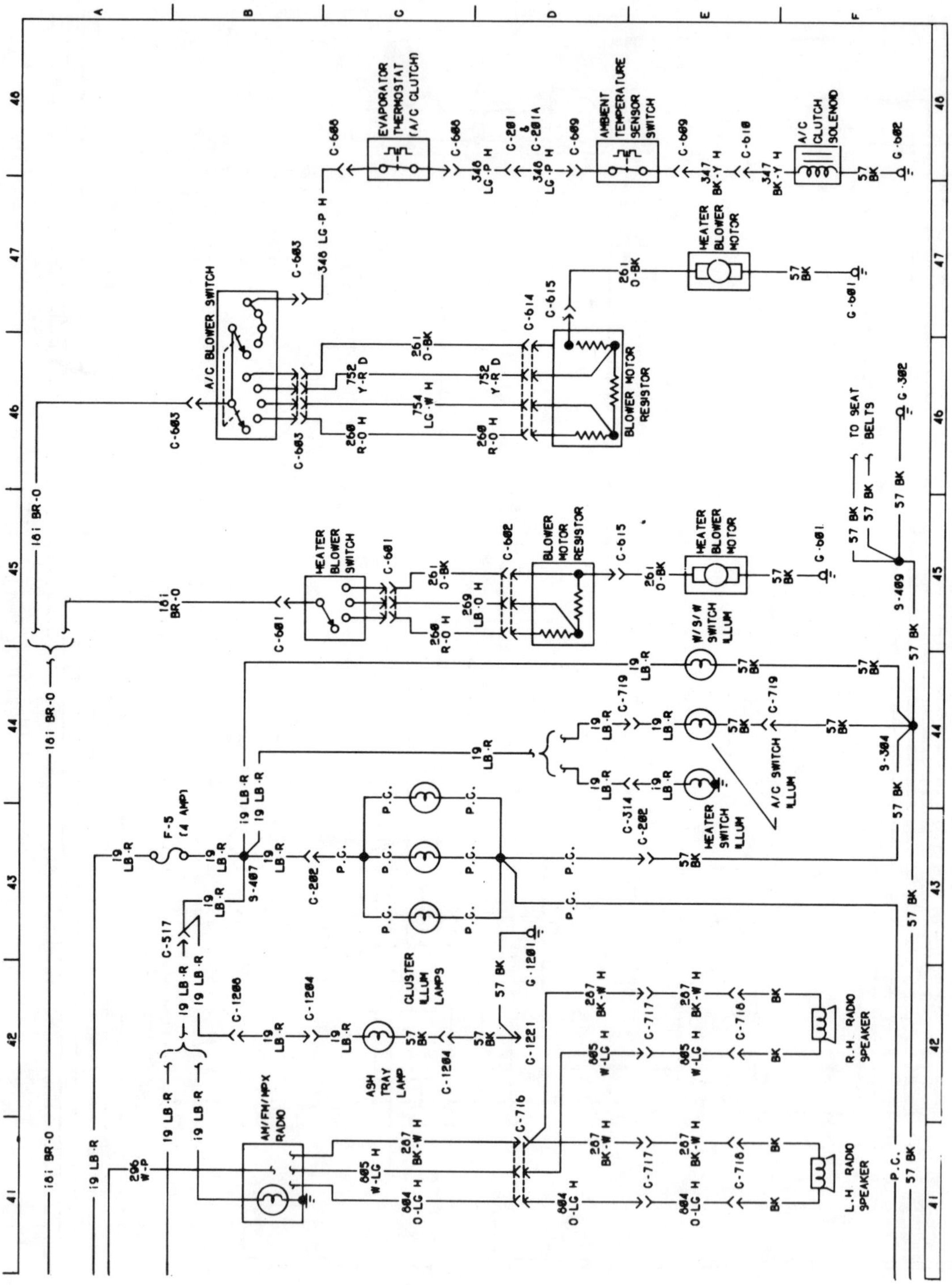

1974 Pinto Part 6

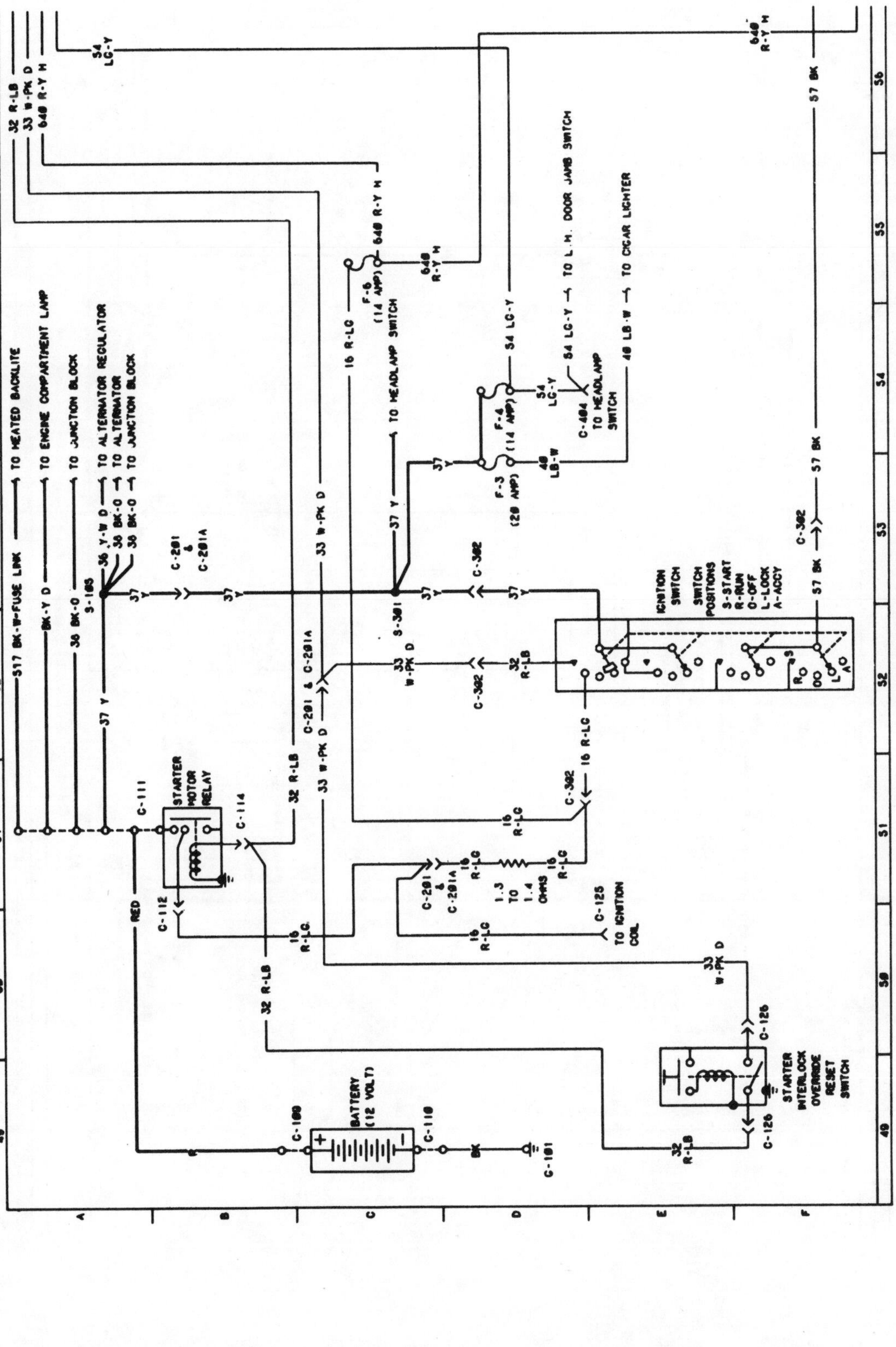

1974 Pinto Part 7

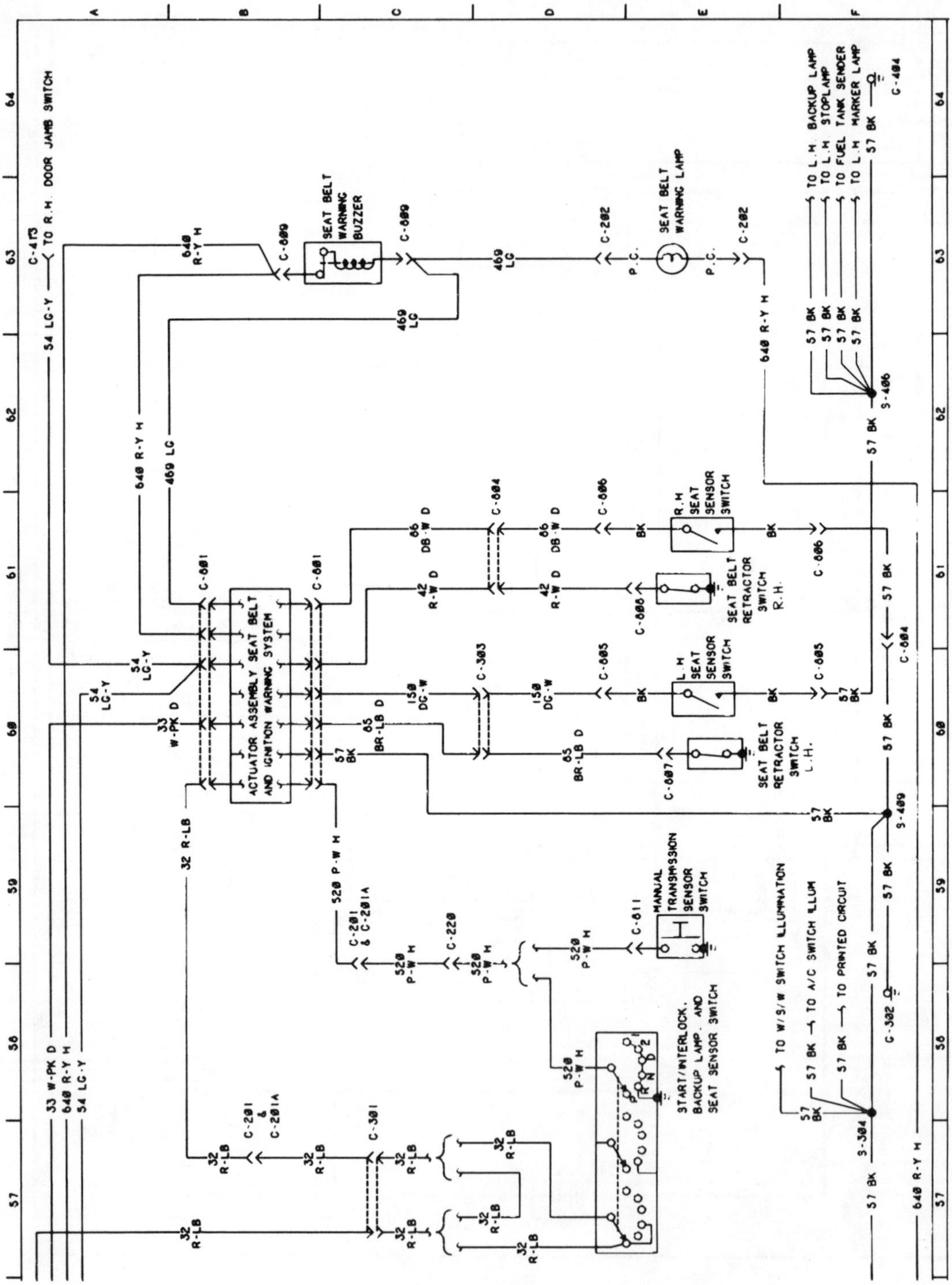

1974 Pinto Part 8

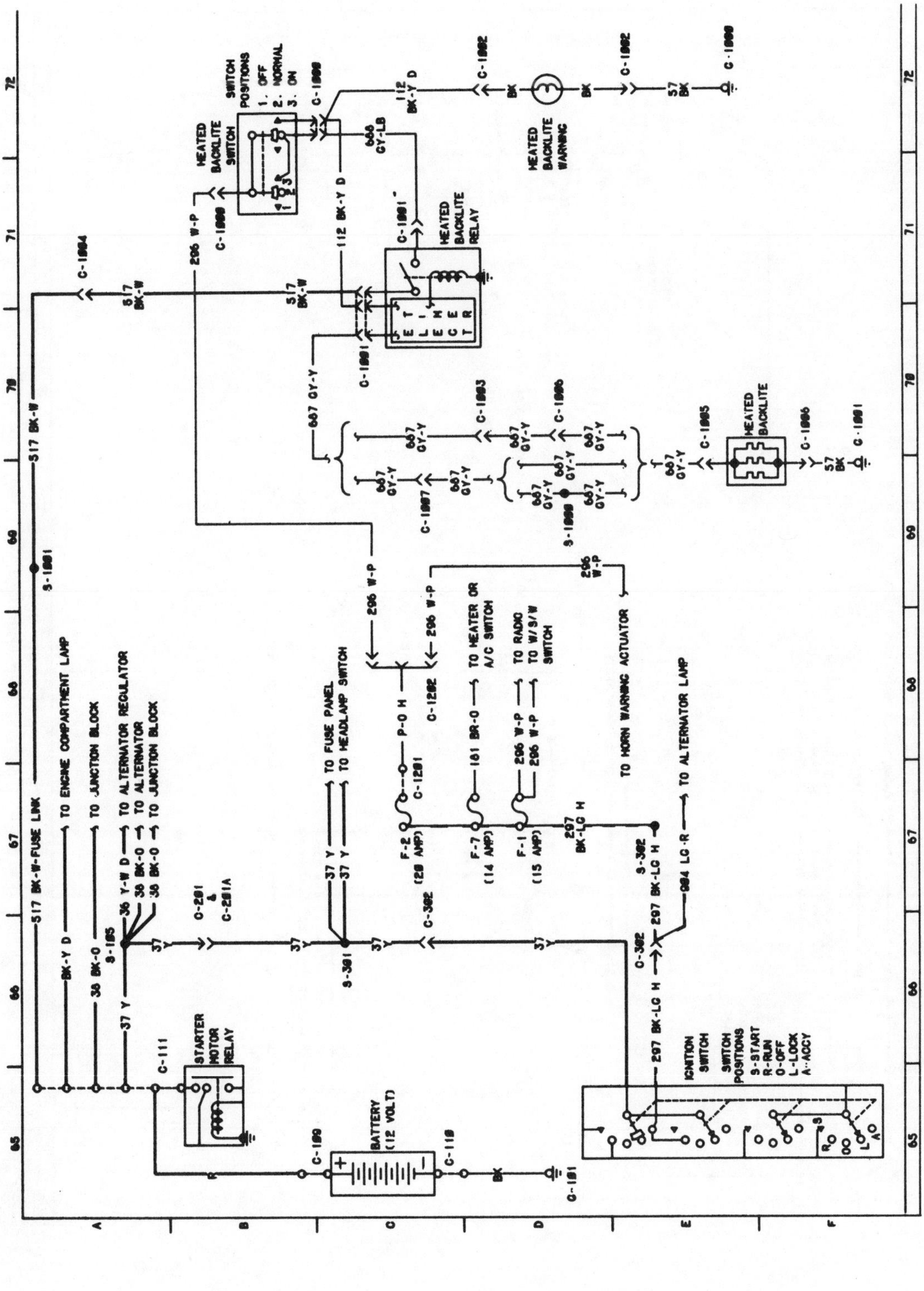

1974 Pinto Part 9

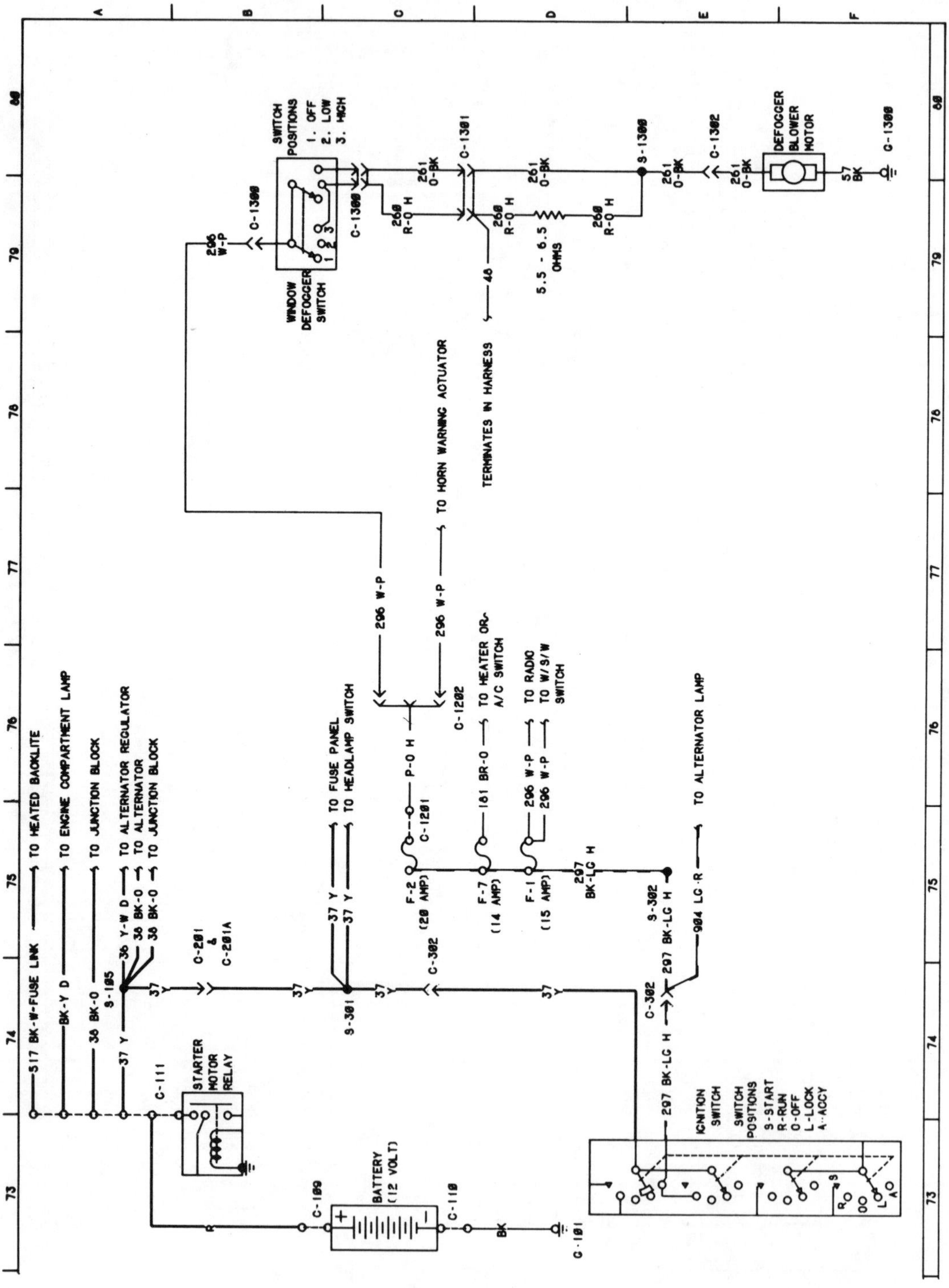

1974 Pinto Part 10

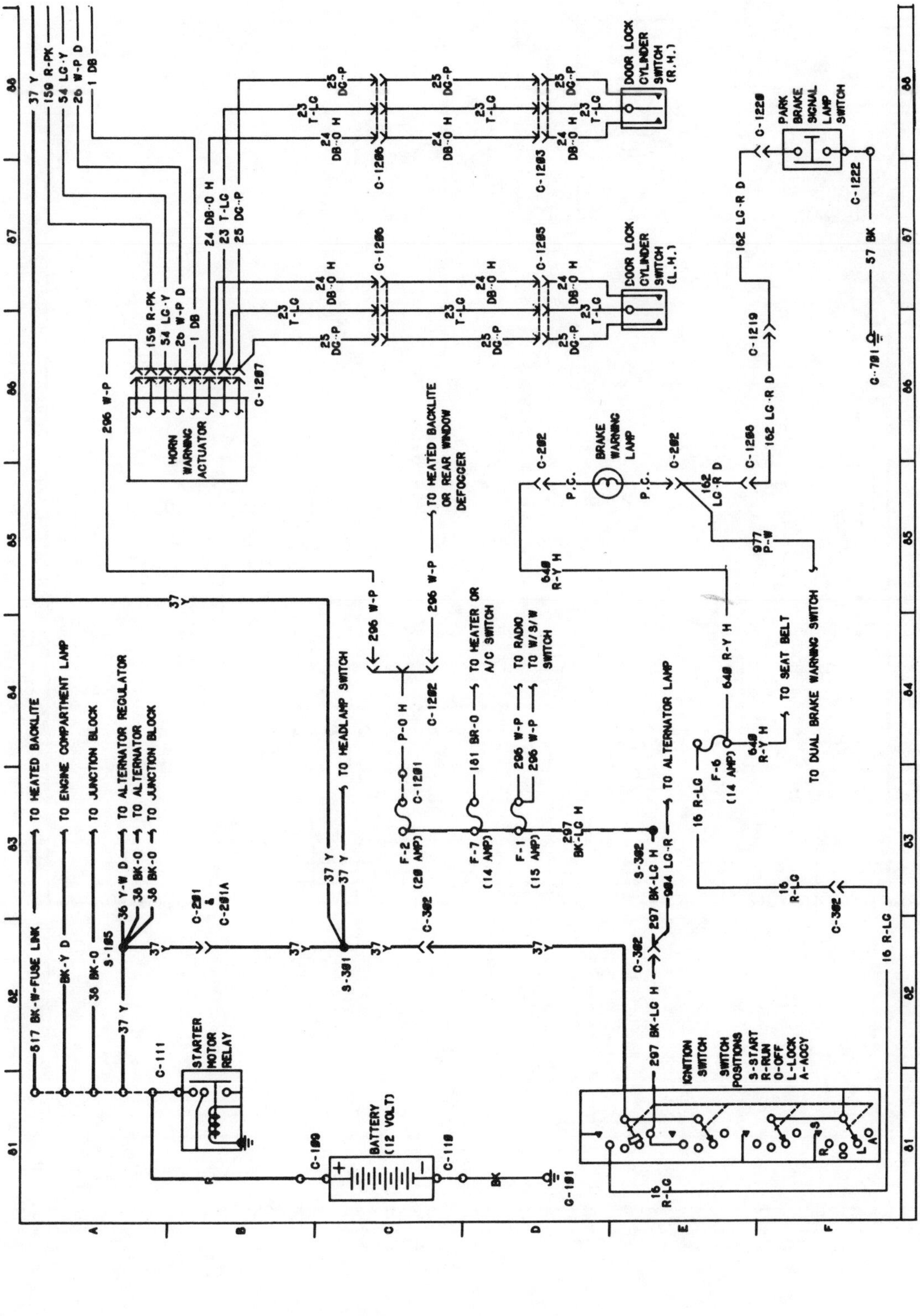

1974 Pinto Part 11

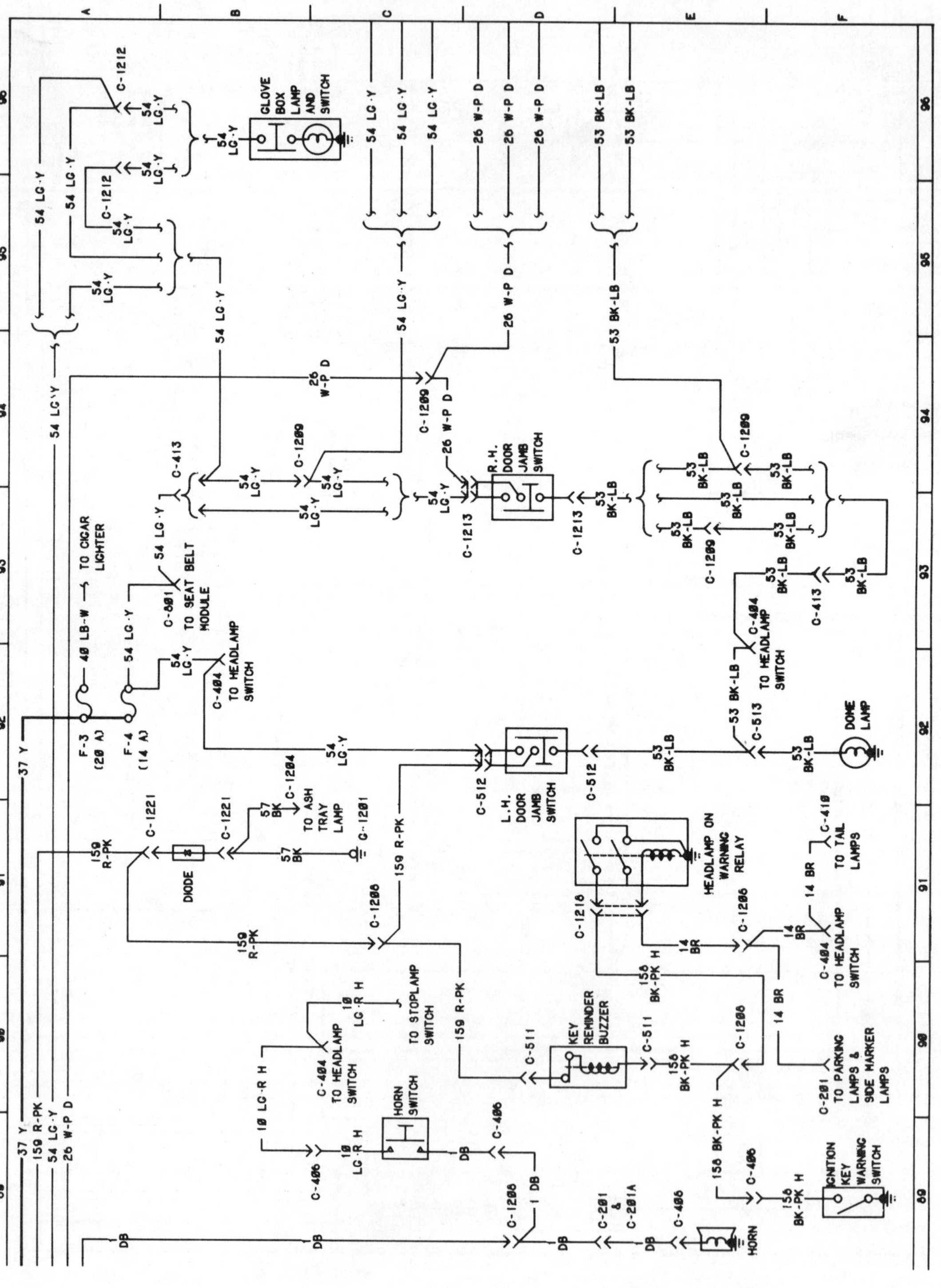

1974 Pinto Part 12

Chapter 6

Clutch and Transmission

Manual Transmission

A four-speed manual transmission is standard equipment on all Pintos. Two different types of manual transmissions are used, one made in Germany and the other made in England. The German transmission is by far the most common. Although the 1600 engine is made in England and the 2000 is made in Germany, there is not a direct relationship between engine and transmission usage.

The shift lever of both transmissions is connected to the transmission inside the transmission case; there is no external linkage.

The clutch housing is integral with the transmission housing. Because of this it is necessary to remove the transmission from the car to replace the clutch.

Removal

NOTE: *Consult the illustration in chapter three for the location of metric bolts.*

1. Place the gearshift lever in Neutral. Raise the car and remove the back-up light switch from the transmission extension housing. The back-up light switch *must* be removed before the shift lever is removed.
2. Loosen the shift lever locknut. Remove the knob and the locknut from the shift lever. Remove the four rubber boot attaching screws and the boot.
3. Compress the corrugated rubber spring, then remove the retaining snap-ring and slide the spring upward on the lever.
4. Bend the shift lever locktabs up, then thread the plastic dome nut from the extension housing.
5. Lift the shift lever from the extension housing.
6. Working from under the hood, remove the upper flywheel housing-to-engine attaching bolts.
7. Raise the vehicle and match-mark the driveshaft and the rear axle pinion.
8. Disconnect and remove the driveshaft. Place rags in the extension housing to prevent the loss of lubricant.
9. Remove the clutch release lever dust cover.
10. Disconnect the clutch cable from the clutch release lever.
11. Remove the starter motor attaching bolts and position the motor out of the way.
12. Remove the speedometer cable-to-transmission attaching screw and remove the cable and gear from the transmission. Plug the opening in the transmission to prevent lubricant spillage.

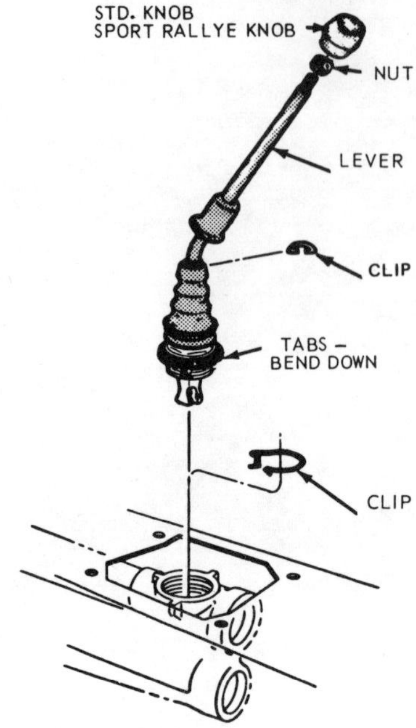

Shift lever components

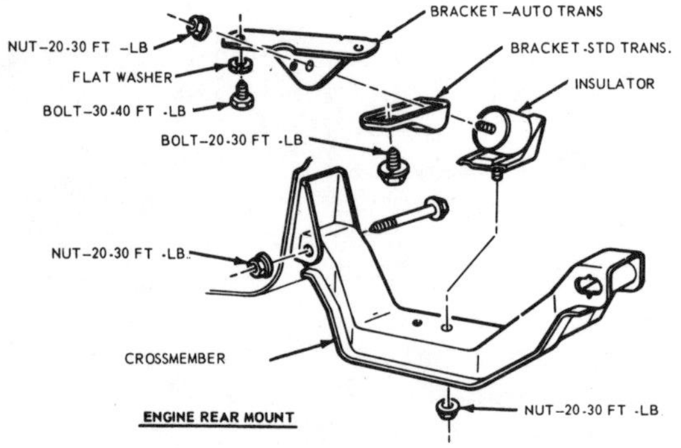

Transmission crossmember

13. Support the rear of the engine with a jack and remove the crossmember-to-body attaching bolts.

14. Remove the bolts that attach the crossmember to the transmission extension housing and remove the crossmember from the car.

15. Lower the engine to gain working room and remove the remaining flywheel housing-to-engine attaching bolts.

16. Slide the transmission rearward and remove it from the car.

Installation

1. Position the transmission assembly on the engine. It may be necessary to put the transmission in gear and turn the output shaft to align the input shaft splines with the splines on the clutch.

2. Make sure the flywheel housing fully engages the dowels on the rear of the engine and install and tighten the transmission attaching bolts while holding the transmission against the engine. Tighten the center attaching bolts first, then lower the car and tighten the upper attaching bolts.

3. Make sure the transmission is in neutral, then install the shift lever. Working inside the car, position the shift lever insulator in a straight-down position on the shift rail.

4. Position the shift lever in the extension housing so the forked end engages the insulator properly.

5. Thread the shift lever dome nut into the extension unit until it seats. Bend the tabs down to lock it in place.

6. Compress the corrugated rubber spring and install the retaining snapring.

7. Install the boot and attaching screws and install the carpet in place.

8. Install the shift knob and locknut.

9. Raise the car and install the backup light switch. The shift lever must be installed before installing the back-up light switch.

10. Raise the engine slightly and install the crossmember.

11. Install the speedometer cable.

12. Install the starter.

13. Align the match marks and install the driveshaft.

14. Fill the transmission with fluid to the bottom of the filler plug hole. Install the filler plug.

15. Lower the car and check the transmission operation.

Transmission Troubleshooting

JUMPING OUT OF HIGH GEAR

1. Misalignment of transmission case or clutch housing.
2. Worn pilot bearing in crankshaft.
3. Bent transmission shaft.
4. Worn high-speed sliding gear.
5. Worn teeth in the clutch shaft.
6. Insufficient spring tension on the shifter rail plunger.
7. Gears not engaging completely.

STICKING IN HIGH GEAR

1. Clutch not releasing fully.
2. Burred or battered transmission main shaft.
3. Frozen synchronizing clutch.

4. Stuck shifter rail plunger.
5. Gearshift lever twisting and binding the shifter rail.
6. Battered teeth on the high-speed sliding gear or on the sleeve.
7. Lack of lubrication.
8. Improper lubrication.
9. Corroded transmission parts.
10. Defective mainshaft pilot bearing.

Jumping out of Second Gear

1. Insufficient spring tension on the shifter rail plunger.
2. Bent or loose shifter fork.
3. Gears not engaging completely.
4. End-play in the transmission mainshaft.
5. Defective mainshaft pilot bearing.
6. Bent transmission shaft.
7. Worn teeth on the second-speed sliding gear or sleeve.
8. Loose or worn bearings on the transmission mainshaft.
9. End-play in the countershaft.

Sticking in Second Gear

1. Clutch not releasing fully.
2. Burred or battered teeth on the sliding sleeve.
3. Burred or battered transmission mainshaft.
4. Frozen synchronizing clutch.
5. Stuck shifter rail plunger.
6. Gearshift lever twisting and binding the shifter rail.
7. Lack of lubrication.
8. Second-speed transmission gear bearings locked will give same effect as gears stuck in second.
9. Improper lubrication.
10. Corroded transmission parts.

Jumping out of Low Gear

1. Gears not engaging completely.
2. End-play in the transmission mainshaft.
3. End-play in the countershaft.
4. Loose or worn bearings on the transmission mainshaft.
5. Loose or worn bearings in the countershaft.
6. Defective mainshaft pilot bearing.

Sticking in Low Gear

1. Clutch not releasing fully.
2. Burred or battered transmission mainshaft.
3. Stuck shifter rail plunger.
4. Gearshift lever twisting and binding the shifter rail.
5. Lack of lubrication.
6. Improper lubrication.
7. Corroded transmission parts.

Jumping out of Reverse Gear

1. Insufficient spring tension on the shifter rail plunger.
2. Badly worn gear teeth.
3. Gears not engaging completely.
4. End-play in the transmission mainshaft.
5. Idler gear bushings loose or worn.
6. Loose or worn bearings on the transmission mainshaft.
7. Defective mainshaft pilot bearing.

Sticking in Reverse Gear

1. Clutch not releasing fully.
2. Burred or battered transmission mainshaft.
3. Stuck shifter rail plunger.
4. Gearshift lever twisting and binding the shifter rail.
5. Lack of lubrication.
6. Improper lubrication.
7. Corroded transmission parts.

Failure of Gears to Synchronize

1. Binding pilot bearing on mainshaft; will synchronize in high gear only.
2. Clutch not releasing fully.
3. Detent springs weak or broken.
4. Weak or broken springs under balls in sliding gear sleeve.
5. Binding bearing on clutch shaft.
6. Binding countershaft.
7. Binding pilot bearing in the crankshaft.
8. Badly worn gear teeth.
9. Scored or worn cones.
10. Improper lubrication.
11. Constant-mesh gear not turning freely on the transmission mainshaft. Will synchronize in that gear only.

Gears Spinning When Shifting into Gear from Neutral

1. Clutch not releasing fully.
2. In some cases an extremely light lubricant in the transmission will cause the gears to continue to spin for a short time after the clutch is released.
3. Binding pilot bearing in the crankshaft.

Clutch

The clutch is a system of parts which, when engaged, connects the engine to the transmission. When the clutch is disengaged (clutch pedal pushed in), the turning motion of the engine crankshaft is separated from the transmission. Since the engine does not produce enough torque at idle to turn the rear wheels and start the car in motion, it is necessary to gradually connect the engine to the rest of the drive train to prevent the engine from stalling on acceleration. It is also much easier to shift the gears within a manual transmission when engine power is disconnected from the transmission.

When the clutch pedal is depressed, a cable attached to the clutch pedal pulls on the clutch release lever. This causes the clutch release bearing, which is attached to the clutch release lever, to press against the release fingers of the pressure plate. This removes the spring pressure of the pressure plate from the clutch disc. Since it was this pressure which was holding the clutch disc against the engine flywheel, the clutch can now move away from the flywheel. If engine power is to be transmitted to the rest of the power train, the clutch must be firmly held against the flywheel (which is attached to, and turns with, the crankshaft). By depressing the clutch pedal you allow the clutch disc to move away from the flywheel, thus isolating engine power from the rest of the drive train.

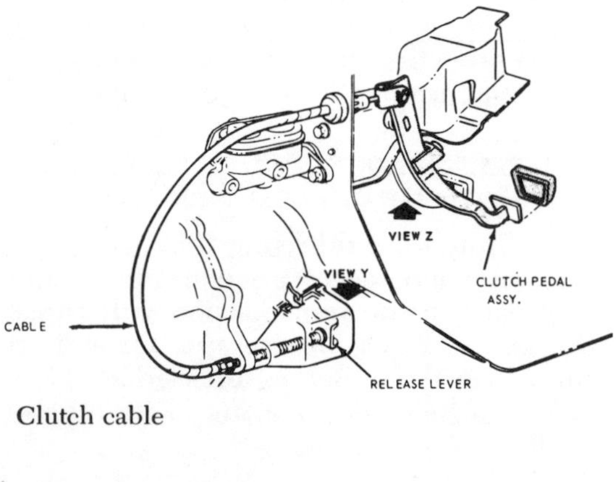

Clutch cable

Clutch Troubleshooting

The following are some symptoms that may accompany clutch troubles.

1. Excessive noise.
2. Clutch chatter or grab.
3. Clutch slip.
4. Clutch drag or failure to release.
5. Pedal pulsation.
6. Low clutch facing life.
7. Gear lock-up or hard shifting.
8. Hard pedal.

Excessive Noise

There are five common sources of clutch noise:

1. Release bearing.
2. Clutch shaft pilot bearing.
3. Transmission pinion shaft bearing.
4. Transmitted engine noises.
5. Clutch linkage noises.

Release Bearing

Release bearing noises vary with the degree of bearing failure. A dry or damaged bearing usually makes a shrill or scraping sound when depressing the clutch pedal to the point of release finger-to-bearing contact. This means that the noise should be audible at the lower end of clutch pedal free-play. Continued use of a car, with the release bearing in this condition, is damaging to the clutch release fingers.

Usual cause of release bearing failure is overwork—caused by riding the clutch. Other causes are not enough pedal free-play, lack of lubricant in the bearing, clutch release fingers worn or out of true.

Pilot Bearing

Clutch shaft pilot bearing noises can be heard only when the bearing is in operation. This is at any time crankshaft speed is different from that of the clutch shaft (clutch disengaged with transmission in gear).

This is a high-pitched squeal, caused by a dry bearing and requires replacement.

Transmission Pinion Shaft Bearing

A rough, or otherwise damaged, transmission pinion (input) shaft bearing noise can be heard only when the clutch is engaged, with the transmission in any

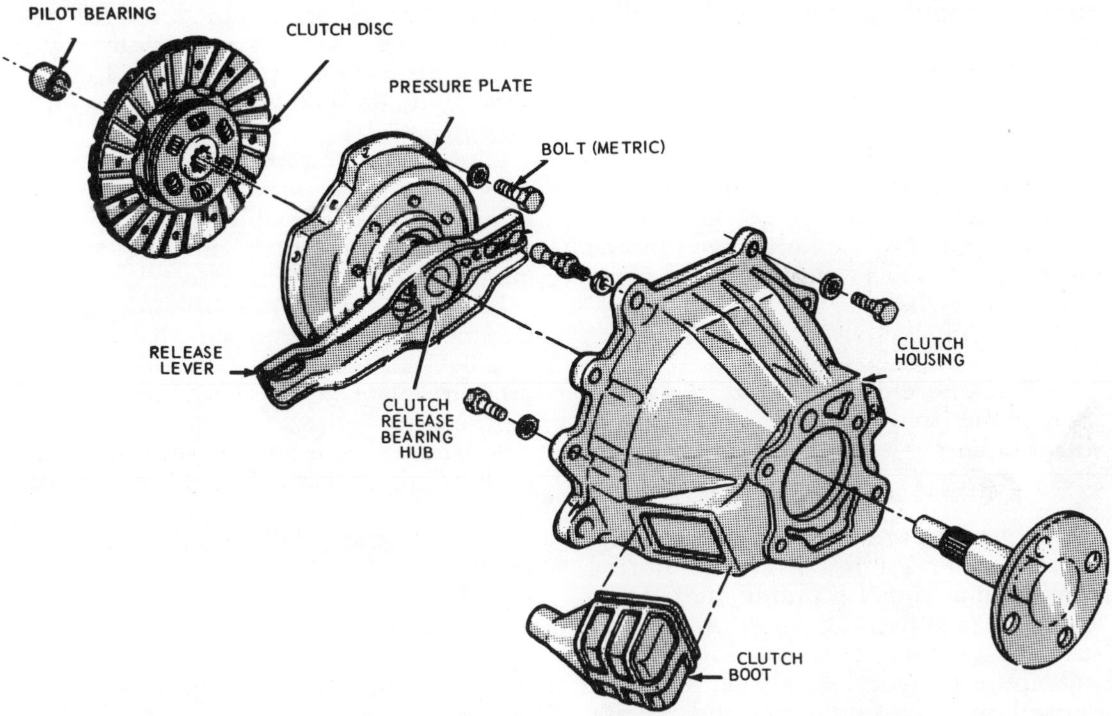

Clutch components

shift position. The noise is usually quite noticeable with the gears in Neutral. This noise should diminish and completely disappear as the transmission pinion gear slows down and stops after clutch release. This noise is easily distinguished from release bearing noise because of the opposite conditions of encounter.

Transmitted Engine Noises

Assuming that the clutch pedal has the required amount of free-play, there should be no objectionable amount of engine noise transmitted to the passenger area via the clutch. Some engine noises are transmitted through the positive pressure of the clutch release bearing and fingers to the clutch housing. Here they are amplified by the shape of the clutch housing and heard in the passenger compartment in the guise of clutch or transmission trouble. Engine noise transmission can usually be modified through clutch pedal manipulation.

Clutch Linkage Noise

Clutch linkage noise is usally a clicking or snapping sound that can be heard or felt in the pedal itself when moving it completely up or down. Locating the cause of trouble and correcting it is a matter of repositioning and lubrication. The trouble may be in the clutch assist spring, the retract spring, the release bearing lever, or even at the release bearing.

Clutch Chatter or Grab

Usually the cause of clutch chatter or grab can be located within the clutch assembly. To correct the trouble will require the removal of the clutch. However, symptoms resembling clutch trouble may be misleading and originate in other areas.

In order to isolate the cause of the problem, we suggest that the following items be checked in this order.

1. Be sure that the clutch linkage is in adjustment and not binding. If necessary, lubricate, align, and adjust the linkage.

2. Check for worn or loose engine or transmission mounts. If necessary, tighten or replace the mounts.

3. Check for wear, looseness, or misalignment of the universal joints. Check the attaching bolts on the clutch pressure plate, transmission, and clutch

housing. Tighten, align, or replace as necessary.

4. Check the freedom of movement of the clutch release bearing on its sleeve. Free up or replace as necessary.

5. Check for oil or grease on the flywheel, friction disc, or pressure plate.

6. Check for trueness of the friction disc, and that the disc hub is not binding on the splines of the transmission input shaft (clutch shaft).

7. Be sure that the disc or the pressure plate is not broken

8. Examine clutch pressure plate and cover plate assembly for cracks or heat discoloration.

Clutch Slip

Clutch slippage is usually most noticeable when pulling away, and during acceleration from a standing start. A severe, but positive, test for slippage is to start the engine, set the parking brake, and apply the service brakes; shift the transmission into high gear and release the clutch pedal while accelerating the engine. A clutch in good condition should hold and stall the engine. If the clutch slips, the cause may be one or more of the following:

1. Improper linkage adjustment (not enough free-play).
2. Broken or disconnected parts.
3. Clutch linkage or lever mechanism binding or broken, not allowing full pressure plate application.
4. Friction disc oil-saturated or excessively worn.
5. Pressure plate worn, springs weak from temper loss or failure (damaging heat will usually cause parts to appear blue).

Clutch Drag or Failure to Release

There are many reasons for clutch drag (spin) or failure to release. The following conditions, therefore, apply to unmodified versions of standard vehicles. Changing the driven plate mass (replacing the standard driven plate with a heavy-duty unit), changing transmission oil viscosity, etc., may influence clutch spin-time. Three seconds is a good, typical, spin-time for the standard transmission and clutch, driven under normal conditions, in temperate zone climates.

The friction disc and some of the transmission gears spin briefly after clutch disengagement, so normal clutch action should not be confused with a dragging clutch.

Clutch drag, failure to release, or abnormal spin-time may be caused by one or more of the following:

1. Improper clutch linkage adjustment.
2. Clutch plate hub binding on the transmission input (pinion) shaft.
3. A warped or bent friction disc or pressure plate; or loose friction material on the driven disc.
4. The transmission input shaft may be binding or sticking in the pilot bearing.
5. Misalignment of the transmission to the engine.
6. Transmission lubricant low or not heavy enough.

Pedal Pulsation

This condition can be felt by applying light foot pressure to the clutch pedal with the engine idling. It may be caused by any of the following:

1. Bent or uneven clutch release finger adjustment.
2. Excessive flywheel run-out due to bent wheel or crankshaft flange; or the flywheel may not be properly seated on the crankshaft flange.
3. Release bearing cocked on transmission bearing retainer.
4. Poor alignment of transmission with the engine.

Low Clutch Facing Life

This sort of complaint warrants a close study of the operator's driving habits. Poor clutch facing wear may be caused by any of the following:

1. Riding the clutch.
2. Drag strip type operation.
3. Continuous overloading, or the hauling of heavy trailers or other equipment.
4. Holding the car from drifting backward on a grade by slipping the clutch instead of using the brakes.
5. Improper pedal linkage adjustment (free-play and pedal height).
6. Rough surface on the flywheel or pressure plate.

7. Presence of oil or water on the clutch facing.

8. Weak pressure plate springs, causing clutch creep or slip.

GEAR LOCK UP OR HARD SHIFTING

This trouble is so closely related to "Clutch Drag or Failure to Release" that diagnosis should be conducted in the same way as given under that heading. If, after checking the items listed and finding that the transmission still locks up or is hard to shift, the trouble probably lies in the transmission cover or shifter assembly, or in the transmission proper. In that case, transmission work is needed.

HARD PEDAL

A stiff clutch pedal or a clutch release that requires abnormal pedal pressure may result from one or more of the following:

1. Dry and binding clutch linkage.
2. Linkage out of alignment.
3. Wrong type clutch assembly (heavy-duty) being used.

Removal

1. Remove the transmission from the car. See "Manual Transmission Removal" earlier in this chapter.
2. Loosen each of the pressure plate-to-flywheel attaching bolts gradually to relieve spring pressure.
3. If the same pressure plate is to be reused, match-mark it with the flywheel so it may be reinstalled in its original position.
4. Remove the clutch disc and pressure plate from the car.

INSPECTION

If the clutch disc, pressure plate, and clutch release bearing have a considerable amount of mileage on them, it is probably smart to replace them all at the same time. This will save you the aggravation of having to yank the transmission out again in a few thousand miles if one of them should fail.

Clutch Disc

The coil springs near the center of the disc are supposed to be loose. Do not replace the clutch because the springs are loose.

If the clutch disc is contaminated with oil or any other foreign substance, it must be replaced. However, you must also locate and repair the source of the leak to avoid repeated clutch failure. If the clutch disc is worn, distorted or if the friction material is loose on the disc it must be replaced.

Pressure Plate

If the face of the plate is worn, scored, or burnt, it should be replaced. If the release fingers are excessively worn, the pressure plate must be replaced. Do not clean the pressure plate in any way other than wiping the face with alcohol.

Release Bearing

The bearing is prelubricated and should not be cleaned with solvent. Inspect the rivets and spring clips on the bearing cover; if they are loose, replace the bearing.

Check the face of the bearing; if it is distorted, replace the bearing.

As a general rule, whenever in doubt about the release bearing, replace it. Release bearings are not that expensive and they make very annoying noises when they go bad.

Pilot Bearing

The pilot bearing is a press fit in the end of the crankshaft. Therefore, if it is loose it must be replaced. If the opening in the center of the bearing is worn out of round it should be replaced.

Do not lubricate the pilot bearing with grease.

If it is necessary to replace the bearing, it can be removed with an expanding type slide hammer.

Flywheel

If the flywheel is grooved or burnt, it is necessary to replace the flywheel or have the surface machined by an automotive machine shop.

Installation

1. Lubricate the pressure plate *lightly* at the pivot points.
2. Position the clutch disc and pressure plate on the flywheel and install the attaching bolts but do not tighten them.
3. Install a clutch alignment (dummy)

shaft to center the clutch disc. These can be bought at any large auto supply store.

4. Tighten the pressure plate attaching bolts alternately and evenly.
5. Remove the dummy shaft.
6. Install the clutch release bearing on the release lever.
7. Install the transmission.
8. Adjust the clutch using the procedure that follows.

Clutch Adjustment

Cars Built Before 10/1/70

1. From beneath the car, pull the clutch cable toward the front of the vehicle until the C-clip can be removed from the cable. Remove the clip.
2. Continue to pull the cable toward the front of the vehicle until all free movement has been eliminated from the clutch release bearing.
3. While holding the cable in the zero free-play position, insert a 0.135 in. spacer against the flywheel boss on the engine side and install the C-clip in the closest possible groove next to the spacer.
4. Remove the spacer and release the cable.

Cars Built After 9/30/70

1. Working beneath the car, loosen the clutch adjusting nut, the front locknut, and the rear locknut (if so equipped).
2. Pull the clutch cable toward the front of the car until all free play is removed from the clutch release lever.

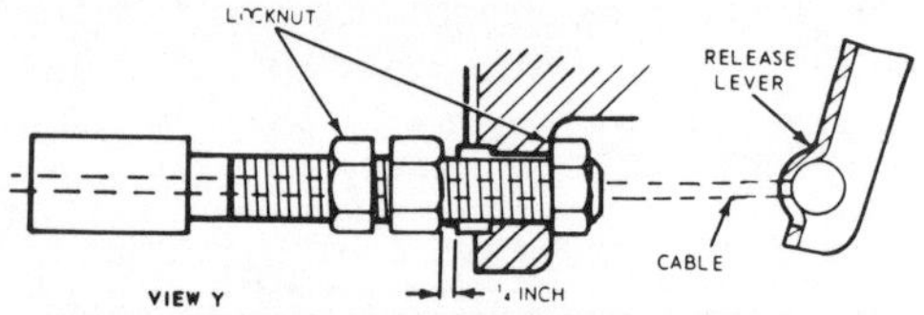

Clutch adjustment

3. Holding the cable in this position, place a ¼ in. spacer against the engine side of the flywheel housing and tighten the adjusting nut finger-tight against the spacer.
4. Hold the adjusting nut so that it maintains its position, then tighten the front locknut against the adjusting nut.
5. Remove the spacer and tighten the rear locknut (if so equipped) against the transmission side of the flywheel housing.

Automatic Transmission

A Ford, C4 automatic transmission is offered as optional equipment on all Pintos with 2000 cc and 2300 cc engines and standard on the 2800 cc V6 engine. While the automatic transmission is a complex unit, there are some adjustments which can be made by the average do-it-yourselfer.

Starting 1975, another transmission was offered as the base automatic transmission, the C3. The C4 was offered as a heavier-duty option.

Adjustments—All Models

All adjustments *must* be performed in the order listed here.

Downshift Linkage Adjustment

Downshift linkage (or kick-down linkage) controls forced downshifting of the transmission into the next lower gear when the gas pedal is pushed to the floor, as in a passing situation. This provides quicker acceleration. Downshift linkage adjustment controls how far the gas pedal must be depressed before the transmission will downshift.

1. Disconnect the kick-down rod return spring from the kick-down rod.
2. Have a friend depress the gas pedal completely to the floor.
3. Move the kick-down rod downward until it contacts its stop and it cannot be moved any farther.
4. Check the clearance between the kick-down adjusting screw and the tab on the top of the kick-down rod. Clearance should be 0.050–0.070 in. to 1972; 0.010–0.080—1973 and later. If the clearance is not correct, turn the adjusting screw inward or outward to correct.
5. Have your friend release the gas pedal and reconnect the kick-down return spring.

Manual Linkage Adjustment

The manual linkage connects the gearshift selector lever to the transmission.

1. Place the transmission selector lever in the Drive position.

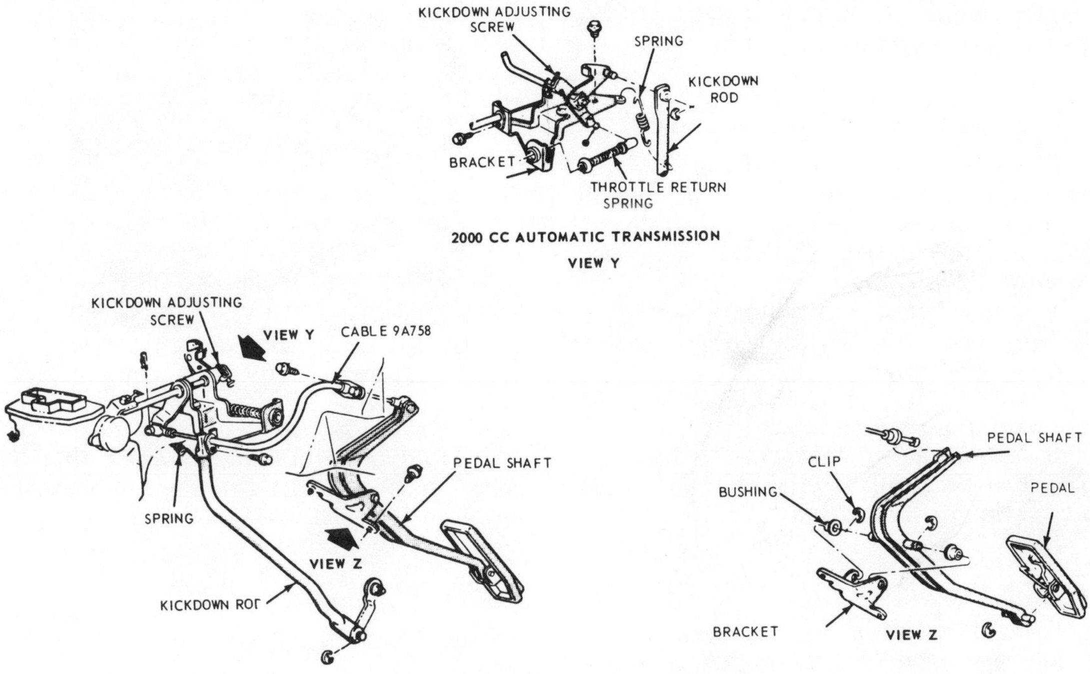

Transmission downshift linkage

2. Raise the vehicle and loosen the manual linkage shift rod attaching nut at the selector lever.

3. Move the transmission manual lever to the Drive position (fourth detent position from the rear of the transmission).

4. Tighten the nut on the manual linkage shift rod to 10–20 ft lbs.

5. Lower the car and check transmission operation.

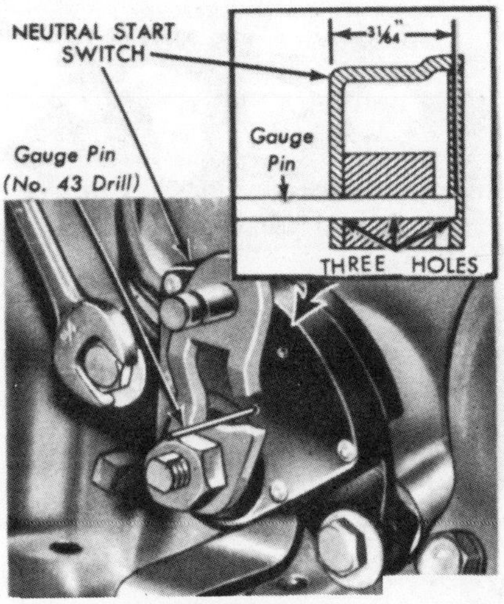

Neutral start switch adjustment

C3 Front Band Adjustment

1. Remove the downshift rod from the transmission downshift lever.

2. Remove and discard the locknut.

3. Install a new locknut and torque the adjusting screw to 10 ft lbs.

4. Back off the adjusting screw *exactly* one and a half turns.

5. Hold the adjusting screw with a wrench and torque the locknut to 35–45 ft lbs.

6. Reinstall the downshift rod on the transmission downshift lever.

Neutral Start Switch Adjustment (C4)

The neutral start switch prevents the engine from starting unless the transmission selector lever is in Park or the Neutral position.

1. Place the transmission selector lever in the Neutral position.

2. Raise the vehicle and loosen the two bolts that attach the Neutral switch to the transmission.

3. Rotate the switch until a gauge pin (shank end of a no. 43 drill bit) can be inserted through the gauge pin holes in the switch. The gauge pin must be inserted a full 31/64 in. into the switch through all three holes in the switch.

4. Tighten the switch retaining bolts to 50–75 in. lbs and remove the pin.

Neutral Start Switch Replacement

1. Raise the car with the transmission in neutral, and, disconnect the downshift linkage rod from the downshift lever. Remove the downshift outer lever retaining nut and the outer lever.
2. Remove the neutral start switch attaching bolts and switch and then disconnect the wires.
3. Install the new switch and adjust it. See the above procedure.
4. Install the downshift outer lever.
5. Connect the downshift linkage rod to the downshift lever.

Band Adjustment

CAUTION: *The torque figures and numbers of turns given in these procedures must be exactly correct to prevent transmission damage.*

Intermediate Band (C4)

1. Wipe clean the area around the adjusting screw on the side of the transmission, near the left-front corner of the transmission.
2. Remove the adjusting screw locknut and discard it.
3. Install a new locknut on the adjusting screw but do not tighten it.
4. Tighten the adjusting screw to *exactly 10 ft lbs.*
5. Back off the adjusting screw *exactly 1¾ turns.*
6. Hold the adjusting screw so that it *does not turn* and tighten the adjusting screw locknut to 35–45 ft lbs.

Low-Reverse Band (C4)

1. Wipe clean the area around the adjusting screw on the side of the transmission, near the right-rear corner.
2. Remove the adjusting screw locknut and discard it.
3. Install a new locknut on the adjusting screw but do not tighten it.
4. Tighten the adjusting screw to *exactly 10 ft lbs.*
5. Back off the adjusting screw *exactly 3 full turns.*

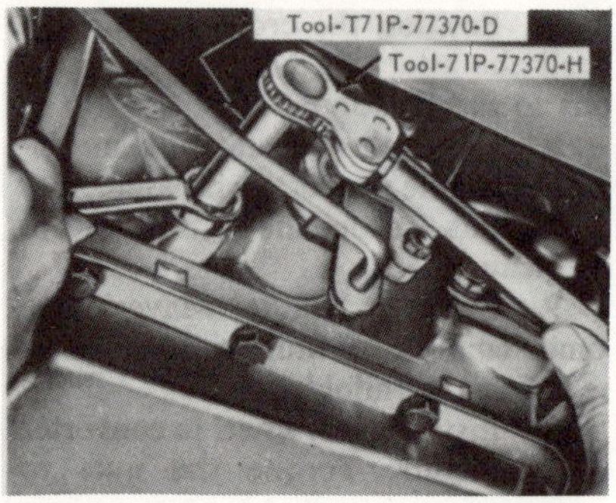

Adjusting intermediate band with special torque wrench and tool

6. Hold the adjusting screw so that it *does not turn* and tighten the adjusting screw to 35–45 ft lbs.

PAN, FLUID, AND FILTER

Removal and Installation

C3 and C4 Models

1. Raise the car up on a lift.
2. Some C4 models require that the transmission fluid filler tube be disconnected to drain the pan; all others can be drained by loosening the pan bolts and letting the fluid drain out when the pan is lowered.
3. After the fluid has drained out, remove the rest of the attaching bolts, the pan and the gasket.
4. Remove the bolts holding the filter in place, remove the filter and replace it. The filter may be reused after cleaning in a nondetergent solution, such as new transmission fluid.
5. Replace the filter and gasket and attach the mounting bolts. Clean the edge of the transmission pan before installing the new gasket; bolt the pan to the transmission, and reattach the fluid filler tube if applicable.
6. Refill the transmission with the proper amount of Type F fluid (see the "Capacities" chart in Chapter 1), and check for leaks around the pan.

CAUTION: *Add a little less than the specified amount of fluid at first, run the engine, shift through all positions, and check the level. It should be between "ADD" and "FULL." The level should be at "FULL" after the transmission is fully warmed up. Be very careful not to overfill.*

Chapter 7

Drive Train

Driveshaft and Universal Joints

The driveshaft is the means by which the power from the engine and transmission (in the front of the car) is transferred to the differential and rear axles, and finally to the rear wheels.

The driveshaft assembly incorporates two universal joints—one at each end—and a slip yoke at the front end of the assembly, which fits into the back of the transmission.

All driveshafts are balanced when installed in a car. It is, therefore, imperative that before applying undercoating to the chassis, the driveshaft and universal joint assembly be completely covered to prevent the accidental application of undercoating to their surfaces, and the subsequent loss of balance.

DRIVESHAFT REMOVAL

1. Mark the relationship of the rear driveshaft yoke and the drive pinion flange of the axle. If the original, yellow alignment marks are visible, there is no need for new marks. The purpose of this marking is to facilitate installation of the assembly in its exact original position, thereby maintaining proper balance of the driveshaft assembly.
2. Remove the four bolts which hold the rear universal joint to the pinion

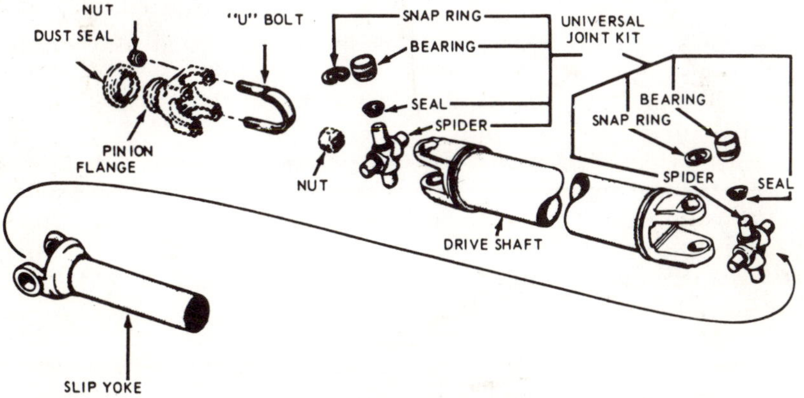

Driveshaft and universal joints

flange. Wrap tape around the loose bearing caps in order to prevent them from falling off the spider.

3. Pull the driveshaft toward the rear of the vehicle until the slip yoke clears the transmission housing and the seal. Plug the hole at the rear of the transmission housing or place a container under the opening to catch any fluid which might leak out.

Universal Joint Overhaul

1. Position the driveshaft assembly in a sturdy vise.

2. Remove the snap-rings which retain the bearing caps in the slip yoke (front only) and in the driveshaft (front and rear).

3. Using a large punch or an arbor press, drive one of the bearing caps in toward the center of the universal joint, which will force the opposite bearing cap out.

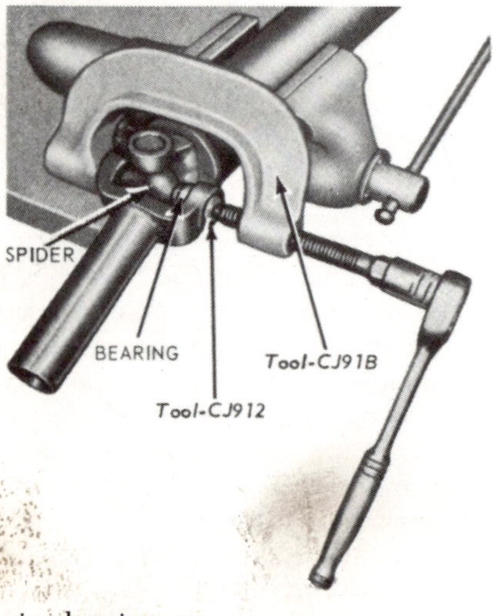

Removing bearing cap

4. As each bearing cap is pressed or punched far enough out of the universal joint assembly so that it is accessible, grip it with a pair of pliers, and pull it from the driveshaft yoke. Then drive or press the spider in the opposite direction in order to make the opposite bearing cap accessible and pull it free with a pair of pliers. Use this procedure to remove all bearings from both universal joints.

5. After removing the bearings, lift the spider from the yoke.

6. Thoroughly clean all dirt and foreign matter from the yoke area on both ends of the driveshaft.

NOTE: *When installing new bearings within the yokes, it is advisable to use an arbor press. However, if this tool is not available, the bearings should be driven into position with extreme care, as a heavy jolt on the needle bearings can easily damage or misalign them, greatly shortening their life and hampering their efficiency.*

7. Start a new bearing into the yoke at the rear of the driveshaft.

8. Position a new spider in the rear yoke and press (or drive) the new bearing cap ¼ in. below the outer surface of the yoke.

9. With the bearing cap in position, install a new snap-ring.

10. Start a new bearing cap into the opposite side of the yoke.

11. Press (or drive) the bearing cap until the opposite bearing—which you have just installed—contacts the inner surface of the snap-ring.

12. Install a new snap-ring on the second bearing cap. It may be necessary to grind the surface of this second snap-ring to facilitate easy entry into its proper position.

13. Reposition the driveshaft in the vise to facilitate work on the front universal joint.

14. Install the new bearing caps, new spider, and new snap-rings in the same manner as you did for the rear universal joint.

15. Position the slip yoke on the spider. Install new bearings and snap-rings.

16. Check both reassembled joints for freedom of movement. If misalignment of any part is causing a bind, a sharp rap on the side of the yoke with a brass hammer should seat the bearing needles, and provide the desired freedom of movement. Care should be exercised to firmly support the shaft end during this operation, as well as to prevent blows to the bearings themselves. Under no circumstances should a driveshaft be installed in a car if there is any bind in the universal joints.

DRIVESHAFT INSTALLATION

1. Carefully inspect the rubber seal in the end of the transmission extension housing. Replace it if it is damaged.

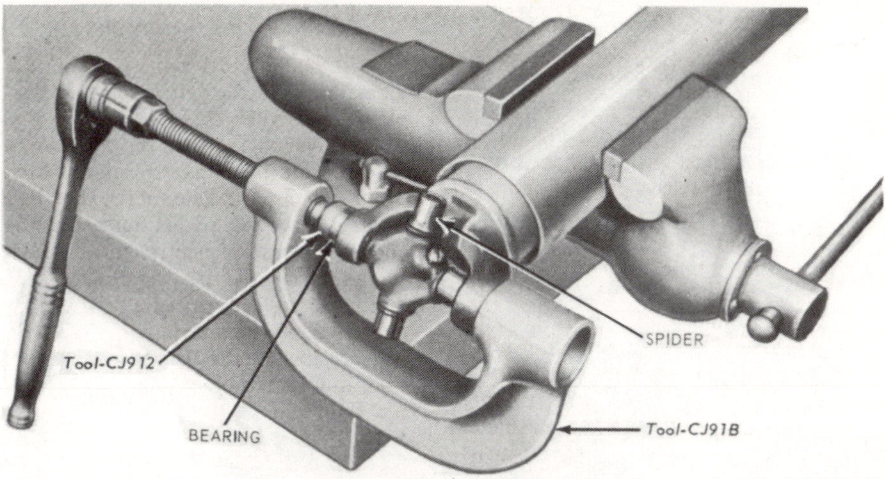

Installing bearing cap

2. Examine the lugs on the axle pinion flange and replace the flange if the lugs are shaved or distorted.
3. Coat the yoke spline with lubricant.
4. Remove the plug which you inserted into the rear of the transmission housing.
5. Insert the yoke into the transmission housing and onto the transmission output shaft. Make sure that the yoke assembly does not bottom on the output shaft with excessive force.
6. Locate the marks which you made on the rear driveshaft yoke and the pinion flange prior to removal of the driveshaft assembly. Install the driveshaft assembly with the marks properly aligned.
7. Install the U-bolts and nuts that attach the universal joint to the pinion flange. Torque the U-bolt nuts to 8–15 ft lbs.

Drive Axle

Pintos use two basic rear axle assemblies: the integral carrier type, used since 1971, and the removable carrier type which is used only with the V6. Procedures for removing the axle shafts and their bearings are the same for both types.

The rear wheels are connected to the differential assembly by axle shafts. The axle shafts are supported in the rear axle housing by bearings and are retained in the housing by bearing retainer plates which bolt to the rear brake mounting plates.

The differential assembly is mounted on two tapered bearings. These bearings are retained in the axle housing by removable bearing caps.

The drive pinion is mounted in the axle on two roller bearings.

An identification tag is attached to one of the inspection plate attaching bolts. The information on this tag must be used when ordering replacement parts.

Axle Shaft and/or Bearing Replacement

NOTE: *Bearings must be pressed on and off the shaft with an arbor press. Unless you have access to one, it is inadvisable to attempt to perform any repair work on the axle shaft and bearing assemblies.*

1. Remove the wheel, tire, and brake drum.
2. Remove the nuts holding the axle retainer plate to the backing plate.
3. Remove the retainer and install the nuts, fingertight, to prevent the brake backing plate from being dislodged.
4. Pull out the axle shaft and bearing assembly, using a slide hammer.

NOTE: *If a slide hammer is not available, the axle can sometimes be pried out using pry bars on opposing sides of the hub.*

If end-play is found to be excessive, the bearing should be replaced. Shimming the bearing is not recommended as this ignores end-play of the bearing itself and could result in improper seating of the bearing.

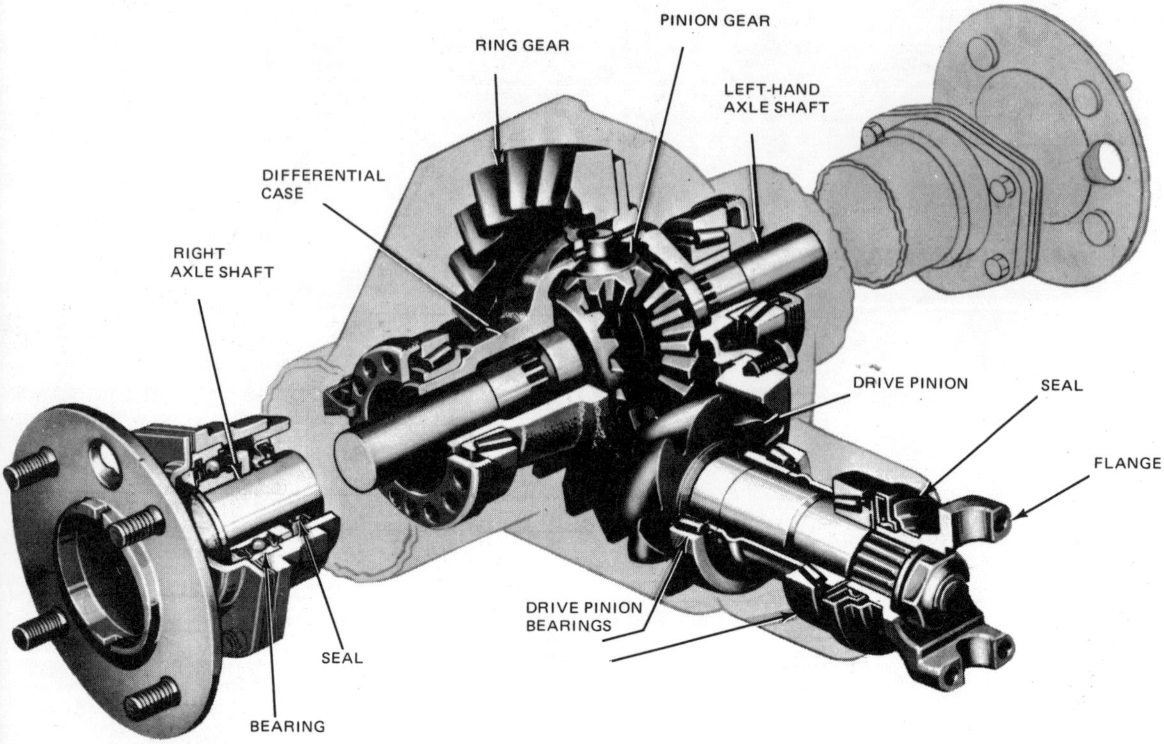

Drive axle assembly

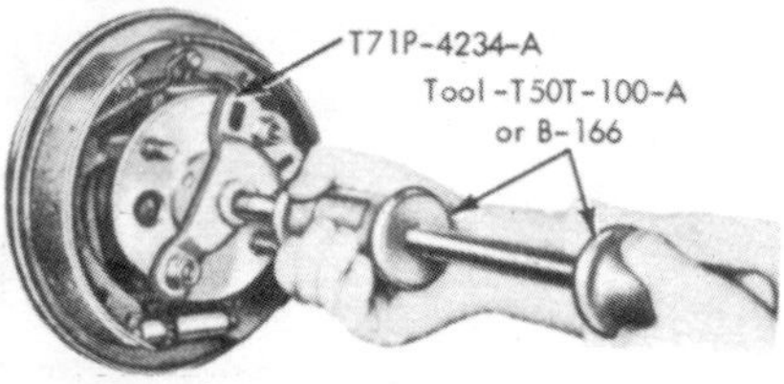

Removing axle shaft

5. Using a chisel, nick the bearing retainer in three or four places. The retainer does not have to be cut, merely collapsed sufficiently, to allow the bearing retainer to be slid from the shaft.
6. Press off the bearing and install the new one by pressing it into position.
7. Press on the new retainer.

NOTE: *Do not attempt to press the bearing and the retainer on at the same time.*

8. Assemble the shaft and bearing in the housing, being sure that the bearing is seated properly in the housing.
9. Install the retainer, drum, wheel, and tire.

Axle Shaft Seal Replacement

1. Remove the axle shaft from the rear axle. See the previous procedure for details.
2. Using a two-fingered seal puller (slide hammer), remove the seal from the axle housing.
3. Clean the recess in the rear axle housing from which the seal was removed.
4. Position a new seal on the housing and drive it into the housing with a seal installation tool.

NOTE: *The right and left axle shaft seals are different and not interchangeable. If the wrong seal is installed on the wrong side of the axle, it will leak.*

5. Install the axle shaft.

Chapter 8

Suspension and Steering

Front Suspension

The front wheels mount to, and rotate on, the spindles. The spindles are attached to the upper and lower control arms by the upper and lower ball joints. A coil spring is mounted between the upper and lower control arms on both sides of the front suspension. A pair of shock absorbers provide suspension dampening. The shocks are attached to the lower control arms and the tops of the spring housings. Additional suspension dampening is provided by a pair of strut bars which attach to the lower control arms and the body of the vehicle.

Upper Ball Joint

INSPECTION

1. Raise the vehicle by placing a floor jack under the lower arm. Do not allow the lower arm to hang freely with the vehicle on a hoist or bumper jack.
2. Have an assistant grasp the bottom of the tire and move the wheel in and out.
3. As the wheel is being moved, observe the upper control arm where the spindle attaches to it. Any movement between the upper part of the spindle and the upper ball joint indicates a bad control arm which must be replaced.

NOTE: *During this check the lower ball joint will be unloaded and may move; this is normal and not an indication of a bad ball joint. Also, do not mistake a loose wheel bearing for a defective ball joint.*

REPLACEMENT

1. Raise the vehicle on a hoist and allow the front wheels to fall to their full down position.
2. Drill a ⅛ in. hole completely through each ball joint attaching rivet.
3. Using a large chisel, cut off the head of each rivet and drive them from the upper arm.
4. Place a jack under the lower arm and lower the vehicle about 6 in.
5. Remove the cotter pin and attaching nut from the ball joint stud.
6. Using a suitable tool, loosen the ball joint stud from the spindle and remove the ball joint from the upper arm.
7. Clean all metal burrs from the upper arm and install the new ball joint, using the service part nuts and bolts to attach the ball joint to the upper arm. Do not attempt to rerivet the ball joint once it has been removed.
8. Have the front end alignment checked.

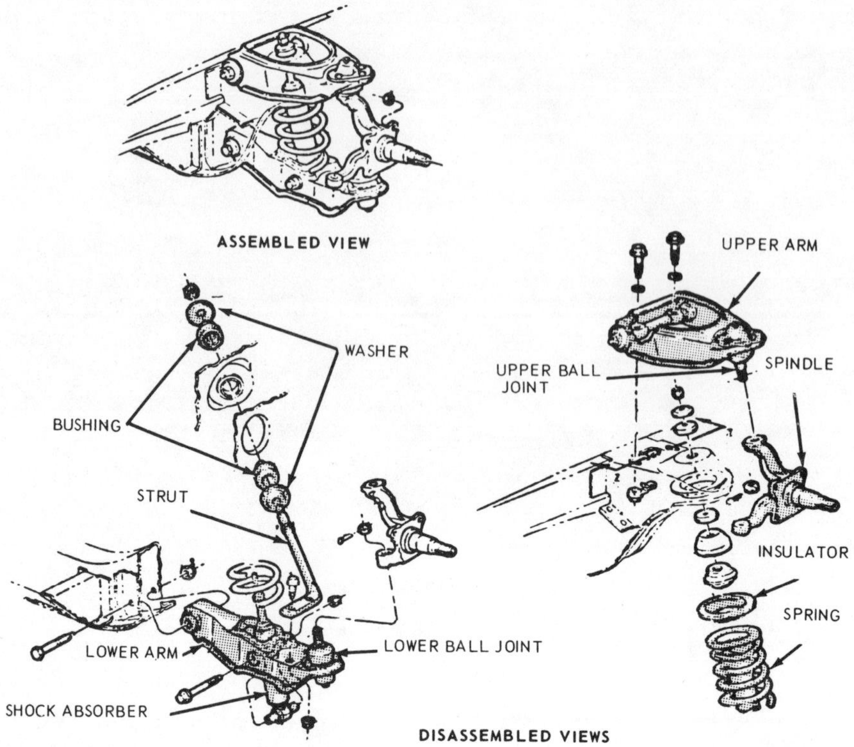

Pinto front suspension

Lower Ball Joint

Inspection

1. Raise the vehicle by placing a floor jack under the lower arm; or, raise the vehicle on a hoist and place a jack stand under the lower arm and lower the vehicle onto it to remove the preload from the lower ball joint.
2. Have an assistant grasp the wheel top and bottom and apply alternate in and out pressure to the top and bottom of the wheel.
3. Radial play of ¼ in. is acceptable measured at the inside of the wheel adjacent to the lower arm.

NOTE: *This radial play is multiplied at the outer circumference of the tire and should be measured only at the inside of the wheel.*

Replacement

1. Raise the vehicle and allow the front wheels to fall to their full down position.
2. Drill a ⅛ in. hole completely through each ball joint attaching rivet.
3. Use a ⅜ in. drill in the pilot hole to drill off the head of the rivet.
4. Drive the rivets from the lower arm.
5. Place a jack under the lower arm and lower the vehicle about 6 in.
6. Remove the lower ball joint stud cotter pin and attaching nut.
7. Using a suitable tool, loosen the ball joint from the spindle and remove the ball joint from the lower arm.
8. Clean all metal burrs from the lower arm and install the new ball joint, using the service part nuts and bolts to attach the ball joint to the lower arm. Do not attempt to rerivet the ball joint once it has been removed.
9. Have the front end alignment checked.

Upper Control Arm

Replacement

1. Raise the vehicle and remove the coil spring. See "Front Spring" later in this chapter.
2. If equipped with drum brakes, remove the tire, wheel, and brake drum as an assembly. If equipped with disc brakes, remove the tire and wheel, remove the caliper attaching bolts, and posi-

tion the caliper out of the way with the brake hose attached. Remove the rotor and hub from the spindle.

3. Remove the cotter pin and attaching nut from the ball joint stud.

4. Using a suitable tool, loosen the upper ball joint from the spindle.

5. Remove the upper arm inner shaft attaching bolts and remove the arm and shaft from the chassis as an assembly.

6. Reverse above procedure to install.

7. Have the front end alignment checked.

Lower Control Arm

Replacement

1. Raise the car and support it with stands placed in back of the lower arms.

2. If equipped with drum brakes, remove the wheel and brake drum as an assembly. Remove the brake backing plate attaching bolts and remove the backing plate from the spindle. Wire the assembly back out of the way.

3. If equipped with disc brakes, remove the wheel from the hub. Remove the caliper from the rotor and wire it back out of the way. Then, remove the hub and rotor from the spindle.

4. Disconnect the shock absorber and remove it. Disconnect the stabilizer bar if so equipped.

5. Remove cotter pins from the upper and lower ball joint stud nuts.

6. Remove two bolts and nuts holding the strut to the lower arm.

7. Loosen the lower ball joint stud nut two turns. Do not remove this nut.

8. Install the spreader tool between the upper and lower ball joint studs.

9. Expand the tool until the tool exerts considerable pressure on the studs. Tap the spindle near the lower stud with a hammer to loosen the stud in the spindle. Do not loosen the stud with tool pressure only.

10. Position the floor jack under the lower arm and remove the lower ball joint stud nut.

11. Lower the floor jack and remove the spring and insulator.

12. Remove the A–arm-to-crossmember attaching parts and remove the arm from the car.

13. Reverse the above procedure to install. If the lower control arm was replaced because of damage, have front end alignment checked.

Front Spring

NOTE: *Be extremely cautious when working with coil springs.*

Removal

1. Raise the front of the car and place safety stands under the frame.

2. Remove the shock absorber.

3. Disconnect the strut bar from the lower control arm.

4. Place a floor jack under the lower control arm.

Removing front spring

5. Remove the nut and bolt that attaches the lower control arm to the front crossmember. Disconnect the stabilizer bar if so equipped.

6. Carefully lower the jack slowly to relieve the spring pressure from the lower arm.

7. Remove the coil spring and upper insulator.

Installation

1. Place the upper insulator on the spring and secure it in place with tape.

2. Position the spring on the lower control arm. Make sure the bottom of the spring properly engages the seat on the lower control arm. The end of the spring must not be more than ½ in. from the end of the depression in the lower control arm.

3. Raise the lower control arm with the floor jack and guide the lower con-

trol arm and the top of the spring into place. Install the lower control arm attaching bolt and nut. Tighten the lower control arm attaching bolt to 75–110 ft lbs.

4. Install the shock absorber after removing the jack.

5. Attach the strut bar to the lower control arm.

6. Remove the safety stands and lower the vehicle.

Front Shock Absorber

Replacement

1. Remove the nut, washer, and bushing from the upper end of the shock. If the shaft of the shock absorber turns while you are trying to remove the attaching nut, hold the shaft in place with an adjustable wrench while removing the nut.

2. Raise the front end of the vehicle and install safety stands.

3. Disconnect the bottom of the shock absorber from the lower control arm. It may be necessary to raise the lower arm to remove the bottom bolt.

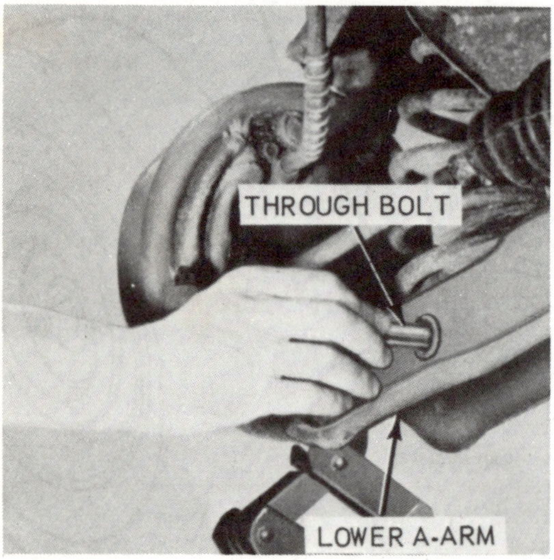

Removing lower shock absorber bolt

4. Remove the shock absorber from under the car.

5. Position the new shock absorber on the lower control arm and install the attaching bolts.

6. Remove the safety stands and lower the car.

7. Connect the top of the shock absorber to the upper spring pad.

Front End Alignment

Front end alignment can only be adjusted on a front end alignment machine. This section is included only for reference.

Camber, Caster and Toe-In Adjustment

Position one Ford tool T71P-3000 A at each end of the upper control arm, pivot shaft with the leg of the tools through the holes in the sheet metal (see illustration). Turn the adjusting bolts until they are solidly contacting the sheet metal and loosen the pivot shaft retaining bolts.

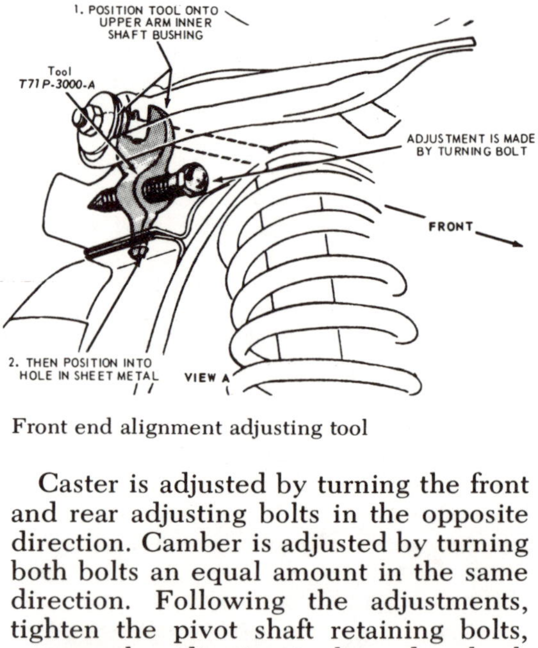

Front end alignment adjusting tool

Caster is adjusted by turning the front and rear adjusting bolts in the opposite direction. Camber is adjusted by turning both bolts an equal amount in the same direction. Following the adjustments, tighten the pivot shaft retaining bolts, remove the adjusting tools, and recheck caster and camber.

Prior to adjusting toe-in, align the straight-ahead marks at the base of the steering wheel and the head of the steering column. Loosen both the clamp at the outer end of the rack bellows and the tie rod jam nuts. Using suitable pliers (i.e. vise-grips), turn the inner tie-rod shafts to adjust toe-in. Turn the shafts an equal amount in the opposite direction, to maintain steering wheel spoke alignment. Following the adjustment, hold the inner shafts with pliers, and tighten the jam nuts.

Front Suspension Troubleshooting

Hard Ride

1. Excessive tire pressure
2. Shock absorbers malfunctioning
3. Broken spring
4. Worn suspension bushings

Car Veers to One Side

1. Unequal tire pressures
2. Incorrect caster, camber, or toe-in
3. Unequal spring rates
4. Unequal shock absorber control
5. Incorrect steering axis inclination (bent spindle)
6. Damaged suspension components or bushings
7. Incorrect tracking
8. Dragging brake
9. Grease on brake lining

Wander

1. Incorrect or unequal tire pressures
2. Incorrect caster or toe-in
3. Excessively worn or damaged suspension components

Hard or Erratic Steering

1. Insufficient tire pressure
2. Lack of lubrication
3. Binding or damaged steering column, steering gear, or linkage
4. Worn or damaged suspension components

Tires Wear in Center

1. Excessive tire pressure

Tires Wear on Both Edges

1. Insufficient tire pressure

Tires Wear Evenly on One Edge

1. Incorrect camber or toe-in
2. Bent or damaged suspension components

Tires Wear Unevenly on One Edge

1. Insufficient tire pressure
2. Incorrect camber or toe-in
3. Out of round wheel and/or tire
4. Loose steering linkage
5. Severe cornering

Tires Wear Unequally

1. Unequal tire pressure
2. Unequal tire size
3. Incorrect toe-in or camber
4. Loose or bent steering linkage

Squeal on Cornering

1. Insufficient tire pressure
2. Incorrect toe-in or camber
3. Severe cornering

Rear Suspension

The rear suspension consists of conventional three-leaf, longitudinal, semi-elliptic springs, located asymmetrically to the rear axle carrier and fastened by U-bolt clamps. Standard telescopic shock absorbers control vertical rebound.

Rear, Shock Absorber Replacement

1. Disconnect the lower end of the shock absorber from the spring plate.
2. Remove the three bolts retaining the shock absorber mounting bracket at the upper end of the shock.
3. Compress and remove shock from car.
4. Transfer the mounting bracket to a new shock.
5. Position the shock absorber on the car and install the attaching parts.

Rear Spring

Removal

1. Raise the rear of the vehicle and position safety stands under the rear axle assembly and the underbody of the car.
2. Disconnect the bottom of the shock absorber from the spring plate.
3. Remove the spring clip plate attaching nuts and remove the spring clip plate.
4. Place a floor jack under the rear axle and raise it just enough to remove the load from the rear springs.
5. Remove the two rear shackle attaching nuts and remove the rear shackle.
6. Remove the nut and bolt that attach the front of the spring to the spring hanger and lower the spring from under the car.

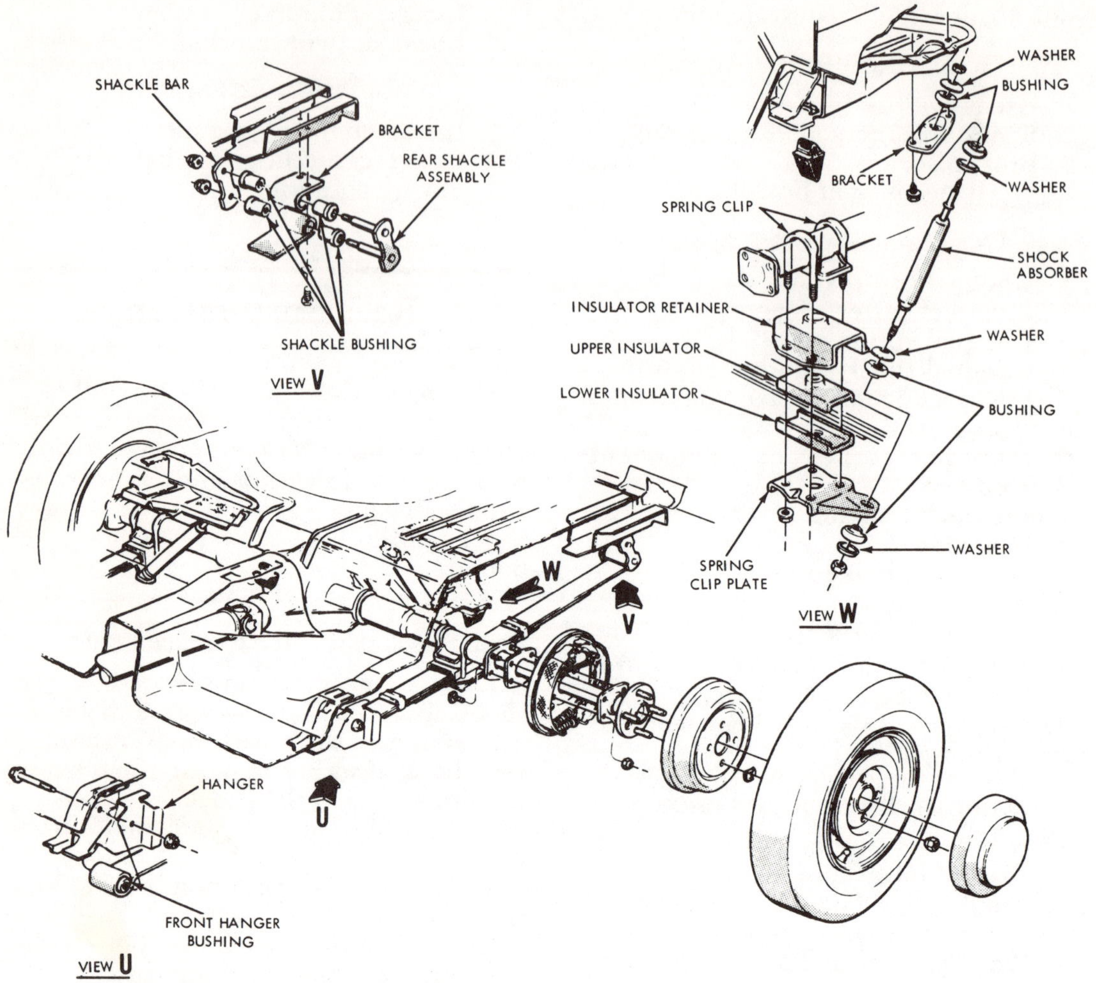

Pinto rear suspension

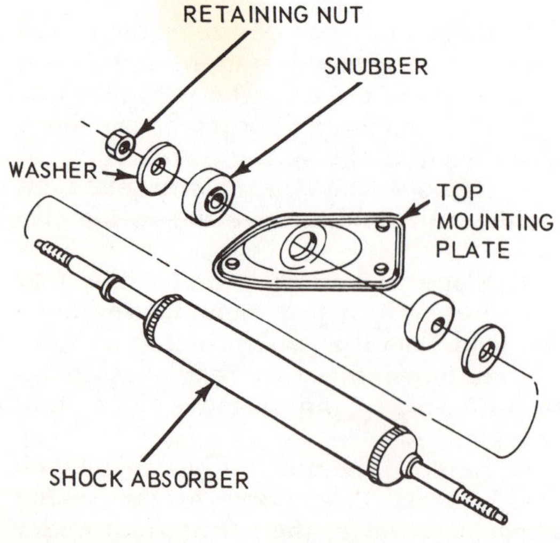

Rear shock absorber mounting brackets

INSTALLATION

NOTE: *All used attaching nuts and bolts that were removed from the vehicle must be discarded and replaced with new parts.*

1. Position the spring under the car and install the rear shackle.
2. Install the rear shackle attaching bolts finger-tight.
3. Position the front eye of the spring in the front hanger and install the front hanger nut, bolt, and washer. Tighten the nut and bolt finger-tight.
4. Lower the rear axle assembly until it rests on the springs.
5. Install the spring clip plate and tighten its attaching nuts.
6. Place safety stands under the rear

Wheel Alignment Specifications

Year	Model	CASTER Range (deg)	CASTER Pref Setting (deg)	CAMBER Range (deg)	CAMBER Pref Setting (deg)	Toe-in (in.)	Steering Axis Inclin	WHEEL PIVOT RATIO (deg) Inner Wheel	WHEEL PIVOT RATIO (deg) Outer Wheel
'71	All Models	1P to 2P	1½P	0 to 1½P	¾P	0 to ¼	8.968	20	18.95
'72	All Models	½N to 3½P	1½P	¼N to 1¾P	¾P	1/16 to 7/16	8.968	20	18.94
'73	All Models	1N to 3P	1P	¼N to 1¾P	¾P	0 to ¼	8.968	20	18.94
'74–'75	Pinto	¾N to 3¼P	1¼P	¼N to 1¾P	¾P	⅛ to ⅜	10.018	20	18.84
'74–'75	Pinto Sta Wag	½N to 3½P	1½P	¼N to 1¾P	¾P	⅛ to ⅜	10.018	20	18.84
'76–'77	Pinto	½P to 2P	1¼P	0 to 1½P	¾P	⅛ to ⅜	10.018	20	18.84
'76–'77	Pinto Sta Wag	¾P to 2¼P	1½P	0 to 1½P	¾P	⅛ to ⅜	10.018	20	18.84

N Negative P Positive

axle assembly and remove them from beneath the body of the car.

7. Lower the car until the springs are in their approximate curb load position.

8. Tighten the rear shackle and front hanger attaching bolts and nuts.

9. Remove the safety stands and lower the car.

Steering

The steering gear is of the rack and pinion type. The gear input shaft is connected to the steering shaft by means of a flexible coupling. A pinion gear, machined on the input shaft, engages the rack and rotation of the input shaft pinion causes the rack to move laterally.

The tie-rod is attached at each end of the rack joint. This allows the tie-rods to move with the front suspension. The gear is sealed at each end with rubber bellows. The steering gear is filled with approximately 5 oz of SAE-90 EP oil at initial assembly and checking or refilling is not required unless fluid leakage is evident or repairs become necessary.

Couplings attaching the tie-rods are retained on the rack, are pinned, and cannot be disassembled in service. Replacement of inner tie-rods, rack, housing, or upper pinion bearing requires installation of a new steering gear assembly.

If the steering linkage, front suspension, and steering column components are in good condition, there should be no more than ⅜ in. free-play in the steering wheel when measured at the rim of the wheel.

If a loud knock is heard when turning the steering wheel from lock-to-lock, the pinion bearing preload should be checked. A faint knock from the steering wheel when driving on very rough roads is normal and not an indication of a steering defect.

CAUTION: *When the front wheels of the vehicle are suspended completely off the ground, do not turn the wheels quickly or forcefully from lock to lock. This could cause a buildup of hydraulic pressure within the steering gear which could damage or blow out the bellows.*

STEERING GEAR

Removal and Installation

1971–72

1. Position the steering wheel in the straight-ahead position and raise the front of the car.

2. Remove the bolts retaining the flexible coupling to the pinion shaft.

3. Remove the two nuts and bolts that retain the steering gear to the mounting pad on the crossmember. Remove the U-clamp attaching bolts.

4. Remove the U-clamp.

5. Remove the cotterpins and loosen the nuts securing the connecting rod ends to the spindle arms.

6. Using a suitable tool, separate the connecting rods from the spindle arms and remove the nuts from the rod ends.

7. Remove the steering gear from the left side of the vehicle.

8. Make certain the steering wheel and the front wheels are in the straight-ahead position.

9. Obtain a 0.050 in. shim having bite-in teeth on both sides. Position the shim on the bolt shanks.

10. File off the bite-in teeth around the two gear mounting bolt holes in the left-side crossmember mounting bracket.

11. Install the steering gear on the mounting bracket so the shim is between the steering and the mounting bracket.

12. Install two new cones and tighten them to 50–65 ft lbs.

13. Install the rubber insulator and U-clamp on the right side of the steering gear.

14. Install the connecting rod ends in the spindle ends and tighten the attaching nuts to 18–30 ft lbs. Install a new cotter pin in the spindle end.

15. Check to be sure the steering gear is centered. When the gear is centered, the bottom bolt which attaches the flexible coupling to the pinion shaft should be straight up and down with the bottom of the bolt pointing downward.

16. Connect the flexible coupling to the pinion shaft and tighten the attaching bolt to 20–37 ft lbs.

17. Remove the safety stands and lower the vehicle.

1973 AND LATER

1. Disconnect the negative battery cable from the battery.

2. Leave the ignition key in the ON position and raise the vehicle on a hoist.

3. Remove the two tie-rod end retaining nuts and cotter pins. Separate the studs from the spindle arms using the ball joint separator (Tool 3290-C).

4. Remove the one bolt retaining the pinion shaft to the flexible coupling.

5. Remove the four bolts (3 bolts—

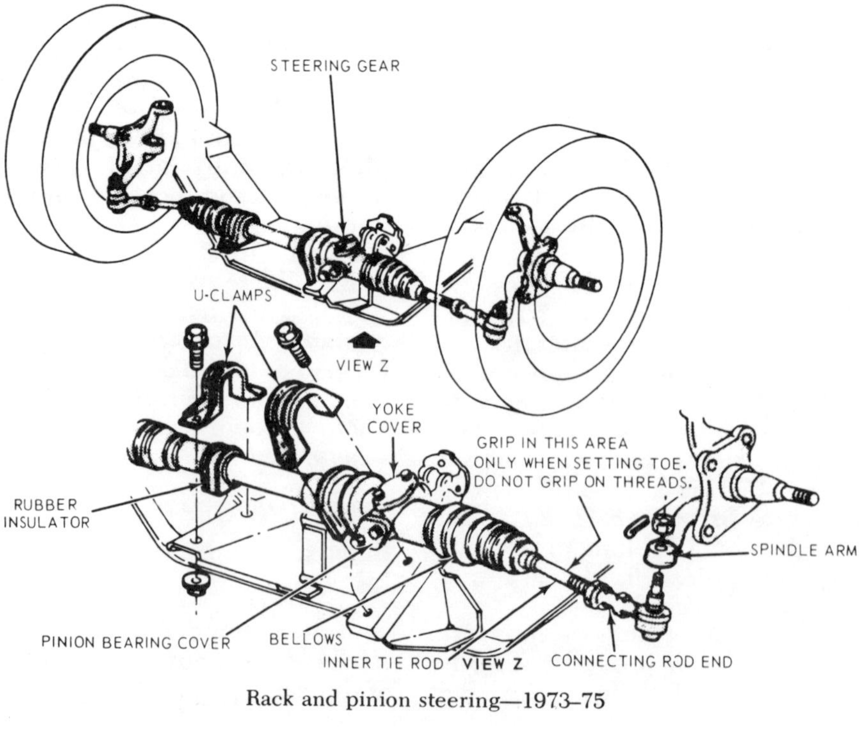

Rack and pinion steering—1973–75

1975 and later) and two nuts (1971–74) right-side only) retaining the steering gear to the crossmember.

6. Turn the front wheels and remove the steering gear assembly from the left-side of the vehicle.

7. Position the steering gear assembly to the chassis and install the one bolt retaining the pinion shaft to the flexible coupling. Tighten to 20–37 ft lbs.

8. Install the four bolts and two nuts (right side only) attaching the steering gear to the crossmember. Torque to 80–100 ft lbs.

9. Connect the tie-rod ends to the spindle arms and install the two retaining nuts and cotter pins after torquing to 35–47 ft lbs.

10. Lower the vehicle and turn the ignition key to OFF position.

11. Connect the negative battery cable to the battery.

12. Check the toe-in and reset if necessary.

Adjustments

There are two adjustments which can be performed on the rack and pinion steering gear: support yoke-to-rack adjustment and pinion bearing preload adjustment. The steering gear assembly must be removed from the car to perform either adjustment.

Support Yoke-to-Rack

1. Remove the steering gear from the car.

2. Mount the steering gear in a soft-jawed vise with the yoke cover up. Clean the exterior of the gear.

3. Remove the yoke cover, gasket, shims, and yoke spring. Clean the yoke cover and support thoroughly.

4. Reinstall the yoke cover on the support yoke.

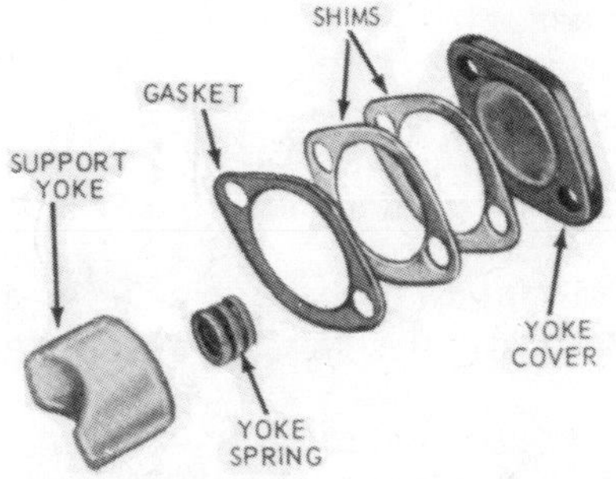

Support yoke arrangement

5. Tighten the yoke cover until the cover just touches the yoke support.

6. Measure the clearance between the cover and support yoke flange.

7. To the clearance figure measured in Step 6, add 0.006 in.

8. Measure the thickness of the shims and gasket that were removed from under the yoke cover in Step 3.

9. Subtract the figure obtained in Step 8 from the figure obtained in Step 7. The remainder from this subtraction is the thickness of the shim that must be added under the yoke cover to obtain the correct support yoke-to-rack adjustment.

10. Remove the yoke cover and install the yoke spring, shims, and gasket re-

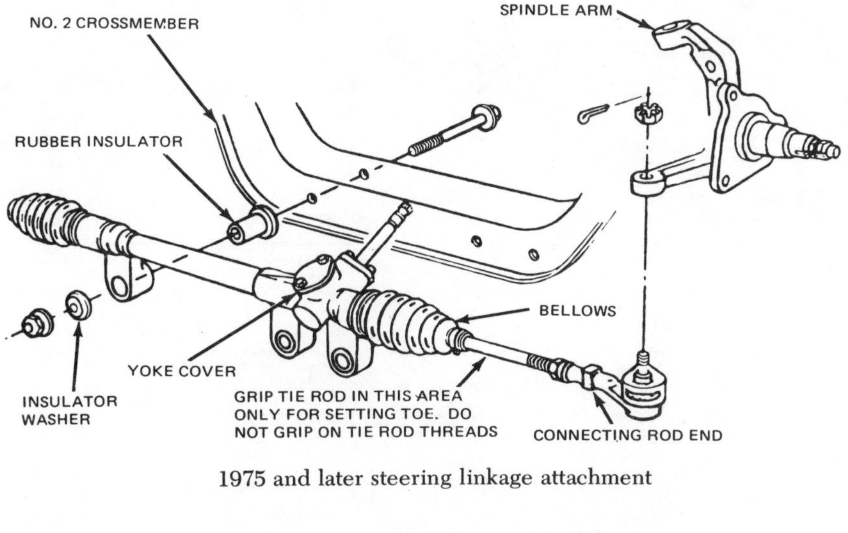

1975 and later steering linkage attachment

moved in Step 3, plus a shim of the correct thickness.

11. Apply sealer to the yoke cover bolts and install the yoke cover.

12. Turn the pinion shaft to ensure proper operation of the gear.

NOTE: *Return the pinion shaft to its centered position before installing it in the car.*

PINION BEARING PRELOAD

1. Remove the steering gear assembly from the car.

2. Mount the steering gear in a soft-jawed vise and clean the exterior of the gear.

3. Remove the pinion cover.

4. Clean the pinion flange area and remove the gasket and shims.

5. Install a new gasket and install shims until the shim pack is flush with the gasket. Check by placing a straightedge on top of the gasket and applying light pressure.

6. Remove the gasket and shims and reinstall the shims in the following order: the thinnest of the select fit shims first, followed by the other select fit

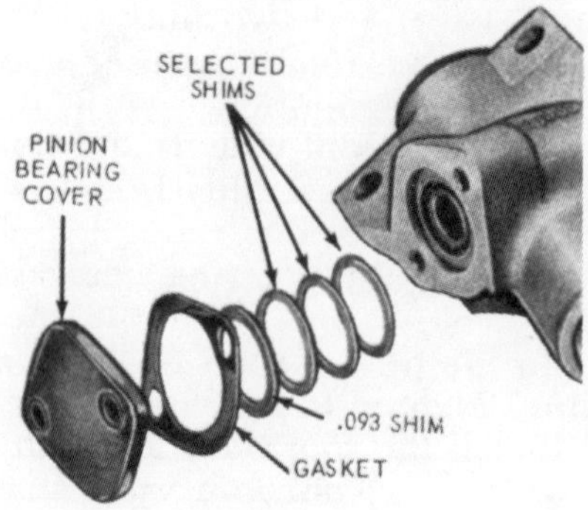

Pinion bearing cover and shims

shims and the 0.093 in. shim next to the cover.

7. To the above shim pack, add a 0.005 in. shim to preload the bearing. Place it in the correct order in the shim pack.

8. Apply sealer to the cover attaching bolts and install the cover and gasket.

STEERING WHEEL

Removal and Installation

1. Disconnect the negative battery cable.

2. On models with a small horn but-

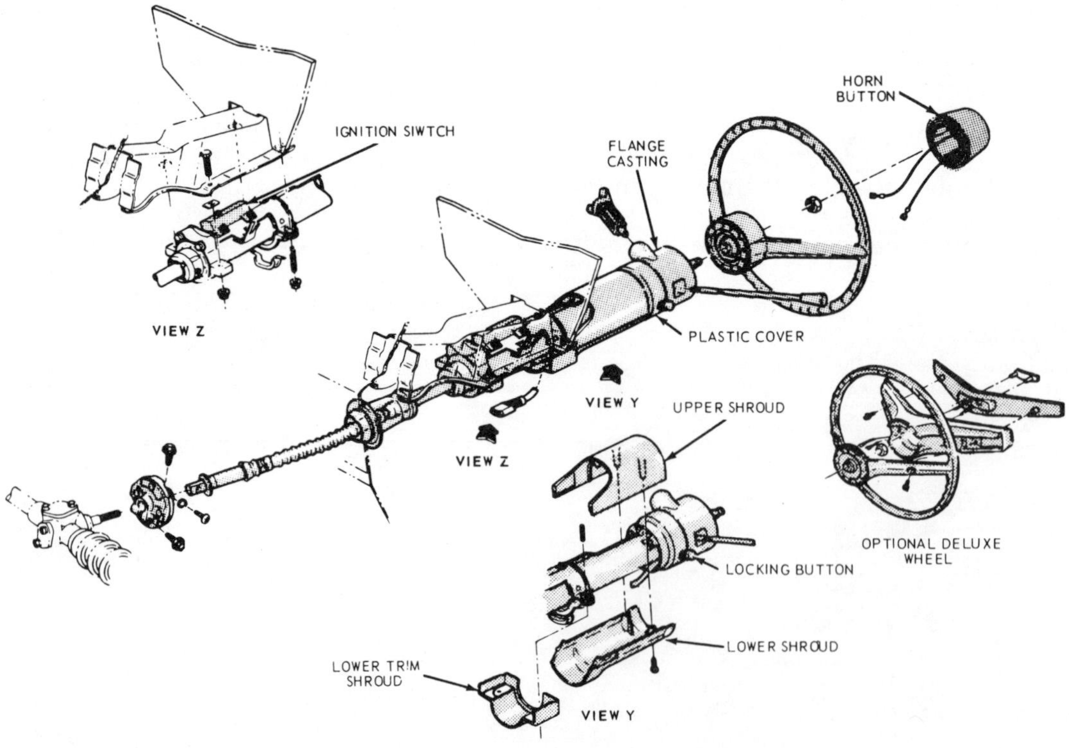

Steering wheel and column installation

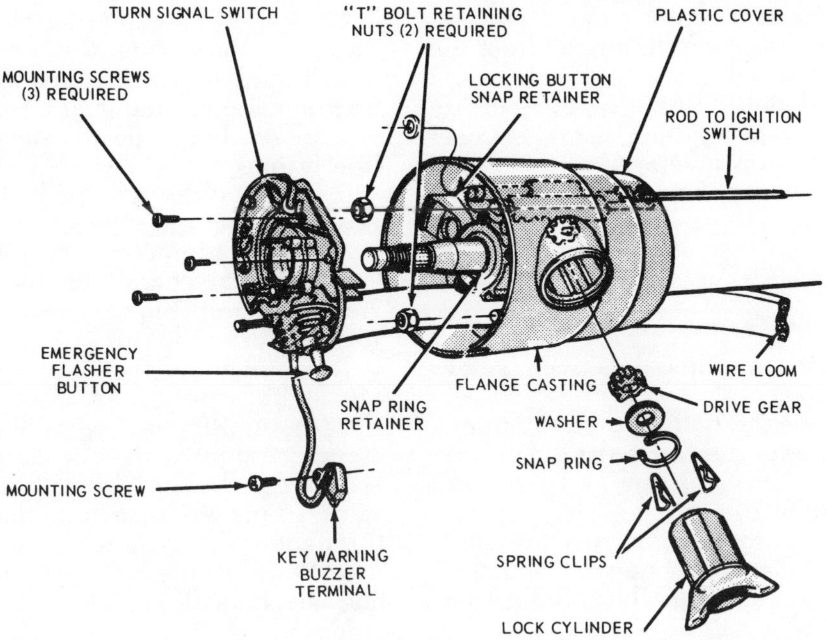

Upper steering column components

ton, remove the horn button by pushing it down and turning in a counterclockwise direction.

3. On a deluxe steering wheel, remove the steering wheel crash pad by removing the two attaching screws from behind the steering wheel. Disconnect the horn wires from the crash pad.

4. Remove the steering wheel attaching nut and, using a puller, remove the steering wheel.

NOTE: *Use only a screw-type steering wheel puller. Using a knock-off type puller or striking the steering shaft in any way could damage the shaft or bearings.*

5. Align the mark on the steering wheel hub and the mark on the steering shaft and install the wheel on the shaft.

6. Install the steering wheel attaching nut and tighten it to 30–40 ft lbs.

7. Install the horn button or crash pad.

TURN SIGNAL AND HAZARD WARNING LIGHT SWITCH AND WIRING

Removal and Installation

1. Remove the steering wheel.

2. Remove the turn signal lever by unscrewing it from the steering column.

3. Snap off the lower steering column shroud.

4. Remove the two screws that attach the upper column shroud and remove it.

5. Disconnect the steering column wiring connectors from the steering column by lifting up on the tabs and removing the connectors from the brackets.

6. Remove the three screws that attach the head of the switch to the top of the steering column.

7. Pull the switch and wire assembly up and out of the steering column. It is often an aid to installation if a thin wire is attached to the connector. When installing the new switch, tie the wire to the connector and pull it down through the column.

8. Position the switch and wires in the steering column and work the wires down the steering column.

9. Secure the wires and connectors to the base of the steering column.

10. Connect the wire connectors at the base of the column.

11. Install the switch head attaching screws.

12. Install the turn signal lever.

13. Install the steering wheel.

POWER STEERING PUMP

Removal and Installation

1. Disconnect the hoses and drain the fluid.

2. Loosen and remove the drive belt and remove the mounting bolts from the front.

3. Installation is the reverse of removal, but on installation, turn the wheel from stop to stop several times with fluid in the pump and recheck and add fluid if necessary.

POWER STEERING GEAR

Removal and Installation

1. Disconnect the negative battery cable.

2. Remove the bolt retaining the flexible coupling to the input shaft. Turn the key to the "On" position and raise and safely support the car.

3. Remove the cotter pins and nuts from the ends of the tie-rods and then separate the studs from the spindle arms.

4. Support the steering gear, and remove the three nuts, washers, and bolts which hold the steering gear to the crossmember. Lower the gear a bit to enable you to reach the power steering pump line fittings.

5. Remove the screw which holds the hose bracket to the gear mounting bracket and remove the hose bracket.

6. Disconnect and plug the two power steering pump lines. Remove the steering gear from the car.

7. Installation is the reverse of removal, but when you're finished, disconnect the ignition coil wire, fill the power steering pump with fluid and move the steering wheel while cranking the starter. This will distribute the new fluid throughout the system.

8. Reinstall the coil wire, start the car, and check for fluid leaks.

Chapter 9

Brakes

Hydraulic System

The hydraulic system is composed of the master cylinder, the brake lines, the brake pressure differential valve, and the wheel cylinders (drum brakes) and/or calipers (disc brakes).

The master cylinder serves as a brake fluid reservoir and as a hydraulic pump. Brake fluid is stored in the two sections of the master cylinder. The front half of the master cylinder holds the fluid that is used to activate the rear brakes. The rear half of the master cylinder holds the fluid that activates the front brakes. This tandem master cylinder is required by federal law as a safety device. Since the front hydraulic system is independent of the rear system, a fluid leak in one system would only cause that system to fail, allowing the other system to stop the car.

When the brake pedal is depressed, it moves a piston mounted in the bottom of the master cylinder. The movement of this piston creates hydraulic pressure in the master cylinder. This pressure is carried to the wheel cylinders or calipers by the brake lines.

On the way to the wheels, the brake fluid passes through the pressure differential valve. The pressure differential valve is an H-shaped valve which is connected between the front and rear brake lines. Each of the brake lines is connected to one of the upright sides of the "H." The brake fluid passes through each of the upright sides inside the valve and leaves at the bottom of the sides where the outgoing brake lines pick up the fluid and carry it on to the wheels. A piston is mounted in the crossbar section of the "H." It is held centered in the valve by the brake fluid in each of the upright sides of the "H." A brake warning light switch is screwed into the crossbar and contacts the piston. If a leak should develop in either the front or rear brake system, fluid pressure in the portion of the pressure differential valve which corresponds to that system would drop. This would cause the piston in the crossbar of the valve to move to-

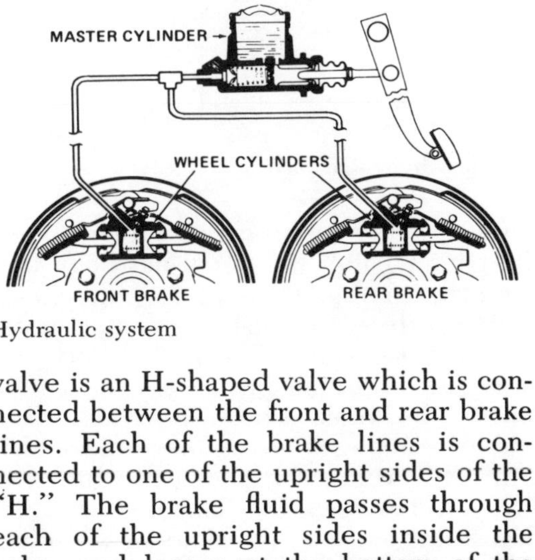

Hydraulic system

ward that section of the valve, since the normal fluid pressure in the other side of the valve would now be dominant. The brake warning light switch would sense this movement and turn the brake warning light on, on the instrument panel. When the failure is repaired and the system bled of air, the piston will recenter itself when the brake pedal is firmly depressed. The brake light on the instrument panel will then go off.

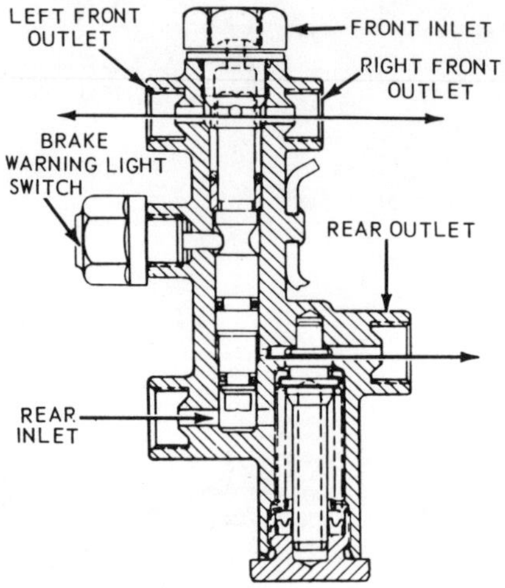

Pressure differential valve

When the hydraulic pressure reaches the wheels, after the pedal has been depressed, it enters the wheel cylinders or calipers. Here it comes into contact with a piston or pistons. The hydraulic pressure causes the piston(s) to move, which moves the brake shoes or pads (disc brakes), causing them to come into contact with the drums or rotors (disc brakes). Friction between the brake shoes and the drums causes the car to slow down. There is a relationship between the amount of pressure that is applied to the brake pedal and the amount of force which moves the brake shoes against the drums. Therefore, the harder the brake pedal is depressed, the quicker the car will stop.

Since a hydraulic system is one which operates on fluids, air is a natural enemy of the brake system. Air in the hydraulic system retards the passage of hydraulic pressure from the master cylinder to the wheels. Anytime a hydraulic component below the master cylinder is opened or removed, the system must be bled of air to ensure proper operation. Air trapped in the hydraulic system can also cause the brake warning light to come on, even though the system has not failed. This is especially true after repairs have been performed on the system.

The wheel cylinders used with drum brakes are composed of a cylinder with a polished inside bore, which is mounted on the brake shoe backing plate, two boots, two pistons, two cups, a spring, and a bleeder screw. When hydraulic pressure enters the wheel cylinder, it contacts the two cylinder cups. The cups seal the cylinder and prevent fluid from leaking out. The hydraulic pressure forces the cups outward. The cups in turn force the pistons outward. The pistons contact the brake shoes and the hydraulic pressure in the wheel cylinders overcomes the pressure of the brake springs, causing the shoes to contact the brake drum. When the brake pedal is released, the brake shoe return springs pull the brake shoes away from the drum. This forces the pistons back toward the center of the wheel cylinder. Wheel cylinders can fail in two ways; they can leak or lock up. Leaking wheel cylinders are caused either by defective cups or irregularities in the wheel cylinder bore. Frozen wheel cylinders are caused by foreign matter getting into the cylinders and preventing the pistons from sliding freely.

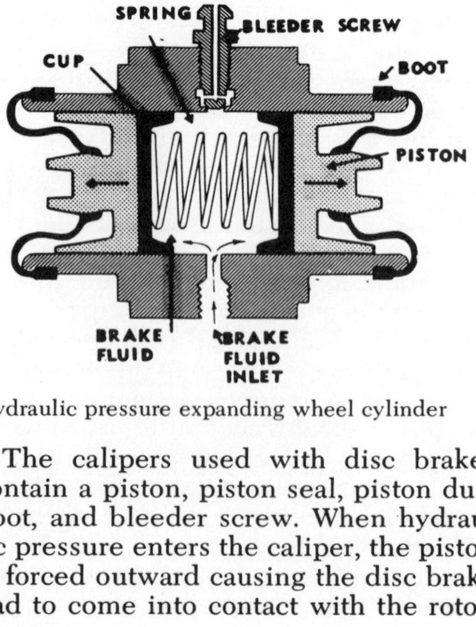

Hydraulic pressure expanding wheel cylinder

The calipers used with disc brakes contain a piston, piston seal, piston dust boot, and bleeder screw. When hydraulic pressure enters the caliper, the piston is forced outward causing the disc brake pad to come into contact with the rotor.

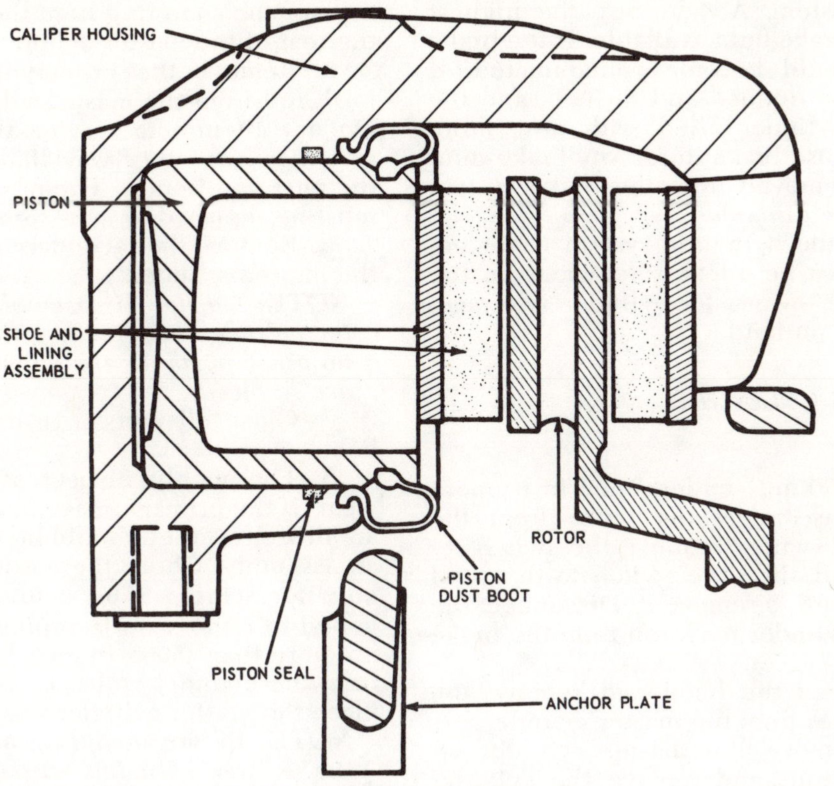

Disc brake assembly

When the brakes are applied, the piston seal, mounted on the caliper housing, becomes slightly distorted in the direction of the rotor. When the brakes are released, the piston seal moves back to its normal position and, at the same time, pulls the piston back away from the brake pad. This allows the brake pads to move away from the rotor. Calipers can fail in three ways, two of these being caused by defective piston seals. When a piston seal becomes worn, it can allow brake fluid to leak out to contaminate the pad and rotor. If a piston seal becomes weak, it can fail to pull the piston away from the brake shoe when the brakes are released, allowing the brake pad to drag on the rotor when the car is being driven. If foreign material enters the caliper housing, it can prevent the piston from sliding freely, causing the brakes to stick on the rotor.

Clean, high-quality brake fluid is essential to the proper operation of the

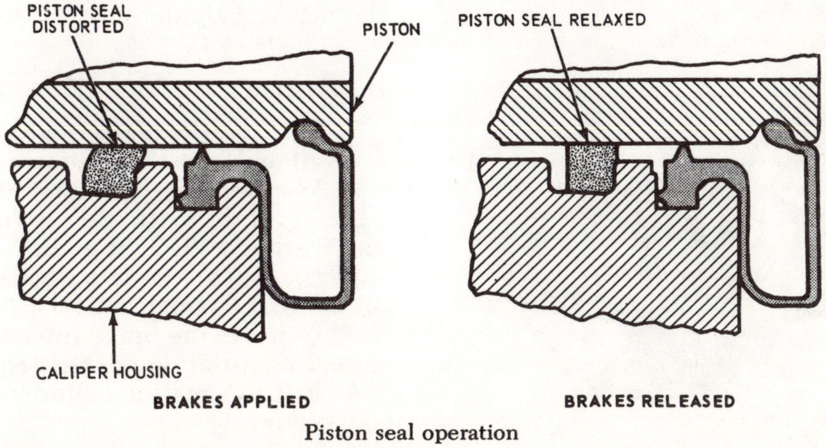

Piston seal operation

brake system. Always buy the highest quality brake fluid available. If the brake fluid should become contaminated, it should be drained and flushed, and the master cylinder filled with new fluid. Never reuse brake fluid. Any brake fluid that is removed from the brake system should be discarded.

Since the hydraulic system is sealed, there must be a leak somewhere in the system if the master cylinder is repeatedly low on fluid.

MASTER CYLINDER

Removal

1. Working under the instrument panel, disconnect the wires from the stoplight switch. Remove the switch retainer and slide the switch to the right and upward to remove it. Disconnect the master cylinder push rod from the brake pedal.
2. Raise the hood and remove the brake lines from the master cylinder.
3. Remove the master cylinder attaching bolts and remove the cylinder from the car.

Overhaul

1. Clean the outside of the master cylinder, and remove the cap and rubber gasket. Drain and discard the fluid that is in the master cylinder.
2. Remove the secondary piston stop bolt from the bottom of the cylinder.
3. Remove the bleeder screw from the cylinder.
4. Depress the primary piston and remove the snap-ring from the groove in the rear of the master cylinder bore.

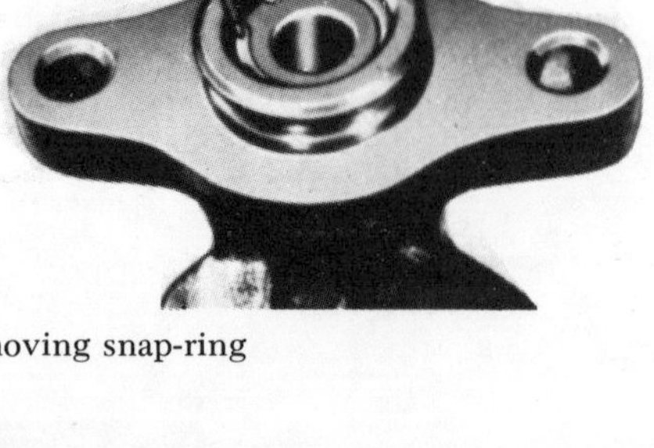

Removing snap-ring

5. Remove the primary piston and push rod from the master cylinder bore. Do not attempt to service the primary piston in any other way than removing the push rod from it. The primary piston must be replaced as an assembly.
6. Remove the secondary piston from the master cylinder.

NOTE: *Do not disassemble the master cylinder any further than this as no other parts for the master cylinder are serviced.*

7. Clean all parts in isopropyl alcohol.
8. Thoroughly inspect all parts for wear. If the primary or secondary pistons are defective, they should be replaced as an assembly. Check the master cylinder bore for scoring. The cylinder can be honed to remove surface blemishes, but no more than 0.003 in. can be removed from the cylinder walls. If in doubt, replace the master cylinder.

NOTE: *Before installing any part in the master cylinder, dip it in clean brake fluid.*

9. Install the secondary piston assembly in the master cylinder.
10. Install the primary piston assembly in the master cylinder.
11. Install the push rod, retainer, and boot, depress the piston, and install the snap-ring.
12. Install the secondary piston stop bolt and O-ring in the bottom of the master cylinder.
13. Install the bleeder screw.
14. Fill the master cylinder with new fluid, depress the push rod, and open the bleeder to remove most of the air from the master cylinder.

Installation

1. Position the master cylinder on the firewall and install the attaching bolts.
2. Working under the instrument panel, coat the push rod's nylon bushing and washer with light engine oil and install the push rod and stoplight switch on the brake pedal.
3. Connect the brake lines to the master cylinder but do not tighten them.
4. Fill the master cylinder with new brake fluid.

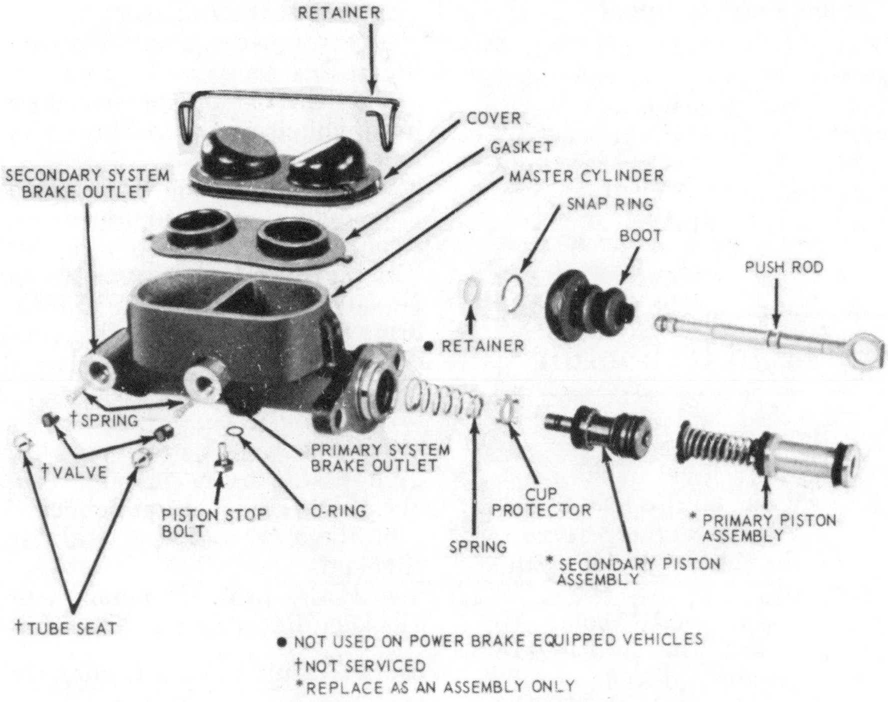

Exploded view of master cylinder

5. Depress the brake pedal several times to bleed the master cylinder.

6. Tighten the brake lines on the cylinder, fill the master cylinder and bleed the brakes at the wheels.

Bleeding the Hydraulic System

NOTE: *If it is known that only one system has air in it, only that system has to be bled since the front and rear hydraulic systems are independent.*

1. Fill the master cylinder with brake fluid.

2. Install a ⅜ in. box-end wrench on the bleeder screw on the right rear wheel.

3. Push a piece of small-diameter rubber tubing over the bleeder screw until it is flush against the wrench. Submerge the other end of the rubber tubing in a glass jar partially filled with clean brake fluid. Make sure the rubber tube fits on the bleeder screw snugly or you may get zapped with brake fluid when the bleeder screw is opened.

4. Have a friend apply pressure to the brake pedal. Open the bleeder screw and observe the bottle of brake fluid. If bubbles appear in the glass jar, it means there is air in the system. When your friend has pushed the pedal to the floor, immediately close the bleeder screw *before he releases the pedal.*

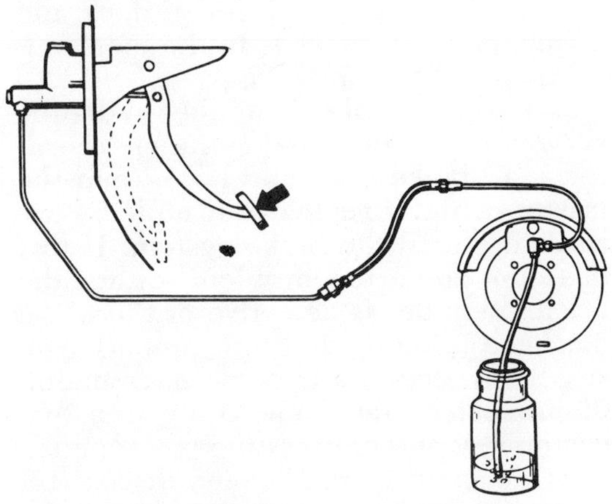

Bleeding brake system

5. Repeat this procedure until no bubbles appear in the jar. Refill the master cylinder.

6. Repeat this procedure on the left rear, right front, and left front wheels, in that order. Periodically refill the master cylinder so it does not run dry.

7. If the brake warning light is on, depress the brake pedal firmly. If there is no air in the system, the light will go out.

Wheel Cylinders and Calipers

Since repair or replacement of these components requires the removal of the brake shoes, the procedures are included in the brake shoe replacement section of this chapter. Wheel cylinders can be found under "Drum Brakes" and calipers under "Disc Brakes."

Brake Troubleshooting

Low or Soft Brake Pedal

1. Check the fluid level in the master cylinder and fill as required to bring it within ¼ in. of the top of the reservoir.
2. Push on the brake pedal with a pumping motion.
   A. If the brake pedal comes up when pumped, or if the fluid level in the master cylinder goes down after pumping, the trouble is in the hydraulic system.
   B. If brake pedal level does not change, the trouble is in the mechanical part of the brakes.
3. If the trouble is in the hydraulic system, check all wheel cylinders or calipers, all brake lines and hoses, and the master cylinder for leaks. If no leaks are present, bleed the brake system. If this does not solve the problem, either the master cylinder is defective or there is a blockage in the hydraulic system. If you suspect a blockage in some component, disconnect a brake line going into that component and depress the brake pedal. Next, reconnect that line and disconnect a line coming out of the component and depress the brake pedal. If fluid went in but did not come out, there is a blockage.
4. If the trouble is in the mechanical system, adjust the brakes. On cars with front disc brakes, adjust the front wheel bearings. If this does not solve the problem, remove the wheels and check for bent, worn, or broken brake shoes or brake attaching parts. If everything else is OK, check for a worn brake pedal or mounting pivot.

Brakes Pull When Applied

1. Check and adjust the air pressure in all of the tires.
2. Adjust the brakes.
3. If the pedal is soft or spongy, bleed the brakes.
4. If the trouble persists, remove the front wheels and inspect the wheel bearings.
5. Remove all the wheels and inspect the brake lining and the drums and/or rotors.

   If the lining is dirty or glazed, it can be sanded and cleaned. Mild glazing of drums can be sanded. If the lining is contaminated, the source of the leak must be found and corrected and the brakes must be replaced. Check all brake attaching parts for condition and tightness. If drums or rotors appear to be out of round, have them checked.
6. Have the front end alignment checked.
7. If the problem persists, there is a blockage in the hydraulic system.

Brake Warning Light Comes On

1. Check the fluid level in the master cylinder and fill to within ¼ in. of the top of reservoir.
2. Bleed the brakes. Do a thorough job since it is possible for small air bubbles to become trapped in the system, in which case they will break loose and turn the light on.
3. If light remains on and the fluid level in master cylinder decreases, repair the leak in the hydraulic system.
4. If the light remains on but the fluid level does not decrease, remove the wire from the switch on the pressure differential valve, the light should go out. If it does not, there is a short in the circuit to the bulb. If it does go out, remove the switch from the valve. Depress the plunger in the switch and check for continuity with a self-powered test light. If the switch is OK, manually center the piston in the pressure differential valve with a small screwdriver. Reinstall the switch and wire. If the light remains on, the pressure differential valve is defective.

Drum Brakes

All Pintos have drum brakes on the rear wheels. Front drum brakes are standard equipment on 1971–73 models, with front discs being optional. In 1974 front disc brakes became standard.

The major components of the system are the drum, the brake shoes, the brake shoe return and hold-down springs, and the automatic adjuster assembly. The rear brakes also incorporate a parking brake mechanism.

When the brake pedal is depressed, and hydraulic pressure is delivered to the wheel cylinder, the wheel cylinder expands to force the shoes against the drum. The primary shoe moves first, contacting the drum and pivoting slightly on its hold-down spring mounting pin. As the top of the primary (front) shoe contacts the drum, the bottom of the shoe moves slightly away from the drum. This movement is transferred through the adjusting screw to the secondary brake shoe, where it aids the wheel cylinder in bringing the secondary shoe in contact with the drum. Friction between the brake shoes and the drum causes the car to slow down and stop. When the brake pedal is released, the brake shoe return springs move the brakes away from the drum. If the lining on the brakes becomes contaminated or if the lining or drum becomes grooved, the engagement of the brakes and the drum will become very harsh causing the brakes to lock up and/or squeal. If the brake shoes on one wheel contact the drum before the same action occurs in the other wheels, the brakes will pull to one side when applied.

The automatic adjuster assembly consists of a cable, cable guide, adjuster lever, automatic adjuster spring, and adjusting screw. The automatic adjuster operates only when the brakes are applied while the car is backing up. When the brakes are applied with the car moving rearward, the movement of the secondary (rear) brake shoe (the automatic adjuster is attached to this shoe) causes the adjuster cable to pull the adjusting lever upward. When the brakes are released, the automatic adjuster spring pulls the adjusting lever downward. As the lever moves downward, it contacts the star wheel on the adjusting screw and pushes it downward. This causes the adjusting screw to unscrew slightly (expand) and move the brake shoes closer to the drum. The adjusting lever then rests on the star wheel of the adjusting screw until the brakes are applied the next time the car backs up. If the brake adjustment is OK, the secondary shoe will not have to move very far to contact the drum. This limited shoe movement will not lift the adjusting lever off the star wheel, thus the brakes will not be adjusted.

The parking brake mechanism in the wheel consists of a parking brake link and lever. The link fits between the two brake shoes. The lever is attached to the parking brake cable and the secondary brake shoe. When the parking brake handle is pulled in the car, the rear brake shoes are moved into contact with the brake drums.

Inspection

1. Raise the front or rear of the car and support the car with safety stands. Make sure the parking brake is not on.

2. If you are going to check the rear brakes, remove the lug nuts that attach the wheels to the axle shaft and remove the tires and wheels from the car. Remove the Tinnerman nuts from the wheel studs with a pair of pliers. Pull the brake drum off the axle shaft. If the brakes are adjusted too tightly to remove the drum, see step four. If you can remove the drum, see step five.

3. If you are going to check the front brakes, the front tire, wheel and brake drum can be removed as an assembly.

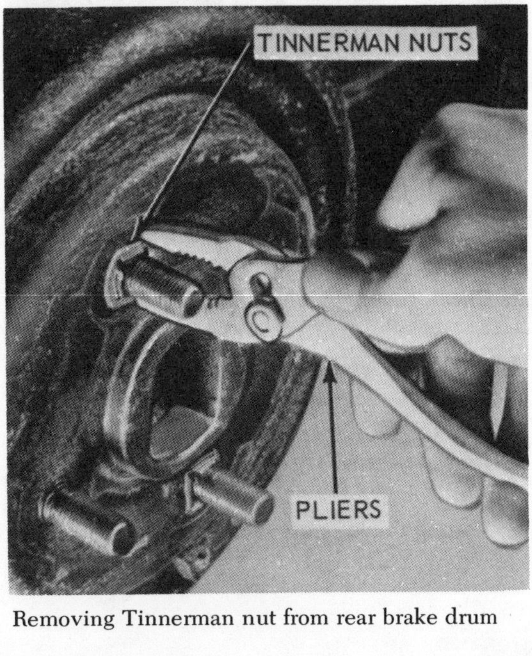

Removing Tinnerman nut from rear brake drum

Remove the hub cap, then either pry the dust cover off the drum hub with a screwdriver or pull it off with a pair of channel-lock pliers. Remove the cotter pin from the spindle. Slide the nut lock off the adjusting nut, then loosen the adjusting nut until it reaches the end of the spindle. Do not remove the adjusting nut yet. Grab the tire and pull it out, toward yourself, then push it back into position. This will free the outer wheel bearing from the drum hub. If the brakes are adjusted too tightly to allow the drum to be pulled off them, go to step four and loosen the brakes, then return here. Remove the adjusting nut, washer, and outer bearing from the spindle. Pull the tire, wheel, and brake drum off the spindle.

4. If the brakes are too tight to remove the drum, get under the car (make sure you have safety stands under the car to support it) and remove the rubber plug from the bottom of the brake backing plate. Shine a flashlight into the slot in the plate. You will see the top of the adjusting screw star wheel and the adjusting lever for the automatic brake adjusting mechanism. To back off the adjusting screw, you must first insert a small, thin screwdriver or a piece of firm wire (coat hanger wire) into the adjusting slot and push the adjusting lever away from the adjusting screw. Insert a brake adjusting spoon into the slot and engage the top of the star wheel. Lift the bottom of the adjusting spoon to force the adjusting screw star wheel downward. Repeat this operation until the brake drum is free of the brake shoes and can be pulled off. See the brake adjustment procedure for an illustration.

5. Clean the brake shoes and the inside of the brake drum. There must be at least 1/16 in. of brake lining above the heads of the brake shoe attaching rivets. The lining should not be cracked or contaminated with grease or brake fluid. If there is grease or brake fluid on the lining, it must be replaced and the source of the leak must be found and corrected. Brake fluid on the lining means leaking wheel cylinders. Grease on the brake lining means a leaking grease retainer (front wheels) or axle seal (rear brakes). If the lining is slightly glazed but otherwise in good condition, it can be cleaned with medium sandpaper. Lift the bottom of the wheel cylinder boots and inspect the ends of the wheel cylinders. A small amount of fluid in the end of the cylinders should be considered normal. If fluid runs out of the cylinder when the

Removing plug from backing plate

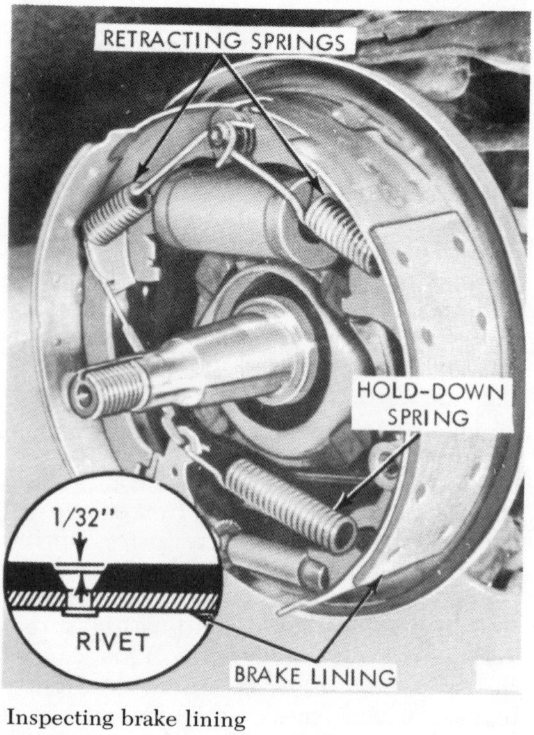

Inspecting brake lining

boots are lifted, however, the wheel cylinder must be rebuilt or replaced. Examine the inside of the brake drum. It should have a smooth, dull finish. If excessive brake shoe wear has caused grooves to wear in the drum, it must be machined or replaced. If the inside of the drum is slightly glazed, but otherwise in good condition, it can be cleaned with medium sandpaper.

6. If no repairs are required, install the drum and wheel. If the brake adjustment was changed to remove the drum, adjust the brakes until the drum will just fit over the brakes. After the wheel is installed it will be necessary to complete the adjustment. See the brake adjustment procedure in this chapter. If a front wheel was removed, tighten the wheel bearing adjusting nut to 17–25 ft lbs while spinning the wheel. This will seat the bearing. Loosen the adjusting nut ½ turn, then retighten it to 10–15 in. lbs.

Brake Shoe Removal

NOTE: *If you are not thoroughly familiar with the procedures involved in brake replacement, disassemble and assemble only one side at a time, leaving the other wheel intact as a reference.*

1. Remove the brake drum. See the above "Inspection" procedure.
2. Place the hollow end of a brake spring service tool (available at auto parts stores) on the brake shoe anchor pin and twist it to disengage one of the brake retracting springs. Repeat this operation to remove the other spring.

CAUTION: *Be careful the springs do not slip off the tool during removal, as they could cause personal injury.*

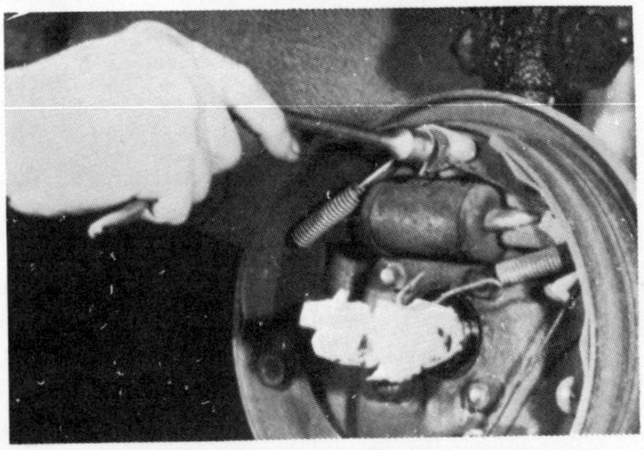

Removing brake retracting springs

3. Reach behind the brake backing plate and place a finger on the end of one of the brake hold-down spring mounting pins. Using a pair of pliers grasp the washer on the top of the hold-down spring that corresponds to the pin that you are holding. Push down on the pliers and turn them 90° to align the slot in the washer with the head on the spring mounting pin. Remove the spring and washer and repeat this operation on the hold-down spring on the other brake shoe.
4. Place the tip of a screwdriver on the top of the brake adjusting screw and move the screwdriver upward to lift up on the brake adjusting lever. When there is enough slack in the automatic adjuster cable, disconnect the loop on the top of the cable from the anchor pin. Grasp the top of each brake shoe and move it outward to disengage it from the wheel cylinder (and parking brake link on the rear wheels). When the brake shoes are clear, lift them from the backing plate. Twist the shoes slightly and the automatic adjuster assembly will disassemble itself.
5. If you are working on rear brakes, grasp the end of the brake cable spring with a pair of pliers and, using the brake lever as a fulcrum, pull the end of the spring away from the lever. Disengage the cable from the brake lever.

Wheel Cylinder Overhaul

Since the travel of the pistons in the wheel cylinder changes when new brake shoes are installed, it is possible for previously good wheel cylinders to start leaking after new brakes are installed. Therefore, to save yourself the expense of having to replace new brakes that become saturated with brake fluid and the aggravation of having to take everything apart again, it is strongly recommended that wheel cylinders be rebuilt every time new brake shoes are installed. This is especially true for cars with high mileage.

1. Remove the brakes.
2. Place a bucket or some old newspapers under the brake backing plate to catch the brake fluid that will run out of the wheel cylinder.
3. Remove the boots from the ends of the wheel cylinders.
4. Push one piston toward the center

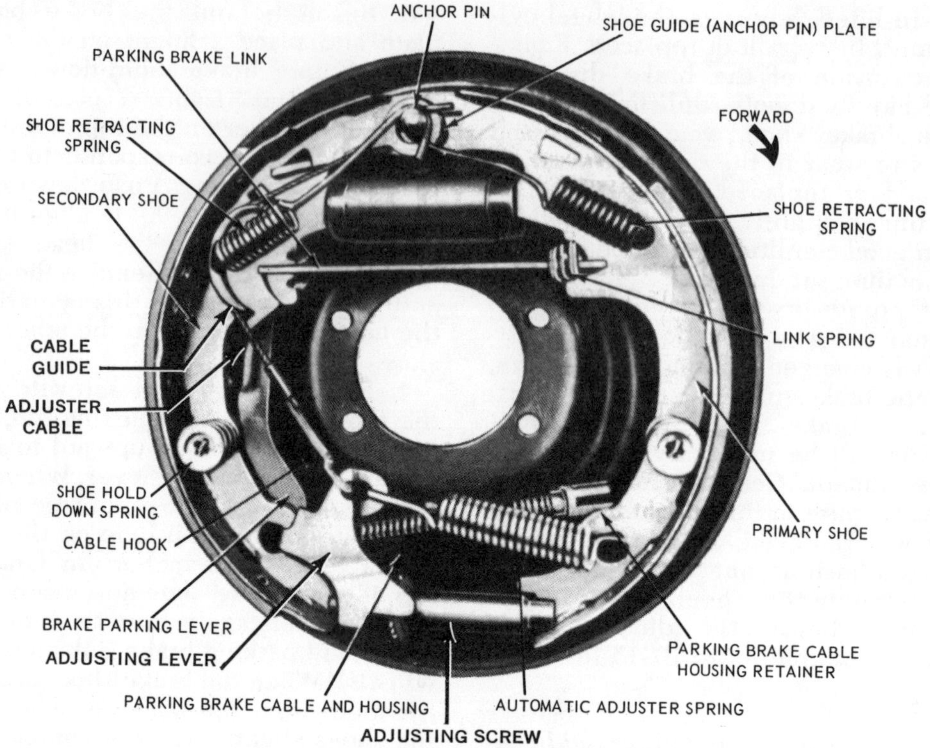

Rear brake assembly

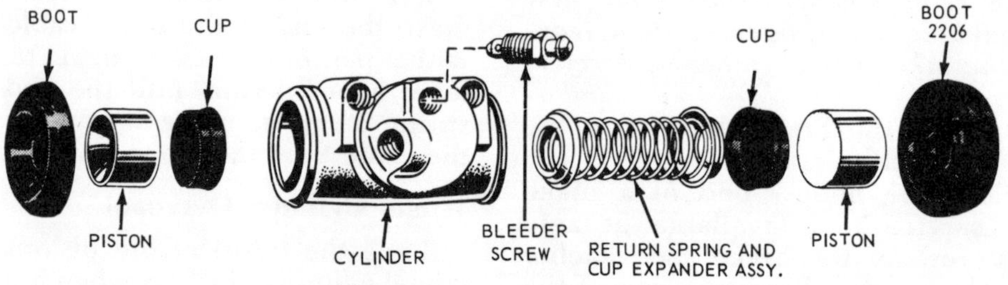

Exploded view of wheel cylinder

of the cylinder to force the opposite piston and cup out the other end of the cylinder. Reach in the open end of the cylinder and push the spring, cup, and piston out of the cylinder.

5. Remove the bleeder screw from the rear of the cylinder, on the back of the backing plate.

6. Inspect the inside of the wheel cylinder. If it is scored in any way, the cylinder must be honed with a wheel cylinder hone or fine emery paper, and finished with crocus cloth if emery paper is used. If the inside of the cylinder is excessively worn, the cylinder will have to be replaced, as only 0.003 in. of material can be removed from the cylinder walls. Whenever honing or cleaning wheel cylinders, keep a small amount of brake fluid in the cylinder to serve as a lubricant.

7. Clean any foreign matter from the pistons. The sides of the pistons must be smooth for the wheel cylinders to operate properly.

8. Clean the cylinder bore with alcohol and a lint-free rag. Pull the rag through the bore several times to remove all foreign matter and dry the cylinder.

9. Install the bleeder screw and the return spring in the cylinder.

10. Coat new cylinder cups with new brake fluid and install them in the cylinder. Make sure they are square in the bore or they will leak.

11. Install the pistons in the cylinder after coating them with new brake fluid.

12. Coat the insides of the boots with new brake fluid and install them on the cylinder. Install and bleed the brakes.

Wheel Cylinder Replacement

1. Remove the brake shoes.

2. On rear brakes, loosen the brake line on the rear of the cylinder, but do not pull the line away from the cylinder or it may bend.

3. On front brakes, disconnect the metal brake line from the rubber brake hose where they join in the wheel well. Pull off the horseshoe clip that attaches the rubber brake hose to the underbody of the car. Loosen the hose at the cylinder, then turn the whole brake hose to remove it from the wheel cylinder.

4. Remove the bolts and lockwashers that attach the wheel cylinder to the backing plate and remove the cylinder.

5. Position the new wheel cylinder on the backing plate and install the cylinder attaching bolts and lockwashers.

6. Attach the metal brake line or rubber hose by reversing the procedure given in step two or three.

7. Install the brakes and bleed the brake system.

Brake Shoe Installation

1. If you are working on rear brakes, the brake cable must be connected to the secondary brake shoe before the shoe is installed on the backing plate. To do this, first transfer the parking brake lever from the old secondary shoe to the new one. This is accomplished by spreading the bottom of the horseshoe clip and disengaging the lever. Position the lever on the new secondary shoe and install the spring washer and the horseshoe clip. Close the bottom of the clip after installing it. Grasp the metal tip of the parking brake cable with a pair of pliers. Position a pair of side cutters on the end of the cable coil spring and, using the pliers as a fulcrum, pull the coil spring back with the side cutters. Position the cable in the parking brake lever.

2. Apply a *light* coating of high-temperature grease to the brake shoe contact points on the backing plate. Position the primary brake shoe on the front of the backing plate and install the hold-down spring and washer over the mounting pin. Install the secondary shoe on the rear of the backing plate.

3. If working on rear brakes, install the parking brake link between the notch in the primary brake shoe and the notch in the parking brake lever.

4. Install the automatic adjuster cable loop end on the anchor pin. Make sure the crimped side of the loop faces the backing plate.

5. Install the return spring in the primary brake shoe and, using the tapered end of a brake spring service tool, slide the top of the spring onto the anchor pin.

CAUTION: *Be careful the spring does not slip off the tool during installation, as it could cause personal injury.*

6. Install the automatic adjuster cable guide in the secondary brake shoe, making sure the flared hole in the cable guide is inside the hole in the brake shoe. Fit the cable into the groove in the top of the cable guide.

7. Install the secondary shoe return spring through the hole in the cable guide and the brake shoe. Using the brake spring tool, slide the top of the spring onto the anchor pin.

8. Clean the threads on the adjusting screw and apply a light coating of high-temperature grease to the threads. Screw the adjuster closed, then open it one-half turn.

9. Install the adjusting screw between the brake shoes with the star wheel nearest to the secondary shoe. Make sure the star wheel is in a position that is accessible from the adjusting slot in the backing plate.

10. Install the short hooked end of the automatic adjuster spring in the proper hole in the primary brake shoe.

11. Connect the hooked end of the automatic adjuster cable and the free end of the automatic adjuster spring in the slot in the top of the automatic adjuster lever.

12. Pull the automatic adjuster lever (the lever will pull the cable and spring with it) downward and to the left and engage the pivot hook of the lever in the hole in the secondary brake shoe.

13. Check the entire brake assembly to make sure everything is installed properly. Make sure the shoes engage

the wheel cylinder properly and are flush on the anchor pin. Make sure the automatic adjuster cable is flush on the anchor pin and in the slot on the back on cable guide. Make sure the adjusting lever rests on the adjusting screw star wheel. Pull upward on the adjusting cable until the adjusting lever is free of the star wheel, then release the cable. The adjusting lever should snap back into place on the adjusting screw star wheel and turn the wheel one tooth.

14. Expand the brake adjusting screw until the brake drum will just fit over the brake shoes.

15. Install the wheel and drum and adjust the brakes. See "Brake Adjustment."

Brake Adjustment

1. Raise the car and support it with safety stands.

2. Remove the rubber plug from the adjusting slot on the backing plate.

3. Insert a brake adjusting spoon into the slot and engage the lowest tooth on the star wheel possible. Move the end of the brake spoon downward to move the star wheel upward and expand the adjusting screw. Repeat this operation until the brakes lock the wheel.

4. Insert a small screwdriver or piece of firm wire (coat hanger wire) into the adjusting slot and push the automatic adjuster lever out and free of the star wheel on the adjusting screw.

5. Holding the adjusting lever out of the way, engage the topmost tooth possible on the star wheel with a brake adjusting spoon. Move the end of the adjusting spoon upward to move the adjusting screw downward and contract the adjusting screw. Back the adjustment off until the wheel spins freely with a minimum of drag. Keep track of the number of turns the star wheel is backed off.

6. Repeat this operation on the other side of the car of the set (front or rear) of brakes that you are adjusting. When backing off the brakes on the other side, the star wheel must be backed off the same number of turns to prevent side-to-side brake pull.

7. Repeat this operation on the other set of brakes (front or rear).

Disc Brakes

The major components of the disc brake system are the brake pads, the caliper, and the rotor (disc). The caliper is similar in function to the wheel cylinder used with drum brakes, and the rotor is similar to the brake drum used in drum brakes.

The major difference between drum brakes and disc brakes is that with drum brakes, the wheel cylinder forces the brake shoes *out* against the brake drum to stop the car, while with disc brakes, the caliper forces the brake pads *in*ward to squeeze the rotor and stop the car. The biggest advantage of disc brakes over drum brakes is that the caliper and brake pads enclose only a small portion of the rotor, leaving the rest of it exposed

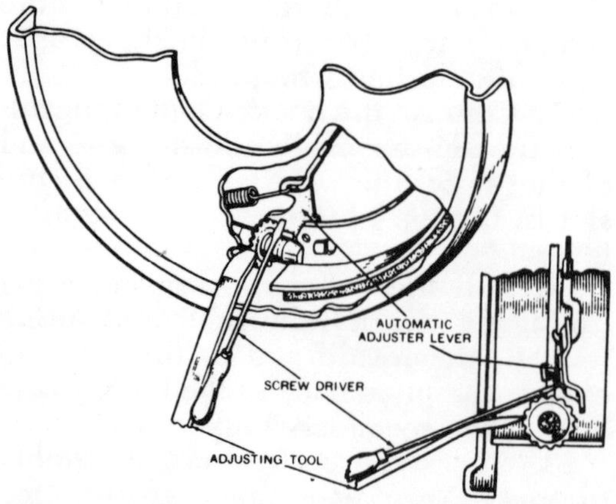

Adjusting brakes

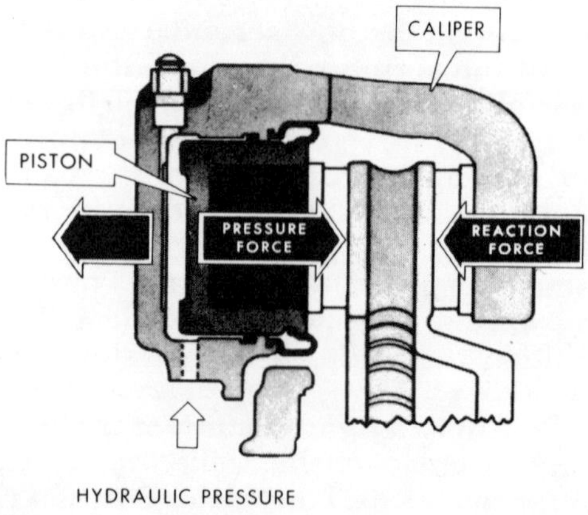

Sliding caliper operation

to outside air. This aids in rapid heat dissipation, reducing brake fade.

The disc brakes used on Pintos are known as sliding caliper disc brakes. The name of this system is derived from the sliding action of the brake caliper on the anchor plate during braking. The plate-like brake rotor is attached to and mounted on the car by the front wheel hub. A brake caliper anchor plate, attached to the front wheel spindle, mounts over the top of, but does not touch, the rotor. The caliper is mounted in the middle of the large opening in the anchor plate. When the brake pedal is depressed, and hydraulic force is generated, the piston in the caliper forces the inboard brake pad inward and into contact with the brake rotor. The caliper now begins to act like a C-clamp, with the inboard shoe and the piston acting as the adjustable screw. Since there is only a small amount of clearance between the brake pads and the rotor, the inboard shoe contacts the rotor almost as soon as the brake pedal is depressed. As the brake pedal is depressed further, it increases the amount of hydraulic pressure sent to the piston in the caliper. Since the inboard shoe is already in contact with the brake rotor, it cannot be moved. As the caliper pushes on the inboard brake shoe, the increased hydraulic pressure forces the back of the caliper housing away from the back of the piston. This causes the caliper to slide inward on the anchor plate and force the outboard brake pad into contact with the rotor. Thus the name sliding caliper. This happens very quickly, so both pads contact the rotor at about the same time.

When the brakes are released, the piston seal in the caliper housing (which was stretched during brake application) returns to its normal position and, in so doing, pulls the piston back away from the brake pad. A very slight wobble in the rotor as the car begins to move pushes the brake pads back so they are not in contact with the rotor. The clearance between the pads and the rotor is very slight, but it is sufficient to prevent brake drag. The same clearance is maintained even when the brake pads wear as the car accumulates mileage and, because of this, disc brakes do not have to be adjusted.

Removal and Inspection

1. Raise the front of the car and support it with safety stands.
2. Remove the hub cap and remove the lug nuts that attach the front wheels to the brake rotor, and remove the front wheels and tires.
3. On 1971–73 models, straighten and remove the two cotter pins from the caliper retaining key. On 1974 and later models, remove the retaining screw from the caliper retaining key with the appropriate allen wrench.

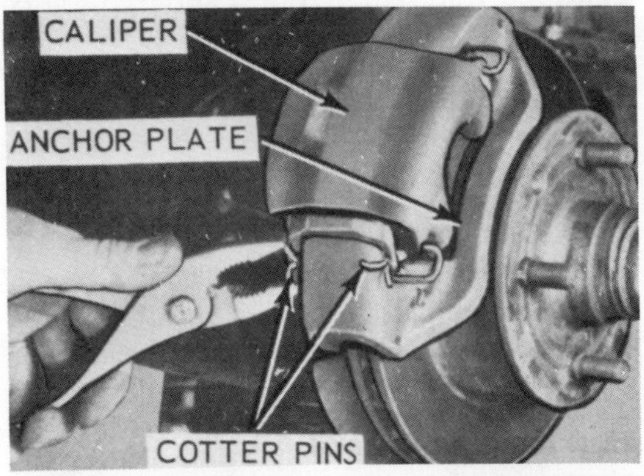

Removing cotter pins

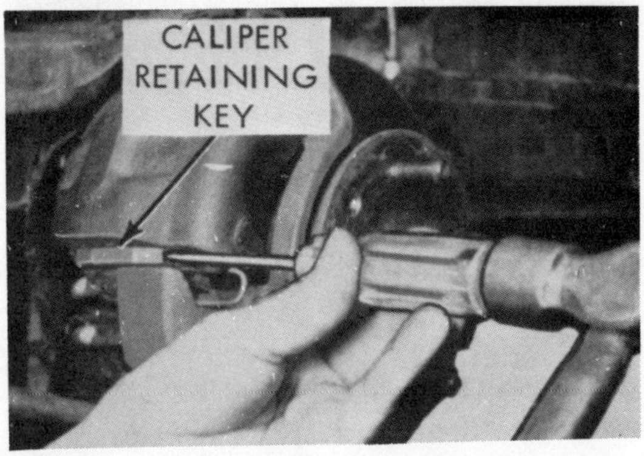

Removing retaining key

4. Carefully drive the caliper retaining key out of the slot between the caliper and the anchor plate.
5. On 1971–73 models, press the caliper assembly inward and upward against the caliper support springs and then lift the caliper assembly away from the anchor plate. On 1974 and later models, lift the caliper assembly away from the anchor plate by pushing the caliper downward against the anchor plate and working the top end up and out of the anchor plate.
6. Inspect the caliper and brake hose

for leaks. If the caliper is leaking it must be overhauled. If the brake hose is leaking or cracked it must be replaced. If the caliper needs to be overhauled, see "Caliper Overhaul" in this chapter.

7. If the caliper and hose are both OK, securely wire them out of the way under the car. Do not allow the caliper to hang on the brake hose.

8. On 1971–73 models, remove the brake pads from the anchor plate. On 1974 and later models, only the inner brake shoe is attached to the anchor plate. To remove the outer shoe which is attached to the caliper, tap lightly on the shoe and it will fall out. On any Pinto, if you are going to reuse the old shoes, don't mix them up because they have to be replaced in their original positions for proper braking. Also, when removing the shoes, there is a small anti-rattle clip attached to the inner shoe which has a tendency to fall off. Make sure that you replace it when replacing shoes.

9. Inspect the brake pads for wear. There must be at least 1/32 in. ('71–'74) or 1/8 in. ('75 and later), of lining above the heads of the rivets. If the lining is cracked or contaminated, it must be replaced. If the lining is slightly glazed, it can be cleaned with medium sandpaper.

10. Inspect the rotor, it should have a smooth, dull finish. If the brake pads are excessively worn and have scored the rotor, the rotor will have to be machined or replaced. To remove the rotor, see "Rotor Removal."

Caliper Removal and Overhaul

Due to the important functions of the piston seal, the relative ease of overhauling a caliper, and the low cost of caliper overhaul kits, it is strongly recommended that the calipers be overhauled whenever the brake pads are replaced.

1. If you have not already done so, remove the front wheels.

2. Disconnect the front brake hose from the metal brake line in the wheel. To do this, loosen the fitting on the metal brake line and pull out the horseshoe clip that attaches the rubber brake hose to the underbody of the car. Loosen the rubber brake hose connection at the caliper and turn the whole brake hose to remove it from the caliper.

3. Remove the caliper from the anchor plate by performing steps 3–5 of "Disc Brake Pad Removal."

4. Remove the piston by applying compressed air to the fluid inlet port with a rubber-tipped nozzle. Place a towel or thick cloth over the piston before applying air pressure to prevent damage to the piston. If the piston is seized in the bore and cannot be forced from the caliper, lightly tap around the outside of the caliper while applying air pressure.

5. Remove the dust boot from the caliper and discard it.

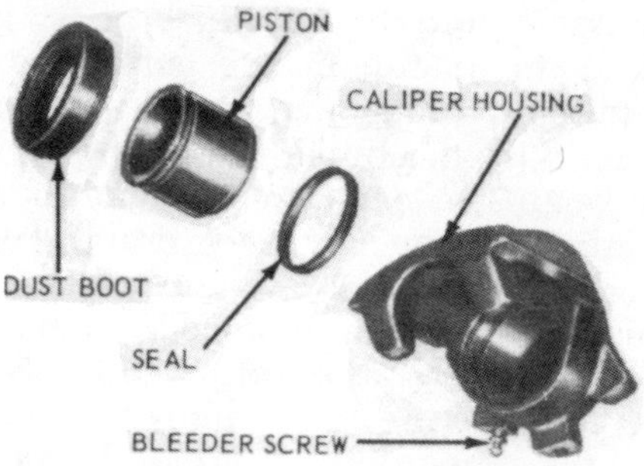

Caliper disassembled

6. Remove the piston seal from the caliper and throw it away.

7. Clean the inside of the caliper and the piston with an isopropyl alcohol. If either the piston or caliper are scored, they must be replaced. Wipe the assembly clean with a lint-free rag.

8. Coat a new piston seal with brake fluid and install it in the caliper. Make sure it is not twisted and that it is seated squarely in the groove.

9. Install a new dust boot by positioning the flange squarely in the outer groove in the piston bore of the caliper.

10. Coat the piston with brake fluid and install it in the caliper. Spread the dust boot over the piston as it is installed in the caliper. Seat the dust cover in the piston groove.

11. Connect the rubber brake hose to the caliper, making sure the copper gasket is installed on the end of the hose.

12. Connect the metal brake line to the end of the brake hose, position the hose, and install the horseshoe clip.

13. Install the caliper on the anchor plate by following the instructions in steps 3–6 of the brake pad installation procedure.

Pad Installation

1971–73

1. Install the pads in the anchor plate. If the original pads are being installed, they must be installed in their original location. If new pads are being installed, either one may be installed in either side.
2. If the caliper was not rebuilt, it will be necessary to compress the piston in the caliper so it will clear the brake pads during installation. To do this, place a block of wood (or suitable substitute) approximately 1¾ in. by 1 in. and ¾ in. thick on the piston. Position a 4 in. C-clamp on the caliper and, using the block of wood, tighten the clamp to bottom the piston in the caliper. The piston will remain in the bottomed position, so the clamp and block can be removed.
3. Install the bottom of the caliper over the brake pads and onto the anchor plate. Push downward on the bottom of the caliper to compress the lower caliper support spring and push downward on the top of the caliper to seat it on the anchor plate.
4. Push upward on the caliper and tap the caliper retaining key into the slot between the caliper and the anchor plate with a hammer.
5. Install two, new, stainless steel cotter pins in the caliper retaining key.
6. Install the front wheel. If the caliper was overhauled it will be necessary to bleed the system. See "Bleeding the Hydraulic System" in this chapter.

1974–77

1. Remove approximately ⅔ of the fluid from the rear reservoir of the tandem master cylinder. Raise the vehicle, taking proper safety precautions.
2. Remove the wheel and tire assembly.
3. Remove the key retaining screw from the caliper retaining key.
4. Slide the retaining key and support spring either inward or outward from the anchor plate. To remove the key and spring, a hammer and drift may be used, taking care not to damage the key in the process.
5. Lift the caliper assembly away from the anchor plate by pushing the caliper downward against the anchor plate and rotating the upper end upward out of the anchor plate. Be careful not to stretch or twist the flexible brake hose.
6. Remove the inner shoe and lining assembly from the anchor plate. The inner shoe antirattle clip may become displaced at this time and should be repositioned on the anchor plate. Lightly tap on the outer shoe and lining assembly to free it from the caliper.
7. Clean the caliper, anchor plate, and disc assemblies, and inspect them for brake fluid leakage, excessive wear or signs of damage. Replace the pads if either of them are worn to within 1/32 in. (⅛ in.—1975 and later), of the rivet heads.
8. To install new pads, use a 4 in. C-clamp and a block of wood 1¾ in. x 1 in. and approximately ¾ in. thick to seat the caliper hydraulic piston in its bore. This must be done in order to provide clearance for the caliper to fit over the rotor when the new linings are installed.
9. At this point, the antirattle clip should be in its place on the lower inner brake shoe support of the anchor plate with the pigtail of the clip toward the inside of the anchor plate. Position the inner brake shoe and lining assembly on the anchor plate with the pad toward the disc.
10. Install the outer brake shoe with the lower flange ends against the caliper leg abutments and the brake shoe upper flanges over the shoulders on the caliper legs. The shoe is installed correctly when its flanges fit snugly against the machined surfaces of the shoulder.
11. Remove the C-clamp used to seat the caliper piston in its bore. The piston will remain seated.
12. Position the caliper housing lower V-groove on the anchor plate lower abutment surface.
13. Pivot the caliper housing upward toward the disc until the outer edge of the piston dust boot is about ¼ in. from the upper edge of the inboard pad.
14. In order to prevent pinching of the dust boot between the piston and the inboard pad during installation of the caliper, place a clean piece of thin cardboard between the inboard pad and the lower half of the piston dust boot.
15. Rotate the caliper housing toward the disc until a slight resistance is felt. At this point, pull the cardboard downward

toward the disc centerline while rotating the caliper over the disc. Then remove the cardboard and complete the rotation of the caliper down over the disc.

16. Slide the caliper up against the upper abutment surfaces of the anchor plate and center the caliper over the lower anchor plate abutment.

17. Position the caliper support spring and key in the key slot and slide them into the opening between the lower end of the caliper and the lower anchor plate abutment until the key semicircular slot is centered over the retaining screw threaded hole in the anchor plate.

18. Install the key retaining screw and torque to 12–16 ft lbs.

19. Check the fluid level in the master cylinder and fill as necessary. Install the reservoir cover. Depress the brake pedal several times to properly seat the caliper and pads. Check for leakage around the caliper and flexible brake hose.

20. Install the wheel and tire assembly and torque the nuts to 70–115 ft lbs. Install the wheel cover.

21. Lower the car. Make sure that you obtain a firm brake pedal and then road-test the car for proper brake operation.

Rotor Removal

See the disc brake portion of the "Wheel Bearing" section in this chapter.

Parking Brake

When the parking brake is applied, the rear brakes of the vehicle are locked against the rear brake drums. The parking brake control lever applies the brakes by mechanical means rather than through the brake hydraulic system as when the foot brake is depressed.

The parking brake system consists of the control lever which is mounted on the transmission tunnel in the floor pan, an equalizer or adjustment rod, which is attached to the control lever, a cable equalizer, which is attached to the rear of the equalizer rod, the brake cables, which connect the equalizer or adjustment rod to the rear brakes, and the parking brake levers and links in the rear brake shoe hardware.

When the control lever is pulled upward, the adjusting rod pulls the cables to the rear brakes tight. This tightening of the cables moves the parking brake levers, which brings the rear brake shoes into contact with the brake drum.

Adjustment

1. Make sure the transmission is in Neutral and the parking brake is fully released.
2. Raise the rear of the car and support it with jack stands.
3. Pry upward on the rear of the parking brake control lever boot to gain access to the adjusting nut.
4. Loosen the locknut on the equalizer rod.
5. Tighten the adjusting nut until the rear brakes drag when the rear wheels are turned by hand.
6. Loosen up the adjusting nut until the rear wheels can be turned freely without dragging.

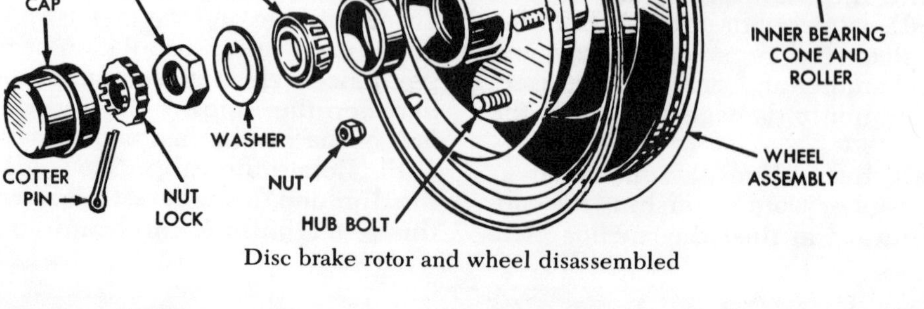

Disc brake rotor and wheel disassembled

7. Tighten the locknut, lower the boot into position, and lower the car.

Front Wheel Bearings

Outer Bearing Removal—Drum Brakes

1. Raise the front of the car and support it with safety stands.

2. Remove the hub cap, then either pry the dust cover off the spindle with a screwdriver or pull it off with a pair of channel-lock pliers. Remove the cotter pin from the spindle. Slide the nut lock off the adjusting nut, then loosen the adjusting nut until it reaches the end of the spindle. Do not remove the adjust nut yet. Grab the tire and pull it out, toward yourself, then push it back into position. This will free the outer wheel bearing from the drum hub. If the brakes are adjusted too tightly to allow the drum to be pulled off, go to step four and loosen the brakes, then return here. Remove the adjusting nut, washer, and outer bearing from the spindle. Pull the tire, wheel, and brake drum off the spindle.

3. If the brakes are too tight to remove the drum, get under the car (make sure you have safety stands under the car to support it) and remove the rubber plug from the bottom of the brake backing plate. Shine a flashlight into the slot in the plate. You will see the top of the adjusting screw star wheel and the adjusting lever for the automatic brake adjusting mechanism. To back off on the adjusting screw, you must first insert a small, thin screwdriver or a piece of firm wire (coat hanger wire) into the adjusting slot and push the adjusting lever away from the adjusting screw. Insert a brake adjusting spoon into the slot and engage the top of the star wheel. Lift the bottom of the adjusting spoon to force the adjusting screw star wheel down. Repeat this operation until the brake drum is free of the brake shoes and can be pulled off.

Outer Bearing and Rotor Removal—Disc Brakes

1. Raise the front of the car and support it with safety stands.

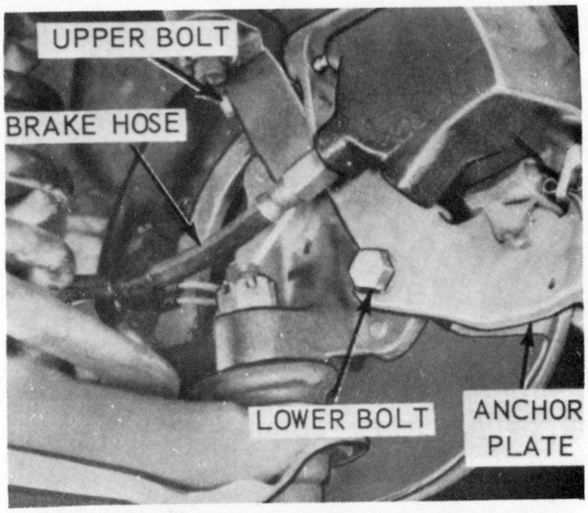

Anchor plate attaching bolts

2. Remove the front wheels.

NOTE: *In order to remove the rotor, the caliper and anchor plate must be removed from the car.*

3. Loosen, but do not remove, the upper anchor plate attaching bolt with a ¾ in. socket.

4. Using a ⅝ in. socket, remove the lower anchor plate attaching bolt.

NOTE: *When the caliper is removed from the car it must be wired out of the way of the rotor. Also, the brake pads will fall out of the caliper if they are not held in place when the caliper is removed. You will have to insert a small piece of wood or a folded piece of heavy cardboard between the shoes to hold them in place. Have a piece of wire and a piece of wood handy before you start the next step.*

5. Hold the caliper in place and remove the upper anchor plate attaching bolt.

6. Slide the caliper and anchor plate assembly off the rotor, inserting the block of wood between the brake pads as they become visible above the rotor.

7. When the anchor plate is clear of the rotor, wire it out of the way.

8. Remove the dust cap from the rotor hub by either prying it off with a screwdriver or pulling it off with a pair of channel-lock pliers.

9. Remove the cotter pin and the nut lock from the spindle.

10. Loosen the bearing adjusting nut until it is at the end of the spindle.

11. Grasp the rotor with a rag and pull it outward, push it inward.

12. Remove the adjusting nut and the outer bearing.

13. Remove the rotor from the spindle.

Inner Bearing Removal—Disc and Drum Brakes

1. Place the rotor or drum and tire on a clean, paper-covered surface with the wheel studs facing upward.

2. Working through the hole in the center of the wheel hub, tap the grease seal out of the rear of the hub with a screwdriver or drift.

NOTE: *Be careful not to damage the inner bearing while knocking out the grease seal.*

3. Remove the grease seal and bearing from under the rotor or drum, and discard the grease seal.

Cleaning, Inspection, and Repacking

1. Clean the inner and outer bearings and the wheel hub with a suitable solvent. Remove all old grease.

2. Thoroughly dry and wipe clean all components.

3. Clean all old grease from the spindle on the car.

4. Carefully check the bearings for any sign of scoring or other damage. If the roller bearings or bearing cages are damaged, the bearing and the corresponding bearing cup in the rotor or drum hub must be replaced. The bearing cups must be driven out of the rotor or drum hub to be removed. The outer bearing cup is driven out of the front of the rotor or drum from the rear and vice versa for the inner bearing cup.

5. Whether you are reinstalling the old bearings or installing new ones, the bearings must be packed with wheel bearing grease. To do this, place a glob of grease in your left palm, then, holding one of the bearings in your right hand, drag the edge of the bearing heavily through the grease. This must be done to work as much grease as possible through the roller bearings and cage. Turn the bearing and continue to pull it through the grease until the grease is packed between the bearings and the cage all the way around the circumference of the

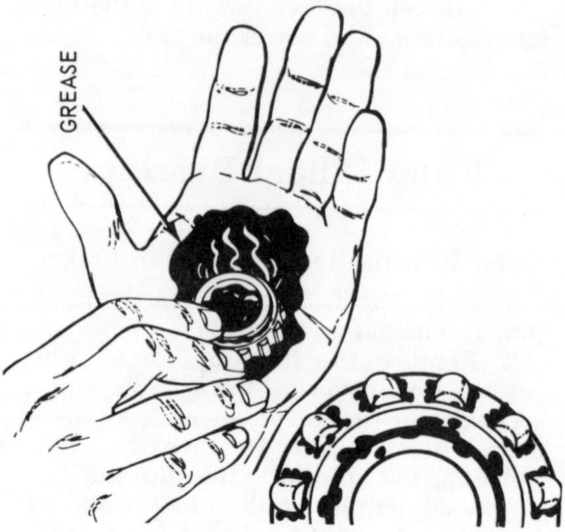

Packing grease in wheel bearing

bearing. Repeat this operation until all of the bearings are packed with grease.

6. Pack the inside of the drum or rotor hub with a moderate amount of grease, between the bearing cups. Do not overload the hub with grease.

7. Apply a small amount of grease to the spindle.

8. Place the drum or rotor, face down, on a protected surface and install the inner bearing.

9. Coat the lip of a new grease seal with a small amount of grease and position it on the drum or rotor.

10. Place a block of wood on top of the grease seal and tap on the block with a hammer to install the seal. Turn the block of wood to different positions to seat it squarely in the hub.

Drum or Rotor Installation and Wheel Bearing Adjustment

1. Position the drum or rotor on the spindle.

2. Install the outer bearing and washer on the spindle, inside the drum or rotor hub.

3. Install the bearing adjusting nut and tighten it to 17–25 ft lbs while spinning the rotor or drum. This will seat the bearing.

4. Back off the adjusting nut one half turn.

5. Tighten the adjusting nut to 10–15 in. lbs.

6. Install the nut lock on the adjusting nut so two of the slots align with the hole in the spindle.

7. Install a new cotter pin and bend the ends back so they will not interfere with the dust cap.

8. Install the dust cap.

9. Install the front tires if they were removed.

10. If the brakes (front, drum) were backed off to remove the drum, adjust them.

Brake Specifications

All measurements are given in inches

	MASTER CYLINDER		*WHEEL CYLINDER*			*BRAKE DISC OR DRUM DIAMETER*		
			Front			*Front*		
Year	*Disc*	*Drum*	*Disc*	*Drum*	*Rear*	*Disc*	*Drum*	*Rear*
'71–'73	.9375	.9375	2.125	1.000	.7187①	9.3	9.0	9.0
'74–'77	.9375	—	2.600	—	.8750	9.3	—	9.0

① .8750 on station wagons

Chapter 10

Body

Doors

DOOR TRIM PANEL

Removal

1. Remove the door handle attaching screw.
2. Remove the window handle attaching screw.
3. Remove the two armrest attaching bolts and the armrest.
4. Insert a screwdriver between the door trim panel and the door, and lift outward on the trim panel to free the attaching clips from the holes in the door.
5. Remove the door panel from the door.

Installation

1. Position the trim panel on the door, making sure the clips align with the holes in the door.
2. Press the trim panel to seat the clips in the holes.
3. Install the armrest.
4. Install the door and window handles.

Front Door Glass Adjustment

1. Remove the trim panel from the door.

Door trim panel removal

2. Remove the weathersheet from the door.
3. Loosen the screw on the rear window run (A in illustration).
4. Loosen the nut on the front window run (B in illustration).
5. Raise or lower the window until the top edge of the glass is about 4 in. above the window opening in the door.
6. Tighten the rear run adjusting

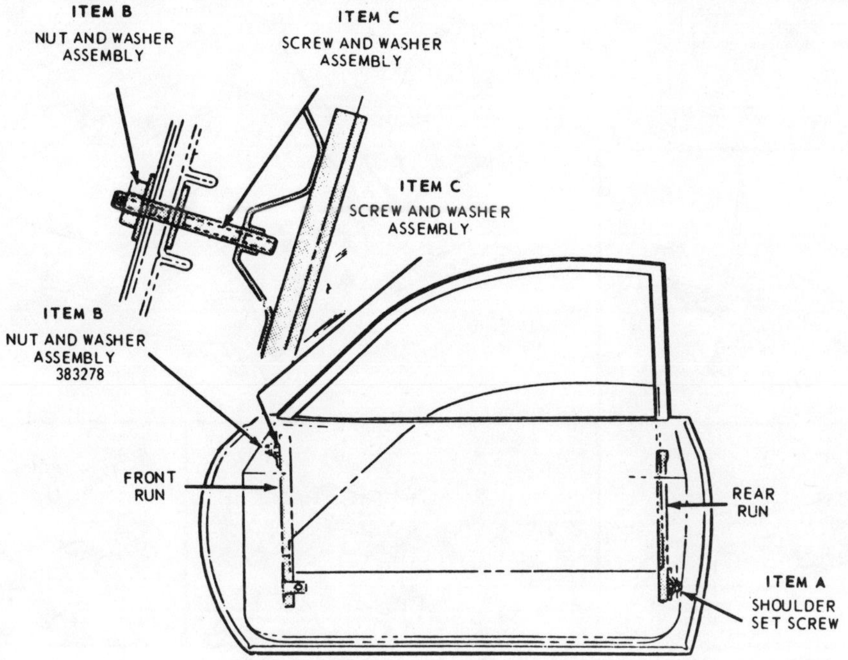

Front door glass adjustment

screw (A), then raise the window to the full-up position.

7. Adjust the front run snugly against the window, then tighten the front run screw (C) while preventing the nut (B) from turning.

8. Loosen the rear run screw and lower the window until the top of the glass is flush with the door glass opening in the door.

9. Position the rear run snugly against the window and tighten the screw.

10. Check the operation of the window to ensure that it does not bind.

11. Install the weathersheet and the trim panel.

Front Door Lock Cylinder Replacement

NOTE: *The key code for the ignition and door locks is stamped on the front door lock cylinder.*

1. Remove the trim panel from the door.
2. Remove the weathersheet from the door.
3. Disconnect the lock button-to-lock cylinder rod at the lock cylinder.

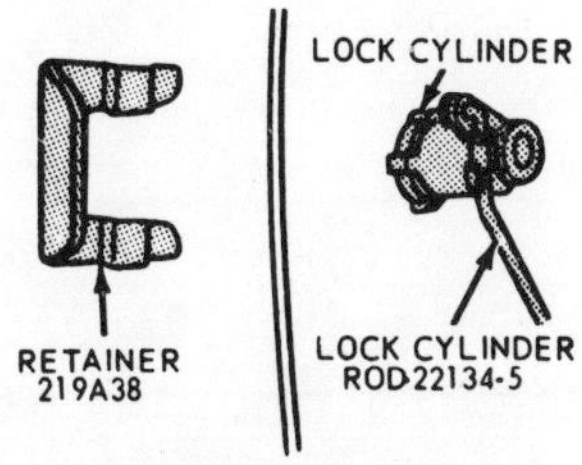

Front door lock cylinder and retainer

4. Remove the lock cylinder retainer clip and remove the cylinder from the door.
5. Transfer the lock cylinder arm to the new lock cylinder.
6. Position the cylinder in the door and install the lock cylinder retaining clip.
7. Connect the lock button rod to the lock cylinder.
8. Install the weathersheet and the trim panel.

Body Molding Replacement

See the illustrations to determine what types of clips are used to attach the molding to the body and either unscrew them or pry them out (push-on type) to remove the molding.

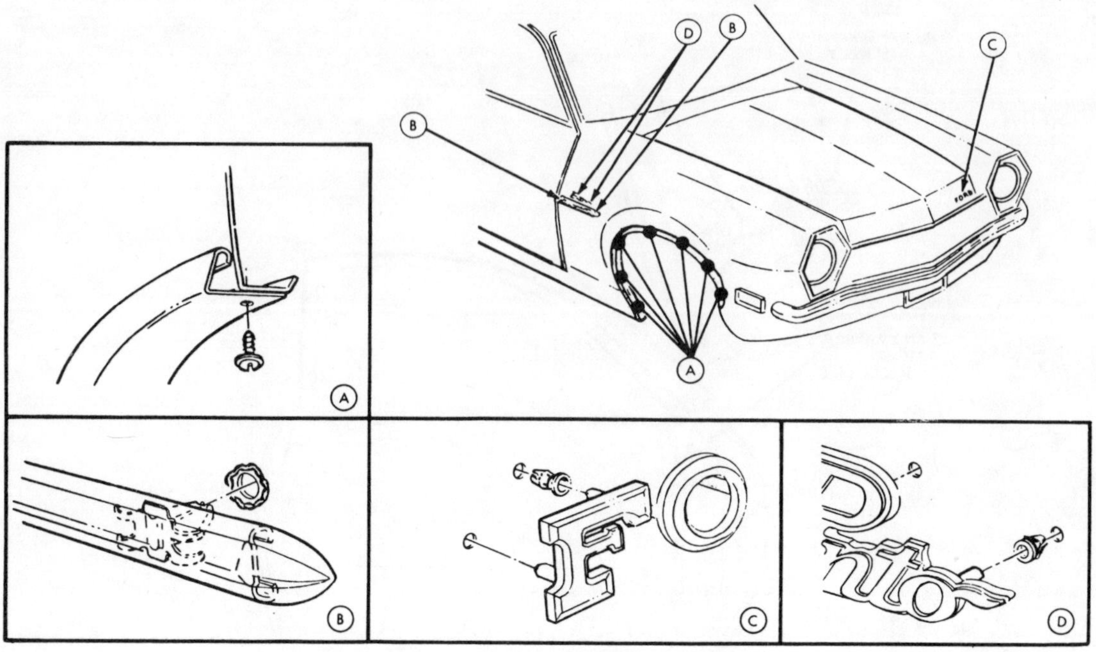

Front fender and hood molding attachment

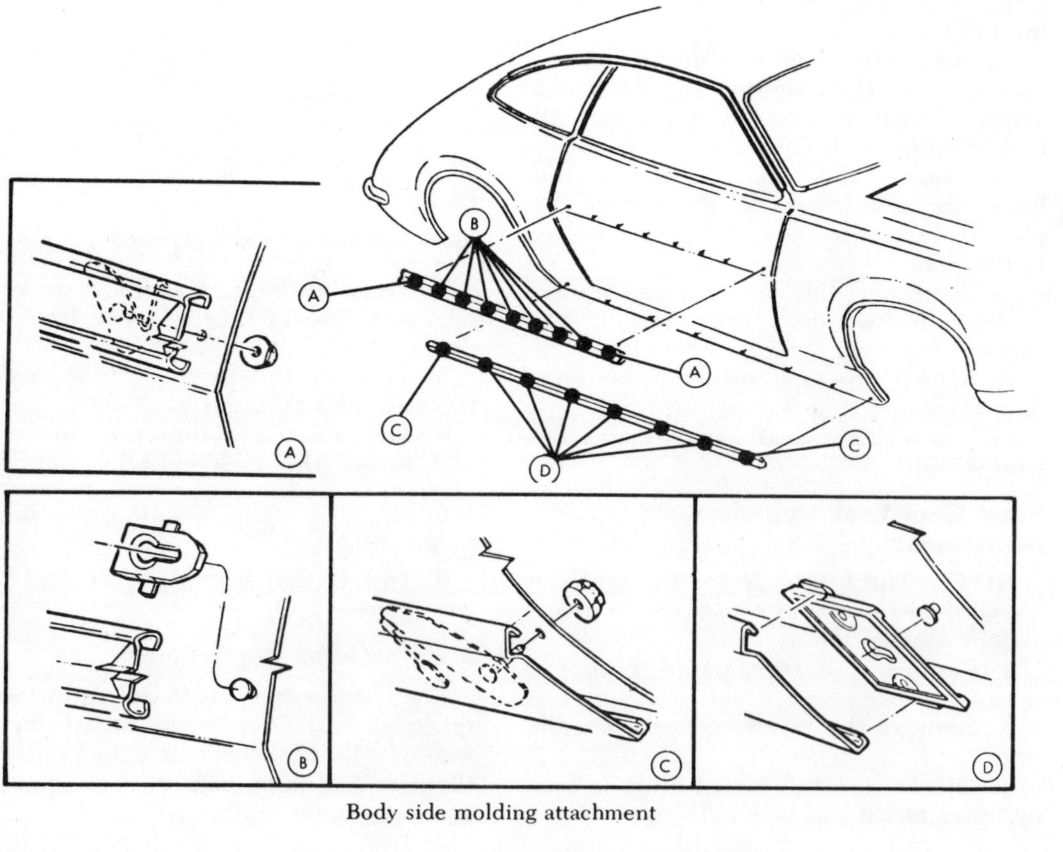

Body side molding attachment

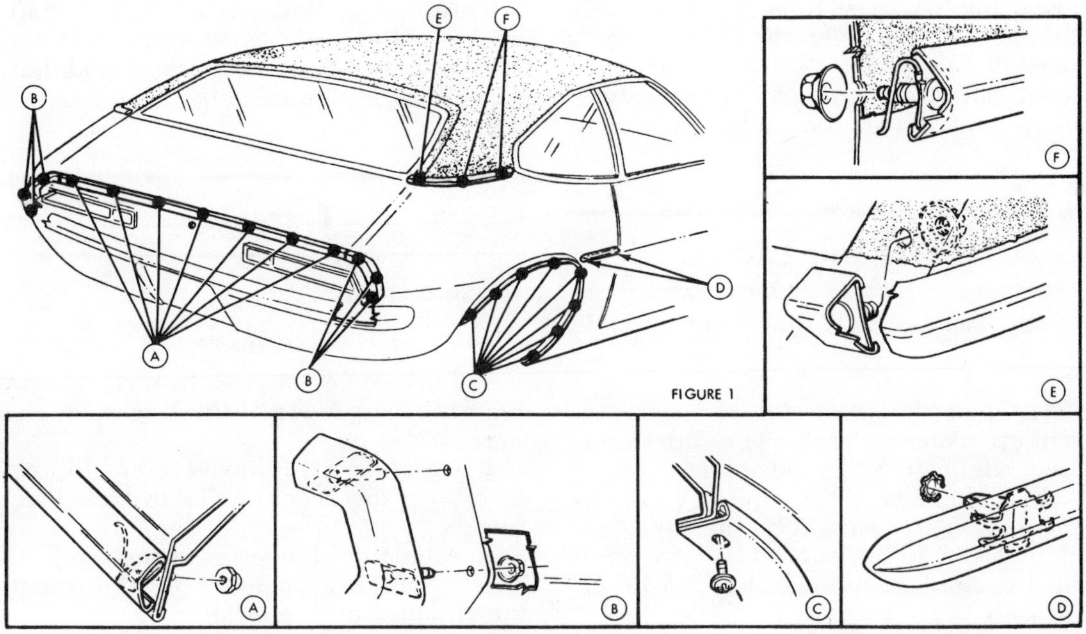

Rear body molding attachment

Hood

Hood Latch Adjustment

HORIZONTAL

Loosen the hood latch bracket-to-hood attaching screws and lower the hood. Move the hood latch bracket as required to align the hood latch hook with the hood latch striker bar. Tighten the screws.

VERTICAL

Loosen the hood latch-to-hood latch bracket attaching screws. Move the hood as required to align the top of the hood with the tops of the fenders. Tighten the screws. Raise or lower the rubber hood bumpers on the radiator support to re-

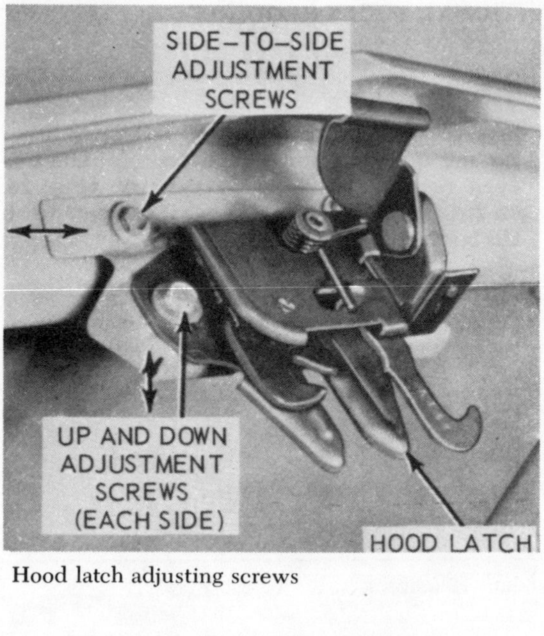

Hood latch adjusting screws

Rubber hood bumper

move any looseness from the hood. Hold the rubber bumper locknut with a wrench and turn the bumper. Close the hood and make sure it locks securely. If it does not, the hood must be readjusted.

Trunk Lid

Hinge Torsion Bar Adjustment

2 Dr. Sedan

1. Open the trunk lid and note the pop-up distance of it. The lid should have adequate finger clearance.
2. If there is not adequate clearance the torsion bars should be increased.
3. If the lid opens with more force than desired, the torsion bar can be decreased.

CAUTION: *Be careful when adjusting the torsion bar as it is under tension and could spring out.*

4. Support the lid in the full open position before adjusting the torsion bar.
5. To adjust, grip the bar with a pipe wrench and move the bar end to another position or notch to increase or decrease tension.
6. Adjust one torsion bar at a time and afterwards the difference in the position of the torsion bar ends, right and left sides must not be more than one slot.

Liftgate

Hinge Adjustment

Hatchback

1. Pull down the weatherstrip across the entire top edge of the liftgate opening.
2. Carefully pull down the headlining to expose the access holes to the hinge nuts.
3. Adjust the hinges as necessary.
4. Apply trim cement to the sheet metal flange and reinstall.
5. Apply rubber cement to the upper surface of the flange and install the weatherstrip.

Station Wagon Tailgate

To adjust for proper weather sealing of the tailgate, you must first remove the torsion bars (those long rods which stretch across the top).

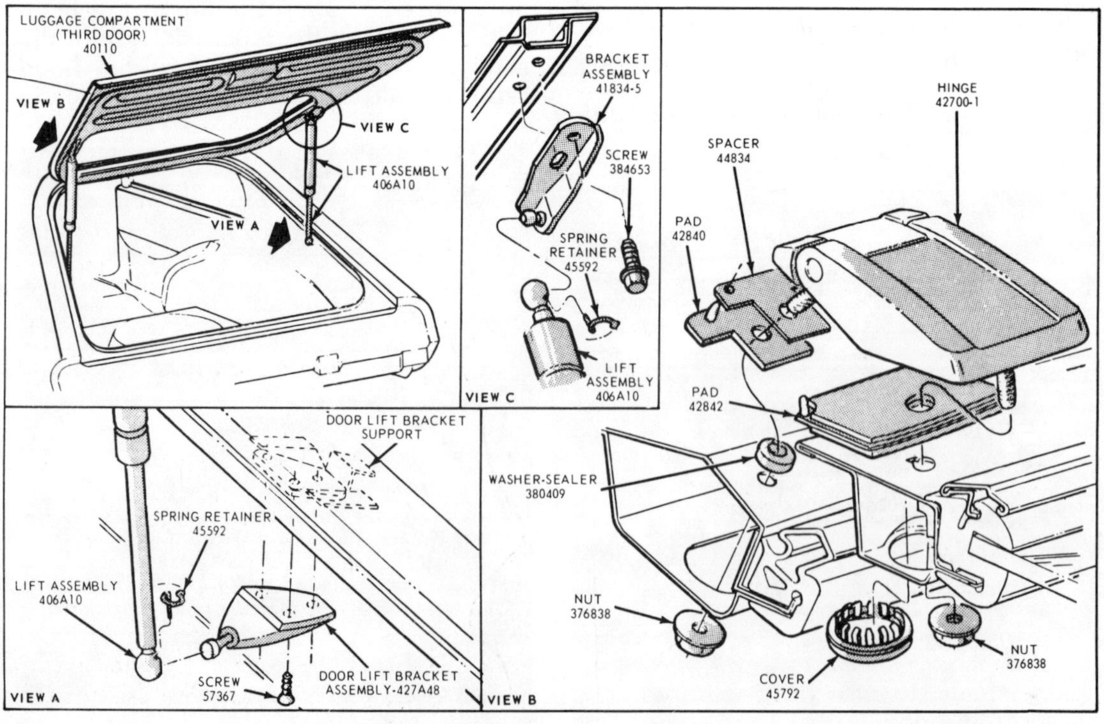

Liftgate hinge adjustment—Hatchback

1. Support the tailgate in the open position.

2. Remove the hinge cover panel and using a pair of vise grips, remove the torsion bar. Be careful to hold the bar securely when removing it as it will be under tension. Mark the bars so that you'll know which side they go on when you replace them.

3. Using a drift, open the hinge slot about ⅛ in. so that the bars can extend in to the fullest amount. The hinge slot is the notch in the hinge which is contacted by the torsion bar.

4. Replace the torsion bars and check the door fit.

Fuel Tank

Removal

1. Raise the vehicle up on a hoist.
2. Drain the fuel from the tank.
3. Disconnect the fuel lines and hoses from the tank assembly.
4. Loosen the retaining straps at the adjusting bolts and remove the tank.

Installation

1. Position the fuel tank and install the retaining straps.
2. Connect all fuel lines, replacing any cracked, split, or dried out hoses.
3. Replace the fuel separator if found to be damaged or inoperative.
4. Tighten the retaining straps securely.

Bumpers

IMPACT ABSORBING FRONT BUMPER

Removal and Installation

1973 AND LATER

1. Remove the bolts connecting the insulator to the reinforcement and remove the bumper assembly.

2. If you are replacing the bumper, transfer the bumper reinforcement, guards, pads, license plate bracket and braces to the new bumper.

3. Position the bumper to the isolators and install the attaching bolts and retaining nuts snug.

4. Adjust the bumper so that the top edge of the bumper is 20.93 inches, (plus or minus 1¼ inches) from the ground.

5. Adjust the bumper for appearance while maintaining the top edge dimension.

6. Tighten the bolts between the isolator and the reinforcement. (See the illustration for torque specifications.)

IMPACT ABSORBING REAR BUMPER

Removal and Installation

1973 AND LATER

1. Remove the two license light attaching screws and let the light hang by the wires.

2. Remove the two bolts attaching each isolator to the bumper reinforcement and remove the bumper assembly.

3. On wagons, remove the stone deflector from the reinforcement.

4. Remove the bolts attaching the reinforcement to the bumper and separate the reinforcement and end brackets from the bumper.

5. If a new bumper is to be used transfer the bumper guards and pads to the new bumper.

6. Check the isolators for fluid leakage. If leakage is found replace the isolators.

7. Position the reinforcement and end brackets to the bumper and install the attaching bolts and nuts. (See the illustration for torque specifications.)

8. On wagons, install the stone deflector on the reinforcement.

9. Position the bumper assembly to the isolators and install the attaching bolts.

10. Adjust the bumper so that the top edge of the bumper is 21.53 inches for the sedan or 21.34 inches for the station wagon (plus or minus 1¼ inches) from the ground.

11. Adjust the bumper for appearance while maintaining the top edge dimension.

12. Tighten the bolts attaching the isolators to the reinforcement. (See the illustration for torque specifications.)

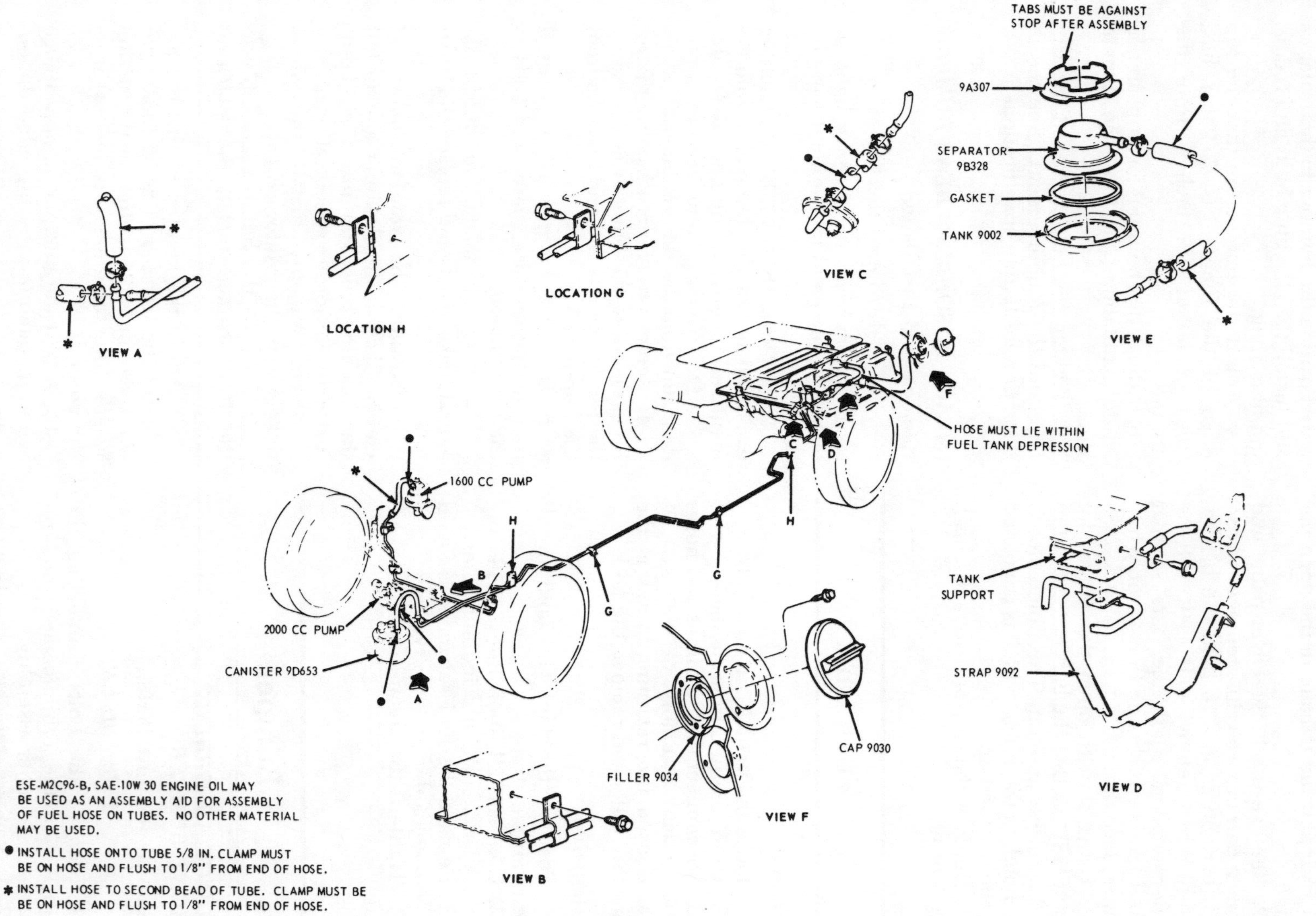

Fuel tank and lines

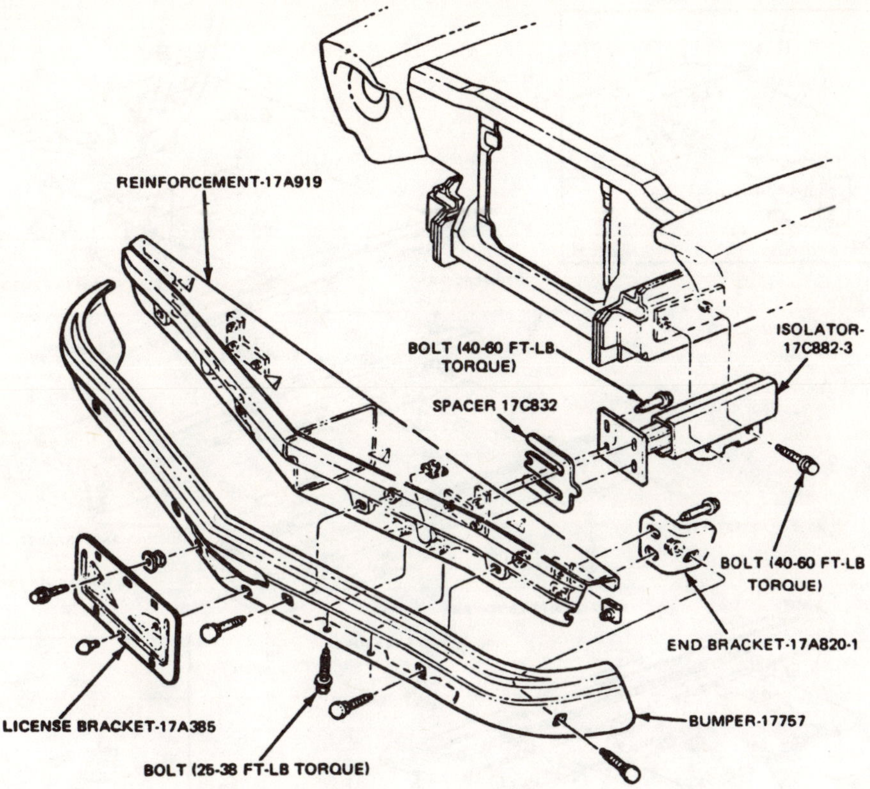

Impact absorbing front bumper

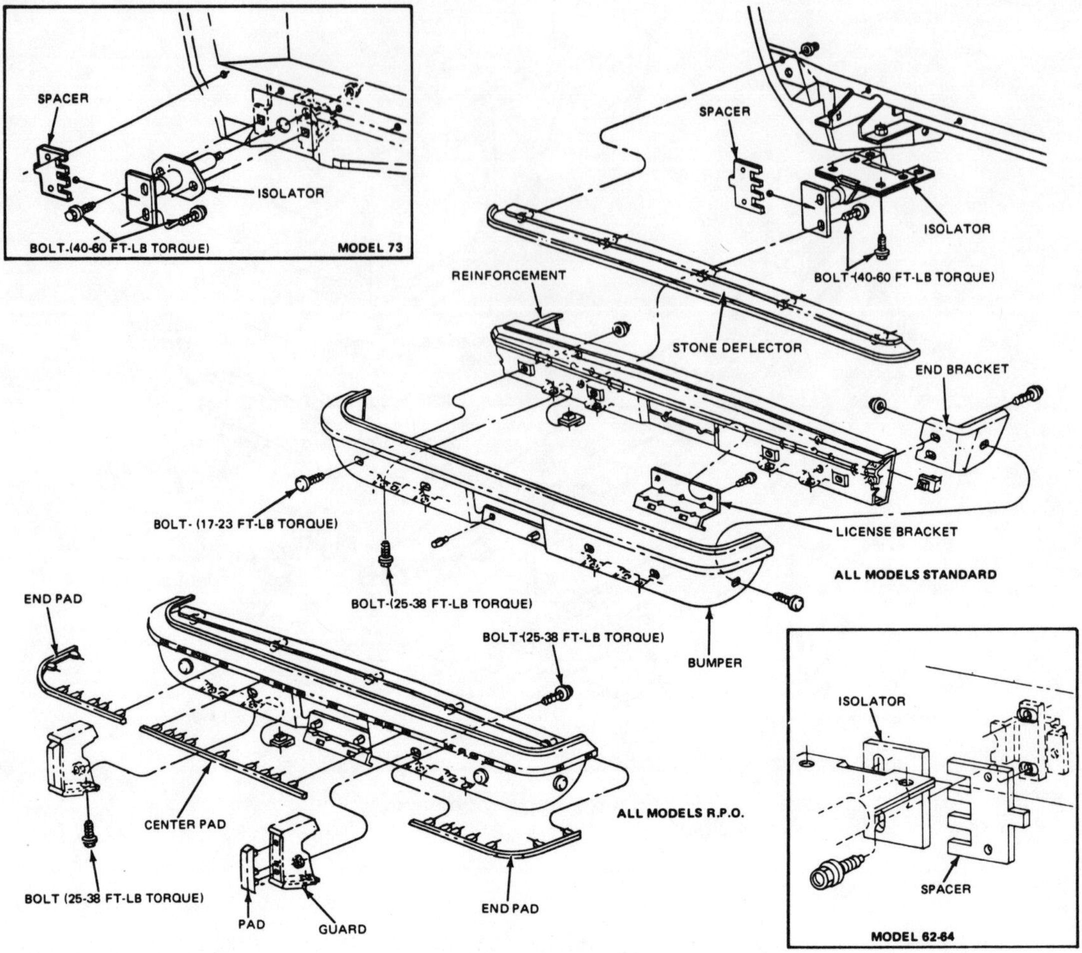

Impact absorbing rear bumper

Appendix

General Conversion Table

Multiply by	*To convert*	*To*	
2.54	Inches	Centimeters	.3937
30.48	Feet	Centimeters	.0328
.914	Yards	Meters	1.094
1.609	Miles	Kilometers	.621
.645	Square inches	Square cm.	.155
.836	Square yards	Square meters	1.196
16.39	Cubic inches	Cubic cm.	.061
28.3	Cubic feet	Liters	.0353
.4536	Pounds	Kilograms	2.2045
4.546	Gallons	Liters	.22
.068	Lbs./sq. in. (psi)	Atmospheres	14.7
.138	Foot pounds	Kg. m.	7.23
1.014	H.P. (DIN)	H.P. (SAE)	.9861
——	To obtain	From	Multiply by

Note: 1 cm. equals 10 mm.; 1 mm. equals .0394″.

Conversion—Common Fractions to Decimals and Millimeters

Inches			Inches			Inches		
Common Fractions	*Decimal Fractions*	*Millimeters (approx.)*	*Common Fractions*	*Decimal Fractions*	*Millimeters (approx.)*	*Common Fractions*	*Decimal Fractions*	*Millimeters (approx.)*
1/128	.008	0.20	11/32	.344	8.73	43/64	.672	17.07
1/64	.016	0.40	23/64	.359	9.13	11/16	.688	17.46
1/32	.031	0.79	3/8	.375	9.53	45/64	.703	17.86
3/64	.047	1.19	25/64	.391	9.92	23/32	.719	18.26
1/16	.063	1.59	13/32	.406	10.32	47/64	.734	18.65
5/64	.078	1.98	27/64	.422	10.72	3/4	.750	19.05
3/32	.094	2.38	7/16	.438	11.11	49/64	.766	19.45
7/64	.109	2.78	29/64	.453	11.51	25/32	.781	19.84
1/8	.125	3.18	15/32	.469	11.91	51/64	.797	20.24
9/64	.141	3.57	31/64	.484	12.30	13/16	.813	20.64
5/32	.156	3.97	1/2	.500	12.70	53/64	.828	21.03
11/64	.172	4.37	33/64	.516	13.10	27/32	.844	21.43
3/16	.188	4.76	17/32	.531	13.49	55/64	.859	21.83
13/64	.203	5.16	35/64	.547	13.89	7/8	.875	22.23
7/32	.219	5.56	9/16	.563	14.29	57/64	.891	22.62
15/64	.234	5.95	37/64	.578	14.68	29/32	.906	23.02
1/4	.250	6.35	19/32	.594	15.08	59/64	.922	23.42
17/64	.266	6.75	39/64	.609	15.48	15/16	.938	23.81
9/32	.281	7.14	5/8	.625	15.88	61/64	.953	24.21
19/64	.297	7.54	41/64	.641	16.27	31/32	.969	24.61
5/16	.313	7.94	21/32	.656	16.67	63/64	.984	25.00
21/64	.328	8.33						

Conversion—Millimeters to Decimal Inches

mm	*inches*	*mm*	*inches*	*mm*	*inches*	*mm*	*inches*	*mm*	*inches*
1	.039 370	31	1.220 470	61	2.401 570	91	3.582 670	210	8.267 700
2	.078 740	32	1.259 840	62	2.440 940	92	3.622 040	220	8.661 400
3	.118 110	33	1.299 210	63	2.480 310	93	3.661 410	230	9.055 100
4	.157 480	34	1.338 580	64	2.519 680	94	3.700 780	240	9.448 800
5	.196 850	35	1.377 949	65	2.559 050	95	3.740 150	250	9.842 500
6	.236 220	36	1.417 319	66	2.598 420	96	3.779 520	260	10.236 200
7	.275 590	37	1.456 689	67	2.637 790	97	3.818 890	270	10.629 900
8	.314 960	38	1.496 050	68	2.677 160	98	3.858 260	280	11.032 600
9	.354 330	39	1.535 430	69	2.716 530	99	3.897 630	290	11.417 300
10	.393 700	40	1.574 800	70	2.755 900	100	3.937 000	300	11.811 000
11	.433 070	41	1.614 170	71	2.795 270	105	4.133 848	310	12.204 700
12	.472 440	42	1.653 540	72	2.834 640	110	4.330 700	320	12.598 400
13	.511 810	43	1.692 910	73	2.874 010	115	4.527 550	330	12.992 100
14	.551 180	44	1.732 280	74	2.913 380	120	4.724 400	340	13.385 800
15	.590 550	45	1.771 650	75	2.952 750	125	4.921 250	350	13.779 500
16	.629 920	46	1.811 020	76	2.992 120	130	5.118 100	360	14.173 200
17	.669 290	47	1.850 390	77	3.031 490	135	5.314 950	370	14.566 900
18	.708 660	48	1.889 760	78	3.070 860	140	5.511 800	380	14.960 600
19	.748 030	49	1.929 130	79	3.110 230	145	5.708 650	390	15.354 300
20	.787 400	50	1.968 500	80	3.149 600	150	5.905 500	400	15.748 000
21	.826 770	51	2.007 870	81	3.188 970	155	6.102 350	500	19.685 000
22	.866 140	52	2.047 240	82	3.228 340	160	6.299 200	600	23.622 000
23	.905 510	53	2.086 610	83	3.267 710	165	6.496 050	700	27.559 000
24	.944 880	54	2.125 980	84	3.307 080	170	6.692 900	800	31.496 000
25	.984 250	55	2.165 350	85	3.346 450	175	6.889 750	900	35.433 000
26	1.023 620	56	2.204 720	86	3.385 820	180	7.086 600	1000	39.370 000
27	1.062 990	57	2.244 090	87	3.425 190	185	7.283 450	2000	78.740 000
28	1.102 360	58	2.283 460	88	3.464 560	190	7.480 300	3000	118.110 000
29	1.141 730	59	2.322 830	89	3.503 903	195	7.677 150	4000	157.480 000
30	1.181 100	60	2.362 200	90	3.543 300	200	7.874 000	5000	196.850 000

To change decimal millimeters to decimal inches, position the decimal point where desired on either side of the millimeter measurement shown and reset the inches decimal by the same number of digits in the same direction. For example, to convert .001 mm into decimal inches, reset the decimal behind the 1 mm (shown on the chart) to .001; change the decimal inch equivalent (.039" shown to .000039").

Tap Drill Sizes

Screw & Tap Size	National Fine or S.A.E. Threads Per Inch	Use Drill Number
No. 5	44	37
No. 6	40	33
No. 8	36	29
No. 10	32	21
No. 12	28	15
1/4	28	3
5/16	24	1
3/8	24	Q
7/16	20	W
1/2	20	29/64
9/16	18	33/64
5/8	18	37/64
3/4	16	11/16
7/8	14	13/16
1 1/8	12	1 3/64
1 1/4	12	1 11/64
1 1/2	12	1 27/64

Screw & Tap Size	National Coarse or U.S.S. Threads Per Inch	Use Drill Number
No. 5	40	39
No. 6	32	36
No. 8	32	29
No. 10	24	25
No. 12	24	17
1/4	20	8
5/16	18	F
3/8	16	5/16
7/16	14	U
1/2	13	27/64
9/16	12	31/64
5/8	11	17/32
3/4	10	21/32
7/8	9	49/64
1	8	7/8
1 1/8	7	63/64
1 1/4	7	1 7/64
1 1/2	6	1 11/32

Decimal Equivalent Size of the Number Drills

Drill No.	Decimal Equivalent	Drill No.	Decimal Equivalent	Drill No.	Decimal Equivalent
80	.0135	53	.0595	26	.1470
79	.0145	52	.0635	25	.1495
78	.0160	51	.0670	24	.1520
77	.0180	50	.0700	23	.1540
76	.0200	49	.0730	22	.1570
75	.0210	48	.0760	21	.1590
74	.0225	47	.0785	20	.1610
73	.0240	46	.0810	19	.1660
72	.0250	45	.0820	18	.1695
71	.0260	44	.0860	17	.1730
70	.0280	43	.0890	16	.1770
69	.0292	42	.0935	15	.1800
68	.0310	41	.0960	14	.1820
67	.0320	40	.0980	13	.1850
66	.0330	39	.0995	12	.1890
65	.0350	38	.1015	11	.1910
64	.0360	37	.1040	10	.1935
63	.0370	36	.1065	9	.1960
62	.0380	35	.1100	8	.1990
61	.0390	34	.1110	7	.2010
60	.0400	33	.1130	6	.2040
59	.0410	32	.1160	5	.2055
58	.0420	31	.1200	4	.2090
57	.0430	30	.1285	3	.2130
56	.0465	29	.1360	2	.2210
55	.0520	28	.1405	1	.2280
54	.0550	27	.1440		

Decimal Equivalent Size of the Letter Drills

Letter Drill	Decimal Equivalent	Letter Drill	Decimal Equivalent	Letter Drill	Decimal Equivalent
A	.234	J	.277	S	.348
B	.238	K	.281	T	.358
C	.242	L	.290	U	.368
D	.246	M	.295	V	.377
E	.250	N	.302	W	.386
F	.257	O	.316	X	.397
G	.261	P	.323	Y	.404
H	.266	Q	.332	Z	.413
I	.272	R	.339		

ANTI-FREEZE INFORMATION

Freezing and Boiling Points of Solutions According to Percentage of Alcohol or Ethylene Glycol

Freezing Point of Solution	Alcohol Volume %	Alcohol Solution Boils at	Ethylene Glycol Volume %	Ethylene Glycol Solution Boils at
20°F.	12	196°F.	16	216°F.
10°F.	20	189°F.	25	218°F.
0°F.	27	184°F.	33	220°F.
−10°F.	32	181°F.	39	222°F.
−20°F.	38	178°F.	44	224°F.
−30°F.	42	176°F.	48	225°F.

Note: above boiling points are at sea level. For every 1,000 feet of altitude, boiling points are approximately 2°F. lower than those shown. For every pound of pressure exerted by the pressure cap, the boiling points are approximately 3°F. higher than those shown.

ANTI-FREEZE CHART

Temperatures Shown in Degrees Fahrenheit
+32 is Freezing

Cooling System Capacity Quarts	Quarts of ETHYLENE GLYCOL Needed for Protection to Temperatures Shown Below													
	1	2	3	4	5	6	7	8	9	10	11	12	13	14
10	+24°	+16°	+4°	−12°	−34°	−62°								
11	+25	+18	+8	−6	−23	−47								
12	+26	+19	+10	0	−15	−34	−57°							
13	+27	+21	+13	+3	−9	−25	−45							
14			+15	+6	−5	−18	−34							
15			+16	+8	0	−12	−26							
16			+17	+10	+2	−8	−19	−34	−52°					
17			+18	+12	+5	−4	−14	−27	−42					
18			+19	+14	+7	0	−10	−21	−34	−50°				
19			+20	+15	+9	+2	−7	−16	−28	−42				
20				+16	+10	+4	−3	−12	−22	−34	−48°			
21				+17	+12	+6	0	−9	−17	−28	−41			
22				+18	+13	+8	+2	−6	−14	−23	−34	−47°		
23				+19	+14	+9	+4	−3	−10	−19	−29	−40		
24				+19	+15	+10	+5	0	−8	−15	−23	−34	−46°	
25				+20	+16	+12	+7	+1	−5	−12	−20	−29	−40	−50°
26					+17	+13	+8	+3	−3	−9	−16	−25	−34	−44
27					+18	+14	+9	+5	−1	−7	−13	−21	−29	−39
28					+18	+15	+10	+6	+1	−5	−11	−18	−25	−34
29					+19	+16	+12	+7	+2	−3	−8	−15	−22	−29
30					+20	+17	+13	+8	+4	−1	−6	−12	−18	−25

For capacities over 30 quarts divide true capacity by 3. Find quarts Anti-Freeze for the 1/3 and multiply by 3 for quarts to add.

For capacities under 10 quarts multiply true capacity by 3. Find quarts Anti-Freeze for the tripled volume and divide by 3 for quarts to add.

To Increase the Freezing Protection of Anti-Freeze Solutions Already Installed

Cooling System Capacity Quarts	Number of Quarts of ETHYLENE GLYCOL Anti-Freeze Required to Increase Protection													
	From +20°F. to					From +10°F. to					From 0°F. to			
	0°	−10°	−20°	−30°	−40°	0°	−10°	−20°	−30°	−40°	−10°	−20°	−30°	−40°
10	1 3/4	2 1/4	3	3 1/2	3 3/4	3/4	1 1/2	2 1/4	2 3/4	3 1/4	3/4	1 1/2	2	2 1/2
12	2	2 3/4	3 1/2	4	4 1/2	1	1 3/4	2 1/2	3 1/4	3 3/4	1	1 3/4	2 1/2	3 1/4
14	2 1/4	3 1/4	4	4 3/4	5 1/2	1 1/4	2	3	3 3/4	4 1/2	1	2	3	3 1/2
16	2 1/2	3 1/2	4 1/2	5 1/4	6	1 1/4	2 1/2	3 1/2	4 1/4	5 1/4	1 1/4	2 1/4	3 1/4	4
18	3	4	5	6	7	1 1/2	2 3/4	4	5	5 3/4	1 1/2	2 1/2	3 3/4	4 3/4
20	3 1/4	4 1/2	5 3/4	6 3/4	7 1/2	1 3/4	3	4 1/4	5 1/2	6 1/2	1 1/2	2 3/4	4 1/4	5 1/4
22	3 1/2	5	6 1/4	7 1/4	8 1/4	1 3/4	3 1/4	4 3/4	6	7 1/4	1 3/4	3 1/4	4 1/2	5 1/2
24	4	5 1/2	7	8	9	2	3 1/2	5	6 1/2	7 1/2	1 3/4	3 1/2	5	6
26	4 1/4	6	7 1/2	8 3/4	10	2	4	5 1/2	7	8 1/4	2	3 3/4	5 1/2	6 3/4
28	4 1/2	6 1/4	8	9 1/2	10 1/2	2 1/4	4 1/4	6	7 1/2	9	2	4	5 3/4	7 1/4
30	5	6 3/4	8 1/2	10	11 1/2	2 1/2	4 1/2	6 1/2	8	9 1/2	2 1/4	4 1/4	6 1/4	7 3/4

Test radiator solution with proper hydrometer. Determine from the table the number of quarts of solution to be drawn off from a full cooling system and replace with undiluted anti-freeze, to give the desired increased protection. For example, to increase protection of a 22-quart cooling system containing Ethylene Glycol (permanent type) anti-freeze, from +20°F. to −20°F. will require the replacement of 6 1/4 quarts of solution with undiluted anti-freeze.